# THE COFFEE CHRONICLES

A DEEP JOURNEY INTO THE ALCHEMY,
OBSESSION, AND GLOBAL EMPIRES OF COFFEE

JOSH LEE

SAND HILL PUBLISHING GROUP

*First published by Sand Hill Publishing Group 2026*

*First edition*

*ISBN (paperback): 979-8-9941034-3-2*
*ISBN (hardcover): 979-8-9941034-4-9*
*ISBN (ebook): 979-8-9941034-5-6*

*For my Dad, who likes his coffee black, any time of the day.*

# CONTENTS

PART V

# RITUALS AND REVOLUTIONS

PART VI

# EMPIRES OF COFFEE

PART VII

# NEW HORIZONS

PART VIII

# APPENDIX

# THE CHRONOLOGY OF COFFEE

**Pre-History – 1400: Biology, Myth, and Early Use**

- **1,000,000–500,000 BCE** *Coffea arabica* evolves in the montane forests of what is now southwestern Ethiopia, likely within the modern Kaffa and Buno regions. A natural hybrid of *Coffea eugenioides* and *Coffea canephora*, it acquires an allopolyploid genome with four chromosome sets, enabling self-pollination while severely limiting genetic diversity—an evolutionary advantage that will later become an agricultural vulnerability.
- **3000–1000 BCE** Wild coffee persists as an understory species beneath dense forest canopy, interacting with human societies ecologically instead of agriculturally. The plant is neither cultivated nor traded, remaining part of a broader foraged landscape.
- **850–900 CE** The legend of Kaldi enters Ethiopian oral tradition, describing a goatherd who observes heightened energy in his flock after they consume red coffee cherries. Though apocryphal, the story reflects early recognition of

coffee's stimulant properties and situates its discovery within pastoral life rather than commerce or empire.

- **900–1300 CE** Among Oromo and other Cushitic-speaking peoples, coffee cherries are crushed, fermented, and mixed with animal fat or butter into compact energy rations. In this "food era," coffee functions as sustenance and ritual substance instead of a beverage, valued for endurance over stimulation.

### 1400 – 1600: Sanctity, Surveillance, and Prohibition

- **1400–1450** Coffee crosses the Red Sea from Ethiopia into Yemen, likely through trade, pilgrimage, and enslaved labor routes. Cultivation becomes concentrated in the Yemeni highlands around Mocha, Sana'a, and Zabid, where altitude and climate prove ideal.
- **1450–1470** Sufi orders, particularly the Shadhiliyya, adopt coffee as a devotional aid, consuming it to sustain wakefulness during *dhikr* and nocturnal prayer. The drink is called *qahwa*, a term previously associated with wine, now reimagined as a substance that sharpens spiritual vigilance rather than dulls it.
- **1475–1500** Written references to coffee as a brewed beverage begin to appear in Yemeni sources, marking the transition of coffee from oral tradition and ritual practice into documented cultural life.
- **1511** The Trial of Mecca unfolds when Governor Khair Beg bans coffee, triggering a formal legal debate over its permissibility under Islamic jurisprudence. Scholars dispute whether roasted beans constitute forbidden "charcoal" and whether coffee's social effects resemble intoxication. The ban is overturned by the Sultan in Cairo, establishing a lasting legal precedent for coffee's consumption.
- **1524** Suleiman the Magnificent formally legalizes coffee throughout the Ottoman Empire, ending regional bans and integrating coffee into imperial economic and social systems.

- **1530s–1540s** Coffeehouses proliferate across Cairo, Damascus, and Mecca, prompting cycles of closure and reopening as authorities oscillate between tolerance and repression. The concern is not intoxication but congregation—coffeehouses foster unsupervised political conversation outside mosque or palace control.
- **1554** The first permanent coffeehouses open in Constantinople, furnished with benches, fountains, and performance spaces. Known as "Schools of the Wise," they suspend social rank and institutional authority, transforming coffee into a civic force as much as a beverage.

## 1600 – 1700: The Seed Escapes

- **1600–1610** Baba Budan commits the first great act of botanical espionage, smuggling seven fertile seeds out of Yemen and planting them in the hills of southern India, creating the first crack in the Arab monopoly.
- **1616** The Dutch East India Company transports a live coffee plant from Mocha or Aden to the botanical gardens of Amsterdam. This single lineage becomes the genetic ancestor of nearly all coffee later grown in the Americas.
- **1645** Europe's first documented coffeehouse opens in Venice, a mercantile gateway between the Ottoman world and Western Europe, accelerating coffee's spread across the continent.
- **1650** A coffeehouse opens in Oxford, preceding London's scene and reinforcing coffee's association with scholarship, debate, and information exchange.
- **1652** London's first coffeehouse opens, soon followed by dozens more that function as information exchanges for news, shipping intelligence, financial speculation, and political gossip.
- **1674** The "Women's Petition Against Coffee" circulates in London, criticizing coffeehouses for emasculating men and disrupting domestic life, revealing coffee's rapid cultural penetration and moral controversy.

- **1688–1698** Lloyd's of London emerges from Edward Lloyd's coffeehouse, embedding coffee in the architecture of modern finance.
- **1683** Following the Ottoman retreat from Vienna, abandoned sacks of green coffee seed the café culture of Central Europe, transforming coffee from an Islamic novelty into a European habit.

## 1700 – 1800: Imperial Transplantation

- **1714** A coffee tree cultivated by the Dutch is presented to King Louis XIV and planted in Paris's Jardin des Plantes, placing coffee under royal and scientific patronage.
- **1723** Gabriel de Clieu transports a cutting from the royal coffee tree to Martinique in a sealed glass enclosure, reportedly rationing his own water to keep it alive. Within decades, millions of Caribbean trees descend from this single specimen.
- **1727** Francisco de Melo Palheta introduces coffee to Brazil after acquiring seeds from French Guiana, marking the origin of what will become the world's dominant coffee economy.
- **1730s–1740s** Coffee overtakes sugar as the most profitable crop in Saint-Domingue, binding global coffee supply directly to plantation slavery and colonial violence.
- **1760s–1780s** Coffee cultivation expands across the Caribbean and Brazil through plantation monoculture, dependent on enslaved labor and intensive land exploitation.
- **1773** In the wake of the Boston Tea Party, coffee becomes a patriotic beverage in North America, symbolically severing colonial ties to British tea and reframed by physicians as both healthful and morally superior.
- **1791** The Haitian Revolution begins, dismantling Saint-Domingue's plantation system and collapsing the world's largest coffee exporter, accelerating Brazil's rise to dominance.

## 1800 – 1900: Industrialization and Epidemiology

- **1820–1850** Brazil consolidates its position as the world's leading coffee producer, supported by plantation slavery, expanding rail infrastructure, and vast tracts of fertile land.
- **1864** Jabez Burns patents the self-emptying drum roaster, enabling consistent large-scale roasting and transforming coffee into a standardized industrial product.
- **1865** John Arbuckle introduces pre-roasted coffee sold in one-pound paper bags sealed with a sugar-and-egg glaze, establishing the first national coffee brand and distancing consumers from roasting.
- **1869** Coffee leaf rust (*Hemileia vastatrix*) is identified in Ceylon, where it devastates plantations and forces the British Empire to abandon coffee in favor of tea.
- **1873** Early chemical decaffeination experiments begin, foreshadowing the industrial manipulation of coffee's stimulant properties.
- **1888** Brazil abolishes slavery, prompting a transition to the *colonato* labor system and large-scale European and Japanese immigration to sustain coffee production.
- **1898–1900** *Coffea canephora*, later known as Robusta, is identified and commercialized in Central Africa, valued for disease resistance, high yields, and elevated caffeine content.

## 1900 – 1950: The Era of Chemistry

- **1901** Spray-drying technology is applied to coffee extract, enabling the large-scale production of soluble coffee powder.
- **1905** Ludwig Roselius commercializes decaffeinated coffee, introducing coffee engineered for restraint rather than stimulation.
- **1908** Melitta Bentz invents the paper coffee filter, removing oils and sediment and redefining brewed coffee toward clarity and acidity.

- **1920** Prohibition begins in the United States, accelerating coffee consumption as alcohol disappears from public life and repositioning coffee as the dominant socially acceptable stimulant.
- **1938** Nestlé launches Nescafé to absorb Brazil's chronic surplus. During World War II, instant coffee becomes a military staple, training consumers to value speed and uniformity over flavor.
- **1948** Achille Gaggia introduces the lever-piston espresso machine, standardizing high-pressure extraction and producing crema, redefining coffee as performance and precision.

## 1950 – 2000: Market Swings and Quality Revolutions

- **1962** The International Coffee Agreement is signed, establishing export quotas to stabilize prices and support producer nations during the Cold War through "caffeine diplomacy."
- **1966** Alfred Peet opens Peet's Coffee in Berkeley, reintroducing dark roasting, freshness, and origin awareness to the American market.
- **1975** A catastrophic frost strikes Paraná, Brazil, killing millions of coffee trees and triggering global price shocks.
- **1982** The Specialty Coffee Association of America is founded, formalizing quality standards, cupping protocols, and professional certification.
- **1989** The International Coffee Agreement collapses, unleashing a free-market crash that drives prices downward and impoverishes millions of smallholder farmers.
- **1995** The Frappuccino is launched, redefining the coffee shop business model by blending coffee with sugar, milk, and ice, dramatically expanding margins and demographics.
- **1999** The term "Third Wave Coffee" enters common usage, reframing coffee as an artisanal product analogous to wine instead of a commodity beverage.

## 2000 – Present: Climate, Capital, and Computation

- **2004** The Q Grader certification program launches, standardizing sensory evaluation and professionalizing coffee quality assessment worldwide.
- **2009** The expiration of single-serve capsule patents accelerates the convenience economy, increasing waste while lowering brew ratios and average cup quality.
- **2010s** Specialty coffee formalizes origin storytelling and direct-trade models, while shifting climate risk and price volatility increasingly onto producers.
- **2019** Luckin Coffee expands rapidly in China, signaling a shift in coffee's center of gravity from the Atlantic world toward Asia.
- **2020s** Rising temperatures and erratic rainfall disrupt flowering cycles and yields, prompting research into hybrids, agroforestry, cellular agriculture, and alternative species such as *Coffea liberica*.
- **2023** Cold brew becomes a dominant format, de-seasonalizing consumption and prioritizing stability and sweetness over acidity and terroir expression.
- **2050 (Projection)** Climate models predict a severe contraction and upward migration of the global coffee "bean belt," with adaptation requiring capital-intensive interventions beyond the reach of most smallholders, threatening the long-term sustainability of the supply chain.

# INTRODUCTION

*At the edge of morning, before the day has fully decided what it will demand of the world, coffee happens.*

*In a quiet shop in Seattle, or Berlin, or Tokyo, the silence is broken by the sharp engagement of a burr grinder. It is a brief, precise sound—dense, brittle seeds being fractured into thousands of uniform particles, creating a geometric increase in surface area. A portafilter locks into the brass group head with a practiced, distinct twist of the wrist. Water, heated to a thermally stable 93°C and driven by a rotary pump generating nine bars of atmospheric pressure, is forced through the compacted bed of grounds.*

*For twenty-five seconds, a complex interplay of thermodynamics and fluid mechanics occurs within the darkness of the steel basket. The superheated water acts as a solvent, stripping lipids, dissolving sugars, and emulsifying oils. It carries acids into solution, balancing the brightness of fruit against the depth of caramelization. Then, a liquid runs dark and glossy, thick as lacquer, into the waiting ceramic cup.*

*The barista hands it across the counter. The transaction is seamless, almost invisible. The consumer takes the cup, feels the radiant heat against their palm, and inhales the volatile aromatics—notes of jasmine, bergamot, or roasted nuts —that are currently escaping the surface. In this moment, the coffee is a source of comfort. It is a tool for alertness, a biological signal that the work of the day can begin. It is an intimate global commodity; we don't just consume it, we internalize it, using it to alter our energy and mood.*

*But this private ritual is built upon a vast, invisible distance.*

### THE VIEW FROM THE HILL

Seven thousand kilometers away, on a steep, terraced hillside in Nyeri, Kenya, the morning is already old. The light is harsh, cutting through the thin air at 1,800 meters above sea level, illuminating the dark, waxy leaves of the *Coffea arabica* trees. Here, the reality of the coffee is not liquid; it is agricultural.

Fingers stained purple with fruit juice strip clusters of SL-28 cherries from a branch. The work is rhythmic, exhausting, and exacting. The harvester moves with a speed born of necessity, yet they must exercise a botanical judgment with every motion. Only the deepest red cherries, the ones that have reached peak maturation and sugar density, will pass inspection at the washing station down the valley. The green cherries are unripe, astringent, and worthless. The black cherries are rot, potential carriers of fungal defects. Only the red ones are paid for.

Once harvested, these cherries will enter a processing chain of industrial scale. They will be weighed on rusted scales, pulped by mechanical discs to strip the skin, and fermented in concrete tanks for twenty-four to forty-eight hours to break down the sugary mucilage layer through enzymatic activity. They will be washed in channels of cold river water, scrubbing the parchment clean, before being laid out on raised drying beds. There, they will rest for weeks, raked hourly by hand to ensure even drying, monitored until their moisture content drops from 60% to the precise 10-12% range required for maritime export.

This is the physical reality of the seed. It is a physical burden of soil chemistry, rainfall patterns, manual labor, and the relentless pressure of the harvest cycle. It is a reality that rarely intersects with the quiet shop in Berlin.

### THE ABSTRACTION OF PRICE

And seven thousand kilometers from both the farm and the café, on a server rack in a New Jersey data center operated by ICE Futures U.S., a number updates in real time.

It is the "C-Price"—the global benchmark for Arabica coffee. This number serves as a digital abstraction, a number largely detached from the sensory quality of the Kenyan cherry or the technical skill of the Berlin barista. This number does not taste the coffee. It does not know if the Nyeri harvest was sweet or savory. It moves in response to rain forecasts in the cerrado of Brazil, currency fluctuations between the U.S. Dollar and the Colombian Peso, and the speculative positions of financial actors who may never handle a single physical sack of beans.

For the producer on the hill, this abstraction becomes concrete. A dip in the C-Price is not a statistic; it is a new roof in Vietnam that goes unbuilt. It is a loan in Honduras that defaults. It is the decision to abandon a farm in Guatemala because the cost of fertilizer exceeds the potential revenue of the harvest. The market dictates the survival of the farm, yet the market operates on a logic that views the bean as a fungible unit of trade, indistinguishable from any other.

These three moments—the extraction, the harvest, and the trade—will never physically meet. The picker will never drink the espresso brewed from their labor. The trader will never touch the tree that anchors the derivative contract. The barista will never see the ledger that determined the price of the beans in the hopper.

But they are all drinking from the same chain. The central paradox of coffee is that it is a product of comfort with a history of consequences. The cup is warm, but the systems that filled it are vast, complex, and often invisible. To understand coffee is to understand how the modern world was made, how biology was bent to the will of empire, how taste was industrialized by science, and how agriculture was financialized by the market.

### The Roots of Alertness

The story of this distance does not begin in a boardroom or a cafe. It begins in the biology of the Ethiopian highlands, the evolutionary cradle of the *Coffea* genus.

Coffee is not native to the Americas, where the vast majority of it is grown today. It is not native to Asia, which is currently reshaping the consumption map. It is the child of the Afromontane forests, where wild

*Coffea arabica* still grows in the shade of ancient canopy trees. In these forests, the plant evolved not to serve humanity, but to defend itself.

The caffeine molecule, 1,3,7-trimethylxanthine, is a bitter alkaloid. It functions in nature not as a stimulant, but as a pesticide—a chemical weapon synthesized by the plant to create a biological barrier against predation. The great irony of the coffee industry is that humanity is simply the mammal that learned to enjoy the poison. We seek out the very compound the plant created to drive consumers away.

For centuries, this plant remained a local secret, consumed by the Oromo people as a foodstuff—balls of crushed cherries mixed with animal fat for stamina during long journeys. It was only when the seed crossed the Red Sea to Yemen in the 15th century that it underwent its first transformation: from food to beverage, and from tribal sustenance to religious technology.

The Sufi mystics of the Shadhili order in Yemen were the first to brew the roasted seeds into a hot liquid, which they called *qahwa*—a poetic term originally used for wine. But where wine dulled the senses, *qahwa* sharpened them. It was used during the *dhikr*, the midnight remembrance ceremonies, to banish sleep and sustain the rhythmic chanting required to reach a state of spiritual ecstasy. Coffee began as a tool for the mind, a way to steal hours from the night and devote them to the divine.

From the monasteries of Yemen, the drink spread to the secular world of the Ottoman Empire, and here it revealed its second power: the ability to build rooms. The coffeehouse, or *kahvehanes*, emerged in Constantinople as a new kind of social space. Unlike the tavern, which was a place of intoxication and chaos, the coffeehouse was a place of sobriety and conversation. Known as the "School of the Wise," it offered a venue where rank and class were suspended in favor of intellectual debate.

These spaces were so effective at generating public opinion that they terrified the Ottoman sultans. Repeated attempts were made to ban the drink, to close the houses, to sew coffee drinkers into leather sacks and throw them into the Bosphorus. But the demand for alertness, and the social connection it fostered, proved stronger than the fear of the state.

The pattern was established: wherever coffee goes, a reconfiguration of social time and space follows.

## THE SEEDS OF EMPIRE

If biology provided the fuel of the industry, empire built the chassis. By the 17th century, the European powers—the Dutch, the French, and the British—had acquired a taste for the "Wine of Islam," but they resented the Ottoman monopoly on the trade. They could not afford to bleed silver and gold to the East for a commodity they could not control. They needed to own the tree.

This geopolitical anxiety triggered one of the greatest eras of botanical espionage in history. The Dutch East India Company (VOC), the first modern multinational corporation, managed to smuggle fertile seeds out of Yemen and transport them to their colonial possessions in Java and Ceylon. They treated the coffee tree not as a mystical gift, but as a unit of production. They cleared rainforests, terraced mountains, and enslaved populations to tend the crop. The Dutch flooded the European market with Javanese coffee, breaking the Ottoman stranglehold and turning a luxury good into a bourgeois staple.

The French followed suit, driven by the obsession of King Louis XIV to cultivate the plant in the Caribbean. The journey of the "noble tree"—a single specimen transported across the Atlantic by the naval officer Gabriel de Clieu—is often romanticized as a heroic voyage of water rationing and storm survival. But the result of that voyage was the establishment of the plantation system in Saint-Domingue (modern Haiti) and later throughout the Americas.

This was the "Great Transformation" of the coffee lands. The complex, shade-loving forest shrub was forced into the full tropical sun to maximize yield. The "Wakefulness" of the Enlightenment thinkers in London and Paris—who sat in coffeehouses discussing democracy, physics, and stock markets—was purchased with the exhausted labor of enslaved people in the colonies. The plantation system turned the coffee tree into a machine for converting soil nutrients and human suffering into cash crops.

We are still living with the ecological and political scars of that decision. The map of modern coffee production—the "Bean Belt" stretching between the Tropics of Cancer and Capricorn—is largely a map of former colonial possessions. The trade routes that move the beans today follow the shipping lanes carved out by the imperial navies of the 18th century. The dependency of the Global South on the export of raw materials to the Global North is a structural legacy of the moment coffee became a seed of empire.

## THE ALCHEMY OF SCIENCE

As the volume of coffee grew, so did the desire to control its quality. The history of coffee is also a history of science—a relentless quest to understand and manipulate the chemistry of the bean.

For centuries, brewing was a crude affair: boiling crushed grounds in water until they surrendered their essence, producing a thick, sediment-heavy liquor. But the industrial age demanded consistency. It demanded a beverage that was clear, reproducible, and refined.

This drive for precision gave rise to the "Alchemy of Aroma." We see it in the kitchen of Melitta Bentz in 1908, a German housewife who, frustrated by the bitter grit of boiled coffee, punched holes in a brass cup and lined it with blotting paper from her son's schoolbook. In doing so, she invented the paper filter, a device that fundamentally altered the taste of coffee by trapping the oils (diterpenes) and sediment, revealing the clean, acidic clarity of the liquid. She did not just invent a method; she invented a flavor profile that would come to define the modern American and Northern European palate.

We see it in the workshops of Milan in the early 20th century, where engineers struggled to harness the power of steam without burning the coffee. The invention of the lever-piston machine by Achille Gaggia introduced the concept of high-pressure extraction. By forcing water through the puck at nine bars of pressure, Gaggia sheared the oils into a stable emulsion, creating *crema*—the golden foam that defines espresso. He changed the physics of the drink, allowing for a concentrated, syrupy extraction that could be prepared in seconds rather than minutes.

And we see it in the laboratories of Switzerland, where chemists at Nestlé faced the challenge of preserving the surplus harvest of Brazil during the Great Depression. Their solution was freeze-drying: a process of dehydrating the brewed coffee at sub-zero temperatures to create a soluble crystal that could be rehydrated instantly. Nescafé was not just a product; it was a triumph of food science, decoupling the consumption of coffee from the ritual of brewing and turning it into a purely functional "soluble fuel" for the post-war era.

Today, this scientific inquiry has reached a granular level. We now understand the specific roles of the 800 volatile compounds created during roasting. We measure the total dissolved solids (TDS) of a brew with refractometers. We analyze the particle distribution of grinders using laser diffraction. Coffee has become an arena where physics, chemistry, and sensory science converge. The bean is no longer just grown; it is engineered, roasted, and extracted with a precision that rivals the pharmaceutical industry.

## THE SHADOW OF THE MARKET

Yet, beneath the botanical complexity and the scientific precision, the "Shadow of the Market" always looms.

Coffee is among the world's most traded agricultural commodities. It's a drink, yes—but also a supply chain and a livelihood system spanning farms, ports, exchanges, and cities. It is the livelihood of twenty-five million farming families, most of them smallholders working less than two hectares of land. But the financial mechanisms that determine their income are vast, opaque, and volatile.

The "C-Market" is the driver of this volatility. It is a system of futures contracts designed to hedge risk, allowing roasters to lock in prices and farmers to secure buyers. But in practice, it has become a casino for global capital. High-frequency trading algorithms and macro-hedge funds speculate on coffee prices as a proxy for commodity inflation or emerging market currency strength. A frost in Brazil causes a panic that spikes the price; a bumper crop in Vietnam causes a surplus that crashes it.

The result is the "Coffee Paradox": a booming global industry worth hundreds of billions of dollars, supported by a production base that is often operating at a loss. The farmer in Ethiopia, the genetic birthplace of the crop, may receive less than five percent of the final retail price of the latte sold in New York. The value is captured not by those who grow the risk, but by those who brand the experience.

We have seen attempts to correct this asymmetry. The "Fair Trade" movement began as a radical attempt to set a price floor, a safety net to protect farmers from the brutality of the free market. "Direct Trade" models emerged in the specialty sector, seeking to bypass the anonymity of the commodity exchange and build relationships based on quality and transparency. But these remain small corrections in a massive system. The fundamental economic structure of coffee remains extractive: cheap raw materials flowing from the periphery to the center, fueling the economies of the consuming nations while leaving the producing nations in a state of perpetual development.

### THE FUTURE OF THE SEED

Finally, the narrative must turn to the horizon. The coffee industry is currently facing a threat that makes all previous challenges—the rust epidemics, the price crashes, the colonial wars—seem minor by comparison.

The "Climate Squeeze" is not a theoretical model; it is an observable reality. *Coffea arabica* is a "Goldilocks" plant. It requires a very specific thermal envelope—between 18°C and 21°C—to thrive. It needs distinct wet and dry seasons to trigger flowering and harvest. As the planet warms, this envelope is shifting. The thermal belt is moving up the mountains, forcing farmers to climb higher in search of cooler air. But mountains are conical; as you go up, there is less land. Eventually, you run out of mountain.

By 2050, roughly half of the land currently suitable for Arabica production may be rendered unproductive. We are already seeing the signs: erratic rainfall in Colombia disrupting the flowering cycles; prolonged droughts in East Africa stressing the trees; the spread of pests like the coffee berry borer into altitudes that were previously too cold for them to survive.

The response to this crisis is the new frontier of coffee science. We are seeing a race to adapt. Agronomists are revisiting the "forgotten species" like *Coffea stenophylla* and *Coffea liberica*, seeking genetic traits of heat tolerance and drought resistance that can be bred into commercial varieties. We are seeing the rehabilitation of Robusta, the hardy, high-yield sibling of Arabica that was long despised by connoisseurs for its harsh, rubbery flavor. In a warming world, the resilience of Robusta may be the only thing that keeps coffee affordable for the masses.

We are even seeing the emergence of "cellular agriculture," where scientists in bioreactors are attempting to grow coffee cells in a nutrient bath, divorcing the production of the beverage from the plant, the soil, and the farmer entirely. This "Ghost in the Machine" raises the profound existential paradox of the Ship of Theseus: if you replace every biological component of the bean with a synthesized replica, at what point does it cease to be coffee? If you synthesize the molecule, do you lose the soul? It forces a confrontation with Goethe's question—posed to the chemist Runge—asking whether the "spirit" of the plant is a chemical reality or a biological history.

## THE ARCHITECTURE OF ATTENTION

Why does this matter? Why devote such scrutiny to a beverage?

Because coffee is not just a drink. It is the fuel of the modern mind. It is a tool that humanity uses to alter the experience of time itself.

Before coffee, the human circadian rhythm was tethered to the sun. We rose with the light and rested with the dark. The introduction of caffeine into the Western diet broke that tether. It allowed us to disconnect work from daylight and attach it instead to the clock. It made the night habitable. It made the long shift possible.

Empires loved coffee because it kept clerks awake to balance the ledgers. Factories loved coffee because it kept workers alert around the spinning jennies and power looms. Armies loved coffee because it kept soldiers marching through fatigue. And modern corporations love coffee because it fuels the 24-hour cycle of global digital commerce.

Coffee helped shape the infrastructure of modern capitalism. It is the chemical foundation of the "Protestant Work Ethic." It is the fluid that lubricates the meetings, the coding sessions, the late-night drives, and the early-morning commutes that define our lives. We drink it to signal to ourselves and to others that we are productive, that we are reliable, that we are "on."

But the ability to buy alertness comes with a shadow. If coffee allows us to disconnect from our body's natural rhythms, the global trade allows us to disconnect from the earth's natural limits. We drink the energy of the tropics in the conference rooms of the north, rarely thinking about the nutrient exchange that makes it possible. We consume the water, the nitrogen, and the labor of the Global South in a paper cup, and then we throw the cup away.

If coffee is a mirror, it reflects not just our taste, but our values. It shows us how we value labor, how we value land, and how we value the connections between us.

### THE PROMISE OF THE CHRONICLE

This book follows coffee through all of its forms—from the gene to the jar, from the cloud forest to the commodity market—not to flatten the story into a clean, simple narrative, but to show why the friction matters.

We will not shy away from the complexity. We will delve into the botany of the *haustoria*, the feeding tubes of the rust fungus. We will unpack the history of the "Peet's Revolt" and the "Green Mermaid" that changed how America drinks. We will analyze the "Terroir Wars" and the search for the perfect soil.

By the end of this account, the reader will understand the connection between the grinder in Berlin and the hill in Nyeri. You will know why a frost in the Minas Gerais region of Brazil changes the price of a latte in Tokyo. You will understand why the label on your bag says "Washed Process" and why that matters for the watershed of a village in Colombia. You will understand why the Robusta bean might be the hero of the 21st century.

You will see the cup not just as a beverage, but as a condensed world: sunlight turned into sugar, sugar turned into aroma, aroma turned into culture, culture turned into capital, and capital turned back into pressure on the land.

The story of coffee is the story of how we connected the world, and the price we paid to do it. It is a seed that learned how to manipulate time. Like every technology that does so, it raises a question that cannot be avoided: what will we do with the hours it gives us—and who will absorb the cost?

The water is hot. The grinder is silent. The extraction begins.

# PART I

## ROOTS IN LEGEND

Every origin story begins in darkness: a time before the world knew what it was missing. Coffee's beginnings survive first as myth—stories of goats, saints, and sudden awakenings—because coffee is the kind of discovery that feels too miraculous to belong only to agriculture. But legend is not the opposite of truth. It is a kind of truth that arrives through memory instead of archives.

In this section, we start where coffee begins: in the Ethiopian highlands and the cultural worlds that held coffee long before it held the planet. We follow it across the Red Sea into Yemen, where coffee becomes a tool of devotion and discipline. Then we watch it step into public life in the Ottoman world, where coffeehouses transform conversation into something powerful enough to provoke bans.

These chapters trace the enduring transformation of a bitter seed into a global tool for wakefulness.

# 1

## DANCING GOATS AT DAWN: THE DISCOVERY MYTH AND THE OROMO PEOPLE

*he air in the Kaffa highlands of southwestern Ethiopia does not behave like the air in most places. At roughly 1,800 meters (6,000 feet) above sea level, the atmosphere is thin, cool, and perpetually saturated with moisture. Mornings do not break here with harsh sunlight; they arrive slowly, as a gray illumination filtering through thick banks of mist that cling to the canopy of the ancient Afromontane forest.*

*This is an ecosystem of intense, saturated green. Deep layers of humus and decaying organic matter blanket stones, fallen logs, and the gnarled roots of massive trees, absorbing the high-altitude humidity like a living sponge. The understory forms a dense tangle of ferns, lianas, and creeping vines. In the shadows of giants like African teak (Milicia excelsa) and Dracaena steudneri grows a slender, easily overlooked shrub, with glossy leaves arranged in opposite pairs and, in season, clusters of jasmine-scented white flowers that mature into bright red cherries.*

*Long before coffee had a written history, the Oromo people of these highlands already knew the plant that grew beneath the forest canopy. The legend later gave that knowledge a name: Kaldi. While Kaldi is likely a composite character or an allegorical figure assembled long after the fact to personalize a centuries-long agricultural relationship, the story captures the essential discovery.*

*His goats, usually sluggish in the damp chill of dawn, were behaving with frantic, unfamiliar energy. They bleated sharply, head-butted one another, sprinted in tight circles, and sprang onto their hind legs. Even the older bucks, typically docile, moved with the vigor of kids.*

*They were not sick. They were stimulated.*

*Kaldi, fearing bewitchment or the work of a forest spirit, approached the glade where they had been grazing. He found them stripping bright red cherries from glossy bushes he had passed countless times without notice. Whether out of curiosity, hunger, or habit, the legend says he plucked a handful of the fruit. He chewed on the skin. It was sweet, faintly vegetal, with a texture like a grape. He sucked the slimy, sugar-rich mucilage from the seeds and swallowed.*

*The legend describes a familiar transformation: fatigue recedes, replaced by sustained mental clarity. His heartbeat quickened—not with fear, but with capacity. He felt a surge of restless energy that demanded movement. And so, in the silence of the cloud forest, the human mirrored the animals. He began to move—an image that would later be remembered as dance.*

## ROME, 1671

This is the legend of Kaldi. It has become the most widely circulated explanatory story of coffee's beginnings, recounted in children's books, printed on the menus of cafes from Brooklyn to Tokyo, and animated in cartoons on the walls of roadside stalls in Addis Ababa. It is a charming, tidy narrative that provides the world with a specific "eureka" moment—a singular point in time where humanity met caffeine.

*The legendary discovery in the Kaffa highlands, where local fauna first interacted with the energizing properties of the wild cherry.*

. . .

But like most origin myths, the story of Kaldi is almost certainly a fiction. There is no contemporary Ethiopian record of a goatherd named Kaldi. The story does not appear in writing until 1671—nearly eight centuries after it was supposed to have occurred. It was recorded not by an African chronicler, but by Antonie Faustus Naironi, a Maronite scholar living in Rome, in one of Europe's earliest treatises on coffee, *De Saluberrima Potione Cahue*. Writing for a European audience still suspicious of coffee as a foreign, possibly Islamic drug, Naironi required an origin story that was pastoral, harmless, and morally neutral. The goats offered a version of coffee's origins that was unintimidating, apolitical, and safely distant from Islam.

To dismiss the Kaldi story as false is to misunderstand the function of myth. Myths are rarely accurate records, but they are often precise descriptions of experience. The story persists because it compresses a biological effect into a single, durable image: the sudden refusal of sleep. It captures what caffeine reliably does to the human body—muting fatigue and extending the capacity for effort—without requiring any understanding of chemistry or physiology. Kaldi himself may be a literary invention, but the landscape assigned to him is not arbitrary. The cloud forests of southwestern Ethiopia are the genetic center of coffee's origin, the only place on Earth where the plant evolved under precisely the conditions that made its chemistry possible.

### THE GENETIC ACCIDENT

Why did coffee begin here, and only here? The answer lies beneath the soil and inside the cell; the biosphere beneath the soil functions as a genetic laboratory.

Scientific analysis of the coffee genome reveals that *Coffea arabica* is the product of a rare and specific "speciation event." Most coffee species, including the hardy *Coffea canephora* (Robusta) and the delicate *Coffea eugenioides*, are diploids—they possess two sets of chromosomes (22 in total).

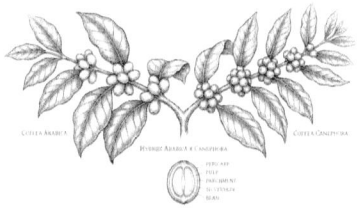

Coffea arabica *emerged as a rare natural hybrid, combining the*
*resilience of* robusta *with the complexity of* eugenioides.

But Arabica is a genetic rarity. Unlike its parents, it possesses four
sets of chromosomes rather than two. Botanists believe that sometime
between 10,000 and 500,000 years ago, a spontaneous hybridization
occurred in these highlands. A Robusta plant (likely contributing disease
resistance and vigor) crossed with a *eugenioides* plant (contributing low
caffeine, high sugar, and flavor complexity). This genetic accident
created a "super-plant" that could survive the cooler, high-altitude
temperatures of the Ethiopian plateau while producing a seed rich in
lipids and sugars.

This specific ecosystem dictates the plant's fragility. Coffee evolved as
an understory shrub, designed by nature to grow in the shade. The
towering *Milicia* and *Ficus* trees of the Kaffa forest act as a thermal blanket, moderating the temperature so that it rarely exceeds 25°C (77°F) or
drops below freezing. This shade canopy also filters the UV radiation,
forcing the coffee tree to ripen its fruit slowly.

This slowness is the secret to quality. A cherry that ripens in direct
sun might turn red in six months. A cherry that ripens in the deep shade
of Kaffa might take nine or ten months. This extended gestation allows
the seed to stockpile complex sugars and nutrients, resulting in a bean of
exceptional density and flavor complexity. When humans later moved
the plant out of the forest and forced it to grow in full sun in Brazil or
Vietnam to maximize yield, they broke a biological contract that had
held for ten thousand years, trading flavor for speed.

But here, in the wild forests of Yayu and Harenna, the contract is still
intact. Ethiopia holds 99.8% of the world's genetic diversity for Arabica
coffee. While a farmer in Brazil might choose between five or six cultivars (Bourbon, Caturra, Mundo Novo), the forests of Kaffa contain thou-

sands of "landraces"—distinct, genetically unique varieties that have never been cataloged, named, or tasted by the outside world. This genetic bank is the industry's only insurance policy against climate change; locked inside these wild trees are likely the genes for drought tolerance and heat resistance that will be needed to save the crop in the coming decades.

## Kaffa vs. Qahwa

Before coffee conquered the world, it had to be named. The etymology of the word "coffee" is a linguistic map of its migration, revealing the complex bridge between African origins and Arab expansion.

One persistent theory suggests the word is derived directly from the geography: Kaffa, the province where the plants grew wild. It is a logical assumption—naming the product after the place, like Champagne, Gouda, or Darjeeling. However, there is a linguistic snag: the indigenous people of Kaffa do not call the plant "coffee" or "Kaffa." They call it *bun* or *buna*.

The more accepted etymological path traces the word through the Arabic term *qahwa*. Originally, *qahwa* was a poetic term for wine, derived from the verb *qahiya*, meaning "to lack an appetite" (referencing wine's ability to curb hunger). When the drink crossed the Red Sea into Yemen and was adopted by Sufi mystics in the 15th century, the term *qahwa* was repurposed. Since alcohol was *haram* (forbidden) in Islam, coffee became the "Wine of Araby"—the permitted stimulation that suppressed physical hunger but stimulated spiritual appetite.

From *qahwa*, the word traveled into Turkish as *kahve*. The Ottoman pronunciation softened the "q" and the "w." From there, Venetian merchants trading in the spice markets of the Levant heard the Turkish word and transliterated it into Italian as *caffè*. The Dutch, the great logistical movers of the 17th century, made it *koffie*. And finally, by 1582, the word entered the English language as coffee. Thus, the word printed on the side of a Starbucks cup today is a ghost of a ghost—an Arabic poetic metaphor for wine applied to an Ethiopian bean, filtered through Turkish pronunciation and Italian spelling. But the indigenous name, *buna*, survives in the Horn of Africa, a reminder that the plant had a name long before the rest of the world tried to label it.

### Oromo: The First Cultivators

While the Kaldi myth suggests a sudden discovery by a lone individual, the reality is that coffee was co-evolved with a culture. Long before monasteries were brewing beverages or Arabs were trading seeds, the indigenous peoples of the Ethiopian highlands, specifically the Oromo people, had woven the coffee plant into the very fabric of their social and spiritual lives. The Oromo did not just "discover" coffee; they domesticated it, though not as a drink.

In the traditional Oromo belief system, known as *Waaqeffannaa*, coffee is considered a sacred plant, a direct gift from *Waaqa* (God). It is written into their creation mythology. One Oromo legend tells of *Waaqa* crying over the death of a beloved, and where his tears fell to the earth, the first coffee trees sprang up. Therefore, to consume coffee is to partake in the divine essence. It is a sacrament.

For centuries, the Oromo usage of coffee had little to do with a roasted, black liquid; instead, coffee functioned primarily as a food source and a ritual object. The plant grew wild around their settlements, and they understood its stimulating properties intimately. The most ancient way of consuming coffee, still practiced in some regions today, is known as *Buna Qalaa* (literally "coffee slaughter" or "coffee sacrifice"). In this ritual, the coffee is not ground. Whole, dried coffee cherries are washed and then pan-cooked in butter—often spiced, clarified butter known as *niter kibbeh*. They are cooked until they are soft, swollen, and savory, releasing a heavy, nutty aroma distinct from the sharp acridity of dry roasting—smelling more like browned butter and toasted grain than an espresso bar. A pinch of salt is added, never sugar. The result is a rich, oily, savory snack that is earthy, fatty, and intensely stimulating. The caffeine is present, but it is delivered alongside a heavy dose of lipids from the butter. *Buna Qalaa* was, and is, used for special occasions— welcoming honored guests, blessings for long journeys, weddings, and religious ceremonies. It is a communal act of breaking bread, where the coffee fruit itself is the sustenance.

. . .

### THE WARRIOR'S RATION

Beyond ritual, the Oromo and other highland tribes utilized coffee as a practical tool for survival in a rugged environment. The Ethiopian highlands are treacherous terrain, a landscape of basalt cliffs and deep gorges that requires immense physical endurance to traverse.

Ancient Ethiopian warriors and nomadic traders developed what was essentially the world's first energy bar. They would take the ripe coffee cherries, crush them—seeds, pulp, skin, and all—and mix the resulting paste with animal fat (usually ghee) to create dense, spherical rations.

*Before it was a beverage, coffee was a solid foodstuff used by Oromo warriors for sustenance during long treks.*

These high-calorie, high-caffeine spheres, sometimes called *goli*, were the perfect travel food. The fat provided long-burning calories for the hike, while the caffeine from the raw coffee fruit provided an immediate and sustained stimulant effect, suppressing hunger and warding off exhaustion during multi-day treks or military campaigns. This usage predates the "invention" of roasted coffee water by perhaps a millennium. It shows a sophisticated understanding of the plant's pharmacological properties long before the chemistry of caffeine was understood by European scientists. It also challenges the Western-centric view of coffee history, which often begins only when the beverage appeared in European cups in the 1600s. For the Oromo, coffee was a technology of survival long before it was a beverage of leisure.

## Bunna Maflat

The transition from eating coffee to drinking it likely happened gradually. There is evidence of teas made from the leaves (*kuti*) or the dried husks (*qishr*) being consumed in the region for centuries. But eventually, the seed took center stage. The Ethiopians developed a brewing ritual that remains one of the most elaborate and hospitable ceremonies on Earth: the *Bunna Maflat* (Coffee Ceremony).

This is not a "drive-thru" experience. It is a slow, deliberate performance of hospitality that can last two to three hours. It is predominantly the domain of women, and it anchors the social life of the village. The ceremony is a sensory masterpiece, designed to engage every faculty of the guest.

It begins with the washing. The hostess takes green, raw coffee beans and washes them in water to remove the silverskin. She then places them on a flat iron pan over a charcoal brazier (*midija*). She roasts the beans by hand, shaking the pan rhythmically to ensure even heat. This is the moment of olfactory transformation. As the beans turn from gray-green to cinnamon to dark brown, the room fills with smoke. The hostess walks around the room with the smoking pan, wafting the aroma toward the guests. This is a blessing; the smoke is believed to carry prayers and goodwill.

Once roasted, the beans are crushed. They are not ground in a burr grinder; they are pounded in a wooden mortar and pestle (*Mukecha* and *zenezena*) until the dense seeds are ground into granules. The rhythmic thumping of the pestle is the heartbeat of the ceremony, a sound that signals to neighbors that coffee is being prepared.

The coarse grounds are then added to a *Jebena*—a bulbous clay pot with a long, slender neck and a spherical base. The water is boiled, and the coffee is brewed. The pouring is an art form. The hostess holds the *jebena* high, pouring the golden-black liquid into tiny, handleless cups (*cini*) in a single, continuous stream without spilling a drop.

*The* Jebena *remains the central vessel of the Ethiopian ceremony, designed to settle grounds naturally before serving.*

The grounds settle at the bottom of the pot, creating a naturally filtered brew that is thick and potent.

The ceremony always involves three rounds of service, each with a specific name and meaning:

- *Abol*: The first cup. It is the strongest, thickest, and most potent. It represents the earth and the heavy matters of life. It is for pleasure and awakening.
- *Tona*: Water is added to the remaining grounds, and the coffee is boiled again. This second cup is weaker and lighter. It represents conversation and friendship.
- *Baraka*: The third cup. It is the weakest, often just "coffee water." But it is the most important. *Baraka* means "blessing." To leave before the third cup is considered rude; one must stay for the blessing.

Throughout the ceremony, snacks are served—traditionally popcorn or roasted barley (*kolo*). Incense (frankincense or myrrh) is burned constantly. It is a multisensory experience: the smell of roast and incense, the sound of the pestle and the pouring, the taste of the strong, sugary brew. In Ethiopia, coffee is the destination, not the fuel for the journey, and the ritual serves as the anchor for the community's time.


### 525 CE: THE AKSUMITE VECTOR

How did this mountain secret escape to the rest of the world? Wild Arabica is native to Ethiopia and neighboring South Sudan's Boma Plateau. It does not grow wild in the Arabian Peninsula; Yemen's coffee would begin as an imported plant, cultivated into a new identity.

The transfer occurred across the Bab-el-Mandeb strait—the "Gate of Tears"—the narrow strip of water separating the Horn of Africa from the Arabian Peninsula (modern-day Yemen). While birds or floating cherries might have carried seeds occasionally, the establishment of coffee as a crop in Yemen required human agency.

One prevailing historical theory points to the Aksumite Invasion of 525 CE. The Kingdom of Aksum, a powerful Ethiopian empire that traded with Rome and India, launched a massive military campaign to conquer the Himyarite Kingdom of southern Arabia (modern Yemen). Led by King Kaleb, a Christian monarch seeking to protect persecuted Christians in Najran, the Aksumite army crossed the Red Sea in a fleet of sewn boats.

These Ethiopian soldiers, administrators, and camp followers brought their culture with them. They brought their food, their rituals, and almost certainly, their *goli* rations. It is highly probable that during the decades of Aksumite occupation (roughly 525–575 CE), Ethiopian soldiers planted coffee seeds in the Yemeni highlands to ensure a steady supply of their stimulant.

The geography of Yemen was similar enough to Kaffa—high altitude mountains, terraced slopes, and mist—that the plants survived. But the climate was drier. The trees could not rely on the wild forest for protection; they had to be cared for. This marked the pivotal shift from wild gathering to agriculture. For the first time, humans were farming coffee rather than simply finding it. When the Aksumites were eventually driven out by the Persians, they left behind a botanical legacy. The "Ethiopian shrub" had taken root in the Yemeni soil, waiting for the moment it would cross the narrow sea to begin its global conquest.

2

---

# NIGHT HYMNS IN MOCHA: YEMEN, SUFI MONASTERIES, AND RELIGIOUS ENDURANCE

T he night air in the port city of Aden, circa 1450, presses against the body. Built within the crater of a dormant volcano at the southern edge of the Arabian Peninsula, the city retains the thermal energy of the Red Sea, releasing it slowly after dark. Stone walls radiate stored heat. The air carries salt, dried fish, and the heavy dampness of the Tihama coastal plain.

Inside the zawiya of the Shadhiliyya Sufi order, the atmosphere is defined by ascetic discipline rather than sensory overload. A circle of men sits on a rush-covered floor, engaged in dhikr—the rhythmic remembrance of God— recited aloud and sustained for hours after sunset. The practice is structured endurance, designed to carry attention beyond the physiological limits of fatigue.

The physical demands of the ritual are exacting. The men sway in unison, a human tide moving to the meter of the chant: La ilaha illa'allah. There is no god but God. The chest heaves; the breath is controlled, hyper-oxygenating the blood. Yet, biology remains a stubborn tether. By the third hour, the body begins to falter. The lower back aches, the eyelids grow heavy, and the "fog of the soul"—sleep—threatens to sever the connection with the Divine. In the medieval Islamic worldview, sleep was considered the brother of death, a lapse in spiritual vigilance. To sleep during the vigil was to miss the subtle whisper of God.

*Tonight, the circle does not break. A servant enters from the shadows, carrying a large, unglazed earthenware bowl. Steam rises from it, carrying a scent entirely alien to the incense-heavy air of the lodge. It smells of earth, charred pits, and something vegetal, like boiled leaves.*

*The bowl is passed hand-to-hand. Each dervish takes a long, deliberate draft. The liquid is dark, opaque, and bitter. There is no sugar—a luxury for the courts of Cairo, not the ascetics of Aden—nor milk. It is a decoction valued purely for its effect.*

*Within twenty minutes, a shift occurs in the room. It is not a shiver of cold, but of reactivation. The fatigue recedes, replaced by sustained mental clarity. The chanting grows louder, more urgent. The sway becomes more vigorous. What later writers would call the "Wine of Islam" has entered the bloodstream.*

*To an outside observer, these men are consuming a beverage. To the Sufi, they are imbibing prayer itself. They utilize a psychotropic tool to overcome the limitations of the human body, turning the biological night into a spiritual day.*

*Early consumption in Yemeni monasteries was a communal act designed to fuel midnight prayers and religious endurance.*

*This moment in the Adeni zawiya marks coffee's first durable transformation. If Ethiopia was the biological cradle where the plant evolved in the wild, Yemen was the place where it was forged into a repeatable system. Here, the red berry was stripped of its local context and reinvented as an intellectual and religious catalyst.*

*It was here that coffee acquired its first contested identity: qahwa. Historically used to refer to wine, the term was appropriated to describe the brew's stimulating properties, sparking a theological firestorm that would eventually turn the sleepy port of Mocha into the wealthiest harbor in the world.*

## SHEIKH AL-SHADHILI

History often compresses complex cultural shifts into the biography of a single figure, and in the oral traditions of Yemen, that figure is Sheikh Ali ibn Omar al-Shadhili. While the historical record is fragmented—dating specific Sufi saints is notoriously difficult due to the blending of hagiography and chronicle—al-Shadhili serves as the essential human anchor for the coffee revolution.

The legends surrounding him circle the same theme: the discovery of vitality in the midst of deprivation. One tradition claims that during a period of ascetic exile in the mountains, al-Shadhili observed birds eating the red berries of wild shrubs and singing with unusual vigor. Another, more grounded tradition suggests he was introduced to the drink by Ethiopian traders and recognized its potential for his order.

The Sufis were the ideal "early adopters" for caffeine. Their practice was athletic, with *dhikr* sessions lasting six, eight, or ten hours. They fasted during the day, resulting in low blood sugar. They required a stimulant that was *halal* (permissible). Alcohol was strictly forbidden by the Quran; it was an intoxicant (*sukr*) that clouded the mind and led to moral looseness. Hashish was known, but it induced lethargy, a state useless for the rigorous discipline of prayer.

Coffee functioned as a theological loophole. It provided the stamina associated with wine without the drunkenness. It sharpened the faculties rather than dulling them, offering a "dry" stimulation.

Al-Shadhili's endorsement functioned as a de facto approval. Because the Saint drank it, the drink became sanctified. It was served with ceremony in the *zawiya* and blessed before being consumed. To drink coffee was to align oneself with the pious. Even today, in parts of the Islamic world, coffee is sometimes called *Shadhiliyya* in honor of the man who first sanctified the buzz. However, by blessing the drink, al-Shadhili inadvertently released it from the monastery. Pilgrims visiting the holy men tasted the black broth, felt the surge of energy, and carried the habit back to their homes. The practice could no longer be contained within the monastery walls.

## 2,000 METERS UP

While the Sufis were refining the brew, the farmers of the Yemeni highlands were solving a different problem entirely - the hostile terrain.

Yemen is not Ethiopia. The Ethiopian highlands are a lush, tropical cloud forest with deep volcanic loam and predictable rainfall. The Yemeni mountains—specifically the Haraz and Bani Matar regions—are jagged, arid skeletons of rock rising from the desert. The sun is scorching, and rainfall is erratic. By all biological logic, *Coffea arabica*, a plant that evolved in the cool shade of the African understory, should perish here.

It survived only because the Yemeni farmers built a landscape to keep it alive. They invented a system of High-Altitude Terraced Farming that remains a marvel of hydro-engineering.

Examining the Haraz mountains today, the landscape appears as a topographic map made of stone. The farmers carved the sheer mountainsides into thousands of step-like fields, reinforcing them with dry-stone walls (*jidar*) built without mortar. These walls, some standing for 500 years, served a dual purpose: they prevented precious topsoil from washing away during rapid flash floods, and they acted as thermal batteries, absorbing heat during the day and releasing it at night to protect the trees from the chill.

*Farmers in the Yemeni highlands engineered elaborate stone terraces to trap moisture and soil in an otherwise hostile environment.*

The masterstroke was the water management. Since there was no canopy to shade the trees, the farmers pushed the cultivation line up—dangerously high. They planted coffee at altitudes of 2,000 to 2,400 meters (6,560–7,870 feet). At this height, they tapped into the Cloud Forest Effect. In the afternoons, as hot air rose from the Red Sea, it hit the cool mountain peaks and condensed into thick, wet fog. This mist shrouded the trees, blocking ultraviolet radiation and bathing the leaves in moisture.

To supplement this, they built elaborate cisterns (called *karif*) carved into the rock high above the terraces. These caught the runoff from sporadic rains, which was then funneled down through gravity-fed sluice gates. Every drop was accounted for.

This struggle for survival fundamentally changed the bean. In Ethiopia, the wild coffee bean is often large and high in moisture. In the stress of the Yemeni mountains, the bean evolved to be smaller, harder, and rounder. The metabolic stress concentrated the sugars and essential oils. This new varietal became known to the world as Mocha. Its flavor profile was distinct from its African ancestor: deep, chocolatey, winey, and spicy. It lacked the delicate floral notes of the wild Geisha, possessing instead a heavy, resinous body that could withstand dark roasting. It was among the first widely recognized coffee cultivars, shaped by human ingenuity in the face of a hostile environment.

Marqaha

For the Sufi, the effect of coffee was not just physiological; it was phenomenological. They developed a specific vocabulary to describe the state of coffee stimulation, which they called *Marqaha*.

*Marqaha* roughly translates to "the state of coffee euphoria." It describes a specific lightness of being, a clarity of thought, and a lifting of the spirit. Unlike the stupor of wine, which drags the soul down into the body, *Marqaha* lifts the soul out of it.

In the *dhikr* ceremonies, coffee was served from a large communal bowl—a chalice of wakefulness. The caffeine acted as a chemical scaffolding for meditation, allowing the dervish to perform rhythmic breathing and chanting for hours without succumbing to biological exhaustion.

However, this state became the subject of intense scrutiny. Conservative scholars asked a dangerous question: If coffee produces a "state change"—altering the mind from its baseline—is it not, by definition, a drug?

The legal debate hinged on the definition of intoxication. The Quran forbids *khamr* (wine/alcohol) because it causes a loss of reason. The Sufi defense was elegant and precise. They argued that coffee did not add a distortion to the mind; it merely removed the barrier of fatigue, revealing the mind's natural potential. Coffee, they claimed, was the *miftah*—the key. It allowed the believer to see God more clearly by keeping the eyes, and the conscience, wide open.

## A New Architecture

As coffee leaked out of the sanctuary and into the secular world, it required a new kind of room. In the early 16th century, first in Mecca and then spreading to Cairo, Damascus, and Aleppo, a new architectural form appeared in the Islamic city: the *Kahvehane* (Coffee House).

Until this moment, public space in the Islamic world was rigidly binary. There was the Mosque (a space for God) and the Souq (a space for commerce). There was no secular space for leisure. The home was private, the domain of the family and women. The street was for transit. The *Kahvehane* broke this binary.

Physically, these early coffeehouses were designed to mimic the mosque. They featured high ceilings, archways, and often a central fountain to cool the air. But the orientation was radical. Instead of facing the *qibla*, the patrons faced each other. Instead of rows of prayer rugs where men knelt in submission, there were raised platforms (*mastabas*) covered in carpets and cushions where men reclined in luxury.

The social structure was even more revolutionary. In the *Kahvehane*, the rigid hierarchies of the Mamluk and Ottoman worlds dissolved. A merchant could sit next to a poet; a soldier could sit next to a scholar. For the price of a penny, anyone could rent a space on the carpet and engage in the conversation. This earned the coffeehouse a dangerous nickname: The School of the Wise (*Madrasat al-Arifin*).

*The layout of the* Kahvehane *encouraged face-to-face conversation, breaking down social hierarchies.*

It was dangerous because it was uncontrolled. In the mosque, the Imam controlled the message. In the coffeehouse, the conversation could go anywhere—politics, gossip, complaints about taxes, criticism of the Sultan. It functioned as an early "information network" fueled by a stimulant.

### THE TRIAL OF 1511

The inevitable collision between the freedom of the coffeehouse and the order of the state occurred in Mecca in the year 1511. It is the first recorded attempt to ban coffee, establishing a pattern of prohibition that would repeat in London, Berlin, and Sweden for centuries.

The antagonist was Khair Beg, the Mamluk governor of Mecca (the *Muhtasib*, or overseer of public morals). Khair Beg, a rigid disciplinarian, viewed the chaotic energy of the coffeehouses with deep suspicion, hearing rumors that satirical verses about his rule were being recited over cups of the black brew.

One night, while walking home from the mosque, Khair Beg observed a group of men huddled in a corner of the mosque courtyard, passing around a vessel, laughing and animated. He assumed it was wine. When his guards seized the bowl, they found it contained coffee.

Khair Beg saw an opportunity. He convened a council of jurists, theologians, and doctors to put the drink on trial. It was a proceeding convened to reach a predetermined verdict. The prosecution's argument relied on medical testimony to bypass theological ambiguity. Two Persian doctors, brothers known for their adherence to Galenic medicine, were brought in as expert witnesses. Galenic medicine held that health was a balance of the four humors. The doctors examined the cold, black liquid and declared it to be "Cold and Dry" in the extreme. They argued that consuming it would unbalance the humors, causing melancholia, insomnia, and eventually, insanity.

Then, the conservative jurists attacked with a legal technicality: the Charcoal Issue. Islamic dietary law forbids eating charred or carbonized foods (*amylum*), as carbonization was seen as a form of impurity. Since coffee beans were roasted until they were dark brown or black, argued the conservatives, they were technically charcoal. Therefore, the drink was *haram* (forbidden).

Khair Beg ruled against the bean. He ordered the stocks of coffee in Mecca to be seized and incinerated in the street. He sent town criers through the streets announcing that anyone caught selling or drinking coffee would be beaten and paraded backward on a donkey.

It was one of the earliest recorded attempts at prohibition. But it failed, and it failed quickly.

The Sultan of Cairo, Al-Ghawri, was Khair Beg's superior. He was also a habitual coffee drinker. When word of the ban reached Cairo, the Sultan was furious—not just at the loss of his drink, but at the impudence of a local governor issuing a *fatwa* on a substance that was widely consumed in the capital. The Sultan issued a counter-decree overriding Khair Beg. He argued that stimulation implied a sharpening of reason, whereas intoxication implied a loss of it. He dismissed the "charcoal" argument as pedantic legalism.

Khair Beg was humiliated. A few years later, he was removed from office on unrelated charges of embezzlement and executed. Coffee had survived its first existential threat. The verdict solidified its status: it was the drink of the believer, the intellectual, and the citizen—not merely a social lubricant. The ban had only succeeded in advertising its potency.

### Sterilization

With the theological green light, demand for Yemeni coffee exploded. By the mid-16th century, coffee had spread to Istanbul, Damascus, and Aleppo. The Ottoman Empire, which conquered Egypt and Yemen in 1517, realized they were sitting on a geopolitical gold mine. The entire world wanted this black powder, and it grew in only one place: the terraced mountains of Yemen.

To control the trade, the Ottomans funneled all coffee exports through a single, desolate port on the Red Sea coast: Al-Makha (Mocha). Mocha was a harsh place. Surrounded by salt flats and baking in the humidity, the city operated less as a natural settlement than as a machine for extraction. But in the 17th century, it became the wealthiest harbor in the Indian Ocean.

*To protect their monopoly, Ottoman authorities boiled or parched coffee beans before export, ensuring no fertile seed left Yemen.*

Ships from India, Egypt, and eventually the Dutch and British East India Companies anchored offshore, unable to enter the shallow harbor. They sent small lighters to the jetty to load thousands of bales of coffee.

The currency of the world flowed into Mocha: Spanish silver dollars, Venetian gold sequins, Indian textiles, and Chinese porcelain.

The Ottomans were ruthless monopolists. They understood that if the seeds escaped Yemen, their monopoly would end. They instituted a policy of Biological Sterilization. Before any coffee bean could be sold to a Christian merchant, it had to be processed. The beans were either steeped in boiling water or parched on hot iron plates.

This killed the germ inside the seed. A "Mocha bean" sold to a Dutchman was a dead commodity; it could be ground and brewed, but it could never be planted.

For nearly two centuries, this informal Ottoman Embargo held. Yemen held a 100% market share of the global coffee trade. The tax revenue from the port of Mocha bankrolled the Ottoman armies in the Balkans and built the pleasure palaces of the Bosphorus.

### DRINKING THE HUSK

There is a final irony to the Yemeni coffee boom. While the world clamored for the bean, the Yemenis themselves largely stopped drinking it. They preferred—and still prefer—*Qishr*.

*While the world demanded the bean, Yemeni locals traditionally consumed Qishr, a spiced tea made from the dried fruit husk.*

*Qishr* is a tea made from the dried husks (the skin and pulp) of the coffee cherry. When the bean is extracted for export, the fruit is left behind. To the European trader, the husk was trash. To the Yemeni farmer, it was a sweeter, lighter, and more digestible stimulant. They brewed the husks with ginger, cinnamon, cardamom, and dates. The result is a golden, spicy, sweet beverage that tastes more like a chai or a mulled cider than an espresso.

The logic was purely economic. The bean was so valuable as an export commodity that it made no sense for a farmer to drink it. By selling the seed and drinking the husk, the Yemenis maximized their profit while still enjoying the caffeine. This bifurcation of culture persists. The West drinks the seed (roasted dark); Yemen drinks the fruit (spiced and light). Visitors to a home in Sana'a today will be offered a cup of amber *qishr* long before seeing a dark roast.

## THE SEED ESCAPES

The Ottoman monopoly on the seed eventually broke. Smugglers—first a Sufi pilgrim named Baba Budan, and later the corporate spies of the Dutch East India Company—would eventually manage to sneak viable germplasm past the guards of Mocha. But the legacy of Yemen remains imprinted on every cup consumed today. The word *Arabica* itself is a tribute to this era. The plant is African (Ethiopian), but science named it *Coffea arabica* because Europe discovered it via Arabia.

The flavor term *Mocha*—now used to describe a mix of chocolate and coffee—comes from the distinct chocolatey notes of the Yemeni bean that dominated the European palate for three centuries. When ordering a "Caffè Mocha," one unknowingly references a dusty, defunct port city on the Red Sea coast where the heat is heavy and the ghosts of the Ottoman tax collectors still watch the horizon. As the sun sets over the ruins of the merchant houses in Mocha today, destroyed by time and civil conflict, the harbor is silted up, but up in the mist-shrouded terraces of the Haraz mountains, the farmers still tend to the descendants of the same trees that Sheikh al-Shadhili blessed six hundred years ago, bridging the sacred origins of the drink with its secular global future.

# 3

## THE WINE OF ISLAM:
## OTTOMAN COFFEEHOUSES
## AND THE FIRST PROHIBITIONS

C onstantinople's Tahtakale district in the 16th century was a sensory
accumulation of charcoal smoke, unwashed wool, roasting chest-
nuts, and the brine of the Golden Horn. This was the commercial
gut of Constantinople, a chaotic hub where the inventory of the Silk Road was
offloaded from galleys and dispersed into the empire's arteries. Into this chaotic
bazaar walked two men from the Arab provinces: Hakem of Aleppo and Shams
of Damascus. They arrived not with the usual silks or uncut gems, but
carrying sacks of hard, green berries and a business model without precedent in
the Ottoman capital.

In a narrow storefront near the spice market, they established a shop that
sold neither alcohol nor food. They sold a thick, black liquid served in porcelain
thimbles, yet their primary product was the space itself. They named it
Kiva Han.

This establishment marked the earliest recorded public coffeehouse in the
imperial city, and its arrival altered the urban acoustic landscape. Inside, the
sound differed entirely from the hushed piety of the mosque or the slur-
heavy noise of the tavern (meyhane). The room hummed with a sharp,
buzzing frequency: the clatter of backgammon dice, the bubbling of water
pipes (nargile), and the rapid-fire exchange of sober men engaged in debate.
For the price of a single copper akçe—roughly the cost of a loaf of bread—a

porter could sit adjacent to a poet, and a janissary could debate a carpet merchant.

They reclined on raised wooden platforms known as peyk, covered in woven kilims that lined the walls. These benches faced inward toward a central marble fountain, designed not just for aesthetics but to cool the air and mask the privacy of conversations with the sound of falling water. Here, they drank what later writers would call the "Wine of Islam," a beverage that did not dull the senses but sharpened them to a fine point. High above on the promontory, within the gated silence of the Topkapi Palace, the Sultan's advisors observed the smoke rising from Tahtakale. They understood that by selling caffeine and seating together, the two Syrians had built an unmonitored information network. In a city ruled by strict protocol, the coffeehouse introduced a politically potent commodity: unsupervised speech.

THE SCHOOL OF THE WISE

The radical nature of the coffeehouse becomes clear when examining the rigid hierarchy of Ottoman social life in the 16th century. Before Kiva Han, a man's geography was triangular: the home, where he ruled over his family; the mosque, where he submitted to God; and the market, where he traded for survival. There was no widely accepted secular public space for leisure. Those not praying, working, or sleeping had nowhere to exist socially.

The coffeehouse filled this vacuum. Within two decades of Hakem and Shams' arrival, the city rapidly filled with imitators. By the late 16th century, chroniclers estimated there were over 600 coffeehouses (kahvehane) in Istanbul alone. They colonized the urban fabric, from the grandiose, marble-floored salons near the Hagia Sophia to the rough, open-air shacks of the Bosphorus fishermen.

The layout of these spaces enforced a new kind of social leveling. Unlike the tavern, where patrons huddled in dark corners to conceal their vice, the coffeehouse was a theater in the round. The peyk benches forced patrons to face one another, turning the room into a forum. In this layout, the strict hierarchy of the empire—where a cobbler would rarely speak to a scribe—began to loosen. Coffee did not erase status, but it softened the choreography of deference. The historian Peçevi, writing

in the 1630s, noted that the coffeehouse was a place where "people of all
sorts, from the lowest to the highest, would gather."

Patrons called it *Mekteb-i irfan*—the "School of the Wise." It was an
accurate title. In the coffeehouse, news traveled faster than the Sultan's
couriers. If a tax collector was corrupt in Anatolia, the coffeehouses of
Istanbul knew it within weeks. If the navy lost a skirmish in the Mediterranean, the critique of the admiral's strategy was being analyzed over
backgammon boards before the official report reached the Vizier. The
coffeehouse had become an early form of the empire's information
network, decentralized, fast, and impossible to edit.

### THE CARBON DISPUTE

The first backlash came from the pulpit rather than the palace. The
conservative religious establishment, particularly scholars who adhered
to strict interpretations of Islamic law, viewed this new habit with suspicion. Their opposition was theological as well as cultural. The *ulema*
(religious scholars) launched a legal inquiry based on the concept of
*bid'ah*—innovation. In their view, anything introduced after the time of
the Prophet Muhammad that altered the body or soul could be treated
as potentially heretical.

Because coffee was not mentioned in the Quran, jurists relied on
*qiyas* (analogical reasoning) to argue against it. They settled on a technicality of *fiqh* (jurisprudence) regarding carbonization. The argument,
championed by early hardliners, posited that Islamic dietary law forbids
the consumption of coal or anything burnt to a state of carbon. Since
coffee beans are roasted until dark and oily, critics argued coffee was
technically "carbonized." To the jurists, this was not a question of chemistry, but of theological impurity—making it akin to eating coal, a viola-
tion of dietary law.

Beyond the chemistry, there was the issue of effect. Critics argued
that coffee was *khamr*—an intoxicant—because it altered the mind. This
culminated in a series of *fatwas* and localized bans. In one instance in
1539, a local governor in Mecca had coffee stocks burned in the streets.
However, the theological argument proved fragile. As jurists themselves
drank the brew to stay awake for midnight prayers (*dhikr*), consensus

shifted. The Chief Mufti eventually issued a counter-ruling: coffee was not coal, because the bean was not reduced to total ash, and it was not *khamr*, because it sharpened instead of clouded the reason. The religious ban collapsed, in part because the scholars themselves adopted the drink. Yet the political danger remained; mosques emptied during evening prayers because men had gathered at the *kahvehane*, transitioning the drink from a religious aid to a social lubricant.

PERFORMANCE AS POLITICS

If the coffeehouse was the stage, the *Meddah* was the lead actor. The *Meddah* was a professional storyteller, a one-man theater troupe who served as the primary entertainment. He would sit on a high stool in the center of the room, armed with only two props: a handkerchief (*makrama*) and a walking stick (*değnek*).

He was a master of mimicry, draping the handkerchief over his head to voice a nagging mother-in-law, then twisting it around his neck to play a pompous tax collector. He used the stick to knock on the floor, simulating a door or a horse's hoof. But the Meddah functioned as more than a comedian; he was the editorial page. In a society with limited literacy, his stories—ostensibly about legendary heroes or corrupt viziers from centuries prior—were thinly veiled codes.

The Meddah *served as both entertainer and political satirist, using stories to critique power within the safety of the coffeehouse.*

When a *Meddah* told a story about a Sultan misled by a greedy advisor in the year 1200, the room understood he was discussing the current Grand Vizier and the price of wheat in 1630. The audience participated in the subversion, laughing too loudly at the wrong lines or cheering for the thief who stole from the treasury. Authorities tried to regulate them, requiring *Meddahs* to submit stories for approval, but improvisation is difficult to censor. A raised eyebrow, a pause, or a slight inflection could turn a loyal script into a scathing critique, institutionalizing satire within the coffeehouse walls.

### 1633: The Fire and the Law

The tension between the state and the street broke in 1633. A massive fire erupted in the Cibali district, allegedly starting in a coffeehouse where a caulker fell asleep with his pipe. Fanned by Bosphorus winds, the blaze spread through the timber-framed city, destroying 20,000 homes and a third of Istanbul.

The Sultan at the time, Murad IV, was a ruler of administrative absolutism who had ascended the throne during a period of anarchy. He was determined to restore order through force. The fire gave him the pretext to declare that the twin habits of coffee and tobacco were drivers of social decay. He issued a decree making the consumption of either a capital crime.

Murad IV enforced this personally. Contemporary accounts describe the Sultan disguising himself as a commoner—shedding his kaftan for rough wool—and stalking the streets of Istanbul at night, carrying an executioner's mace. He prowled the alleyways of Tahtakale and Galata, testing the air. If he caught the scent of roasting beans or tobacco smoke seeping from under a shuttered door, the response was immediate. Chroniclers suggest that significant numbers of men were executed during Murad's reign for the crime of gathering to drink coffee. Coffeehouses were demolished, pots were smashed, and for a few years, the social hum of Istanbul was silenced, merging the crackdown on caffeine with a broader suppression of dissent.

·   ·   ·

### THE SPY IN THE CORNER

Murad IV died in 1640, and with his death, the absolute ban began to waver. His successors realized that while prohibition costs money, consumption yields revenue. The Ottoman state pivoted from eradication to regulation, placing heavy taxes on imports. But if the state could not kill the coffeehouse, it would monitor it. This era gave birth to the *Hafiye*—the secret police.

*Sultan Murad IV personally enforced the prohibition of coffee, viewing the beverage as a catalyst for sedition.*

The *Hafiye* were the eyes of the Sultan. They were paid informants who spent their days sitting in coffeehouses, sipping slowly, and listening. They scanned the room for keywords: the name of the Vizier, complaints about grain prices, or mentions of the Janissary corps. The presence of the *Hafiye* changed the texture of Ottoman conversation. The carefree roar of the early 1500s was replaced by a culture of sophisticated paranoia. A Turkish idiom from this era warns: "Beware, the walls have ears."

Patrons developed coded language, using metaphors and lines from the poetry of Hafez and Rumi to express political discontent, relying on shared cultural context to convey meaning a spy might miss. The coffee-house became a game of strategy, a place where intelligence was proven by saying everything without saying anything explicitly. Owners were made complicit, held legally responsible for speech in their shops. Every proprietor became a bouncer of ideas, quieting patrons who spoke too loudly or too specifically.

### THE JANISSARY ENTERPRISE

By the 18th century, the coffeehouse evolved again, moving from a center of debate to a center of paramilitary power. The Janissaries were the Sultan's elite infantry, the backbone of the Ottoman military machine. As the empire stagnated, the Janissaries mutated from a disci-plined fighting force into a powerful, armed political class that terrorized the palace.

They began to dominate the coffee trade. The Janissary corps was divided into regiments (*ortas*), and each regiment acquired coffeehouses as bases of operation. They marked their territory by painting regi-mental insignias—stylized symbols like tents, anchors, or crossed spoons—on the doors and walls.

*The Barracks of Influence: Inside a Janissary Kahvehane.*

A Janissary coffeehouse functioned as a clubhouse for the regiment, where they ran protection rackets from corner tables. If a shopkeeper required a loan or needed a rival intimidated, they went to the Janissary *kahvehane*. The institution that began as a "School of the Wise" had hardened into a barracks of organized influence. The connection was so strong that when Sultan Mahmud II finally dismantled the Janissary corps in 1826, he also ordered the demolition of their coffeehouses, understanding that to break their power, he had to dismantle their gathering places.

### RITUALS OF THE PALACE: THE KAHVECIBAŞI

While the Janissaries utilized coffee for commerce, the palace elevated it to state ceremony. Inside the Topkapi, brewing was refined into a precise ritual. The role of *Kahvecibaşı* (Chief Coffee Maker) was created—a position of genuine influence. He commanded a corps of forty assistants known as the *kahveciler ocağı*.

Beans were roasted daily in palace kitchens to ensure peak freshness, and water was fetched from specific springs prized for their mineral content and "sweetness." Service was a display of imperial wealth; the *Kahvecibaşı* entered the Sultan's presence carrying a tray draped in velvet. Coffee was served in a *fincan*—a small porcelain cup without a handle—which sat inside a *zarf*, a jeweled metal holder that protected the fingers from the heat. For the Sultan, the *zarf* was often filigreed gold, studded with diamonds.

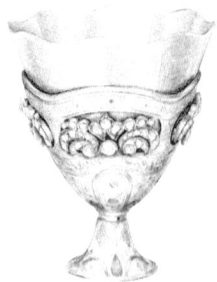

*The* zarf *allowed the drinker to hold the hot porcelain cup, evolving into a display of imperial wealth and craftsmanship.*

This role offered unique access. The *Kahvecibaşı* was among the few permitted near the Sultan when he was unmasked and unguarded. He held the Sultan's drink and therefore his safety. It is no coincidence that several Grand Viziers began their careers as Chief Coffee Makers;

managing the Sultan's caffeine was a stepping stone to managing his empire.

## THE SHERBET OF THE HAREM

The public coffeehouse was strictly male. For a woman to be seen in a *kahvehane* was a social impossibility. But that did not mean Ottoman women were excluded from coffee. They moved the ritual to the spaces they controlled: the home and the bathhouse.

In the *hammam*, coffee became the social lubricant of the female sphere. Lady Mary Wortley Montagu, wife of the British ambassador, described the scene in 1717: hundreds of women, nude or draped in towels, reclining on marble slabs, sipping coffee served on floating wooden trays. Here, the politics were domestic but no less high-stakes. Mothers scouted wives for their sons, and intelligence about the palace, neighbors, and markets flowed freely.

In the home, coffee service became a test of household competence. When a suitor's family visited, a potential bride was expected to roast beans on a flat pan without burning them and grind them to dust in a brass hand-mill. She brewed in a copper *cezve* over charcoal, managing the heat so a thick foam (*kaimaki*) rose to the top. A cup without foam signaled a careless host. While legends persist that Ottoman law granted women the right to divorce husbands who failed to provide coffee, court records more accurately reflect that coffee was listed alongside wheat and oil as an essential component of *nafaka* (maintenance). A husband who could not keep the coffee pot full was a husband failing in his basic economic duties.

## THE SIEGE

By 1680, the Ottoman Empire was saturated with coffee. It was fuel for the army, solace for the mystic, and an obsession of the court. But to the west, beyond the Danube, the drink remained largely a medicinal curiosity. That changed with the mobilization of the imperial military machine.

In 1683, the Ottoman army, led by Grand Vizier Kara Mustafa Pasha, marched toward Vienna. It was a massive force—over 150,000 strong—intent on breaking the gateway to Western Europe. Essential to their logistics were hundreds of heavy sacks of green coffee beans, transported to keep the troops alert through the cold watches of the siege. As the army consolidated its lines around the city walls, the sacks were piled in the encampments—a vast supply of caffeine sitting on the doorstep of Christendom. The seed had traveled from the mountains of Ethiopia to the gates of Europe, carried not by wind or water, but by the logistics of empire.

# 4

## BAPTIZING COFFEE: EUROPE'S MORAL PANIC

The fog in Venice does not roll in; it rises. In the winter months, the damp, bone-chilling mist known as the *nebbia* clings to the Istrian stone of the Rialto Bridge, obscuring the dark waters of the Grand Canal. It is weather that demands warmth—a cold that seeps through wool and linen. For centuries, the Venetians had relied on heavy Malvasia wine and hot broth to stave off the Adriatic chill. But in the late sixteenth century, on the docks of the Dogana da Mar—the Customs House pointed like a ship's prow toward the basin of San Marco—a different kind of warmth was being unloaded.

A merchant galley, fresh from the Levant, rocked gently against the wooden pilings. Its hold was filled with familiar treasures of the East: bales of silk from Damascus, pepper from India, cloves from the Moluccas. But tucked away in the manifest, often listed under "medical drugs" alongside opium and rhubarb, were sacks of a hard, gray-green seed. The dockworkers who hauled these sacks knew them only as *caveé* or *bunna*—a strange commodity that Ottoman consumers boiled into a bitter black brew.

Venice was the hinge of the world, the turnstile between the Christian West and the Islamic East. Its merchants were pragmatic, cosmopolitan, and famously greedy. They had seen the Ottoman pashas drinking this "black broth" in Cairo and Istanbul; they had watched Turkish sentries sip it to *remain vigilant during long sieges. Now, they were bringing it to the Piazza San Marco. But this new substance would be put on trial before it could be sold. To the doctors of the University of Padua, it was a dangerous medical novelty that threatened the theory of humors; to the priests of Rome, it was the "Wine of Infidels," a foreign custom believed to corrupt the soul of Christendom. Before coffee could become ordinary, it had to survive Europe's moral panic.*

### "Black Water, As Hot As They Can Suffer"

Coffee entered Europe through Venice because the *Serenissima Repubblica* occupied a rare geopolitical position: a Christian power whose survival depended on trading with the perceived enemy. While the rest of Europe was locked in religious wars and crusading fervor against the Ottoman Empire, Venice was doing business with it. This economic entanglement created a hesitation in the rest of Europe— adopting coffee meant sending silver directly into the treasury of the Sultan.

Venetian ambassadors, known as *baili*, lived in luxury in the Pera district of Istanbul. They sent detailed reports to the Senate, not just on troop movements, but on the shifting cultural habits of their neighbors. In 1585, the magistrate Gianfrancesco Morosini wrote a dispatch to the Senate that contained one of the first official European descriptions of the drink:

"They sit constantly, and for entertainment they drink a black water, as hot as they can suffer, which is extracted from a seed they call Caveé."

Morosini noted that the drink made men "witty" and "awake." For Venetians, who prized sharp wits and long working hours, this was intriguing. Venice was a city of spies, glassblowers, and arbitrageurs— professions that demanded sustained focus. Wine, the staple drink of Europe, dulled the senses and softened afternoons into stupor. This "black water" promised the opposite. It was a tool for alertness.

But the Venetians were not reckless consumers. They thought empirically. Before they drank it for pleasure, they needed to understand it scientifically. This task fell to Prospero Alpini, a physician and botanist at the University of Padua, the intellectual engine of the Venetian Republic.

Alpini had spent years in Cairo as the personal physician to the

Venetian consul, George Emo. While there, he had not just observed the coffee plant; he had studied it with the rigor of a biologist. In 1592, he published a widely cited text, *De Plantis Aegypti* ("The Plants of Egypt"). It was the first time a European audience saw a botanical drawing of the coffee bush.

*Prospero Alpini's 1592 sketches introduced the coffee plant to European science, initially classifying it as a medicinal drug.*

Alpini's description was purely clinical, stripping the plant of its Sufi mysticism and presenting it as a collection of active properties. He noted the Egyptians used it to treat "obstructions of the liver" and to induce menstruation. Crucially, he translated the Arabic preparation method into a European context, describing the taste as "bitter and similar to chicory."

Because of Alpini's classification, coffee's first home in Italy was not the café, but the apothecary. It was a high-priced pharmaceutical, sold by the ounce and kept in painted majolica jars labeled Buna. Doctors prescribed it for headaches, digestion, and an expanding list of ailments. At nearly three lira per ounce—roughly a day's wage for a laborer—it belonged to the wealthy and anxious, serving as a prescription rather than a social lubricant.

. . .

## The Problem of Pleasure

As the "medicinal" use of coffee spread from the apothecaries of Venice to the aristocracy in Rome, the Church took notice. To the conservative Catholic clergy of the early 1600s, coffee was culturally suspect.

The objection was grounded in theology. Coffee was associated with the Ottoman Empire, Christendom's chief rival, and was often framed as the "Wine of Islam." Some clerics argued—by a logic both literal and polemical in its intent—that Satan had forbidden wine to Muslims because wine, in the Catholic Mass, became the blood of Christ, and had instead offered coffee as a bitter substitute: a black potion that mimicked communal ritual while producing wakefulness instead of reverence.

Furthermore, coffee was a stimulant. It agitated the body and the mind. In early modern Catholic moral thought, the ideal state of the soul was calmness, submission, and reverence. A drink that caused "wakefulness," "witty conversation," and "loquacity" was suspicious. It read as a potion for conspirators.

By 1600, a group of clerical advisors petitioned Pope Clement VIII to formally ban the drink. They wanted coffee declared *haram* for Christians—a dark import from the Islamic world, an unholy indulgence dressed up as medicine. They argued that allowing the so-called "Devil's Brew"—a term used sparingly in the archives but potent in the cultural imagination—into Rome would open a door in the Holy City. The stakes were high: the memory of the Battle of Lepanto (1571), where the Holy League had barely held off the Ottoman navy, was still fresh. Drinking the enemy's broth felt like a betrayal of the dead.

## Legend vs. Record: The Baptism

The story of what happened next is one of the most famous anecdotes in culinary history, though it sits precariously on the line between fact and hagiography. It must be acknowledged that the "Baptism" story is likely apocryphal, a convenient myth constructed to explain a massive cultural shift, yet its symbolic importance remains undeniable.

The legend goes that Pope Clement VIII, a devout but intellectually curious man, refused to condemn something he had never experienced. He ordered a pot of steaming coffee to be brought to his chambers in the Vatican. The smell was likely shocking to the papal court—acrid, roasted, and alien compared to the sweet frankincense of the cathedral or the floral notes of Italian wine.

The Pope lifted the cup—likely a porcelain bowl without handles—and took a sip. The priests held their breath, waiting for the condemnation that would banish the bean from Europe forever. Instead, Clement smiled. According to the tradition, he declared: "This Satan's drink is so delicious that it would be a pity to let the infidels have exclusive use of it. We shall cheat Satan by baptizing it."

*Pope Clement VIII's legendary approval of the "Devil's Brew" opened the floodgates for coffee consumption in Christendom.*

No surviving papal bull or decree confirms this specific quote. Like the story of Kaldi and the goats, the "Baptism of Coffee" functions as an explanatory myth. However, the effect of Clement's papacy on coffee is undeniable. Whether he literally blessed a pot with holy water or simply gave his tacit verbal assent, Clement VIII refused to ban the drink. In doing so, he transformed coffee from a Muslim threat into a Christian commodity. He gave the pious permission to drink. This moment marked the turning point. Once the Vatican shrugged, the moral panic dissolved, replaced quickly by something far more powerful: demand.

## Speziali vs. Acquacedratari

With the blessing of the Pope, the demand for coffee exploded. But this created a new conflict, fought not in the heavens, but in the narrow, cobblestone streets of Venice. It was a guild war.

Initially, coffee remained the domain of the *Speziali* (Apothecaries). They sold the roasted beans as a high-priced drug, arguing that because Prospero Alpini had classified it as a medicine, it fell under their strict guild monopoly. If a customer wanted coffee, they had to go to a pharmacist, describe their symptoms, and pay a premium.

But a new group of street vendors, known as the *Acquacedratari* (Lemonade and Citron Water Sellers), saw an opportunity. These vendors walked the Piazza San Marco selling cold drinks—lemonade, orgeat (almond syrup), and iced water—during the sweltering Venetian summers. They realized that their business died in the winter. Coffee was the perfect seasonal counterweight: a hot, black stimulant to sell when the fog rolled in.

The *Speziali* sued. They dragged the *Acquacedratari* before the Venetian magistrates, the *Giustizia Vecchia*, arguing that these "water peddlers" were practicing medicine without a license by dispensing a potent botanical drug.

The trial was a battle over definition. Was coffee a cure, or a food? The magistrates looked at how it was actually consumed. People weren't drinking it only when sick; they drank it to talk, to wake up, to negotiate, to linger. In a landmark ruling, the *Giustizia Vecchia* sided with the *Acquacedratari*. Coffee was declared a "foodstuff" and a "beverage," rather than a controlled substance.

This legal ruling marks the moment coffee was liberated from the medicine cabinet. It allowed the *Acquacedratari* to set up permanent structures. Wooden shacks appeared in the Piazza, then small shops. These evolved into the first *Botteghe del Caffè*.

. . .

## 1645: THE FIRST SHOP

In 1645, one of the earliest recorded European coffeehouses (outside Ottoman lands) opened in Venice. This simple shop sat under the arcades of the Procuratie Vecchie on the north side of Piazza San Marco.

It was called a *bottega del caffè*. Unlike Ottoman *Kahvehanes*, often carpeted and built for lingering, Venetian shops adapted to the city's cramped, vertical geometry. They were small, narrow, sometimes standing-room only—built for quick intake before business, a precursor to the modern Italian bar culture of drinking *al banco*.

But they quickly evolved. By 1763, a census recorded 218 coffee shops in Venice. The most famous, Caffè Florian, opened in 1720 and still stands today. These places became the living rooms of the city.

The Venetian coffeehouse developed a unique culture that differed from the later "Penny Universities" of London. In London, the coffeehouse was a place of news and sedition; in Venice, it was a place of theatrical observation. It was one of the rare places where the rigid class structure of the Republic softened. Senators in their crimson robes stood next to playwrights, gondoliers, and foreign merchants. They were "neutral ground" in a city of strict hierarchy.

## THE WAR OF THE HUMORS

While the Pope had settled the religious debate and the magistrates had settled the commercial one, the medical debate raged on for decades. The arrival of coffee threw European medicine into chaos because it did not fit the ancient models.

Seventeenth-century medicine was still tethered to the Greek theory of Humoral Pathology, popularized by Galen. The body was a balance of four humors: Blood (hot/moist), Phlegm (cold/moist), Yellow Bile (hot/dry), and Black Bile (cold/dry). Health was equilibrium; illness was an excess of one fluid.

Coffee was a nightmare to classify. It was physically hot, yet it could be cooling by inducing sweat. It was a liquid, yet it was a potent diuretic, making it "drying." This specific quality—"hot and dry"—was particularly feared in Northern Europe.

According to Galenic theory, Northern Europeans possessed bodies that were naturally 'cold and moist,' a biological mirror of their damp, chilly climates. To the 17th-century physician, this internal dampness was vital—it was the fluid of life. Physicians feared that introducing a substance as intensely 'hot and dry' as coffee would act like a kiln. The medical literature of the time is filled with genuine horror: the belief that coffee would literally desiccate the body, evaporating the spinal fluid and drying out the brain like a prune left in the sun. They warned that the heavy coffee drinker would eventually become a walking skeleton, their mind turned to dust by the 'furnace' of the roasted bean.

The medical community split into two vicious camps. The Pro-Coffee Camp argued that Europe was suffering from a plague of "moist" diseases—dropsy, lethargy, drunkenness, and catarrh (phlegm). Coffee, being a powerful drying agent, was the perfect antidote. It "dried up the mists of the brain." It cured the "drunken hangover." A pamphlet from 1671 claimed coffee could "comfort the memory" and "prevent the Sleepiness which usually happens after Meat."

The Anti-Coffee Camp, led by doctors like Simon Paulli (physician to the King of Denmark), argued the opposite. In his 1665 treatise *Commentarius de Abusu Tabaci et Herbae Thee*, Paulli warned that the extreme dryness of coffee would cause men to become impotent ("effeminating the body") and women to become barren. He famously called coffee "a kind of syrup of soot," leveraging the anxiety about ingesting a dark substance from the "torrid zones" of the earth.

The debate was settled not by science, but by experience. People drank it, and they felt clearer. The empirical evidence of the "morning buzz"—an unmistakable physiological lift—outweighed the dusty theories of Galen. The populace realized that "drying out the mists of the brain" actually felt like clarity.

## THE SILVER AND THE GLASS

One of Venice's distinct contributions to coffee culture was the refinement of the vessel. The material culture of the drink had to be reinvented for European hands and Venetian vanities.

The Turks drank from *fincan*—small porcelain cups without handles. Because porcelain conducts heat, the Turks often held these cups in metal holders called *zarfs*. When the drink arrived in Venice, the city faced a material conflict. Venice was the capital of glass, not porcelain. The artisans of Murano were producing the finest, clearest crystal in Europe, and Venetian aristocrats initially wanted to show off the color of the drink—that deep, resinous hazelnut hue.

But there was a physics problem: boiling coffee shattered delicate Murano glass (thermal shock), and even if the glass survived, it was too painful to hold.

Venice's solution reflected its characteristic opulence. Drawing on the Ottoman concept of the zarf, wealthy Venetians began serving coffee in delicate glass cups set into ornate silver holders. The metal frame allowed the hot, handle-less glass to be held comfortably while turning the act of drinking coffee into a display of craftsmanship and status. The transparency of the glass showcased the drink itself, while the silver elevated it to an object of luxury.

*The Venetian adaptation of the Ottoman zarf. A silver frame protected the drinker's fingers from the heat, while a replaceable Murano glass liner showcased the coffee's dark color.*

However, glass remained impractical for the high-volume rough-and-tumble of the street-side *botteghe*. As the craze grew, Venice was forced to import—and eventually manufacture—porcelain. By the 1700s, the Cozzi factory in Venice was churning out *chicchere* (coffee cups) painted with flowers, landscapes, and carnival scenes. Yet, they did add one distinctly European innovation to the ceramic cup, a feature the Turks had deemed unnecessary but the hurried Venetians required: the handle.

·   ·   ·

## "THE THEATER OF REALITY"

The coffeehouse became so central to Venetian life that it became a character in the theater. In 1750, the great Venetian playwright Carlo Goldoni wrote *La Bottega del Caffè* (The Coffee Shop). The entire play takes place in a single square in Venice, centered around Ridolfo's coffeehouse.

In the play, the coffeehouse becomes a kind of panopticon for the city. It is where characters go to observe others without being seen. Ridolfo, the coffee shop owner, is the all-knowing confidant. He knows who is gambling, who is cheating on their wife, and who is bankrupt.

Goldoni's play captured the sociological truth of the *bottega*. It functioned as a system of constant observation. In a city as small and dense as Venice (population roughly 140,000 squeezed onto islands), privacy was non-existent. The coffeehouse was where reputations were made and destroyed. It was a "theater of reality" where the mask of the Carnival was often slipped off, revealing the true face of the debtor or the lover. Unlike the tavern, where drunkenness blurred the truth, the coffeehouse was a place of hyper-clarity. Everyone was awake. Everyone was watching.

## THE INNOVATION OF MILK

As coffee embedded itself in Italian life, the beverage itself began to change. The Italians respected the Turkish method, but they found it harsh. The bitterness of cheaper market blends could be aggressive to palates raised on sweet wine.

In the Caffè Florian, coffee began to be served on a silver salver, accompanied by a glass of water and a small pitcher of milk. This was the birth of the *Caffè Latte*.

*Caffè Florian: The oldest coffeehouse in continuous operation in the world, established 1720.*

The Turks almost never put milk in coffee; to them, it was a corruption of the flavor profile, masking the spices and the roast. But the Europeans, with their love of dairy and their belief in milk as a "nutritive" substance, found that a small addition of fat softened the bitterness and rounded out the texture. The Capuchin friars in Vienna would later lend their name to the *Cappuccino* (because the color of the coffee-and-milk resembled the brown of their monastic robes), but the practice of mixing dairy and caffeine began in these early Italian experiments. It was a way to domesticate the "wild" taste of the Orient, making it softer, creamier, and more European.

### THE END OF THE MIDDLEMAN

For the first fifty years of the craze, Venice enjoyed a lucrative monopoly. Every bean in Europe passed through Venetian hands, bought from Ottoman merchants in Mocha or Alexandria, shipped to the Dogana, taxed, and then resold to Paris, London, and Vienna.

But the price was exorbitant. The Ottomans knew they had the Europeans hooked, and they gouged them. By 1690, a pound of coffee in Venice cost the equivalent of a week's wages. The Venetian merchants, usually the most prescient navigators of capital, committed a fatal strategic oversight. They were content to remain the masters of the *dock*, forgetting that the true power lay in the *dirt*. They treated coffee as a cargo to be taxed rather than a crop to be possessed.

To the north, the Dutch—a newer, hungrier maritime power—were watching. They saw the rivers of silver flowing from Europe into the Ottoman treasury, and they realized that the middleman is always vulnerable. They didn't want to buy the sack; they wanted to own the tree.

They realized that buying coffee from the Ottomans was a losing proposition. The real money was in ownership.

While the Venetians were busy debating the humors, serving coffee in St. Mark's Square on silver trays, and watching Goldoni plays, Dutch spies were already infiltrating the port of Mocha. They weren't looking for beans to roast; they were looking for seeds to plant.

Venice had baptized the bean, giving it the moral and cultural passport to travel the West. But Venice would not own the future of coffee. The era of the Mediterranean trade was ending. The era of the Colonial Plantation was about to begin.

Today, Venice is a museum city—sinking slowly into the lagoon. But standing at the counter of a modern *bottega*, sipping an espresso, one is participating in the oldest continuous coffee ritual in the Western world. The Pope's baptism was more than a religious loophole; it was the moment Europe chose sobriety over stupor. By legitimizing coffee, the Church inadvertently poured the foundation for a new way of thinking. This clear, bitter liquid would fuel the long hours of the scientists, philosophers, and revolutionaries of the coming century. The "Devil's Brew" did not corrupt Christendom; it catalyzed it. By swapping the morning haze of ale for the sharp clarity of caffeine, the Church inadvertently poured the chemical foundation for the very intellectual rigor that would eventually challenge its own dogmas during the Enlightenment.

5

# PENNY UNIVERSITIES: COFFEE AND CAPITALISM

T he smell of London in the mid-seventeenth century was a dense, suffocating miasma of coal smoke, open sewers, unwashed wool, and stale beer. London was a city that consumed alcohol with the regularity of breathing. Because the water from the Thames was little more than diluted sewage—polluted by the tanneries of Southwark and the butchers of Fleet Street—men, women, and children drank "small beer" or gin from morning until night. The average Londoner consumed roughly three liters of beer a day. The city functioned under a persistent, mild fog of alcohol, a chemical haze that dulled the senses, lowered the heart rate, and encouraged a certain bovine passivity.

But in a narrow, cobbled alleyway off Cornhill, known as St. Michael's Alley, a new scent began to cut through the rot. It was sharp, roasted, and pungent—the smell of burning vegetable matter. It drifted from a wooden shed run by a man named Pasqua Rosée. Rosée is often described in legends as a simple servant, but the archival record suggests he was a man of significant cosmopolitan agency. A Greek (or possibly Armenian) speaker from the Ottoman lands, he had traveled the Levant with his employer, the merchant Daniel Edwards. When they returned to London in 1651, Edwards' friends were so enamored with the dark, sobering drink he served that they began visiting *his home at all hours, disrupting his family life. Edwards' solution was to set Rosée up in a shed outside the churchyard of St. Michael's.*

*There, Rosée wore Turkish robes and a turban, a piece of theatrical branding designed to emphasize the exoticism of the product. He spent his days pounding dried berries into powder and boiling them in copper pots. The drink he served was thick, gritty, and black as ink. It was served in small bowls, unaccompanied by food. To the ale-soaked Englishmen who gathered to gawk, it looked like poison. One observer famously described it as "syrup of soot and the essence of old shoes." But those who dared to pay the single penny for a bowl found something miraculous: the fog lifted. For the first time in centuries, London was waking up.*

A City of Small Beer

The arrival of Pasqua Rosée's stall in 1652 marked the beginning of a neurological revolution in England. Comprehending the impact of coffee requires understanding the biological rhythm of the pre-caffeinated Englishman. Ale and wine are depressants. They mimic the neurotransmitter GABA, which inhibits brain activity. They are sedatives that make the afternoon sluggish and the evening blurry. Coffee is the opposite. It acts as an antagonist to adenosine, the chemical that accumulates in the brain throughout the day to signal fatigue. By blocking adenosine receptors, coffee creates a chemically induced state of alertness. It is a vasoconstrictor and a stimulant. It sharpens the focus, accelerates the heart, and creates a sense of urgent clarity.

As the habit spread from St. Michael's Alley to Fleet Street and the Strand, the effect on the city's productivity was palpable. Writers, merchants, and scientists who had previously conducted business in taverns—where deals grew fuzzier with every pint—moved their operations to the coffeehouses. The coffeehouse became the antithesis of the alehouse. The alehouse was for singing, fighting, and forgetting. The coffeehouse was for reading, debating, and remembering. It was, as the contemporary handbills proclaimed, a place where "one can be made sober for a penny." This sobriety was intellectual as well as physical. The drink provided the chemical clarity necessary for the complex mathematics of the upcoming Financial Revolution and the rigorous empiricism of the Scientific Revolution. The Enlightenment was a movement of physiology as much as ideas—a cerebral awakening fueled by a chemical shift; Europe had to sober up before it could smarten up.

### RULES ON THE WALL

The London coffeehouse was truly radical because of its democracy. In 17th-century England, society was rigidly stratified. A Duke did not dine with a draper. A scholar did not converse with a fishmonger. But the coffeehouse operated under a unique set of bylaws known as the "Rules of the Coffee House." These were often framed and hung on the wall, printed in bold type, serving as a social constitution for the space. The rules explicitly dismantled the class system for anyone who crossed the threshold. One 1674 version read: "First, gentry, tradesmen, all are welcome hither, and may without affront sit down together."

The key rule was equality of seating. "Pre-eminence of place, none here should mind, but sit in the next chair that he can find." If a Peer of the Realm walked into a coffeehouse and the only empty seat was next to a rat-catcher or a bankrupt poet, the Peer sat next to him. There were no reserved booths, no VIP sections. Furthermore, anyone who paid the entrance fee of one penny had the right to speak and be heard. If a man started a debate about the King's navy or the price of wool, anyone in the room could jump in with a counter-argument. This egalitarianism earned the coffeehouse its famous nickname: The Penny University.

*Inside the 'Penny University': A 17th-century London coffeehouse where a single penny bought a cup of coffee, the latest news, and a seat at the table regardless of social standing.*

It was said that a man could learn more in a week sitting in a coffee-house for a penny than he could in a year at Oxford for a thousand pounds. It was an open-source education system. Patrons paid their penny at the bar—where a "coffee-man" or a "boy" (often a young apprentice) presided over the great boiling pots—and took their bowl into the fray.

By 1663, there were over 80 coffeehouses in London. By the turn of the century, estimates ranged from 500 to 2,000. They were everywhere. However, patrons did not simply go to "a coffeehouse." They went to *their* coffeehouse. The network was highly specialized. For a clergyman, the destination was Child's in St. Paul's Churchyard. For a poet or a play-wright, the destination was Will's in Covent Garden, where the poet laureate John Dryden held court. (Dryden, violating the spirit of the rules, did have a specific armchair by the fireplace in winter and by the balcony in summer, which no one else dared to sit in). For a Tory politi-cian, the destination was the Cocoa Tree. For a Whig, it was the St. James's. But the most consequential nodes in this network were the houses dedicated to science and money.

DISSECTING THE DOLPHIN

For the men of science—the "Virtuosi" as they were called—the node was The Grecian in Devereux Court. The Royal Society, founded in 1660, was the official body of British science. But their formal meetings at Gresham College were often stuffy, bureaucratic affairs managed by committees. The real work happened afterwards, when members like Isaac Newton, Edmond Halley, and Hans Sloane would walk down to The Grecian to argue over coffee. The atmosphere was hands-on and notoriously messy. In the coffeehouse, science became a spectator sport.

One famous evening in the 1690s, a debate erupted between the scientists over the anatomy of a dolphin. Was it a fish or a mammal? How did its lungs work? In a tavern, this argument would have ended in a fistfight or a wager. In The Grecian, it ended in dissection. The scien-tists actually hauled a dead dolphin onto a table in the middle of the coffeehouse. While the other patrons sipped their coffee and smoked their clay pipes, Halley and his colleagues cut the creature open, exam-

ining the ventricles of the heart to prove the circulation of blood. This
was the spirit of the Penny University: empirical, public, and verifiable.

*The Grecian coffeehouse served as an informal laboratory for the Royal
Society, where Isaac Newton and his peers dissected nature amidst the
smoke and caffeine.*

It was at The Grecian that Newton likely refined his arguments for
the *Principia*. The caffeine-fueled environment encouraged "mechanical
philosophy"—a way of viewing the universe not as a divine mystery, but
as a machine that could be taken apart, understood, and debated over a
bowl of black broth. The transparency of the coffeehouse reinforced the
transparency of the scientific method: nothing was to be taken on faith;
everything had to be shown on the table.

EXCHANGE ALLEY

While the scientists dissected dolphins at The Grecian, the
merchants were dissecting debt at Jonathan's Coffee House in Exchange
Alley. In the 1690s, King William III needed massive amounts of money
to fight wars against France. The government began issuing debt (bonds)
and granting charters to joint-stock companies. The official Royal
Exchange was too polite and dignified for the rowdy mob of brokers
buying and selling these papers. So, the brokers were kicked out. They

moved across the street to a cluster of coffeehouses in a labyrinth of lanes: Jonathan's, Garraway's, and Sam's.

At Jonathan's, the "stockjobbers" created a market. This was not a refined financial institution; it was a brawl. Men stood on tables, shouting prices. Behind the bar, a blackboard listed the current price of stocks—the world's first ticker. The coffeehouse environment created the mechanisms of modern finance. Because the brokers were drinking coffee, they were awake, hyper-alert, and capable of complex mental arithmetic. They developed "Time-Bargains"—the precursors to modern futures and options contracts. A merchant could pay a premium today to buy a stock at a fixed price six months from now.

But the speed of information in the coffeehouse also fueled mania. The most catastrophic example was the South Sea Bubble of 1720. The South Sea Company was a trade monopoly that promised immense riches from Spanish America. In reality, it was a Ponzi scheme. But the atmosphere of Jonathan's fueled the viral spread of FOMO (Fear Of Missing Out). Rumors spread through the room like a contagion. "The King of Spain has granted a new port!" "Dividends will be 50%!" Peers of the realm, scullery maids, and even Isaac Newton himself crammed into Jonathan's to buy shares. The price went from £100 in January 1720 to £1,000 in August. Bogus companies sprang up to take advantage of the frenzy. There was a subscription for a company "for carrying on an undertaking of great advantage, but nobody to know what it is." People bought it. When the bubble burst in September 1720, Jonathan's was the scene of ruin. The stock crashed back to £100. Newton lost £20,000 (millions in today's money), leading him to famously remark, "I can calculate the motions of the heavenly bodies, but not the madness of people." The crash led to the "Bubble Act," which regulated the market, but the precedent was set. Jonathan's was the stock exchange. It wasn't until 1773 that the brokers finally raised enough money to build their own building, which they creatively named "New Jonathan's" before eventually rebranding it as the London Stock Exchange.

## PIN AND CANDLE

A few streets away, near the Tower of London, sat a coffeehouse run by a man named Edward Lloyd. Lloyd catered to a specific crowd: captains, shipowners, and mercantile traders whose fortunes floated on wood and canvas. These men faced a terrifying variable: risk. Sending a ship to the Levant or the Indies was not commerce so much as a wager. Storms, privateers, war, and simple navigation errors could turn a voyage into a total write-off. A place that could trade reliable information—and share that risk—was worth more than the coffee itself.

To mitigate this, they developed the mechanism of Marine Insurance. In the 1680s, there were no massive insurance corporations. Insurance was a personal bet between individuals. A merchant would write the name of his ship, its cargo, and its destination on a piece of paper. He would bring it to Lloyd's and put it on a table. Wealthy individuals—sitting in the booths drinking coffee—would look at the paper. If they liked the odds, they would write their name under the details (hence the term "Underwriter") and the amount they were willing to cover. If the ship sank, they paid. If it returned, they kept the premium. Edward Lloyd acted as a data broker rather than an insurer. He hired a network of "runners" to visit every dock in London and bring back news of arrivals, departures, and shipwrecks. He published this intelligence in a newsletter called *Lloyd's List*, which is still published today.

The most dramatic ritual at Lloyd's was the "Candle Auction". When a captured French prize ship or a damaged cargo needed to be sold quickly, the auctioneer would not use a gavel. He would light a short stub of a candle—usually just an inch long. He would insert a metal pin into the side of the wax, a fraction of an inch from the top. Bidding began. The coffeehouse would fall silent, eyes fixed on the flame. As the wax melted, the flame drew closer to the pin. The bidding would become frantic as the pool of wax widened. The psychological pressure of the melting wax was intense. It was a visible timer that could not be argued with. The moment the flame reached the pin, and the pin fell onto the table with a tiny clink (or the flame sputtered out), the auction was over.

*The "Candle Auction" at Lloyd's: bidding continued only as long as the flame burned, ending the moment the pin dropped.*

The last bid made before the pin dropped was final. This high-tension, caffeine-fueled mechanism allowed millions of pounds of merchandise to move with brutal efficiency. From this coffeehouse grew Lloyd's of London, the insurance market that today underwrites everything from oil rigs to satellites.

### "Useless Corpses"

There was one demographic notably absent from the Penny University: Women. Unlike the alehouse, where women often served as barmaids or drank alongside men, the London coffeehouse was an exclusively male domain. It was a "monastery of the mind." Men would spend hours there, neglecting their work and their families, returning home wired and talkative late at night. This stood in stark contrast to the burgeoning café culture in Paris and Venice, where women were increasingly welcomed into the social fabric of the coffeehouse, allowing for a mixed-gender public sphere that London stubbornly rejected.

In 1674, the wives of London struck back. They published a scathing, satirical pamphlet titled *The Women's Petition Against Coffee*. It is a masterpiece of vitriol that reveals the deep sexual anxiety provoked by the new drug. The women argued that coffee was turning their virile, ale-drinking husbands into effeminate, chattering "Frenchmen."

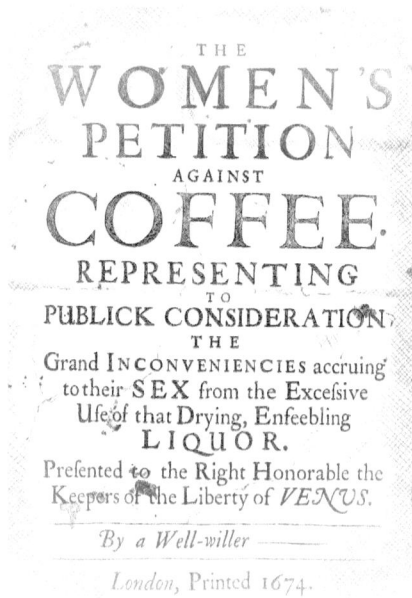

THE

# WOMEN'S
## PETITION
### AGAINST
# COFFEE.
### REPRESENTING
TO
## PUBLICK CONSIDERATION
THE
Grand INCONVENIENCIES accruing
to their SEX from the Excesive
Use of that Drying, Enfeebling
LIQUOR.
Presented to the Right Honorable the
Keepers of the Liberty of VENUS.

*By a Well-willer* ————

*London,* Printed 1674.

*The Women's Petition Against Coffee: Arguing the bean was 'desiccating
the male seed' and ruining English masculinity.*

They attacked the drink's effect on the libido, claiming that the drying
nature of coffee (a reference to the Galenic humors) was desiccating the
male seed. The pamphlet accused the drink of turning Englishmen into
"mere Cock-sparrows." It complained that coffee had "so Eunucht our
Husbands, and cripple our more kind Gallants" that they had become as
"unfruitful as those Deserts whence that unhappy Berry is said to be
brought." They famously referred to their husbands as "useless corpses"
who carried nothing but a "nose" (a reference to the snuff taking that
often accompanied coffee). The men responded with *The Men's Answer to
the Women's Petition*, arguing that coffee actually improved their stamina
by keeping them awake and making their "spirits" rise. But the gender
divide remained. While continental coffeehouses evolved, the London
coffeehouse remained a fraternity. It would take another century—and
the rise of Tea—for women to claim an equal place in the British hot
beverage culture.

. . .

THE KING'S PANIC

The only person who hated coffeehouses more than the wives was King Charles II. The King had been restored to the throne in 1660 after the chaos of the Civil War and Cromwell's republic. He was terrified of sedition. He knew that the plot to kill his father (Charles I) had been hatched in taverns, but the new plots were being hatched in coffeehouses. His spies—a network of informants paid to drink coffee and listen—reported that men were openly criticizing the Crown, debating republicanism, and mocking the King's mistresses. The coffeehouse was a "Seminary of Sedition." It was an uncontrolled media environment where news traveled faster than the royal censors could catch it.

On December 29, 1675, Charles II issued a Proclamation for the Suppression of Coffee Houses. The text was explicit. It stated that coffeehouses were the resort of "idle and disaffected persons" and that they had produced "very evil and dangerous effects" by spreading "false, malicious, and scandalous reports." He ordered every coffeehouse in London to close its doors by January 10th. He banned the sale of coffee, chocolate, sherbet, and tea in public.

It was a massive political miscalculation. The backlash was instantaneous and universal. It wasn't just the radicals who were angry; it was the King's own base. The Tories, the merchants, and the aristocrats all loved their coffee. They relied on it for news, for insurance, and for stock prices. To close the coffeehouses was to shut down the commercial operating system of London. Petitions flooded the palace. The King's ministers warned him that he might face another revolution. The mechanism of the coffeehouse had become too integrated into the economy to be removed. On January 8, 1676—two days before the ban was set to take effect—Charles II backed down.

He "indefinitely postponed" the ban. It was a humiliation for the Crown, but a victory for the bean. It proved that the Coffee House was now a "Fourth Estate," a power center that even the Monarchy could not dismantle.

By the King.

# A PROCLAMATION

FOR THE

## Suppreſſion of Coffee-Houſes.

CHARLES R.

God ſave the King.

*LONDON.*

Printed by the Aſſigns of *John Bill* and *Chriſtopher Barker*, Printers to the Kings moſt Excellent Majeſty. 1675.

*The document that almost caused a revolution: King Charles II's order to close the 'commercial operating system' of London.*

## THE INFORMATION NETWORK

The coffeehouse was also the physical infrastructure of the mail system. Before street addresses were standardized, if a writer wished to reach a man in London, they didn't write to his house (which might be hard to find in the unplanned sprawl). They wrote to his coffeehouse. A letter addressed to "Mr. Isaac Newton, c/o The Grecian Coffee House" would be delivered there and pinned to a board behind the bar or tucked into a wooden rack. Men "checked their inbox" by visiting their favorite coffeehouse daily.

This created a primitive form of "Packet Switching." Runners—young boys paid a pittance—would carry bags of mail and newsletters from Will's to the Grecian to Lloyd's multiple times a day. The system was incredibly fast; a runner could navigate the crowded lanes from the Temple Bar to the Royal Exchange in under fifteen minutes, ensuring that stock prices and shipping news propagated across the entire commercial district within the hour. Foreign newspapers were translated aloud by linguists hired by the coffeehouse owners. If a ship arrived in Dover with news from France, the letter would be rushed to the coffee-houses first. It was a physical network of intelligence, buzzing with data packets moving at the speed of a running boy.

## The Retreat to Privacy

So why did the Golden Age end? By 1750, the London coffeehouse began to die out, replaced by a new institution: the Private Gentlemen's Club. The egalitarianism that made the coffeehouse great eventually killed it. As the British Empire grew and the merchant class became fabulously wealthy, the "Rules of the Coffee House" became irksome. The upper classes grew tired of sitting next to the fishmonger and the noisy stockjobber. They wanted privacy. They wanted exclusivity. Famous coffeehouses like White's and Boodle's installed doormen. They instituted membership fees and ballots. They stopped letting the public in for a penny. They became "Members Only" clubs, where a man could be sure he was surrounded only by his peers.

Simultaneously, the British East India Company began pushing a different drug: Tea. Tea was easier to make at home (no roasting or grinding required). It was socially acceptable for women. It moved the caffeine ritual from the rowdy, masculine public sphere of the coffee-house to the polite, domestic sphere of the drawing room. The "Penny University" closed its doors. The open debate ended, and the class system reasserted itself. But the damage—or rather, the progress—was done. In those hundred years of caffeine-fueled meritocracy, England had invented the stock market, the insurance industry, the free press, and Newtonian physics. Many modern institutions trace their origins to a coffee-stained table in a London alley.

# PART II

## SEEDS OF EMPIRE

Coffee did not conquer the world by accident. It was carried—sometimes lovingly, often violently—by empires that understood the value of controlling both plants and people.

This section follows coffee as it is smuggled, transplanted, and scaled. The bean becomes a colonial prize, guarded like a weapon and stolen like one. It moves through botanic gardens and naval ships, into islands and mountains where the work of cultivation is rarely romantic. Coffee becomes entangled with sugar, slavery, and the economics of extraction. It also becomes political: drinks change with revolutions, and revolutions change what the world drinks.

By the end of these chapters, coffee is no longer only a story of origin. It is a story of ownership.

# 6

## THE SEVEN SEEDS: BREAKING
## THE OTTOMAN MONOPOLY

*he Customs House at the port of Al-Makha (Mocha) in the mid-17th century operated primarily as a biological sterilization facility. Every bag of green coffee beans destined for export was subjected to a rigorous and paranoid inspection designed to ensure that Yemen remained the sole producer of the commodity. Ottoman guards, armed with scimitars and acting on the Sultan's strict edicts, oversaw a process designed to prevent agricultural theft. Before a single sack could be loaded onto a Dutch fluyt or an Indian dhow, the beans had to be processed to neutralize the germ. Sometimes they were steeped in boiling water; other times they were parched on hot iron plates. This thermal shock turned the living seed into a dead commodity. A Mocha bean could be ground, brewed, and drunk, but it could never be planted.*

*For two hundred years, this Ottoman Embargo held. The Ottomans understood the concept of intellectual property long before the term existed. They knew that if a single viable seed escaped the terraced mountains of Yemen, their monopoly—which poured tax revenue into the treasury in Istanbul—would evaporate. The penalty for smuggling live plants was death. Yet, around the year 1600, a lone figure walked through the gates of the port. He was not a merchant or a soldier; he was a pilgrim. He wore the rough, dusty robes of a Sufi mystic returning from the Hajj. His name was Baba Budan. The guards, perhaps deferring to his holy status, or perhaps simply careless in the relentless*

*heat of the Red Sea coast, did not conduct a strip search. If they had, they*
*would have found the seeds of a global industry secured against his skin.*


## THE PILGRIM'S BELT

Baba Budan is a figure who straddles the line between history and myth. In the oral traditions of Karnataka, he was a Sufi saint from India named Dada Hayat who had undertaken the treacherous journey to Mecca. On his return journey, he traveled through the Yemeni highlands. There, in the mosques and zawiyas where the Shadhili order practiced their *dhikr* (remembrance of God), he encountered the "Wine of Islam." For a mystic, the drink served as a functional tool for prolonged prayer, a chemical bridge to the divine that allowed the faithful to keep vigil long into the night. Baba Budan believed that such a gift belonged to all the faithful, not just the Arabs. The Ottoman monopoly, to him, was not just economic greed; it was spiritual hoarding.

Legend says that Baba Budan resolved to take the "holy bean" back to his homeland in India. He knew the risks. He knew that if caught, he could be beheaded. So, he improvised. He selected seven fertile, red coffee cherries—fresh from the tree, the mucilage still sticky and sweet. He knew that a pocket or a saddlebag was a death sentence; the Ottoman guards at the port searched luggage with the thoroughness of men protecting a state secret. Instead, he strapped the seeds directly to his abdomen, binding them tight against his skin with a rough cloth sash.

This placement was a masterstroke of both espionage and biology. As he walked past the scimitars of the customs agents, the seeds were invisible, but they were also alive. The constant warmth of his skin acted as a living incubator, maintaining the humid, tropical microclimate the embryos needed to survive the arid desert crossing. Every bead of sweat produced by his fear or the heat of the journey served to keep the mucilage moist. He was not just smuggling cargo; he had become a human greenhouse, carrying the genetic future of the global coffee industry inches from his navel.

*Baba Budan broke the Ottoman monopoly by securing fertile seeds against his skin for the journey to India.*

The number seven was not accidental. In Islam, seven is a sacred number—the seven heavens, the seven verses of the Al-Fatiha, the seven circumambulations of the Kaaba during the Hajj. By taking seven seeds, he was turning the act of smuggling into a religious talisman. He walked out of Yemen and survived the sea voyage across the Indian Ocean—a journey of weeks where the sweat and heat of his body kept the seeds warm and moist, acting as a living incubator. This was crucial because coffee seeds are recalcitrant; unlike grain, they lose viability rapidly if their moisture content drops below a critical threshold. When he arrived back in his home village in the princely state of Mysore, he walked up into the Chandragiri Hills. There, near a mountain cave that would become his shrine, he planted the seven seeds, and they successfully took root.

### THE FIRST ESTATE: CHIKMAGALUR

The trees associated with Baba Budan's legend are among the earliest documented coffee plantings outside Africa and the Arabian Peninsula. They found a second home in the red laterite soil and heavy monsoon rains of the Western Ghats, where coffee could be grown not as contraband, but as agriculture. This region, now known as Chikmagalur ("The Town of the Younger Daughter"), became the cradle of Indian coffee.

The specific variety he planted—an ancient Arabica lineage—is still known by botanists today as "Old Chikmagalur."

Unlike the arid, rocky terraces of Yemen, where coffee struggled for water and grew in harsh sunlight, the Indian mountains were lush, tropical jungles. The microclimate of Chikmagalur, with its distinct wet and dry seasons and high-altitude coolness, allowed the trees to thrive without irrigation. The coffee here had to adapt. It grew in the shade of giant fig, jackfruit, and silver oak trees. This created a new agricultural model: Shade-Grown Coffee. The shade protected the coffee from the intense tropical sun, slowing down the maturation of the cherry. This slower growth allowed the beans to develop more sugar and density. The soil, rich with decaying leaves and spiced by nearby pepper vines and cardamom plants, imparted a distinct flavor profile: heavy, spicy, chocolatey, and low-acid.

For decades, this Indian coffee remained a local secret. It was a backyard crop, consumed by the locals and the pilgrims who visited Baba Budan's shrine. It didn't immediately dismantle the Ottoman monopoly because there was no export infrastructure. The seeds were free, but they were isolated. To turn this botanical breach into a global industry, it would take a different kind of smuggler—not a mystic, but a corporation.

## THE CORPORATE SPY

While Baba Budan was planting seeds for God, the Dutch East India Company (Verenigde Oostindische Compagnie, or VOC) was looking for seeds for profit. The VOC was the most powerful economic engine the world had ever seen. It was the first multinational corporation, the first to issue stock, and it possessed its own private army and navy. It operated with a scale and ruthlessness that eclipsed many national governments, controlling the spice trade (nutmeg, cloves, pepper) with an iron fist. But by 1690, the Dutch directors (the "Heeren XVII" or Gentlemen Seventeen) had realized that the spice market was saturated. They needed a new commodity. They looked at the coffee trade in Mocha, where they were paying exorbitant prices to Ottoman middlemen, and decided they wanted to own the means of production. Rather than buying coffee, they intended to grow it.

*Merchant-explorer Pieter van den Broecke presents a coffee seedling to the "Heeren XVII" (Gentlemen Seventeen). After failed attempts to grow the plant in cold Amsterdam greenhouses, the VOC decided to move production to their colony in Java.*

Their point man was Pieter van den Broecke, a merchant-explorer who had visited Mocha as early as 1616. He was one of the first Europeans to taste the drink and, crucially, to see the tree. He managed to steal a few seedlings, but his early attempts to cultivate them in the cold greenhouses of Amsterdam failed. The Dutch climate was too harsh; the plants froze and died. The VOC realized they needed a tropical laboratory. They looked to their new colony in the East Indies: Java (modern-day Indonesia).

### THE MALABAR TRANSFER

The Dutch didn't get their production-scale seeds from Yemen. The security there was still too tight. Instead, they got them from India. In 1696, Adrian van Ommen, the Dutch Commander of Malabar (the southwest coast of India, near where Baba Budan had lived), secured coffee seedlings from the local descendants of Baba Budan's trees. This is the crucial link in the chain: the Sufi mystic broke the seal, and the Dutch corporation widened the breach.

Van Ommen sent the seedlings to Batavia (Jakarta), the headquarters of the VOC in Asia. They were planted in the garden of the Governor-General, Willem van Outhoorn, at a profound estate called Kedawoeng. The first crop was a disaster. In 1699, a massive earthquake and flood hit Batavia, washing away the young trees. Undeterred, the Dutch simply ordered more seeds from Malabar. This time, they moved the plantations to higher ground, into the volcanic foothills of West Java, in the Preanger region.

The result was a rapid agricultural expansion. The volcanic soil of Java, combined with the humid equatorial heat, acted like a super-fertilizer. The trees grew faster and produced more fruit than they ever had in Yemen. By 1711, the first commercial shipment of "Java Coffee" arrived in Amsterdam. It was 894 pounds (405 kg). By 1724, the VOC was shipping 2 million pounds (approx. 907,000 kg) a year.

## "Tasted of Tears"

The success of Java coffee was built on a system of brutal exploitation that makes the Ottoman monopoly look benign. The Ottomans had taxed the farmers; the Dutch enslaved them. The VOC instituted the *Cultuurstelsel* (Cultivation System). They forced the local Javanese regents (princes) to deliver a fixed quota of coffee beans every year as a form of tax. The regents, in turn, forced their peasants to clear the rainforests and plant coffee instead of rice.

This resulted in a humanitarian catastrophe; the peasants, forced to tend the Company's coffee trees, had no time to grow food for their families, and famines swept through Java. The price of coffee in Amsterdam was inversely proportional to the caloric intake of the Javanese farmer. This exploitation remained largely hidden from the European public until 1860, when a former colonial administrator named Eduard Douwes Dekker (writing under the pseudonym Multatuli, Latin for "I have suffered much") published a novel called *Max Havelaar: Or the Coffee Auctions of the Dutch Trading Company*. It was the *Uncle Tom's Cabin* of coffee. The book exposed the hypocrisy of the Dutch bourgeoisie, who grew rich on coffee profits while the Javanese starved. Multatuli famously wrote that the coffee served in Amsterdam "tasted of tears." The book caused a political storm in the Netherlands, eventually leading to the reform (though not the immediate end) of the Cultivation System, and the phrase "A Cup of Java" entered the English lexicon as a synonym for coffee.

## The Grandfather Tree

While the plantations of Java churned out the commodity, the VOC did something else—something scientific—that would shape the genetics of coffee for the next three centuries. In 1706, a single, healthy coffee plant was dug up from the Javanese estate and put on a ship to Amsterdam. It was treated like royalty. It was kept on deck, shielded from the salt spray, and watered daily. It arrived in Amsterdam and was planted in the Hortus Botanicus, the city's botanical garden. It was placed in a heated greenhouse.

This single tree—let's call it the Amsterdam Patriarch—is the genetic father of almost every coffee tree in the Western Hemisphere. Because *Coffea arabica* is self-pollinating (autogamous), you only need one tree to start a world. The botanists at the Hortus successfully harvested seeds from this patriarch and began to clone it. This tree is the historical bottleneck. Before this moment, coffee had the genetic diversity of the Ethiopian forests and the Yemeni terraces. After this moment, the coffee that would conquer the world was essentially a clone of a clone of a single plant that survived a boat ride in 1706.

### THE SURINAME DETOUR

Before coffee reached the Caribbean, it made a crucial logistical pit stop in South America. In 1718, the Dutch took seeds from the Amsterdam Patriarch and transported them to their colony of Suriname (Dutch Guiana) on the northeast coast of South America. This was the first time the coffee plant touched the soil of the Americas. The Suriname plantations were wildly successful, but they were guarded with the same paranoia as the Yemeni mountains. The Dutch instituted the death penalty for anyone caught smuggling seeds out of Suriname. They wanted to keep the American monopoly for themselves. But, as history shows, coffee wants to travel.

### THE KING'S TOY

Meanwhile, in Europe, coffee diplomacy was at work. In 1714, the Mayor of Amsterdam, trying to curry diplomatic favor and end the hostilities of the War of the Spanish Succession, gifted a healthy offspring of the Amsterdam Patriarch to King Louis XIV of France. Louis

XIV, the Sun King, was not a man who liked to be outdone by Dutch merchants. He received the tree at his palace. But the French winters were cruel. The King commissioned the construction of the first modern heated greenhouse (the *Serre*) at the Jardin des Plantes in Paris specifically to keep this coffee tree alive. It became a celebrated object. Aristocrats would visit the garden to look at the "Noble Tree" (*L'Arbre Noble*). It was a curiosity, a status symbol. But one man looked at that tree and saw something else. He saw the potential for a French empire. His name was Gabriel de Clieu.

## THE GLASS CASE

De Clieu was a French naval officer stationed in Martinique, a French colony in the Caribbean. He was visiting Paris on leave in 1723. He knew that Martinique had the perfect climate for coffee. He just needed a seed. He asked the Royal Botanist for a cutting from the King's tree. The Botanist refused. The tree was royal property; it was not for common sailors. De Clieu did not give up. While some accounts suggest a "Dutch Spy" level heist, it is possible this narrative was a literary invention of De Clieu's own memoirs to heighten his prestige. Regardless of the method—bribery or theft—he smuggled a seedling aboard his ship.

To protect the plant, he constructed a glass case to house it on deck. This device was an antecedent to the Wardian Case, designed to trap moisture and protect the leaves from the corrosive salt spray while allowing sunlight to penetrate. The fraught voyage back to Martinique was a nightmare. The ship was attacked by Tunisian pirates (De Clieu fought them off, reportedly saber in hand). Then, the ship hit the "Horse Latitudes"—a zone of dead calm. They drifted for weeks. Water ran out.

The crew went on strict water rations. De Clieu kept his "green passenger" alive by dividing his own daily allowance. The melodrama of his memoirs emphasizes the sacrifice, but the botanical reality was a calculation of investment. He arrived in Martinique with the plant shriveled and yellow, but alive. He planted it in his garden, surrounded it with thorns, and set a guard to watch it 24/7.

*Once on land, the first tree in Martinique was guarded like a prisoner of state to prevent theft by rivals.*

It grew. Within two years, it bore fruit. De Clieu distributed the seeds to his friends. Within 50 years, there were 18 million coffee trees on Martinique.

## THE BRAZILIAN SEDUCTION

The Dutch had Suriname. The French had Martinique. The Portuguese, who controlled the massive territory of Brazil, had nothing. They watched their neighbors getting rich and grew desperate. In 1727, the Governor of Brazil dispatched a charming, dashing army officer named Francisco de Melo Palheta to French Guiana. His official mission was to mediate a trivial border dispute between the French and the Dutch. His secret mission was to get some coffee seeds by any means necessary.

The French Governor in Guiana, Claude d'Orvilliers, was under strict orders not to let a single seed leave the colony. He refused Palheta's requests. So, Palheta turned to Plan B: **Social Engineering**. He focused his attentions on the Governor's wife, Madame d'Orvilliers. He was a man of great charm and military bearing. During the weeks of the diplomatic negotiations, he wooed her at state dinners and garden walks. Whether it was a genuine romance or a calculated act of espionage, it worked.

On the day of Palheta's departure, a state banquet was held. As he prepared to board his ship back to Brazil, Madame d'Orvilliers presented him with a parting gift: a large, beautiful bouquet of flowers. She handed it to him in front of her husband. The Governor smiled, seeing only a polite gesture. He did not know that buried deep inside the bouquet, hidden among the blooms, were viable coffee seedlings (or, by some accounts, a handful of fertile red cherries).

*The Brazilian coffee empire began with an act of espionage disguised as a romantic gesture in French Guiana.*

Palheta bowed, took the flowers, and sailed for Brazil. He planted the seeds in the state of Pará. From that illicit bouquet grew the Brazilian coffee industry, which today produces one-third of the world's coffee supply. The entire economy of Brazil was founded on a bouquet of stolen flowers given by a Governor's wife to her lover.

### THE GENETIC BOTTLENECK

This sequence of heists—Baba Budan to India, Dutch to Java, Java to Amsterdam, Amsterdam to Paris, Paris to Martinique, and Guiana to Brazil—reveals a terrifying scientific reality. Almost all the coffee in the Americas (the Typica variety) is descended from that one tree in the Amsterdam greenhouse. The genetic diversity of Latin American coffee is effectively zero. It is an inbred lineage. The billions of trees in Brazil and Colombia are all clones of the Amsterdam Patriarch.

This is why coffee is so susceptible to diseases like Leaf Rust (*Hemileia vastatrix*). It has no genetic variation to fight back. The "Great Heist" of the 18th century succeeded in spreading the crop to every corner of the tropics, but it created a fragile empire—a monoculture built on a single, lonely seed. By 1730, the Ottoman monopoly was dead. Yemen went from being the only producer to a minor player. The center of gravity had shifted to the colonial empires of the Dutch, the French, and the Portuguese. The port of Mocha began its slow decline into the silted ruin it is today. But in the hills of India, the shrine of Baba Budan still stands. Pilgrims—both Hindu and Muslim—still climb the mountain to leave offerings. They don't leave gold or flowers. They leave small sachets of coffee beans, a tribute to the man who realized that a seed, like a prayer, is meant to be scattered.

# 7

# THE GLASS CASE: DE CLIEU TO MARTINIQUE

T he winter of 1723 in Paris was a gray misery of sleet and coal smoke that coated the gargoyles of Notre Dame in ice. The city was a landscape of frozen mud and shivering stone, but inside the royal greenhouses of the Jardin du Roi (the King's Garden, now the Jardin des Plantes), the air was thick, humid, and smelled of the tropics. The source of this artificial summer was a marvel of 18th-century engineering: the Serre, one of the first glass-paned hothouses of its kind in Europe, heated by coal-fired stoves that required constant stoking to maintain a temperature that would not kill the King's most exotic treasures.

Inside this crystal palace, surrounded by Swiss Guards and tended to by the royal botanist Antoine de Jussieu, stood a celebrity. It was a tree, roughly 1.5 meters (five feet) tall, with glossy, dark green leaves and clusters of white, jasmine-scented flowers. This was the Arbre Noble—the Noble Tree. It was the direct offspring of the "Amsterdam Patriarch," the plant gifted to Louis XIV by the Mayor of Amsterdam a decade earlier. It was the only coffee tree in France, and in the eyes of the state, it was not a plant; it was a diplomatic asset.

Standing outside the glass, pressing his face against the condensation on the pane, was Gabriel de Clieu. Neither courtier, scientist, nor diplomat, De Clieu was a naval officer—a Captain of Infantry stationed in the colony of Martinique. De Clieu was a man of the Enlightenment—pragmatic, patriotic, and obstinate. While Jussieu looked at the tree and saw a botanical specimen to be cataloged—a trophy of the King's reach—De Clieu looked at it and saw an economy.

He knew that the sugar plantations of Martinique were struggling. The soil was exhausting under the monoculture of cane, and the island needed a diversification of assets. He knew the soil of the Caribbean was chemically identical to the volcanic loam of Java where the Dutch were making millions. He intended to acquire a cutting. But taking a tropical plant from a heated Parisian greenhouse and transporting it 6,500 kilometers (4,000 miles) across the Atlantic on a wooden sailing ship was not just a crime against the Crown; it was a logistical impossibility.

De Clieu began through official channels. He petitioned the Regent of France (Louis XV was still a boy) and the Royal Academy of Sciences. He argued that introducing coffee to the French West Indies would break the Dutch monopoly and fill the coffers of the state. His logic was sound—mercantile and strategic—but the bureaucracy was immovable. The head of the Jardin, Monsieur de Chirac, was a jealous guardian. He viewed the coffee tree as a scientific curiosity to be studied, not a crop to be commercialized. He flatly refused to cut a slip from the royal plant for a "mere colonial captain." To Chirac, the tree was a symbol of prestige; to cut it was to diminish it.

De Clieu, however, was not a man who accepted refusal. In his memoirs, published decades later in the Année Littéraire, he is coy about the details, but historical consensus suggests a raid. He didn't break in himself; he used the leverage of the bedroom. He enlisted the help of a lady of the court—some sources say it was a mistress of Monsieur de Chirac, others say a rival noblewoman—to exert pressure. Whether by seduction, bribery, or a quiet entry into the greenhouse facilitated by a compromised guard, the result was the same. One night in May 1723, De Clieu obtained a small, rooted cutting from the Noble Tree.

He had the prize. Now, he had to keep it alive in a wooden world of salt and rot.

THE WARDIAN PROTOTYPE

De Clieu was a sailor. He understood the Atlantic, and he knew that the environment of a ship was hostile to terrestrial life. The primary killer was salt. Ocean spray contains sodium chloride, which is lethal to *Coffea arabica*. If salt water lands on the leaves, it creates a hypertonic environment, drawing moisture out of the plant cells through osmosis, causing immediate chemical burns and leaf drop. Beyond the salt, the physical force of the winds in the Bay of Biscay would fracture a delicate sapling, and the shifting temperatures—from the freezing gales of the north to the scorching heat of the Tropic of Cancer—would shock the root system into dormancy or death.

He needed a life-support system. De Clieu commissioned a custom-built vessel for his passenger. It was a heavy wooden box with a wedge-shaped glass front—essentially a portable greenhouse.

*De Clieu engineered a sealed microclimate to protect the plant from salt spray and dehydration during the Atlantic crossing.*

This device was a visionary precursor to the Wardian Case, the sealed terrarium invented by Dr. Nathaniel Ward a century later that would eventually allow the British to transport tea from China and rubber from Brazil. De Clieu, however, was improvising the technology 100 years early, relying on intuition instead of established botany.

The design of De Clieu's box was ingenious, functioning as a proto-Wardian case long before the term existed. The glass front allowed the plant to photosynthesize, capturing the sunlight essential for sugar production. But the key innovation was the microclimate it created. The sealed environment established a closed hydrological loop. As the plant "breathed" through the stomata on the undersides of its leaves (transpiration), water vapor would rise, hit the cool glass, condense, and drip back down into the soil—a miniature water cycle that recycled ninety percent of the plant's moisture. This meant the plant needed significantly less fresh water than if it were exposed to the desiccating trade winds—a crucial feature on a ship where fresh water was more valuable than rum and strictly rationed.

*Gabriel de Clieu, who guarded the original sapling day and night before distributing its seeds to found the island's coffee industry.*

The construction required precision. The wood had to be tarred to prevent rot from the sea air, but the tar could not touch the soil, lest it leach toxic chemicals into the roots. The glass had to be thick enough to withstand a rogue wave but clear enough to admit the weak light of the lantern-lit cabin. To combat the motion of the ship, the box was heavily weighted at the bottom with lead ingots. This lowered the center of gravity, ensuring that as the ship pitched and rolled in heavy seas, the box might slide across the floorboards, but it would not tip over, preserving the integrity of the root ball.

With his "green passenger" secured in its glass stateroom, De Clieu boarded the merchant ship *Le Dromadaire* at the port of Nantes. He did not check the plant into the cargo hold, where rats and darkness would have killed it in days. He kept it in his cabin, fastened to the floorboards, sleeping next to it like a father watching a feverish child.

## "A Man Who Spoke Dutch"

The voyage of *Le Dromadaire* reads less like a botanical log and more like a fraught voyage. De Clieu writes in his journal that he was not the only one interested in the plant. There was a fellow passenger on board —De Clieu never names him, referring to him only as a man who "spoke Dutch" and seemed envious of the potential glory the plant represented.

Historians have long debated the identity of this antagonist. Was he a corporate spy for the Dutch East India Company (VOC)? It is possible. The Dutch were fiercely protective of their monopoly, executing smugglers in Java and guarding the price of coffee in Amsterdam. Their intelligence network was vast. A French officer carrying a live specimen of the "Money Tree" to the Caribbean would have been a high-priority target for sabotage.

However, modern historians suggest this "Dutch Spy" might be a literary invention of De Clieu's memoirs—a narrative device to heighten the heroism of his struggle and personify the geopolitical stakes. Alternatively, he may have been a rival French officer or a jilted lover of the noblewoman who helped De Clieu, seeking petty revenge.

Whatever his motive or reality, the tension in the cabin escalated into psychological warfare. De Clieu claimed this man tried to sabotage the plant repeatedly. On one occasion, the man "accidentally" stumbled during a swell, falling onto the box and attempting to fracture the glass frame with his elbow. On another, De Clieu caught him attempting to pour a flask of liquid into the soil. Had it been seawater, the sodium would have sterilized the soil and killed the roots within hours.

The paranoia was palpable. De Clieu stopped sleeping for more than an hour at a time. He moved the glass case to different spots in his cabin every night to throw off his cabin-mate. He began carrying his sword at all times, even when wiping condensation from the glass leaves. The coffee tree had become a VIP under assassination threat, and De Clieu found himself in the position of a bodyguard protecting a head of state.

## Corsairs and Calms

As the ship sailed south past the coast of Spain and toward North Africa, a new threat appeared on the horizon: The Barbary Pirates.

A Tunisian corsair vessel, faster and more heavily armed than the lumbering merchantman *Dromadaire*, closed in. The pirates of the Barbary Coast were notorious not just for cargo theft, but for human trafficking. They wanted the crew. Being captured meant a life of rowing in a galley or hard labor in the stone quarries of Algiers.

The *Dromadaire* prepared for battle. Cannons were run out; muskets were loaded. De Clieu, a trained infantry officer, took his post on the deck. But before he joined the fight, he secured the glass case in the safest part of the ship—likely the carpenter's hold deep below the waterline—padding it with wool blankets to dampen the shock of cannon fire. The reverberations of a broadside can shatter glass as easily as a hammer; De Clieu had to insulate the box from the ship's own defense.

The battle was brief but intense. Cannon fire was exchanged, damaging the rigging and sending splinters of oak flying across the deck. The French crew managed to repel the boarding party, killing several pirates and dismasting the corsair ship enough to make an escape. De Clieu survived the skirmish, but he didn't check his own wounds first. He ran to check the box. The glass was intact. The plant was shaken, perhaps a few leaves torn by the vibrations, but alive.

The pirate attack was dramatic, but the real danger was the silence that followed.

The ship entered the Horse Latitudes—a band of high pressure in the mid-Atlantic notorious for dead calms. The wind died. The sails hung limp, slapping uselessly against the masts. The *Dromadaire* drifted aimlessly for weeks. The sea became a mirror of oil, reflecting the brutal tropical sun until the horizon disappeared in a haze of heat.

On a sailing ship, time is measured in water. As the voyage stretched from weeks into a month of stagnation, the water barrels began to run dry. The cooper checked the levels daily, his face growing grimmer. The water that remained was "ropey"—thick with algae and crawling with weevils. Finally, the captain issued the dreaded order: strict rationing.

The crew was reduced to roughly 0.5 liters (a pint) of water a day. Then half a pint. In the tropical heat, this was barely enough to sustain life. Men's lips cracked; tongues swelled in their mouths. The psychological strain of thirst began to set in, a delirium that makes rational thought difficult. The kidneys begin to shut down, concentrating urine into a dark, toxic sludge. The blood thickens, straining the heart.

The coffee plant, a tropical organism accustomed to the humidity of a greenhouse and the regular watering of the royal botanists, began to wilt. Its leaves turned yellow and drooped. The closed-loop system of the glass case was efficient, but not perfect. It was slowly drying out. The plant was entering survival mode, shedding leaves to reduce surface area and minimize water loss. If it lost too many, it would not have the energy to recover.

This is the moment that defined Gabriel de Clieu's mission. In his diary, he wrote: *"Water was lacking to such an extent that for more than a month I was obliged to share the scanty ration of it which was allowed me with the plant upon which my happiest hopes were founded and which was the source of my delight."*

It was a calculated investment instead of a melodramatic gesture. De Clieu would take his meager cup of stagnant, slimy water. He would drink half—barely enough to keep his kidneys functioning and prevent circulatory collapse. He would pour the other half into the soil of the glass case.

It was an act of supreme discipline. A dehydration headache is blinding; the instinct to drink is primal. To pour life-saving fluid into a box of dirt while your own throat burns requires a singular focus. De Clieu was betting his life that this stick of wood was worth more than his own comfort. He was keeping the tree alive with his own suffering, managing the moisture levels with the precision of a lab technician rather than the flair of a hero.

## Le Prêcheur

When the *Dromadaire* finally limped into the harbor of Saint-Pierre, Martinique, the plant was a skeleton. It had lost most of its leaves. It looked like a dry twig stuck in mud. The salt air and the heat of the arrival threatened to finish what the voyage had started.

De Clieu rushed it ashore. He did not plant it in the humid lowlands of the capital, where the heat might scorch the weakened sapling. He took it to his own estate in Le Prêcheur, a region with rich volcanic soil (andosol) and cooler mountain air—conditions that mimicked the Ethiopian highlands where the species had originated.

He planted it with the ceremony of a coronation. But the danger wasn't over. De Clieu feared that his "Dutch" rival or local thieves might try to steal the precious specimen now that it was on land. He ordered a hedge of thorns—likely acacia or bougainvillea—to be planted in a tight circle around the coffee tree. He then set up a 24-hour guard rotation. For the first two years, that single tree was watched by armed men day and night.

In 1726, three years after the voyage, De Clieu's tree produced its first harvest: roughly 1 kilogram (two pounds) of bright red cherries.

De Clieu did not hoard the seeds. This differentiates him from the Dutch. The Dutch wanted a corporate monopoly; De Clieu wanted a colonial industry. He distributed the seeds from that first harvest to his friends, fellow officers, and the religious orders (specifically the Dominicans and Jesuits) on the island. He gave them strict instructions on how to plant and tend them. The multiplication was exponential.

- 1726: One tree.
- 1730: A few hundred trees.
- 1777: 18,791,680 coffee trees on the island of Martinique.

The topology of the island changed. The forests were cleared, replaced by neat rows of glossy green shrubs. Martinique became wealthy. The coffee from the "De Clieu stock" was high quality—the Typica variety—and fetched high prices in the cafes of Paris. De Clieu was hailed as a hero. He was eventually made Governor of Guadeloupe.

## THE CODE NOIR

The story of De Clieu's heroism cannot be told without acknowledging the machinery that made his vision possible. De Clieu brought the seed, yet the labor fell to others. The "delight" he felt in sharing his water ration was a prelude to centuries of labor for the workers who would harvest the fruit of his sacrifice.

The explosion of coffee in the Caribbean was fueled by the Transatlantic Slave Trade. Coffee cultivation is incredibly labor-intensive. Unlike sugar, which is cut and burned in a brutal but seasonal cycle, coffee requires year-round, meticulous attention. The cherries do not ripen all at once; they must be picked by hand, one by one, only when perfectly red. If a green cherry is picked, it ruins the roast. If a ripe cherry is missed, it rots and attracts beetles.

The 18 million trees in Martinique were not tended by French yeomen. They were tended by enslaved Africans kidnapped from Senegal, Benin, and the Congo.

The legal framework for this system was the *Code Noir* (The Black Code), a decree signed by Louis XIV in 1685 that defined the conditions of slavery in the French empire. It was a systematic document that regulated the treatment of humans as "movable property." Article 22 specifically mandated the food rations for enslaved people, detailing the cassava flour and salt beef they were owed—rations often withheld by cruel masters.

The coffee plantation, or *habitation*, was a different kind of environment compared to the sugar plantation. It was often cooler, located in the mountains, and lacked the dangerous, industrial boiling houses of the sugar mills. But the surveillance was total. Because coffee required precision picking, the overseers were relentless. A missed cherry was seen as an act of sabotage.

To clear the land for De Clieu's seeds, enslaved workers had to hack through dense tropical jungle on steep volcanic slopes, often facing the deadly fer-de-lance pit viper, which infested the underbrush. They terraced the hillsides by hand to prevent erosion, hauling stones to build retaining walls that still stand today. They carried heavy baskets of cherries down slippery mud paths, the weight of the harvest bearing down on their spines.

De Clieu is remembered for the water he sacrificed on the ship. But the wealth that De Clieu unlocked for France was built on a foundation of coerced labor. The coffee tree in Martinique was a symbol of botanical triumph, but it was also an instrument of captivity.

## THE COCOA WIND

Just as De Clieu's tree was maturing, a catastrophic event occurred that would decide the fate of the island's agriculture. Until this point, the primary crop of Martinique (besides sugar) was Cocoa. The French court was addicted to hot chocolate, and the cocoa groves were lucrative.

But *Theobroma cacao* is a brittle tree. It has shallow roots and weak branches that snap easily under pressure. *Coffea arabica*, by contrast, is a shrub-like tree with a deep taproot and flexible wood that bends rather than breaks.

On November 7, 1727, a massive "tempest"—historically recorded as a hurricane accompanied by a seismic event—struck Martinique. It was a chaotic double-blow of wind and earth. The destruction was total. The cocoa groves were flattened. The trees were uprooted or snapped in half like matchsticks. The planters were ruined.

*The hurricane of 1727 destroyed the brittle cocoa groves of Martinique, clearing the way for the resilient coffee tree to take over.*

But when De Clieu went out to check his coffee tree in Le Prêcheur, it was standing. The wind had stripped its leaves, but the trunk held. The deep taproot had anchored it against the storm.

This was the proof the islanders needed. The cocoa was dead; long live coffee. The planters, desperate for a crop that could survive the violent Caribbean weather, flocked to De Clieu for seeds. The hurricane had inadvertently cleared the land for the coffee revolution, proving that the new crop was not just valuable, but resilient.

### GENETIC BOTTLENECK

Gabriel de Clieu died in Paris in 1774, a celebrated man. A botanical garden in Martinique (the *Jardin de Balata*) honors him today with a monument. It depicts him not with a sword, but holding a potted plant.

But his true monument is the genetic landscape of the Americas.

If you drink a cup of coffee from Jamaica (Blue Mountain), the Dominican Republic, Mexico, or Costa Rica, you are likely drinking the great-great-grandchild of the plant that traveled in the glass case. Botanists call this lineage the "Noble Wave".

However, this triumph contains a hidden, catastrophic weakness. Because almost all the coffee in the Caribbean and Central America descended from that single cutting (or the very few related plants that came via Suriname), the genetic diversity of the region is almost zero. This phenomenon is known as a genetic bottleneck.

A wild forest of coffee in Ethiopia is a library of genetic defenses—some trees resist heat, some resist bugs, some resist mold. But the coffee of the Americas was a clone army. Every tree was identical. It meant that if a disease evolved to kill one tree, it possessed the key to kill them all.

De Clieu's glass case protected the plant from the salt and the wind, but it could not protect it from the future. The genetic uniformity he unleashed created an industry that was incredibly productive but terrifyingly fragile—a vulnerability that would come due centuries later when the fungal spores of leaf rust finally crossed the Atlantic. The "Noble Tree" was a mother to billions, but it was a mother that passed on a fatal susceptibility to every single one of its children.

# 8

## HAITI'S CRUCIBLE: COFFEE AND REVOLUTION

T he approach to Saint-Domingue from the Atlantic offered a deceptive tranquility. Viewed from the quarterdeck of a merchant brig in 1788, the colony appeared as a lush geological anomaly rising from the Caribbean Sea. The Massif du Nord dominated the horizon, a serrated spine of green peaks that seemed to scrape the underbelly of the tropical clouds. Below, the coastal plains of the Plaine du Nord were a masterpiece of agricultural geometry, a grid of sugar cane shimmering like verdant glass under the relentless sun, interrupted only by the smoking chimneys of the boiling houses.

However, the true engine of the colony's wealth lay in the jagged elevations. Here, the primordial canopy had been systematically cleared, replaced by millions of coffee trees clinging to slopes so precipitous that the terrain itself seemed to reject human habitation. This was the "Pearl of the Antilles," the economic reactor of the French Empire. By the eve of the Haitian Revolution, this sliver of Hispaniola—no larger than the state of Maryland—was an economic outlier that out-produced entire continents. It supplied roughly 40% of the sugar and, crucially, 60% of all the coffee consumed in the Western world.

The revenue generated by Saint-Domingue surpassed the combined output of all the British West Indies and the thirteen American colonies. But the soil of the colony was fertilized with inputs more potent than nitrogen: the forced *labor of 500,000 enslaved Africans. The colony functioned as a pressure vessel with the valve welded shut, containing the volatile chemistry of extreme wealth extraction and systemic misery. In the cool, mist-shrouded coffee groves of the high country, the structural integrity of this vessel was beginning to fail.*

## THE MOUNTAIN MACHINE

While sugar remained the undisputed monarch of the Caribbean economy, coffee was its ascendant challenger. Sugar was an industrial crop demanding massive capital, flat topography, expensive crushing mills, dangerous boiling houses, and armies of livestock. It was the province of the *Grands Blancs*—the aristocratic elite who managed their estates like feudal fiefdoms.

Coffee offered a different economic trajectory. It thrived on the "waste land"—the steep mountainsides where cane could not take root. It required no steam engines or blast furnaces; it demanded only a drying patio, a mortar, and human kinetic energy. This accessibility fostered a distinct demographic of colonist: the *Petits Blancs* (Little Whites). These were often marginalized Frenchmen—discharged soldiers, sailors, or younger sons displaced by primogeniture—who arrived in the colony to carve a fortune out of the limestone and basalt. They ascended into the mountains, cleared the high-altitude forests, and planted the seeds descended from Gabriel de Clieu's stolen cutting.

By 1789, the scale of this transformation was total. The colony hosted over 3,000 distinct coffee plantations, known as *habitations caféières*. The output statistics illustrate a frantic expansion: In 1755, Saint-Domingue exported 7 million pounds (3.1 million kg) of coffee. By 1789, that figure had escalated to 77 million pounds (34.9 million kg).

To sustain this yield on such hostile terrain, the planters engineered sophisticated infrastructure that rivaled the aqueducts of Europe. They carved extensive terracing systems into the mountainsides to prevent soil erosion during the violent tropical storms. Intricate hydraulic systems captured mountain streams, funneling water through stone sluices to wash the depulped beans and power the mills. These were not simple farms; they were agro-industrial complexes perched on the edge of gravity.

*The French engineered sophisticated hydraulic infrastructure in the mountains of Saint-Domingue to process massive volumes of coffee.*

The demographic reality of the coffee districts differed significantly from the sugar plains. Sugar plantations consumed lives with mechanical efficiency, often exhausting workers within seven to ten years. Coffee plantations were physically less lethal but psychologically more compressed. They were smaller, remote, and intimate in their tyranny. A coffee planter might own only 20 or 30 enslaved people, living in immediate proximity to them in the high mountain mists, miles from the nearest garrison. This proximity did not breed empathy; it bred a specific, paranoid severity.

To extract 77 million pounds of coffee from a mountainous wilderness required a system of absolute control. The harvest season, or *la cueillette*, was a grueling logistical operation. Coffee cherries ripen asynchronously, necessitating that workers return to the same tree five or six times, harvesting only the fruit at peak maturity. The processing was equally labor-intensive. Once harvested, the cherries were depulped and laid out on massive masonry platforms called *glacis* to ferment and dry. Enslaved workers were compelled to turn the beans constantly with wooden rakes to prevent fungal rot, traversing the hot stone barefoot for hours under the supervision of the whip.

### THE CODE AND THE GARDEN

To manage this population, the French Crown relied on the *Code Noir* (The Black Code). Promulgated by Louis XIV in 1685, the Code was theoretically a legal framework meant to regulate the treatment of enslaved people, mandating Catholic baptism and specific food rations. In the isolation of the coffee slopes, however, the Code functioned as a system of authorized brutality rather than protection.

The legal text of the *Code Noir* stripped the enslaved of all juridical agency. Article 28 declared that enslaved people could not own property; anything they possessed belonged legally to their masters. Article 38 codified the punishment for fugitives: the cutting of ears and branding with the fleur-de-lys for the first attempt, hamstringing for the second, and death for the third. On the *habitations*, planters supplemented these laws with sadistic innovations. They utilized iron masks to prevent workers from eating the sugar cane or coffee fruit during the harvest. They poured boiling wax on limbs as punishment for lethargy. This violence was structural; when 30,000 white colonists attempt to subjugate 500,000 enslaved people, terror becomes the primary administrative tool.

Yet, the coffee plantation contained a flaw in its design. Unlike the sugar gangs, who worked under the constant, panoptic gaze of an overseer in open fields, coffee work was dispersed among the dense foliage of the trees. Furthermore, because coffee cultivation required less contiguous land than sugar, the topography allowed for the existence of *jardins à nègres* (negro gardens).

These were small, marginal plots of land on the steep peripheries of the plantation where the enslaved were permitted to cultivate their own subsistence crops—yams, manioc, and plantains—to supplement the insufficient rations provided by the masters. These gardens provided the enslaved with a critical resource: a degree of economic autonomy and a valid reason to travel between plantations to trade their surplus. In the Sunday markets, amidst the exchange of vegetables, information circulated. The coffee slopes transformed into a covert communication network, linking the disparate plantations into a unified web of resistance.

·  ·  ·

## MACKANDAL'S TOXICOLOGY

Before the insurrection utilized machetes, it deployed botany. The mountains of Saint-Domingue harbored communities of escaped slaves known as Maroons. These fugitives inhabited the inaccessible peaks, raiding plantations before receding into the cloud forests. In the 1750s, a Maroon leader of significant intellect emerged: François Mackandal.

A one-armed strategist and a powerful *Houngan* (Vodou priest), Mackandal analyzed the asymmetry of the colonial power structure. He recognized that a conventional military confrontation with the French army was premature. Instead, he initiated a campaign of asymmetrical warfare targeting the domestic sphere.

Mackandal organized a vast, clandestine network of household slaves across the North Province. He instructed them in the application of tropical toxicology, specifically the extraction of cyanide from the root of the bitter cassava (*Manihot esculenta*) and the identification of toxic fungi indigenous to the coffee groves.

The ensuing "Poison Panic" of 1757 paralyzed the colony. It commenced with the livestock; cattle, horses, and mules expired in the fields without visible injury. The vector then shifted to the dining tables of the *Grands Blancs*. Planters would succumb to convulsions and respiratory failure during meals. Entire families were extinguished. The terror was psychological and pervasive; every vessel of water and every plate of food represented a potential threat. Mackandal was eventually betrayed, captured, and burned at the stake in the public square of Le Cap in 1758. However, the legend persisted that his spirit escaped the flames, transforming into a mosquito. His legacy was the tactical realization that the colonial infrastructure was vulnerable from within.

## AUGUST 14, 1791

The structural collapse arrived three decades later, in the summer of 1791. The French Revolution had erupted in Paris two years prior, and the "Declaration of the Rights of Man and of the Citizen" had proclaimed that "men are born and remain free and equal in rights."

This ideology traveled to Saint-Domingue on the very vessels transporting luxury goods and newspapers. The white planters argued the

Declaration applied exclusively to Europeans. The *Gens de Couleur Libres* (wealthy mixed-race landowners) argued it applied to free men of all races. The enslaved population observed the fracturing of the white power structure and concluded that the Rights of Man would not be granted, but must be seized.

On the night of August 14, 1791, a cadre of slave drivers and coachmen —the operational elite of the enslaved workforce—converged in a forest clearing known as Bois Caïman (Alligator Woods). They were led by Dutty Boukman, a foreman and *Houngan* of imposing physical stature.

The gathering functioned as both a strategic war council and a spiritual unification. Amidst a torrential tropical storm, the conspirators sacrificed a black pig, drinking the blood to seal a pact of absolute secrecy and total commitment.

*The meeting at Bois Caïman initiated the revolution, transforming the plantation labor force into an insurgent army.*

Boukman delivered an invocation that rejected the colonial theology which had been utilized to pacify them:

"The God of the white man calls him to commit crimes; our God asks only good works of us. But this God who is so good orders revenge! He will direct our hands; he will aid us. Throw away the image of the God of the whites who thirsts for our tears and listen to the voice of liberty which speaks in the hearts of all of us."

This was the commencement of a revolution.

. . .

## LANDSCAPE OF EXTRACTION

One week later, on the night of August 22, the horizon of the North Province began to glow. It was a coordinated offensive of terrifying precision. At a prearranged signal, 100,000 enslaved men and women mobilized. They utilized the implements of their labor—machetes, pruning hooks, and cane knives—as munitions of war.

They incinerated the cane fields. They dismantled the sugar mills. They torched the coffee warehouses. The insurrection aimed to erase the infrastructure of their enslavement. The sky over Le Cap turned opaque with soot. Naval observers miles offshore reported that the atmosphere carried the scent of caramelizing sugar and roasting coffee—a sensory testament to the destruction of the colony's capital assets.

The coffee plantations in the mountains were particularly susceptible. Isolated by geography and surrounded by dense forest, the planters had no avenue of retreat. The *Petits Blancs* who had enforced their rule with the whip were overwhelmed on their own drying patios. The geometric order of the plantation was rapidly reclaimed by the insurgent terrain.

The destruction of the coffee infrastructure was deliberate. To the insurgents, the coffee tree was a mechanism of torture instead of a botanical asset. Demolishing the processing mills and the *glacis* was an act of dismantling the engine that had consumed their labor.

## MILITARIZED BOTANY

From this chaotic upheaval emerged a military intellect of the highest order: Toussaint Louverture.

Toussaint, a former slave who had secured his freedom years prior, presented a paradox: a revolutionary who understood the mechanics of capitalism. He was a coffee enthusiast who had operated a small coffee plot prior to the revolution. Physically slight and reserved, he possessed a strategic acumen that consistently outmaneuvered the French generals dispatched to subdue him.

Toussaint recognized that scorching the earth was a tactic of desperation instead of a strategy of governance. To secure a permanent victory, Haiti required an army, and an army required munitions. Munitions required capital, and in Saint-Domingue, capital was synonymous with exports.

By 1801, Toussaint had unified the island, drafting a constitution that abolished slavery in perpetuity. However, he then implemented a policy that alienated many of his followers: he mandated the return of the former slaves to the plantations.

Toussaint understood the grim economics of sovereignty. He knew that for Haiti to survive as a black republic in a hemisphere dominated by slave-holding powers, it required a functional economy. He instituted the system of *Fermage* (farming). The workers were legally free and entitled to a share of the profits—typically one-quarter—but they were prohibited from leaving the land. It was a system of militarized agriculture, enforcing productivity with the discipline of a regiment.

Under Toussaint, the coffee industry began to stabilize. The trees were pruned; the mills were rehabilitated. He operated on the conviction that the discipline of the coffee harvest was the discipline of the state. He sought to demonstrate to the global powers that black labor did not require the coercion of chattel slavery to be productive. However, in Paris, Napoleon Bonaparte had calculated a different future.


THE WAR OF EXTERMINATION

Napoleon, as First Consul of France, found the existence of a colony ruled by black generals intolerable. He required the revenue of Saint-Domingue to finance his expansionist ambitions in Europe. In 1802, he authorized the largest naval expedition in French history, dispatching his brother-in-law, General Charles Leclerc, with 40,000 veteran troops to reconquer the island and—secretly—reinstate slavery.

The conflict that ensued was characterized by brutal repression. The French tactics were indiscriminate. They utilized improvised gas chambers, burning sulfur in the holds of ships to suffocate prisoners. They imported combat dogs from Cuba to hunt insurgents in the rough terrain.

The Haitians responded with a policy of *Koupe Tèt, Boule Kay*—"Cut

Heads, Burn Houses." Toussaint's lieutenant, Jean-Jacques Dessalines, issued the directive: "Burn the cities! Shoot down the white men! Poison the wells!"

The coffee plantations transformed into theaters of guerrilla warfare. The dense architecture of the coffee groves provided ideal concealment for Haitian sharpshooters. The French columns, maneuvering in heavy woolen uniforms, were decimated by invisible adversaries. However, the French encountered a biological antagonist far deadlier than the insurgents: Yellow Fever.

The mosquito *Aedes aegypti* proliferated in the water cisterns of the plantations and the stagnant pools of the lowlands. As the French troops penetrated the interior, they began to succumb to the pathogen. The symptoms were horrific: high fever, jaundice, and the vomiting of black, coagulated blood. General Leclerc himself died of the virus.

Of the 40,000 troops Napoleon dispatched—the veterans of the Rhine—approximately 32,000 perished. It was a catastrophic failure of colonial ambition. The terrain of the coffee mountains had effectively neutralized the *Grande Armée*.

### CITADEL LAFERRIÈRE

On January 1, 1804, Dessalines declared independence. He renamed the colony "Haiti," reclaiming the indigenous Taíno designation for "Land of Mountains." It stood as the first black republic in the world and the only nation in history born of a successful slave insurrection.

Yet, the Haitians remained acutely aware of the threat of French revanchism. To guarantee their sovereignty, Toussaint's successor, King Henri Christophe, commissioned the construction of a fortress of immense scale.

The Citadel Laferrière sits atop the 3,000-foot (914-meter) Bonnet à l'Evêque mountain. It remains the largest fortress in the Americas. Its limestone walls rise 130 feet (40 meters) and are 13 feet (4 meters) thick. The structure was erected by 20,000 conscripted workers hauling massive stones and hundreds of heavy cannons up a sheer mountain ascent over a period of fifteen years.

*Citadel Laferrière: King Henri Christophe built the massive Citadel to protect the newly free nation—and its valuable coffee crop—from French reinvasion.*

The Citadel was designed to protect the coffee. Christophe understood that the Haitians could not defend the coastline against a naval bombardment. His strategy was a scorched-earth retreat: burn the coastal cities and withdraw the population into the mountains—into the coffee country. The Citadel was the stronghold where they would stage their final defense, subsisting on stockpiled grain and water, training their cannons on the mountain passes.

The mortar of the Citadel is locally rumored to be mixed with the blood of the workers who died building it—along with molasses and lime to ensure adhesion. It stands today as a UNESCO World Heritage site, a colossal stone sentinel guarding the coffee fields below. It is a physical manifestation of the reality that Haitian sovereignty was not granted; it was constructed.

### THE JEFFERSONIAN BLOCKADE

Haiti was free, but it was geopolitically isolated. The success of the Haitian Revolution terrified the slave-holding powers of the Atlantic World, particularly the United States.

Thomas Jefferson, then President of the United States and a slaveholder, viewed the revolution with horror. He feared the "contagion of liberty" would metastasize from Haiti to the American South. He referred to the revolutionaries as "cannibals of the terrible republic."

Rather than engaging in trade with the new democracy, Jefferson imposed a crushing embargo. The United States refused to recognize Haiti's independence—a diplomatic stance that would persist until 1862, during the American Civil War. They severed trade relations.

This isolation was economically devastating. Haiti possessed coffee —thousands of tons of it—but the markets of the Western world were sealing their ports. The nation became a pariah state. This enforced isolation eventually compelled them to negotiate with their former oppressors.

## 150 MILLION FRANCS

In 1825, French warships returned to the harbor of Port-au-Prince. They did not arrive to invade; they arrived to extort. With cannons primed, they issued an ultimatum to the Haitian president, Jean-Pierre Boyer: Pay reparations or face immediate naval bombardment and re-invasion.

The French did not demand reparations for the centuries of slavery, torture, and resource theft. They demanded reparations *from* the former slaves to compensate the French planters for their lost "property"—a legal term that encompassed both the land and the human bodies they had once owned.

The demand was 150 million gold francs. This was an astronomical sum, equivalent to roughly ten times Haiti's annual revenue at the time.

Fearing re-invasion and strangled by the American embargo, the Haitian government acquiesced. To service this crushing debt, the Haitian state was forced to tax its only viable asset: peasant-grown coffee.

For the next 122 years—until 1947—Haiti remitted payments to France. The coffee that Haitian peasants harvested in the mountains was effectively expropriated by the state to pay the descendants of their former masters. The "Independence Debt" crippled Haiti's infrastructure development. Schools remained unbuilt; roads remained unpaved; hospitals were not established. The surplus wealth of the coffee harvest was systematically siphoned to Parisian banks. The wealthiest colony in the hemisphere was engineered into the poorest nation through financial attrition.

· · ·

## THE BRAZILIAN VACUUM

The collapse of Saint-Domingue's output during the revolution and the subsequent strangulation of its economy created a seismic shift in the global market. In the span of a few years, the world's primary supplier of coffee effectively went offline.

The market reacted with predictable volatility. Prices spiked. Traders in London, Amsterdam, and Hamburg scrambled to secure supply. The question facing the mercantile world was urgent: Where would the coffee come from?

The answer lay to the south. In Brazil, the seeds planted by Francisco de Melo Palheta were proliferating. Brazil possessed vast tracts of land. It possessed a climate analogous to Haiti. And, crucially, it maintained the institution of slavery.

As Haiti secured its freedom, Brazil entrenched its commitment to bondage. The collapse of Saint-Domingue was the direct catalyst for the expansion of the Brazilian slave trade. Between 1800 and 1850, millions of Africans were transported to Rio de Janeiro to work the expanding coffee *fazendas*, filling the supply vacuum created by the Haitian Revolution.

History transferred the burden of production. The whip that was broken in Haiti was taken up in Brazil. The global coffee economy migrated to a new host, prioritizing the volume of the harvest over the liberty of the harvester.

## FERAL TREES

Today, the coffee industry in Haiti is a remnant of its 18th-century dominance. Soil erosion, exacerbated by deforestation and centuries of intensive farming without capital investment, has denuded much of the mountains.

However, in the deep valleys of the Massif du Nord, one can still encounter wild coffee trees thriving in the understory.

*The* Kafe Tyòt—*feral descendants of the colonial plantations—still grow in the Haitian mountains, a living legacy of the revolution.*

These are the *Kafe Tyòt*—feral descendants of the French plantations. They grow without pruning, without synthetic fertilizers, and without masters.

Haiti stands as the martyr of the coffee narrative. It is the only nation that paid for its coffee with its blood, and subsequently paid for its freedom with its coffee. The Citadel continues to loom over the valleys, a silent testament to the price of the morning cup. In the soil of those mountains, the roots of the trees remain entangled with the history of the men and women who refused to function as components of a machine.

# 9

# LIBERTY BREW: BOSTON QUITS TEA

T he wind off the harbor on the night of December 16, 1773, did not just bite; it gnawed with a damp, penetrating chill that settled into the marrow of the city. The temperature hovered near freezing, likely around 32°F (0°C), turning the moisture on the cobblestones into a slick, treacherous glaze. But inside the Green Dragon Tavern on Union Street, the atmosphere was pressurized, heated by the crush of bodies and the opaque smoke of clay pipes.

A copper dragon, oxidized to the color of a bruised sea, hung above the door, the metal groaning on its hinges with every gust of the winter gale. To the British regulars patrolling the streets outside, the Green Dragon was merely a public house—a place for mechanics to drink flip and complain about the weather. But to the men inside, crowded into the tallow-lit back rooms, it was the specific locus of a rebellion.

The mood was not raucous. It was vibrantly tense, possessing the sort of quiet that precedes a detonation. At the rough-hewn tables sat the Freemasons of St. Andrew's Lodge and the loose confederation of artisans known as the Sons of Liberty. Paul Revere was present, his hands stained with the silver and copper of his trade. Dr. Joseph Warren, the physician who would later suffer a fatal ballistic wound at Bunker Hill, spoke in low tones. They were drinking, but not heavily. They were waiting.

*A mile away, at Griffin's Wharf, three ships—the Dartmouth, the Eleanor, and the Beaver—strained against their hawsers. Their holds were packed with 342 chests of cured leaves from the Fujian province of China. The deadline to unload this cargo and pay the duty was midnight. If the clock struck twelve without a resolution, the Royal Customs officials would seize the tea, sell it at auction, and the tax would be paid by the vendors, cementing Parliament's right to levy it.*

*The men in the Green Dragon were drinking ale, cider, and increasingly, a bitter, muddy decoction poured from pewter pots. It was coffee. In the winter of 1773, this black liquid was ceasing to be a mere beverage. It was transforming into a political weapon.*

### THE MATHEMATICS OF INSURRECTION

To understand why grown men would paint their faces with soot and risk hanging over dried leaves, one must look past the schoolbook simplicity of "taxation without representation" and examine the ledger. The crisis of 1773 was born of a corporate bailout instead of a price hike.

The British East India Company, the world's first true corporate monopoly, was rotting from the inside. By early 1773, the Company sat on an unsold inventory of 17 million pounds (approx. 7.7 million kg) of tea decaying in London warehouses—enough to supply the entire British Empire for a year. They were effectively bankrupt, owing the British government £400,000 per year in contract payments they could not meet.

The Company was "too big to fail." Many members of Parliament held stock in it. If the Company collapsed, the liquidity of the Empire would evaporate. The solution was the Tea Act of May 1773. The Act was a piece of legislative engineering designed not to punish the colonies, but to clear the warehouse.

The Act allowed the Company to bypass the traditional London wholesale auctions and the middlemen, shipping directly to consignees in America. Even with the hated three-penny tax added, this East India tea would be cheaper than the smuggled Dutch tea the colonists had been drinking for years. This was the trap. Lord North, the Prime Minister, gambled that the American consumer would vote with their purse.

He assumed that the colonist was a *Homo economicus* first and a patriot second.

"They have no idea of the American mind," Samuel Adams argued in the smoky recesses of the tavern. He saw the cheap tea for what it was: a "poisoned gift." If the colonists bought the tea because it was cheap, they implicitly accepted Parliament's right to tax them. It was a seduction. To drink the King's tea was to accept the King's shackles, gilded though they might be.

### "Mohawks" at the Waterline

The signal came shortly after 6:00 PM. A message arrived at the Old South Meeting House, where thousands had gathered: Governor Hutchinson would not grant the ships a pass to leave. Samuel Adams stood and declared, "This meeting can do nothing more to save the country."

It was a code.

Back at the Green Dragon and surrounding safehouses, the "Mohawks" prepared. The disguise was deliberate and symbolic. Mechanics, merchants, and apprentices smeared their faces with coal dust and red ochre. They wrapped themselves in old blankets. By dressing as the indigenous people of the continent, they were visually shedding their British identity. A Briton would respect property law; a "savage" of the American wilderness—in their racialized theater—would not.

*The Green Dragon Tavern served as the headquarters of the rebellion,*
*where coffee began to displace tea as the drink of patriotism.*

They moved with the discipline of a militia. This was a tactical raid.

When they boarded the *Dartmouth*, they demanded the keys to the hatches from the mate. They did not harm the crew. They did not loot the cabins. They sought only the cargo.

The physical labor of the destruction is often glossed over in historical summaries. A chest of Bohea tea weighed roughly 360 pounds (163 kg); a chest of fancy Hyson, slightly less. These were lead-lined, canvas-covered heavyweights designed to survive ocean crossings. The men rigged block and tackle to hoist them from the hold to the deck, the ropes singing with tension.

Under the cold moonlight, the harbor echoed with the thwack-crunch of hatchets fracturing wood. The air filled with the floral, tannic dust of smashed tea.

But there was a problem: the tide. It was low water. As the tea was shoveled overboard, it didn't drift away. It piled up. The water was so shallow that the mounds of wet leaves began to rise above the surface like haystacks, threatening to spill back onto the decks.

Men had to jump from the gunwales into the freezing muck of the harbor. Waist-deep in brine and sludge that was rapidly cooling toward 32°F (0°C), they beat the piles of tea with oars and shovels, churning it into the saltwater to ensure it was ruined. It was grueling, mechanical work.

*The low tide at Boston Harbor required patriots to jump into the freezing mud to ensure the tea was submerged and destroyed.*

By 9:00 PM, 342 chests—92,000 pounds (41,730 kg) of tea—had been destroyed. In modern currency, they had destroyed nearly $1.7 million worth of corporate property. As the men marched back to their homes, shaking the tea dust from their blankets, they cleaned their shoes. They checked their pockets. One man, Charles O'Conner, had been caught earlier stuffing tea into the lining of his coat. He was stripped, removed from the ship, and the coat was nailed to the whipping post in Charlestown as a warning.

This was a moral purge. To keep a single leaf was theft. To destroy it all was politics.

## THE CULINARY SHIFT

The repercussions were immediate. Parliament closed the port of Boston, placing the city under martial law. In response, the colonies did something extraordinary: they turned the breakfast table into a battlefield.

A boycott was declared. But to understand the agony of this decision, one must understand the biology of the 18th-century colonist. They were a population habituated to tea.

Tea was the metronome of the day. It was the warmth in a drafty house, the social lubricant of the parlor, the safe hydration in a world of questionable water. To give it up was not just a political stance; it was a physiological shock.

In early 1774, a collective withdrawal headache descended upon New England. The "caffeine crash" was real. Diaries from the period mention lethargy, irritability, and a desperate craving for something hot and stimulating.

To fill the void, the rural population turned to "Liberty Teas." Newspapers published recipes for these patriotic substitutes, extolling their virtues with a desperate cheerfulness. They were brewed from ribwort, strawberry leaves, currant leaves, sage, and the marsh ledum plant (Labrador tea).

They were, largely, undrinkable.

The *New Hampshire Gazette* claimed that "Four-Leaved Loose-Strife" was "much more healthful" than Bohea. But the reality was a cup of hot, grassy water that tasted of hay and disappointment. More importantly, these herbal concoctions lacked the one molecule the colonists craved: caffeine.

The failure of Liberty Tea cleared the path for the only viable alternative. There was another dark liquid, possessed of a different kind of bitterness, that offered the same neurochemical kick. Coffee did not just arrive; it was drafted into service.

John Adams, writing to his wife Abigail in July 1774, captured the transition in a moment of domestic comedy that masked a cultural seismic shift. He had stopped at a tavern in Falmouth and asked the landlady for a cup of tea.

"No, sir," she scolded him. "We have renounced all tea in this place. But I'll make you coffee."

Adams drank it. "I have drank coffee every afternoon since," he wrote, "and I have borne it very well."

### The French Connection

If the colonists weren't buying tea from the British, where were they getting the coffee? They certainly weren't buying it from British merchants in Yemen or Jamaica. The coffee of the American Revolution was smuggled. It came from the French and Dutch West Indies—specifically Saint-Domingue (Haiti), Martinique, and Suriname. But moving beans from a French port to a blockade-runner's hold required more than just will; it required a specific kind of naval architecture.

The smuggling trade birthed a new kind of American speed. The merchants of the mid-Atlantic began utilizing "pilot boats"—sharp-hulled, schooner-rigged vessels built in the shipyards of Chesapeake Bay. These were the ancestors of the famous Baltimore Clippers. They were small, shallow-draft, and raked at the mast, capable of sailing closer to the wind than the clumsy, square-rigged British patrol sloops.

The trade was simple and lucrative: "Flour for Beans."

The French colonies in the Caribbean were rich in sugar and coffee but perpetually starving for grain. The American colonies had a surplus of wheat. A Philadelphia merchant could load a schooner with Pennsylvania flour, slip past the Royal Navy patrols at night, and make the run to

Cap-Français in Saint-Domingue. There, he would trade the flour for bags of green coffee beans, which were technically illegal to import without British duty.

This "West India Trade" became the lifeline of the American caffeine habit. This trade created a loop of rebellion: American wheat fed the French colonies; French coffee fueled the American resistance. When a housewife in Boston roasted a batch of beans, she was completing a supply chain that relied on the fastest ships and the boldest captains in the Atlantic.

The physical journey of the bean was fraught. These pilot boats had to navigate the treacherous shoals of the Caribbean and the patrols of the Royal Navy. The coffee they carried was often packed in hemp sacks, absorbing the humidity of the hold. By the time it reached the docks of Boston or Philadelphia, the green beans had often faded to a pale yellow, their moisture content fluctuating with the sea air. This was not the carefully climate-controlled shipping of the modern era; it was a rough, high-stakes transit where the cargo was as volatile as the politics that demanded it.

### THE MEDICAL PIVOT: DR. RUSH'S PRESCRIPTION

The revolution needed science to legitimize the switch. It wasn't enough for tea to be politically toxic; it had to be physically toxic, too. The patriots needed a biological mandate to abandon the leaf.

Enter Dr. Benjamin Rush, the most prominent physician in the colonies and a signer of the Declaration of Independence. Rush was a master of political medicine. He recognized that to change a nation's habits, one had to appeal to its hypochondria.

In his influential essays and *Sermons to Gentlemen upon Temperance and Exercise*, Rush launched a calculated critique of tea. He did not merely call it unpatriotic; he called it a slow poison. He argued that tea possessed a 'direct tendency to weaken the tone of the stomach' and, more damningly, to induce 'trembling of the nerves.'

To the 18th-century mind, 'nerves' were not merely a medical condition; they were a moral failing. A nervous man was effeminate, porous, and incapable of the stoic self-governance required for republicanism.

By framing tea as a cause of physical frailty, Rush was engaging in a brilliant piece of biological propaganda. He was coding tea as the drink of the submissive subject—a fluid that literally dissolved the backbone—while framing coffee as the fuel of the citizen. It was a binary choice: drink tea and tremble, or drink coffee and fight.

Coffee, by contrast, Rush framed as a "cordial restorative." It was robust. It aided digestion. It cleared the fog of the mind and prepared the body for industry. This was propaganda wrapped in Latin. Rush and his colleagues successfully medicalized the boycott, telling the colonists that switching to coffee wasn't just good for liberty—it was necessary for the "vigorous constitution" required to win a war.

This medical pivot was crucial because it addressed the Galenic humor theory still prevalent at the time. Tea was seen as cooling and potentially weakening to the constitution if over-consumed. Coffee, with its "heat," was viewed as a stimulant that fortified the blood. For a nation preparing for war, the choice was clear: drink the beverage that builds a warrior, not the one that creates a nervous invalid.

## KITCHEN CHEMISTRY: THE SKILLET ROAST

For the urban elite who frequented coffeehouses, the switch was seamless. But for the average household—the domain of the "Daughters of Liberty"—coffee was a culinary stranger. In 1774, you did not buy roasted coffee. You bought green beans, hard as pebbles and smelling of raw vegetation. The burden of transforming these seeds into a drink fell entirely on the women of the house.

The process was smoky, inconsistent, and laborious. A housewife would place the green beans into an iron skillet or a spider pot over the open hearth. She was locked in a physical battle with the fire. The heat of a wood hearth is erratic, spiking and dipping with every draft. To prevent the precious beans from turning to charcoal, she had to keep them in constant, frantic motion, her arm aching as the iron skillet grew heavy.

*Before industrial roasting, American families struggled with the "Janus roast"—beans burnt on one side and raw on the other.*

The result was often a 'Janus roast'—beans that were charcoal-black on one side and raw-green on the other. This wasn't the sweet, caramelized aroma of a modern café; it was a blue, choking haze of burning chaff that clung to hair and clothes, a daily olfactory reminder of the price of rebellion.

Once roasted, the beans had to be ground. Few households owned the dedicated conical burr mills found in coffeehouses. Instead, the beans were fractured in a mortar and pestle, resulting in a chaotic mix of dust and boulders.

Then came the brewing. There were no filters. No percolation. The grounds were dumped into a pot of water and boiled. To clarify the muddy suspension, women used folk chemistry. They added crushed eggshells, which (being alkaline) helped settle the acidic grounds and reduce bitterness through basic chemistry. Some added a piece of dried fish skin (isinglass) to bind the floating particulates, a trick borrowed from beer brewing.

The resulting cup was often thick, gritty, and harsh. To make it palatable, it was cut with milk, molasses, or even cider. But it was hot, it was dark, and most importantly, it woke you up. It was a rough draft of a beverage, but it tasted like virtue.

. . .

WAR FUEL: THE SOLDIER'S RATION

When the war turned from boycotts to bullets in 1775, coffee was officially enlisted. The Continental Congress, advised by military logistics officers, designated coffee (or chocolate) as a standard part of the ration.

General George Washington, a man who ordered coffee by the hundreds of pounds for Mount Vernon, understood its value for morale. In the freezing misery of winter encampments, alcohol made men drunk and disorderly; tea was unavailable and unpatriotic; water was dysenteric. Coffee was warmth and alertness.

At Valley Forge, supply chains collapsed. The official ration of "one ounce of coffee per man per day" became a cruel fiction.

Desperate soldiers became chemists of necessity. They foraged for chicory root, roasting it until it was black and brittle. They burned rye and barley. In a pinch, they roasted dried peas. These substitutes were boiled into a dark "coffee" that provided heat, if not stimulation.

*In the freezing encampments of the Revolution, coffee substitutes like chicory and roasted rye became critical for warmth when the real bean was scarce.*

It was in these encampments that the myth of the "Cup of Joe" finds its spiritual, if not linguistic, origin. While the specific etymology relating to Josephus Daniels or G.I. Joe is anachronistic, the bond between the American infantryman and his coffee was forged in the snow of Pennsylvania. The soldier learned to rely on the black brew not just for warmth, but for the psychological continuity of a ritual in the midst of chaos.

### THE QUAKER DILEMMA AND THE MERCHANT'S COFFEE HOUSE

The transition was not universal. In Philadelphia, the powerful Quaker merchants viewed the Boston Tea Party not as heroism, but as vandalism. To a Quaker, property was sacred. Destroying inventory was a sin, regardless of the tax status.

*Boston Tea Party, Boston Harbor, December 16, 1773.*

The Sons of Liberty had to wage an internal marketing war. They used the Committees of Correspondence—the information network of the 18th century—to shame holdouts. They published "Blacklists" of merchants who continued to sell tea.

In New York, the battleground was the Merchant's Coffee House on Wall Street. For decades, it had been the neutral ground of commerce. But by 1775, neutrality was treason. The radical Whigs took over the main floor, shouting down Loyalists. The coffeehouse ceased to be a place of polite exchange and became a partisan echo chamber.

When the British occupied New York, the tables turned, and British officers drank claret in the same booths where patriots had plotted. But the coffeehouse itself remained the center of gravity. It was the place where news was read, where spies listened, and where the temperature of the city was taken.

.   .   .

### THE PERMANENT STAIN

The War of Independence ended in 1783, but the tea habit never fully returned. The psychological break was permanent. While the British Empire doubled down on tea—planting vast estates in their new colony of India to break the Chinese monopoly—the Americans looked West, their saddlebags packed with green coffee beans.

The boycott of 1773 created a cultural vacuum that coffee rushed to fill. It changed the American palate. We became a nation of roasters, not steepers. We came to prefer the high-impact hit of the bean over the slow infusion of the leaf. The line from the Green Dragon Tavern to the neon sign of a 24-hour diner is direct and unbroken. The "bottomless cup" is a uniquely American concept, rooted in the idea that this black fuel is a birthright, a democratic necessity that should be cheap, abundant, and hot.

But there is a final, darker irony to this patriotic pivot. The colonists rejected the tea of the East India Company because they viewed it as a product of tyranny. But the coffee they replaced it with was the product of Slavery.

As detailed in the accounts of Haiti's Crucible, the Caribbean coffee that filled the cups of the Sons of Liberty was harvested by enslaved Africans living under the brutal *Code Noir*. The "Liberty Brew"—as they sometimes ironically called coffee—was grown by people who had no liberty. Thomas Jefferson wrote the Declaration of Independence—asserting that all men are created equal—while drinking coffee picked by men who were legally property. This dissonance was the original sin of the American cup, a bitterness that sugar could not hide.

In 1773, in the smoky warmth of the Green Dragon, nobody was thinking about the supply chain. They were thinking about the King. They raised their tankards of black broth, toasted to 'No Taxation Without Representation,' and drank.

# 10

# BRAZIL'S MACHINE: THE INDUSTRIALIZATION OF NATURE

I n 1850, the view from the ridge of the Serra do Mar presented a vast, intentional landscape of extraction. Standing on that granite spine, which rises 800 meters (2,600 feet) straight up from the Atlantic Ocean to wall off the Brazilian interior, a traveler would have smelled the revenue before they saw it. The air was thick with the acrid, oily smoke of burning mahogany and rosewood, a haze that signaled the conversion of biomass into capital. Below, to the east, lay the port of Santos, a fever-ridden archipelago of mud and yellow fever where ships waited in lines three miles long, their masts looking like a leafless forest in the harbor. To the west lay the Paraíba Valley, a corridor of the Atlantic Rainforest that had stood undisturbed for fifty million years. Now, it was being systematically dismantled.

In the clearings, stretching toward a horizon obscured by particulate haze, were lines of emerald green shrubs planted with a geometric precision that offended the chaotic logic of the jungle. This was the Mar Verde, the "Green Sea." Deep within this ocean of leaves stood the Casa Grande, the Great House. Inside, a man in a white linen suit and a silk cravat drank coffee from Limoges porcelain. He was a Barão do Café (Coffee Baron), a title likely purchased for 15 contos de réis from the Emperor of Brazil. He was American-style royalty in a kingdom built on caffeine.

Outside his window, the source of his title was visible in the vibrating heat.

*Hundreds of Black men and women, stripped to the waist, moved through the rows under the supervision of the feitor (overseer). They were the biological workforce of the 19th century. Brazil had become the heir to Haiti's throne, but it had scaled the operation to a monstrous size. This was the industrialization of nature—a machine turning virgin soil into cheap, abundant fuel for the factories of Europe and America.*

FILLING THE VACUUM

Nature abhors a vacuum, but the global market exploits it. When the Haitian Revolution dismantled the coffee fields of Saint-Domingue in the 1790s, the global market entered a state of acute withdrawal. The price of coffee on the London exchange spiked. The consumers of Paris, Vienna, and Philadelphia required a steady supply, and the destroyed mills of Haiti could no longer provide it. Brazil, a slumbering giant of a Portuguese colony, awakened to the opportunity. The seeds that Francisco de Melo Palheta had secured from the French Guiana in 1727 had been languishing in the gardens of the north for decades, treated as botanical curiosities. But as prices rose, the coffee trees began to migrate south. They found their perfect geoclimatic lock in the Vale do Paraíba, a depression sandwiched between Rio de Janeiro and São Paulo.

The climate here was a mirror of coffee's Ethiopian birthplace: hot, wet summers for growth and dry, cool winters for harvest. But unlike the terraced hills of Yemen or the smallholder plots of Java, the land here was treated as an infinite resource. The Portuguese crown granted massive tracts of land (*sesmarias*) to anyone with the capital to clear the forest. The result was the First Coffee Boom (1830-1880). It was a rush for wealth, but the wealth grew on branches. In 1800, Brazil exported a modest 1,700 bags of coffee. By 1840, that number had swelled to 1.3 million bags. By 1880, Brazil was producing more coffee than the rest of the world combined. This was the moment coffee transitioned from a luxury good to a caloric necessity for the Western working class.

## THE ARISTOCRACY OF THE BRANCH

This sudden accumulation of wealth calcified into a new social class: the Coffee Barons. Unlike the fading sugar lords of the Brazilian northeast, who were bound by tradition and declining soil fertility, the coffee planters of the south were aggressive, modern capitalists wrapped in feudal trappings. They constructed palaces in the jungle, importing French architects to raise opera houses in Manaus and Rio. They sent their sons to study civil law at the Sorbonne and procured pianos from Steinway in New York for their daughters.

The Emperor of Brazil, Dom Pedro II, legitimized their power through a transaction-based honors system. A wealthy planter could acquire a Barony—becoming the Baron of Rio Bonito or the Baron of Nova Friburgo—in exchange for significant financial contributions to the state or the funding of a local militia unit. These titles cemented a rigid hierarchy where the planter acted as the local law. The Barons controlled the politics of the Empire, ensuring the state invested in infrastructure that solely benefited the flow of beans: roads, ports, and a militarized police force dedicated to retrieving runaways. They operated under the delusion that the boom was a permanent state of affairs, treating the land not as a partner, but as a disposable battery. They planted trees until the soil was exhausted—usually a cycle of twenty to thirty years—and then, rather than fertilizing or resting the earth, they simply moved west, burning more forest. It was a nomadic, predatory agriculture that left a wake of "dead hills" and ghost towns.

## THE GEOLOGY OF THE GREEN SEA

As the coffee frontier pushed westward, leaving the Paraíba Valley behind, it encountered a geological anomaly that would supercharge the industry: the *Terra Roxa* (Purple Earth). To the untrained eye, the soil appeared blood-red, but chemically, it was a miracle of decomposition. Millions of years ago, massive volcanic eruptions in the Paraná Basin spilled basalt lava across the region. Over eons, this basalt weathered into a clay-rich latosol, exceptionally high in iron oxides, which gave it the distinct reddish-purple hue.

This soil possessed physical properties perfectly suited for *Coffea arabica*. It was porous and deep, allowing the coffee tree's taproot to penetrate up to 3 meters (10 feet) down to access water reserves during the dry season. Chemically, it was naturally fertile, rich in phosphorus and potassium. In the Paraíba Valley, trees might yield fruit for twenty years before exhaustion; in the *Terra Roxa* of Western São Paulo, trees could produce heavy yields for forty years or more without fertilizer. This geological lottery win allowed for a scale of planting previously unimaginable. By the early 20th century, the state of São Paulo alone hosted over 1.5 billion coffee trees. The canopy cover was so extensive that, from a high elevation, the curvature of the earth seemed to be carpeted in green velvet.

## BURNING THE ATLANTIC

To create the Green Sea, the Barons had to dismantle the Green Forest. The *Mata Atlântica* (Atlantic Forest) was one of the world's most biodiverse biomes, a dense, triple-canopy jungle filled with jaguars, tapirs, and thousands of endemic plant species found nowhere else on earth. The coffee planters engaged in a systematic removal using a technique called *coivara* (slash-and-burn).

*The expansion of the "Green Sea" was fueled by the slash-and-burn destruction of the Atlantic Rainforest to fertilize the soil.*

The scale of the destruction was immense. Enslaved workers were ordered to fell massive hardwoods—centuries-old peroba and jacaranda trees—and set them alight. The burning was strategic; the ash provided a temporary, potent injection of potash and calcium for the young coffee plants.

Travelers in the 1860s reported that the smoke was often so thick it obscured the sun in Rio de Janeiro, casting a perpetual, copper-colored twilight over the capital. Once the forest was removed, the soil—exposed to the torrential tropical rains—began to erode. The nutrients were extracted by the hungry coffee trees within a generation. When the land's fertility collapsed, the Barons moved on. Today, less than 7% of the original Atlantic Forest remains. The Brazilian coffee empire was built on an environmental graveyard.

### THE ECONOMICS OF LABOR

The "Green Gold" (*O Ouro Verde*) had a human cost that exceeded the environmental one. Brazil was the largest importer of enslaved Africans in the history of the transatlantic trade—absorbing nearly 5 million people, ten times the number brought to the United States. While Britain banned the slave trade in 1807 and abolished slavery in 1833, and the United States fought a Civil War to end it in 1865, Brazil maintained the institution. In fact, the coffee boom accelerated the trade. Between 1800 and 1850, as coffee prices rose, over 1.5 million Africans were shipped to Brazil specifically to work the coffee *fazendas*.

The life of a coffee slave in the Paraíba Valley was a brutal exercise in caloric math. Unlike sugar cane, which had a defined harvest "season," coffee required year-round maintenance. The holing (digging pits for trees), weeding, and pruning were endless tasks. The "holing" was particularly grueling; a slave was expected to dig a designated quota of pits per day in heavy clay soil. The planters calculated the depreciation of human life with cold rationality. It was widely understood among the Barons that it was more economically efficient to work a "piece" (as enslaved people were listed in ledgers) to death in seven years and purchase a replacement than to provide the food, rest, and medical care necessary for survival into old age.

When the British Royal Navy finally forced Brazil to stop the Transatlantic Slave Trade in 1850 (the Eusébio de Queirós Law), the supply of labor was constricted. The price of an enslaved person doubled overnight. The planters turned to the "Internal Slave Trade," purchasing enslaved people from the declining sugar plantations of the north and marching them south to the coffee fields. This migration was driven by the "Hollow Frontier"—a nomadic agricultural model where coffee exhausted the soil in one region, forcing the entire industry to move south in search of fresh nutrients. As the nutrients in the north collapsed, the "Green Sea" had to consume new forests to survive. This constituted a second Middle Passage, this time on land, driven entirely by the global demand for breakfast.

## The San Paulo Railway

As the coffee frontier moved inland, away from the coast, the Barons faced a logistical bottleneck: the Serra do Mar. For decades, coffee was transported down the steep, muddy mule tracks (*tropeiros*) on the backs of donkeys. A *tropa* (mule train) could take weeks to navigate the treacherous mudslides to Santos. It was slow, expensive, and severely limited the volume of export. The Barons required a train. However, 19th-century steam locomotives could not climb a granite wall with a 10% grade.

The solution was imported from Britain. The Barons hired British engineers to build the São Paulo Railway (SPR). Completed in 1867, it was an engineering marvel that defied the physics of the era. Because the grade was too steep for wheel-on-rail traction (which slips at anything over 2-3%), the engineers constructed a massive funicular system known as the "Endless Rope."

The mechanics were terrifyingly elegant. The ascent was divided into four distinct inclines, each roughly 2 kilometers (1.2 miles) long. At the top of each incline sat a stationary steam engine house—massive brick bunkers housing 150-horsepower engines. These engines did not move; they turned giant drums wound with endless steel cables. The trains themselves were hooked onto this cable by a specialized "loco-break" (brake van). The system operated on a counterweight principle: as a train full of coffee descended the mountain, its weight helped pull the train full of coal or immigrants ascending the mountain.

The friction was immense. The cables, thick as a man's arm, hummed with a tension that could sever a limb if they snapped—a constant fear for the brakemen.

*The "Endless Rope" system of the São Paulo Railway overcame the coastal escarpment, unlocking the interior for massive export volume.*

To stop a runaway train on a 10% grade, the brake vans were equipped with rail-gripping pincers that could bite directly into the iron track. This railway, dubbed "The Iron Serpent," connected the interior plateau of Jundiaí and São Paulo city directly to the port of Santos. The economic effect was instantaneous. The cost of transport dropped by 90%. The volume of coffee arriving at the port exploded from thousands of bags to millions. The bottleneck was broken.

LONDON IN THE JUNGLE

The British did not just bring steel; they brought their atmosphere. To service the steam engines and the cables, they built an entire town on top of the foggy ridge of the Serra do Mar. They named it Paranapiacaba ("Place Where You See the Sea"). It was a surreal slice of Victorian England transplanted into the Brazilian jungle. The station master's house was a replica of a British cottage, complete with a Big Ben-style clock tower that chimed the hour through the rainforest mist. The British engineers formed cricket clubs and held tea parties while jaguars prowled the perimeter. Today, Paranapiacaba stands as a preserved relic, the fog still rolling in over the brickwork, a haunting monument to the era when London bankers and Brazilian slaveholders joined forces to conquer gravity.

## IMPORTING THE CRISIS

With the railway in place, the coffee frontier jumped over the exhausted lands of the Paraíba Valley and landed in the *Oeste Paulista* (Western São Paulo). Here, in the *Terra Roxa*, the planters found the Holy Grail of agriculture. The epicenter of this new boom was Ribeirão Preto, which soon became known as the "California of Coffee."

By the 1880s, the "human engine" was failing. The abolitionist movement, led by intellectuals like Joaquim Nabuco, was gaining ground. Slaves were revolting, burning crops, and fleeing the *fazendas* in mass exoduses. On May 13, 1888, Princess Isabel signed the *Lei Áurea* (The Golden Law), abolishing slavery in Brazil. It was the last country in the Western Hemisphere to do so. The Barons predicted economic collapse. Who would harvest the coffee?

The answer came from Europe. Italy was in the throes of a unification crisis. Poverty and overpopulation were driving peasants off their land. The state of São Paulo, flush with coffee money, launched a massive propaganda campaign in Italy: "Come to Brazil! A land of gold and opportunity!" They subsidized the passage across the Atlantic. Between 1880 and 1930, over 1.5 million Italians immigrated to Brazil, primarily to the coffee fields.

## THE HOSPEDARIA

The transition from ship to plantation occurred at the *Hospedaria de Imigrantes* (Immigrant Hostel) in the Brás neighborhood of São Paulo. It was a massive brick complex, part hotel, part hospital, part processing center, designed to accommodate 3,000 people at a time. For the Italian peasant arriving after a month at sea, the experience was sensory overload. The air smelled of carbolic acid and strong coffee. Upon entry, families were separated. Men went to one shower block, women to another. Their clothes were taken to be fumigated in steam chambers to kill lice and cholera. Doctors moved down lines of naked immigrants, checking eyelids for trachoma and skin for rashes. Rejection meant deportation, a terrifying prospect for families who had sold everything to purchase their ticket.

*The* Hospedaria de Imigrantes *processed millions of workers, replacing slave labor with European immigrants bound for the coffee fields.*

Once cleared, they were ushered into the massive refectory. Here, many Italians tasted Brazilian coffee for the first time—strong, heavily sweetened, and served with hard bread. It was the fuel of their new life. In the central courtyard, agents from the *fazendas* shouted out names and offers, bargaining for muscle. "Who has a family of five? Who has strong sons?" The contracts were signed—often with an 'X' by illiterate fathers —and the families were loaded directly onto the trains waiting at the hostel's private platform, shipped west to the purple earth.

### Life Under Contract

The system that replaced slavery was called the *Colonato*. It was a hybrid of serfdom and sharecropping, designed to keep the workforce anchored without chains. An Italian family would be contracted to tend a specific number of coffee trees—usually 2,000 to 5,000. They were paid a small annual wage for weeding and received a piece-rate for the harvest. Crucially, they were allowed to grow their own food (beans, corn, potatoes) between the rows of coffee.

This system was an accounting triumph for the planter. By allowing the workers to grow their own food, the planter did not have to spend cash to feed his workforce. It was a hard life. The *colonos* lived in rows of whitewashed brick houses on the plantation, often just yards from where the slave quarters had stood. They woke before dawn to the sound of the plantation bell. However, unlike the slaves, the Italians possessed mobility. Many left the fields after a few years, moving to the city of São Paulo to open shops and factories. They infused the city with pizza, labor union politics, and a distinct Italian-Paulista dialect. The coffee money, filtering through immigrant hands, built the modern metropolis of São Paulo.

## "I Am Colonel Schmidt"

The scale of this new era is best personified by one man: Francisco Schmidt. Schmidt was not a Baron by birth. He was a German immigrant who arrived in Brazil poor. Through ruthless business acumen and strategic marriages, he began acquiring land in the Ribeirão Preto region just as the *Terra Roxa* boom began. By the 1910s, Schmidt was the single largest coffee grower in the world. He owned 60 plantations. He had 7 million coffee trees. His workforce numbered in the thousands. Schmidt ran his primary estate, the Fazenda Monte Alegre, like a sovereign state.

The social structure of Monte Alegre was total. Schmidt built a church on the property where his workers were married and their children baptized, ensuring the priest preached loyalty to the estate. He built schools, a cinema, and a hospital. But this benevolence was a cage. Schmidt paid his workers not in Brazilian Real, but in *vales*—private currency tokens minted by the plantation. These tokens could only be spent at the *armazém* (company store) owned by Schmidt himself. The prices at the store were inflated, ensuring that at the end of the harvest, many workers owed more money than they had earned. This debt peonage kept the labor force specifically tied to Schmidt's land, unable to leave until their debts were cleared.

Schmidt was known as the "King of Coffee" (*O Rei do Café*). When offered a title by the waning monarchy, he famously refused to purchase a Barony, stating, "I am Colonel Schmidt, and that is enough." His mansion in the middle of the plantation featured a ballroom with chandeliers imported from Austria. He was the prototype of the agro-industrial tycoon, proving that coffee had moved from the age of aristocrats to the age of corporations. Under men like Schmidt, coffee farming transformed. In the *Oeste Paulista*, trees were planted in endless, straight lines that vanished into the horizon. This was the birth of Mass Production. The Brazilians were not just growing coffee; they were manufacturing it. They disregarded the delicate nuances of flavor, as the Yemenis or Ethiopians did. They prioritized volume. They stripped the branches— ripe, green, and black cherries all together—to process them quickly. This flooded the world with cheap, low-grade coffee (Santos 4), making the beverage affordable for the working class in Europe and America for the first time.

## Coffee with Milk

The power of the coffee growers was so absolute that it defined the political structure of the new Brazilian Republic. This era is known to historians as the *Política do Café com Leite* (Coffee with Milk Politics). It was a power-sharing agreement between the two most powerful states: São Paulo (Coffee) and Minas Gerais (Dairy). For forty years (1889-1930), the Presidency of Brazil alternated between them. But by 1900, Brazil was a victim of its own success. The *Terra Roxa* was so fertile, and the planting so aggressive, that the trees were producing more coffee than the world could drink.

In 1906, a bumper crop threatened to crash the global price. A collapse would bankrupt the Barons and destroy the Brazilian economy. So, the Barons did something that changed the history of global commodities. They invented Price Supports.

## VALORIZATION: THE TRAP

Meeting in the town of Taubaté, the governors of the coffee states signed the Treaty of Taubaté. The plan was simple but radical: "Valorization." The concept was to divorce the price of coffee from the supply of coffee. The state of São Paulo did not have the cash to execute this, so they turned to the masters of global finance. They secured massive loans from British banking houses like J. Henry Schröder and the Rothschilds, using the future tax revenue of coffee exports as collateral.

With this borrowed gold, the Brazilian government entered the market as a buyer of last resort. They purchased millions of bags of surplus coffee and locked them away in warehouses in Santos, New York, and Le Havre. By artificially removing this supply from the market, they forced the global price to stay high. It worked—temporarily. The price stabilized, and the loans were serviced. The Barons grew rich. But the scheme created a catastrophic "moral hazard." Because the government guaranteed to buy the coffee at a profitable price, the planters had no incentive to stop planting. In fact, the logic of the market was inverted: the more you planted, the more the government had to buy. Brazil began to accumulate a mountain of coffee. By the 1920s, the warehouses in Santos held millions of bags of unsold beans. The government was drowning in debt to finance a product that nobody was drinking. They were paying interest to British bankers to store rotting beans in American warehouses. It was a bubble of epic proportions, waiting for a pin.

## WALL STREET OF BEANS

All this coffee flowed through one bottleneck: Santos. By the 1920s, Santos had transformed from a fever swamp into the "Wall Street of Beans." The city smelled of roasting beans, salt water, and jute. The streets were paved with cobblestones brought as ballast in European ships. The heart of the city was the *Bolsa Oficial de Café* (Official Coffee Exchange), a palace built in 1922. It featured marble floors, stained glass windows depicting the colonization of Brazil, and a massive auction pit. Here, the "Coffee Kings"—brokers and exporters—sat in high-backed wooden chairs arranged in a semicircle. They shouted bids, deciding the price of breakfast for the entire planet.

The wealth in Santos was staggering. Exporters built mansions along the beachfront, and the city became a cosmopolitan hub of gambling and trade. But the entire edifice rested on the artificial dam of Valorization. Behind the marble facade of the exchange, the surplus in the warehouses was growing, bag by bag, year by year.

## OCTOBER 1929

The party ended in October 1929. The Wall Street Crash triggered the Great Depression. American and European consumers, suddenly destitute, stopped buying coffee. Demand evaporated overnight. But the trees in Brazil—protected by years of Valorization and biological lag—were still producing billions of cherries. The price of coffee collapsed from 22 cents a pound to 8 cents. The credit markets froze, and the Brazilian government could no longer borrow money from the Rothschilds to buy the surplus. The dam broke.

The new president, Getúlio Vargas, faced a nightmare scenario. The warehouses were bursting. The new crop was arriving. He made a desperate decision. To save the price, he had to destroy the product. It is one of the most enduring, apocalyptic images of the Great Depression. Starting in 1931, the Brazilian government burned 78 million bags of coffee.

The logistics of destruction were complex. Coffee beans contain moisture and oils that make them difficult to burn efficiently. The government had to mix the beans with tar and kerosene to get them to ignite. They used coffee beans as fuel for steam locomotives instead of coal, the smell of roasting coffee pervading the passenger cars. They built massive bonfires in the fields, the smoke drifting over the cities for months. They dumped millions of tons into the ocean, turning the waters off Santos black and killing the fish.

*During the 1930s collapse, Brazil destroyed 78 million bags of coffee,*
*burning beans in locomotives and bonfires to save the price.*

This destruction was a tragedy of waste. The labor of millions of Italian immigrants, the legacy of millions of slaves, and the nutrients of the ancient Atlantic Forest were all converted into smoke. The "Green Gold" had turned to ash.

ASH AND CONCRETE

The crash of 1929 broke the political power of the Coffee Barons. The *Café com Leite* republic fell. Brazil began to force-march toward industrialization, desperate to move away from being a single-crop economy. But the physical footprint remains. An aerial view of the state of São Paulo today reveals a landscape defined by the choices of the 19th century. The railroads, the sprawling metropolis of São Paulo, and the denuded, eroded hills are the scars of the boom.

Brazil remains the world's largest coffee producer, growing a third of the planet's supply. But the era of the Barons—the time when a single man could stand on his veranda and look out over a million trees that he owned like a feudal lord—is gone. It was swept away by the very forces of mass production and global finance that the Barons helped create. They built a machine too big to control, and in the end, it consumed them. The permanent alteration of the global price structure due to Brazil's volume remains the governing law of the modern coffee industry; the sheer weight of Brazilian production dictates the baseline price for every farmer on earth.

# 11

# ARBUCKLE'S EMPIRE: BRANDING THE CAN

I n the winter of 1864, the prevailing scent of the American landscape was not the crisp pine of the wilderness or the ozone of the prairie; it was the acrid, heavy smell of burning organic matter.

In a Union Army encampment outside Petersburg, Virginia, the air hung low and gray, thickened by the smoke of a thousand campfires. A young infantryman, his uniform stiff with the red clay of the trenches, crouched over a flickering flame. In his hand, he held a blackened tin skillet, the metal warped from months of thermal abuse. Inside rattled a handful of green coffee beans, hard as river pebbles and pale as dry bone, which he had been issued as part of his daily ration.

His task was a culinary paradox that required the finesse of a chef amidst the squalor of a siege: he had to roast the beans evenly without carbonizing them—a feat requiring constant agitation and precise heat control—while exposed to the elements. If he ceased shaking the pan for ten seconds to dodge the whine of a sniper's bullet or wipe the sweat and soot from his eyes, the beans resting on the hot metal would scorch into charcoal, while those on top remained raw, grassy, and vegetal. Once sufficiently darkened, he would crush them with the butt of his musket or a smooth rock found in the mud, dump the resulting grit into a pot of boiling water, and consume the sludge. It was bitter, *smoky, and often thick with sediment, but to the exhausted soldier, it was the necessary fuel for survival.*

*Five hundred miles (800 km) away, in the rapidly industrializing heart of Pittsburgh, Pennsylvania, a man named John Arbuckle stood in the storeroom of his wholesale grocery business on Liberty Street, observing a similar struggle. He watched housewives arriving to purchase raw green beans from the bulk barrels, their faces etched with the anticipation of the drudgery awaiting them at home. He observed the profound inconsistency of the product; one week a family might drink a perfect, aromatic brew, and the next week they would endure burnt water or a sour, under-developed extraction.*

*Arbuckle looked at the green bean and saw a failure of imagination. Outside his warehouse door, the world was undergoing a rapid standardization. The Bessemer process was transforming the unpredictable alchemy of iron into consistent, structural steel; the railroads were unifying track gauges to allow seamless transit across the continent. Yet, coffee remained stuck in the pre-industrial age of the kitchen skillet, tethered to the variable skill of the individual roaster. Arbuckle realized that the profit lay not merely in the commodity itself, but in the service attached to it. He was about to take the soldier's inconsistent sludge and transmute it into a marker of consistency, inventing the modern concept of the Brand along the way.*

### The Culinary Anarchy of 1860

It helps to understand the culinary labor of the 1850s in order to grasp the magnitude of the revolution that occurred in the 1870s. Before the Civil War, coffee was almost exclusively sold in its green, unroasted state. Consumers purchased it by the pound or kilogram, scooped from a burlap sack that often served as a home for mice, weevils, or dust from the warehouse floor.

The technology of the home roast was primitive and demanding. While wealthy estates might possess a cylinder roaster that could be turned with a crank over a stove, the average American household relied on a "spider"—a cast-iron skillet with legs designed to stand over coals— or simply a shovel held over the hearth. The process was a sensory trial. Roasting coffee releases heavy, oily smoke containing chaff and particulate matter that clings to curtains, hair, and clothing. It was a chore usually delegated to the women of the household, a weekly ritual of standing before a roaring stove for forty minutes, shaking a heavy pan until their arms ached, eyes watering from the fumes.

The resulting beverage was frequently described by European visitors as a "vile decoction." American coffee was notoriously inconsistent, swinging wildly between the raw acidity of under-roasted beans and the acrid bitterness of carbon. Furthermore, the chemistry of the bean presented a logistical trap. Once roasted, coffee begins to stale immediately. Oxygen attacks the volatile oils and aromatics, turning the flavor flat and eventually rancid within a week. A household could not roast a month's supply at once for convenience; they were forced to roast constantly, in small batches, to maintain drinkability.

John Arbuckle marketed time as much as the product itself. In the mid-19th century, the American kitchen was a factory of manual labor where women were responsible for manufacturing soap, candles, clothing, and bread from raw materials. When Arbuckle eventually launched his pre-roasted coffee, his appeal was structural. He implied that a modern household should not be enslaved to the skillet. By purchasing pre-roasted beans, a family saved not just the physical labor, but the fuel —wood or coal—and the time required for cleaning the soot from the kitchen. It was one of the first true "Convenience Foods" in American history, anticipating the logic of the 20th-century frozen dinner by eighty years.

### THE CAFFEINE RATION

The catalyst for this industrial shift was the American Civil War (1861-1865). It was the first conflict in history where caffeine played a strategic, logistical role.

The Union Army recognized early in the conflict that coffee was essential for morale and physical stamina. In 1832, President Andrew Jackson had substituted coffee for the traditional rum ration, but it was Lincoln's army that institutionalized the dependency. The official ration was massive: roughly 36 pounds (16 kg) of coffee a year per soldier.

Soldiers became obsessive about their brew. They referred to it as "black water" or "essence of old shoe," yet they consumed quarts of it daily. Diaries from the era are filled with references to coffee, often ranking it above food, pay, or safety in importance. One soldier wrote home, "Nobody can 'soldier' without coffee." When supply lines were severed, men were known to search the saddlebags of fallen Confederate soldiers, not for gold or currency, but for the precious green beans.

The government, overwhelmed by the logistics of feeding two million men, attempted to solve the roasting problem with industrial technology. They issued "Essence of Coffee"—an early, disastrous attempt at instant coffee. It was a thick, molasses-like liquid packed in a can, allegedly brewed from concentrated coffee. The soldiers despised it, believing it was adulterated with chicory, sawdust, and grease. They frequently discarded the cans in the roadside ditches of Virginia, preferring to starve rather than consume the sludge.

The army also experimented with the Sharps Carbine Coffee Mill. The Sharps Rifle Company designed a version of their standard-issue carbine with a hand-cranked coffee grinder built directly into the buttstock of the weapon. The concept was that a soldier could engage the enemy, then detach the stock, pour beans into a slot in the wood, and grind his morning cup.

*The Sharps Carbine Coffee Mill was a rare hybrid of weaponry and culinary tool designed for Union cavalry.*

While mechanically ingenious, fewer than one hundred were likely made, and historians debate if they ever saw combat or were merely prototypes. It remains one of the strangest hybrids of weaponry and culinary tools in history, a symbol of the desperate desire to secure a reliable cup amidst chaos.

When the war ended in 1865, millions of men returned to their homes and farms. They were habituated to high caffeine consumption, but they were weary of the campfire roast. They were a market primed for a better, more consistent method.

## THE PHYSICS OF THE ROAST

Arbuckle faced a physics problem. He knew that pre-roasted coffee existed—commercial roasters in New York were selling to local hotels—but it was a failure as a shipped product because of the staling rate. If he roasted coffee in Pittsburgh and shipped it to St. Louis, it would be rancid long before it reached the consumer's pot.

He needed a preservative. He needed a seal.

In 1868, Arbuckle patented a process that utilized a specific glazing agent. He discovered that if he coated the beans in a mixture of egg white, Irish moss (a gelatinous seaweed), and sugar during the final seconds of the roast, the mixture would caramelize and form a hard, airtight varnish around the bean.

This glaze accomplished three things, transitioning the bean from an agricultural product to an industrial one:

1. **Preservation:** It sealed the porous structure of the bean, trapping the volatile aromatics inside and preventing oxygen from entering. This extended the shelf life from days to months, allowing for long-distance shipping.
2. **Clarification:** When the consumer eventually ground the beans and brewed them, the egg coating acted as a "clarifying agent" (similar to fining a wine), binding with the floating particulates and chaff, causing the grounds to settle rapidly to the bottom of the pot. This resulted in a clearer, less gritty cup.
3. **Weight:** Crucially for Arbuckle's profit margins, the sugar and egg added mass to the coffee. He was effectively selling sugar at the price of coffee, a margin boost that allowed him to undercut competitors.

He dubbed his new process "Ariosa." The name was a composite code: A (Arbuckle) - RIO (Rio de Janeiro, the source of the beans) - SA

(Santos, the other source). It sounded exotic, musical, and undeniably modern.

## THE SPIRAL OF JABEZ BURNS

Arbuckle possessed the chemistry, but he required the mechanics to scale it. Hand-roasting, or even batch roasting in small cylinders, could not produce enough volume to feed a nation.

He partnered with an inventor named Jabez Burns. In 1864, Burns had patented the "Self-Emptying Coffee Roaster," a machine that serves as the mechanical ancestor of every industrial roaster used today.

Before Burns, roasters were large, clumsy cylinders that had to be stopped and manually dumped—a slow process that often resulted in scorched beans or burned workers. Burns invented a double-helix screw-flange system inside the drum. It functioned on the principle of the Archimedes screw. During the roast, the internal veins mixed the beans for even heat distribution, tumbling them constantly through the hot air.

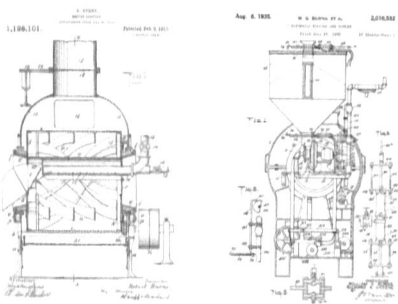

*Jabez Burns' self-emptying roaster allowed coffee to transition from a kitchen chore to a factory product.*

When the roast was complete, the operator simply opened a gate while the drum continued to turn. The internal veins reversed their function relative to the gate, pushing the beans out into the cooling tray in a continuous, fluid stream.

This was the "Ford Model T" moment for coffee. It allowed for continuous, industrial-scale roasting without stopping the engine. Arbuckle bought the rights and constructed a massive factory in Brooklyn, New York. The air over the East River began to smell of roasted nuts and caramel. The facility was a fortress of brick, humming with the sound of steam engines turning the massive Burns drums, capable of roasting thousands of pounds an hour. No longer a kitchen craft, it had become heavy industry.

### THE FLYING ANGEL AND THE PEDDLER

Arbuckle did not just sell coffee; he invented the modern concept of CPG (Consumer Packaged Goods). Before Arbuckle, a customer bought generic "coffee." After Arbuckle, they bought Arbuckle's.

He refused to sell his beans in bulk barrels where they could be mixed with inferior products, corn, or stones by unscrupulous grocers. He packaged them in one-pound (0.45 kg) paper bags. This was a radical departure. The bag was lined to protect the glaze and prevent moisture ingress. It was bright yellow with bold red lettering, featuring a trademark image: a Flying Angel hovering over a map of the world.

This was the first time a commodity had been de-commoditized. The consumer was buying a consistent industrial standard rather than a raw agricultural product. A bag of Ariosa purchased in a general store in Maine tasted exactly the same as a bag bought in a trading post in Texas. The yellow bag became a marker of consistency.

*Arbuckle's was the first national coffee brand, bringing a standardized product—and a peppermint stick—to every corner of the country.*

To distribute this new product, Arbuckle built a "peddling network" that bypassed traditional supply chains. He employed a fleet of salesmen who traveled by rail and wagon, penetrating deep into the rural hinterlands. More than order-takers, they were evangelists for the brand. They taught grocers how to display the bags, creating the first "point of sale" displays. The coffee traveled from the Brooklyn docks to railheads in St.

Louis and Kansas City, and from there, into the saddlebags and wagons of the expanding West.

## "Cooky" and the Chuck Wagon

Ariosa conquered the cities, but its legend was forged in the American West. In 1866, a Texas cattleman named Charles Goodnight invented the mobile logistics hub known as the Chuck Wagon. Facing a cattle drive from Texas to New Mexico without any towns for resupply, Goodnight took a surplus Army Studebaker wagon and reinforced it with iron axles to withstand the rough terrain.

On the back of the wagon, he built a "Chuck Box"—a cabinet with drawers and shelves that folded down into a worktable.

*The Chuck Wagon became the mobile café of the American West, fueled almost exclusively by Arbuckle's Ariosa.*

In the center of that box, the most accessible drawer was always reserved for coffee. Goodnight understood that coffee was the fuel of the drive. Cowboys worked 18-hour days in the saddle, battling stampedes, river crossings, and rustlers. They required hot, black stimulants constantly. The "Cooky" (the camp cook) would keep a pot boiling on the fire 24 hours a day.

Arbuckle's Ariosa became the exclusive supplier to this mobile fleet. The reason was logistical: the egg glaze made the beans almost indestructible. They did not rot in the humidity, they did not stale in the heat, and the rectangular one-pound paper bags were easy to stack in the Chuck Box like bricks.

The yellow bag became as essential to the cowboy as his saddle. In the lexicon of the West, the word "coffee" was often replaced by the word "Arbuckle." A cowboy wouldn't ask for a cup of coffee; he'd say, "Pour me a cup of Arbuckle." It was brewed strong—"strong enough to float a horseshoe," as the saying went. If a traveler stumbled upon a camp, the first offer was always a cup. It was the primary sign of hospitality in a lawless land.

## The Peppermint Strategy

John Arbuckle was a system builder who understood human psychology. He knew that even with pre-roasted beans, there was still one barrier: the grinding.

Grinding coffee on the trail or in the kitchen was a hated chore. The hand-cranked box mills were slow, tiring, and loud. Arbuckle needed to incentivize the labor.

So, he added a bribe. Inside every bag of Ariosa coffee, Arbuckle included a single stick of peppermint candy.

This candy stick became a currency on the range. The "Cooky" would shout, "Who wants the candy?" The cowboy who volunteered to crank the coffee grinder received the peppermint stick. It turned a chore into a contest. This was one of the earliest examples of a "prize in the box" marketing strategy. It created a fierce loyalty. Cowboys would refuse to buy other brands because they wanted the candy. It was a simple sugar stick, but on the dusty Chisholm Trail, where luxuries were non-existent, it was a rare and coveted treat.

## Encyclopedia of the Poor

Arbuckle's innovation extended to the packaging itself. He realized that the paper bag could be monetized as a loyalty device. He printed a signature on the side of every bag and told customers: "Cut out this signature and mail it to us." This was the birth of the national Loyalty Program. Arbuckle published a catalog of "Premiums."

- 15 signatures = A handkerchief.
- 60 signatures = A razor.
- 100 signatures = A pair of lace curtains.
- 150 signatures = A pair of scissors or a pocket knife.

For the rural poor, especially in the Reconstruction South and the developing West where cash was scarce, Arbuckle signatures were a form of currency. Women would save them for years to "buy" wedding gifts or household tools. The yellow bag became a ubiquitous feature of the American pantry, not just for the drink, but for the dream of the catalog.

To further cement the brand, Arbuckle began inserting Lithographed Trading Cards into the bags. These were detailed, full-color cards depicting animals, famous generals, and exotic countries. This sparked a cultural phenomenon. When Arbuckle's rival, the Woolson Spice Company (owned by the Sugar Trust), launched Lion Coffee, they fought back with their own cards. Arbuckle had the "Flying Angel." Lion had the "Lion's Head."

It became the first "collectible war" in American history. Children drove the purchasing decisions of their parents, demanding specific brands to complete their sets of "Wild Animals" or "Famous Battles." The companies escalated their content, printing maps and serialized stories on the cards. For many Americans living in isolated rural communities, these cards were their only window to the wider world. They were the "Encyclopedia of the Poor." Arbuckle was essentially running an educational publishing house inside a coffee factory, using the backs of coffee bags to teach a generation of Americans geography and zoology.

### The War of the Titans: Coffee vs. Sugar

By the 1890s, John Arbuckle was fabulously wealthy. He was the "Coffee King." But his ambition led him into a collision with the "Sugar King"—Henry Havemeyer.

Havemeyer ran the Sugar Trust—the American Sugar Refining Company—which by 1892 had consolidated most of the nation's refineries and controlled roughly 98% of U.S. sugar refining. He was a quintessential monopolist who crushed competition with predatory pricing.

The conflict began over the glaze. Arbuckle purchased massive amounts of sugar for his Ariosa coating. He demanded a wholesale discount commensurate with his volume. Havemeyer refused, treating Arbuckle as a captive customer. Arbuckle, a stubborn Scotsman, decided to expose the vulnerability of the monopoly. He announced that if Havemeyer would not sell him cheap sugar, he would build his own sugar refinery.

Havemeyer retaliated with the brute force of a monopolist who had never been told 'no.' He famously announced that if Arbuckle was going into sugar, the Sugar Trust would go into coffee. He purchased the Woolson Spice Co. (makers of Lion Coffee) and weaponized it.

This was the Great Coffee War, a clash of Gilded Age titans that turned the grocery aisle into a battlefield. Havemeyer dropped the price of Lion Coffee to levels that defied economic logic, selling below cost and subsidizing the losses with his sugar empire's deep pockets. His goal was not competition; it was extermination. He intended to bleed Arbuckle dry until the Scotsman was forced to sell.

But Arbuckle refused to blink. He responded with a counter-subsidy, using his new sugar refinery profits to slash the price of Ariosa. It was a race to the bottom, a game of financial chicken where the American consumer was the winner, purchasing high-grade coffee for pennies while two multi-millionaires set their fortunes on fire to spite one another.

It was a battle of billionaires fought in the grocery aisle. For the consumer, it was a golden age; coffee became incredibly cheap. But Arbuckle had a secret weapon: The Smyser Weighing Machine.

Arbuckle had employed a team of engineers to design a machine that could fill, weigh, and seal bags automatically. Havemeyer was still packing Lion Coffee largely by hand. The Smyser machine was a marvel of clockwork gears and chutes, capable of packing 18,000 bags a day with a skeleton crew.

The efficiency gap was too large for even the Sugar Trust to over-come. After years of bleeding millions of dollars, Havemeyer conceded. He settled with Arbuckle. Arbuckle kept his sugar refinery (beating the Trust), and Havemeyer retreated from the coffee business. The Coffee King had defeated the Sugar Monopoly through superior automation.

### THE RISE OF THE CUP TESTERS

Arbuckle dominated the East and the Midwest, but the geography of the United States was too vast for a single brand to hold absolute sway.

In San Francisco, a carpenter named James Folger had arrived during the Gold Rush of 1849. He realized, much like Levi Strauss, that the true wealth lay not in the mines, but in supplying the miners. He started J.A. Folger & Co., roasting coffee for the prospectors.

Folger pioneered a different approach to quality. While Arbuckle relied on the heavy "Rio" beans—which were harsh, medicinal, and iodine-like—Folger began sourcing milder beans from Central America and the Pacific. More importantly, he introduced Cup Testing. Before purchasing a shipment of beans, Folger would roast a sample, grind it, and taste it. This sensory quality control was a radical step up from the "buy it all and glaze it" strategy of Arbuckle.

Meanwhile, in Nashville, Tennessee, the Cheek-Neal Coffee Company was attempting to create a high-end blend for the finest hotel in the South: The Maxwell House Hotel. Joel Cheek, the founder, blended smooth, mild Central American beans. It was served at the hotel's restaurant to the Southern aristocracy. The brand received its most significant marketing boost from a legend involving President Theodore Roosevelt. When Roosevelt visited the Maxwell House in 1907, he allegedly finished his cup and declared it was "Good to the Last Drop." Whether the quote is apocryphal or not, the slogan endured. Maxwell House positioned itself as the "aristocrat" of coffees, distinct from the working-class Ariosa.

## THE VACUUM SHIFT

Arbuckle's empire was built on the whole bean. The egg glaze preserved the bean, but once it was ground, the clock started ticking. The next technological leap would render the egg glaze and the Arbuckle supremacy obsolete.

In 1900, vacuum packaging was perfected by R.W. Hills (of Hills Bros. in San Francisco). Hills discovered that if roasted coffee was ground, placed in a metal tin, and the air was mechanically removed, it would remain fresh for months without a glaze.

This was the death knell for Ariosa. The consumer preferred the convenience of pre-ground coffee. They no longer wished to crank the mill, even for a peppermint stick. The vacuum tin offered "roastery freshness" with zero labor. One simply opened the can and poured. Arbuckle's refused to adapt quickly enough, clinging to the whole bean and the paper bag, convinced that the "glaze" was their unassailable advantage. By the 1920s, the vacuum-packed tins of Maxwell House and Folgers were ascending.

## THE LEGACY OF THE AISLE

John Arbuckle died in 1912. His company eventually faded, absorbed by larger conglomerates. The yellow bags with the Flying Angel disappeared from the shelves.

However, his legacy is the modern supermarket aisle. Every time a consumer sees a brand logo, a loyalty card, a "prize inside," or a vacuum-sealed bag, they are interacting with the ghost of Arbuckle. He took a raw product of nature—inconsistent, perishable, and difficult—and transformed it into a reliable industrial grocery item.

He taught America how to drink coffee. He moved the roasting from the kitchen hearth to the factory floor. And in doing so, he fueled the settlement of the West. The cowboy, the homesteader, and the factory worker were all powered by the yellow bag. The era of coffee as an agricultural product was ending; the era of coffee as a standardized industrial fuel had begun.

# PART III

# FROM BLOSSOM TO BEAN

To understand coffee's history, you have to understand its biology—because the plant is not a neutral backdrop to human ambition. It is a fragile living thing with preferences, limits, and enemies.

In this section, we step inside the coffee tree: its species, its genetics, its vulnerabilities, and the ecological systems that make good coffee possible. We look at what fermentation and processing actually do, why "washed" and "natural" aren't just methods but flavor philosophies, and how disease has repeatedly redrawn the coffee map.

Coffee tastes like culture, but it grows like ecology. And ecology does not negotiate.

# 12

---

# THE BIOLOGICAL FACTORY:
# ARABICA'S GENETIC PARADOX

H overing inside the white, star-shaped flower of a *Coffea arabica* tree offers a vantage point into a biological factory of extraordinary complexity. The air is heavy with a scent reminiscent of jasmine and orange blossom—a perfume evolved to signal readiness. Below, the ovaries of the plant wait to swell into the fruit known as a "cherry." Above, the anthers are dusted with pollen. Yet, unlike many flowering plants that rely entirely on the chaotic intervention of wind or insect, this flower possesses a capability for self-reliance.

It is a self-pollinating fortress, capable of replicating its own DNA to ensure survival in the deep shade of the Ethiopian understory. Should the insects disappear or the wind die down, this flower retains the ability to fertilize itself, snapping shut its genetic code to produce an offspring that is a near-perfect photocopy of the parent.

This biological solitude constitutes the central paradox of high-quality coffee. The very trait that allows Arabica to produce such consistent, refined flavor—its genetic purity—is also the trait that renders it uniquely vulnerable. The modern coffee industry drinks from a genetic monoculture, and the crop faces a profound susceptibility to pathogens. To understand the liquid in the cup, one must look beyond the barista and examine the chromosome. This is *not merely the history of humans drinking coffee; it is the history of the plant inventing itself.*

### THE ACCIDENT OF BIRTH

Taxonomically, coffee belongs to the order *Gentianales*, family *Rubiaceae*. Botanists refer to this as the "Madder Family," a massive clan containing 13,000 siblings ranging from the medicinal *Cinchona* (the source of quinine) to the ornamental Gardenia. However, within this cosmopolitan family, the genus *Coffea* represents a distinct evolutionary anomaly. And the king of the genus, *Coffea arabica*, is a genetic accident.

*Arabica* stands as the only tetraploid species in the genus. It possesses four sets of chromosomes (44 total), compared to the two sets (22) found in almost all other species, including *Coffea canephora* (Robusta) and *Coffea eugenioides*. This chromosomal difference acts as a significant reproductive barrier, isolating *Arabica* on its own genetic island.

In 2024, genomic researchers finally mapped the family tree, pinning down the "Big Bang" of coffee. Somewhere between 10,000 and 500,000 years ago—a relatively brief window in evolutionary time—in the borderlands between southern Ethiopia and South Sudan, two distinct species converged:

- **The Father:** *Coffea canephora* (Robusta)—tough, bitter, and adapted to the hot lowlands.
- **The Mother:** *Coffea eugenioides*—delicate, low-caffeine, and shrub-like, possessing high sugar content but low physiological vigor.

In a rare botanical event, these two species merged. Instead of splitting their DNA to form a typical hybrid, the resulting plant kept the full genetic code of both parents.

The result was a genomic super-plant. It possessed the sensory complexity and sweetness of the mother (*eugenioides*) and the structural vigor of the father (*canephora*). However, because this event occurred so recently and likely involved a very small number of individual trees, every *Arabica* tree on Earth today descends from that tiny, inbred population.

The genetic diversity of the world's commercial coffee crop is estimated to be less than 1.2%. Compared to rice, corn, or soy, *Arabica* is essentially a genetic monolith. This uniformity explains why a single disease, such as *Hemileia vastatrix* (coffee leaf rust), can sweep through a farm in Brazil and a farm in Kenya with equal devastation. Biologically, they are the same tree.

## UNDERGROUND ENGINEERING

The life of this tree begins in the dark. Beneath the leaf litter of the forest floor, the root system of a coffee plant operates as a masterpiece of hydraulic engineering, designed to solve a specific problem: survival through a four-month dry season without shedding leaves.

The system anchors itself with the taproot. This thick, central spike drives straight down into the earth, piercing the laterite clay to reach depths of 3 to 4.5 meters (10 to 15 feet). Its purpose is foundational as well as nutritional. The taproot hunts for the deep, ancient water tables that sustain the tree when the surface soil turns to dust. This deep anchorage allows coffee to survive on the volcanic slopes of Guatemala or the arid plateaus of the Cerrado in Brazil.

*The central taproot acts as a hydraulic anchor, driving deep into the earth to access water tables during the dry season.*

Radiating outward from the taproot are the lateral roots. These grow horizontally, remaining close to the surface—often within the top 30 centimeters (12 inches) of soil. These are the "feeders."

Upon brushing away the topsoil in a forest in Jimma, Ethiopia, one reveals a white web of these feeder roots. Covered in millions of micro-scopic root hairs, they do not work alone. They connect into a fungal network called mycorrhizae. In a symbiotic exchange, the fungi accept sugars produced by the coffee leaves. In return, the fungi extend the reach of the roots by magnitudes, dissolving minerals like phosphorus and zinc from the surrounding rock and feeding them directly into the tree's vascular system.

This "Human Layer" interaction—where a farmer must nurture the invisible fungi to feed the visible tree—represents the frontier of modern agronomy. When a farmer utilizes excessive fungicide or tills the soil too aggressively, they sever this connection. The tree may appear healthy above ground, but below, it has been disconnected from its nutrient network.

## 100,000 STOMATA

Above the soil, the leaf acts as the engine room. The *Coffea arabica* leaf is an evolution in efficiency: dark green, glossy, and elliptical. Its shine comes from a thick, waxy cuticle that acts as a shield, preventing water loss and reflecting the UV radiation that would otherwise scorch the cellular machinery.

But the real work happens in the shadows. On the underside of a single leaf, roughly 300,000 to 450,000 microscopic valves, called stom-ata, regulate the plant's breathing. These valves manage a dangerous trade-off: to perform photosynthesis, they must open to inhale Carbon Dioxide ($CO_2$). However, the moment they open, the plant bleeds precious water vapor through transpiration.

Because Arabica evolved in the cool, misty understory of Ethiopia, it plays a conservative game. It creates a phenomenon known as "midday depression." When the sun hits its peak between 10:00 AM and 2:00 PM, the tree panics. To preserve moisture, it slams the stomata shut. Photo-synthesis halts. The factory effectively goes offline.

This biological shutdown is the scientific argument for the "Shade Strategy" (explored in Chapter 16). The canopy isn't just a sunscreen; it is an operational requirement. By keeping the air cool, shade trees trick the coffee leaf into keeping its valves open, keeping the sugar factory running during the hottest hours of the day.

This physiological limit explains why "Shade Grown" is not merely a marketing term; it is a biological preference. When a coffee tree grows under a canopy of banana or *Inga* trees, the ambient temperature drops, and humidity remains higher. The stomata remain open for longer periods. The tree creates more carbohydrates. More sugar translates to higher density in the seed, which eventually manifests as higher acidity and complexity in the cup.

When agriculture drags *Arabica* into the full sun of a monoculture to maximize yield, the tree reacts to the stress. It does not "decide" to produce more; it is triggered biologically to over-produce flowers and fruit in an effort to ensure reproduction before potential system failure. The farmer obtains more coffee, but the biological machinery runs at a fever pace, often sacrificing the nuance of flavor for the volume of the crop.

CHEMICAL WARFARE

Why does the coffee plant produce caffeine? It did not evolve to assist a human in maintaining focus. From the plant's perspective, mammals are largely irrelevant. The target audience for caffeine ($C_8H_{10}N_4O_2$) is much smaller. Caffeine is an alkaloid poison, a biological weapon evolved for specific defensive purposes.

First, it acts as an insecticide. To a beetle, a borer, or a slug, caffeine is a neurotoxin. If a pest bites into a coffee leaf or seed, the bitter alkaloid paralyzes its nervous system or kills it outright. This chemical defense explains the genetic split between *Arabica* and *Robusta*. *Robusta* evolved in the hot, insect-heavy lowlands of the Congo Basin. To survive, it adapted to produce nearly double the caffeine content of *Arabica* (2.7% versus 1.5%). *Arabica*, residing in the cooler, high-altitude mountains where insect pressure was lower, adapted by lowering its chemical shields—and consequently, its bitterness.

Second, caffeine acts as an herbicide. When coffee leaves and cherries fall to the ground and decompose, they release caffeine into the soil. This caffeine inhibits the germination of other seeds. The coffee tree effectively alters the soil chemistry around it to prevent competitors from utilizing its water resources. It is allelopathy—chemical territorialism.

However, the plant also utilizes caffeine as a manipulator. While high doses kill insects, low doses present in the nectar act pharmacologically on pollinators. When a bee consumes this nectar, the trace caffeine triggers the reward memory centers in the bee's brain. A bee that consumes caffeinated nectar is significantly more likely to remember that specific flower's scent and return to it than a bee consuming plain sugar water. The coffee plant secures loyalty through chemistry.

THE CHERRY: ANATOMY OF A DRUPE

Botanically, the "bean" is a misnomer. Coffee is the seed of a fruit. Specifically, it is a drupe (stone fruit), structurally identical to a peach, a date, or a cherry.

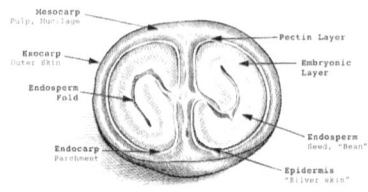

*The coffee "bean" is actually the seed of a drupe, protected by complex layers of skin, mucilage, and parchment.*

To understand processing, one must understand the layers of this fruit. If one were to bite into a ripe coffee cherry on a farm in Colombia, the layers would appear as follows, from the outside in:

- **Exocarp (Skin):** Thick, bitter, and transitioning from green to yellow to "blood red" (or purple) as it ripens.
- **Mesocarp (Mucilage):** This is the functional layer for processing. It is a thin, slimy, translucent flesh rich in pectin and sugars (fructose and glucose). It tastes of watermelon,

honeysuckle, and cucumber. This sugar layer provides the fuel for fermentation.

- **Parenchyma (Parchment):** A tough, fibrous hull that protects the seed. Upon drying, it resembles paper.
- **Endosperm (The Seed):** The prize. Hard, dense, and blue-green, it is packed with lipids, carbohydrates, and proteins—the precursors to flavor.
- **Silverskin:** A microscopic, papery membrane that clings tightly to the seed, serving as the final wrapper.

Typically, two seeds reside inside every cherry, growing flat sides together. However, in approximately 5% of cherries, a genetic variation occurs. Only one ovule fertilizes. The seed possesses no partner to push against, so it grows round and solitary, filling the entire fruit. This is known as a Peaberry (or *Caracol*). Once discarded as mutants, they are now sold as premiums, prized because their round shape allows them to roll smoothly in a roasting drum, heating more evenly than their flat-sided siblings.

## THE LIBRARY OF FLAVOR: VARIETIES

If *Arabica* is the species, "Variety" (or Cultivar) is the dialect. Because *Arabica* is self-pollinating, distinct lineages have developed over centuries. These varieties function as the wine grapes of the coffee world —the Pinot Noirs and Cabernets of the bean belt. A farmer's choice of variety constitutes the single most important decision in the planting process, determining the quality ceiling and the risk floor.

Typica: The genetic baseline. This tall, spindly tree is the lineage the Dutch transported from Yemen to Java and the Caribbean. It produces a clean, sweet cup, but it is low-yielding and genetically frail, susceptible to nearly every common pathogen.
Bourbon: The mutation. French colonists planted *Typica* on the island of Bourbon (now Réunion) in the Indian Ocean. In the volcanic soil, the plant mutated. The resulting tree grew slightly shorter, bushier, and 20-30% more productive. It produces a

distinctively sweet, buttery cup. Many of the celebrated coffees of Rwanda and El Salvador are Bourbons.

**SL-28:** The Drought King. In the 1930s, Scott Laboratories in Kenya operated under the British colonial government to identify a tree capable of surviving the dry African savannah. They selected a drought-resistant variety from Tanganyika (now Tanzania). The result, SL-28, is legendary for its flavor profile—characterized by blackcurrant, tomato, and phosphoric acidity. While it is the gold standard of Kenyan coffee, it remains susceptible to major diseases.

**Caturra:** The Dwarf. Discovered in Brazil in 1937, this is a natural mutation of *Bourbon* that is short and stocky. It revolutionized industrial farming because the trees could be planted at high density and harvested without ladders. It remains the workhorse of Latin America.

**Pacamara:** The Giant. A hybrid created in El Salvador by crossing *Pacas* (a mutation of Caturra) and *Maragogype* (a giant-bean mutation of Typica). The resulting beans are massive, often requiring special grading screens. The flavor profile is equally outsized, often presenting savory, herbal, and chocolate notes.

## The Monster and the Queen

Beyond the standard library lie two extremes: the survivor and the celebrity.

### The Survivor: Catimor.

For a century, botanists attempted to solve the "Arabica Paradox": obtaining the flavor of Arabica with the resilience of Robusta. Due to the chromosomal mismatch (44 vs 22), natural breeding was impossible. However, in 1927, on the island of Timor, nature circumvented the rules. A spontaneous hybrid occurred. The "Timor Hybrid" possessed 44 chromosomes and resistance to Leaf Rust.

Scientists crossed this tough hybrid with the high-yielding *Caturra* to create *Catimor*.

This variety is the tank of the coffee world. It resists rust, yields massive crops, and grows low and fast. For decades, it was a pariah in the specialty world. Buyers criticized it for a "herbal" or "woody" aftertaste—the genetic footprint of its *Robusta* ancestry. Today, through improved processing, Catimor is improving, but it remains the industry's defining trade-off: a variety engineered to withstand the biological realities of the farm, often at the expense of the sensory nuance demanded by the cup.

**The Queen: Geisha.**

In the taxonomy of roots and cherries, one variety stands apart. Geisha (or Gesha) is an heirloom variety collected from the forests of Ethiopia in the 1930s by British colonial expeditions. It was sent to a research station in Costa Rica, then to Panama. For decades, it was ignored. It was a scraggly, low-yielding tree with brittle branches that broke in the wind. Farmers found it impractical.

In 2004, the Peterson family of Hacienda La Esmeralda in Panama made a discovery that shifted the industry's trajectory. They noticed that the *Geisha* trees, planted high on a wind-swept ridge, remained free of fungus while their neighbors succumbed. Curious, they harvested the *Geisha* separately and cupped it.

The flavor was perplexing. It did not taste like traditional coffee. It presented notes of Earl Grey tea, jasmine, honeysuckle, and bergamot. They entered it into the "Best of Panama" competition. The judges, stunned, initially suspected the Petersons had adulterated the brew with fruit juice. It broke the scoring scale. That year, the coffee sold for roughly $21 per pound ($46 per kilogram)—a record. In 2024, top lots of Panama Geisha sell for over $10,000 per pound ($22,000 per kilogram).

*Geisha* proved that the genetic library of *Coffea arabica* still holds secrets. It was not a hybrid; it was a pure, ancient lineage that had maintained its floral complexity through isolation. It reminded the world that coffee is, at its heart, a fruit.

. . .

## THE VAULT IN THE JUNGLE

The fragility of *Arabica*—its lack of genetic diversity—is a ticking clock. Climate change brings new pests, hotter droughts, and new diseases. If the world's coffee is all descended from the same few parents, a single mutation in a pathogen could threaten the entire industry. The insurance policy against this collapse is located in Turrialba, Costa Rica.

Here, at the CATIE (Tropical Agricultural Research and Higher Education Center), lies the "Doomsday Vault" of coffee. In a field of 10 hectares, researchers maintain a living library of nearly 2,000 different coffee accessions. There are trees here that grow 6 meters (20 feet) tall. There are trees with purple leaves. There are trees that produce caffeine-free beans naturally (*Coffea charrieriana*). There are trees from the wild forests of Ethiopia that have never been named.

This is the "Human Layer" of botany. Scientists like Dr. William Solano spend their lives walking these rows, measuring yield, testing for disease resistance, and searching for a gene that might allow *Arabica* to survive a 2°C rise in global temperature.

## THE RESURRECTION: STENOPHYLLA

One of the most promising candidates for the future is not a new lab creation; it is a ghost. In 2018, botanists Dr. Aaron Davis and Jeremy Haggar entered the humid forests of Sierra Leone searching for a lost species: *Coffea stenophylla*.

It had not been seen in the wild since 1954 and was presumed extinct. After weeks of searching, they found it—a slender tree with black fruit and narrow leaves. *Stenophylla* is remarkable because of its habitat. It grows in hot, lowland conditions—similar to *Robusta*—but it possesses a flavor profile comparable to high-altitude *Arabica*. Blind taste tests conducted in London placed it alongside top-tier Ethiopian coffees. It tolerates temperatures 6°C (11°F) higher than *Arabica*.

This black-fruited plant suggests that the future of the *Rubiaceae* family lies not in the laboratory, but in returning to the wild roots.

. . .

## THE ARCHITECTURE OF FLAVOR

Ultimately, every sip of coffee is a translation of biology. The acidity —the sparkle on the tongue—originates from the citric and malic acids stored in the cellular vacuoles of the seed to power germination. The body—the weight in the mouth—comes from the lipids and long-chain sugars stored in the endosperm to feed the embryo. The aroma is derived from the nitrogen-rich alkaloids and proteins evolved to poison insects.

The *Rubiaceae* family did not evolve these compounds for human consumption. It evolved them to survive millions of years of fungal attacks, insect predation, and competition for sunlight in the East African rift. Humans are merely the mammals that discovered that burning the seed and soaking it in water extracts the plant's chemical will to live.

However, the plant remains fragile. As the world moves into an era of climate volatility, the "biological factory" is under siege. The clone army of *Arabica* faces a war it cannot win alone. To survive the next century, it will require the genes of its wild cousins, the stewardship of the farmers who tend the soil, and the preservation of genetic diversity to secure the future.

# 13

## THE CONCRETE SPECIES: ROBUSTA'S REVENGE

I n the taxonomy of desire, *Coffea arabica* is traditionally cast as the poet: difficult, fragile, and capable of exquisite complexity. *Coffea canephora* —known to the world as *Robusta*—is the engineer: tough, functional, and indispensable. If Arabica is a violin, vibrating with high-frequency acidity and delicate floral notes, Robusta is the rhythm section, providing the deep, structural bass notes that hold the composition together.

For most of the last century, the specialty coffee industry has treated Robusta as a horticultural embarrassment. It was the filler, the adulterant, the caffeine kick concealed within the opaque granules of instant coffee that sat in the back of the pantry. Coffee textbooks often dismissed it in a single paragraph, typically describing its flavor profile with adjectives ranging from "woody" to the distinct and unappealing "burnt rubber and raw peanut". But this dismissal ignores a fundamental economic and biological reality. Without Robusta, the global coffee machine would grind to a halt. It is the shock absorber of the market, powering the instant coffee industry, creating the thick, persistent crema on an Italian espresso, and providing the daily caffeine fix for billions of consumers who cannot afford the price premium of high-altitude Arabica.

More importantly, Robusta represents the future of the genus. As the "Bean Belt" warms and the fragile Arabica species retreats further up the mountains *in search of cooler air, Robusta is standing its ground. It is the genetic tank that possesses the resilience to save the industry from climate collapse. To understand the future of coffee, we must shift our gaze from the misty cloud forests of the Andes and Ethiopia to the hot, humid lowlands where this "concrete species" thrives.*

## THE BUREAUCRATIC DISCOVERY

While Arabica's history is wrapped in the romance of Sufi mystics and Ethiopian goatherds, Robusta's entry into the global consciousness was decidedly bureaucratic, classified by the rigorous botanical infrastructure of colonial expansion.

The species was not fully scientifically classified until 1897, when Lucien Linden, a Belgian botanist, received shipments of a strange, broad-leafed coffee plant from the Belgian Congo (now the Democratic Republic of the Congo). Linden was not looking for flavor; he was looking for viability. At the turn of the 20th century, the coffee world was in a state of panic. The fungal plague of Leaf Rust (*Hemileia vastatrix*) had recently annihilated the massive Arabica plantations of Sri Lanka (Ceylon) and was marching inexorably across the Dutch East Indies. The colonial powers—the Dutch in Java, the French in Indochina, and the British in Uganda—were desperate for a replacement crop that could survive the onslaught.

Linden saw the commercial potential immediately. The plant he examined was a monster compared to the delicate Arabica shrub. In the wild, it grew as a 10-meter (33-foot) tall tree in the sweltering heat of the equatorial basin. It did not require the cool, temperate mists of the Ethiopian highlands. It laughed at the pests that decimated Arabica. Linden marketed it not for its sensory complexity, but for its constitution, naming it *Robusta* as a testament to its vigor. It offered an engineering solution to a biological problem.

The adoption was rapid and transformative. Robusta was planted aggressively across the colonial tropics, saving the economies of Java and Madagascar from total collapse. It allowed the French to turn Vietnam into a plantation powerhouse, laying the groundwork for a geopolitical shift that would reverberate a century later. It was the industrial solution for an era of industrial extraction. The fact that the resulting beverage lacked the acidity and sweetness of Arabica was secondary; in the age of mass production, volume and reliability were the only metrics that mattered.

### THE CHROMOSOMAL FORTRESS

Why is Robusta so tough? The answer lies in its genome. As noted, *Coffea arabica* is an allotetraploid with four sets of chromosomes, while *Coffea canephora* is a diploid with only two sets. While Arabica invests its metabolic energy in producing complex sugars and lipids to attract pollinators, Robusta invests its energy in armor.

This defensive strategy is anchored by three biological pillars: caffeine, root architecture, and genetic diversity.

First, Robusta is a chemical fortress. Its seeds contain nearly twice the caffeine content of Arabica, ranging from 2.2% to 2.7% by weight, compared to Arabica's 1.2% to 1.5%. As discussed in previous chapters, caffeine is a bitter alkaloid poison evolved to paralyze and kill insects. Because Robusta evolved in the hot, insect-dense lowlands of the Congo basin, it required a heavier caliber weapon to survive. This high caffeine concentration makes the tree virtually immune to the Coffee Berry Borer and many destructive nematodes. However, this defense mechanism dictates the flavor profile. Caffeine is intensely bitter. When one drinks a cup of Robusta, they are tasting the plant's successful defense against predation.

Second, the root system of *Coffea canephora* is a marvel of hydraulic efficiency. While Arabica relies on deep taproots to seek water, Robusta develops a dense, mat-like system of feeder roots that spread laterally just beneath the soil surface.

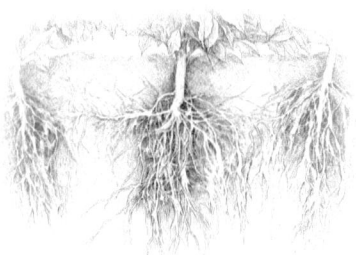

*Robusta relies on a shallow, aggressive net of feeder roots to scavenge nutrients in poor tropical soils.*

This architecture allows the tree to aggressively scavenge nutrients from the nutrient-poor laterite soils common in the tropics. It is a feeder-heavy system designed for rapid uptake, allowing the tree to grow fast and produce fruit in as little as two years, compared to Arabica's three or four. This root efficiency is what allows Robusta to thrive in lower altitudes where evaporation rates are higher and soil quality is lower.

Third is the pollination gamble. Unlike the lonely, self-pollinating (*autogamous*) Arabica, Robusta is *allogamous* (cross-pollinating). A Robusta tree cannot fertilize itself; it requires wind and insects to bring pollen from a genetically distinct neighbor to produce fruit. This promiscuity is a brilliant survival strategy in the wild. It ensures high genetic diversity within a single population, meaning that if a disease strikes, the natural variation increases the odds that some trees will survive. For the farmer, however, this genetic diversity creates a chaotic crop. Every tree in a Robusta field is genetically unique, meaning the cherries ripen at different rates, have different bean sizes, and taste slightly different. It resists the industrial demand for uniformity, forcing farmers to manage a field that is biologically heterogeneous.

## The Taste of Pyrazines

If one were to place a high-quality washed Arabica and a commercial grade Robusta side-by-side on a cupping table, the sensory difference would be stark. The Arabica would release volatile aromas of fruit, flowers, and caramelized sugar. The Robusta would emit scents of wet earth, raw peanuts, and perhaps a hint of burnt wood.

This distinction is not merely a matter of agricultural snobbery; it is a matter of organic chemistry. Robusta beans contain significantly lower levels of sucrose and lipids (fats) than Arabica. Lipids and sugars are the crucial precursors to the volatile compounds that create fruity and acidic aromas during the Maillard reaction in roasting. With less sugar to caramelize, the Robusta bean follows a different chemical pathway in the roaster.

Instead of fruit esters, Robusta is rich in chlorogenic acids (CGAs) and amino acids that degrade into pyrazines. Pyrazines are the molecules responsible for earthy, nutty, and roasted flavors. When roasted dark, Robusta does not just become bitter; it becomes heavy. It produces a thick, syrupy mouthfeel that coats the tongue. This "body" is its redeeming quality in the eyes of traditional espresso blenders. While it lacks the "high notes" of acidity—the violin—it provides the "bass notes" of body—the drum. This is why, for decades, Italian espresso blends have strategically relied on 20% to 40% Robusta. It stabilizes the emulsion, giving the espresso the punch required to cut through the milk in a cappuccino.


## DOI MOI: THE VIETNAM MIRACLE

The most significant event in the modern history of Robusta did not occur in its African birthplace, but in Southeast Asia. The rise of Vietnam as a coffee superpower is a case study in state-directed agricultural engineering.

Following the devastation of the Vietnam War and the subsequent failure of collectivized farming, Vietnam faced an economic crisis in the 1980s. The country was one of the poorest in the world, and food insecurity was rampant. In 1986, the government initiated a series of radical economic reforms known as *Doi Moi* ("Renovation"). The central tenet was to shift from a centrally planned economy to a "socialist-oriented market economy," opening the country to global trade and encouraging private enterprise.

The government looked to the Central Highlands—specifically the red-earth plateau of Buôn Ma Thuột in Dak Lak province—and decided it would become the engine of national recovery. They bet the economy on coffee. However, they did not bet on the fussy, high-altitude Arabica. They bet on the yield and resilience of Robusta.

The government offered land rights, seedlings, and fertilizer subsidies to anyone willing to migrate to the highlands and farm. Millions of Vietnamese responded, moving from the coastal lowlands to the plateau. They applied an intensive, almost industrial logic to smallholder farming. Utilizing the *Canephora* root system's ability to absorb massive nutrient loads, farmers used heavy irrigation and fertilizer application to force the trees into hyper-production.

The results were statistically staggering. In 1990, Vietnam produced roughly 1.2 million bags of coffee (each bag weighing 60 kg or 132 lbs). By 2000, Vietnam produced 15 million bags. Today, it produces nearly 30 million bags annually, making it the second-largest coffee producer in the world after Brazil and the undisputed global king of Robusta.

## THE HUMAN ENGINE OF DAK LAK

To understand the scale of this machine, one must observe the harvest in Dak Lak province. It operates with a distinct rhythm from the romanticized hand-picking of Central America. The harvest here is an exercise in efficiency. Because Robusta cherries attach tightly to the branch—another trait of its toughness—farmers often wear thick gloves and strip the entire branch in a single motion. Ripe red cherries, unripe green ones, and leaves fall onto the tarp below.

The trees are pruned aggressively, kept short and stocky to maximize the energy diverted to fruit production rather than vegetative growth. While a hectare of Arabica in Ethiopia might yield 400 to 600 kilograms (880 to 1,320 lbs) of green coffee, a hectare of high-intensity Robusta in Vietnam can yield 3,000 to 4,000 kilograms (6,600 to 8,800 lbs). The sheer weight of the biomass is overwhelming. During the harvest, coffee is dried on every available flat surface—patios, basketball courts, and the paved shoulders of the highway. Driving through the Central Highlands in November is a sensory experience of navigating a tunnel of drying beans.

*In high-volume Robusta farming, efficiency dictates "strip picking,"*
*collecting ripe and unripe fruit simultaneously.*

This efficiency is the primary reason a jar of instant coffee costs $8 rather than $40. Vietnam democratized caffeine, turning what was once a luxury good into a global utility. However, this miracle came with environmental costs. The aggressive irrigation required to sustain such high yields has severely depleted the groundwater tables in the highlands, forcing farmers to dig deeper wells every year. It is a race against the aquifer, a tension between immediate economic output and long-term ecological viability.

### CREMA: THE ITALIAN SECRET

While Vietnam powered the instant market, Robusta maintained a quieter, more glamorous life in Europe. In Southern Italy, particularly in Naples and Sicily, Robusta is not viewed as an additive, but as a structural necessity. The Neapolitan espresso culture prizes a beverage that is short, dark, and viscous—"like oil."

Arabica alone cannot produce this specific texture. Its oils are too delicate, and its cell structure too porous. Robusta, conversely, possesses a dense, rigid cellular structure. When roasted, this density traps massive amounts of carbon dioxide within the bean. When extracted under 9 bars of pressure (130 PSI) in an espresso machine, this trapped $CO_2$

expands violently, creating the thick, hazelnut-colored foam known as *crema*.

*Robusta's dense cellular structure traps more carbon dioxide during roasting, creating the thick, persistent crema prized in Italian espresso.*

A shot of 100% Arabica often yields a thin, fleeting crema that dissipates within a minute. A blend containing 30% Robusta will produce a "tiger-striped" crema capable of supporting the weight of a spoonful of sugar for several seconds. For decades, Italian roasters like Lavazza navigated this balance with secrecy and skill. They utilized high-quality "Washed Robusta" from India or Uganda to add body and caffeine without introducing the "burnt rubber" defects associated with lower-grade commercial crops. They treated Robusta not as a filler, but as a civil engineer treats steel reinforcement in concrete—invisible, but essential for structural integrity.

## THE INSTANT ENGINE

If espresso represents the art of Robusta, Instant Coffee (Soluble Coffee) represents the industry. Roughly 35-40% of the world's green coffee is converted into soluble granules. This process is chemically violent. The coffee is roasted, ground, brewed into a concentrated liquor, and then either spray-dried in hot towers or freeze dried in vacuums.

This industrial processing strips away the volatile aromatics that make Arabica special. If one were to take a delicate, floral Panamanian Geisha and subject it to the spray-drying tower, the jasmine notes would evaporate instantly. It would be a financial waste. Robusta, however, is perfectly suited for this abuse. Its heavy body and high caffeine content survive the thermal shock of the factory. Its harsh flavors can be mitigated by the steam extraction process. The "neutrality" of commercial Robusta becomes an asset here; it provides the generic "brown coffee flavor" that the mass market expects.

The instant coffee market acts as the "floor" of the global coffee economy. When consumers purchase a jar of Nescafé or Folgers Crystals, they are purchasing the output of the Vietnamese miracle. It is a product of logistics and chemistry, prioritizing shelf stability and solubility over terroir.

### CLIMATE RESILIENCE: THE 2-DEGREE SHIFT

The conversation surrounding Robusta is currently undergoing a radical shift. It is no longer solely about cheap filler; it is about survival. Climate models predict that by 2050, roughly 50% of the land currently suitable for Arabica farming will become unsuitable due to rising temperatures and erratic rainfall patterns. Arabica is a thermally sensitive plant; it begins to suffer physiological stress at temperatures consistently above 23°C (73°F).

Robusta, by contrast, is comfortable in temperatures up to 30°C (86°F). As the "Cool Zone" moves up the mountain and eventually disappears off the peak, farmers are left with a binary choice: abandon coffee cultivation entirely, or switch to Robusta.

In countries like Uganda and India, this shift is already underway. Farmers are grafting Robusta onto drought-resistant rootstocks to survive the dry seasons. But they are also changing their agricultural practices. They are realizing that the "burnt rubber" flavor often associated with Robusta is not inherent to the seed, but a result of the processing. When Robusta cherries are strip-picked, the inclusion of unripe green cherries creates astringency. When they are dried on dirty patios, the beans absorb off-flavors.

Farmers are discovering that if they treat Robusta with the same protocols used for specialty Arabica—picking only ripe red cherries, fermenting them carefully to remove the mucilage, and drying them on raised beds—the flavor profile transforms.

.  .  .

### FINE ROBUSTA: THE NEW FRONTIER

This realization has birthed the "Fine Robusta" movement. A small but dedicated cadre of farmers and roasters are attempting to rehabilitate the species. They are applying specialty protocols to *Coffea canephora*, seeking to eliminate the "phenolic" defects (the rubbery notes) and highlight the bean's inherent sweetness.

When treated with this level of care, high-quality Robusta sheds its rubbery notes, revealing flavors of dark chocolate, toasted grain, hazelnut, and even black tea.

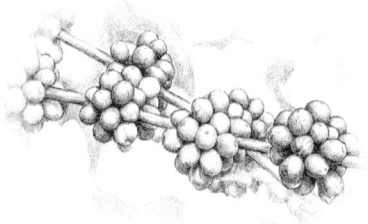

*Unlocking the soul of the plant. By shedding old defects and applying specialty protocols, Fine Robusta reveals the berry's true elegance: a sophisticated profile of toasted grain and rich chocolate. A species, rehabilitated.*

While it lacks the citric acidity of Arabica, it offers a profound, bass-heavy sweetness and a creamy body that Arabica cannot replicate. In 2010, the Coffee Quality Institute (CQI) launched a "Q Robusta" grading system, parallel to the famous Q Arabica system. This created a standardized language for quality. If a farmer could produce a Robusta that scored above 80 points on this scale, they could sell it for a premium, breaking the cycle of commodity pricing.

We are seeing the emergence of "Single Origin Robustas" from the Kaapi Royale estates in India, the high-altitude regions of Uganda, and the Amazonian regions of Ecuador. These are coffees that challenge the Arabica monopoly. They ask the consumer to broaden their palate, to accept that "acidity" is not the sole metric of quality, and to appreciate the heavy, comforting warmth of a well-crafted Robusta.

.   .   .

## THE HYBRID FUTURE

The ultimate destiny of Robusta, however, might not be in the cup, but in the laboratory. Geneticists are increasingly viewing Robusta not as a separate crop, but as a genetic library for Arabica. The goal is *Introgression*: breeding the rust-resistance and heat-tolerance genes of Robusta into the flavor profile of Arabica.

We witnessed early attempts at this with the Timor Hybrid, a natural cross discovered in the 1920s. But modern breeding is far more precise. The "F1 Hybrids" being developed today, such as the Centroamericano variety, are Arabica trees that have been fortified with specific Robusta genes. They taste like Arabica, but they grow with the vigor of Robusta. In a sense, the species are reuniting. Since Arabica was born from a collision between Robusta and *Eugenioides* eons ago, breeders are simply closing the evolutionary loop to prepare for a hotter planet.

## THE NECESSARY ANCHOR

Robusta is often cast as the villain of the coffee story—the cheap, bitter antagonist to Arabica's hero. But this narrative is a failure of perspective. Robusta is the proletariat of the coffee world. It performs the heavy lifting. It thrives in the heat. It bears the burden of the global caffeine addiction so that Arabica can remain a luxury.

Without the millions of bags of Robusta flowing out of Vietnam and Brazil, the price of coffee would skyrocket, making it a beverage accessible only to the elite. As we look toward a hotter, more volatile century, the "Concrete Species" may be the only thing standing between us and a world without coffee. It is a necessary component of a warming world, ensuring that the ritual of the morning cup survives the changing climate. It may not always be the coffee we want, but it is, undeniably, the coffee we need.

# 14

---

# CONTROLLED DECAY: THE
# ART OF FERMENTATION

S tanding on the raised drying beds of Yirgacheffe, Ethiopia, under the relentless midday sun, the air is heavy, sweet, and laced with the scent of fermentation. Millions of whole coffee cherries, shifting from crimson to purple-black, bake in the heat, creating a landscape that resembles vast carpets of raisins. Here, the process is passive and elemental, a slow dehydration fueled by solar radiation where the fruit withers around the seed, imparting sugars into the bean through a long, osmotic interaction. Four thousand miles away, in the volcanic highlands of Huila, Colombia, the sensory experience is radically different. The air smells of fresh water, wet stone, and a sharp, yogurty tang. There is the rhythmic hum of machinery—a depulper stripping the skin off the fruit in a rapid spray of water. The naked, mucilage-covered beans are then submerged in concrete tanks to rest in a dark, aqueous environment where solar radiation is replaced by microbiology.

These two scenes represent the fundamental divide in the coffee industry: the Natural (Dry) process and the Washed (Wet) process. To the uninitiated, these appear to be mere agricultural chores. To the coffee industry, however, they represent opposing philosophies of flavor: a debate over whether the character of coffee should derive from the surrounding fruit or the pure genetic expression of the seed.

. . .

## THE TICKING CLOCK

A coffee cherry, once severed from the branch, is a dying organism. It acts as a globe of water, sugar, and nutrients suddenly cut off from its metabolic life support. Like any fruit—a strawberry left on the counter or a grape crushed in a vat—it immediately begins to decompose. The coffee farmer's primary objective is to manage this decomposition with exacting standards. The goal of all coffee processing is to remove the fruit layers—specifically the exocarp (skin) and mesocarp (mucilage)—and dry the seed to a stable moisture content of roughly 10-12% to prevent rotting during transit. Yet, the specific methodology used to achieve this removal fundamentally alters the chemical architecture of the bean.

The critical layer in this equation is the mesocarp, known colloquially in the industry as "mucilage" or "honey." It is a sticky, pectin-rich hydrogel that clings tenaciously to the parchment surrounding the bean. This layer is loaded with carbohydrates, primarily fructose and glucose, and maintains a high water content. The mucilage serves as a petri dish; the moment the cherry's skin is compromised—either by mechanical depulping or natural degradation—the native yeast and bacteria living on the skin and in the ambient air initiate a feeding frenzy. They consume the available sugars and excrete metabolic byproducts: organic acids (lactic, acetic), alcohols (ethanol), and esters (flavor compounds). This process is fermentation, and it is inevitable. The question is not whether coffee ferments, but rather how, where, and for how long the process is allowed to continue. The different processing methods are, in essence, different systems of throttling this microbial activity to curate a specific flavor profile.

## SUN AND RISK: THE NATURAL PROCESS

The Natural Process, also known as the Dry Process, represents the original method of coffee preparation. It mirrors the techniques used by the Sufis of Yemen in the 15th century, who dried cherries on the stone roofs of Aden, and it remains the dominant method in Ethiopia and the vast, industrial savannas of Brazil. The concept is deceptively simple: the cherry is harvested and placed directly in the sun without removing the skin or the mucilage. However, "simple" does not imply easy; a Natural coffee represents a high-stakes agricultural gamble.

*The Natural process dries the fruit intact on the seed, a high-risk method that imparts intense sweetness and body.*

Because the fruit flesh remains intact, the cherry acts as a sealed vessel containing water and sugar, making it highly susceptible to mold and uncontrolled rot. The mesocarp is roughly 80% water, creating an ideal breeding ground for filamentous fungi like *Aspergillus* and *Penicillium*. If rain falls on the drying beds, or if the layer of cherries is spread too thick (exceeding 5-10 cm / 2-4 inches), the internal humidity spikes. The cherries do not dry; they compost. This failure leads to the most feared defect in the coffee world: Phenolic Taint, often referred to as "Rioy" flavor in Brazil. A single phenolic bean, contaminated by the metabolic waste of uncontrolled fungal growth, can imbue an entire pot of coffee with the taste of iodine, medicinal bandages, or damp basement walls.

To prevent this defect, farmers must manage the drying patio with the care of a nursery. The cherries are turned constantly using wooden rakes—often every thirty to sixty minutes during peak sun—to promote even dehydration and consistent airflow. The process is slow, typically lasting three to five weeks depending on ambient humidity and temperature, which commonly range between 25 and 35 degrees Celsius (77–95°F).

During this prolonged drying phase, a significant transformation takes place within the fruit. Fermentation occurs intracellularly as the cell walls of the cherry begin to break down. Sugars and aromatic precursors from the mucilage migrate through the semi-permeable parchment layer and diffuse into the porous structure of the green coffee bean itself, permanently altering its chemical composition.

The resulting flavor profile is distinct and powerful. Naturals are often described as the "fruit bombs" of the coffee world, characterized by heavy body, low acidity, and intense flavors of blueberry, strawberry, and dried fig. They frequently possess a winey quality due to the production of ethanol and acetic acid during the long drying phase. For decades, the specialty coffee industry viewed Naturals as inferior, interpreting their wild flavors as a mask for poor quality or inconsistent sorting. However, the rise of specialty Ethiopian Naturals in the mid-2000s shifted that paradigm, proving that when executed with precision, the Natural process can yield some of the most complex and distinctive coffees available.

### THE ARCHITECTURE OF WATER: THE WASHED PROCESS

The Washed Process, or Wet Process, emerged as an industrial solution to a climatic problem, though it would eventually become the gold standard for purity. In the mid-19th century, as coffee cultivation expanded into the high-humidity environments of Central America, Colombia, and Java, farmers encountered a logistical wall.In a Colombian cloud forest, the persistent moisture prevents whole cherries from drying before they succumb to rot. The "Natural" method was essentially impossible in these regions. The solution was to remove the water-hoarding fruit immediately upon harvest.

In the Washed process, the harvested cherries are first deposited into water tanks to siphon off the "floaters"—unripe or defective cherries that lack density. The viable cherries are then fed into a depulper, a mechanical device that forces the cherry against a metal grate, popping the seed out of its skin like a pit from a peach.

*The depulper mechanically strips the skin, preparing the beans for the fermentation tanks of the Washed process.*

However, the beans emerge from this machine encased in that sticky, stubborn mucilage. This layer is insoluble in water; one cannot simply rinse it off. It must be biologically degraded. This is achieved via Wet Fermentation, where the beans are submerged in concrete tanks of clean water for a duration ranging from 12 to 72 hours.

In the tank, an invisible biological sequence unfolds. The water creates an anaerobic (oxygen-poor) environment at the bottom and an aerobic one at the top. Specific bacteria, primarily *Lactobacillus* (the genus responsible for yogurt and sauerkraut) and *Pediococcus*, along with yeasts like *Saccharomyces*, begin to thrive. These microbes consume the pectin in the mucilage, breaking down the polysaccharide chains that give the substance its adhesive quality. The fermentation here is subtractive, aiming to cleanly and efficiently remove the fruit rather than add flavor to the bean. The microbes act as a biological scrubbing mechanism.

The farmer monitors this tank with watchful precision. They must track the pH levels carefully. As the bacteria produce lactic acid, the pH of the water drops. It begins around neutral (7.0), but as it approaches 5.5, the mucilage structure weakens. If the pH drops below 4.5, the seeds themselves can be damaged, leading to "sour" or "onion" flavor defects in the final cup. Traditionally, the farmer determines the endpoint of fermentation by tactile sensation. They insert a wooden pole or their hand into the tank; if the beans feel slimy, the process continues. If the beans feel rough and "squeaky" against the friction of the hand, the mucilage has successfully dissolved. Once fermentation is deemed complete, the sluice gates are opened. The beans are washed thoroughly in fresh water channels, known as *correos*, to remove the degraded mucilage and metabolic byproducts.

*In the fermentation tank, microbes digest the sticky mucilage layer, a process that must be timed perfectly to avoid spoilage.*

The result is parchment coffee that is pristine, white, and clean. While the process is industrial in its efficiency, the result is artisanal in its expression. The flavor profile of a Washed coffee stands in direct contrast to a Natural. It is defined by clarity and transparency—a method designed to get out of the way and let the terroir speak.

Because the fruit is removed early in the process, the consumer tastes the genetics of the seed and the mineral composition of the soil. Washed coffees are characterized by high acidity, light-to-medium body, and articulate, transparent flavors. They present notes of citrus, florals, stone fruits, and tea. They are the "white wines" of the coffee world—crisp, clean, and intellectually complex.

·  ·  ·

## THE STINKER IN THE BATCH

Fermentation is a biological bell curve; while most beans ferment perfectly, every tank contains outliers. Perhaps a bean became lodged in a corner of the tank where water circulation was poor, or perhaps it was already over-fermented on the tree. When a bean over-ferments, the microbial population shifts dangerously. The beneficial bacteria die off, replaced by putrefactive microbes that produce nasty, potent compounds. They create butyric acid (the smell of vomit) and propionic acid (the smell of rancid onions).

A single bean infected with these compounds is known as a **"Stinker."** It is visually undetectable; once roasted, it looks identical to the good beans. But in the grinder, it acts as a flavor grenade. One Stinker can overpower an entire pot of delicate floral coffee, instantly turning it into a cup that tastes of sewage or swamp water.

This risk necessitates the use of "channel graders" at Washed processing stations—workers who stand by the washing channels with wooden paddles, pushing the coffee against the current. The lighter, potentially defective beans float and are skimmed off, a manual firewall against the chaos of bacterial decay.

## THE MIDDLE PATH: HONEY PROCESSING

Occupying the space between the extremes of Natural (Sun) and Washed (Water) is a spectrum of hybrid methods known as Honey Processing, or Pulped Natural. This method originated in Brazil in the 1990s as *Cereja Descascada* (Peeled Cherry) to conserve water, but it was refined and branded by Costa Rican farmers in the 2000s. In this method, the cherry is depulped to remove the skin, but instead of washing off the mucilage in a fermentation tank, the beans are moved directly onto drying beds with the sticky "honey" still clinging to the parchment.

The classification of Honey coffee depends entirely on the percentage of mucilage left on the bean and the drying time:

- **White Honey:** Approximately 80-90% of the mucilage is removed mechanically using a high-pressure demucilager.

The beans are dried quickly in full sun. The flavor profile is close to a Washed coffee—clean and acidic.
- **Yellow Honey:** About 50% of the mucilage remains. The beans are dried over roughly 8 days. The result is balanced, with enhanced sweetness.
- **Red Honey:** Roughly 75% of the mucilage is left intact. These beans are often dried in the shade to slow the evaporation, taking up to 12 days. The flavor is fruity and syrupy.
- **Black Honey:** Almost all the mucilage is left on the bean. These are dried very slowly under heavy shade or plastic tarps for up to 30 days. The resulting cup tastes very close to a Natural, with heavy body and intense sweetness.

The Honey process represents a compromise in the most effective sense. It utilizes significantly less water than the Washed process but dries faster and with less risk of spoilage than the Natural process. Flavor-wise, it attempts to thread the needle, offering the sweetness and body of a Natural with some of the acidity and clarity of a Washed coffee.

### The Myth of the Civet

The most famous—and controversial—method of fermentation occurs not in a tank or on a patio, but inside a digestive tract. *Kopi Luwak*, or Civet Coffee, originated in Indonesia. The Asian Palm Civet (*Paradoxurus hermaphroditus*), a small, cat-like nocturnal mammal, consumes ripe coffee cherries. In the wild, the civet is a selective forager, choosing only the sweetest fruit. It masticates the cherry, digesting the soft outer pulp, but swallows the parchment-covered seed whole.

The bean travels through the civet's digestive tract for approximately 24 hours, subjected to a unique chemical bath. The gastric acids and proteolytic enzymes of the civet penetrate the porous parchment. This constitutes a form of Enzymatic Fermentation. These enzymes break down the storage proteins within the bean into shorter peptide chains and free amino acids. Since proteins are responsible for much of the bitterness in roasted coffee, this breakdown results in a cup that is incredibly smooth, syrupy, and devoid of bite.

Kopi Luwak *relies on the digestive enzymes of the civet cat to ferment the beans—a curiosity that became a controversial luxury fad.*

Historically, this was a scavenger's coffee, gathered from the forest floor by colonial laborers who were forbidden from picking fresh coffee from the trees. However, in the 1990s, it transformed into a luxury fad, commanding prices upwards of $600 per pound. This demand drove a humanitarian and ecological crisis. Farmers began trapping wild civets and force-feeding them coffee cherries in battery cages. These stressed and malnourished animals produced inferior coffee. Today, *Kopi Luwak* is largely considered a fraud—cruel to animals and culinarily uninteresting compared to a well-processed washed coffee. Yet, it proved a scientific point that would inspire the next generation of processors: biology can alter flavor in ways machines cannot.

## THE THIRD WAVE OF FERMENTATION

For centuries, fermentation was viewed by farmers primarily as a risk management strategy—a necessary step to remove mucilage without ruining the bean. In 2015, Australian barista Sasa Sestic won the World Barista Championship in Seattle using a coffee processed via a technique borrowed from winemaking: Carbonic Maceration. This victory marked the beginning of the "Third Wave of Fermentation," where farmers moved from passive observation to active manipulation.

"Anaerobic Fermentation" became the industry buzzword. Instead of using open concrete tanks, farmers began sealing cherries—either whole or depulped—in airtight stainless steel barrels or plastic grain bags equipped with one-way valves. These valves allow the carbon dioxide produced during fermentation to escape while preventing oxygen from entering. By depriving the environment of oxygen, the farmer fundamentally shifts the microbial population. Aerobic bacteria, such as *Acetobacter* (which creates sharp, vinegary flavors), die off. In their place, anaerobic yeasts thrive. These yeast strains, operating under metabolic stress, produce wild, exotic esters that do not exist in traditional processing.

Specifically, fermentation creates esters through the reaction of alcohols and acids. For example, the interaction of ethanol and acetic acid produces ethyl acetate, which smells of green apple and pear. Under anaerobic conditions, different precursors are available, leading to the formation of isoamyl acetate (banana) or ethyl butyrate (pineapple). The results can be polarizing; anaerobic coffees often taste like bubblegum, cinnamon, artificial grape, or lactic funk. To traditionalists, they taste "fake" or "adulterated." To the modern market, they taste exciting and new.

Carbonic Maceration takes this logic a step further. Whole cherries are placed in a sealed stainless steel tank which is then injected with carbon dioxide, purging all oxygen. This forces fermentation to happen inside the intracellular structure of the fruit before the skin even breaks. It creates intensely juicy, bright, candy-like flavors, reminiscent of a Beaujolais Nouveau wine.

## The Designer Yeast

The final frontier of processing is the transition from "Wild" to "Cultured" fermentation. Traditionally, coffee fermentation relied on indigenous yeasts—the wild microbes floating in the jungle air or residing on the tank walls. While romantic, this method is inconsistent, explaining why coffee from the same farm might taste like jasmine on Tuesday and onions on Friday. Sophisticated producers are now borrowing directly from the winemaker's playbook by using Starter Cultures.

Farmers can purchase freeze-dried packets of specific yeast strains, often *Saccharomyces cerevisiae* strains isolated for Champagne or Sauvignon Blanc production, or non-Saccharomyces yeasts like *Torulaspora delbrueckii*. By inoculating the tank with a dominant, known yeast, they can "design" the flavor profile. If a producer desires more floral notes, they might add a yeast strain known for producing terpene esters. If they want a creamy mouthfeel, they might introduce a specific strain of *Lactobacillus*. This practice removes the variable of luck. A farmer in Panama can now produce a coffee that tastes consistently like peaches, not because the soil smells like peaches, but because the commercial yeast they introduced produces the exact chemical compound for peach flavor. This practice remains controversial; purists argue it violates the sanctity of terroir by "flavoring" the coffee. However, strictly speaking, it is simply applied microbiology, transforming the fermentation tank from a bucket into a precision bioreactor.

### THE COST OF CLARITY

Discussion of processing is incomplete without addressing the environmental cost. The Washed process became the gold standard for quality in the 20th century because it was replicable and clean, but it demands a high environmental price. Traditional wet milling uses massive amounts of fresh water; archaic systems can require up to 20 liters (5.2 gallons) of water to process a single kilogram (2.2 lbs) of parchment coffee.

Furthermore, the "wastewater" or effluent that exits the fermentation tanks is toxic to aquatic life. It is highly acidic (pH 4.0) and loaded with organic matter, resulting in a staggering Biological Oxygen Demand (BOD). If this water is discharged directly into rivers—as it was for decades—it strips the oxygen from the waterways, killing fish and destroying local ecosystems. Modern "Eco-Mills" now utilize centrifugal demucilagers that scrub the beans mechanically with very little water (less than 1 liter per kg), though these machines require significant capital investment and electricity. The environmental burden of the Washed process is a major driver pushing farmers back toward Naturals and Honey processes, which require almost no water.

### THE TERROIR OF PROCESS

The explosion of processing methods has complicated the concept of terroir, or the taste of place. Fifty years ago, a coffee could be identified by its origin genetics and soil; a Kenyan coffee tasted like blackcurrant due to the SL-28 variety and the phosphoric soil. Today, that map is blurred. A farmer in Colombia can take a standard Caturra variety, process it using an extended anaerobic natural method with champagne yeast, and produce a cup that mimics a blueberry-bomb Ethiopian. We are entering an era where the hand of the maker is as visible as the land itself. We are not just drinking the seed; we are drinking the history of its transformation. Every cup serves as a testament to biological management, a record of how the farmer navigated the delicate relationship between the honey of the fruit and the husk that protects the bean. Processing has become the primary driver of flavor differentiation in the modern market.

## 15

# RUST ON THE LEAVES: THE COLLAPSE OF CEYLON AND THE SHIFT TO TEA

I n the spring of 1869—over a century before the Black Frost of 1975 would reshape Brazil—the British Empire functioned on a steady intake of caffeine, and the island of Ceylon (now Sri Lanka) served as its primary source. To comprehend the magnitude of the impending collapse, one must first visualize the profound confidence of the era. Ceylon was more than a farming colony; it was a "Planter's Raj," a tropical aristocracy constructed upon the labor of Tamil workers and the absolute monoculture of Coffea arabica.

The British planters resided in sprawling bungalows characterized by wide verandas, maintaining cricket lawns manicured from the jungle landscape. They referred to coffee as "The Golden Bean." By 1868, the island exported over 45 million kilograms (100 million pounds) of coffee to London. The Oriental Bank in Colombo operated with vast credit surpluses, and land prices in the Kandyan highlands exceeded those in the home counties of England. It was a bubble of biological optimism, predicated on the assumption that nature was a static resource to be harvested indefinitely.

Then, on a humid morning in May, G.W.H. Thwaites—the director of the Royal Botanic Gardens at Peradeniya—received a specimen from a concerned planter in the Madulsima district. It consisted of a handful of coffee leaves. On the upper surface, the foliage appeared punctuated by chlorotic yellow spots, sickly and pale against the deep waxy green. Thwaites turned them over. On the underside, the leaves were coated in a fine, orange-yellow powder, resembling turmeric dust or the pollen found on a moth's wing.

Thwaites scraped the dust with a scalpel and placed it under his microscope. He observed thousands of kidney-shaped spores, spiny on the convex side and smooth on the concave. He sent the specimens to England, where the Reverend M.J. Berkeley analyzed the dust and named the organism Hemileia vastatrix. The nomenclature was a dark biological descriptor: Hemileia ("Half-Smooth") for the physical shape of the spore, and vastatrix ("Devastating") for the potential he feared it possessed.

His categorization proved prescient. Within fifteen years, the "Golden Bean" industry had effectively collapsed. The 160,000 hectares of coffee trees in Ceylon were denuded, their leaves accumulating like snow on the plantation floors. The Oriental Bank failed, erasing the life savings of thousands. Planters who had previously imported pheasant and champagne found themselves destitute in ruined fields. The processing machinery rusted into the jungle floor, reclaimed by the vines. Desperate for a crop that would survive, the remaining agriculturalists removed the dead coffee skeletons and planted tea bushes in their place. This fungal invasion remains the primary reason the United Kingdom is a nation of tea drinkers today; The shift represented a biological surrender as much as a change in palate. The Empire had lost the war against the spore.

### THE NATURE OF THE BIOTROPH

Coffee Leaf Rust, known throughout the Latin American world as *La Roya*, operates as a constantly mutating, insidious pathogen that targets the immune system of the plant. Unlike blights that kill tissue instantly, rust is a parasite. It colonizes the tree to feed on it, keeping the host alive while draining its resources. As a biotroph, it requires a living host to survive, creating a parasitic relationship that drains the plant's resources over time. This makes it a far more complex adversary than a simple rot; it is a biological hijacker.

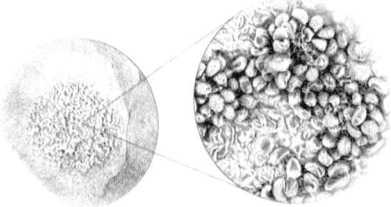

Hemileia vastatrix: *The microscopic fungal spore that devastated the coffee empires of the 19th century.*

To understand the severity of rust, the perspective must shift to the microscopic level.

The infection begins with a single urediniospore. Microscopic and spiny, it functions like a burr, latching onto the waxy cuticle of a coffee leaf or the leg of a passing insect. Once attached, it plays a waiting game. Possessing a built-in hygrometer, the spore stays dormant until it detects two specific triggers: darkness and liquid water.

When the conditions are met, the invasion unfolds like a heist:

1. **The Search:** The spore germinates, extending a biological probe that crawls across the leaf. Using touch sensitivity, it feels the ridges of the surface, hunting for a stoma—the microscopic breathing pore of the plant.
2. **The Breach:** Upon finding the open door, the fungus forms a pressurized battering ram called an appressorium and forces its way into the leaf's interior.
3. **The Theft:** Inside the chamber, the fungus weaves a web between the plant's cells. It inserts feeding tubes, known as *haustoria*, directly into the cellular walls. It doesn't kill the cell immediately; it taps the line, siphoning off the sugar meant for the coffee cherry.

These haustoria function as parasitic interfaces. Crucially, they do not rupture the cell membrane, which would kill the cell and stop the nutrient flow. Instead, they indent the membrane, siphoning off the sugars and nutrients the coffee tree produced for its fruit. The tree is effectively being consumed from the interior, its energy redirected from growing cherries to feeding the fungus.

On the surface, the farmer observes a yellow spot, indicating the loss of chlorophyll and the cessation of photosynthesis in that zone. As the fungus matures, it requires an exit strategy to reproduce. It erupts back through the underside of the leaf, rupturing the plant's epidermis to release a cloud of approximately 300,000 fresh orange spores, ready to infect neighboring trees.

The plant, detecting the systemic attack and nutrient loss, reacts with a defense mechanism known as abscission. It severs the nutrient flow to the infected leaf and drops it. A rust-infected tree eventually resembles a skeleton, standing denuded with branches stripped of foliage. Without leaves, photosynthesis ceases. Without photosynthesis, the cherries on the branch stop ripening; they shrivel into black, empty husks known as "palote." The tree eventually dies of carbohydrate exhaustion, starving to death in the sunlight.


## THE TRANSATLANTIC BREACH

For a century, the Atlantic Ocean functioned as a biological firewall. Rust destroyed the coffee industries of Asia and Africa in the late 19th century, forcing the Dutch in Java and the French in Vietnam to abandon delicate Arabica cultivars in favor of the robust, rust-resistant *Canephora* (Robusta). However, the Americas—Brazil, Colombia, and Central America—remained a "Rust-Free Zone." This biological isolation allowed Latin America to develop into the coffee garden of the world. Farmers cultivated delicate, heirloom varieties like Typica and Bourbon without the need for heavy fungicides or resistant hybrids. They operated in a golden age of epidemiological ignorance.

Then, in 1970, the barrier failed. Spores of *Hemileia vastatrix* were discovered in the state of Bahia, Brazil. The vector of transmission remains a subject of debate. Some theories suggest the spores were transported on cacao seedlings imported from West Africa; others point to high-altitude jet streams capable of carrying dust from Angola across the Atlantic. Regardless of the method, the firewall was breached.

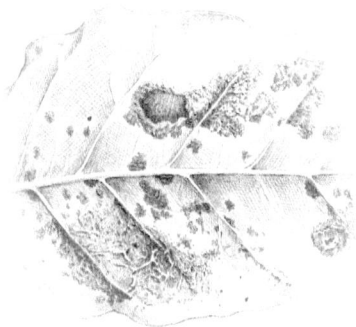

*Coffee leaf rust: (A) Chlorotic spots and spore masses on the lower leaf; (B) Severe defoliation contrasting with resistant plants.*

The disease migrated north with formidable speed, moving from farm to farm, carried by migrant pickers, transport trucks, and trade winds. It reached Nicaragua in 1976, Mexico in 1981, and crossed into Colombia by 1983.

Unlike the total collapse in Ceylon, the industry in the Americas did not vanish. The survival was due to the fact that agricultural scientists had analyzed the history of the blight. They understood that stopping the wind was impossible, so they attempted to alter the farm environment.

This realization launched the era of "Technification." Governments in Brazil and Colombia advised farmers to remove shade trees. The logic was based on ultraviolet radiation: direct sunlight is lethal to fungal spores. By removing the humid canopy, the leaf surface dries more rapidly, preventing the spore from germinating. Farmers cleared the forest and planted high-density rows of coffee in full sun. They saturated the soil with synthetic nitrogen to force the trees to generate new foliage faster than the fungus could destroy it. It was a strategy of outrunning the pathology—growing faster than the dying.

While this approach maintained production levels, it created a "Chemical Trap." The new, full-sun technified farms were metabolically stressed and biologically vulnerable. They required massive applications of Copper Sulfate fungicide to keep the rust at bay. The arrival of rust transformed coffee farming into a chemical-intensive industrial process.

. . .

### THE BLUE STAIN: A CHEMICAL DEPENDENCE

For the last forty years, the primary weapon against *Hemileia vastatrix* has been copper. Visitors to coffee farms in Central America during the rainy season often encounter laborers navigating the rows with 20-liter backpack sprayers, coating the trees in a fine blue mist.

*To combat rust, farmers rely on copper fungicides, a chemical shield that must be reapplied constantly during the rainy season.*

Copper functions as a contact fungicide, acting as a shield. It kills the spore on the leaf surface before the germ tube can penetrate the stoma. However, it possesses a fatal flaw: it is not systemic. It does not enter the plant's vascular system. This creates a logistical crisis in coffee regions, where afternoon rains are common. Precipitation washes the copper off the leaf and into the soil, necessitating re-application. In years with high rust pressure, a farm might require 10 to 15 spray cycles per season.

The environmental consequences are significant. Copper is a heavy metal that does not biodegrade. It accumulates in the soil profile. Over decades, toxic levels of copper reduce populations of earthworms and beneficial mycorrhizal fungi, which the tree relies on for nutrient uptake. The industry is essentially poisoning the soil microbiome to protect the tree canopy.

Furthermore, the fungus is evolving. Much like bacteria developing resistance to antibiotics, *Hemileia vastatrix* is developing tolerance to fungicides. There are now over 50 known "races" (strains) of rust. Every time scientists release a new chemical protocol, the rust mutates to circumvent it. It is an evolutionary arms race, and the fungus possesses the advantage of speed.

## THE 2012 EPIDEMIC

The catastrophe that had been building for decades materialized in 2012. It was a convergence of biology, meteorology, and economics—a perfect storm that triggered a severe correction in the market.

Three critical factors aligned to create the crisis. First, the weather patterns shifted. The year 2012 was unusually warm in Central America. Crucially, the diurnal temperature range narrowed, meaning nights remained warm. Rust thrives in warm nocturnal conditions. The incubation period of the fungus shortened from 30 days to 20 days, allowing the pathogen to reproduce at an accelerated rate.

Second, the market collapsed. Simultaneously, the price of coffee on the New York C-Market crashed. Farmers in Honduras, Guatemala, and El Salvador faced liquidity crises. They were receiving prices below the cost of production.

Third, the neglect set in. Due to financial constraints, many farmers made a fatal calculation. They reduced fertilizer application and skipped fungicide sprays, hoping to conserve capital for one season. They assumed the trees could weather a year of austerity.

They were wrong. The trees, malnourished and unprotected, lacked any immune defense. The result was the 2012-2014 Central American Leaf Rust Epidemic, the worst phytosanitary crisis in the history of the Americas. In Honduras, entire mountainsides transitioned from green to orange, and finally to the gray of dead wood. In El Salvador, production plummeted by 60% in a single year. In Guatemala, 70% of the national crop was lost.

This was not merely an agricultural statistic; it was a humanitarian disaster. Coffee serves as the primary employer in rural Central America and acts as the region's social safety net. When the coffee trees died, employment vanished. An estimated 1.7 million jobs disappeared across the region. Smallholder farmers, living harvest-to-harvest, watched their primary asset disintegrate. They sold tools, then livestock. Facing hunger and debt, many abandoned their land.

### The Sociological Vector

There is a direct causal link between the orange dust on a leaf in the highlands of Santa Bárbara, Honduras, and political shifts at international borders. Sociologists studying migration patterns from 2014 to 2016 identified a high correlation between municipalities most severely impacted by *La Roya* and regions with the highest rates of out-migration.

In a shelter in Tapachula, Mexico, in 2015, a farmer named Carlos from western Honduras recounted the dissolution of his livelihood. "First the leaves fell," he stated. "Then the cherries dried up. I tried to prune them, to see if they would grow back. But the wood was dead. I owed money for the fertilizer. The bank said they would take the land. So I left."

Rust acts not just as a biological event, but as a sociological engine. It depopulates villages and fractures family units. It demonstrates that coffee is not merely a beverage; it is the structural beam of the rural economy in the Global South. When that beam fractures, the entire edifice is compromised.

### The Fortress in the Andes: CENICAFÉ

While Central America suffered, one nation remained largely secure. The front line of the defense against rust is located in a laboratory in the mountains of Chinchiná, Colombia, known as CENICAFÉ. Functioning as the central intelligence agency of coffee science, CENICAFÉ is funded by the Colombian Coffee Growers Federation (FNC) and employs hundreds of geneticists, agronomists, and pathologists with a singular directive: protect the crop.

In the 1980s, scientists at CENICAFÉ recognized that Caturra, the traditional variety of Colombia, was vulnerable. It possessed zero genetic resistance to rust. To secure the future, they initiated a massive breeding program, seeking a genetic donor. They located the solution in the

Timor Hybrid. As noted previously, this was a natural cross between Arabica and Robusta found on the island of Timor, carrying the dominant "T-Gene" for resistance.

The scientists spent twenty years crossing Caturra with the Timor Hybrid. They utilized a process of backcrossing—breeding the offspring back with the Arabica parent five times—to eliminate the harsh "Robusta flavor" while retaining the "Robusta armor." The result was a variety named Castillo.

CENICAFÉ's strategy was innovative. They understood that releasing a single genetic clone would allow the rust to eventually mutate and defeat it. Instead, they created a "Multiline Variety." A bag of Castillo seeds is not a monoculture of one plant; it is a composite of multiple resistant genetic lines. Some lines are resistant to Rust Race I, others to Race II, and others to Race III. When a farmer plants a field of Castillo, they are establishing a genetic puzzle. If a spore lands on Tree A, it might infect it. However, if the spore travels to Tree B, it may encounter a different immune profile that blocks infection. This strategy creates a form of "herd immunity" for plants.

## THE DEBATE ON QUALITY

In 2008, the Colombian Federation launched a "Renovation" program, offering loans and subsidies to farmers to replace their traditional Caturra trees with the resistant Castillo. This initiative triggered a conflict within the industry regarding flavor.

Baristas and roasters in the United States and Europe initially rejected Castillo. They claimed it possessed sensory defects—notes of rubber or asphalt reminiscent of Robusta—and mourned the loss of the sweet, fruit forward Caturra. They accused the Federation of prioritizing volume over quality. However, the Federation maintained its position, arguing that a tree scoring 90 points on a quality scale is useless if it is dead. "No hay café sin vida" ("There is no coffee without life") became the pragmatic mantra.

When the 2012 rust epidemic devastated the Andes, the Federation's strategy was vindicated. Caturra trees died by the millions, while Castillo trees survived, retaining their foliage and fruit. Colombia's production dipped but recovered rapidly, reaching record highs by 2015. The "Castillo Gamble" effectively saved the Colombian economy. Furthermore, as the trees matured and farmers refined their processing techniques, the flavor profile improved. In blind tastings today, high-quality Castillo often scores indistinguishably from Caturra. The rust epidemic forced the specialty industry to reconcile its preferences with the biological reality of survival.

### THE BIOTECH FUTURE: F1 HYBRIDS

The battle has now advanced to the next generation of trees: F1 Hybrids. Traditional breeding, like the development of Castillo, is a slow process, often taking 25 years to stabilize a variety. This timeline is insufficient relative to the accelerating pace of climate change.

Biotech companies and institutes such as World Coffee Research are developing "Formula 1" trees. These are created by crossing two genetically distant parents—for example, a wild Ethiopian landrace (for floral flavor) and a rust-resistant Catimor (for resilience)—through manual pollination. The resulting first generation of offspring (F1) exhibits "Hybrid Vigor" (heterosis). These trees grow 30% faster, yield 40% more fruit, and possess high disease resistance. Varieties such as *Centroamericano* and *Starmaya* are currently being introduced in Central America, offering high cup quality—scoring over 90 points—while resisting rust infection.

However, a complication exists. F1 Hybrids are genetically unstable for propagation. Farmers cannot save the seeds from the fruit to replant, as the offspring will revert to a mix of the parents' traits (genetic segregation). This shifts the power dynamic of coffee farming. For centuries, farmers controlled their own genetics by saving seeds from their best trees. With F1 Hybrids, they must purchase cloned seedlings from a specialized lab or nursery for every new planting cycle. This represents a shift toward a subscription model of agriculture, similar to the corn and soy industries. It offers protection from the spore, but integrates the farmer more deeply into the commercial biotech supply chain.

.   .   .

## THE PERMANENT EPIDEMIC

The rust is not disappearing; it is ascending. Historically, *Hemileia vastatrix* was limited by a "thermal ceiling." It could not survive at altitudes above 2,000 meters (6,560 feet) due to low temperatures, which caused the spores to go dormant. This created a sanctuary at high altitudes where the highest quality coffee was cultivated.

As global temperatures rise, that ceiling is lifting. In 2019, active rust infections were documented at 2,400 meters (7,870 feet) in the Cusco region of Peru. The safe zone is shrinking. The "Rust Wind" is no longer a singular event; it has become a chronic condition. The modern coffee farmer is not just cultivating beans; they are managing a continuous, low-level biological insurgency. They inspect their fields daily, turning over leaves to check for orange dust, aware that the wind carries a persistent threat.

When Thwaites identified the first spores in 1869, he viewed it as a local anomaly. He was mistaken. It was the harbinger of a permanent conflict between the human demand for a homogeneous agricultural product and nature's chaotic imperative to decompose it. The arrival of rust fundamentally altered the economics, sociology, and chemistry of the coffee world, transforming it from a passive agrarian pursuit into a complex, high-stakes management of biological risk.

# 16

# SHADE CANOPY: COFFEE'S FOREST

I n the highlands of western El Salvador, on the slopes of the Apaneca-Ilamatepec range, the distinction between a farm and a forest is intentionally blurred. Entering Finca Himalaya at 6:00 A.M. creates an immersion into a cathedral of noise. Rather than the mechanical hum of agriculture, the air is filled with the chaotic, overlapping frequencies of biology. Above the coffee trees, which stand chest-high and glossy, rises a secondary tier of banana palms and citrus. Above those, towering twenty meters into the mist, spread the massive, umbrella-like branches of the Inga trees. And everywhere, there is movement.

Turquoise-browed motmots swing their pendulum tails from the lower branches. Tennessee warblers, having flown 4,800 kilometers from the Appalachian Mountains, dart through the upper canopy hunting for caterpillars. Digging a hand into the soil reveals a substance that does not feel like dirt; it feels like a damp sponge, black and thick with decaying leaves, smelling of fungi and geosmin.

This is "Shade Coffee"—an agroforestry system that views the coffee tree not as a solitary factory, but as a citizen of a vertical village.

Fly 3,200 kilometers south to Minas Gerais, Brazil, and the architecture changes fundamentally. Here, the coffee grows in vast, undulating monocultures that stretch to the horizon. There is no canopy. There are no vertical tiers.

*The coffee trees are exposed to the full, blinding intensity of the tropical sun. The soil is often red dust, held in place not by root systems but by topography. The silence is profound, broken only by the wind or the distant roar of a mechanical harvester.*

*This is "Sun Coffee." It is a system designed on the logic of the assembly line: maximum solar intake, maximum chemical input, maximum yield.*

*For the last half-century, the coffee industry has been engaged in a structural debate between these two philosophies. It is a tension between biology and chemistry, between the slow resilience of the forest and the rapid efficiency of the plantation. To understand why the cup of coffee on your desk tastes the way it does—and whether it will still be available twenty years from now— requires an understanding of the roof under which it was born.*

### 1970: THE TECHNIFIED MISTAKE

To understand why shade matters, we have to understand why the industry attempted to eliminate it.

For centuries, all coffee was shade coffee. It was an agronomic necessity. *Coffea arabica* evolved in the Kaffa understory of Ethiopia, programmed by evolution to thrive in dappled light. When the Dutch and French moved the plant to the Caribbean and Latin America in the 18th century, they mimicked this structure, planting shade trees (often nitrogen-fixing legumes) to keep the cash crop from scorching.

Then came the Green Revolution.

In the 1970s and 80s, facing the dual threats of fungal disease and global price instability, national coffee institutes—funded by U.S.AID and the FAO—began a massive campaign of "Technification." The logic was borrowed from the corn and wheat fields of Iowa: remove the competition, increase the density, and pump in the nutrients.

The shade trees were targeted as inefficiencies. Agronomists argued that the Inga and Erythrina trees were competitors, extracting water, light, and nutrients that belonged to the coffee. They occupied valuable square footage that could be utilized for production.

*A traditional shade farm mimics a forest, utilizing vertical tiers of vegetation to regulate temperature and light.*

The pitch to farmers in Colombia, Costa Rica, and Honduras was seductive and mathematical:

- **Traditional Shade:** 1,500 trees per hectare. Yield: 500–700 kg (1,100–1,500 lbs).
- **Technified Sun:** 5,000–8,000 trees per hectare. Yield: 1,500–2,000 kg (3,300–4,400 lbs).

It appeared to be a miracle of efficiency. Governments incentivized the removal of trees. In Colombia, the Federación Nacional de Cafeteros (FNC) made loans contingent on farmers removing their shade trees and planting high-yield, dwarf varieties like Caturra in full sun. In Central America alone, an estimated 2.5 million acres of shade coffee were converted to sun monoculture between 1990 and 2010.

The yields did increase significantly. However, the agronomists had failed to account for the metabolic cost.

When an Arabica tree is exposed to 100% solar radiation, its photosynthetic machinery is pushed into overdrive. The stomata (pores on the leaf surface) remain open, transpiring water furiously to cool the leaf. The plant flowers excessively, setting more fruit than its skeletal structure can support. This leads to a condition known as "overbearing dieback." The tree essentially exhausts itself, cannibalizing its own tissue to ripen the cherries.

To keep a sun-grown tree alive, the farmer must intervene with external inputs. The soil, stripped of organic leaf litter, requires heavy doses of synthetic nitrogen (urea) to replace what the forest used to provide. Without the canopy to buffer the humidity, the trees require irrigation. Without birds and bats to consume the insects, the trees require pesticides.

The "Technified" farm was not a self-sustaining ecosystem; it was a synthetic input-dependent system. The farmer had traded a low-input, low-yield biological asset for a high-input, high-yield chemical dependent. As long as oil prices (and thus fertilizer prices) remained low, the calculation held. But when the cost of inputs rose, or when the market price of coffee crashed, the sun farmer was left with a depleted field and significant debt.

### THE NITROGEN ENGINE

In the surviving shade farms of Veracruz, Mexico, or Jinotega, Nicaragua, the farmers do not view the canopy merely as a sun-block. They view it as a fertilizer factory as much as a sun-block.

The dominant tree in Latin American coffee culture is the *Inga* (commonly called Guama or Ice Cream Bean). It is chosen not for its timber, but for its root system. The Inga is a legume, a member of the Fabaceae family, which possesses a biological advantage: nitrogen fixation.

Examining the roots of an Inga tree reveals small, pinkish nodules. Inside these nodules live colonies of *Rhizobia* bacteria. These bacteria perform a chemical conversion that industrial humanity requires 500°C (932°F) and 200 atmospheres of pressure to replicate: they pull inert nitrogen gas from the atmosphere and break its triple bond, converting it into ammonia, a form of nitrogen that plants can metabolize.

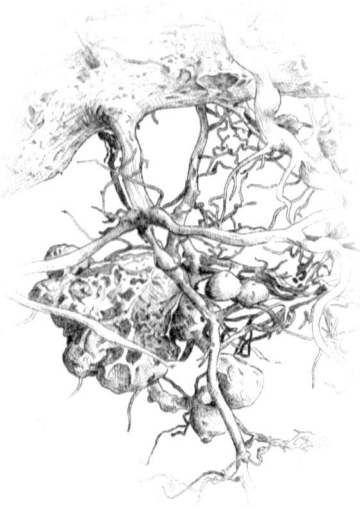

*The roots of the Inga tree house nitrogen-fixing bacteria, creating a
natural fertilizer factory beneath the soil.*

The Inga functions as a nutrient pump. It draws nitrogen from the air
and phosphorus from the deep soil, integrating them into its leaves.
Because the Inga is semi-deciduous, it continually sheds these nutrient-
rich leaves onto the coffee below.

- **The Leaf Litter:** In a well-managed shade farm, the ground is
  covered in a 5–10 centimeter (2–4 inch) layer of decomposing
  organic matter. This mulch suppresses weeds (reducing
  herbicide costs) and traps moisture.
- **The Slow Release:** As the leaves decay, they release their
  nitrogen slowly, in synchronization with the coffee tree's
  needs.

A 2009 study in the journal *Agroforestry Systems* quantified this relationship. It found that a density of 200 Inga trees per hectare could
contribute up to 150 kg (330 lbs) of nitrogen to the soil annually. To
purchase that quantity of nitrogen in bags of synthetic urea would cost a
farmer hundreds of dollars. Far from extracting from the coffee, the
shade tree fuels it.

. . .

## "Exclosure": The Birds as Mechanism

The most visible casualty of the Sun Coffee revolution was not the soil, but the sky.

In the late 1980s, ornithologists at the Smithsonian Institution recorded a precipitous decline in North American migratory songbirds. Populations of Baltimore Orioles, Wood Thrushes, and Tennessee Warblers were collapsing. The cause, they discovered, was not in the suburbs of Maryland, but in the wintering grounds of Central America.

These birds are "neotropical migrants." They spend their summers in the U.S. and Canada but fly south to the "Bean Belt" for the winter. For millennia, the mid-elevation forests of the Andes and Central America were their habitat. When those forests were cleared for Sun Coffee, the birds arrived to find a monocultural expanse unable to support them.

A Sun Coffee monoculture creates a biodiversity deficit. It creates a "hard edge" where the forest stops and the farm begins. A shade coffee farm, by contrast, functions as a "soft edge," a buffer zone that mimics the structural complexity of the forest. Smithsonian researchers established that a traditional shade farm can host over 150 species of birds—numbers comparable to undisturbed primary rainforest.

For the farmer, however, biodiversity is often viewed as a luxury. "Bird-friendly" is a marketing term; they need to know if the biological presence translates to financial gain.

Enter the "Exclosure Experiment".

In a landmark study in Jamaica's Blue Mountains, researchers Matt Johnson and Thomas Sherry wrapped entire coffee trees in nylon netting, physically preventing birds from accessing them, while leaving adjacent control trees accessible. They monitored the insect populations.

*Scientists used netting to prove that without birds, pest populations on coffee farms explode.*

The results challenged the "inefficiency" argument. On the netted trees, the population of the Coffee Berry Borer (*Hypothenemus hampei*)— a beetle that drills into the fruit and ruins the crop—surged.

The birds were performing specific agricultural labor:

- **Warblers** were gleaning leaf-miners and caterpillars from the foliage.
- **Migratory Orioles** were acting as heavy artillery, consuming larger weevils.

The study calculated that the birds were responsible for reducing borer infestation by nearly 50%. By translating the saved crop into market value, they estimated the birds were worth approximately $75 to $310 per hectare to the farmer.

When farmers removed the shade to "modernize," they effectively eliminated their pest control system. They replaced the foraging of the warblers with Endosulfan and Chlorpyrifos—neurotoxic insecticides that contaminated the water table and posed risks to workers, all to perform a function the birds had provided at no cost.

## THE NIGHT SHIFT: CHIROPTERA

If the birds control the day, the bats control the night. This represents a critical, often overlooked frontier of coffee research.

For decades, the role of bats in coffee was neglected. However, a 2014 study published in *Science*, led by researchers at the University of Michigan, used DNA barcoding to analyze the guano of bats living in Mexican shade coffee farms.

The results were significant. The bats were consuming massive quantities of arthropods, specifically the nocturnal moths whose larvae infest coffee leaves.

The mechanism is "top-down limitation." During the day, parasitic wasps and birds hunt. At dusk, they retire, and the moths emerge to lay eggs. In a sun farm, this creates a safe window for pests. In a shade farm, the air is patrolled by insectivorous bats navigating by echolocation.

The study utilized similar "exclosure" nets, but opened them only during the day (to allow birds) or only at night (to allow bats). They found that in the wet season, the bats were even more effective at pest control than the birds.

Bats, however, are selective regarding habitat. They do not roost in coffee bushes. They require hollows in old-growth trees, or the dense, folded leaves of heliconias and bromeliads to sleep during the day. A sun farm offers no shelter. By removing the "useless" non-coffee vegetation, the farmer effectively evicts the night shift.

## THE THERMOSTAT: PHYSICS OF THE CANOPY

While nutrients and pests are critical, the most immediate physical impact of shade is on temperature. This is the mechanism of the "Buffer."

Coffee is a plant with narrow thermal tolerances. It prefers temperatures between 18°C and 21°C (64°F–70°F). It cannot tolerate frost, but it also ceases metabolic function in extreme heat. When leaf temperatures exceed 24°C (75°F), photosynthesis slows. Above 30°C (86°F), the plant undergoes thermal stress, closing its stomata to preserve water, effectively halting sugar production.

In a sun farm, the leaf temperature often exceeds the ambient air temperature by several degrees due to direct radiation. The plant diverts energy to survival—heat dissipation—rather than fruit development.

The shade canopy acts as a macro-climate controller.

- **Solar Attenuation:** A typical Inga canopy blocks 20% to 40% of solar radiation. This keeps the leaves in their optimal photosynthetic range for more hours of the day.
- **Radiative Buffering:** At night, the canopy acts as an insulator, trapping ground heat and preventing temperatures from dropping too drastically.

This dampening effect—reducing the peaks of heat and the troughs of cold—is becoming the single most valuable asset in the era of climate change. As the "Bean Belt" warms, the lower altitudes are becoming inhospitable to Arabica. Farmers in sun-grown regions are observing their crops scorch and their yields become erratic. Farmers with shade cover are measuring ambient temperatures 3°C to 5°C (5°F–9°F) cooler than their neighbors. The shade tree functions as a cooling system powered by sunlight.

### The Yield Tradeoff

If shade provides nitrogen, pest control, and thermal protection, why is it not the universal standard? Why did Brazil dominate the global market with Sun Coffee?

We must address the "Yield Gap".

A well-managed sun farm in Brazil, mechanized and chemically fertilized, can produce 2,500 to 4,000 kg of green coffee per hectare. A traditional organic shade farm in Mexico might struggle to produce 800 kg.

Shade trees compete for resources. They occupy physical space. Their roots, while deep, can compete for surface water during extreme droughts if not managed correctly. Furthermore, excessive shade acts as a contraceptive for coffee yield—the plant requires a signal of light intensity to trigger heavy flowering.

This creates the central economic dilemma for the producer:

1. **The Sun Strategy:** High volume, high input costs, shorter tree lifespan (12–15 years), high risk of environmental degradation.
2. **The Shade Strategy:** Low volume, low input costs, longer tree lifespan (25–30 years), high resilience.

For the smallholder farmer—the family with three hectares in Guatemala—the Sun Strategy often becomes a debt trap. They are encouraged to maximize yield, but they lack the cash reserves to purchase the necessary fertilizers when prices spike. They end up with "passive sun" coffee—trees exposed to the sun but starved of nutrients. This results in the worst possible outcome.

The Shade Strategy operates more like an annuity than a lottery ticket. It provides a lower, but more stable, income. Furthermore, the shade trees themselves function as a bank account. When coffee prices crash, the farmer can harvest avocados, mangoes, or citrus from the canopy. In times of financial urgency, they can harvest the timber itself, selling *Cordia* or *Cedrela* wood for cash. The sun farm is a monoculture of risk; the shade farm is a diversified portfolio.

THE RUST PARADOX

There is, however, one area where the shade advocates must concede ground to the technicians: *Hemileia vastatrix*, the Coffee Leaf Rust.

As detailed previously, rust is a fungus. Fungi require moisture to germinate. A spore of *Hemileia* needs a film of water on the leaf for roughly 24 to 48 hours to penetrate the plant.

Shade trees increase humidity. They block the wind that would otherwise dry the leaves after a rainstorm. In a dense, unmanaged shade forest, the humidity stays at saturation point for too long, creating an incubator for rust.

During the severe rust epidemic of 2012–2014, which destroyed half the crop in Central America, many farmers blamed the trees. They entered the fields with chainsaws, "opening the roof" to let the sun sterilize the fungus.

This led to a nuanced agronomic rule: Active Canopy Management. Shade is not a static installation. It requires pruning. The farmer must regulate the shade percentage like a dimmer switch—heavier in the dry season to conserve water, lighter in the wet season to allow airflow and suppress rust. The target is often 40% shade, not full darkness. It is a labor-intensive process, requiring the farmer to monitor the canopy as closely as the crop.

### The Ant and the Scale: A Mafia in the Trees

It is also important to view the biodiversity of the shade farm without romanticism. Not all interactions in the shade are benevolent.

In many shade farms, one will find coffee branches coated in a sticky, black substance. This is "sooty mold," a fungus that grows on the sugary excrement of the Green Scale insect (*Coccus viridis*).

The Green Scale extracts sap from the coffee phloem. Examining them closely reveals they are not alone. Swarming over the scales are aggressive ants, often of the *Azteca* species.

This is a symbiotic protection racket. The scales provide the ants with sugar (honeydew). In exchange, the ants act as bodyguards. They attack anything that attempts to consume the scales—including the beneficial ladybugs and parasitic wasps. They will even attack the hands of the coffee pickers.

*A complex symbiosis: ants protect the scale insects from predators in exchange for the sugary honeydew they excrete.*

The shade trees provide the nesting sites for these ants. A sun farm, devoid of permanent nesting structures, rarely suffers from this specific ant-scale complex. It is a reminder that nature is not a moral system designed to assist the farmer; it is a competitive chaos. The shade farmer must manage these "disservices" alongside the services.

CERTIFICATION WARS: THE FROG VS. THE BIRD

In the grocery aisle, this complex agronomy is flattened into a sticker. Consumers want to "save the rainforest," and certifications have attempted to monetize that desire. However, the standards vary significantly.

The two dominant players represent the tension between "perfect" and "good enough."

**Smithsonian Bird-Friendly (The Gold Standard):** This is the strictest environmental certification in coffee. To earn the "Bird-Friendly" seal, a farm must be 100% Organic certified first. Then, it must meet rigorous biophysical criteria:

- Canopy height must be at least 12 meters (40 feet).
- Shade cover must be at least 40%.
- The canopy must include at least 10 different species of woody trees.

It is scientifically robust. Purchasing Bird-Friendly coffee genuinely funds a forest habitat. However, the criteria are so stringent (and the market for it so niche) that few farms can achieve it.

**Rainforest Alliance (The Green Frog):** This is the dominant certification. It appears on bags at supermarkets and fast-food chains. Their approach is pragmatic. They do not require organic certification; farmers can use synthetic fertilizers and some pesticides. Their shade requirements are more lenient (typically requiring 15% to 40% native tree cover, but with exceptions for "technified" systems).

Critics label it "Shade Lite." Proponents argue it is a vital entry point. By setting an achievable standard, they encourage large-scale agricultural operations to plant some trees, rather than none.

The difficulty is that the consumer often cannot distinguish the difference. A bag featuring an illustration of a toucan might originate from a farm that hasn't supported a toucan population in a decade.

### Taste Mechanism: The Bean as Battery

Does all this biology translate to the cup? Is "shade" a flavor? The answer, supported by biochemistry, is yes. The mechanism is maturation time. In a sun farm, the high radiation accelerates the cherry's ripening cycle. The fruit turns red quickly, often before the seed inside has fully developed. It is a "forced" ripeness.

In a shade farm, the lower temperatures slow the metabolism of the tree. The cherry remains on the branch for two to four weeks longer. This extended hang-time is crucial. It allows the plant to deposit more nutrients into the seed.

- **Sugars:** The sucrose content in shade-grown beans is measurably higher.
- **Acidity:** The slower respiration rate preserves malic and citric acids that would otherwise be metabolized due to heat stress.
- **Density:** Shade-grown beans are physically harder and denser.

When a roaster places a sun-grown bean and a shade-grown bean of the same variety into the drum, they behave differently. The sun bean is often softer, more porous; it roasts rapidly and can taste flat or "woody." The shade bean is a dense battery of potential energy. It absorbs heat efficiently and unfolds with complex fruit notes, structure, and body. The "Shade Taste" is defined by patience.

## THE FUTURE: RE-GREENING THE BELT

Looking toward 2050, the trend is reversing. The "Technified" era is increasingly viewed as a historical anomaly, a failed experiment in forcing a forest shrub to function like corn.

We are observing the rise of "Insetting"—where major roasters, concerned about supply chain stability, are paying farmers to plant trees. In Colombia, the same FNC that once mandated deforestation is now distributing millions of native tree saplings. They are establishing "Biological Corridors"—strips of forest connecting fragmented landscapes, allowing genetic migration for flora and fauna.

It is a recognition that the coffee farm of the future cannot resemble the coffee farm of the 1990s.

Back in Finca Himalaya in El Salvador, the sun has crested the canopy. The mist is evaporating. The noise of the birds has settled into a steady hum. The Inga trees are shedding their leaves, a silent, continuous rain of fertilizer. The system is functioning. It is slower. It is more difficult to harvest. But it is resilient.

The choice between sun and shade is not merely about birds or insects. It is a choice regarding the definition of agriculture itself. Is a farm a machine for extraction, independent of its environment? Or is it an ecology, a participant in the local loop of water, carbon, and life? The canopy suggests that for Arabica to survive the volatile century ahead, it requires the protection of the forest from which it came.

# 17

# TERROIR WARS: THE ALTITUDE PARADOX

S tanding on the ridge of the Inga Aponte region in Nariño, Colombia, at exactly 2,200 meters (7,217 feet) above sea level, the human body begins to register the altitude. The air is thin, containing roughly 20% less oxygen than the air at sea level, forcing the lungs to work harder with every step. It is piercingly cold. When the sun vanishes behind the galeras—the local term for the jagged volcanic peaks—the temperature undergoes a rapid thermal shift, dropping near freezing within an hour. The farmers here wear heavy wool ruanas to inspect their crops, their breath misting in the twilight, a visual testament to the atmospheric density that defines their livelihood.

The coffee trees on this ridge look nothing like the lush, manicured hedges found in low-altitude commercial brochures. They are stunted, gnarled, and compact, expending every ounce of energy to maintain structural integrity against the wind and the cold. The cherries they produce are small, dense, and hard as river pebbles. But inside those compact seeds lies a flavor profile of sparkling acidity, intense sweetness, and complex floral notes that mimic jasmine and bergamot. This is not the taste of a happy tree; this is the taste of metabolic stress. This is the taste of the high Andes.

Three thousand miles southeast, in the vast Cerrado Mineiro of Brazil, the landscape tells a different story. This is a flat savannah sitting at a comfortable 900 meters (2,950 feet). The air is warm, thick, and humid. The sun beats down on endless rows of mechanically harvested trees that grow fast, leafy, and lush. The beans harvested here are large, soft, and porous. When roasted, they taste of chocolate, nuts, and caramel—comforting, consistent, but lacking the electric, fruit-forward profile of the high-altitude bean. They provide the bass notes of the coffee orchestra, while Nariño provides the violins.

This stark divergence is not accidental; it is the direct result of the most critical, debated, and expensive variable in coffee quality: Terroir. For centuries, the wine industry claimed ownership of this word, the mystical French concept of "somewhereness"—the idea that the soil, the slope, and the wind imbue the grape with a signature that cannot be replicated elsewhere. In the coffee trade, this concept was ignored for generations. Coffee was treated as a fungible commodity, a monolithic "brown flavor" indistinguishable by origin. But in the last twenty years, coffee has surpassed wine in its obsession with geography. The industry has entered the era of the Terroir Wars, where a difference of fifty meters in elevation or a slight shift in soil pH can multiply the price of a pound of beans by a factor of ten. The flavor is derived from soil composition and atmospheric physics rather than magic.

## THE CALCULUS OF COLD

In the specialty coffee industry, the acronym MASL (Meters Above Sea Level) is often printed on bags like a badge of rank, or perhaps a warning label. A bag might proudly display "1,850 MASL," signalling to the buyer that this is not ordinary coffee. But height itself is not the flavor maker; height is merely a proxy for temperature.

The governing principle here is the Adiabatic Lapse Rate. Think of the atmosphere as a heavy blanket; the higher you climb, the thinner the blanket becomes, and the less heat it can hold. In the troposphere, for every 1,000 meters you climb, the ambient temperature drops by approximately 6.5°C (11.7°F). This physical law creates a vertical climate map.

Coffee is a tropical plant, specifically from the *Rubiaceae* family, but the Arabica species is biologically paradoxical: it is a tropical plant that intolerant of high heat. Its genetic code, evolved in the cool, shaded understory of the Ethiopian forests, dictates an optimal temperature range of 18°C–21°C (64°F–70°F). In the equatorial tropics, where sea-level temperatures can easily exceed 30°C (86°F), the only way to find this "Goldilocks" thermal zone is to climb the mountain.

However, flavor isn't just about the average temperature; it's about the swing. This is the **Diurnal Temperature Range**. At high altitudes, the air is thin and holds less moisture. Without that moisture to act as an insulating blanket, heat escapes rapidly into space the moment the sun sets.

This creates a massive gap between the heat of the day and the freeze of the night. This thermal shock triggers a biological switch in the tree, forcing it to choose between growing leaves or hoarding energy:

- **Day:** The coffee tree photosynthesizes, converting sunlight into complex sugars (sucrose and fructose) to fuel its fruit.
- **Night:** The cold shocks the tree's metabolism into near-dormancy.

This is the secret mechanism of quality. In a warm environment (low altitude), the tree continues to respire at night, consuming the sugars it created during the day to fuel vegetative growth—new leaves, longer branches, and trunk expansion. It effectively "burns" its own flavor reserves to grow larger. In a cold environment, the tree shuts down at sunset, banking the sugars instead. These stored carbohydrates are packed into the seed as a survival mechanism for the next generation. When the roaster eventually applies heat to that seed, those conserved sugars undergo Maillard reactions and caramelization, creating the sweetness and acidity prized by the market. The cold night is the vault where flavor is saved.

### WHY HARD BEANS FRACTURE

The physical manifestation of this altitude-induced stress is density. A coffee bean grown at 2,000 meters matures with agonizing slowness. It might take ten or eleven months to ripen from flower to harvest, compared to six or seven months at low altitude. This slow maturation allows the tree to pack more cellular material, lipids, and carbohydrates into the same volume of space. The cellular structure of a high-altitude bean is tight, complex, and chaotic.

This creates a distinct physical property known as the "Hard Bean" or "Strictly Hard Bean." If one were to take a raw green bean from a high-altitude Kenyan farm and bite it, the risk of fracturing a tooth is real. If dropped on a glass table, it sounds like a marble—a sharp, high-pitched *ping*. The cellular walls are reinforced, packed tightly together to withstand the elements.

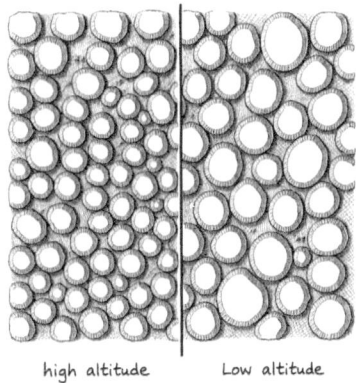

high altitude        Low altitude

*High-altitude beans develop a dense, chaotic cellular structure that acts as a thermal battery during roasting*

Conversely, a low-grown bean is porous. Under a microscope, the cell walls are further apart, with larger air pockets between the structures. If one bites a raw Brazilian bean from the lower plains, it crunches like a raw peanut or soft wood. If dropped, it sounds dull—a hollow *thud* rather than a ping. This is a "Soft Bean."

For the roaster, this density reading is the primary instruction manual for the roast profile. A high-density bean acts like a thermal battery. It can absorb massive amounts of conductive and convective heat energy without scorching. A roaster can push it hard in the drum, using high temperatures to develop complex fruit acids and aromatics. The bean fights back against the heat, allowing for a longer, more aggressive development. A low-density bean is delicate; if a roaster applies that same thermal energy, the cellulose will burn before the center of the bean is cooked, resulting in an ashy, hollow cup. The "snap" of a fine acidity is the sensory result of this structural density. Because the hard bean can withstand intense thermal pressure without scorching, the roaster can develop the sugars while preserving the vibrant fruit acids that a softer bean would lose.

## ZONING THE MOUNTAIN

Because altitude correlates so strongly with market value, govern-ments have codified the Adiabatic Lapse Rate into national law. The grading systems of Central America are not based on taste, but on an altimeter reading, creating a rigid hierarchy of value based on verticality.

In Guatemala, the hardest bean generates the highest tax revenue and export price. The government created the SHB (Strictly Hard Bean) grade. To qualify for this stamp—and the higher price per pound that comes with it—the coffee must be grown above 1,350 meters (roughly 4,400 feet). Below that lies the HB (Hard Bean) zone (1,220–1,350 meters), and below that is Prime and Extra Prime.

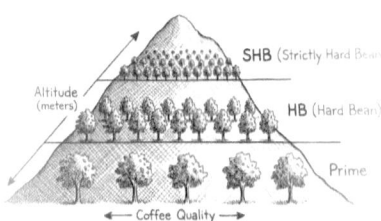

*Coffee grading systems in Central America are strictly tied to altitude,*
*equating elevation with quality.*

This creates a bizarre bureaucratic reality where a farmer whose land sits at 1,340 meters produces "Hard Bean," while a farmer ten meters uphill produces "Strictly Hard Bean." The flavor difference across that ten-meter gap might be negligible, but the market price gap is substan-tial. This bureaucratic ladder creates a vertical real estate market where elevation is the primary driver of land value. In Costa Rica, one can often visually trace the contour lines on the mountainside: above the line, the coffee is pruned and managed for specialty markets; below the line, it is harvested for volume commercial blends. The mountain is zoned by the laws of thermodynamics and the laws of the export board.

## Magma and Ash: The Soil Engine

If altitude provides the climate, soil provides the diet. The best coffee in the world almost invariably grows on the slopes of volcanoes—past or present. From the Blue Mountains of Jamaica to the highlands of Panama and the Great Rift Valley of Kenya, the dominant soil type is Andosol (volcanic soil). But why do volcanoes make good coffee? It is a matter of drainage and mineral availability.

Coffee trees suffer from a condition known as "wet feet." If the roots sit in standing water, the oxygen supply is cut off, and the roots begin to rot within days. Volcanic soil, composed of ash, pumice, and tephra, is highly porous. It drains water instantly, preventing rot, yet retains just enough moisture in the microscopic pores of the pumice for the root hairs to access during dry spells.

*Volcanic soil offers perfect drainage and mineral content, essential for high-quality Arabica.*

More importantly, volcanic ash is a mineral cocktail, rich in the specific nutrients coffee trees crave:

- **Magnesium (Mg):** This is the central atom of the chlorophyll molecule. A soil rich in magnesium allows for more efficient photosynthesis, even on cloudy days, turning sunlight into sugar with greater efficacy.
- **Potassium (K):** This mineral regulates the stomata—the breathing pores on the leaf—and controls the turgor pressure of the cells. High potassium levels in the soil correlate directly with the perception of citric acidity in the brewed cup.
- **Zinc (Zn):** Essential for the synthesis of growth hormones and internode elongation.

When a consumer drinks a cup of coffee from Antigua, Guatemala, situated in a valley ringed by three volcanoes, they are tasting the mineral output of the *Volcán de Fuego*. The smoky, spicy, chocolate notes often attributed to that region are not just poetic metaphors; they are the chemical signature of the sulfur and magnesium in the magma.

The most dramatic example of soil influencing flavor occurs in Kenya. Kenyan coffee is famous for its screamingly high acidity—flavors of blackcurrant, tomato, and grapefruit that make the sides of the tongue salivate. This is largely due to Phosphoric Acid. The soils around Mount Kenya are incredibly rich in phosphorus due to specific ancient volcanic activity, and they are naturally acidic (low pH). The coffee tree absorbs this phosphorus and concentrates it in the bean. Unlike citric acid (which tastes like lemons) or malic acid (which tastes like green apples), phosphoric acid is an inorganic acid—the same acid found in cola beverages. It adds a "sparkle" or a savory, vibrating sensation to the tongue. You cannot replicate a Kenyan coffee in Brazil, no matter what seed you plant. One could take the exact SL-28 variety seed from Kenya and plant it in the Cerrado, but without the phosphorus-rich volcanic loam, the bean will not synthesize that specific acid profile. It will taste flat. The soil is the limiting reagent.

## 2004: THE GEISHA SHOCK

For decades, the industry treated terroir as a general guideline. But in 2004, a specific event turned terroir into a combat sport. This is the "Blind Tasting" that changed the world.

The setting was the "Best of Panama" auction, a competition designed to showcase the country's beans. For years, Panama was known for solid, but unremarkable, traditional coffees. The judges—seasoned buyers from the U.S. and Japan—sat before a row of white cups, moving through the routine of slurping, spitting, and marking scores. Then they reached a specific lot from the Peterson family at Hacienda La Esmeralda.

The room went quiet. The flavor in the cup did not resemble coffee in the traditional sense. It possessed the aromatic profile of jasmine perfume, bergamot, and sweet honeysuckle. It tasted like a refined Earl Grey tea. Some judges initially assumed there was a mistake—that the producers had added flavorings or that the sample had been contaminated. Others recognized it for what it was: a botanical revelation. One judge famously remarked, "It was like seeing the face of God in a cup."

The coffee was the Geisha variety (covered in Chapter 12), but the variety alone was not the cause. The Petersons had discovered that this specific Ethiopian variety, when planted at the very top of their farm—above 1,600 meters in a specific wind-protected canyon called Jaramillo—mutated in flavor. At 1,400 meters, Geisha was good. At 1,700 meters, subjected to the stress of the wind and the cold, it became a masterpiece. The terroir had unlocked a genetic expression that had remained dormant at lower elevations.

That year, the coffee sold for $21 a pound—a record-breaking price when the commodity market was hovering around $0.70. This moment launched the "Altitude Wars." Farmers realized that specific microclimates could generate exponential value. It was no longer sufficient to say "Panama Coffee." The market now demanded the valley, the elevation, and the side of the hill.

## MICROLOT MATHEMATICS

Today, the obsession with terroir has led to the rise of the Microlot. Roasters no longer just buy from a region; they buy from a specific coordinate. Farmers have realized that the **Aspect**—the compass direction the slope faces—changes the flavor chemistry.

- **East-Facing Slope:** These trees catch the gentle morning sun. The dew dries quickly, reducing mold risk, and photosynthesis starts early in the day. Because the morning sun is less intense, the trees undergo less heat stress. These slopes often produce brighter, more floral, and delicate coffees.
- **West-Facing Slope:** These trees endure the harsh afternoon sun. The heat stress is higher, causing the tree to close its stomata to conserve water. To protect themselves, the trees often produce more mucilage (sugar) around the seed as a hydration buffer. These slopes often produce sweeter, fruitier, but less acidic coffees.

*The direction a slope faces determines solar intensity, altering the chemical composition of the cherry.*

A sophisticated farmer in Colombia might now harvest the east slope on Tuesday and sell it as a "Floral Microlot," then harvest the west slope on Thursday and sell it as a "Natural Fruit Microlot." It is the same seed, the same soil, the same farm. But the angle of the sun creates a different chemical product. This is the granularity of modern terroir.

## THE "POTATO" CURSE

However, volcanic terroir has a dark side. Terroir is not just soil and sun; it is also the ecology of pests. In the Great Lakes region of Africa—specifically Rwanda and Burundi—the terroir produces one of the most tragic flavor defects in the world.

The soil here is rich and volcanic, producing incredible sweetness. But this specific ecology is also the natural habitat of the Antestia Bug (*Antestiopsis*). The Antestia bug is a variegated beetle that feeds on the coffee cherry. When it punctures the skin of the fruit to drink the sap, it introduces a bacteria into the seed. This bacteria produces a chemical compound called Isopropyl Methoxypyrazine.

This molecule is incredibly potent. Even a few parts per trillion are detectable by the human nose. And it smells exactly, unmistakably, like raw, peeling potato.

This is the "Potato Defect." It is the curse of Rwandan coffee. A farmer can do everything right—grow the coffee at high altitude, pick it perfectly, process it cleanly—but if one infected bean makes it into a sixty-kilo bag, it acts as a ticking time bomb. The defect is invisible to the naked eye. It lies dormant until the consumer grinds the beans. Suddenly, the kitchen fills with the scent of old earth and starch. Because of this specific biological terroir, Rwandan coffee often sells at a discount, despite its high quality. The "somewhereness" of Rwanda includes the bug. It is a haunting reminder that nature is not always benevolent to the farmer.

## DISTANCE FROM THE SUN

There are exceptions to the altitude rule. If one examines a map of premium coffee, two outliers appear: Kona (Hawaii) and the Galapagos Islands. Both grow coffee at relatively low altitudes (600–800 meters), yet they are considered specialty grade and command high prices. How do they circumvent the physics of the lapse rate?

They utilize the Latitude Algorithm. The further one moves away from the Equator (Latitude 0°), the cooler the air becomes at sea level.

- **Colombia (Latitude 4°N):** Deep in the tropics. To find the cool 20°C air, one must climb to 1,800 meters.
- **Hawaii (Latitude 19°N):** Subtropical. The air is naturally cooler. One can find that same 20°C temperature at just 600 meters.

This creates the concept of Effective Altitude. A farm in Kona at 600 meters produces coffee that behaves biologically like a farm in Colombia at 1,500 meters. They are trading height for distance from the sun. Furthermore, they utilize Maritime Cooling. The trade winds in Hawaii blow cool air constantly across the islands. In the Galapagos, the Humboldt Current brings freezing cold water from Antarctica up to the equator, creating a cool, misty microclimate at sea level.

These "Maritime Coffees" have a distinct signature. Because the cooling is gentle (wind and mist) rather than aggressive (high-altitude night freeze), the beans are softer than Andean beans. They produce a mild, smooth, low-acid cup—the classic Kona profile. They lack the jagged complexity of the high mountain, offering instead a round, polite sweetness that appeals to a broad demographic.

THE NITROGEN TRAP

While nature dictates the baseline of terroir, humans can—and do—attempt to hack it. The most common tool for altering terroir is Nitrogen.

Nitrogen is the fuel for leaf growth. It is the gasoline of the plant world. In an effort to increase yields, commercial farmers often bombard their soil with urea-based fertilizers. There is a trap here. If a farmer applies too much nitrogen to force growth, the tree responds by producing lush foliage and massive beans. The yields look impressive. But the flavor becomes "grassy," "herbal," or "vegetal."

The bean becomes packed with proteins and amino acids rather than simple sugars. When roasted, these proteins do not caramelize; they burn. High-quality terroir management often means starving the tree just enough. The goal is to keep the tree on the verge of hunger, so it prioritizes reproduction (the seed) over vegetative growth (the leaf). This leads to a cruel irony in the coffee market. The farmer who fertilizes heavily gets more bags of coffee per hectare, but a lower price per bag because the flavor is diluted. The farmer who restricts fertilizer gets fewer bags, but a higher quality score. Terroir is not just what is in the soil; it is what the farmer chooses not to put in the soil.

### THE LUNGS OF THE HARVEST

We must not discuss the romance of the mountain without discussing the lungs of the people who climb it. Harvesting coffee at 2,000 meters is physically grueling labor that defies modern industrial logic. The air is thin. The slopes are often pitched at 45-degree angles. In regions like Huehuetenango or Nariño, pickers often tie ropes around their waists, anchoring themselves to the trees to avoid tumbling down the ravine.

A picker might carry a basket that weighs 15 kilograms (33 lbs). When full, they must haul it up the vertical slope to the weighing station. They do this ten, twenty times a day. The "brightness" in the cup—that sparkling acidity utilized in marketing campaigns—is the direct result of this extreme physical exertion. The terroir of the high mountain is a hostile workplace. Machines cannot operate here; tractors would tip over. Every single cherry from a high-altitude microlot was reached by a human hand and carried by a human back. The premium price of high-altitude coffee pays for the hazard of the geography as much as the flavor.

### THE MOVING MOUNTAIN

The most terrifying aspect of altitude terroir is that it is finite. As the planet warms, the "Goldilocks Zone" is moving up the mountain. Farmers who used to grow premium Arabica at 1,200 meters are now finding their beans are ripening too fast. The heat is accelerating the maturation, stripping the bean of its density and acidity. The flavor is flattening out. Even worse, pests like the Coffee Berry Borer—a beetle that used to die in the cold air of the highlands—are now surviving at higher elevations. The frost line is retreating.

To chase the cool air, farmers are planting higher. But mountains are shaped like pyramids. There is less land at the top than at the bottom.

- At 1,500 meters, there is arable land.
- At 2,200 meters, there is scrubland (often protected *páramo* ecosystems that act as water reservoirs).
- At 2,500 meters, there is only rock.

We are running out of altitude. This phenomenon is leading to a potential extinction of flavor profiles. The sparkling, high-acid, dense coffees of the future may simply not exist because there is no land high enough to produce them. We can move wine grapes from France to England as the climate warms, but we cannot move a tropical mountain.

### The Uncopyable Signature

You can clone a Geisha tree in a lab. You can buy the exact Probat roaster used by a world champion. You can synthesize water with the perfect magnesium-to-calcium ratio. But you cannot copy Terroir. You cannot fake the angle of the sunlight hitting the western slope of the *Volcán de Fuego* at 4:00 PM. You cannot fake the specific phosphorus content of the Kenyan rift. You cannot fake the misty afternoon cloud cover of the Blue Mountains.

Terroir is the one unscalable variable. It is the reason why coffee will never be fully commoditized like aluminum or corn. As we move into the next chapter, we will see how roasters take these hard, dense, mineral-rich seeds and apply fire to them. But the roaster is only revealing what the mountain already created. The flavor was derived from the soil composition, the thin air, and the metabolic stress of the tree long before the harvest began. Roasting can only reveal potential; it cannot create what the terroir didn't provide.

# PART IV

## THE ALCHEMY OF AROMA

Coffee is one of the rare foods that becomes itself only through transformation. The cherry is sweet. The seed is bitter. The cup is something else entirely.

This section is about that metamorphosis: the controlled violence of heat in the roaster, the geometry of grinding, the physics of pressure, the quiet power of paper and water chemistry, and the chemistry of caffeine —the molecule that turned coffee into modernity's favorite drug.

You can drink coffee without knowing any of this. But once you understand the alchemy, the cup stops feeling accidental. It starts feeling designed.

# 18

# CONTROLLED DESTRUCTION: THE THERMODYNAMICS OF FLAVOR

T he room carries the scent of wet hay and warm iron, a sensory prelude to the transformation about to occur. It is 5:00 AM in a converted warehouse in Seattle's industrial district, and the air vibrates with a low, rhythmic thrum—the mechanical heartbeat of a machine that resembles a steam locomotive more than a culinary instrument. It is a vintage Probat UG-22, a cast-iron apparatus forged in Emmerich, Germany, in 1958. It weighs nearly 1,814 kilograms (4,000 lbs). It possesses no touchscreen, no U.S.B ports, and no automation. It operates on physics and intuition.

Standing before the machine is a roaster we'll call Maya. She cooks like a chef and manages reactions like a chemist, yet she is neither. Her hand rests on the "tryer," a brass scoop inserted into the spinning drum, monitoring the tactile vibrations of 20 kilograms (45 lbs) of green coffee beans tumbling inside. The temperature gauge, a needle twitching on a dial, reads 198°C (388°F). The atmosphere is taut with anticipation. She waits for a specific sound.

Suddenly, the process announces itself. A sporadic, sharp popping, distinct and crisp, like dry twigs snapping underfoot. Pop. Snap. Crack.

This is the First Crack. This audible signal indicates that the coffee seed has finally surrendered its structural integrity to the thermal load. Inside the drum, thousands of beans are simultaneously fracturing, expanding in size, and *releasing a pressurized ghost of steam and carbon dioxide. In this rapid exothermic reaction, the raw agricultural product transforms, and the culinary ingredient emerges. The olfactory profile of the room shifts instantly from the scent of baking bread to something sharper, fruitier, and more intricate—the aroma of caramelized sugar and volatile acids.*

*To the observer, roasting coffee appears deceptively simple: heat is applied until the green seeds turn brown. However, to the physicist, the roaster acts as a pilot navigating a chaotic cascade of thermodynamics. Over the course of twelve minutes, the operator must steer a batch of beans through a precise curve of heat energy, managing the creation of over 800 volatile aromatic compounds. If the landing window is missed by fifteen seconds, the coffee may taste like ash. If the batch is pulled ten seconds too early, it will taste like sour grass. More than mere cooking, this process acts as the controlled evolution of a seed using heat.*

### 1864: The Invention of Consistency

For the majority of coffee's history, roasting was a smoky, domestic chore subject to the vagaries of an open flame. In the Ethiopian highlands, the *mahmas*—a perforated iron pan—was held over a fire, the beans tossed by hand until they blackened. In the Ottoman coffeehouses of the 16th century, beans were roasted daily in shallow metal ladles, often scorching the exterior while leaving the interior raw. The result was a cup that was frequently acrid, always dark, and wildly inconsistent. Coffee could not ascend to the status of a global industrial commodity until the variable of fire could be standardized.

The turning point occurred during the American Civil War. In New York City, an inventor named Jabez Burns observed the chaotic process of manual roasting and identified an engineering deficiency. The beans required constant motion and immediate removal from the heat source upon completion. In 1864, Burns was granted U.S. Patent No. 42,306 for the "Improved Coffee Roaster".

His invention introduced the "self-emptying" machine. It featured a screw flange inside the drum—a double helix of metal that churned the beans back and forth to prevent scorching, and then, when the rotation was reversed, ejected the finished coffee out the front into a cooling tray.

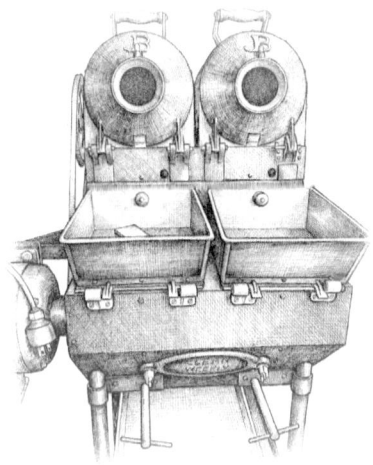

*Jabez Burns' self-emptying drum roaster revolutionized the industry by allowing for continuous, uniform batch roasting*

Burns wrote in his trade catalog that it was the only roaster allowing the operator complete control over every bean. This invention did for coffee what the cotton gin did for textiles. It standardized the application of heat. By creating a machine that could roast distinct batches identically, Burns paved the way for the branded empires of Arbuckle and Folgers. Yet, the machine was only the vessel. The true revolution lay in understanding the invisible chemistry occurring inside the drum.

### The Charge and the Turn

A modern roast begins with a calculation of energy storage. Before a single bean enters the machine, the roaster must "soak" the drum with heat, pre-heating the cast iron to a specific target—usually between 204°C and 215°C (400°F–420°F). This creates thermal momentum. When the hopper gate is opened—a moment technically known as the Charge —the ambient temperature coffee falls into the high-temperature environment. The thermal shock is immediate. The temperature probe in the drum plummets, tracing a steep checkmark on the roaster's digital log.

The bottom of this curve is known as the Turning Point. It is a mechanical illusion. The beans do not actually stop heating up and "turn"; they absorb heat from the moment they contact the metal. The Turning Point simply marks the moment the thermal mass of the cold beans equalizes with the cooling thermocouple probe. For the roaster, however, it serves as the starting gun.

For the first four to five minutes, the process is purely Endothermic —the beans absorb energy. The green beans are dense, rock-hard matrices of cellulose, water, and chemical precursors. They contain roughly 10–12% moisture. The roaster's primary objective during this phase is to boil the beans rather than brown them.

This is the Drying Phase. The drum acts as a conductive engine, transferring heat from the steel walls to the beans, while hot air (convection) rushes through the pile. The water inside the cellular structure turns to vapor and pushes outward. Visually, the change is unappetizing. The beans fade from a vibrant jade green to a sickly, pale yellow. The smell is vegetal—reminiscent of steaming broccoli, wet dog, or damp cardboard. This is the scent of chlorophyll degrading. If the roaster rushes this phase by applying excessive heat, the water trapped inside will boil with too much force, fracturing the cell walls before the flavors can develop. If the process is too slow, the beans steam in their own moisture, breaking down the precious chlorogenic acids and resulting in a "flat" or "baked" cup profile.

## MAILLARD'S BROWNING

Around 149°C (300°F), the chemistry shifts. The beans transition from pale yellow to a golden tan. The smell of wet grass vanishes, replaced by the comforting aroma of baking bread and toasted grain. The beans have entered the Maillard Reaction.

Discovered by French chemist Louis-Camille Maillard in 1912, this is the same alchemy that browns a seared steak or gives a baguette its crust. It is the engine of flavor creation. Under heat, simple sugars (like glucose) collide with amino acids, fusing together to spawn hundreds of new flavor compounds:

- **Melanoidins:** Large, brown molecules that give coffee its color and its heavy, syrupy body.
- **Pyrazines:** The compounds responsible for nutty, earthy, and roasted aromas.
- **Ketones:** The molecules that provide buttery, caramel notes.

The roaster is now walking a tightrope. They must extend this phase long enough to build body and sweetness, but not so long that they flatten the delicate fruit notes that make the coffee unique.

Riding the back of the Maillard reaction is a secondary process called Strecker Degradation. Maya pulls the tryer again, bringing the sample to her nose.

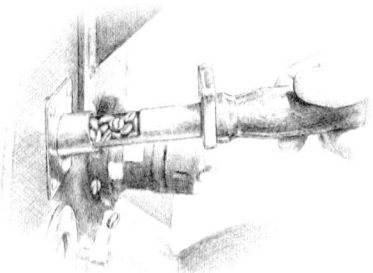

*The tryer allows the roaster to physically smell and inspect the beans during the roast without interrupting the thermal cycle.*

A minute ago, the beans smelled like hay; now, they smell of toast. In another thirty seconds, they will smell of fruit. This shift is caused as amino acids interact with the dicarbonyls produced by Maillard browning, fracturing into aldehydes. These aldehydes are the high notes of the sensory symphony—the floral jasmine in a washed Ethiopian, the green apple in a Colombian, the berry jam in a Kenyan. But for the roaster, they are a fleeting target. These compounds are highly volatile.

They are created in the heat, but they are also destroyed by the heat. A difference of thirty seconds in the Maillard phase can shift a coffee from tasting like fresh apricots to tasting like apricot jam, and finally to burnt toast.

### THE PHYSICS OF THE FIRST CRACK

As the temperature climbs past 193°C (380°F), the roast moves from chemistry back to physics. The bean is now a pressure vessel. The water inside the cellulose matrix has turned to superheated steam. Simultaneously, the breakdown of sugars generates carbon dioxide. The internal pressure within the bean spikes to nearly 25 atmospheres—roughly the same pressure found in the boiler of a steam locomotive. The cellulose walls, already weakened by the thermal load, can no longer contain the force.

The First Crack is a structural failure of the bean. The seed physically expands, doubling in volume within seconds. It sheds its papery outer skin—the "chaff" or silverskin—which flies off into the roaster's exhaust cyclone.

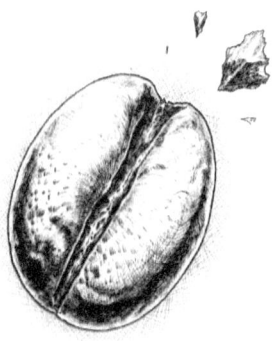

*The "First Crack" is a physical expansion caused by steam pressure,*
*signaling the bean has become porous and edible.*

Thermodynamically, the environment changes instantly. The reaction shifts from Endothermic (absorbing heat) to Exothermic (releasing heat). The cracking beans, acting like thousands of tiny thermal reservoirs, dump their stored energy back into the drum. This is the most critical moment for the roaster. If they do not anticipate this energy release and reduce the gas burner before the crack starts, the roast temperature will skyrocket—a defect known as a "flick." The result is "roasty" flavors that mask the bean's origin. The roaster must intercept the rising thermal momentum, reducing the energy input just as the beans begin to generate their own heat.

This marks the birth of Light Roast, often referred to as City Roast. At the end of First Crack, the coffee retains high acidity, the enzymatic fruit flavors are intact, and the sugar development is just beginning.

### DEVELOPMENT: THE DYNAMICS OF FLAVOR

Following the structural shift of the First Crack, the roast enters the Development Phase. The timer counts down the final seconds as the sugars rapidly caramelize. Sucrose breaks down, losing its sweetness but gaining complexity—turning into bitter-sweet compounds, caramel, and eventually carbon. The acids are also degrading. Citric acid, responsible for lemon notes, and Malic acid, responsible for apple notes, break apart. The roaster balances a three-way equation:

1. **Acidity:** Decreases with time.
2. **Body:** Increases with time.
3. **Bitterness:** Increases with time.

Stopping the roast 45 seconds after First Crack might yield a bright, tea-like cup with lemon acidity but thin body. Stopping it at 90 seconds might yield a chocolate-forward cup with heavy body but muted acidity. This is where the "Roast Curve" becomes a visual gospel. Modern roasters use software like Cropster or Artisan, which plots the temperature in real-time on a laptop screen. They monitor the Rate of Rise (RoR) —the derivative of the temperature curve. They look for a smoothly declining RoR. If the line crashes to zero, the coffee stalls and tastes baked. If it flicks upward, the coffee tastes charred. The goal is a precise, aerodynamic deceleration into the drop temperature.

This phase is often misunderstood as merely a "darkening" period, but it is actually a period of solubility management. The longer the development, the more porous the bean structure becomes, making it easier for water to extract flavor during brewing. A very light roast, developed for a short period, is dense and difficult to extract, often requiring hotter water and finer grinds to unlock its potential. A darker roast is more porous, surrendering its solubles easily. Thus, the roaster designs flavor while engineering the mechanics of the future brew.

SECOND CRACK: THE COLLAPSE

If the roaster maintains the heat, the temperature will breach 224°C (435°F). The cellulose matrix, already fractured by the First Crack, begins to carbonize. The oils trapped deep within the seed liquefy and migrate to the surface, giving the beans a glossy sheen.

Then comes a new sound: Snap-crackle-pop. This is Second Crack. It is quieter, faster, and more frantic than the first, resembling milk being poured into cereal. This is the sound of the bean's structural collapse. At this stage, Pyrolysis—burning—takes over.

Chemically, the sugars are incinerated into pure carbon. The unique "origin character"—the specific fingerprint of the Ethiopian soil or the Colombian altitude—is obliterated by the fire. In terms of flavor, the geography is erased, replaced by the generic but comforting architecture of the "Roast Taste"—smoke, ash, tobacco, dark chocolate, and spice. This is the realm of Vienna, French, and Italian roasts, where the voice of the roaster drowns out the whisper of the farmer. While specialty purists often view Second Crack as a failure—a masking of the agricultural reality—it served a vital historical function. By incinerating the acids, dark roasts created a low-acid, predictable product that paired perfectly with milk and sugar, offering a comforting consistency that delicate light roasts could not provide. But for decades, this was the "strong" coffee standard. The dark roast creates a uniform product. A low-quality bean from Brazil and a high-quality bean from Kenya will taste almost identical if taken deep into Second Crack: they will both taste like fire.

However, the Second Crack has a utility. By breaking down the cellulose so thoroughly, the roast reduces the acidity to near zero. For consumers with sensitive stomachs or those who grew up on the bitter, strong coffee of the diner era, this roast level provides a comforting, low-acid consistency. It is a flavor profile built on texture and bitterness rather than aromatic complexity.

## CONDUCTION VS. CONVECTION: THE MACHINE WARS

The flavor of the coffee is determined not just by the bean, but by the physics of the machine that heats it. The Drum Roaster—like the Probat, Diedrich, or Giesen—relies on a mix of conduction and convection. The beans spend part of their time tumbling against the hot steel drum and part of their time falling through hot air. The conductive heat creates a searing effect, often leading to coffee with heavier body and deeper, more bass-note sweetness.

In the 1970s, a chemical engineer named Michael Sivetz declared opposition to the drum. Sivetz, an iconoclast from Oregon, argued that hot metal was the enemy. He claimed that contact with the drum scorched the beans and coated them in their own oils, creating a "tarry" taste that the industry had accepted as normal. His solution was the Fluid Bed Roaster, or Air Roaster. Inspired by industrial drying technologies, Sivetz designed a machine that levitated the beans on a high-velocity fountain of hot air. The beans never touched metal; they floated in the heat.

The result was coffee of piercing clarity. Without the conductive searing, the acidity became pronounced. The flavors were "clean," almost clinical. While the traditional drum roasters called it "thin" and "sour," Sivetz called it "pure." Today, the debate has largely settled into a détente. The vast majority of specialty roasters still use drums, preferring the complexity and mouthfeel they provide, but they operate them with high airflow to mimic the cleanliness of the fluid bed. New technologies, such as the Loring Smart Roaster, have bridged the gap completely by eliminating the burner from the drum environment entirely, recirculating hot air to roast via pure convection while maintaining the tumbling action of a drum.

·   ·   ·

## The Agtron Truth

The definitions of "Dark" or "Light" are subjective. The human eye is notoriously unreliable; lighting conditions, bean size, and surface texture can deceive a roaster into thinking a batch is lighter than it really is. The industry standard for objective measurement is the Agtron Scale.

The Agtron is a spectrophotometer—a machine that fires Near-Infrared energy at a sample of roasted coffee and measures the reflection. Light beans reflect energy (resulting in a high number), while dark beans absorb energy (resulting in a low number). The scale typically runs from 0 to 100:

- **Agtron 95:** Very Light (Nordic style).
- **Agtron 55:** Medium (Standard Specialty).
- **Agtron 25:** French Roast (Traditional Dark).

A skilled roaster analyzes two numbers: the Whole Bean reading and the Ground reading. If a bean reads 55 on the outside but 75 on the inside after grinding, it reveals a flaw. The roaster cooked the shell but left the core raw—a defect common in "fast" roasting where high heat is applied too quickly. A master roaster seeks a tight spread between these numbers, ensuring the heat has penetrated fully to the center of the seed, developing flavor evenly from core to crust. This internal development is crucial for extraction; an under-developed core will taste grassy and astringent, regardless of how brown the outside looks.

## The Quench: Water vs. Air

For Maya, the roast does not end when the beans leave the drum. At 204°C (400°F), the beans are still cooking, coasting on their own internal thermal momentum. If they are not stopped instantly, they will drift from a perfect Medium into a Dark roast within seconds. This process is known as the Quench.

In specialty roasting, the beans are dumped into a "cooling tray"—a circular bin with a rotating agitator and a massive suction fan underneath. Room temperature air is pulled rapidly through the bean pile, halting the cooking process in under four minutes. This is "Air Quenching."

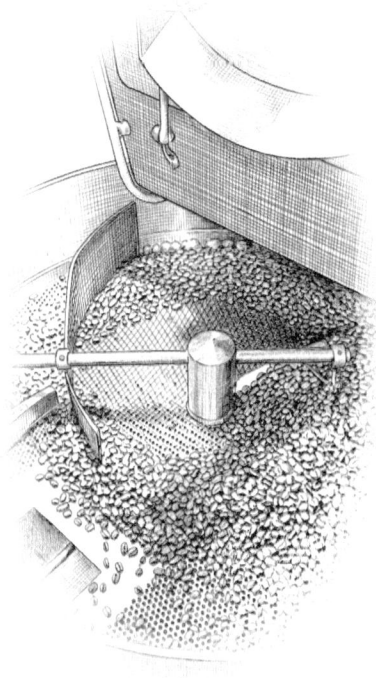

*Rapid cooling is essential to stop the exothermic reaction and lock in the desired roast profile.*

However, in the world of industrial commodity coffee—the domain of the gigantic continuous roasters supplying supermarket brands—there is a different method: Water Quenching. In this process, water is sprayed directly onto the hot beans while they are still inside the roaster or immediately upon exit. The water flashes to steam instantly, sucking the heat out of the beans through evaporative cooling. It is fast and efficient.

It is also profitable. Coffee is sold by weight. Roasting causes moisture loss—a 45 kg (100 lb) bag of green coffee yields only about 38 kg (84 lbs) of roasted coffee, a 16% shrinkage. By spraying water on the beans, industrial roasters can add 1% to 2% of that weight back. In an industry trading millions of pounds, water quenching effectively means selling water for the price of coffee. For the purist, it is a degradation of quality, as it reduces shelf life and oxidizes the surface oils. For the shareholder, it is a dividend.

## THE SMOKE AND THE AFTERBURNER

Roasting is an industrial process that produces significant byproducts. The transformation of seed to ingredient releases a plume of Chaff (particulate matter), Carbon Monoxide, and Volatile Organic Compounds (VOCs). In an urban setting, a roastery cannot simply vent this acrid blue smoke into the neighborhood.

Enter the Afterburner. Mounted on the exhaust stack, the afterburner is a thermal oxidizer. It blasts the roaster's exhaust with a dedicated natural gas flame, raising the temperature to over 600°C (1100°F). At this extreme temperature, the smoke particles and VOCs are incinerated instantly. The air that leaves the chimney is invisible, odorless, and scrubbing-clean heat. The irony is palpable: to produce a "green" product, the roaster must burn twice the fossil fuel—once to roast the coffee, and once to burn the smoke.

## THE MAILLARD TRADE-OFF

As Maya opens the door of the Probat, the beans cascade out into the cooling tray—a waterfall of mahogany brown. The cooling fan roars to life, sucking the smoke away. She leans over the tray, smelling the sweet, caramelized aroma of the finished batch. She checks the curve on her laptop. The line is smooth, a perfect declination. The First Crack occurred at 198°C (388°F). The drop was at 206°C (404°F). Total time: 11 minutes, 14 seconds.

The ultimate paradox of her profession is that she has created flavors the coffee plant never intended. The jasmine, the blueberry, the chocolate, and the caramel—none of these exist in the raw seed. The *Coffea arabica* plant packed the seed with sugar and protein solely to feed a germinating embryo in the soil. It did not design them to taste good.

Maya, and the thousands of roasters like her, have hijacked that biological battery. Through the application of fire and the precision of airflow, they have forced those molecules to rearrange into new configurations, turning potential energy into sensory pleasure. The roast profile dictates the balance between acidity and bitterness. She opens the hopper gate for the next batch. The temperature drops. The curve resets. The seed transforms.

# 19

## GRIND GEOMETRY: FRACTURE AND FINES

High-speed imagery of a coffee grinder in operation, slowing time to 10,000 frames per second, reveals a chaotic event: a study in fragmentation. A roasted coffee bean, desiccated and brittle, enters the crushing chamber of two serrated steel discs spinning at 1,400 revolutions per minute. The bean fractures rather than slices. It breaks apart under compressive force. Shards of cellulose separate from the main body, colliding with the steel teeth and fracturing again in a cascade of kinetic energy. The sound filling the room is the noise of thousands of beans shattering at once. In this fraction of a second, the coffee bean ceases to be a seed and becomes a powder. While this transformation is the most aggressive act in the coffee ritual, but it is also the most mathematically precise.

This reduction is necessary because of a fundamental principle of physics: extraction is a function of surface area. Water, acting as a solvent, cannot dissolve the center of a dense solid. If whole beans were submerged in hot water, the fluid would merely strip the outer layers of the cellulose matrix. It would take weeks to brew a cup, and the result would be thin, astringent, and largely tasteless. To access the flavor—the lipids, carbohydrates, and organic acids locked within the cellular structure—the surface area must be exponentially increased. One object must become ten thousand objects. More than a tool for making things smaller, the grinder is a geometric multiplier determining *how the solvent interacts with the solute. If the roaster is the architect of flavor potential, the grinder is the engineer that determines how much of that potential can be realized.*

## THE PEUGEOT REVOLUTION

Before the electric hum of the modern café, the reduction of coffee was achieved through the manual percussion of the mortar and pestle. For centuries, coffee was pulverized, a method that produced a chaotic mixture of dust and large chunks. The goal was simply to break the bean, not to measure it. However, as the 19th century brought the Industrial Revolution to the European kitchen, the need for uniformity arose.

In 1840, in the Doubs region of eastern France, the Peugeot brothers —Jean Pierre and Jean-Frédéric—were not yet associated with the automobile industry. Their manufactory specialized in saws, springs, and tools requiring hardened steel. They applied their metallurgical expertise to the culinary arts, patenting a coffee mill mechanism that differed radically from the crude crushers of the past. The Peugeot mill utilized a grooved, case-hardened steel mechanism that did not merely smash the bean; it cracked and sheared it. It was durable, adjustable, and introduced a new standard of consistency.

The mechanism they perfected—a conical burr spinning inside a fixed ring—remains the blueprint for hand grinders nearly two centuries later. It introduced the concept of the "particle target." By adjusting a tension screw, the operator could dictate the gap between the burrs, thereby dictating the geometry of the grounds. This was the moment coffee moved from being a raw ingredient to being an engineering challenge. The Peugeots understood that the specific manner in which a bean breaks determines the specific manner in which it tastes.

## THE MATHEMATICS OF SURFACE AREA

To understand why the Peugeot brothers' invention matters, and why modern specialty coffee demand grinders that cost as much as small motorcycles, one must examine the mathematics of surface area, specifically the Square-Cube Law. Consider the mathematics of surface area.

Imagine a single coffee bean simplified as a perfect cube, measuring exactly 1 centimeter on each side.

- **Volume:** 1 cubic centimeter.
- **Surface Area:** 6 square centimeters.

If that cube is bisected along every axis, it yields 8 smaller cubes. The total volume remains exactly the same (1 cm³), but the surface area doubles to 12 cm².

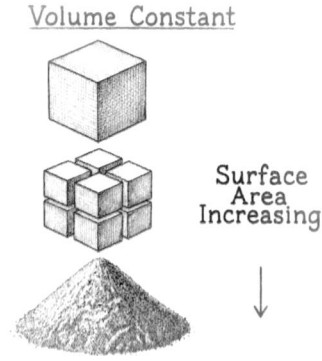

*The Square-Cube law dictates that grinding exponentially increases the surface area available for water extraction.*

If this process continues—grinding the bean down to the size of espresso particles, roughly 250 microns in diameter—the contact area increases exponentially. A single dose of espresso (18 grams or 0.63 oz) contains approximately 3.5 million individual particles. If the surface area of those microscopic shards were unfolded and laid flat, they would cover the surface of a small dining table.

This massive increase in surface area exposes the soluble compounds to the water. The finer the grind, the larger the surface area, and the faster the extraction. This geometric multiplier explains why espresso, with its flour-like consistency, extracts fully in 30 seconds, while a French Press, utilizing a coarse sea-salt consistency, requires four minutes of immersion. The brewer is trading time for geometry.

. . .

## Fracture Mechanics: Brittle vs. Ductile

The physics of grinding is dictated by the roasting process that precedes it. Green coffee is ductile; it is rubbery, dense, and tough. Attempting to grind a green bean results in the shredding of the material, clogging the machine with fibrous pulp. Roasting acts as a drying agent, driving moisture content down from 11% to roughly 1% and crystallizing the cellulose structure. The roasting process creates a pressurized internal environment that leaves the bean porous and fragile.

When a steel burr impacts a roasted bean, the fracture propagates through the path of least resistance. This fracture occurs in two distinct modalities:

1. **Intergranular Fracture:** The break occurs between the cells, separating them without rupturing the cell wall.
2. **Transgranular Fracture:** The break cuts directly through the cell walls.

This distinction is critical to the sensory experience. Inside the microscopic cells of the coffee bean reside the oils and volatiles—the flavor itself. If the grinder shears the cell wall (transgranular), it releases the oils immediately. This creates the intense aroma that fills a coffee shop, but it also exposes those oils to oxidation instantly. If the grinder breaks the bean along the cell boundaries (intergranular), the cells remain intact, protecting the flavor until the hot water bursts them during the brew. A sharp, high-quality grinder tends to slice cleanly, optimizing the release. A dull mechanism crushes and mashes, creating a chaotic mix of structural damage and "bleeding" the flavor out before the water makes contact.

## The Propeller of Chaos

The most common grinder in the Western household is the blade grinder, a device that operates less like a tool and more like a crime scene. Structurally, it is a small motor spinning a dull metal propeller inside a plastic cup. Strictly speaking, it functions as a blender rather than a grinder. It does not cut; it bludgeons.

When the user presses the lid, the blade spins at 20,000 RPM, impacting the beans with random, violent force. The resulting sound is a high-pitched scream of shattering cellulose that changes pitch as the beans are reduced to rubble. Inside the chamber, a chaotic lottery takes place: one bean is pulverized into microscopic dust (fines) that will instantly over-extract and choke the brew, creating a bitter, muddy sludge. Right next to it, another bean is merely cracked in half, leaving a massive, jagged 'boulder' that will remain virtually raw in the water, contributing a sour, grassy astringency. It is a machine that engineers bitterness and sourness simultaneously, ensuring the cup fails in two directions at once.

It reduces some unlucky particles to a microscopic powder (fines) that will instantly over-extract and choke the brew, while leaving others as massive, jagged boulders that remain virtually raw in the water. It is a machine that creates bitterness and sourness simultaneously, ensuring the cup fails in two directions at once.

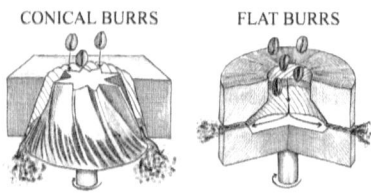

*Conical burrs crush beans gradually for texture; flat burrs shear them quickly for clarity.*

The particle size distribution of a blade grinder is essentially flat—a chaotic spread of every possible size. Furthermore, the blade spins at such high revolutions per minute (RPM) that the friction generates significant heat. This heat transfer begins to cook the volatile oils before brewing even commences, stripping the coffee of its delicate top notes. In the geometry of the grind, the blade grinder acts as a blunt instrument where a precision tool is required. It is the primary reason why home-brewed coffee often tastes bitter and sour simultaneously: the dust over-extracts (bitter) while the large fragments under-extract (sour).

## THE BURR CIVIL WAR: CONICAL VS. FLAT

The specialty coffee industry has long abandoned the blade for the burr—two abrasive surfaces that crush the coffee at a precise distance. However, within the realm of burrs, a debate regarding geometry persists: Conical versus Flat.

> **Conical Burrs** consist of a cone spinning inside a ring. They act like an auger, crushing the beans gradually as gravity pulls them into the narrowing gap. This crushing action creates a "bimodal" distribution—a mix of large particles and fine dust. In the cup, this chaos creates texture. The fines thicken the liquid, resulting in the heavy body and rich mouthfeel prized in traditional espresso.
>
> **Flat Burrs** operate on centrifugal force. Two identical rings sit parallel to each other, shearing the beans between their teeth as they are flung outward. This geometry produces a "unimodal" distribution—a bell curve with one tall, narrow peak. Because the particles are so uniform, they extract at the exact same rate. This yields high clarity and flavor separation, the preferred geometry for modern "Third Wave" coffee that seeks to highlight fruit and acidity over body.

For years, the industry operated under the assumption that flat burrs were superior simply because they were more consistent. However, taste is subjective. The Italian espresso tradition relies on the body provided by conical burrs. The modern Nordic light-roast tradition relies on the clarity provided by flat burrs. The geometry chosen dictates the style of coffee produced.

### The Bell Curve and Laser Diffraction

Regardless of the expense of the machinery—even the Mahlkönig EK43, the German standard-bearer of flat burrs—no grinder can create perfectly identical particles. When a grinder is set to "Medium," it does not produce thousands of particles that are all exactly 800 microns wide. It produces a chaotic mix of boulders, rocks, sand, and dust. This chaos —not grind size alone—is the true antagonist of flavor.

If these particles are measured with a laser diffraction analyzer—a laboratory instrument that passes a laser beam through a cloud of coffee dust to measure the angle of light scattering—the result is a Bell Curve, known as the Particle Size Distribution (PSD).

- **The Mode:** The peak of the curve, representing the target size.
- **The Tails:** The particles that are smaller (fines) or larger (boulders) than the target.

This curve defines the quality of the grinder. A superior grinder generates a very narrow, tall peak, indicating that 90% of the particles are close to the target size. An inferior grinder generates a wide, flat curve, producing large chunks and microscopic dust simultaneously. This inconsistency is the antagonist of flavor.

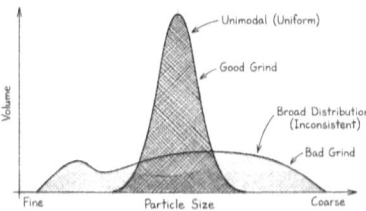

*A superior grinder produces a narrow particle distribution (unimodal), minimizing both dust and boulders.*

The boulders under-extract; the water cannot penetrate to the center, contributing sour, grassy flavors. The fines over-extract; they dissolve instantly, contributing bitter, astringent, and dry sensations. A poor grind guarantees a cup that is flawed in two directions at once.

. . .

### THE MIGRATION OF FINES

Of all the particles produced, the "fines" are the most contentious. These are particles smaller than 100 microns—essentially the consistency of flour. In the physics of percolation brewing, fines function as hydrodynamic impediments.

In a gravity-fed brew method, such as a V60 or Chemex, water moves downward through the coffee bed. However, the fines are so small they are buoyant. As the water drains, the fines detach from the larger grounds and migrate downward, settling at the very bottom of the filter paper in a phenomenon known as fines migration. This creates a layer of silt that blocks the pores of the paper, clogging the brew. The flow rate stalls. The water remains in contact with the slurry for too long, leading to over-extraction. This explains why a cheap grinder ruins a pour-over; it produces such a high volume of dust that the filter becomes impermeable.

### THE ESPRESSO DILEMMA: RESISTANCE

However, context is paramount. In espresso preparation, fines are not the villain; they are the hero. Espresso brewing involves forcing water through a puck of coffee at 9 bars of pressure—roughly nine times atmospheric force. If the coffee were composed of perfectly uniform spheres, the water would rush through the interstitial spaces in seconds. It is the fines—jamming into the gaps between the larger particles—that create the necessary hydraulic resistance.

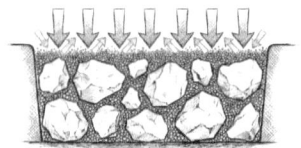

*In espresso, microscopic fines act as mortar between larger grounds,*
*creating the resistance needed to build 9 bars of pressure*

The fines form the mortar in the brick wall of the espresso puck. Without fines, modern espresso would not be possible; the water would channel through the path of least resistance, and the crema would never form. This dichotomy—fines being detrimental to filter coffee but essential for espresso—illustrates why many coffee shops utilize two entirely different grinders for the two methods. The "perfect" grind is relative to the physics of the brewing method.

## THE ALIGNMENT IMPERATIVE

The pursuit of geometric perfection leads coffee professionals into maintenance routines that resemble precision engineering. One can possess the most expensive flat burrs in the world, machined from tool steel or coated in Red Speed titanium, but if they are not aligned, they are ineffectual.

Alignment refers to the parallelism of the two burrs, and it is best understood through the analogy of a car's tires. If your wheels are misaligned by a fraction of a degree, the tire doesn't roll true; it drags, wearing out unevenly and vibrating the chassis.

In a grinder, the stakes are similar but microscopic. The gaps involved are often as small as 200 microns. If the bottom burr is tilted by even 20 microns—the width of a fine human hair—the geometry fails catastrophically. On the 'low' side of the tilt, the gap gapes open, letting massive boulders pass through untouched. On the 'high' side, the steel teeth clash together, pulverizing the beans into choking dust. You are essentially brewing with two different grind sizes simultaneously, guaranteeing a cup that is both sour and bitter.

To rectify this, baristas perform the "Marker Test." The grinder is dismantled, and the cutting edge of the burrs is colored with a dry-erase marker. The machine is reassembled, and the burrs are spun by hand until the faintest sound of metal-on-metal contact is heard. Upon inspection:

- If the marker is erased from the entire circumference, the burrs are aligned.
- If the marker is only erased on one side, the burrs are tilted.

To correct the tilt, microscopic shims made of aluminum foil are placed under the low side of the burr. This process of calibration, performed with office supplies and kitchen foil, ensures that when the bean fractures, it fractures symmetrically.

## THE INDUSTRIAL ROLLER: THE PERFECT GRIND

To witness the closest approximation of "perfect" geometry, one must leave the boutique coffee shop and enter the industrial factory. Mass-market coffee—the vacuum brick or the commercial pod—is not ground on burrs. It is ground on Roller Mills.

A roller mill consists of pairs of giant, corrugated steel cylinders, often several feet in length. The beans pass through a cascade of three or four stages:

1. **The Cracker:** The top rollers break the bean into chunks.
2. **The Reducer:** The middle rollers break chunks into grit.
3. **The Finisher:** The bottom rollers smooth the grit into powder.

Because the beans are crushed between rollers rather than rubbed between burrs, there is almost zero friction. Consequently, the heat generation is negligible. More importantly, the particle distribution is incredibly tight. The resulting particles are almost perfect tetrahedrons. This technology produces a "cleaner" taste than any shop grinder, but the machinery is cost-prohibitive for small businesses and occupies significant floor space. The specialized coffee world is constantly attempting to replicate the quality of the "Roller Grind" with smaller, cheaper burr sets, but the physics of the roller  crushing without rubbing—is difficult to replicate on a countertop.

## STATIC ELECTRICITY AND THE ROSS DROPLET

Grinding is an energy conversion process. Electrical energy (motor) is converted into kinetic energy (spin), which is then converted into mechanical energy (fracture). As the dry coffee particles rub against each other and the plastic chute at high speeds, they exchange electrons. This is the Triboelectric Effect.

The coffee grounds become statically charged. They cling to the discharge chute of the grinder. They scatter onto the counter in a cloud of chaff and dust. They adhere to the burrs. This is not merely a sanitation issue; it causes retention. If 20.0 grams of beans are input, only 19.5 grams might be output. The missing 0.5 grams remains stuck inside the machine, only to be dislodged during the next use, mixing stale, oxidized coffee into the fresh brew.

To combat this, enthusiasts utilize the Ross Droplet Technique (RDT). Popularized in 2005 by David Ross, a home-barista enthusiast, this method involves a simple intervention. The handle of a spoon is run under water and used to stir the beans prior to grinding. That minute amount of moisture—milligrams of water—increases the surface conductivity of the beans, allowing the static charge to dissipate. The retention drops to near zero. The physics of static electricity is neutralized by a single drop of water.


## The Retention Ghost

For decades, commercial espresso grinders were designed with large "hoppers" holding three pounds of beans. They were engineered for speed rather than precision. Inside these machines lies a reservoir of old coffee. The chute between the burrs and the basket often creates a backlog of 5 to 10 grams of ground coffee.

When a customer orders an espresso in a café where the grinder has been idle for twenty minutes, that shot is composed of those 10 grams of "retention." It is stale, oxidized, and flavorless. This engineering oversight birthed the "Single Dosing" movement in the 2010s. New grinder designs —such as the Niche Zero or the Weber HG-1—featured straight-through chutes and gravity-fed pathways to achieve zero retention (<0.1 g).

The ritual shifted. Instead of filling a hopper, the user weighs exactly 18.0 grams of beans, inputs them, and retrieves exactly 18.0 grams of powder. It forces the grinder to be empty every time. This ensures that every particle in the basket was ground seconds ago, not hours ago. It is the pursuit of freshness through the elimination of dead space.

. . .

THE MICRON SCALE

To communicate effectively about grind size, the industry requires a unit of measurement more precise than "fine" or "coarse," which are subjective descriptors. The standard unit is the Micron (micrometer).

- **1500 - 1000 microns:** Coarse Sea Salt consistency. Used for French Press and Cold Brew. Low surface area, slow extraction.
- **800 - 600 microns:** Beach Sand consistency. Used for Pour Over and Drip. Medium surface area.
- **300 - 200 microns:** Table Salt consistency. Used for Espresso and Moka Pot. High surface area, rapid extraction under pressure.
- **< 100 microns:** Flour consistency. Used for Turkish Coffee. Extreme surface area.

A veteran barista can observe a pile of grounds on their palm and estimate the micron size by touch, calibrating their sensory perception to the physics of dissolution. However, at the extreme lower end of the scale, the rules of physics appear to invert.

THE TURKISH PARADOX

At the bottom of the micron scale lies Turkish Coffee (Ibrik). Here, the coffee is ground into a dust—less than 50 microns. It possesses the tactile quality of talcum powder. According to standard brewing theory, this should result in a disastrous cup. The surface area is nearly infinite. The coffee should over-extract instantly, becoming bitter and astringent.

Yet, Turkish coffee is sweet, thick, and rich. This is due to the Saturation Limit. Because the ratio of coffee to water is so high (1:10, compared to 1:16 for drip), the water quickly becomes saturated with dissolved solids. It simply cannot hold any more coffee. The extraction naturally stalls before it can pull out the harsh, woody tannins from the cell walls. Furthermore, the sugar often added during brewing increases the viscosity and acts as a buffer. Turkish coffee demonstrates that if the geometry is pushed to its absolute limit, the rules of linear extraction loop back around, creating a unique exception to the dogma that fines are detrimental.

### THE SIEVING CONTROVERSY

If grinders are inherently imperfect, producing boulders and fines that compromise the cup, the logical conclusion for some is to correct the result manually. This line of reasoning led to the rise of precision sieving systems, such as the Kruve Sifter, in the mid-2010s.

The user pours their ground coffee into a stack of metal sieves with calibrated holes (e.g., 400 microns and 800 microns). They agitate the stack manually.

- The **Fines** fall through the bottom (under 400).
- The **Boulders** remain on the top (over 800).
- The **Middle** represents the "Goldilocks" zone—perfectly uniform particles.

In theory, brewing with this middle section should yield the perfect cup. Initially, it creates a tea-like, incredibly clear brew. However, there is a caveat: complexity. Many coffee professionals found that "perfectly" sieved coffee tasted one-dimensional. It lacked body. It lacked depth. It appears that a degree of chaos is necessary for a full sensory experience. The fines provide body and texture; the boulders provide slow-release acidity. By purifying the geometry, the soul of the coffee was inadvertently removed. The controversy continues: does the industry desire mathematical perfection, or complex imperfection?

### THERMAL ARCHITECTURE

There is one final variable in the grinder: Friction. Grinding is a mechanical process, and friction generates heat. In a high-volume café during the morning rush, a grinder might operate continuously. The burrs can reach temperatures of 60°C or 70°C (140°F - 158°F).

This heat is transferred directly to the coffee grounds. Since coffee volatiles are highly unstable, this heat begins to denature the chemical compounds before they even reach the water. It strips away the delicate floral top notes—the jasmine and bergamot—leaving only the heavier caramel and chocolate notes. Industrial grinders utilize cooling fans or even liquid-cooled jackets to maintain low burr temperatures. The objective is to fracture the bean without adding thermal energy to the system.

### THE GATEKEEPER

Ultimately, the grinder acts as the gatekeeper of the coffee chain. One can procure the most expensive Geisha beans from a high-altitude farm in Panama. One can roast them on a computerized Loring roaster with a flawless profile. One can brew them with pristine, mineralized water. But if those beans are processed through a cheap blade grinder, the chain is broken. A chaotic geometry is created that no amount of brewing skill can rectify.

The grind is the promise. It is the moment where the potential energy of the bean is unlocked and distributed, particle by particle, waiting for the water to complete the reaction.

# 20

# PAPER AND PURITY: THE INVENTION OF CLARITY

I n the early months of 1908, the definition of coffee was sediment. In a cramped, four-room apartment in Dresden, Germany, a thirty-five-year-old housewife named Melitta Bentz sat before a brass pot with a look of calculating dissatisfaction. To drink coffee at the turn of the twentieth century was to engage in a struggle with particulate matter. The brewing methods of the era—the aggressively boiling percolator, the decoction of the Turkish ibrik, or the linen sack that grew rancid with mold after a week of use—all produced a beverage that was more foodstuff than drink. It was opaque, heavy, and bitter, the bottom of every porcelain cup coated in a thick sludge of grounds that stuck to the teeth and ruined the final sip.

Bentz appreciated the stimulation of caffeine, but she rejected the mechanics of its delivery. Her husband, Hugo, was a department store manager, and their mornings were fueled by a brew that tasted of tar and over-extraction. The prevailing wisdom of 1908 held that to make coffee strong, one had to boil it. This thermal intensity extracted the harsh tannins and woody fibers of the bean, masking any delicate acidity or sweetness behind a wall of astringency. Bentz, however, possessed a mind that refused to accept domestic inconveniences as laws of nature. She began to experiment with the materials at hand, looking for a way to separate the essence from the matter.

She took a brass cup and, using a hammer and a masonry nail, punctured the bottom with a series of jagged holes. It was a crude sieve. When she poured coffee through it, the water rushed past too quickly, and the finer grounds followed. She needed a liner, something disposable that could arrest the solids but release the liquid. She looked to her son's schoolbag. Inside was a notebook of heavy, absorbent blotting paper—a material designed to soak up excess ink from fountain pens. It was a matrix of cellulose fibers, dense and thirsty. She tore out a sheet, trimmed it into a rough circle, and pressed it into the bottom of her punctured brass cup. She filled the makeshift basket with ground coffee and poured hot water from a kettle, not boiling, but just off the boil—approximately 93°C (200°F).

The liquid that dripped into the jug below was a revelation. Rather than black, it was a deep, translucent mahogany. There was no sludge. There was no surface slick of oil. When she tasted it, the aggressive bitterness that defined German coffee was absent. The paper had trapped the sediment and the diter-penes, leaving only the soluble aromatics. In that quiet moment of kitchen engi-neering, Melitta Bentz had done more than invent a gadget; she had fundamentally altered the sensory architecture of coffee. She had decoupled "strength" from "weight," proving that coffee could be powerful without being heavy. She had popularized the method of Filtration.

## The Patent and the Pfennigs

Melitta Bentz was an instinctual industrialist as much as an inventor, operating within the rising tide of German functionalism. While the Bauhaus movement—with its maxim "form follows function"—was still a decade away, the intellectual climate of Germany was already shifting toward rational design and hygiene. Bentz's invention fit perfectly into this emerging ethos: it was clean, efficient, and mathematically precise. On June 20, 1908, the Imperial Patent Office in Berlin granted her utility model protection (*Gebrauchsmuster*) for a "Coffee Filter with a Domed Underside.

*Melitta Bentz's first prototype was a simple brass cup modified with
masonry nails and lined with blotting paper from a school notebook.*

The capital required to launch the revolution was exactly 72 Pfen-
nigs. With this small sum, she and Hugo registered the company M.
Bentz in the commercial register of Dresden. The family apartment was
converted into a production line. Her husband took a leave of absence to
demonstrate the device in shop windows; her sons, Willy and Horst,
delivered the cartons using a handcart. The brilliance of the business lay
not in the brass holder, which was a durable good, but in the paper.
Bentz had applied the "razor and blade" economic model to the breakfast
table. You bought the filtration device once, but you bought the paper
forever.

The public response was immediate. At the 1909 Leipzig Trade Fair,
amidst a sea of industrial machinery and textiles, the Bentz family sold
1,200 coffee filters. They marketed the device with a promise that
resonated with the German obsession for order: "No more sieve! No
more grounds in the cup!" By 1912, they had moved out of the apartment
and into a factory employing fifteen workers. By 1929, the demand was so
great that the company relocated to Minden, where the Melitta Group
remains headquartered today, a global empire built on a circle of blotting paper.

### THE PHYSICS OF THE CELLULOSE TRAP

The reason paper filtration changed the flavor of coffee so drastically
becomes clear when looking at the microscopic interaction between the
bean and the wood pulp. Brewing coffee is a solvent extraction, but
filtering it is an act of physical adsorption. Paper filters are composed of
cellulose fibers woven into a chaotic, non-woven web. This web acts as a
selective gatekeeper, discriminating based on size and polarity.

First, the paper addresses the solids. The interstitial spaces in a standard paper filter are roughly 10 to 15 microns wide. This is small enough to trap the "fines"—the microscopic dust created during grinding. In a French Press or metal filter, these fines pass into the cup, creating turbidity and continuing to extract bitterness as the coffee cools, a phenomenon known as "fines migration." Paper removes them entirely, stopping extraction the moment the water drips through.

Second, and perhaps more importantly for the flavor profile, the paper addresses the lipids. Coffee beans are rich in oils, specifically diterpenes known as cafestol and kahweol. These oils carry the heavy body, the mouthfeel, and a significant portion of the aroma. However, cellulose fibers are lipophilic, or oil-loving. As the coffee emulsion passes through the paper, the oils physically adhere to the fibers, trapped in the web of pulp.

*Paper filters physically trap the oils (diterpenes) that carry cholesterol and heavy mouthfeel, resulting in a cleaner cup.*

This lipid entrapment is the defining characteristic of paper-filtered coffee. It creates a cup that is distinct in its lack of viscosity. By stripping away the coating of fat, the paper unmasks the naked acidity of the bean. Fat molecules have a tendency to coat the tongue, physically blocking the proton receptors responsible for detecting acidity. When the fat is removed, the citric brightness of a washed Ethiopian or the malic crispness of a Guatemalan becomes perceivable. Melitta didn't just filter the grounds; she filtered the texture, shifting the beverage from a savory, heavy experience to an aromatic, tea-like one.


## The Lipid Shield: A Health Accidental

Decades after Melitta Bentz altered the mechanics of brewing, medical science discovered an accidental physiological benefit to her invention. In the late 20th century, epidemiological studies, particularly in Scandinavia where boiled coffee remained popular, began to notice a troubling correlation: populations that drank large amounts of unfiltered coffee exhibited significantly higher levels of serum cholesterol.

The culprits were identified as the very lipids the paper filter was designed to trap: cafestol and kahweol. These diterpenes are among the most potent cholesterol-elevating compounds found in the human diet. They function by disrupting the body's homeostasis in the liver. Specifically, cafestol is an agonist for the farnesoid X receptor (FXR) and acts to suppress the synthesis of the LDL receptor. When the liver has fewer LDL receptors, it cannot effectively clear Low-Density Lipoprotein (the "bad" cholesterol) from the bloodstream, leading to accumulation in the arteries.

A daily habit of unfiltered coffee—whether French Press, Turkish, or Scandinavian boiled—can raise cholesterol levels by up to 8% over time. However, the paper filter acts as a medical shield. Because the cellulose fibers are so effective at binding lipids, paper-filtered coffee contains negligible amounts of cafestol and kahweol. The oil stays in the trash, not in the artery. In her quest for a grit-free cup, Melitta Bentz had inadvertently created the heart-healthiest way to consume caffeine, saving millions from arterial plaque simply because she disliked the texture of grounds in her mouth.


## Mid-Century Chemistry: The Chemex

If Melitta Bentz brought filtration to the kitchen table, Dr. Peter Schlumbohm brought it to the laboratory. A German chemist with a doctorate from the University of Berlin, Schlumbohm emigrated to New York in the 1930s. He was a flamboyant eccentric, a man who viewed the

American kitchen as a disorganized chemistry set in need of rationalization. Schlumbohm viewed the separation of solid from liquid as a chemical process instead of a culinary art.

In 1941, Schlumbohm patented the Chemex. It was a masterpiece of Bauhaus reductionism: a modified Erlenmeyer flask made of heat-proof borosilicate glass, adorned only with a wooden corset and a leather tie. It had no moving parts, no pumps, and no electricity. It was so visually striking that it was added to the permanent collection of the Museum of Modern Art (MoMA) merely two years after its invention.

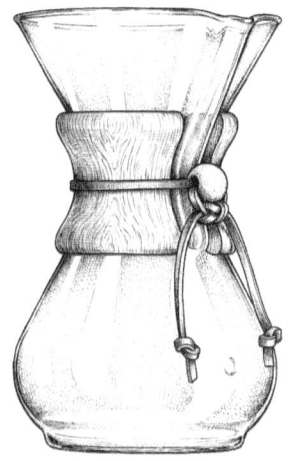

*Dr. Peter Schlumbohm's Chemex applied laboratory glass design to the kitchen, using heavy bonded paper for maximum purity.*

But the secret of the Chemex lay in the paper. Schlumbohm leveraged his laboratory connections to develop a proprietary filter paper that was 20% to 30%heavier than the standard Melitta gauge. He called it "bonded" paper. This ultra-thick cellulose mat possessed a tighter grain and a higher retention rate. It filtered out everything—every micron of sediment, every globule of oil, and even some of the heavier color compounds.

The resulting beverage was coffee of unparalleled purity. It shone with a reddish-gold hue and tasted less like a roasted seed and more like a fruit tea. The Chemex pushed the logic of filtration to its extreme limit: if removing some solids was good, removing all solids was better. It polarized the coffee world. To its devotees, it was the only way to taste the true "origin character" of a bean, unencumbered by the "noise" of oil and grit. To its detractors, it was sterile, a brew so stripped of its fats and fibers that it lost the soul of coffee.

## THE AUTOMATION OF BREWING

For sixty years, the "pour-over"—the act of manually pouring hot water over a paper cone—was the standard for filtered coffee. But in the post-war American economy, convenience began to displace ritual. The housewife was leaving the kitchen for the workforce, and the patience for a three-minute manual brew was evaporating. Enter Vincent Marotta and Samuel Glazer, two Ohio entrepreneurs who looked at the Melitta cone and asked a typically American question: "Why can't a machine do this?"

They hired engineers from Westinghouse to automate the pour. In 1972, they launched Mr. Coffee. It was the first successful automatic drip coffee maker for the home. The machine utilized a simple, gravity-defying mechanism known as the thermosyphon or bubble pump. Water flowed from a reservoir into a heated aluminum tube. As the water boiled, bubbles of steam rose, pushing slugs of hot water up a vertical tube and showering them over a basket lined with a ruffled paper filter.

With baseball legend Joe DiMaggio as their spokesman, Mr. Coffee conquered the countertop. By 1979, the percolator was effectively extinct in the United States. The automatic drip machine—built entirely around the concept of paper filtration—became the standard appliance in every American home. Melitta's invention had been automated, but in the process, it had been degraded. The machines often poured water too fast and too cool (rarely reaching the necessary 90°C–96°C range), and the "basket" shape of the filter encouraged uneven extraction. The clarity of the paper remained, but the precision of the hand was lost. This era solidified the paper filter not as a tool of gourmet precision, but as a commodity of convenience.

### Dioxins and the Bleach Panic

In the late 1980s, the paper filter faced an existential crisis, not from a rival technology, but from environmental toxicology. For decades, consumers had preferred white filters. White signaled purity, hygiene, and cleanliness. To achieve this, manufacturers bleached the brown wood pulp using elemental chlorine gas.

Environmental scientists discovered that this bleaching process produced trace amounts of dioxins, specifically TCDD (2,3,7,8-Tetrachlorodibenzo-p-dioxin), one of the most toxic carcinogenic compounds known to science. While the amount of dioxin leaching into a single cup of coffee was infinitesimally small, the cumulative effect of billions of bleached filters decomposing in landfills presented a genuine environmental hazard.

A massive consumer boycott ensued, particularly in Europe. The industry scrambled to reinvent the chemistry of whiteness. This led to two new standards: ECF (Elemental Chlorine Free), which used chlorine dioxide derivatives, and TCF (Totally Chlorine Free), which utilized oxygen, ozone, or hydrogen peroxide to bleach the pulp. Today, almost all high-quality white filters are oxygen-bleached and safe. However, the scare created a permanent market fissure. A segment of consumers switched to Brown (Unbleached) filters, believing them to be more "natural." This was a sensory error. Unbleached paper contains lignin, the organic polymer that gives wood its structure. When hot water hits lignin, it releases a distinct flavor profile: cardboard, wet paper bag, and wood pulp. The "natural" choice was, ironically, the one that tainted the flavor of the coffee the most, proving that in coffee, "processed" is often synonymous with "clean."

## THE GEOMETRY OF FLOW

By the early 2000s, a new generation of coffee professionals—the "Third Wave"—began to rebel against the mediocrity of the automatic machine. They looked backward to move forward, resurrecting the manual pour-over. But they approached it not as a chore, but as a performance of hydrodynamics.

The Melitta cone had a design flaw for the modern barista: the small hole at the bottom restricted the flow rate. The device controlled the speed, not the user. In 2004, Hario, a Japanese heat-proof glass manufacturer (the name translates to "King of Glass"), released the V60. It resembled a Melitta cone, but with three critical modifications that transformed brewing into a skill: a steep 60-degree slope, a massive aperture at the bottom, and spiraling ribs that ran from top to bottom.

The large hole meant that if a barista poured water fast, it drained fast. If they poured slow, it drained slow. The V60 offered total control. But the true innovation was the ribs. If a wet paper filter sticks flat against the smooth wall of a funnel, it creates a vacuum seal, stopping the flow. The V60's spiral ribs lifted the paper off the glass, creating air channels.

*The spiral ribs of the V60 prevent the paper from sealing against the wall,
allowing air to escape and water to flow freely.*

This allowed air to escape as water entered, ensuring a continuous, unchoked drawdown. This device birthed a new ritual: The Bloom. Baristas realized that fresh coffee releases carbon dioxide ($CO_2$) when hit with hot water. This gas pushes water away, causing uneven extraction. The new protocol required pouring a small amount of water, waiting 30 to 45 seconds for the bed to "bloom" and de-gas, and then continuing. It was a dance of chemistry and gravity, performed over a paper cone.

As the obsession with precision grew, engineers began to analyze the flaws of the conical filter. They discovered a hidden variable: Bypass. When water is poured into a V60 or Chemex, not all of it passes through the coffee grounds. Water, seeking the path of least resistance, often travels horizontally, hits the paper wall, and runs down the side of the filter, exiting the bottom without ever extracting flavor from the bean. In a standard pour-over, bypass can account for 20% to 30% of the liquid in the cup. This effectively dilutes the coffee with plain water.

This realization fractured the design philosophy of the 2020s. The romantics accepted bypass as part of the profile; it softened the extraction, creating a gentle, tea-like elegance. The engineers, however, declared war on it. New devices like the NextLevel Pulsar or the Tricolate utilized a "Zero Bypass" architecture. These were flat-bottomed cylinders with impermeable walls. The water had no choice but to travel vertically through the entire bed of coffee. The result of Zero Bypass brewing is an extraction yield that borders on the scientific limit—24% to 26% of the bean's mass dissolved into the water, compared to the 18% to 20% of a standard drip. The flavors are intense, saturated, and structurally dense. It is the furthest possible evolution from Melitta's brass pot, yet it relies on the same fundamental component: a circle of cellulose.

## Melitta's Legacy

Melitta Bentz died in 1950, shortly after seeing her company recover from the devastation of World War II. She had lived to see her invention transition from a kitchen hack to a global industrial standard. But her legacy is not found in the patents or the corporate headquarters in Minden. It is found in the expectation of the modern drinker.

Before 1908, humans drank the whole bean—oils, fines, and all. We accepted grit as the price of admission to wakefulness. Melitta separated the essence from the matter. She proved that the best part of the coffee was the liquid, not the solid. Every time a barista in a boutique café creates a "clean" cup of Geisha, or a shift worker in a diner drinks a cup that doesn't leave a mudslide in the mug, they are unknowingly paying tribute to a frustrated housewife in Dresden. She took a piece of her son's homework and taught the world that coffee didn't have to be a food. It could be a beverage.

# 21

# 9 BARS: THE HYDRAULIC FORCE

T he event takes exactly thirty seconds. It begins with a silence, followed by the engagement of a rotary pump, a low mechanical hum that vibrates through the countertop. Inside the machine, water heated to exactly 93.5°C (200.3°F) is released from a copper boiler. It travels through a stainless steel tube, passes a restrictor valve, and meets a compressed puck of coffee with a force of nine atmospheres—roughly 130 pounds per square inch (PSI). This is a pressurized extraction rather than a gentle steeping.

Under this immense pressure, the water does not merely wash over the grounds; it penetrates the microscopic pores of the cellulose structure. It shears oils away from the fiber. It strips carbohydrates and lipids that would never dissolve under the gentle gravity of a drip brew. It creates an emulsion—a suspension of oil droplets and carbon dioxide bubbles trapped in a web of liquid surface tension.

When the liquid hits the porcelain cup, it does not splash; it settles, heavy and syrupy, capped by a layer of hazelnut-colored foam known as crema.

This beverage, espresso, is the most chemically complex preparation of coffee on the planet. It is also the most unforgiving. In a standard drip brew, the water has three or four minutes to correct a barista's mistakes. In espresso, the extraction is rapid and instantaneous. Every error in grind size,

*every milligram of inconsistency in the dose, and every degree of tempera-*
*ture fluctuation is magnified. To understand why we subject a fruit seed to*
*this kind of industrial processing, one must look backward—not to the*
*romance of the Italian piazza, but to the factory floors of Milan at the turn*
*of the 20th century. Espresso was originally invented for speed rather than*
*flavor.*

## THE SOLUBLE CEILING

Before dismantling the machine, we must define the target.What is
being extracted?

A roasted coffee bean is a deceptive object. To the naked eye, it looks
solid. Under a microscope, it is a honeycomb of woody material.
Roughly 70% of the bean is cellulose and insoluble fiber. This is the
structural scaffolding of the seed. This material is impervious to heat
and pressure, remaining in the portafilter as the 'spent puck' destined for
the trash. The flavor reservoir is the remaining 30%. This soluble mass
contains everything the drinker desires—and everything they fear. It
includes fruit acids, caramelized sugars, caffeine, lipids, proteins, and
melanoidins. However, this reservoir does not dissolve all at once. The
compounds liberate themselves from the bean in a strict, chemical hierarchy based on their solubility.

Sensory scientists map this timeline of extraction to visualize the
flavor progression. It is often called the "Salami Shot" technique because
the extraction is sliced into distinct phases:

1. **The Acid Shock (0–15% Extraction):** The first compounds to
   wash out are light molecules: organic acids (citric, malic) and
   salts. If a cup is pulled away after just five seconds, the liquid
   is dark, viscous, and intensely sour. It tastes like concentrated
   lemon juice and soy sauce. It is undrinkable.
2. **The Sweet Middle (15–18% Extraction):** As the water
   continues to flow, it begins to dissolve heavier sugars and
   Maillard reaction byproducts. This is where the sweetness
   and caramel notes reside. The liquid lightens in color, and the
   taste softens.

3. **The Golden Balance (18–22% Extraction):** This is the target zone. The sugar balances the acid. The body rounds out. The flavor becomes transparent and distinct.

4. **The Cellulose Wall (22%+ Extraction):** If the water continues to flow, it runs out of desirable compounds. It begins to break down the stubborn, heavy materials: lignin, tannins, and roast byproducts. The flavor turns instantly dry, ashy, and medicinal, coating the tongue like uncoated aspirin.

The objective of espresso is to halt the process exactly inside that narrow 18–22% window—but to do so in twenty-five seconds, using a ratio of water-to-coffee that is incredibly tight.

LOCKHART'S BOX

The mathematical definition of this "good" coffee was codified not in Italy, but in New York City in 1952. Dr. Earl Lockhart, the Scientific Director of the Coffee Brewing Institute (CBI), was tasked by the Pan-American Coffee Bureau to fix a national crisis: American coffee was inconsistent, weak, and often boiled to bitterness. Lockhart conducted thousands of sensory tests, feeding different brews to consumer panels. He plotted the results on a graph with two axes:

1. **Strength (Total Dissolved Solids or TDS):** How concentrated is the liquid?

2. **Extraction Yield:** What percentage of the bean mass was removed?

A clear shape emerged from the data. The panels consistently preferred coffee that sat in a "Golden Cup" zone: a Strength between 1.15% and 1.35% TDS, and an Extraction Yield between 18% and 22%. This became the Control Chart, the governing document of coffee brewing for the next seventy years. It demonstrated that "strong" coffee (high TDS) could still be "sour" (under-extracted) if the water hadn't done its work. It proved that "weak" coffee (low TDS) could be "bitter" (over-extracted) if one used too much water on too little coffee.

However, Lockhart designed his chart for filter coffee—the gentle drip brew. Espresso breaks Lockhart's geometry. An espresso is not 1.35% TDS; it is 8% to 12% TDS. It is a flavor concentrate. Because the concentration is ten times higher, the acids are ten times more potent. This means the margin for error in espresso is almost non-existent. If one misses the extraction target by 1% in a drip brew, the drinker might not notice. In espresso, that 1% difference is the gap between a fruit bomb and a caustic, sour failure.

## STEAM AND SPEED: 1901

The machine that would eventually conquer the world began as a steam engine. In 1901, Luigi Bezzera, a Milanese inventor, filed a patent for a "process of preparing and immediately serving coffee beverage." Bezzera's innovation was logistical rather than culinary. He wanted to shorten the coffee break for factory workers.

At the time, brewing coffee meant boiling grounds in water for minutes. Bezzera built a massive, vertical boiler heated by a gas flame. It resembled a locomotive engine standing on end. When the operator opened a valve, steam pressure forced boiling water through a bed of coffee packed into a brass handle. It was fast. A cup could be produced in seconds. But it was flawed. To generate the pressure needed to move water through a compact cake of coffee, the water had to be boiling—well over 100°C (212°F). The steam scorched the grounds on contact. The resulting beverage was black, thin, and intensely bitter. It was caffeine delivery, stripped of pleasure.

In 1903, Desiderio Pavoni bought Bezzera's patent and began manufacturing the machines commercially. For forty years, "espresso" meant steam-pressure coffee. It was a drink of the railway station and the factory gate—functional, harsh, and rapid.

## BREAKING THE SPRING: THE GAGGIA REVOLUTION

The flavor changed in 1947. Achille Gaggia, a café owner who had spent years tinkering with prototypes in the back of his shop, filed a patent for a new mechanism that would eliminate the steam. Gaggia's insight was simple: decouple temperature from pressure. He needed water at 90°C (194°F)—hot, but not boiling—to extract the coffee without burning it, but he needed high pressure to do it quickly. Steam could not do both; if the temperature was lowered, the pressure was lost.

Gaggia replaced the steam drive with a spring-loaded piston. The barista would pull a long lever down, compressing a massive steel spring inside the group head. This action opened a valve, allowing hot water from the boiler to flood the coffee puck at line pressure. This was the "pre-infusion" phase. Then, the barista released the lever.

The spring expanded. As it uncoiled, it drove a piston downward, forcing the water through the coffee.

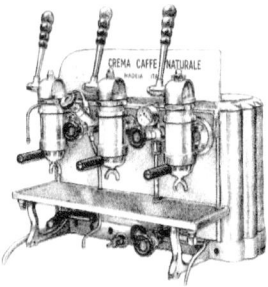

*Achille Gaggia's lever mechanism used a powerful spring to generate high pressure independent of steam temperature.*

The physics of the spring were distinct. It generated roughly 8 to 10 atmospheres of pressure—9 bars. This was a quantum leap from the 1.5 bars of the steam machines. At 130 PSI, the water acted differently. It sheared the insoluble oils out of the coffee matrix and emulsified them with the carbon dioxide gas trapped in the roast.

The result was crema.

When Gaggia first served this new liquid at his bar in Milan, customers were suspicious. They saw a layer of rusty scum floating on top of their coffee. They asked him to scrape it off. Gaggia, a brilliant marketer, refused. He erected a sign in his window: *"Caffè crema di caffè naturale"* (Cream coffee from natural coffee). He claimed the foam was proof of quality, evidence that the "heart" of the coffee had been extracted.

The lever machine changed the taste as well as the texture. The high pressure extracted heavy body and sweetness that steam never could, while the lower temperature (90°C vs 100°C) spared the delicate aromatics. The "bitter" espresso of the steam age faded. The "rich" espresso of the modern age was born.

### THE E61 AND THE THERMOSYPHON

The lever machine had a weakness: it was exhausting. Baristas—*macchinisti*—required significant physical strength to cock the springs hundreds of times a day. If a sweaty hand slipped, the lever could snap back with bone-fracturing force. Furthermore, the pressure profile was fixed by the spring's tension; it started high and trailed off as the spring expanded.

In 1961, the next evolution arrived. The Faema E61, designed by Ernesto Valente, replaced the barista's muscle with an electric volumetric pump. The pump was relentless. It could deliver a flat 9 bars of pressure for as long as the button was held. But the E61's true genius was thermal. Valente introduced the thermosyphon, a plumbing loop that constantly circulated hot water from the boiler through the brass group head, even when the machine was idle.

This solved the "first shot" problem. In older machines, the group head would cool down between orders, sucking the heat out of the next brew and making it sour. The E61 kept the extraction path thermally locked at the target temperature. The E61 set the standard that defines espresso today:

- **Pressure:** 9 bars (generated by a pump).
- **Temperature:** 93°C / 199°F (stabilized by thermal mass).
- **Time:** 25–30 seconds.
- **Volume:** ~30–60ml.

## GEOLOGY OF THE PUCK

With the machine established, attention turns to the extraction itself. What happens inside the basket during those thirty seconds?

When the barista tamps the coffee, they are creating a resistor. The puck is a compressed column of soil, packed with thousands of particles of varying sizes. The goal is to make the water flow through this soil evenly, extracting flavor from every particle at the same rate. This is a problem of fluid dynamics known as Percolation. Unlike immersion brewing (such as the French Press), where water and coffee sit together in equilibrium, percolation is an active erosion. Fresh water is constantly entering the system, hungry for solids.

## THE CHANNELING THREAT

Water, like electricity, seeks the path of least resistance. If the barista distributes the grounds unevenly—leaving a low-density air pocket on the left side of the basket—the high-pressure water will find it. It will drill a hole through that weak spot, a phenomenon known as a channel.

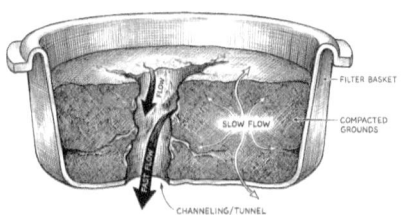

*Channeling occurs when high-pressure water finds a weak spot, over-extracting one area while leaving the rest dry.*

Inside that channel, the flow rate skyrockets. The water assaults those few grams of coffee, stripping them of everything they have, pulling out bitter tannins and harsh wood notes. Meanwhile, the rest of the puck remains dense and dry, barely touched by the water, contributing nothing but sour acid.

The resulting shot is a schizo-extraction. It tastes of vinegar and ash simultaneously. A refractometer might read a perfect "average" extraction, but the average is a lie. Half the puck was starved, and the other half was drowned.

## FINES MIGRATION

Even if the distribution is perfect, the puck is unstable. As water rushes through, it drags the smallest particles—"fines"—downward. These microscopic dust specks migrate to the bottom of the basket and lodge themselves in the holes of the filter basket. This phenomenon obstructs the flow rate. This is why espresso extraction is non-linear. The flow starts fast, then chokes slightly as the fines settle, then speeds up again as the puck erodes and loses mass. The barista watches the stream, looking for the "blonding point"—the moment the stream turns from dark caramel to pale yellow, signaling that the desirable solids are gone and only cellulose water remains.

## THE MODERN ERA: PROFILING AND TURBO SHOTS

For fifty years, the 9-bar standard was unchallenged. But in the late 2010s, a new generation of machines revisited the rules of physics. Companies like La Marzocco, Slayer, and Decent Espresso introduced Flow Profiling. Instead of subjecting the puck to a sudden 9 bars of pressure, these machines allowed the barista to manipulate the flow rate.

Imagine a "Pre-Infusion" stage: The machine gently saturates the puck at 2 bars for ten seconds. The water swells the grounds, healing small cracks and evening out the density. Only then does the pressure ramp up to 9 bars. This technique reduces channeling and allows for much finer grinds, which in turn exposes more surface area and creates higher extraction yields.

Then came the Turbo Shot. In 2020, a team of researchers and baristas challenged the industry with a paper proposing a counter-intuitive method. Instead of grinding fine and brewing at 9 bars for 30 seconds, they ground coarser—much coarser—and pulled the shot in just 15 seconds at only 6 bars of pressure. The logic was grounded in physics. By grinding coarser, they reduced the surface area but drastically improved the evenness of the flow. There was zero channeling.

Every particle was washed equally. The result was a shot with lower strength (lighter body) but incredibly high sweetness and clarity. It tasted less like traditional espresso and more like a fruit concentrate.

### IMMERSION VS. PERCOLATION: THE GREAT SCHISM

To fully grasp the "efficiency" of the espresso engine, one must briefly contrast it with its opposite: the French Press (Immersion).

In an immersion brew, the water and coffee sit together. As the water dissolves solids, it becomes saturated. The extraction power fades over time. It is a self-limiting process. One can leave a French Press plunging for ten minutes, and it will rarely become bitter because the water simply cannot hold any more solids. It reaches equilibrium.

Espresso is the opposite. Because fresh water is constantly pushed through, the concentration gradient is always at maximum. The water never gets "full." If a shot runs for 60 seconds, the water will continue to strip material until it is dissolving the paper taste of the cellulose itself. This makes espresso efficient—one can extract 20% of the flavor in 30 seconds—but it also makes it volatile. There is no safety brake. The barista's hand on the switch is the only thing preventing the cup from becoming unpalatable.

### PRESSURE AS AN INGREDIENT

We often list the ingredients of coffee as beans and water. In espresso, Pressure is the third ingredient. Pressure changes the solubility of gases. It forces carbon dioxide (a byproduct of roasting) to dissolve into the liquid. When the liquid leaves the machine and returns to atmospheric pressure in the cup, that gas comes out of solution. It forms tiny bubbles that get trapped in the oil emulsion.

This is Crema.

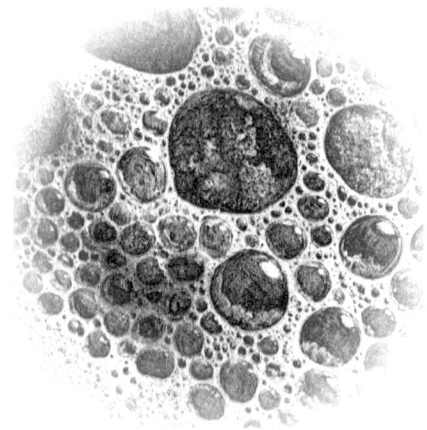

*High pressure emulsifies insoluble oils and CO2, creating the defining foam of espresso.*

For years, Italians judged espresso by the thickness of this foam (the "sugar test"—does a pouch of sugar rest on the crema before sinking?). Today, sensory scientists know that crema itself is not flavor-positive. It is composed of $CO_2$ (sour/bitter) and suspended fines (dry). It is essentially a polyphasic foam of bitterness.

Modern specialty baristas often stir the crema into the shot to integrate the flavor, or scrape it off entirely to access the sweeter liquid beneath. Yet, the industry cannot abandon it. Crema acts as a lid, trapping volatile aromatics in the cup that would otherwise evaporate instantly. It is the aroma-guard of the espresso.

## THE LIMITS OF THE MACHINE

We have reached a point where the machine is more precise than the agricultural product it consumes. A modern espresso machine can control temperature to within 0.1°C (0.18°F). It can verify flow rate to the milliliter. But the bean is chaos. It is a seed from a tropical fruit, processed on a farm, dried on a patio, and roasted in a drum. Its density changes as it ages. Its gas content drops every hour after grinding.

The barista's job is to mediate between the perfection of the machine and the inconsistency of the bean. They use the variables of Grind, Dose, and Yield to align the chaos into the Golden Cup window.

If the shot tastes sour (underextracted):

- Grind Finer (increase surface area).
- Increase Yield (push more water through to grab the sugars).
- Increase Temperature (add energy to the solvent).

If the shot tastes bitter (over-extracted):

- Grind Coarser (decrease surface area).
- Decrease Yield (stop the water sooner).
- Lower Temperature (reduce solvent energy).

This is the "dialing in" ritual performed every morning in every café on earth. It is a negotiation with physics. The machine offers the power —the 9 bars, the 93°C—but the barista provides the judgment.

## The Ghost in the Pipes

There is one final variable that the machine cannot control, yet it dictates the success of every extraction described in this chapter. It is the solvent itself. Water is not merely $H_2O$. It is a solution of minerals— calcium, magnesium, bicarbonates. In the high-pressure environment of the espresso boiler, these minerals do more than just dissolve coffee. They coat the heating elements with scale. They buffer the acids. They can destroy the machine from the inside out. The espresso engine is a precision instrument, but if one puts sand in the fuel tank, it will not run. To understand the final piece of the extraction puzzle, one must leave the mechanics of pressure and enter the chemistry of the water supply. Espresso is a magnifier; it amplifies both the quality and the defects of the bean. It requires not just engineering, but elemental purity.

# 22

# SOLVENT: MINING THE BEAN

T he revolution in modern coffee did not begin in a bustling café in Melbourne or on a misty farm in the Chiriquí province of Panama. It began in a quiet, sterile laboratory at the University of Bath in 2014, born from a friction between two distinct worlds: the sensory and the molecular.

On one side of the lab bench stood Maxwell Colonna-Dashwood, a UK Barista Champion and proprietor of Colonna & Small's in Bath. He was a professional whose career—and the solvency of his business—depended on the ability to replicate flavor with decimal-point precision. He had spent years dialing in roast curves and grind sizes, obsessing over the geometry of burrs and the thermodynamics of extraction. Yet he was haunted by a ghost in the machine. He could take the exact same coffee, brew it with the exact same equipment in two different cities, and taste two completely different beverages.

On the other side stood Dr. Christopher Hendon, a theoretical chemist. Hendon's days were usually spent in the abstract realm of computational materials science, modeling metal-organic frameworks for renewable energy storage. To him, coffee was a complex solution of organic compounds dissolved in a solvent. He viewed the barista's problem not as a curse, but as a variable to be solved through essential chemistry.

Between them on the cupping table sat three white porcelain bowls. Each bowl contained exactly 12 grams of the same coffee—a washed Gesha from Panama, roasted to a delicate light brown. Each bowl had been brewed with water heated to exactly 96°C (204.8°F). To the naked eye, the liquid in the bowls was identical: a clear, amber tea, steaming gently under the fluorescent lab lights.

Colonna-Dashwood dipped his silver cupping spoon into the first bowl. He slurped loudly, aspirating the liquid to coat his palate. He paused, analyzing the volatile compounds hitting his retronasal olfaction. "Bright," he noted. "Lemon zest, jasmine, high acidity. It sings. This is the coffee I bought."

He rinsed the spoon and dipped into the second bowl. Immediately, his expression shifted. "Chalky," he said. "Flat. The fruit is dead. It tastes like cardboard and aspirin."

He dipped into the third. "Sour," he grimaced. "Vinegary. Aggressive. No sweetness whatsoever. It's hollow."

The coffee was the same. The roast was the same. The temperature was the same. The only variable was the mineral composition of the water. The first bowl used water synthesized with a precise ratio of magnesium sulfate and a calculated bicarbonate buffer. The second used hard tap water drawn from the limestone-heavy aquifers of the Thames Valley. The third used pure distilled water.

This experiment, which would eventually culminate in their seminal co-authored paper "The Role of Dissolved Cations in Coffee Extraction," exposed the coffee industry's most significant blind spot. For centuries, the trade had obsessed over the genetics of the seed, the thermodynamics of the roast, and the geometry of the grind. Engineers had built machines costing $30,000 to control pressure profiles. Yet the industry largely ignored the solvent that comprises 98.5% of the final beverage.

We treated water as a neutral canvas, a passive void into which coffee flavor is painted. This is a chemical lie. Water acts as an active ingredient rather than a neutral canvas. It acts as a solvent binder. Depending on the mineral content hidden within that clear liquid—the microscopic constellation of magnesium, calcium, sodium, and bicarbonate ions—it will choose to extract different compounds from the bean. You cannot make good coffee with bad water, no matter how much you paid for the beans.

·  ·  ·

## THE MYTH OF PURITY

The first instinct of the perfectionist is purification. If tap water contains "junk"—chlorine from the municipal treatment plant, rust from Victorian-era iron pipes, algae blooms, or trace pharmaceuticals—logic suggests the solution is subtraction. Why not use Distilled Water or Reverse Osmosis (RO) water? Why not strip the solvent down to pure $H_2O$ and ensure nothing interferes with the coffee?

This is a fatal error in brewing physics. Pure water is a terrible solvent for coffee.

To understand why, we must look at the molecule itself. Water is a polar solvent. The oxygen atom hugs the electrons, creating a partial negative charge, while the two hydrogen atoms remain positive. This "dipole moment" makes water desperate to dissolve things; it wants to surround charged particles and pull them into solution.

When ultra-pure water hits coffee grounds—whose surface area we analyzed in Chapter 19—it acts with aggressive hygroscopy. It is "hungry." Because it has no dissolved solids of its own, it attacks the exposed cellular structure indiscriminately. It strips out soluble compounds too quickly, pulling not just the pleasant oils and sugars, but also the harsh, dry distillates that usually remain trapped in the cellulose.

The result is a cup that is paradoxically sharp yet hollow—an aggressive sourness lacking any roundness or body.

Furthermore, flavor needs a vehicle. Many of the aromatic compounds in coffee—the aldehydes and ketones that smell like flowers or fruit—are volatile. In a complex solution, mineral ions act as anchors. They help bind these compounds to the liquid, allowing them to reach your palate rather than flashing off into the atmosphere the moment the coffee is brewed. Without minerals, the flavor has no structure.

There is also a mechanical failure to consider. Modern espresso machines, from the workhorse La Marzocco Linea to the precision Slayer, utilize electronic sensors to detect water levels in the boiler. These sensors rely on the conductivity of the water to close a circuit. Pure distilled water is an electrical insulator; without dissolved ions to carry the charge, the circuit remains open. Fill a commercial espresso machine with pure water, and it will often sit there in silence, refusing to turn on, believing its boilers are empty. To brew coffee, we need impurities. But we need a very specific kind of impurity.

### CATION EXCHANGE: THE FLAVOR SELECTORS

In the lexicon of water chemistry, general hardness refers to the concentration of multivalent cations dissolved in water. While water may contain trace amounts of iron, copper, or other metals, for the coffee brewer the chemistry of flavor extraction is dominated by two ions: magnesium and calcium.

These ions are the primary agents of extraction. Many coffee flavor compounds—such as citric acid, malic acid, and a range of aromatic esters—are electron-rich. They are often negatively charged or polar. Magnesium and calcium, by contrast, carry a positive charge. As water passes through the coffee bed, these cations interact electrostatically with the flavor molecules, binding to them and drawing them into solution.

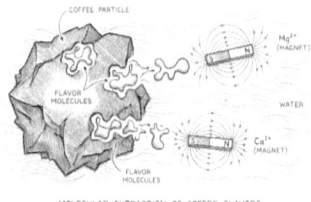

MOLECULAR EXTRACTION OF COFFEE FLAVORS

*The Pull of Extraction: Divalent ions lock onto flavor molecules like chemical hooks, stripping them from the bean matrix more effectively than water alone.*

However, they do not pull with equal strength. This is where the physics of Charge Density becomes the defining factor of the morning cup. The difference lies in how these two minerals interact with the organic compounds in the bean.

**Magnesium is the King of extraction.** Think of magnesium as a small, powerful magnet. Because of its high charge density, it exerts a strong pull on organic acids, ripping them away from the grounds and into your cup. A magnesium-rich water will produce a cup that is vibrant, articulate, and complex. It emphasizes the "top notes"—the delicate florals that distinguish a Geisha from a Caturra. Magnesium pulls fruit.

**Calcium is the Heavy.** A larger, bulkier ion, calcium binds readily to heavier compounds. While it aids in extraction, it creates a different sensory profile. High-calcium water tends to produce coffee with a creamy mouthfeel and heavy body, but it can mask the delicate florals. If the calcium levels are too high, the coffee takes on a distinct "chalky" texture, blurring the image of the roast. Calcium pulls body.

The ideal water for modern specialty coffee—where we prize distinct varietal character and acidity—is magnesium-rich. We want the fruit, not just the weight. But getting magnesium without calcium is geologically rare; in nature, they almost always travel together, dissolved from dolomite or limestone bedrock.

### THE BUFFER: THE ACIDITY THROTTLE

While the cations—primarily magnesium and calcium—determine how much flavor is extracted from the coffee grounds, a different chemical property governs how that flavor is ultimately perceived in the cup. This property is alkalinity, often referred to as carbonate hardness, or KH.

It is crucial to distinguish between alkalinity and pH. pH describes the state of the water at a specific moment—whether it is acidic or basic. Alkalinity, by contrast, describes the water's ability to resist changes in pH. It functions as a chemical buffer. In most municipal water supplies, this buffering capacity comes primarily from dissolved bicarbonate ions.

The chemistry of the cup can be imagined as a battlefield. A light-roast Ethiopian coffee is prized for its acidity—the sparkling lemon notes of citric acid, the crisp apple character of malic acid, the wine-like tartness of tartaric acid. When brewed, such a coffee becomes a mild acid solution, rich in volatile and organic acids that define its brightness and complexity.

If the brewing water has high alkalinity—above roughly 80 parts per million—it behaves like a dissolved antacid tablet. The bicarbonate ions immediately react with the coffee's acids, neutralizing them through a rapid chemical reaction in which acid is converted into water and carbon dioxide. The sparkle disappears. The coffee tastes flat, dull, and muddy. The chemical information is still present—the acids were successfully extracted by the cations—but the buffer has silenced them. One cannot taste an acid that has already been neutralized.

At the opposite extreme, if the brewing water has very low alkalinity, there is nothing to restrain the acids. The pH of the beverage plunges. The coffee becomes sharply sour, thin, and aggressive, lacking the roundness and structure that make a cup feel balanced and complete.

This places the barista on a narrow, high-stakes tightrope. The water must contain enough buffering capacity to prevent vinegar-like sourness, yet little enough to allow desirable acidity to shine. For modern light roasts, the ideal target lies within a remarkably narrow window—around 40 parts per million of alkalinity. Darker roasts, which possess lower natural acidity and higher concentrations of bitter pyrolysis compounds, can tolerate—and often benefit from—a higher buffer, which helps smooth their rougher edges.

## GEOGRAPHY AS DESTINY

The history of roasting styles is, at its core, a history of hydrology. We often wonder why specific regions developed such entrenched preferences for how coffee should taste. Why is New York City famous for its "bright" breakfast blends, while London, Paris, and Rome historically preferred dark, heavy roasts?

It is not a matter of sophisticated versus unsophisticated palates. It is a matter of bedrock. New York City tap water flows from the Catskill Mountains. It travels over insoluble granite bedrock. Because granite does not donate minerals or carbonate buffers to the flow, NYC water is naturally "soft"—it has low mineral content and, crucially, very low alkalinity. It is the perfect solvent for light roasts. The lack of buffer allows the delicate acids of a breakfast blend to shine without being neutralized. A light roast tastes sweet and bright in Manhattan. This same soft water chemistry is what allows the gluten in bagel dough to form its characteristic chew without becoming tough, cementing the city's dual culinary legacy.

Contrast this with London. The city sits atop a massive basin of limestone and chalk. Its water is "hard," loaded with calcium and massive amounts of bicarbonate. If an 18th-century Londoner tried to brew a light roast with Thames water, the bicarbonate would annihilate the acidity, leaving a cup that tasted like flat, chalky dirt.

The solution was not chemistry, but fire. European roasters learned, through trial and error, that roasting darker destroys acidity and creates bitter compounds (phenylindanes and lactones). When you brew a dark roast with high-alkalinity water, the buffer neutralizes the acids you didn't want anyway, while the calcium amplifies the body. The bitterness cuts through the chalk.

The "Italian Espresso" profile and the "Scandinavian Light Roast" are evolutionary adaptations to the geology of the pipe. We roasted to match our water.

## THE SCALE CONFLICT

Within the café ecosystem, a quiet cold war plays out between two factions: the barista and the technician.

The barista wants minerals. Magnesium and calcium make coffee taste alive. They enhance extraction, amplify sweetness, and give the cup weight and texture. For optimal flavor, the barista aims for a total dissolved solids level of roughly 150 parts per million—enough mineral content to produce a rich, syrupy brew.

The technician, by contrast, despises minerals. Or more precisely, the technician despises calcium carbonate, better known as limescale.

The conflict stems from a peculiar and counterintuitive property of calcium carbonate known as retrograde solubility. Most solids dissolve more readily in hot water—sugar disappearing into tea is the familiar example. Calcium carbonate behaves in the opposite manner: it becomes *less* soluble as temperature increases. When water is heated inside an espresso machine boiler to approximately 125°C (257°F), dissolved calcium precipitates out of solution, crystallizing into a rock-hard white crust that coats heating elements and internal surfaces.

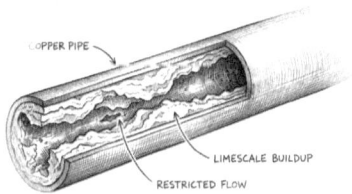

*Calcium carbonate precipitates out of hot water, forming limescale that insulates heating elements and blocks valves.*

Scale is the primary killer of commercial espresso equipment. It insulates heating coils, forcing them to overheat and fail. It clogs precision gicleurs—flow restrictors often no wider than 0.6 millimeters—causing erratic pressure and unpredictable extraction. It jams solenoid valves, leading to leaks, pressure faults, and sudden shutdowns. A scaled machine is a dying machine, and for a busy café, the cost of downtime can climb into the thousands of dollars per day.

To prevent this, traditional cafés long relied on ion-exchange softeners. These systems are packed with resin beads charged with sodium ions. As hard water passes through, the resin captures calcium and magnesium and releases sodium in their place. The result is technically "soft" water—water that will never form scale. The technician is satisfied. The warranty remains intact.

But the flavor suffers. Sodium does not contribute meaningfully to extraction; instead, it produces a dull, flattened cup, often with a faintly saline edge. Worse still, bicarbonate ions typically remain untouched by the softening process, leaving the water with high alkalinity but little extraction power. The result is coffee that is chemically stable yet sensorially lifeless.

This is the central dilemma of café water treatment: safe for the machine, bad for the coffee.

## PITTING CORROSION

There is a villain in water chemistry even more destructive than scale: chloride.

Often confused with chlorine—the disinfectant gas used by munici-palities—the chloride ion is a corrosive agent commonly found in coastal aquifers and in regions where road salt infiltrates groundwater supplies. It is invisible, tasteless at low concentrations, and profoundly dangerous to espresso equipment.

Chloride is the nemesis of stainless steel. High-end espresso boilers are typically constructed from 316L stainless steel, a durable alloy that includes molybdenum to improve corrosion resistance. Its protection depends on a thin, passive layer of chromium oxide that forms naturally on the metal's surface, sealing it against rust. Chloride ions possess a rare and insidious ability: they can penetrate this protective film.

Once inside, they initiate pitting corrosion. Instead of causing uniform surface damage, chlorides carve microscopic holes deep into the metal, attacking the boiler from the inside out. Unlike limescale—which can be removed through descaling—pitting is irreversible. It is structural cancer. A boiler compromised by chloride corrosion cannot be repaired; it must be replaced.

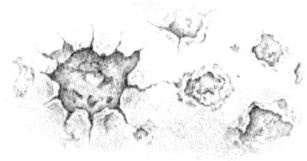

*Chlorides penetrate the protective oxide layer of stainless steel, causing irreversible structural damage known as pitting.*

For cafés operating in high-chloride regions—such as Los Angeles or coastal Florida—standard filtration is insufficient. Carbon filters remove taste and odor, but they do not remove dissolved ions. In these environ-ments, cafés are forced to adopt the nuclear option of water treatment: reverse osmosis.

· · ·

### REVERSE OSMOSIS: THE BLANK SLATE

For the serious café, the gold standard of water treatment is reverse osmosis with remineralization. This approach begins from a sober admission: natural water is too variable to be trusted. Reverse osmosis does not refine water—it erases it. The system acts as a factory for solvent.

The process begins with what might be called *the strip*. Incoming water is forced, under high pressure—typically between 60 and 80 psi—through a semi-permeable membrane. The pores of this membrane are small enough to allow water molecules to pass through, yet too small for dissolved minerals, chlorides, bacteria, or viruses.

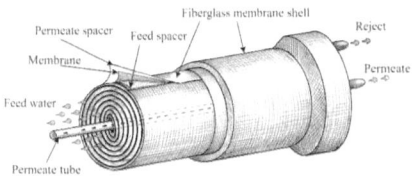

*Reverse Osmosis strips water to a blank slate, requiring remineralization to become a viable coffee solvent.*

The result is known as permeate: water reduced to nearly zero total dissolved solids. It is pure, chemically hungry, and completely flavorless. It is also inefficient. Traditional reverse osmosis systems may waste eleven to fifteen liters of water for every 3.7 liters (one gallon) of purified output—a serious sustainability concern for the modern café.

Because this stripped water is too aggressive for brewing—and can even be mildly corrosive due to its eagerness to bind with ions—the system must reintroduce minerals in a controlled way. Lower-end installations rely on a blend valve or bypass, which allows a measured portion of filtered tap water to mix back into the permeate stream. The flaw is obvious: if the source water contains high chloride levels, blending it back in simply reintroduces the original threat. The patient is reinfected.

Superior systems avoid blending altogether. Instead, the purified water passes through a remineralization cartridge—a canister filled with crushed calcite or magnesium-based media. As the slightly acidic RO water flows through, it dissolves these minerals in precise, predictable amounts. The café gains full control.

With this approach, even a shop located in the harshest hard-water environment can dial in an exact target—say, 120 parts per million of total dissolved solids—ensuring that the espresso tastes exactly as the roaster intended, regardless of what flows from the city pipes.

### DIY Chemistry: The Water Recipe

In 2016, the discrepancy between "roastery water" and "customer water" reached a breaking point. A roaster might profile a coffee perfectly in Portland (soft water), ship it to a customer in Las Vegas (hard water), and receive a complaint that the coffee was ash. The roaster had no control over the final ingredient.

The solution appeared in the form of a white powder. Companies like Third Wave Water and Global Customized Water began selling remineralization sachets. The premise was "Deconstruct, then Reconstruct." The user buys a gallon of Distilled Water—the blank canvas—and dumps in the sachet. Instantly, the water is transformed into the SCA (Specialty Coffee Association) ideal.

For those unwilling to buy pre-made sachets, the "Water Recipe" movement, popularized by Matt Perger of Barista Hustle and the research of Christopher Hendon, turned the kitchen sink into a chemistry lab. They published open-source recipes that allow any enthusiast to dial in their water with pharmaceutical precision.

Here is the framework for the modern "Water Chef." Note the precision; we are no longer cooking, we are compounding.

### Phase 1: The Concentrates

First, the brewer creates two separate bottles of concentrate. One never adds dry powder directly to a kettle; it is too difficult to measure 0.1g accurately on a standard kitchen scale.

- **Buffer Concentrate:** Dissolve 1.68g of Sodium Bicarbonate (Baking Soda) in 1L of distilled water. This is the "Acidity Throttle".

- **Hardness Concentrate:** Dissolve 2.45g of Magnesium Sulfate (Epsom Salts) in 1L of distilled water. This is the "Flavor Claw".

**Phase 2: The Recipe**

To make one liter of brewing water, these concentrates are mixed into distilled water.

- **The "SCA Standard" Replica:**
  - 940g Distilled Water
  - 40g Hardness Concentrate
  - 20g Buffer Concentrate
- **The "Bright" Profile:**
  - 900g Distilled Water
  - 75g Hardness Concentrate
  - 25g Buffer Concentrate

This specific ratio yields a water with high magnesium hardness for fruit extraction and low alkalinity to let the acidity pop. The beauty of the system is its elasticity. Brewing a dark roast? Increase the Buffer to 40g. Brewing a delicate Gesha? Drop the Buffer to 15g. The home brewer is no longer a victim of their municipality; they are a chemist.

VISCOSITY AND TEXTURE

Water chemistry alters more than just flavor; it changes the tactile physics of the liquid. We often describe coffee as having "body" or "mouthfeel," assuming these are properties of the bean's oils and lipids. While true, the water ions play a massive role in how we perceive texture.

A coffee brewed with high calcium content feels physically "thicker" and "creamier" on the tongue. This is likely due to the interaction between calcium ions and the Mucin proteins in human saliva.

Saliva is a lubricant. Astringency—that drying, sandpaper sensation on the roof of the mouth often associated with black tea or red wine—is caused by polyphenols (tannins) binding to the proteins in saliva, causing them to aggregate and stripping away the lubrication. Calcium ions help precipitate these tannins before they hit the palate, potentially smoothing out the finish.

Conversely, water softened with sodium feels "slick" or "slimy." Pure distilled water feels "hollow" or "thin," as if the liquid passes through the mouth without registering weight. When a roaster notes "syrupy body" on a bag, they are implicitly assuming the consumer is using water with enough mineral structure to support that weight. Without the minerals, the syrup is just water.

## THE BOTTLED WATER ROULETTE

Many consumers, intimidated by the prospect of mixing sulfates and bicarbonates, pivot to bottled water. "I'll just buy spring water," they think. "It comes from nature, so it must be good."

This is a gamble. The label "Spring Water" is a geological descriptor, not a flavor profile. The mineral content of spring water varies wildly depending on the source aquifer, leading to a game of "Bottled Water Roulette."

Evian: Sourced from the French Alps, Evian is the heavyweight champion of hardness. It has a high mineral content and is loaded with bicarbonate (often over 300 ppm). It is excellent for hydration, but it will absolutely kill the acidity of a light roast, turning it flat and muddy.

Fiji: Contains unusually high silica content. While silica does not extract flavor the way magnesium does, it creates a unique, silky mouthfeel that some brewers prize for espresso. However, its isolation makes it an ecological burden to ship.

**Crystal Geyser (Alpine Source):** This is often the "Goldilocks" choice for American brewers. It is generally soft, with enough magnesium to extract but low enough alkalinity to preserve acid. However, Crystal Geyser bottles from different sources (Weed, California vs. Olancha, California) have different chemistries, adding another layer of randomness to the morning ritual.

**Poland Spring:** Varies by source, but generally balanced enough for drip coffee, though often lacking the magnesium punch needed for high-end specialty.

Roasters are now forced to publish "Recommended Water" lists, explicitly warning customers that if they brew a premium Panama Gesha with high-bicarbonate water, they are essentially throwing money down the drain.

## THE LANGELIER SATURATION INDEX

For the engineer or the café owner, the ultimate arbiter of water quality is not taste, but the Langelier Saturation Index (LSI). This is a calculated number used to predict whether water will precipitate calcium carbonate (scale) or dissolve it (corrosion). It is the formula that keeps the technician up at night.

The formula balances pH, temperature, and hardness to predict the water's behavior. Think of it like a traffic light for the boiler:

- **Positive (> 0):** The water is "full." It will drop its mineral load, forming scale that clogs the machine.
- **Negative (< 0):** The water is "hungry." It will eat existing scale, but eventually, it will start eating the metal of the boiler itself (corrosion).
- **Zero:** Equilibrium.

This creates a chemical standoff between the chef and the mechanic. The water that makes the coffee sing—rich in magnesium and calcium —is the same water that calcifies the boiler, effectively slowly strangling the machine with stone. Conversely, the water that keeps the machine pristine often renders the coffee flat and lifeless. This forces a compromise. Most cafe owners, fearing the repair bill more than the mediocre cup, unknowingly choose machine longevity over peak flavor, running softeners that keep the LSI negative but strip the coffee of its character. The best cafes invest in complex blending valves to hover the LSI at exactly +0.3—just enough mineral content to taste great, but not enough to scale rapidly.

## The Water Sommelier

The obsession with water has birthed a new, specialized figure in the culinary world: the Water Sommelier. Men like Martin Riese have made careers out of tasting water menus, distinguishing between the salty minerality of Vichy Catalan and the glacial smoothness of Berg.

While it is easy to view the idea of a "water menu" as the height of culinary pretension, it represents the final frontier of the specialty mindset. We have deconstructed the bean, the roast, and the milk. Water was the last variable to fall.

In the future, we may see "terroir-specific" water sachets. Imagine buying a bag of Kenyan coffee that comes with a sachet of minerals designed to replicate the water chemistry of the Nyeri washing station where it was processed. Or a "Melbourne Water" profile sold in New York so one can taste the coffee exactly as the roaster intended.

## The Ceiling of Flavor

For centuries, we assumed the coffee bean was the painting and the water was merely the white wall upon which it hung. We thought the wall was invisible.

We now know the wall has a color. If the water is hard, the wall is dark gray; one must paint with the bold, heavy strokes of a dark roast to be seen at all. If the water is soft, the wall is bright white; one can paint with the translucent watercolors of a light roast.

The modern coffee revolution is, in large part, a story of seizing control of the canvas. By stripping water back to zero and rebuilding it mineral by mineral—adding 40 ppm of magnesium here, 20 ppm of bicarbonate there—we are finally seeing the coffee bean as it truly is. We see it naked, vulnerable, and unadulterated by the random geology of the city pipe. We have learned that the "Universal Solvent" is not universal at all. It is a local variable, and it is the hidden ingredient that defines the ceiling of flavor.

# 23

# THE WHITE CRYSTAL: ISOLATION, ADDICTION, AND THE CHEMISTRY OF WAKEFULNESS

I n the first week of October 1819, a carriage navigated the cobblestones of Weimar, Germany, carrying a demonstration that balanced precariously between scientific breakthrough and professional suicide. Inside sat Friedlieb Ferdinand Runge, a twenty-five-year-old medical student from the University of Jena. He was a man of the new century—materialist, analytical, and chemically curious—traveling to meet a relic of the old.

He was there to see Johann Wolfgang von Goethe. At seventy years old, Goethe was the titan of German letters, the author of Faust, and a Privy Councillor. But he was also a celebrity scientist of the Romantic tradition, a man who believed that the poet's eye could discern truths in nature that the mechanic's tools missed. Goethe had heard rumors of this student who was performing borderline forbidden experiments with nightshade (Atropa belladonna), extracting the plant's essence to manipulate biological systems.

Runge did not disappoint. Standing in Goethe's study, a room lined with mineralogical specimens and botanical drawings, the student produced a live cat. With the dispassionate precision of a modern toxicologist, Runge applied a single drop of concentrated hemlock extract to the animal's eye. Within moments, the pupil dilated into a massive, encompassing black orb, while the other remained reactive to the light. It was a piece of scientific theater: a *visceral demonstration that the "spirit" of a plant could be chemically isolated and wielded like a precision instrument.*

*Goethe was mesmerized. "That is the way the world is caught," he reportedly murmured, observing the chemical manipulation of the animal's nervous system. But the poet had a different botanical mystery in mind. He went to a wooden cabinet inlaid with ivory and retrieved a small, decorative box. He opened it to reveal a handful of rare Arabian Mocha beans—a luxury item in post-Napoleonic Europe, prized for their aroma and their scarcity.*

*"You have shown me the poison in the nightshade," Goethe told the young chemist. "Now, find me the soul of the coffee."*

*Goethe, a prodigious coffee drinker, suspected that the beverage's ability to sharpen the mind was not magic, nor was it a nutritional property of the oil or the fiber. He believed it was a specific chemical entity waiting to be found. He handed the box to Runge. That exchange—a poet handing a box of agriculture to a chemist—marked the end of the mystical age of coffee and the beginning of the pharmacological age. Runge returned to his laboratory in Jena, and within months, he had done what centuries of imams, sultans, and popes could not. He stripped the coffee bean of its mystery and found the engine inside.*

## THE ISOLATION

Runge's laboratory in Jena was a primitive environment by modern standards, a place of open flames, hand-blown glassware, and noxious fumes. To find Goethe's "soul," Runge had to dismantle the physical body of the bean.

He began by roasting the Mocha beans and grinding them to a fine powder, then brewing a strong decoction, creating a thick, dark slurry rich in oils, acids, and solids. He knew from his work with belladonna that plant alkaloids—nitrogen-based compounds that trigger physiological effects in humans often reacted with heavy metals. Runge treated the coffee solution with lead acetate. The heavy lead ions bound to the tannins and organic acids in the brew, creating a thick, insoluble precipitate that sank to the bottom of the beaker like river silt.

Runge filtered off the liquid, which was now clarified and freed from the dark coloring agents. He then gently evaporated the remaining water over a flame, watching the solution reduce to a syrup. As the steam cleared and the liquid cooled, something remarkable occurred. Delicate, silky white crystals began to precipitate out of the solution. They formed long, needle-like structures, resembling frost on a windowpane.

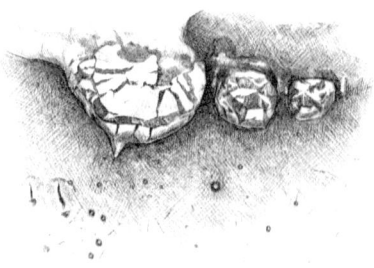

*In 1820, Friedlieb Runge isolated the active principle of coffee: pure, white, bitter crystals of caffeine.*

They were odorless. When Runge placed a few grains on his tongue, they were intensely, purely bitter. He called the substance *Kaffebase*. A year later, fellow chemists, confirming the discovery, refined the name to *Coffein*. In 1821, Runge published his findings, describing a substance that was chemically stable, water-soluble, and physiologically potent. He had isolated the molecule 1,3,7-trimethylxanthine. Its chemical formula is $C_8H_{10}N_4O_2$.

This was the moment coffee stopped being just a crop and became a delivery system. Runge proved that the "wakefulness" of the Sufi night vigils and the "wit" of the London coffeehouses were not atmospheric, spiritual, or caloric qualities. They were the result of a specific white powder—a bitter alkaloid—interacting with the human central nervous system. The bean served as the packaging for the crystal payload.


CONVERGENT EVOLUTION

What Runge did not know—what he could not know without the periodic table, which wouldn't be organized for another fifty years—was that he had isolated one of nature's most successful chemical weapons.

As we saw in the forests of Kaffa (Chapter 12), the coffee tree does not produce caffeine to help humans process data or navigate morning traffic; it produces it as a chemical weapon. To an insect, caffeine is not a stimulant; it is a potent neurotoxin. When a bug takes a bite of a caffeine-rich leaf or cherry, the molecule causes unregulated calcium release in the insect's muscles. This leads to rapid tremors, paralysis, and eventual death. It is a natural pesticide, evolved to protect the nutrient-rich cherry.

But the coffee tree utilizes this molecule for offense as well as defense. As coffee cherries ripen and fall to the forest floor, they decompose, leaching caffeine into the humus. Caffeine is allelopathic—it inhibits the germination of rival seeds. By poisoning the soil around its base, the coffee tree ensures that no competing plants can steal its sunlight or water. The "buzz" humans perceive is simply the mammalian body processing a dose of poison too small to be lethal, but large enough to trigger systemic alarm bells.

Runge's discovery sparked a continental treasure hunt. If caffeine was the active principle of coffee, chemists reasoned, what was the active principle of tea? For centuries, Europeans had debated the relative merits of the two drinks. Tea was seen as cerebral, feminine, and temperate; coffee as aggressive, masculine, and radical. Surely, they contained different drugs.

In 1827, the French chemist Oudry analyzed tea leaves and isolated a crystal he named *Theine*. Shortly after, chemists analyzing the South American drink yerba maté found a compound they named *Mateine*. Others investigated the guarana berry from the Amazon and identified *Guaranine*.

For decades, the scientific community believed these were distinct substances. They built elaborate theories on why *Theine* produced a gentle focus while *Caffeine* produced a kinetic rush. It wasn't until 1838 that the Dutch chemist Gerardus Johannes Mulder performed a rigorous elemental analysis of all of them. The result was a shock to the Victorian medical establishment. They were identical. There is no such thing as *Theine*. There is no *Mateine*. It is all caffeine.

This realization revealed a stunning example of convergent evolution. Three completely unrelated plants—a flowering bush in China (*Camellia sinensis*), a fruit tree in Ethiopia (*Coffea arabica*), and a holly tree in South America (*Ilex paraguariensis*)—had independently evolved the exact same molecular formula to kill pests. Humans, in our global wandering, had identified every single plant that produced this specific molecule and built civilizations around them. We domesticated these plants for their drug as much as their taste.

### THE ADENOSINE ANTAGONIST

How does the crystal work? For 150 years after Runge's discovery, this remained a black box. It wasn't until the 1980s that neurobiologists finally mapped the mechanism. What they found overturned the common wisdom about energy.

We say that coffee "gives" us energy. In a physics sense, this is incorrect. A cup of black coffee contains roughly two calories (8.4 kilojoules). It provides no fuel for the metabolic fire. Instead, caffeine works by receptor blockade. It doesn't step on the accelerator; it cuts the brake lines.

The mechanism revolves around a molecule called adenosine. Adenosine is a byproduct of cellular work. Every second a human is awake, neurons fire, and as they burn adenosine triphosphate (ATP) for fuel, they produce adenosine as metabolic waste. This adenosine drifts through the brain, seeking specific receptors on nearby neurons, primarily the A1 and A2A receptors. When adenosine docks into these receptors, it sends a biochemical signal to slow down neural activity. It is the brain's fatigue counter. The longer one is awake, the more adenosine accumulates, and the more "sleep pressure" occurs. It is a gradual, biological dimmer switch.

Enter Runge's white crystal.

Caffeine is a molecular mimic. Structurally, it is a purine, almost identical to adenosine. It is similar enough to slide perfectly into the brain's adenosine receptors, but with one critical difference: caffeine fits the lock, but it does not turn the key.

It creates a blockade. When you drink a double espresso, you flood your brain with millions of these impostors. They park in the receptors and refuse to leave. The real adenosine—the chemical signal for fatigue —bounces off the caffeine blockade, unable to deliver its message.

The brain, unaware of the mounting fatigue, keeps the engine running at maximum speed. This blockade triggers a secondary cascade: by jamming the A1 receptor, caffeine prevents the brain from regulating dopamine, allowing the "feel-good" neurotransmitter to flow freely.

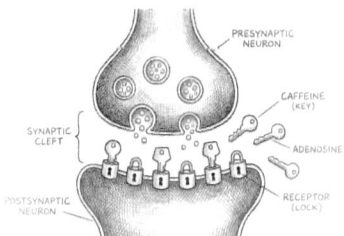

*Caffeine functions by "jamming" adenosine receptors, preventing the brain from receiving the chemical signal for fatigue.*

Dopamine is the neurotransmitter of reward and focus. With the "brakes" of adenosine removed, dopamine flows more freely, creating the sensation of elevated mood and sharpness. Simultaneously, the pituitary gland, detecting rapid neural firing despite the prolonged wakefulness, assumes an emergency is underway. It triggers the adrenal glands to release adrenaline (epinephrine). The heart rate increases; the liver releases stored glucose into the bloodstream; the airways dilate. The "jolt" of the morning cup is a chemically induced state of fight-or-flight response.

## THE HALF-LIFE

Once the crystal enters the bloodstream, it begins a race against the liver. This race is governed by a variable that dictates the rhythm of modern sleep cycles: the half-life.

The primary assassin of caffeine in the human body is a liver enzyme named CYP1A2. This enzyme's sole function regarding caffeine is to hunt down the molecule, rip off its methyl groups, and break it down into smaller metabolites: paraxanthine (84%), theobromine (12%), and theophylline (4%).

For the average human, the CYP1A2 enzyme requires approximately five to six hours to reduce the caffeine concentration in the blood by

50%. This mathematics is deceptive and often misunderstood. If a person consumes a large drip coffee (containing 200mg of caffeine) at 4:00 PM to power through the end of the workday, the decay rate is unforgiving.

- At 4:00 PM: 200mg.
- At 10:00 PM: 100mg (still equivalent to a shot of espresso).
- At 4:00 AM: 50mg.

When the individual attempts to sleep at midnight, their brain is still bathed in as much caffeine as if they had just consumed a small coffee. They may fall asleep—exhaustion eventually overpowers the receptor blockade—but the quality of that sleep is chemically compromised.

Caffeine acts as a destroyer of "slow-wave" sleep, the deep, restorative phase where the brain cleanses itself of metabolic waste (the glymphatic system). With caffeine active in the receptors, the brain struggles to reach these deep valleys of rest. The sleeper wakes up the next morning feeling groggy and unrefreshed, not realizing that the "brain fog" is a lingering effect of the previous afternoon's coffee. The natural solution is another cup. The loop is closed.

However, the CYP1A2 enzyme is not consistent across the species. In the early 2000s, geneticists identified two primary variants of the gene that controls this enzyme, revealing why coffee serves as a tonic for some and a torment for others:

1. **The CYP1A2*1A Allele:** The "Fast Metabolizers." These are the genetic lottery winners of the coffee world. Their livers produce a voracious version of the enzyme that clears caffeine rapidly. They can consume a cappuccino after dinner and sleep soundly.

2. **The CYP1A2*1F Allele:** The "Slow Metabolizers." These individuals possess a sluggish enzyme. Caffeine loiters in their system for ten, twelve, or fourteen hours. For them, a single cup in the morning creates a stimulation that lasts all day, but a second cup at noon guarantees insomnia.

This genetic variance explains the polarized reaction to coffee. When one person claims, "Coffee focuses me," and another claims, "Coffee induces anxiety," they are not describing different beverages. They are describing different livers.

## SANKA AND SOLVENTS

While Runge was the first to find the crystal, a German merchant named Ludwig Roselius was the first to build an empire on removing it. The invention of decaffeination is a story born of paranoia.

In 1902, Roselius was running his coffee trading firm in Bremen when his father died unexpectedly. The doctors offered a vague diagnosis of "caffeine poisoning." Roselius, grief-stricken and guilty, became convinced that the family business had killed his father. He dedicated his resources to a strange new goal: separating the flavor from the poison.

His breakthrough was accidental. A shipment of Roselius's beans was soaked in seawater during a storm. When he roasted and tested them, he found they still tasted like coffee, but the "kick" was gone. The salt water had leached out some of the alkaloid. This gave him the clue: caffeine is water-soluble, but it requires a solvent to be fully extracted from the hard cellular matrix of the green bean.

In 1905, Roselius patented the first commercial decaffeination process. He steamed the green beans to open their pores, swelling the cellulose structure. He then rinsed them with a chemical solvent to bind with and dissolve the caffeine. The solvent he chose was benzene.

Benzene is an effective solvent. It is also a potent carcinogen, known to suppress bone marrow function and cause leukemia. Today, it is banned in almost every consumer application. But in 1906, it was simply a tool of industrial chemistry. Roselius launched his product under the name *Kaffee HAG* in Germany and later *Sanka* (a contraction of the French *sans caféine*) in France and the United States.

Sanka became a global phenomenon, instantly recognizable by its orange label. For decades, millions of health-conscious consumers drank benzene-treated coffee, believing they were making the safer choice. It wasn't until the late 20th century that the industry switched to safer agents—first methylene chloride (which is still used, as it acts specifically on caffeine and evaporates at 104°F / 40°C during roasting), and eventually the "Swiss Water Process," which uses osmosis and carbon filters to scrub the caffeine without harsh chemicals.

*The universal convention of distinguishing the decaf pot is a silent nod to
Sanka, the brand that originally set the standard for coffee service.*

But the legacy of Roselius remains. The orange handle on the decaf
pot in every American diner is a nod to the Sanka branding, a ghost of
the man who declared war on Runge's crystal.

## UNITED STATES V. FORTY BARRELS

Once Roselius proved caffeine could be removed, a strange economic
inversion occurred. Decaffeination plants create caffeine as a waste product. By the 1910s, decaf facilities were accumulating tons of pure white
caffeine powder. They needed a buyer.

They found one in Atlanta.

The Coca-Cola Company had been under siege. In 1911, the U.S.
government launched a landmark lawsuit against the soft drink giant,
titled *United States v. Forty Barrels and Twenty Kegs of Coca-Cola*. The
government's charge was that the caffeine added to the soda was "inju-
rious to health," specifically to the health of children.

The trial, held in Chattanooga, Tennessee, was a media circus. The
government brought in expert witnesses who testified that caffeine
caused "neuropathic volatility" and moral degeneration in boys. Coca-
Cola's defense team needed to prove that caffeine was a harmless stimulant. They hired a psychologist named Harry Hollingworth to conduct
one of the first double-blind behavioral studies in human history.

Hollingworth's data was rigorous. He administered caffeine caps and
placebos to subjects and measured their motor skills and mental acuity.
His findings were clear: in moderate doses, caffeine improved perfor-

mance. It increased the speed of typing and reduced errors. It did not cause madness; it caused efficiency.

Coca-Cola won the scientific argument, though they eventually settled the case by agreeing to reduce the caffeine content slightly. But the symbiotic relationship was sealed. For the rest of the 20th century, the caffeine removed from coffee beans in decaf plants was sold to soft drink manufacturers. The coffee drinker's desire to sleep subsidized the soda drinker's desire to wake up.


SYNTHETIC GENESIS

However, in the 1950s, the demand for soda exploded. The "Baby Boom" generation was thirsty. There was not enough decaf coffee being produced in the world to supply the caffeine needed for every bottle of Coke, Pepsi, and Dr. Pepper. The natural supply chain broke.

So, the chemists went back to the drawing board. They figured out how to synthesize Runge's crystal from scratch, bypassing the plant entirely. Using a process involving urea (a component of fertilizer) and chloroacetic acid, industrial chemists created a pathway to build $C_8H_{10}N_4O_2$ in the lab. This is known as the Traube synthesis, named after the chemist Wilhelm Traube.

Today, the caffeine market is bifurcated:

- **Natural Caffeine:** Extracted from decaf coffee or tea processing. This is expensive and finite. It is often sold to "premium" energy drink brands or supplement companies who want a "natural source" claim on the label.
- **Synthetic Caffeine:** Produced in massive pharmaceutical factories, primarily in China (specifically in the industrial hubs of Shijiazhuang and Shandong). It is cheap, pure, and infinite. This is the fuel of the mass-market soda and energy drink industry.

The human brain cannot distinguish the difference. The adenosine receptor does not care if the blockade molecule came from a misty hillside in Colombia or a vat of urea in Shandong. The geometry is identical. But the source matters for the scale. Synthetic caffeine detached the drug from the crop. It allowed the "energy" market to grow beyond the limitations of agriculture, paving the way for the Monster and Red Bull cans that line convenience store shelves today. It democratized the stimulant, making it cheaper than water.

## THE LETHAL DOSE

The ubiquity of caffeine raises the question: Can it kill? Theoretically, yes. Practically, almost never—provided it is consumed as a beverage.

The LD50 of caffeine—the lethal dose required to kill 50% of the population—is roughly 150 to 200 milligrams per kilogram of body weight. For an average adult male weighing 80 kg (176 lbs), this translates to about 10 to 12 grams of pure caffeine.

To obtain this dose from brewed coffee, one would need to drink roughly 75 to 100 cups in rapid succession. This is physically impossible. The volume of liquid (nearly 20 liters or 5 gallons) would cause gastric rupture or acute water intoxication (hyponatremia) long before the caffeine toxicity became fatal. Furthermore, the body possesses a violent safety valve for caffeine poisoning: emesis. If a person attempts to drink that much coffee, the stomach will eject it before the lethal dose can be absorbed into the bloodstream.

However, Runge's isolation of the pure crystal removed this safety valve. When caffeine is sold as a pure anhydrous powder—often marketed to bodybuilders as a pre-workout booster or to students as a nootropic—the liquid buffer is gone.

A single teaspoon of pure caffeine powder is equivalent to 28 cups of coffee. A tablespoon is equivalent to 75 cups—a lethal dose.

In the last decade, there have been tragic cases of teenagers and athletes accidentally overdosing on powdered caffeine. The specific cause of death is cardiac arrhythmia. The massive influx of caffeine causes the ryanodine receptors in the heart muscles to lock open, dumping calcium into the cells. The heart begins to beat so fast it simply flutters (ventricular fibrillation), unable to pump blood effectively. It is a stark reminder that what acts as a pleasant ritual in the cup is a deadly neurotoxin in the jar.

## NASA AND THE SPIDER

Perhaps the most famous visual representation of caffeine's power over the nervous system came not from a human medical trial, but from an arachnid.

In 1995, NASA researchers were investigating the toxicity of various drugs. They exposed common house spiders (*Araneus diadematus*) to marijuana, chloral hydrate (a sleeping pill), Benzedrine (speed), and caffeine, then observed their web-spinning ability.

The results were a striking visualization of pharmacokinetics. The marijuana spider spun a reasonable web but appeared distractible, leaving the outer rim unfinished. The Benzedrine spider spun a web with great zest but no planning—a jagged, hole-filled mess. But the caffeine spider was a catastrophe.

The web produced under the influence of caffeine was not even recognizable as a web. It was a series of disjointed, chaotic strands, completely lacking the geometric symmetry of a normal spiral. It looked like the work of a creature that had lost its fundamental understanding of space, tension, and structure.

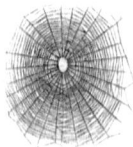 

*NASA experiments demonstrated that caffeine disrupts the central nervous system's ability to organize complex tasks.*

The images of the "caffeine webs" became a viral sensation, published in magazines and textbooks worldwide. They were amusing to the public, but to neurobiologists, they were a warning. They visualized the "neuropathic volatility" that the government had feared in 1911.

They demonstrated that caffeine does not just speed up the brain; it reorganizes the way the brain processes reality. It prioritizes output over structure, speed over symmetry.

## THE DRUG THAT BUILT THE MODERN WORLD

Goethe's request in 1819 was prophetic. He asked for the "soul" of the coffee because he sensed that the beverage was more than a foodstuff. He was right.

The isolation of caffeine changed the trajectory of human history. Before 1820, the human relationship with stimulants was agricultural. We were tethered to the harvest. We drank the tea that grew that year; we brewed the coffee that the ships brought in. The potency varied with the weather, the soil, and the roast. The stimulant was organic, variable, and tied to the rhythm of the earth.

After 1820, the relationship became chemical. Once caffeine was a white powder, it could be measured, dosed, and added. It could be divorced from the ritual of the coffeehouse and injected into the work-flow of the factory. It allowed for the creation of the "coffee break" as an industrial tool, transforming fatigue from a signal to sleep into a problem to be solved.

Friedlieb Runge died in obscurity in 1867. He was a difficult man who burned bridges with his colleagues and failed to patent his discoveries. While others built fortunes on the synthetic dye industries that sprang from his other chemical work (he also discovered aniline dyes), Runge died poor.

There is no statue of Runge in the town square of Jena. But his monument is everywhere. It is in the hiss of the espresso machine in Milan, the crack of the energy drink can in Tokyo, and the headache one feels if the morning brew is skipped. Every day, billions of humans replicate his experiment in their kitchens. We use hot water to perform a crude extraction, pulling those same white crystals out of the cellulose matrix, hoping to borrow just enough poison to make it through the day.

The poet asked for the soul. The chemist handed him a molecule. And for the last two hundred years, the modern world has been running on nothing else.

# PART V

## RITUALS AND REVOLUTIONS

Coffee has always been more than a beverage. It is a social arrangement.

In this section, we return to coffee as a ritual—Ethiopian ceremony, European coffeehouses, the invention of places built for lingering. Then we follow coffee through war and convenience, through instant coffee and mass culture, into waves of reinvention where taste becomes identity and cafés become a kind of civic architecture.

Revolutions do not always arrive with banners. Sometimes they arrive with a cup, a table, and the permission to stay.

# 24

## THE CLAY HEARTH: ETHIOPIA'S LIVING RITUAL

T he air in the living room of a concrete row house in the Addis Ababa neighborhood of Bole is dense, not with the smell of cooking food, but with the heavy, resinous scent of burning frankincense. It hangs suspended in the slanted afternoon light, a blue-gray haze that acts as the first signal of the ritual. The resin hisses on the red coals of a ceramic brazier, releasing distinct plumes of incensole acetate—a psychoactive compound known to activate ion channels in the brain that lower anxiety—into the lungs of everyone present. The biology of the room is being altered before the chemistry of the cup even begins.

Seated on a low, three-legged wooden stool is the matriarch of the family. Her white cotton dress, the habesha kemis, glows against the shadows of the room, embroidered with the tibeb patterns that trace her lineage to the highlands of the north. She moves deliberately, for in this context, speed is considered a social error. Before her, spread across the linoleum floor, is a carpet of fresh green grasses and yellow flowers called ketema. In a city of four million people, where Chinese-funded construction cranes dominate the skyline and the exhaust of blue Lada taxis chokes the Ring Road, the ketema serves as a terraforming act. It transforms a domestic floor into a meadow, signaling that this space has been removed from the timeline of the street.

In her hand, she holds a shallow iron pan called a menkeshkesh. She shakes *it with a rhythmic, hypnotic clack-swish motion. Inside the pan, green coffee beans are in a state of agitation. They turn from pale jade to yellow, then to cinnamon, and finally to a deep, glistening oil-black. She does not use a timer; she uses her nose and the sound of the crack. When the smoke billows, thick and pungent, she stands and walks the circle of guests, waving the pan so the smoke wafts over them. This is the magyet—the blessing of the smoke, an invitation to inhale the spirit of the coffee before the liquid is ever tasted.*

*This is the Bunna Maflat—the Ethiopian Coffee Ceremony. In a global economy where coffee culture is defined by speed, extraction efficiency, and paper cups passed through drive-thru windows, the Ethiopian ceremony stands as a structural counterpoint. This process is a slow, three-hour meditation designed for communal reinforcement, not productivity. To say "I don't have time for coffee" in Ethiopia is to say "I don't have time for you". It is the social anchor of the nation, a ritual that has survived the fall of the Solomonic dynasty, the Red Terror of the Derg regime, and the frantic modernization of the twenty-first century.*

### THE GENETIC LIBRARY IN THE PAN

Before the fire is lit, the raw material in the bowl demands attention. In Brazil or Vietnam, a farmer looks out at a field and sees a monoculture: rows of Caturra, or vast hedges of Robusta. These are industrial crops, selected for yield, uniformity, and machine harvestability. They are biological clones, vulnerable to the same pathogens and requiring the same chemical inputs.

In Ethiopia, the biology is distinct. The beans washing in the woman's bowl are likely what Western importers classify as "Ethiopian Heirloom," masking a staggering complexity. These are landraces— thousands of distinct genetic varieties that evolved naturally in the forests of Kaffa, Sidama, and Yirgacheffe over millennia. A single hectare of forest in southwestern Ethiopia might contain more genetic diversity than the entire coffee sector of Colombia.

When the hostess washes the green beans, scrubbing away the silver skin and dust with cool water, she is handling a genetic library. In recent decades, the Jimma Agricultural Research Center (JARC) has attempted to catalogue this diversity. Researchers trek into the cloud forests, identifying varieties resistant to Coffee Berry Disease and bestowing them with utilitarian names like 74110 and 74112—named after the harvest of 1974, when a major expedition identified them. These berries are often smaller and denser than their commercial cousins abroad. They are the ancestors of the modern coffee world—ancient, untamed, and possessing floral and citrus precursors that do not exist anywhere else in the genus *Coffea*.

However, an economic irony exists in this bowl. The highest grade of these beans—the Grade 1 specialty lots washed to perfection and dried on raised beds—are almost entirely exported. They are destined for roasteries in Seattle, Melbourne, and Tokyo, where they will sell for $25 (approx. 23€) a bag or more. The beans remaining in the Addis Ababa living room are often the "domestic consumption" grade. These are the beans that were rejected at the washing station: too small, too oddly shaped, or slightly chipped. Yet, through the alchemy of the ceremony, this "lower quality" green coffee will produce a cup that rivals the finest specialty brew. The quality is not just in the bean; it is in the pan.

## Pyrolysis by Hand: The Melange Mechanism

To a modern Western roaster, obsessed with computerized airflow profiles, rate-of-rise curves, and variable drum speeds, the Ethiopian method appears imprecise. Roasting beans on a flat iron pan over an open charcoal brazier relies almost entirely on conductive heat. The hot metal touches the cellulose of the bean directly, unlike the convective heat (hot air) used in modern drum roasters.

The physics of the *menkeshkesh* are unforgiving. The risk is scorching. If the hand stops moving for even three seconds, the face of the bean turns to carbon while the interior remains raw and grassy. But the hostess does not stop. She maintains a constant agitation, tossing the beans in the air to cool them, then returning them to the iron. She is manually modulating the thermal energy, acting as the drum, the airflow, and the cooling tray all at once.

*Hand-roasting over charcoal requires constant agitation, resulting in a
complex mixture of roast levels in a single batch.*

The result is a "Melange" roast—considered a technical flaw in industrial roasting, yet a deliberate feature here. Because the heat transfer is
uneven, the finished batch contains a spectrum of roast levels in the
same pan:

- **The Black Beans:** Some beans hit the iron hard and darken
  to an oily level, exceeding 240°C (464°F). These provide the
  heavy body, the bass notes, and the smoky intensity that cuts
  through sugar.
- **The Brown Beans:** These reach a standard medium roast,
  approximately 218°C (425°F), developing the Maillard reaction
  sugars and caramel notes.
- **The Cinnamon Beans:** Some beans, protected by their
  neighbors or floating in the agitation, barely reach the first
  crack at roughly 196°C (385°F). These light-roast beans
  preserve the citric acidity and the volatile floral aromatics—
  jasmine, bergamot, lemon—that would be destroyed by a
  darker roast.

When these are ground and brewed together, they create a cup with
the visceral punch of a dark roast and the high-frequency brightness of a
light roast. It is a full-spectrum flavor profile that a singular, computerized roast curve struggles to replicate. It is the taste of the fire itself.

### CRUSHING THE CELL STRUCTURE

Once the beans are roasted to a dark, oily shine, they are dumped into a small clay pot to cool. Then comes the sound that defines the Ethiopian afternoon, echoing from corrugated tin roofs and mud-walled compounds alike: the *Mukecha* and *Zenezena*.

The *Mukecha* is a heavy wooden mortar, waist-high and worn smooth by years of use. The *Zenezena* is the heavy metal or wooden pestle. Rather than being sliced by burrs, the beans are crushed by impact. Thump. Thump. Thump. The woman establishes a rhythm, often singing quietly to maintain the tempo. This is a percussive act, not a mechanical one.

*The rhythmic crushing of the* Mukecha *creates a mix of fines and coarse chunks, essential for the body of the ceremonial brew.*

Particle distribution matters here. A modern espresso grinder aims for a "unimodal" distribution—every particle the same size to ensure even extraction. The *Mukecha* creates a "bimodal" or even "trimodal" distribution: a chaotic mix of coarse chunks and fine powder. Western brewing theory suggests this leads to a muddy cup, bitter from the fines and sour from the boulders. But in the context of the ceremony, this "inconsistent" grind is structurally necessary. The fines provide the heavy, mud-like body that anchors the sugar, while the coarse chunks release their flavor slowly over the three consecutive boiling cycles. The powder settles at the bottom of the pot, creating a sediment layer that clarifies the liquid above it.

FLUID DYNAMICS OF THE JEBENA

The ground coffee is poured into the *Jebena*. This is the most iconic object in Ethiopian material culture, a silhouette as recognizable as the Eiffel Tower is to France. It is a spherical clay pot with a long, narrow neck, a handle, and a pouring spout. The base is round, meaning it cannot stand flat on a table; it must rest on a woven ring (*matot*) or nestle directly into the coals.

Water is added to the grounds in the pot, and the mixture is set on the charcoal. This is an immersion brew (like a French Press) combined with decoction (boiling). However, the design of the *Jebena* is a feat of vernacular engineering that manages fluid dynamics without moving parts.

1. **The Convection Cycle:** The spherical base encourages convection currents. As the water boils at the bottom, it rises up the sides, cools slightly, and falls down the center. This keeps the grounds in constant agitation, ensuring full saturation without the need for a spoon.

2. **The Condenser Neck:** As the coffee foams up—the release of $CO_2$ known as the bloom—it hits the long, narrow neck. The foam is compressed and pushed back down by the cooler ceramic, preventing boil-over and trapping the volatile aromatics inside the pot. The neck acts as a reflux condenser, returning the most flavorful vapors back into the liquid.

3. **The Settling Tank:** When the brewing is done, the pot is moved to the woven ring and tilted at an angle. The spherical shape allows the heavy grounds to settle perfectly into the curved bottom belly of the pot, leaving the liquid above clear. The spout acts as a weir, drawing only the clarified coffee from the top layer.

A new *Jebena* is useless; it tastes of dust and earth. It must be "seasoned"—boiled with coffee grounds, oil, and sometimes milk for days until the porous clay is saturated with coffee oils.

*The design of the* Jebena *traps grounds in its spherical belly, allowing clear coffee to decant from the neck.*

Like a cast-iron skillet, a *Jebena* accumulates memory. It imparts a deep, earthy flavor to the brew that a glass or steel pot simply cannot replicate. If a *Jebena* breaks, it is treated with genuine sadness, a disruption of the family lineage.

## ORIGINS: FROM ENERGY BAR TO HOLY WATER

While the ceremony today is a liquid ritual, the history of coffee in Ethiopia begins with solids. Long before the *Jebena* was fired in a kiln, the Oromo people of the highlands were consuming coffee as food. Warriors and travelers would crush the ripe red cherries—fruit and seed together—and mix them with animal fat to create dense, calorie-rich spheres. These were the original energy bars. The fat provided the fuel for long marches, while the caffeine provided the stamina and focus. In some regions, this tradition persists as *Buna Qalaa*, a ceremonial dish of coffee cherries roasted in butter.

The transition to a liquid brew is intimately tied to the spiritual history of the region. In the eastern city of Harar, a walled city of white limestone and narrow alleys, Sufi mystics adopted coffee in the 15th century. They called it *qahwa*. It was not a leisure drink; it was a tool for *zikr*—the midnight prayers and chanting rituals that required sustained wakefulness. The communal circle, the passing of the cup, the incense—

these elements of the modern ceremony echo the structure of those early Sufi gatherings.

When the drink spread to the Christian Orthodox highlands, it was initially viewed with suspicion as a "Muslim drink". However, its utility was undeniable. The church eventually embraced it, and today, the ceremony is practiced with equal fervor by Christians and Muslims alike. The term for the third cup, *Baraka*, is a direct loan word from Arabic, signifying "divine grace" or "blessing," a linguistic fossil of its Sufi origins.

### ABOL, TONA, BARAKA: THE STRUCTURE OF TIME

One does not drink a single cup of coffee. That would be transactional. The ceremony is structurally divided into three rounds, using the same grounds. Water is added to the *Jebena* between each round and reboiled. This progression is the clock by which the social gathering is measured.

1. **Abol (The First)** The first cup is the strongest. It is thick, oily, and buzzing with caffeine and soluble solids. It represents the pleasure of the senses and the breaking of the ice. This round is named after Abol, the first goat herder in some legends, or simply "The First". It is the cup of awakening. The flavor is intense—earthy, winey, and often heavily sweetened with sugar to balance the roast bitterness.

2. **Tona (The Second)** Water is added to the remaining wet grounds. The resulting brew is weaker, more diluted, but the conversation has thickened. The caffeine has hit the bloodstream. Tongues loosen. This is the round where business is discussed, where gossip is exchanged, where the news of the neighborhood is dissected. The *Tona* is the cup of discourse. In the absence of a free press during various regimes, the *Tona* round was often the true newspaper of the people.

3. **Baraka (The Third)** The "Blessing". This cup is thin and watery, a shadow of the Abol. But spiritually, it is the most important. To leave before the *Baraka* is to reject the blessing

of the house. It represents the resolution, the peace, and the departure. By the time the *Baraka* is poured, the guests have been sitting for nearly two hours. The aggressive energy of the caffeine has smoothed out. The problems raised during the *Tona* have been resolved or shelved.

## THE INSTRUMENT OF PEACE: THE SHIMGILIT

The ceremony serves a function far deeper than hospitality; it is a critical piece of Ethiopia's informal legal system. In the rural highlands, and even in the crowded neighborhoods of Addis, the coffee ceremony acts as a mechanism for *Shimgilit*—conflict resolution by elders.

If two neighbors are fighting over a property line, or if a marriage is strained, the elders might call for a coffee ceremony. The mechanism is time. It is impossible to maintain high-octane anger while a woman spends forty-five minutes roasting beans by hand in front of you. The ritual forces a "cooling off" period. The scent of the frankincense triggers a Pavlovian response of sanctity; one cannot scream in a room that smells like a church.

By the time the *Abol* is poured, the tension has lowered. By the *Tona*, the grievances are aired in the presence of witnesses. By the *Baraka*, a solution—or at least a truce—is expected. The phrase *Bunna Tetu* ("Come drink coffee") is often a code for "Let's make peace." The ceremony creates a containment field where social friction can be lubricated by the shared ritual of consumption.

## OLFACTORY ENGINEERING: THE SCENT BUBBLE

The presence of frankincense (*Boswellia*) is not decorative; it is a crucial piece of sensory engineering. Ethiopia is one of the world's few sources of high-grade frankincense, harvested from the gnarled trees in the Tigray and Amhara regions.

When the resin hits the coals, it releases a complex smoke dominated by terpenes. Scientifically, this smoke does two things. First, it masks the acrid smells that might exist in a rural home shared with livestock or cooking fires, purifying the space. Second, it creates a powerful "episodic memory" trigger.

For an Ethiopian child, the smell of roasting coffee is inextricably linked to the smell of incense. The brain wires these two inputs together. Years later, the scent of frankincense alone can trigger a physiological relaxation response, lowering the heart rate and preparing the mind for connection. The smoke creates a "scent bubble"—a physical demarcation that separates the sacred space of the ceremony from the profane space of the outside world. Inside the bubble, the rules are different. Time moves slower.

### Vignette: The Portable Homeland

Four thousand miles away, on the sixteenth floor of an apartment complex in Silver Spring, Maryland, it is snowing. The windows are sealed against the cold. Inside, a fire alarm has been temporarily covered with a plastic shower cap—a necessary hack for the diaspora.

Here, imagine a young woman named Haimanot performing the ceremony for her two American-born daughters. She is not in a village in Sidama; she is in the suburbs of Washington D.C., home to the largest Ethiopian population outside of Africa. The challenge of maintaining the ritual here is a logistical feat.

The green coffee beans were bought at an Ethiopian specialty market on U Street. The *Jebena* was carried in a suitcase, wrapped in three layers of towels, guarded like a crown jewel during the transatlantic flight. The *ketema* grass is missing—replaced by a green rug or sometimes skipped entirely. But the roast is the same. The smoke is the same.

For the diaspora, the ceremony is an act of resistance against assimilation. In a country that runs on "to-go" cups and 15-minute breaks, the three-hour ceremony is a defiant assertion of identity. Haimanot teaches her daughters how to hold the *cini* (small cups) without burning their fingers, how to compliment the hostess (*Konjo Bunna*—Beautiful Coffee), and how to wait.

"Watch the fire," she tells them, switching from English to Amharic. "We are not the kind of people who rush". The ceremony becomes a portable homeland, a way to fold the sensory experience of the Rift Valley into a suitcase and unfold it in a high-rise.

## The Texture of Hospitality

Coffee in Ethiopia is never drunk alone, and it is never drunk empty. It is always accompanied by the "snack". Surprisingly to many Western-ers, the traditional pairing is not a sweet pastry, but popcorn (*fanidisha*).

*Popcorn is the standard accompaniment to the ceremony, providing a textural contrast to the heavy, sweet coffee.*

The white, fluffy popcorn contrasts visually with the black coffee and the green grass on the floor. It is sprinkled with sugar. In other regions, large loaves of round bread called *himbasha*—decorated with wheel-like patterns—are torn and shared. Or *kolo*, roasted barley grains mixed with peanuts, is placed in bowls.

One chews the crunchy barley between sips of the smooth, sugary coffee. It is a texture study: the dissolve of the sugar, the grit of the grounds at the bottom of the cup, the crunch of the grain, the heavy oil of the brew.

In the southern regions, among the Gurage and Oromo, the texture changes further. They may add *niter kibbeh*—a clarified butter spiced with cardamom, fenugreek, and nigella seeds—directly into the cup. The fat floats on top, an oily golden slick. When one drinks, the butter coats the lips and tongue, mitigating the bitterness of the roast and slowing the absorption of caffeine. It is savory, rich, and dense—a meal in a cup.

### Addis Ababa, 2024: The Charcoal Economy

Back in Addis Ababa, the ceremony is facing the pressures of the modern world. The city is expanding outward at a breakneck pace. A chain called Kaldi's Coffee—often called the "Ethiopian Starbucks"—has sprung up, with bright green logos, espresso machines, and Wi-Fi. Young entrepreneurs meet there for macchiatos, checking stock prices on their phones, their laptops glowing on the tables.

But even here, the pull of the *Jebena* is inescapable. In the corner of these modern glass-walled cafes, one will often find a traditional station: a woman sitting on a stool with a charcoal stove, offering the traditional brew alongside the cappuccinos. The modern Ethiopian consumer wants the Wi-Fi, but they also crave the incense.

There is also an ecological cost. The ceremony runs on charcoal. As the population of Addis booms, the demand for charcoal has led to deforestation in the surrounding acacia woodlands. The government has attempted to regulate charcoal production, driving up prices. For a poor family, the daily ceremony is becoming an expensive luxury. Some have switched to electric hotplates or electric *Jebenas*, but the purists scoff. "Electric fire has no taste," they say. The connection to the earth, they argue, requires the burning of wood.

### The Final Grounds: A Circular End

When the *Baraka* is finished, and the last cup is drained, the ceremony is not quite over. The wet grounds remaining in the *Jebena* are not thrown in the trash. In the circular economy of the Ethiopian household, nothing is wasted.

The grounds might be mixed with honey to make a scrub for the skin, an exfoliant that smells of the morning's roast. Or, more commonly, they are poured into the soil of the garden to nourish the next generation of plants. The *ketema* grass, now flattened by the feet of the guests, is swept up and used as fodder for the goats or compost for the earth.

The guests rise. The incense has burned down to gray ash. The caffeine is humming in the blood, a chemical reminder of the bond just reaffirmed. They step out of the heavy, scented air of the living room and back into the noise of the street. They are armed against the chaos of the world by three tiny cups of black oil. They have been blessed, they have been heard, and they have been slowed down. In the birthplace of coffee, the bean is not a fuel for work; it is the work itself.

# 25

# THE PAPER PARLIAMENT: VIENNA'S EMPIRE OF TIME

I t is January 1913, and the air inside Café Central is heavy enough to possess a physical texture. It is a warm, suspended fog composed of cigar smoke, damp wool drying on brass hooks, the savory steam of goulash, and the pervasive, dark-roasted anchor of coffee. Outside, the wind whips around the Herrengasse, carrying the bite of an Austrian winter where temperatures drop to -5°C (23°F). But inside, under the soaring vaulted ceilings supported by reddish marble pillars, the calendar has stopped. The soundscape is a gentle, rhythmic symphony: the dry click of billiard balls from the back room, the crisp rustle of broadsheet newspapers being turned on wooden sticks, the murmur of political conspiracy, and the delicate chime of silver spoons against porcelain.

At one table, a man with a neatly trimmed beard and intense, darting eyes is writing furiously; it is Leon Trotsky, born Lev Bronstein, biding his time as a refugee before he attempts to reshape Russia. At another, Peter Altenberg, the bohemian poet who lists the café as his legal address, is composing a sketch on the back of a receipt, having just woken from a nap on the banquette. Moving through this chaos with the detached elegance of a tuxedoed penguin is the Herr Ober—the head waiter. He balances a silver tray loaded with water glasses and cups of Melange, his face a mask of professional discretion. He knows every regular's name, their preferred table, their political leanings, and *exactly how long they can be left undisturbed before needing a fresh glass of water.*

*More than a place to consume caffeine, it acts as a "democratic club," as the writer Stefan Zweig described it, "open to everyone for the price of a cheap cup of coffee." In a city characterized by cramped, unheated apartments and rigid social stratification, the coffeehouse became the city's erweitertes Wohnzimmer —the extended living room. It was an institution built on a fundamental paradox: it was a place of intense public privacy, where one went to be alone in the company of others, and where the greatest luxury on offer was not the drink, but the space to linger.*

### THE MYTH OF THE BLUE BOTTLE

Every great institution requires a founding mythology, and Vienna's begins in the smoke of the 1683 siege. For two months, the Ottoman army had encircled the city, starving its inhabitants and battering its walls. The stalemate was broken only by the arrival of the Polish King Jan III Sobieski, whose cavalry swept down from the Kahlenberg hills to rout the Ottoman forces. In the chaotic retreat, the Ottomans left behind a city of tents, oxen, camels, and five hundred sacks of strange, green beans. The Viennese soldiers, ignorant of the commodity, assumed it was camel feed and prepared to throw it on the fire.

They were stopped by Jerzy Franciszek Kulczycki, a Polish-Lithuanian officer and spy who had lived in the Ottoman world. He knew exactly what the sacks contained. As a reward for his heroism—he had slipped through enemy lines in Turkish garb to coordinate with the relief forces—Kulczycki was granted the coffee and a license to serve it. He opened the *Hof zur Blauen Flasche* (House under the Blue Bottle). While the Armenian Diodato opened the first shop, Kulczycki became the protagonist of the city's coffee mythology, largely because of what he did to the liquid itself.

He realized quickly that the Viennese palate, accustomed to beer and wine, rejected the sludge-heavy, unfiltered brew preferred by the Turks. It was too bitter, too gritty, too foreign. In a moment of culinary adaptation that would secure coffee's future in the West, Kulczycki strained the grounds. Then, he added a dollop of honey. Finally, and most crucially,

he added milk. By softening the black brew with dairy, he invented the
*Kapuziner*—so named because the brown color of the coffee mixed with
milk resembled the brown robes of the Capuchin monks. This drink was
the ancestor of the cappuccino, and the moment coffee ceased to be an
exotic Eastern stimulant and became a comforting Western staple.

## The Economics of Warmth

To understand why the Viennese coffeehouse flourished, one must
look beyond the beverage to the boiler room. In the 18th and 19th
centuries, Vienna was a city of extreme housing density. Apartments
were small, dark, and notoriously difficult to heat. Coal and wood were
expensive; keeping a private room warm for an entire day was a luxury
few students, writers, or artists could afford. The coffeehouse offered a
solution: centralized heating. For the price of a single *Melange*—roughly
equivalent to a few cents today—a patron bought not just a drink, but
twelve hours of warmth.

The café owners understood this implicit contract. They invested
heavily in massive ceramic stoves (*Kachelöfen*) that radiated a steady,
comforting heat throughout the high-ceilinged rooms. This economic
reality dictated the social behavior. Patrons did not frequent the café
merely to socialize; they went to survive the winter. This explains the
presence of the "coffeehouse writer." It was not just a romantic affectation; it was a practical necessity. Peter Altenberg, the poet who famously
lived at Café Central, didn't write there because he liked the noise. He
wrote there because his rented room was freezing. The café provided
light, heat, furniture, and stationery. The coffee was merely the admission ticket to a fully serviced office.

## The Lease and the Water Glass

The economic model of the Viennese coffeehouse defies modern
capitalism. In a modern Starbucks or a Parisian brasserie, the table is
real estate that must be turned over. The waiter is trained to clear plates
quickly, to bring the check unasked, to subtly signal that your time is up.
In Vienna, this is a capital offense. The soul of the institution rests on the

"rent" paid by the first cup. Once a patron orders a *Melange* or a *Schwarzer*, they effectively sign a lease on that table for the remainder of the day.

This contract is enforced by the ritual of the water glass. Every coffee, no matter how small, is served on a silver tray with a glass of tap water, usually with a spoon balanced across the rim. Beyond hydration, this water serves as a symbol of hospitality. It signifies that the guest is not a customer to be processed, but a resident.

*The glass of water is the symbol of the "rent" paid by the customer; as long as it is full, the patron may stay.*

The water itself is a point of immense civic pride. Since 1873, Vienna has been supplied by the First Vienna Mountain Spring Pipeline (*Erste Wiener Hochquellenwasserleitung*), which brings crystal-clear spring water directly from the Alps, 90 kilometers away, to the city taps without pumps, powered only by gravity. When a waiter serves that glass, he is serving the Alps.

The most crucial rule—one that foreign tourists often misunderstand—is the refill. A good busboy, or *Piccolo*, will circulate through the room with a pitcher. As long as the guest remains, the water glass is kept full. A waiter would never ask, "Would you like another coffee?" To do so would be an insult, implying the guest is only welcome if they continue to pay. The full water glass is the silent signal: *You may stay.* How did the cafés survive on such low turnover? Historically, they relied on high margins for the coffee itself, low labor costs, and the sheer volume of regulars who, while they sat for hours, would eventually order a meal, a cognac, or a cigar. But primarily, the coffeehouse sold something intangible: heat and light. In the drafty, dark winters of the early 20th century, the price of a coffee was cheaper than heating one's own apartment.

### Design of Indolence

By the mid-19th century, the coffeehouse had evolved a distinct architectural vernacular designed to solve a specific problem: how to make a customer comfortable enough to stay for six hours, but not so comfortable that they fell asleep. Unlike the Italian espresso bar, which would later be designed for vertical speed, the Viennese coffeehouse was engineered for horizontal endurance.

The tables were small, round, and surfaced in marble. This was a strategic choice. Marble was cool to the touch, easy to wipe clean of cigar ash and spilled cream, and durable enough to withstand decades of banging fists during political debates. More importantly, the marble table was a stage. Mirrors were essential. In the grand cafés of the Ringstrasse era, mirrors were not merely decorative; they were tools of social surveillance. Positioned along the walls behind the plush velvet banquettes, they allowed patrons to observe the room without turning their heads. A writer could watch a rival enter; a debtor could spot a creditor; a suitor could watch a beloved. The coffeehouse was a theater where everyone was both audience and performer, and the mirrors ensured no entrance went unnoticed.

But the most critical piece of technology in the room was the chair. In 1859, a German-Austrian cabinet maker named Michael Thonet perfected a technique for bending solid beech wood using high-pressure steam. The result was the No. 14 Chair. It was a miracle of industrial design.

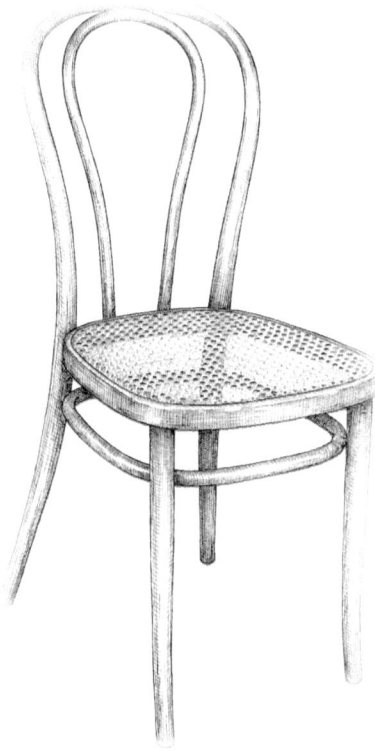

*The Thonet No. 14 chair defined the aesthetic of the coffeehouse: lightweight, durable, and designed for lingering.*

Consisting of only six pieces of wood, ten screws, and two washers, it was elegant, virtually indestructible, and affordable. For the coffeehouse owner, it offered a logistical superpower: lightness. A waiter could lift a No. 14 with one finger to reconfigure a table arrangement for a sudden influx of poets. For the export market, it was the first flat-pack furniture; Thonet could fit thirty-six disassembled chairs into a single one-cubic-meter crate. By 1930, he had sold fifty million of them. The Thonet chair became the visual signature of the coffeehouse, its curved back embracing the spine while the woven cane seat allowed air to circulate. It kept the sitter cool during heated arguments and long afternoons. It was a chair engineered for loitering.

.   .   .

## "Ornament and Crime"

While most coffeehouses were temples of plush velvet, gold leaf, and heavy drapes—a style known as Ringstrasse Historicism—one architect dared to strip the coffeehouse naked. In 1899, Adolf Loos, the firebrand of Austrian architecture who would later famously declare that "Ornament is Crime," designed the Café Museum. Located near the Secession building, it was a shock to the system. Loos ripped out the stucco. He banished the velvet. He installed simple brass rails, plain green walls, and unadorned bentwood chairs. The lighting was harsh and exposed, stripping away the romantic gloom.

The Viennese public was horrified. They nicknamed it "Café Nihilism." They said it looked like a waiting room for a train station or a prison. But the artists loved it. It was clean. It was modern. It was honest. The Café Museum became the headquarters for the Secessionist painters like Gustav Klimt and Egon Schiele, who were trying to break free from the suffocating decoration of the past. Loos had proven that the coffeehouse didn't need to be a palace; it just needed to be a neutral container where the mind could breathe.

## The Paper Parliament

If the water glass provided the lease, the newspaper provided the window. Before the internet, the coffeehouse was the world's information hub. A respectable house subscribed to hundreds of newspapers from around the globe—the *Times* of London, *Le Figaro* of Paris, the *Frankfurter Zeitung*, and local broadsheets like the *Neue Freie Presse*. In an era of strict censorship and high subscription costs, knowledge was expensive. A single subscription to a foreign paper might cost as much as a month's rent. The coffeehouse aggregated this cost. By buying one coffee, a student gained access to the entire world's press.

These were not flimsy tabloids but massive, ink-heavy broadsheets. To keep them organized and prevent them from disintegrating under the hands of a hundred readers, they were clamped into long, polished wooden sticks—*Zeitungshalter* (newspaper holders). The newspaper stick dictated the choreography of the room. It required two hands to hold. It forced the reader to sit upright. It created a visual barrier, a temporary wall behind which one could hide. The smell of newsprint, old wood, and stale tobacco became the olfactory signature of the era.

*The* Zeitungshalter *allowed patrons to read broadsheets without damaging them, turning the café into a library.*

The selection of papers was a political statement. The Café Central carried the radical press; the Café Landtmann (preferred by Freud) carried the conservative sheets. The waiter's job was to curate this flow. A skilled *Herr Ober* would slide the *Neue Freie Presse* onto a regular's table before he even sat down, the wooden handle making a satisfying thwack against the marble. This "Paper Parliament" was where public opinion was forged. It was a pre-digital internet, a place where news was consumed, debated, and often written, all within the same cloud of smoke.

This environment incubates what the sociologist Jürgen Habermas would later identify as the "Public Sphere". Operating as a "third space" distinct from the private home or government institution, the coffee-house allowed private individuals to come together to debate public matters. In an empire where the parliament was often paralyzed by ethnic infighting and bureaucratic inertia, the *Kaffeehaus* became the true forum of political discourse. Arguments that began over the text of a morning editorial often spiraled into pamphlets, manifestos, and move-ments. The newspaper stick was not just a reading aid; it was the scepter of this civic function.

## THE WAITER'S FIEFDOM

The figure who managed this delicate ecosystem was the *Herr Ober* (Head Waiter), but his role was far more complex than mere service. In the golden age of the coffeehouse, the waiter system was a unique micro-economy. The *Herr Ober* was essentially an independent contractor. In many establishments, he was not paid a salary by the owner. Instead, he

had to "buy" the food and drink from the kitchen counter with his own
cash (or tokens) and then resell it to the customer. His income was
derived entirely from the *Trinkgeld* (tip). This created a bizarre alignment
of incentives: the waiter was technically a freelancer operating within
the café's walls. Beneath the *Herr Ober* was a strict military hierarchy:

- The *Zahlkellner* (Pay Waiter): The only one authorized to
  handle money. He carried a massive leather wallet and was
  the final authority on the bill.
- The *Speisenträger* (Food Carrier): Allowed to bring food but
  forbidden to take orders or money.
- The *Piccolo* (Apprentice): Usually a teenage boy, responsible
  for clearing ash, refilling water, and running errands. A *Piccolo*
  might be sent to a nearby tobacconist, or even to the library to
  check a fact for an arguing patron.

This system bred a specific type of character: the omniscient, slightly
arrogant, paternal waiter. He acted as the host rather than a servant. He
knew the intricate social webs of the room. He knew that the gentleman
at Table 4 was avoiding the gentleman at Table 9. He knew which newspapers to reserve for whom. There is a famous story of a Viennese waiter
who, upon seeing a regular customer enter after a ten-year absence (perhaps due to exile or war), simply nodded, walked to the kitchen, and
returned with the man's usual order, saying only, "The Herr Doctor was
away for a while."

### BRONSTEIN AND THE CHESS PLAYER

If the coffeehouse was a living room, it was also a laboratory. Between
1890 and 1938, an astonishing percentage of the 20th century's intellectual architecture was drafted on Viennese marble. The epicenter was
Café Central. It was known as the "Chess School" because of the intense,
smoky games played in the upper arcade, but the real game was history.
The proximity of future antagonists in this single room is dizzying.

At one table, Sigmund Freud might be found sipping a black coffee,
taking a break from his consulting room at Berggasse 19 to observe the

neuroses of the public. A few tables away sat Leon Trotsky, then known as Bronstein, arguing dialectics and playing chess with such ferocity that he often forgot to eat. Trotsky was a fixture. He lived in Vienna from 1907 to 1914, and the Central was his office. He wrote articles for *Pravda* there, played endless games of chess against the café owner, and held court with fellow dissidents. He was so embedded in the furniture that he became a local joke.

There is a famous, perhaps apocryphal, anecdote that captures the establishment's blindness to the fire in its midst. When Count Leopold Berchtold, the Austrian Foreign Minister, was warned in 1914 that war could trigger a revolution in Russia, he reportedly scoffed: "And who will lead this revolution? Perhaps Herr Bronstein sitting over there at the Café Central?" It was a fatal underestimation. The coffeehouse allowed these figures to exist on the margins, surviving on cheap coffee and free heat while they formulated theories that would dismantle the very empire that sheltered them. Tragically, the same space also hosted a failed artist from Linz named Adolf Hitler. In 1913, he was scraping by in Vienna, selling watercolors and absorbing the virulent anti-Semitism of the city's populist mayor, Karl Lueger. The coffeehouse was a neutral container; it amplified the psychoanalysis of Freud and the modernism of Loos, but it also incubated the hatreds that would eventually burn the coffeehouses down.

## A ROOM OF ONE'S OWN (KIND OF)

For much of the 19th century, the coffeehouse was a masculine preserve. While there were no explicit statutes barring women, social codes were rigid. A "respectable" woman did not enter a coffeehouse alone. To do so was to invite suspicion; a woman sitting alone with a newspaper was assumed to be a radical, a revolutionary, or a prostitute. So, where did the women go? They went to the *Konditorei*.

Establishments like Demel, Sluka, or Gerstner were the female domain. Here, the architecture was lighter—Rococo pastels, gold leaf, and mirrors—and the menu focused on hot chocolate and cream cakes rather than strong coffee and cigars. The *Konditorei* was a safe public space for socialization without male chaperones. It wasn't until the interwar period of the 1920s, with the rise of the "New Woman" and the collapse of imperial etiquette, that the gender barrier shattered. Women began to claim the marble tables, the cigarettes, and the newspaper sticks for themselves, integrating the *Wohnzimmer* for the first time.


JURISPRUDENCE OF JAM

In Vienna, coffee is the vehicle, but *Mehlspeise* (pastry) is the destination. And no pastry has generated more litigation than the Sachertorte. This dense chocolate cake, coated in apricot jam and encased in a hard chocolate glaze, sparked a legal battle that lasted longer than the Second World War. The combatants were two pillars of Viennese society: the Hotel Sacher and the Café Demel.

The Hotel Sacher was founded by the son of Franz Sacher, the apprentice chef who allegedly invented the cake in 1832 for Prince Metternich. Café Demel was the Imperial and Royal Court Confectionery, the "Chanel of chocolate," which had once supplied the Emperor himself. The dispute exploded in 1954 but was rooted in a decades-old argument over ownership. Demel claimed they had purchased the rights to the "Original" name from a destitute grandson of Franz Sacher in the 1930s. The Hotel Sacher claimed birthright.

The "Cake War" was fought in the Austrian courts for nine years. Judges, culinary historians, and chemistry experts were called to testify. The argument did not hinge on taste, but on engineering.

- The Sacher Argument: The apricot jam belongs in the middle, sandwiching two layers of sponge, as well as under the icing.
- The Demel Argument: The jam belongs only under the icing, on top of a solid, single sponge, as per the original 1832 method.
- The Mechanism: The use of butter versus margarine was analyzed. The specific gravity of the chocolate was debated.

In 1963, the court finally delivered its verdict. It ruled in favor of the Hotel Sacher. Only they had the right to the phrase "The Original

Sachertorte." Demel was forced to rebrand their product as the "Eduard Sacher Torte."

*The legal definition of the* Sachertorte *hinged on the engineering of the jam layer.*

Today, tourists line up for hours in the wind to eat the legally sanctioned cake at the Hotel, while locals often whisper that the Demel version—moister, denser, and free of the sponge-splitting jam layer—is the superior feat of engineering. In Vienna, sugar is a matter of law.

### THE STAMMTISCH

While the coffeehouse was theoretically open to all, it possessed a rigorous internal geography. This was physically manifested in the *Stammtisch*—the Regulars' Table. In every traditional café, the best table —usually situated in a corner with a commanding view of the entrance but protected from the draft of the door—was permanently reserved. A small metal sign, often engraved with the word *Stammtisch* or simply *Reserviert*, sat upon the marble.

A stranger could not sit there. Even if the café was entirely empty and the *Stammtisch* was the only free surface, it remained forbidden. It belonged to a specific tribe: the local chess club, a cabal of politicians, or a circle of critics. Membership was by invitation only. It was a social anchor. The *Stammtisch* served a vital psychological function in a disjointed city. It was a standing appointment. If you belonged to a *Stammtisch*, you never needed to make a plan. You simply arrived at 4:00

PM, knowing your community would be there. It was the original "third place"—not home, not work, but the anchor of identity.

### Taxonomy of Foam

To the uninitiated, the Viennese coffee menu is a baffling code. You cannot simply order "a coffee." You must specify the precise ratio of milk, foam, and water. Historically, waiters at the most fastidious houses carried a color chart, a paint-swatch of browns, so patrons could point to the exact shade they desired.

- *Kleiner Schwarzer* (Little Black): A simple, single espresso. The base unit of time.
- *Verlängerter* (Lengthened): An espresso diluted with an equal amount of hot water. It mirrors the Americano, but is smoother.
- *Melange*: The standard. Half coffee, half steamed milk, topped with milk foam. It differs from a cappuccino in the roast (lighter) and the milk texture (softer).
- *Einspänner* (One-Horse Carriage): A strong black coffee served in a glass handle-mug, topped with a massive, insulating dollop of cold whipped cream and dusted with powdered sugar.

The *Einspänner* is a functional drink, not a dessert. It was designed for the *Fiaker* drivers—the coachmen of Vienna. They needed to hold the reins with one hand and their coffee with the other. The cold cream acted as a lid, keeping the coffee underneath hot for nearly an hour, while the thick glass handle kept their frozen fingers warm. It was an ergonomic solution to the problem of winter work.

- *Fiaker*: The boozy cousin of the *Einspänner*, spiked with rum or kirsch (cherry brandy). A morning drink for the working class, an evening drink for the poets.

## BUCHTELN IN THE BUNKER

The First World War shattered the empire; the Second World War nearly destroyed the city. The Jewish intelligentsia—the writers, critics, and wits who were the nervous system of coffeehouse culture—were murdered or exiled. The Anschluss of 1938 turned the cafés into sites of exclusion and terror. The "democratic club" was suddenly closed to half its members. By 1945, Vienna was a gray ruin, divided into occupation zones. In this bleak landscape, the coffeehouse had to reinvent itself. It could no longer be a palace of imperial nostalgia. It had to become a shelter.

This era belongs to Café Hawelka. Opened in 1939 by Leopold and Josefine Hawelka, it survived the war to become the headquarters of the post-war avant-garde. Unlike the polished Central, Hawelka was dark, smoky, and cluttered. The walls were plastered with posters; the air was thick with the acrid smoke of Gitanes. It became the living room for the Vienna Group of surrealists, who had no money but plenty of time.

The heart of Hawelka was not the coffee, but the *Buchteln*. These are sweet yeast buns filled with *Powidl* (plum jam). Every evening at roughly 10:00 PM, Josefine Hawelka would pull a fresh tray from the oven. The scent of baking yeast would cut through the cigarette smoke, acting as a dinner bell for the hungry artists. It was a ritual of survival. Hawelka proved that the coffeehouse did not need marble or mirrors to function; it only needed warmth and a matriarch.

## THE INTANGIBLE HERITAGE

By the 1960s, the Viennese coffeehouse seemed destined for extinction. The speed of the Italian espresso bar and the efficiency of American commerce made the idea of sitting for three hours over a single cup seem obsolete, even decadent. Many historic cafés were gutted, renovated with Formica, or turned into car showrooms. But the city realized, just in time, that it was losing its distinct social technology. A massive restoration effort began in the 1990s. In 2011, UNESCO officially added "Viennese Coffeehouse Culture" to its list of Intangible Cultural Heritage. The designation citation contained a line that perfectly summarized three centuries of history: These are places where time and space are consumed, but only the coffee is found on the bill.

Today, if you walk into the back room of Café Sperl or Landtmann, past the tourists taking selfies with their Sachertorte, you will still find him. He is an old man in a wool coat. He is reading a newspaper clamped into a wooden stick. His *Melange* is lukewarm. He has not moved in two hours. And silently, without a word, a waiter in a tuxedo slides a fresh glass of water onto his table. The lease is renewed. The coffeehouse provided the infrastructure for the intellectual life of the city, not through the quality of its coffee, but through the generosity of its void.

# 26

# SOLUBLE FUEL: THE WAR ON SLEEP

T*he entrenchment near Bastogne was less a shelter and more a geological indentation in the frozen topography of the Ardennes, a depression in the snow packed firm by the boots of the 101st Airborne. It was December 1944, and the ambient temperature had plummeted to -10°C (14°F), a thermal range where shivering ceased to function as an effective warming mechanism. A soldier we'll call Private First Class Miller sat at the base of the pit, knees drawn to his chest, his respiration visible in short, rhythmic plumes. The artillery barrage had paused, leaving a heavy silence that amplified the sound of timber cracking in the frost and the distant, mechanical idle of Panzer engines.*

*Miller's hands were stiff, manipulating objects with the clumsiness of wooden blocks wrapped in wet wool, yet they managed to execute the most critical logistical ritual of the night. He manipulated his K-ration box, bypassing the tin of "pork luncheon meat"—a sodium-rich cylinder of processed protein—to locate the primary objective. It was a small, foil-laminated envelope, dimensions roughly equivalent to a playing card, secured within the accessory packet. He compromised the seal with his teeth, discarding the foil onto the frozen substrate. Into his canteen cup, stained dark from oxidation and residue, he decanted a few ounces of water melted over a smudge pot. The water was not boiling; it was tepid, holding suspended ash particles. He dispensed the brown powder from the packet into the fluid. It did not bloom or resist saturation like traditional grounds. It dissolved with immediate chemical compliance, an oily, dark suspension dispersing into the gray water like ink.*

*He consumed the mixture in two rapid swallows. The flavor profile was dominated by charred metal, scorched caramel, and a chemical sharpness reminiscent of a galvanic battery. It was objectively the poorest quality coffee he had ever encountered, yet as the caffeine successfully antagonized his adenosine receptors, temporarily staving off the lethargy of hypothermia, Miller registered a perceptible thermal shift in his chest. This functioned more as a logistical necessity than a culinary beverage. It was the only variable in the Ardennes Forest that tethered him to a reality where domestic infrastructure existed, where morning was signaled by a kitchen table rather than a mobilization order.*

*To the Quartermaster Corps, this slurry was cataloged as "Coffee, Soluble." To the infantry shivering in the Belgian woods or perspiring in the humidity of Guadalcanal, it was simply "Joe." It served as the metabolic fuel of the American military apparatus, a substance that transformed the biological requirement of sleep into a deferrable option. However, the trajectory of that packet into Miller's possession is not merely a narrative of combat; it is the account of how the U.S. military, in a calculated effort to maintain the alertness of eleven million personnel, dismantled the traditional culture of coffee and reconstructed it through the lens of industrial efficiency.*

### The Arithmetic of Survival

When the United States mobilized for the Second World War in December 1941, the War Department confronted a supply chain equation that failed to reconcile. The modern mechanized army was a resource-intensive entity, consuming petroleum, munitions, and steel at rates that challenged the predictive models of Washington planners. Yet the human component of that machine—the infantryman—possessed a metabolic requirement deemed as critical as aviation fuel for a B-17 bomber: caffeine.

General Edmund B. Gregory, the Quartermaster General, operated with a singular focus on shipping physics. His mandate was to transport immense tonnages of materiel across two oceans while hostile naval forces attempted to intercept the tonnage. In his logistical ledgers, coffee represented a distinct inefficiency. A coffee bean is, structurally, a vessel of dead weight. It is a cellular matrix of cellulose and lignin—wood fiber —serving only as a container for the soluble lipids and alkaloids required for consumption. To ship roasted, whole-bean coffee to forward operating bases necessitated transporting thousands of tons of cellulose that would become refuse the moment the brewing process concluded.

During World War I, the military had attempted to ship roasted beans to the expeditionary forces in France. The outcome was a logistical failure. Pulverizing beans in a muddy trench under indirect fire proved impractical. When the Army attempted shipping pre-ground coffee, the product oxidized within weeks. Oxygen degrades flavor rapidly; once the protective cellulose structure of the bean is compromised, the volatile aromatics fracture and dissipate, turning rancid in the humid atmosphere of cargo holds. By the time the coffee reached the Somme, it was frequently reduced to a flavorless dust.

Gregory's analysts computed the requirements in early 1942, and the data presented a severe bottleneck. To supply the projected force structure with fresh roasted coffee would require shipping capacity equivalent to three Liberty ships every month, dedicated exclusively to beans. A Liberty ship possessed a cargo capacity of approximately 10,000 tons. Allocating 30,000 tons of monthly capacity to a commodity that was 98% water by weight upon consumption was strategically indefensible.

In a conflict where tonnage functioned as the currency of survival— where every cubic meter of cargo hold was weighed against crates of blood plasma, .30-06 ammunition, or tank treads—shipping "waste" was prohibited. The directive from the War Department was unambiguous: Devise a method to transport the caffeine without the cellulose matrix. The objective shifted from flavor preservation to delivery efficiency, effectively conscripting the coffee bean into the industrial war effort.

## ATOMIZING THE BEAN

The concept of "instant" coffee was not a wartime innovation. It had existed as a technological novelty since 1901, when Satori Kato, a Japanese chemist, introduced a soluble powder at the Pan-American

Exposition. It was subsequently commercialized by George Constant Washington, an inventor who observed coffee particulates accumulating on the spout of a silver carafe. However, early iterations of instant coffee, produced by boiling coffee into a dense sludge and dehydrating it on heated rollers, resulted in a severe degradation of quality. The intense thermal contact incinerated the delicate volatile compounds—the aldehydes and ketones that constitute the coffee's aromatic profile—leaving a residue that tasted of carbon and ash.

By the late 1930s, a new methodology had emerged, driven by the surplus crisis in Brazil. Overwhelmed by excess inventory, Brazil had resorted to incinerating millions of bags of coffee in locomotive furnaces to stabilize global prices. The Brazilian government engaged Nestlé to develop a preservation method that would salvage the inventory rather than destroy it. Nestlé's lead chemist, Max Morgenthaler, dedicated seven years to refining a technique known as spray-drying.

The physics of spray-drying were elegant, mechanical, and industrial. The process initiated with extraction. Unlike a gravity-fed percolation, the industrial method utilized massive stainless steel pressure vessels. Water was forced through the coffee grounds at temperatures significantly exceeding the boiling point, often reaching 175°C (347°F). At this thermal extreme, the water did not merely extract oils; it hydrolyzed the cellular structure of the bean, fracturing the wood fibers into fermentable sugars and astringent tannins. This increased the yield—the percentage of solid material extracted from the bean—from the standard 20% to nearly 50%. While economically advantageous, this hydrolysis introduced harsh, woody flavors into the concentrate.

Once this viscous, black concentrate was synthesized, it required dehydration. Morgenthaler designed a silo, five stories in elevation, containing superheated air circulating in a cyclonic vortex. At the apex of the tower, high-pressure hydraulic nozzles atomized the liquid coffee concentrate into a microscopic mist. The pressure at the nozzle aperture exceeded 172 bar (2,500 psi).

*Morgenthaler's soluble coffee technique used high heat and pressure to preserve natural flavor and extend shelf life.*

As the microscopic droplets entered the tower, they encountered the cyclonic current of air heated to between 200°C and 260°C (400°F–500°F). The surface-area-to-volume ratio of the mist was immense, facilitating near-instantaneous evaporation. In a fraction of a second, the water flashed into steam, and the remaining coffee solids formed tiny, hollow spheres. These spheres descended to the collection hopper at the base of the tower like a brown precipitate. Because the phase change from liquid to gas occurred so rapidly, the coffee solids were not "cooked" in the traditional sense of prolonged conduction. However, the initial high-pressure extraction had already altered the chemical baseline.

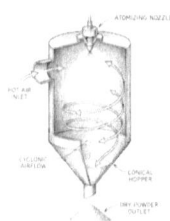

*Spray drying uses cyclonic heat to instantly dehydrate coffee mist, creating the "beads" of instant coffee.*

Nestlé launched the product as "Nescafé" in 1938. Upon the outbreak of war, the U.S. government bypassed commercial negotiation; they commandeered the technology. The War Production Board issued Limitation Order L-82, effectively nationalizing the instant coffee production capacity of the United States. Competitors such as Maxwell House and

Chase & Sanborn were compelled to adopt the spray-drying methodology immediately.

The consequence was a frantic industrial mobilization. In New Jersey
and New York, massive stainless steel drying towers were constructed
with urgency, operating on a continuous twenty-four-hour cycle. The
atmosphere inside these facilities was saturated with a fine, hygroscopic
dust that coated the respiratory tracts of the workforce—predominantly
women—who managed the packaging of the powder into the newly
engineered foil-laminated packets.

*The foil-laminated packet allowed coffee to survive the humidity of the
jungle and the damp of the trenches.*

The military specification for "Coffee, Soluble, Type C" prioritized
shelf-stability and solubility above all other metrics. If the powder
dissolved in cold water and delivered a measurable dose of caffeine, it
met the standard.

### GREEN HELL AND HOBO THERMODYNAMICS

The tactical deployment of this "Soldier's Fuel" varied significantly
based on the theater of operations. In the Pacific, the interaction with
coffee was defined by the "Green Hell" environment. On islands such as
Peleliu, Guadalcanal, and New Guinea, the biosphere was actively
hostile. Relative humidity remained near 90%, and ambient temperatures rarely descended below 29°C (85°F).

For the Marines of the 1st Division, consuming a hyper-heated
beverage in such conditions appeared counter-intuitive. Yet, consumption rates were high. A prevailing theory of "thermoregulation" existed

among the troops—unsupported by formal medical doctrine but adhered to in the field. The hypothesis suggested that ingesting boiling coffee would induce a systemic diaphoretic response (sweating). Once the skin was saturated with perspiration, even minimal airflow—a rarity under the triple-canopy jungle—would facilitate evaporative cooling. It was a severe method of thermal management, combating heat with heat, but in the delirium of the tropics, it provided a perceived physiological benefit.

However, the primary utility of coffee in the Pacific was chemical masking. Potable water was the scarcest commodity in the theater. Sources were often stagnant creeks, muddy shell craters, or canvas lister bags exposed to direct solar radiation. To mitigate the risk of dysentery and cholera, all water required treatment with Halazone tablets. Halazone, a chlorine-based compound, rendered water bacteriologically safe but imparted a nausea-inducing flavor profile similar to a mixture of swimming pool water and medicinal alcohol.

Troops discovered that the only substance potent enough to neutralize the taste of Halazone was the concentrated bitterness of the "Type C" powder. The heavy tannins, the metallic edge of the hydrolysis, and the scorched caramel notes of the spray-drying process were aggressive enough to mask the chlorine. For a Marine on Okinawa, the sensory experience of victory was not a clean cup of Arabica; it was a specific, metallic cocktail of chlorine, iodine, and scorched coffee solids, consumed from an aluminum cup that retained the odor of gun oil.

In the European Theater, the challenge was not humidity, but thermodynamics. The standard issue M-1910 canteen cup, constructed of aluminum, presented a thermal conductivity problem. Aluminum transfers heat rapidly, causing the vessel to become searingly hot upon contact with boiling water, blistering the lips, while simultaneously losing thermal energy to the freezing air. A soldier possessed a window of perhaps three minutes to consume the beverage before it reverted to a cold, brown sludge.

*The aluminum M-1910 cup conducted heat rapidly, forcing soldiers to*
*drink their "Joe" quickly before it froze.*

Soldiers became practitioners of "hobo thermodynamics." They fabricated "Benghazi Burners" from discarded ration cans, filling them with sand saturated in gasoline. These improvised stoves produced a soot-heavy flame capable of boiling water in five minutes. More enterprising soldiers utilized small quantities of Composition C-4 explosive. C-4 possessed high stability and would not detonate without a blasting cap; instead, it combusted with a clean, intense white heat that could bring a canteen cup to a boil in thirty seconds. The risk was not detonation, but toxicity—the fumes were noxious, and soldiers reported that coffee heated over C-4 induced a headache rivaling severe alcohol withdrawal.

When light discipline on the front lines prohibited open flames, soldiers resorted to "chuting." This technique involved tearing the packet and depositing the dry, granular powder directly onto the tongue, followed by a swig of cold water. The powder would coagulate in the oral cavity, adhering to the palate and gums, forming a bitter paste before dissolving. This was a crude, functional energy delivery system, stripped of all ritual. It delivered a rapid caffeine spike, often inducing tachycardia and tremors within minutes. Stripped of the pretense of pleasure, it functioned as a pharmacological intervention instead of a meal.

Through this widespread usage, the moniker "Joe" solidified. While etymologists debate the origins—some tracing it to Josephus Daniels, the Navy Secretary who banned alcohol—the war codified the meaning. Coffee was "Joe" for the "G.I. Joe." It was the common soldier's consumable, stripped of the aristocratic associations of tea or wine. It was a tool of masculine endurance, the substance consumed prior to executing difficult objectives.

. . .

RATIONING THE HOME FRONT

While the military absorbed vast quantities of instant coffee, the civilian population faced a supply shock that altered American domestic life. In 1942, German U-boats began targeting the slow, heavy freighters transporting coffee from Brazil. The Atlantic supply chain fractured.

In response, the Office of Price Administration issued Ration Order 12. The directive was severe: every citizen over the age of fifteen was restricted to one pound (0.45 kg) of coffee every five weeks.

The mathematics of this ration were punitive. A standard pound of coffee yields approximately 40 to 50 cups depending on dilution. Distributed over 35 days, this allowed for barely more than one cup per day. For a nation accustomed to unrestricted consumption, this constituted a crisis. "Coffee panics" erupted in retail environments across the Midwest. Lines extended around city blocks upon rumors of fresh inventory. Hoarding became a widespread behavior, with households concealing tins of Maxwell House, preserving them for significant events.

To extend their limited supplies, American kitchens utilized "extenders." This euphemism covered a range of botanical substitutes. Chicory root, a staple of New Orleans culinary tradition, was the most common additive, contributing body and a dark hue, but also a woody, earthy bitterness. Others utilized roasted barley, which provided a malty sweetness devoid of caffeine. The most extreme measures involved mixing in roasted soybeans, which introduced an oily, vegetal characteristic to the brew.

However, the most detrimental practice—one that would imprint a lasting scar on the American palate—was the "re-brew." Consumers would retain the wet, spent grounds from the morning preparation, add a minimal quantity of fresh grounds, and boil the entire mixture again for the evening consumption.

Scientifically, this practice is disastrous for flavor integrity. The desirable compounds in coffee—the organic acids and fruit notes—extract early in the brewing process. Prolonged boiling of spent grounds extracts the breakdown products of the cellulose structure: heavy tannins and long-chain carbohydrates. The result is a brew that is intensely bitter, astringent, and lacking in nuance. It coats the tongue and desiccates the oral mucosa.

This is the invisible legacy of the war: It conditioned an entire generation to equate "strong coffee" with "bitter coffee." The American palate was systematically desensitized. The subtle acidity of a high-altitude bean was no longer a marker of quality; it was interpreted as weakness. The preferred profile became one that tasted of prolonged extraction in an iron vessel. By the conclusion of rationing, the American consumer had largely forgotten the taste of fresh coffee, learning instead to value the burn.

## THE RISE OF THE COFFEE BREAK

As the war concluded and the industrial machine shifted back to civilian production, a new sociological phenomenon emerged, rooted in the logistical habits of the war: the Coffee Break. This was not merely a pause in work; it evolved into a contested labor right.

During the war, factories running 24-hour shifts to produce munitions found that providing coffee breaks increased aggregate output and reduced accident rates. The caffeine maintained vigilance during the "graveyard shift." Post-war, as veterans returned to the assembly lines and office blocks, they carried the expectation of this ritual with them.

In 1952, the Pan-American Coffee Bureau launched a targeted advertising campaign with the slogan, "Give Yourself a Coffee Break—and Get What Coffee Gives to You." The campaign was designed to institutionalize the morning and afternoon pause. It succeeded beyond the wildest projections of the advertisers. The "coffee break" became a battleground in union negotiations. The United Auto Workers (UAW) and other major labor organizations began to include specific clauses in their contracts guaranteeing two 15-minute breaks per shift.

In a famous 1964 threat of a wildcat strike, the UAW nearly halted production at Chrysler plants—not over wages, but because the company attempted to limit the coffee break. The result was that coffee became legally encoded into the American workday. It was no longer a leisure activity; it was a negotiated condition of employment, a fuel stop required to keep the human machinery of capitalism functioning.

### Diner Culture and the Bottomless Cup

When the eleven million servicemen returned in 1945, they brought with them a specific set of consumption habits conditioned by years of combat. They were acclimated to coffee that was:

1. Instantaneous.
2. High temperature (approx. 85°C/185°F).
3. Available in infinite volume.

This demand reshaped the American culinary landscape. The "Diner" exploded in popularity as the secular community center of the post-war era. These establishments offered a promise of normalcy. But to satisfy the returning GIs, diner operators could not utilize delicate brewing methods or limited serving sizes. They required volume.

This necessity led to the dominance of the Percolator and the Glass Carafe on the hot plate. The physics of the diner coffee system are designed for durability rather than quality. In a percolator, boiling water is continuously cycled up a central tube and sprayed over the grounds repeatedly. This recirculation effectively boils the coffee. As demonstrated by the "re-brew" during rationing, this process strips the coffee of subtlety.

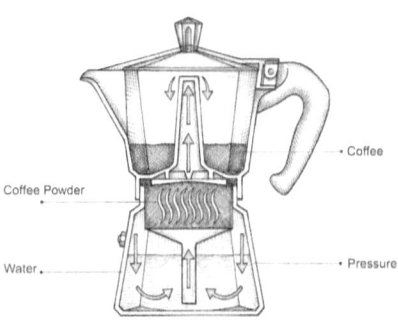

*The percolator recirculates boiling water through the grounds, stripping away nuance in favor of "strong" bitterness.*

Once brewed, the coffee resided in a glass carafe on a heating element maintained at 85°C. At this temperature, chemical degradation continues. The acids decompose into quinic acid (which tastes sour) and the oils oxidize into rancid polymers. Coffee that has remained on a heating element for an hour possesses a chemically distinct profile from fresh coffee; it is thicker, tarrier, and carries notes of burnt rubber.

To sustain this business model, and to finance the concept of the "Bottomless Cup," diners were forced to compromise on inputs. They could not utilize expensive Arabica beans. They utilized blends heavy with Robusta—the cheaper, heartier, more bitter species. They brewed it with a high water-to-coffee ratio to maximize margin.

The returning soldiers did not object. To them, weak, hot, brown water was the flavor of security. It was the taste of absence—the absence of conflict. The sheer abundance of it—the server refilling the cup without prompt—was a symbol of American economic victory. The bottomless cup was a statement to the world: The deprivation was over, and the resources were now limitless.

### Flavor Buds and Marketing

The United States exited the war possessing a massive surplus of spray-drying infrastructure. Towers that had produced caffeine for the

Normandy invasion now sought a civilian market. They found it in the burgeoning suburbs.

The coffee conglomerates—Maxwell House, Folgers, Nescafé—pivoted their massive wartime production to the domestic sector. They marketed instant coffee aggressively, utilizing the GIs' acceptance as validation. "Good enough for our boys overseas" evolved into "Good enough for your breakfast table."

The 1950s are often romanticized as a golden age of American prosperity, but for coffee, it was an era of profound degradation. The war had inadvertently solved the most significant problem facing large food conglomerates: inconsistency. Coffee is an agricultural product; it fluctuates from harvest to harvest. But by extracting coffee to exhaustion and converting it into a stable powder, roasters created a fungible commodity. They could blend cheap, bitter Robusta beans from Vietnam or Africa with a minimal fraction of mild Arabica, process it through the high-pressure hydrolyzers, and the result was uniform: a flat, brown, predictable cup.

To vend this chemically stripped product, advertisers adopted the lexicon of the Space Age. "Old fashioned" brewing was framed as domestic drudgery. The new method was instant. "Flavor buds!" the advertisements proclaimed. It was rapid, sanitary, and "scientific." By 1960, nearly one-third of all coffee consumed in the United States was soluble. The art of roasting had been displaced by the science of solubility. The connection between the consumer and the agricultural origin was severed. Coffee originated from a jar, not a tree.


PROJECT HIGH VACUUM

While spray-drying dominated the 1950s, the technology of the war offered one final contribution to the industry: Freeze Drying.

During the conflict, the National Research Corporation (NRC) had been tasked with a critical objective: transporting penicillin and blood plasma to the front lines. Both substances were heat-sensitive; thermal drying caused plasma to coagulate and rendered penicillin inert. The NRC developed high-vacuum technology to dehydrate these biological materials without thermal damage.

Post-war, the NRC sought commercial applications for their high-vacuum pumps. Initially applied to orange juice (resulting in the Minute Maid brand), they eventually turned their attention to coffee. The process, scientifically known as Lyophilization, was fundamentally different from the mechanical violence of spray-drying.

The mechanism involved navigating the "triple point" of water—the precise pressure (0.006 atm) and temperature (0.01°C) where water can exist as solid, liquid, and gas simultaneously.

The process functioned in three distinct phases:

1. **Freeze:** The coffee concentrate is frozen into a solid slab of dark ice, locking the molecular structure in place.
2. **Vacuum:** The ice is granulated and placed in a vacuum chamber. The pressure is reduced to near-vacuum levels.
3. **Sublimation:** Mild heat is applied, but due to the vacuum, the ice does not melt into liquid water. It transitions directly from solid to vapor.

Because the water never reverts to a liquid phase, it does not wash away the aromatics. Because the temperature never reaches the threshold to burn the coffee, the volatile oils—those responsible for floral or fruity notes—are preserved within the crystal matrix.

In 1965, Nestlé launched Taster's Choice, the first mass-market freeze-dried coffee. It was hailed as a technological marvel. It was visually distinct—angular, gold crystals rather than fine brown dust. While superior to spray-dried options, possessing detectable aroma, it remained a shadow of the fresh bean. It was the final victory of convenience over character, solidifying the concept that coffee was a factory-produced good rather than an agricultural yield.

THE LOGISTICS OF LEGACY

The rise of instant coffee was a transaction of values. The culture traded flavor for function, and the complexity of the bean for the certainty of the caffeine. It would require forty years for the American palate to recover from the conditioning of the war, to relearn that coffee could be a fruit rather than merely a fuel. The artisanal movement of the late 20th century was, in many respects, a direct counter-revolution against the "Type C" standardization of the 1940s.

But for a specific generation, in the freezing mud of Europe or the sweltering heat of the Pacific, the finest cup of coffee in the world was not a Geisha varietal brewed with precision. It was five grams of scorched powder, dissolved in a tin cup, consumed under the threat of imminent danger. It was warm, bitter, and—for the brief interval before the shelling resumed—it was sufficient. The war had industrialized coffee, prioritizing shelf-life over flavor, and in doing so, it built the logistical foundation for the global commodity market that followed.

# 27

# PEET'S REVOLT: THE DARKER PATH

N orth Berkeley, California, in the spring of 1966 was a neighborhood defined by two distinct and warring smells. On the days when the wind blew up from Sproul Plaza, the neighborhood carried the acrid, peppery bite of tear gas, the chemical signature of the Free Speech Movement and the anti-war protests that were turning the university into a staging ground for the counterculture. On quieter days, the air was saturated with the sweet, resinous drift of marijuana smoke rising from the Victorian apartments along Telegraph Avenue. But on the morning of April 1st, at the corner of Walnut and Vine Streets, a third smell introduced itself to the neighborhood— one that would eventually outlast the protests, the politics, and the tear gas.

It was heavy, deep, and deeply caramelized. It was an aroma of such intensity that passersby stopped mid-stride, confused by a sensory signal their postwar American brains couldn't quite decode. To a population raised on the thin, metallic steam of instant coffee or the weak percolator brew of the local diner, this new smell was almost alarming. It smelled of earth, carbon, volatile oils, and heat. It smelled, to the uninitiated, like a controlled industrial process occurring in a retail space.

Inside the nondescript storefront at 2124 Vine Street, a man in a starched white lab coat stood over a black cast-iron machine, listening intently to the sound of seeds fracturing. He was not a hippie. He was not a student radical.

*He was a forty-six-year-old Dutchman with the bearing of a Calvinist school-master and a face that seemed carved from teak. His name was Alfred Peet. He regarded the chaos of the 1960s with a mixture of amusement and European detachment, but he regarded the coffee in the United States with unmitigated, professional disgust.*

*He was roasting coffee the way his father had roasted it in the Netherlands and the way his grandfather had roasted it before that: by pushing the bean to its thermal limit, navigating the narrow margin between flavor development and carbonization. To the average American in 1966, coffee was a pale, brownish liquid scooped from a tin can, percolated until dead, and served as a caffeine delivery system to wash down eggs and bacon. It was the "swill" of the previous era—the industrial byproduct of the war years and the supermarket price wars. What Alfred Peet was pulling out of his roaster was something else entirely. It was oily. It was almost black. It smelled of smoke, spice, and soil. By planting his flag in Berkeley, amidst the professors, the radicals, and the connoisseurs, he accidentally ignited a movement that would eventually conquer the world. The "Peetniks"—the loyal disciples who would soon line up around the block for his beans—were the first foot soldiers of the American coffee renaissance.*

### THE MERCHANT OF ALKMAAR

Every revolution requires an outsider to see the rot in the system, someone whose sensory baseline is calibrated differently than the locals. For the American Second Wave, that outsider was Alfred Peet. Born in Alkmaar, Netherlands, in 1920, Peet did not grow up viewing coffee as a grocery item; he grew up viewing it as a craft. His father ran a small "brandery"—a local roast-and-grind shop that was as common in the pre-war Netherlands as a bakery is in France. In the Dutch model, fresh-ness was the primary metric. Households bought bread fresh daily; they bought cheese fresh; and they bought coffee fresh, often while it was still warm from the roaster.

Peet's education was sensory and mechanical rather than academic. As a teenager, his job was to crawl inside the industrial roasting drums to scrub them clean of carbon buildup, a claustrophobic task that inti-mately acquainted him with the residues of the roasting process. He spent hours sorting green beans by hand, training his eye to spot the defects: the "stinkers" (fermented beans), the stones, the twigs, and the insect-damaged shells. In the Peet household, coffee was not a beverage; it was a discipline.

But the true forging of Alfred Peet happened after the Second World War. Following the liberation of Europe—and a stint in a German labor camp that stripped him of any patience for trivialities or incompetence —he left the gray skies of the Netherlands for the humidity of Indonesia. Working in the tea and spice trade in Java and Sumatra, Peet learned the agricultural reality of the crop. He saw the volcanic soil, the labor of the pickers, and the complex, often chaotic supply chains that moved the product to Europe. He learned to distinguish the smell of a clove drying in the sun from the scent of nutmeg in the hull. He learned the difference between tea harvested in the mist of the morning and tea harvested in the heat of the afternoon.

Most importantly, he developed a taste for the heavy, brooding coffees of the archipelago: Sumatra Mandheling, Sulawesi Kalossi, and Java Blawan. These beans were visually unappealing by commercial standards. They were often misshapen, blue-green, and uneven in size. But they possessed a heavy, syrupy body and earthy spice notes—cedar, mushroom, pipe tobacco—that could withstand aggressive heat. When Peet immigrated to the United States in 1955, arriving in San Francisco to work in the import trade, he brought this specific colonial knowledge with him.

What he found in America horrified him. He famously told a colleague that the coffee being served in American diners was "dishwa-ter." But it wasn't just a casual insult; it was a technical assessment of a broken system. He realized that if he wanted a decent cup—a cup that tasted like the Indonesia of his memories—the existing supply chain couldn't provide it. He wasn't trying to be an entrepreneur; he was trying to solve a personal supply problem. He opened his store not to liberate the masses, but because he refused to drink the alternative.

### The Economics of the Loss Leader

Appreciating Peet's dissatisfaction—and the shift in standards implied in this chapter—requires that we understand the formidable enemy he was fighting. In the 1950s and 60s, the American coffee market was an oligopoly controlled by the "Big Three": Maxwell House (General Foods), Folgers (Procter & Gamble), and Hills Bros. These companies were engaged in a fierce price war, battling for the loyalty of the post-war housewife. The supermarket had become the new battlefield of American commerce, and coffee was the weapon of choice. It was the quintessential "loss leader." Grocery stores would sell coffee below cost—sometimes for as little as 49 cents a pound (approx. $1.08/kg)—to lure customers into the store, hoping they would buy high-margin items like cereal or soap once they were there.

To make a profit at these artificially suppressed prices, the "Big Three" had to weaponize chemistry and economics against the bean itself. They systematically dismantled quality in favor of consistency and shelf-life.

First, there was the botanical shift. Following the massive Brazilian frost of 1954, the price of Arabica beans spiked. To keep the cost of a can under a dollar, the Big Three began cutting their blends with Robusta beans from Africa and the newly recovering French Indochina. Robusta (*Coffea canephora*) is a hardy plant that grows at lower altitudes. It is resistant to disease, high in yield, and cheap. It is also bitter, rubbery, and contains nearly double the caffeine of Arabica. By 1960, the average American can was a chemically harsh cocktail of cheap Robusta beans, masked by industrial processing.

Second, there was the "water weight game." Coffee loses mass as it roasts—water evaporates, and organic matter turns to gas. A dark roast might lose 20% of its weight. A light roast loses only 12–14%. The industrial accountants realized that if they roasted the beans very lightly—barely past the First Crack—and then "quenched" them with a heavy spray of water to cool them down, they could seal water weight inside the bean. They were effectively selling water to the consumer at the price of coffee. The result was a high-acid, sour, thin liquid that required milk and sugar to be palatable.

Finally, there was the vacuum tomb. The invention of the "Key Can" allowed roasters to grind coffee, vacuum pack it, and ship it to a ware-house where it could sit for months, or even years. While the vacuum prevented mold, it did not preserve the volatile aromatics. The moment the can was opened with that signature hiss—a sound marketing agencies trained Americans to associate with freshness—the stale, dead aroma of pre-ground coffee was released. The result was a product designed for logistics, not for human consumption. Alfred Peet looked at this industrial landscape and saw fraud. He saw companies selling water, wood fiber, and marketing jingles disguised as coffee. When he opened his store, he did not advertise. He did not have a jingle. He simply opened the door and let the smell drift out.

### MECHANISM: THE PHYSICS OF THE SECOND CRACK

The defining characteristic of Peet's revolution was the roast profile. To understand why Peet's coffee tasted so radically different—and why it polarized the public—we must look at the thermodynamics of the roasting drum. Coffee roasting is a two-stage chemical drama. The first stage is endothermic: the green beans absorb heat, drying out and turning from grassy green to hay-yellow. Then comes the "First Crack," an audible popping sound like popcorn, caused by steam pressure breaking the cellular structure of the seed. Most American industrial coffee in 1966 stopped right here, or shortly after. The beans were light brown, highly acidic, and retained their enzymatic flavors—which, in low-quality coffee, meant grassy, peanutty, or grain-like notes.

Peet went further. He pushed the roast into the Second Crack.

This is a more distinct, snapping sound, akin to dry twigs breaking underfoot. It signals the fracturing of the bean's cellulose matrix as carbon dioxide tries to escape. At this stage, typically around 435°F to 445°F (224°C to 230°C), a process called pyrolysis takes over. The sugars inside the bean (sucrose) aren't just caramelizing; they are breaking down into complex new compounds. The long-chain carbohydrates fracture.

Crucially, the internal lipids—the coffee oils—migrate from the center of the bean to the surface.

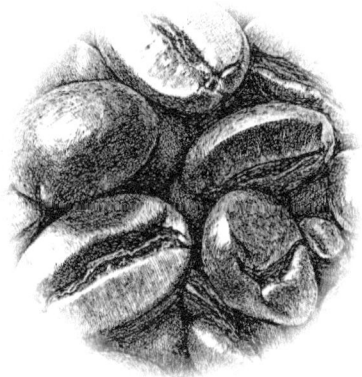

*Peet's "deep roast" pushed the beans until their internal oils migrated to the surface, creating a shiny, black appearance*

This is why Peet's beans looked different: they were shiny, coated in a dark, slick sheen of oil, whereas Folgers beans were dry and matte. This style became known as "deep roasting," though his detractors simply called it "burnt." But it wasn't burnt—or at least, not when Peet did it. He was a master of the machine. He operated a Probat UG-22, a German-built roaster that he treated with more respect than he treated most people. He knew exactly how to manipulate the gas flame and the airflow to caramelize the sugars without carbonizing the bean into ash. He was aiming for the "sweet spot" where the acidity (the sharp, sour notes) burned off, replaced by the bittersweet compounds of roast character.

The result was a cup of coffee that had immense "body"—a viscosity and mouthfeel that Americans had never experienced. It was rich, spicy, and smoky. It lingered on the tongue. For a generation raised on thin, tinny blends, tasting a Peet's Sumatra for the first time was a physiological shock. It was like switching from light beer to a Guinness, or from milk chocolate to 90% cacao. It possessed a pungent intensity that demanded attention.

### The Temple of Vine Street

The store Peet opened in Berkeley was aggressively un-modern. In an era of chrome diners, neon signage, and space-age plastics, "Peet's Coffee, Tea & Spices" looked like a merchant's warehouse from the 19th century. There were no tables. There were no chairs. There was certainly no Wi-Fi or electrical outlets. There was no espresso machine hissing in the corner—Peet actually disliked espresso, considering it a "fast food" method that rushed the extraction and prioritized speed over flavor. The aesthetic was wood, glass, and burlap. Large teak bins held the beans, labeled with their specific geographic origins—Sumatra Mandheling, Guatemala Antigua, Sulawesi Kalossi—rather than marketing buzzwords.

*The Peet's aesthetic focused on the raw ingredient, displaying beans in bulk bins like spices or grain.*

The centerpiece of the room was the roaster itself, which Peet operated in full view of the customers behind a waist-high counter. This was a radical act of transparency. In the industrial model, roasting happened in massive, windowless factories in New Jersey or New Orleans, using continuous roasters that processed thousands of pounds an hour. Peet turned the manufacturing process into theater. Customers could watch the beans turn from green to yellow to brown; they could smell the smoke; they could hear the cracks. They could see the sweat on Peet's forehead as he pulled the "tryer"—a small sampling scoop—to check the bean color against the ambient light.

The air inside the shop was a physical force. It smelled of cardamom, tea leaves, and the overwhelming, smoky punch of dark-roasted coffee. This sensory environment acted as a filter: if a customer didn't like strong smells, they didn't belong there. Peet presided over this domain with an intimidating, autocratic authority. He did not believe in the American maxim that "the customer is always right." In Alfred Peet's shop, the customer was usually wrong, and it was Peet's job to correct them.

If a customer asked for a pound of coffee ground for a percolator, Peet would scowl. He might lecture them on why the percolator was a barbaric instrument that boiled coffee to death, extracting only bitterness and tannins. He would suggest, strongly, that they buy a French press or a chemically bonded paper filter cone. If they asked for decaf, he might suggest they drink water. If they asked for low-fat milk, he would look at them as if they had asked for motor oil. "I don't sell coffee to people who don't know how to drink it," he was known to say. He once refused to sell beans to a customer because they admitted they were going to keep the coffee in the freezer, a practice Peet believed killed the flavor.

This curmudgeonly attitude, paradoxically, was his greatest marketing asset. In a counterculture that rejected corporate slickness and fake smiles, Peet's gruff authenticity was magnetic. He was the "anti-salesman," dispensing truth as much as product. In a world of "Mad Men" advertising, Peet was the stern European mentor telling you to eat your vegetables—or in this case, to drink your coffee black.

## THE MAJOR'S BLEND

One specific interaction captures the collaborative nature of the shop. Among the loyal customers was a retired army officer named Key Dickason. Dickason was a connoisseur who loved the dark, heavy roasts, but he was always tinkering, asking Peet to mix different percentages of beans a little more Guatemala for acidity, a little more New Guinea for body. Peet, usually resistant to input, respected Dickason's palate. They spent weeks refining a specific blend, roasting and cupping, roasting and cupping. Finally, they hit upon a combination that Peet agreed was exceptional. It was rich, smooth, and incredibly potent. When Peet put it on the menu board, he didn't call it "Peet's Special." He named it Major Dickason's Blend.

It became the store's bestseller and remains the signature blend of the company to this day. But the story illustrates a key shift: coffee was moving from a static product to a participatory culture. The customers weren't just consumers; they were constituents. They felt ownership over the shop.

### THE FIRST SIP

Standing in the shop on Vine Street in 1968, a representative student from UC Berkeley—let's call him David—would have experienced a profound disruption of his culinary expectations. He is twenty years old, wearing surplus army fatigues, surviving on dining hall food and instant Maxwell House made with hot tap water. He wanders into the shop because he smells the smoke from three blocks away. He waits in line for twenty minutes. When he reaches the front, he is intimidated by the man in the white coat. He buys a quarter-pound of the Sumatra. He takes it back to his shared apartment. He follows Peet's strict instructions, written on a small pamphlet: boil the water, wait thirty seconds so it's not boiling (200°F/93°C) to avoid scorching the grounds, and pour it over the grounds in a Chemex flask.

*Peet taught his customers to brew manually, rejecting the electric percolator in favor of the chemist's flask.*

The first sip is disorienting. David is used to coffee that hits the high notes—sour, metallic, thin. This liquid is heavy. It sits on the tongue with the weight of cream, even though it's black. It doesn't taste like "coffee" in the way he understands the word. It tastes like dark chocolate, pipe tobacco, and wet soil. There is no acidity to make his mouth pucker. Instead, there is a lingering aftertaste—a finish—that stays with him for twenty minutes. This was the "Peet's epiphany." It wasn't just that the coffee was stronger; it was that it was a completely different beverage category. It transformed coffee from a utility (caffeine) into an experience (flavor). Once a consumer crossed that threshold, they could never go back to the can. They were ruined for Folgers forever.

### THE TRIBE OF THE PEETNIKS

Berkeley provided the perfect soil for Peet's seeds to germinate. The university town was filled with academics, writers, and students who had traveled to Europe and knew what coffee could be. But more importantly, the neighborhood of North Berkeley was coalescing into what would later be called the "Gourmet Ghetto." Just a few blocks away, Alice Waters would soon open Chez Panisse, championing fresh, local ingredients. The Cheese Board Collective was selling Gruyère and sourdough. Peet was the anchor of this culinary awakening.

Drinking Peet's coffee became a signifier of cultural capital. If a resident had a grease-stained bag of Peet's beans on their kitchen counter, it meant they were in the know. It meant they cared about quality over convenience. It meant they were willing to grind their own beans every morning—a ritual Peet insisted upon, calling pre-ground coffee "dead on arrival." These loyalists became known as "Peetniks." They treated the store on Walnut Street as a shrine. On Saturday mornings, the line would stretch down the block. But unlike the modern café queue, where people stare at their phones, the line at Peet's was a social event, a salon of the intelligentsia. Professors argued about the Vietnam War; hippies discussed the Grateful Dead; physicists from the Lawrence Berkeley Lab scribbled equations on napkins while waiting for their pound of Garuda Blend.

Peet himself stood behind the counter, often wearing a tie beneath his lab coat, measuring out beans on a brass balance scale. He educated his customers one by one. He taught them the vocabulary of flavor: "winy," "earthy," "full-bodied." He was raising the coffee literacy of an entire city, creating a market where none had existed.

## THE PILGRIMS FROM SEATTLE

The impact of Alfred Peet would have remained a local Berkeley phenomenon—a quirky footnote in Bay Area history—if not for three young men who walked into his shop in March of 1970. Jerry Baldwin (an English teacher), Zev Siegl (a history teacher), and Gordon Bowker (a writer) were friends from Seattle. They were looking for a business idea. They loved coffee, but Seattle in 1970 was a desert of instant powder and diner swill. They had heard rumors about the Dutchman in Berkeley who roasted the "real stuff".

They made the pilgrimage. Alfred Peet did not just sell them beans; he adopted them as apprentices. For the summer of 1970, the Seattle trio essentially interned at Peet's. It was a transfer of knowledge that would reshape the global economy. Peet taught them how to "cup" coffee—the loud, slurping aspiration technique used to spray coffee over the palate to aerate it and detect subtle notes. He taught them how to listen to the roaster. He showed them the importance of the Second Crack. When they asked what roaster to buy, Peet told them to buy a Probat from Germany—the Mercedes-Benz of roasters. He warned them that it was expensive, but that using anything else was a waste of time and money.

*Alfred Peet insisted on the Probat UG-22; he believed only the conductive heat of a vintage German cast-iron drum could penetrate the beans deeply enough to achieve his 'spicy' roast profile.*

When they returned to Seattle to open their store in Pike Place Market in 1971, they named it Starbucks (after the first mate in *Moby-Dick*). But the DNA of the store was 100% Alfred Peet. Consider the early Starbucks model: No espresso bar, as they sold only whole beans, tea, and spices; the aesthetic of bins, wood floors, and burlap sacks; and most importantly, the roast. For the first year, they didn't even roast their own coffee. Alfred Peet roasted the beans in Berkeley, packed them onto a truck, and shipped them north to Seattle. When they finally started roasting, they copied Peet's profile exactly. They roasted dark, oily, and heavy. It is one of the great ironies of business history: Starbucks, the company that would later become the symbol of corporate globalization and automated espresso, began as a humble homage to a grumpy Dutchman's uncompromising standards.

### THE BREAKUP AND THE SCHISM

The relationship between Peet and his apprentices followed the classic arc of master and student: admiration, emulation, and eventually, friction. As Starbucks grew, the founders began to tinker. They wanted to expand. They started experimenting with slightly lighter roasts—though still very dark by industry standards—and eventually, the addition of the espresso bar.

In 1984, the Starbucks founders—Baldwin and Bowker—actually bought Peet's Coffee when Alfred decided to retire. For a brief period, the two companies were siblings. But the cultures were diverging. Starbucks was becoming faster, more commercial. Peet's remained the stubborn guardian of the dark roast. The defining split happened in 1987. Howard Schultz, a former employee of Starbucks who had been captivated by the espresso bars of Milan, convinced the original founders to sell him the Starbucks name and assets. Baldwin and Bowker, preferring the serious, whole-bean model of Peet's, kept the Berkeley company and sold the Seattle startup.

This moment cleaved the coffee world in two. Starbucks went on to become the "Third Place"—a social hub focused on milk-based beverages, speed, and ubiquity. Peet's remained the "Church of the Bean"—focused on freshness, sourcing, and the deep roast. While Starbucks conquered the suburbs, Peet's held the moral high ground of the connoisseur, at least for a while.


### Legacy: The Bridge to the Third Wave

Alfred Peet was the singular force that initiated the Second Wave. Historians of the industry divide coffee history into three waves: the First Wave of commodity coffee and vacuum cans (Folgers, Maxwell House); the Second Wave of enjoyment, origins, dark roasts, and the café experience (Peet's, Starbucks); and the Third Wave of coffee as fruit, light roasts, and terroir transparency (Blue Bottle, Intelligentsia). Peet proved that Americans would pay a premium for quality. He proved that freshness mattered. He proved that coffee could be an artisanal product, not just a grocery staple.

However, Peet himself remained ambivalent about the industry he spawned. He sold his business in 1979 and retired to a quiet life, watching from a distance as "specialty coffee" exploded into a multi-billion dollar industry. He was often critical of the direction it took. He hated the trend of flavored coffees—"Hazelnut is for squirrels," he might have grumbled —and he viewed the 20-ounce latte as an abomination that drowned the flavor of the coffee in milk and sugar. To Peet, the bean was the point. Everything else was a distraction.

Alfred Peet died in 2007, but if one visits North Berkeley today, the original store on Vine Street is still there. It has been renovated, and the company is now part of a massive conglomerate (JAB Holding Company), but a small museum in the back corner pays tribute to the founder. The roasting machines have been moved to a factory in Alameda to meet federal air quality regulations, but the smell remains in the cultural memory. Every time a consumer walks into a high-end coffee shop today —whether it's a minimalist Third Wave lab or a corner Starbucks—they are walking into a space that exists because Alfred Peet cleared the ground. He was the bridge. He stood in the wreckage of the post-war industrial food system and built a raft of quality. He re-introduced the concept of "origin" to the American consumer, reminding them that coffee was an agricultural product grown by people, not a powder manufactured by a corporation.

. . .

THE GRINDER

There is a story often told by old Peetniks that encapsulates the man and the movement. It is a story about boundaries. In the early days, a customer returned a pound of beans to the Vine Street shop. He was irate. He slammed the bag on the counter and complained that the beans were so oily they had clogged his electric blade grinder. He wanted a refund.

Alfred Peet looked at the shiny, black beans. He looked at the customer's cheap grinder, a device that chopped beans unevenly and heated them up, destroying the volatiles. He pushed the bag back across the counter. "There is nothing wrong with the coffee," Peet said, his voice flat and final, echoing off the wooden bins. "There is something wrong with your grinder. Buy a better one."

He refused the refund. The customer left, angry. But a week later, he was back in line. He had bought a burr grinder. He had tasted the difference. He understood, finally, that the coffee didn't bend to the consumer; the consumer had to rise to the level of the coffee. This was the Peet philosophy: The standard is the standard. You meet the coffee on its own terms, or you drink tea.

# 28

# THE GREEN MERMAID'S EMPIRE: SCALING THE SECOND WAVE

T he revelation did not occur in a boardroom in Seattle, nor did it manifest among the coffee plantations of Brazil. It took place on a wet Tuesday morning in Milan, in September 1983.

Howard Schultz, the thirty-year-old director of marketing for a small Seattle bean retailer, walked into a compact espresso bar near the Duomo. He was in Italy for the Milan trade fair, a plastics salesman turned coffee enthusiast who was attempting to understand the soul of the product he was selling. At the time, his employer, Starbucks, was a respected but strictly utilitarian seller of whole beans. They were "Peetniks"—disciples of the Dutch roaster Alfred Peet—who adhered to the rigid belief that coffee was a dry good to be scooped, weighed in pounds (0.45 kg), and brewed at home.

What Schultz observed inside that Milanese bar arrested his attention. It was a theater of social interaction as much as a retail store.

The space was tight, filled with the scent of fumo (cigarette smoke) and zucchero (burnt sugar). The barista—a term Schultz had rarely encountered in the American lexicon—operated with the fluidity of a craftsman. He locked the heavy brass portafilter into the group head with a sharp, mechanical engagement, pulled the lever, and watched the espresso emulsify into the cup like warm honey. Steam hissed from the wand as milk was aerated into a velvety micro-foam.

*However, the mechanics were secondary to the sociology. The barista knew the customers' names. He greeted them with a thunderous "Buongiorno!" Men in tailored suits stood shoulder-to-shoulder with factory workers at the marble counter, consuming their caffè in two swift gulps, exchanging news, and leaving Lira coins on the bar. Schultz realized that in the United States, coffee was a commodity—a grocery item consumed in the isolation of a kitchen. In Italy, coffee was a public event, a social lubricant, and a destination.*

*He returned to Seattle with the fervor of a convert. He convened with the owners of his company—Jerry Baldwin, Zev Siegl, and Gordon Bowker—and argued that their model was incomplete. They should not merely be selling beans; they should be selling the beverage and the Italian piazza experience. The founders rejected the premise. To them, coffee was a serious agricultural product; serving frothy milk drinks in paper cups seemed a dilution of the brand, akin to fast food.*

*That refusal provided the friction that ignited the Second Wave. Schultz eventually departed, established his own Italian-style chain called Il Giornale, and two years later, in 1987, returned to acquire his former bosses' assets for $3.8 million. He merged the two companies, retained the name of the bean shop —Starbucks—and initiated a project that would fundamentally alter the culinary landscape of the United States. He intended to teach a nation of percolator users to speak Italian.*

## SOCIOLOGY OF THE THIRD PLACE

Explaining the meteoric rise of Starbucks in the 1990s requires looking past the caffeine and examine the real estate strategy. Schultz's approach was not purely culinary; it was deeply sociological. He intuitively leveraged a concept formalized by the sociologist Ray Oldenburg in his 1989 book, *The Great Good Place.*

Oldenburg argued that for a healthy society to function, humans require three distinct environments. The First Place is the home— private, domestic, and familial. The Second Place is the workplace— structured, hierarchical, and productive. The Third Place is the anchor of community life. It is neutral ground where individuals gather to relax, converse, and exist free from the obligations of hosting. In 18th-century

London, this role was filled by the penny university; in France, the bistro; in Vienna, the *Kaffeehaus*.

In late-20th-century America, however, the Third Place had largely eroded. Pub culture was declining, church socials were fading, and the shopping mall had become a sterile temple of transactional commerce. The American suburb had become a lonely archipelago of single-family homes connected only by highways.

Schultz constructed Starbucks to fill this vacuum. The design of the stores was deliberate and calculated. Wright Massey, the head of the creative team in the mid-1990s, developed a visual language based on the four elements: earth, fire, water, and air. The stores featured organic curves, avoiding sharp angles that felt institutional. Round tables were selected specifically because a square table with an empty chair emphasizes the customer's solitude, whereas a round table feels complete even with a single occupant.

The sensory landscape was engineered for retention. Soft jazz playlists were curated by a dedicated team, eventually leading Starbucks to acquire a music management company. The aroma of roasting beans was paramount—so much so that for years, Schultz prohibited the sale of cooked breakfast sandwiches because the scent of burning cheese overpowered the olfactory signature of the coffee.

Unlike a diner, where a server creates subtle pressure to order and vacate the table, Starbucks sold "rent" in the form of a $3 latte. For the price of a cup of milk and espresso, a customer purchased the right to occupy a public space for two hours with a laptop or a book. It was an affordable luxury. In a decade defined by corporate downsizing and economic anxiety, the "Third Place" became the collective living room of the American middle class. By the time Starbucks went public on June 26, 1992, at $17 a share, it was not merely selling a beverage; it was selling belonging.

## REAL ESTATE: THE CLUSTER STRATEGY

While the sociology attracted customers, a formidable real estate strategy ensured they had few alternatives. During the aggressive expansion of the late 1990s and early 2000s, Starbucks utilized a tactic known as "clustering."

Conventional retail wisdom suggests that stores should be spaced out to maximize the catchment area and avoid cannibalizing sales. Starbucks inverted this logic. They deliberately opened stores within blocks of each other—sometimes directly across the street. In Vancouver, the intersection of Robson and Thurlow famously featured a Starbucks on opposite corners.

*The "Cluster Strategy" involved saturating a neighborhood to reduce wait times and block competitors.*

The logic was threefold. First, it reduced wait times. If the line at Store A extended out the door, the customer could walk fifty feet (15 meters) to Store B. Second, it acted as a billboard. The sheer density of the green logo created a perception of dominance and reliability. Third, and most critically, it created a barrier to entry for competitors.

Independent coffee shops struggled to compete with Starbucks on real estate. Landlords preferred Starbucks due to its "credit tenant" status. A lease signed by a multi-billion dollar corporation is a bankable asset; a lease signed by a local café is a risk. Starbucks used this leverage to secure the premier corners, paying rents that independent operators could not sustain. They would often pay above-market rates to lock in a prime location, viewing the operational loss as a marketing expense.

This strategy was famously satirized, yet the humor masked a brutal efficiency. By saturating a market, Starbucks lowered its own logistics costs—a delivery truck could service ten stores in one hour—and effectively blocked rival chains from establishing a foothold. They did not just acquire the customer; they secured the pavement.

·  ·  ·

## LINGUISTIC ENGINEERING

If the furniture drew people in, the language kept them there. One of Schultz's most significant gambits was the introduction of a new vernacular. When Starbucks began its aggressive expansion, the average American ordered coffee in two sizes: "cup" or "mug."

Schultz introduced a hierarchy that defied local logic but enforced a specific culture: Short (8 oz / 236 ml), Tall (12 oz / 354 ml), Grande (16 oz / 473 ml), and Venti (20 oz / 591 ml). He insisted on Italian names for the drinks: Cappuccino, Latte, Macchiato. Initially, this appeared pretentious, a barrier to entry for the uninitiated. However, Schultz understood the psychology of the "in-group." By requiring customers to learn a new vocabulary, he created a sense of sophistication. Ordering a "half-caf, non-fat, no-foam Venti latte" became a ritualistic act. It allowed the customer to feel like a connoisseur, an initiate in a club of modern, cosmopolitan drinkers.

The "Latte" served as the gateway for this revolution. Americans, generally speaking, did not enjoy the taste of dark-roasted espresso. It was too bitter and intense for a palate accustomed to weak filter coffee. However, the latte—which is essentially twelve ounces of warm, sweet milk flavored with two ounces of espresso—was palatable. It was comfort food. It served as a bridge that allowed a nation of sugar-habituated soda drinkers to transition into coffee consumers without initially acquiring a taste for black coffee.

## PHYSICS OF THE DARK ROAST

As the chain expanded from Seattle to Chicago and New York, Schultz and his roasting team faced a problem of physics. Critics and Third Wave connoisseurs often deride Starbucks as "Charbucks," claiming the beans are burnt. The signature "Pike Place Roast" and the espresso blend are indeed extremely dark, often exhibiting oils on the surface of the bean, indicating a breakdown of the cellular structure.

This is a necessity of scale instead of an accident. Roasting coffee is akin to cooking a steak. A Light Roast highlights the intrinsic flavor of the bean. If the bean is high quality, it tastes of the terroir—the soil, the altitude, the rainfall. However, if the bean is inconsistent, those flaws are magnified. A Dark Roast tastes of the process. It tastes of carbon, smoke, and caramelization.

Starbucks roasts dark for two strategic reasons rooted in standardization. The first is the erasure of terroir. When purchasing millions of pounds of coffee from twenty different countries, the beans will inherently vary; a crop from Sumatra tastes different in 1995 than in 1996. By roasting deeply—into the "Second Crack" where the cellulose structure of the bean fractures and pyrolysis occurs—the delicate, variable acidity is burned off, and the flavor of the origin is replaced with the flavor of the roast. A dark roast Sumatra tastes remarkably similar to a dark roast Brazil, ensuring that a customer in Boston receives the exact same flavor profile as a customer in San Diego. The second reason is the milk factor. The primary product of the Second Wave is not coffee, but the Latte, which is 80% milk. To make the coffee flavor cut through twenty ounces of hot, fatty dairy and vanilla syrup, a "punch" is required. Delicate, floral notes vanish in milk, but bitter, smoky, carbon notes survive. The dark roast is engineered to compete with the milk and maintain presence.

To measure this, the industry uses the Agtron scale, which utilizes near-infrared light to measure the color of ground coffee. A typical Third Wave roaster might target an Agtron of 55 or 60 (medium-light). Starbucks espresso often registers much lower, in the 30s or 40s. It is a roast designed not for the cupping table, but for the syrup pump.

## INDUSTRIAL DESIGN: THE SOLO TRAVELER

While Schultz was engineering the atmosphere, another silent revolution was occurring in the customer's hand. The "Second Wave" was not just about sitting in the café; it was about taking the café with you. In the early 1980s, the technology for mobile coffee was primitive. Lids were flat plastic discs with a tear-back tab that often leaked and splashed hot liquid. Crucially, they blocked the nose, preventing the drinker from smelling the coffee, which diminished flavor perception significantly.

In 1984, Jack Clements of the Solo Cup Company designed the Solo Traveler lid. It was a masterpiece of industrial design that is often overlooked. Clements engineered a dome with a raised rim (the "loft") that accommodated the foam of a cappuccino. Crucially, he created a recess in the lid—a depression that made room for the drinker's nose and upper lip. He elevated the drinking hole, allowing the liquid to flow smoothly rather than glugging.

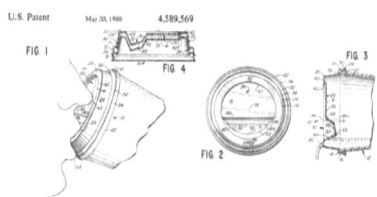

*The industrial design of the Traveler Lid enabled the "walking coffee" culture of the 1990s.*

This lid enabled the "Walking Coffee" culture. Suddenly, the paper cup with the mermaid logo became a fashion accessory. It was a status symbol carried through the streets of Manhattan, signaling that the bearer was busy, caffeinated, and had disposable income. The Solo Traveler lid transformed coffee from a stationary beverage into a mobile lifestyle component.

### FACTORY FLOOR: THE BARISTA ALGORITHM

As the Green Mermaid marched across the map, Schultz faced the ultimate enemy of the artisan: scale. Alfred Peet could roast every batch himself because he operated one store. Starbucks had a thousand, then ten thousand.

In the early days, Starbucks used manual La Marzocco Linea espresso machines. These were beautiful, temperamental machines manufactured in Florence. The barista had to grind the beans, tamp the puck with exactly 30 pounds (13.6 kg) of pressure, lock it in, and time the extraction by eye. It was theater, but it was inconsistent. A poor barista produced a poor drink. Furthermore, the training time for a new employee was weeks.

In the late 1990s, driven by the need for speed and consistency, Starbucks made the fateful decision to switch to super-automatic machines —first the Verismo 801, and later the Mastrena. These machines were marvels of Swiss and German engineering. They ground the beans, tamped them, pulled the shot, and ejected the spent puck at the push of a single button.

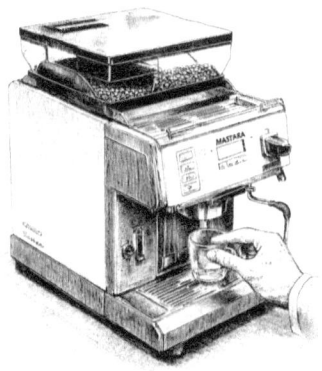

*The switch to push-button Mastrena machines prioritized speed and consistency over the theater of hand-pulled espresso.*

This shift eliminated the variable of human error, but it also removed the romance. The barista was no longer a chef; they were an assembly line operator.

The reality of working in a Second Wave shop became one of extreme Taylorism—the scientific management of labor. Starbucks introduced a system called "Lean," borrowed from the Toyota manufacturing method. Everything was timed. A barista was expected to produce a drink every 45 seconds. The layout of the floor was optimized to minimize footsteps. Syrups were placed in a specific order; fridge doors were designed to close automatically to save seconds.

The "Playbook" dictated exactly where a barista should stand. One partner was the "Plant," rooted at the espresso machine. Another was the "Customer Support," running a cyclic timer to brew fresh coffee, wipe tables, and restock milk every 8 to 10 minutes. This efficiency came at a physical cost. The repetitive motion of pumping syrup bottles led to a surge in Repetitive Strain Injuries (RSI). "Barista Wrist" became a documented occupational hazard. The emotional labor was equally taxed. The company required "The Starbucks Experience"—greeting every customer and making eye contact—even when the queue was substantial and the mobile order printer was generating tickets continuously. The barista was positioned between the demand for artisanal connection and the reality of industrial throughput.

### THE FRAPPUCCINO PIVOT

If the Latte was the gateway, the Frappuccino was the catalyst for mass adoption. The story of its invention highlights the tension between Seattle purism and California commercialism.

In the summer of 1993, Dina Campion, a district manager in Southern California, noticed a concerning trend. During heat waves, traffic in her stores plummeted. Customers were requesting cold drinks and leaving when told Starbucks only served hot espresso or iced lattes, which many found too bitter.

Campion and a store manager named Dan Moore began experimenting with a blender. They mixed strong coffee, sugar, milk, and a bonding agent to prevent separation. They sent the results to Seattle. The leadership initially rejected it. Schultz is famously quoted as saying, "We are not in the ice cream business." To the Peetnik roots of the company, a coffee slushy was an abomination, more akin to mall food than Italian tradition.

But Campion persisted, supported by the sales data. The test stores in Santa Monica were doing double the business of the rest of the region. Around the same time, Starbucks acquired a high-end Boston chain called The Coffee Connection for roughly $23 million. The owner, George Howell—who would later become a pioneer of the Third Wave for his focus on light roasts—had trademarked a drink called the "Frappuccino."

Starbucks appropriated the name, applied it to Campion's recipe, and launched it nationwide in 1995. It was a massive commercial success. In the first week, they tracked over 200,000 drinks. By the end of the year, the Frappuccino accounted for over 10% of total sales. Suddenly, Starbucks was not just for adults requiring a morning stimulant; it was for teenagers, for non-coffee drinkers, for people who desired a milk-shake that conveyed adult status.

*The blended ice drink transformed the coffee shop into a destination for sugar and youth culture.*

The Frappuccino fundamentally changed the demographics of the coffee shop, shifting the caloric center of gravity from the beverage to the dessert. It drove the stock price upward, even as it diluted the brand's claim to coffee seriousness.

## 2008: THE AUSTRALIAN CRASH

By the turn of the millennium, Starbucks appeared invincible. It had conquered North America, Europe, and Asia. Then, in 2000, it entered Australia.

The executives in Seattle assumed success was inevitable. Australia was a wealthy, English-speaking, Western nation with high disposable income. They utilized a "blitzkrieg" strategy, opening 84 stores rapidly, clustering them in major cities to dominate the landscape. It was a miscalculation. In 2008, Starbucks Australia was forced to close 61 of its 84 stores, losing $143 million.

The failure stemmed from the fact that Australia already possessed a sophisticated coffee culture. Following World War II, massive Italian and Greek immigration to cities like Melbourne and Sydney had introduced the espresso machine decades before Schultz went to Milan. The Australians had spent forty years perfecting their own drink: the Flat White. This was a smaller, stronger beverage—usually a double ristretto shot with micro-foamed milk, less airy than a cappuccino but more textured than a latte.

The Australians were accustomed to high-quality, medium-roast Arabica, served by skilled owner-operators who maintained personal relationships with their clientele. When Starbucks arrived with its sugary syrups, its dark roast, and its automated machines, the Australian market viewed it as a degradation of quality. It was a "simulated Italian" experience attempting to replace the authentic culture they already possessed. The failure in Australia proved that the Second Wave model worked best in vacuum markets—places like the U.S. or China that had no pre-existing coffee culture. In markets where the palate was already educated, the Green Mermaid struggled.

### CONQUEST OF TEA: THE CHINA STRATEGY

If Australia was a failure of arrogance, China was a triumph of adaptation. Entering China in 1999 was considered a high-risk endeavor. This was a nation with 5,000 years of tea history, where coffee was often viewed as bitter, Western medicine.

Belinda Wong, who eventually led the China division, understood that they could not just sell coffee; they had to sell status. In a rapidly modernizing China, the rising middle class desired symbols of their arrival. A white paper cup was a badge of cosmopolitanism.

However, the true innovation lay in the Human Resources strategy. In Chinese culture, the family unit is paramount. Parents were often skeptical of their children working as "baristas"—it was perceived as a low-status service job. Starbucks realized that to retain talent, they had to win over the parents. They launched the "Starbucks China Family Forum," large conventions where executives thanked the parents of their employees. They offered health insurance not just to the workers, but to their aging parents—a critical benefit in a country with a strained social safety net. They began referring to staff exclusively as "partners," a term that carried significant weight in this context.

On the product side, they adapted the menu. They introduced drinks like the "Red Bean Green Tea Frappuccino." They built stores that were larger, designed for groups, acknowledging that Chinese social life happens in collectives, not in the solitary mode of the American laptop worker. The crown jewel of this strategy opened in December 2017: the Shanghai Reserve Roastery. Spanning 30,000 square feet, it was an immersive coffee amusement park featuring copper casks two stories high and augmented reality tours. By 2020, Starbucks was opening a new store in China every 15 hours. They had successfully convinced the world's largest tea-drinking nation to adopt coffee.

## THE INVISIBLE HAND: C.A.F.E. PRACTICES

As Starbucks grew to 30,000 stores, it became the largest purchaser of high-quality Arabica coffee in the world. This scale created a moral and logistical problem: How does one ensure ethical sourcing when buying 3% of the world's entire coffee supply?

In response to protests in the early 2000s regarding fair trade, Starbucks did not just adopt the Fair Trade label; they created their own standard: C.A.F.E. Practices (Coffee and Farmer Equity). Developed in partnership with Conservation International, this was a points-based system. Farmers were graded on transparency (showing how much of the price reached the grower), social responsibility (no child labor, minimum wage standards), and environmental leadership (water conservation, shade trees).

If a farm scored high enough, Starbucks paid a premium above the "C-market" price (the commodity price of coffee on the New York Stock Exchange). For millions of farmers, this was a lifeline. Starbucks offered a stable, high-volume buyer who paid better than the local middleman.

However, critics argued that C.A.F.E. Practices was a method for the corporation to control the standards without third-party oversight.

While it undoubtedly raised the floor for agronomy standards globally —teaching farmers how to prune for yield and manage wastewater—it also locked them into the Starbucks ecosystem. The driving force of the "Second Wave" was not just the latte; it was the vertical integration of the global supply chain, from the hillside in Costa Rica to the drive-thru in Kansas.

## THE RETURN OF THE FOUNDER

By 2007, the company faced a crisis. The relentless pursuit of growth had led to a dilution of the "Starbucks Experience." Stores were often unkept. The smell of breakfast sandwiches masked the coffee. The espresso machines were automated, and the baristas were poorly trained. The stock price dropped 42% in a single year.

Schultz, who had stepped down as CEO eight years earlier to serve as Chairman, returned to the helm in January 2008. His first act was unprecedented in the history of American retail. On the afternoon of Tuesday, February 26, 2008, he closed every single Starbucks in the United States—7,100 stores—for three hours.

The cost was estimated at $6 million in lost sales. Critics labeled it a publicity stunt. But for Schultz, it was a necessary recalibration. Inside the locked doors, 135,000 baristas were retrained. They were taught to steam milk again. They were taught the story of the bean. They were instructed to pour out any espresso shot that had been sitting for more than ten seconds, as the crema dissipates and the flavor degrades.

Schultz banned the breakfast sandwiches until the recipe could be changed to reduce the smell. He redesigned the stores to bring the grinders back to the front. He attempted to re-inject the "soul" into the machine he had built. The company stabilized and then grew again. But the "soul" was different now. It was a corporate soul, a form of managed authenticity. The training did not return them to the artistry of the manual La Marzocco; it simply made them better operators of the Mastrena.

### THE LEGACY OF THE WAVE

There is a detail in the Starbucks logo that illustrates the trajectory of the Second Wave. The original logo, taken from a 16th-century Norse woodcut, showed a twin-tailed siren. She was topless, raw, and slightly menacing. She was a seductress of the sea, meant to represent the exotic danger of the coffee trade.

When Schultz took over, he sanitized the image. He covered her chest with flowing hair. He changed the color from brown (earthy, agricultural) to green (fresh, corporate). In 2011, he removed the words "Starbucks Coffee" from the ring entirely, leaving only the face. The Mermaid had become so ubiquitous she no longer needed to state what she was selling. She wasn't selling coffee anymore; she was selling reliability.

Alfred Peet's disciples had started a fire, and Howard Schultz had built a factory on top of it.

But in the shadows of the Green Mermaid, a new movement was stirring. Independent roasters were beginning to look at the Starbucks cup —with its dark-roasted beans, its sugary syrups, and its push-button automation—and ask the same question Schultz had asked in Milan twenty years earlier: Is this truly the best we can do?

Schultz had solved the problem of access. He had democratized espresso. He had provided America a place to sit. But he had sacrificed the nuance of the bean for the scalability of the brand. The stage was set for the Third Wave, a movement that would reject the "Third Place" living room in favor of the laboratory, rejecting the comfort of the latte for the clarity of the single-origin pour-over.

Yet, the artisans of the Third Wave owe their existence to the Mermaid. Howard Schultz did not roast the most complex coffee in history, but he achieved something more significant: He built the pipeline. He trained the American palate to pay $4 for a drink. He established the infrastructure of consumption that the future artisans would inherit. Without the scalability of the Second Wave, the precision of the Third would have had no market to serve. Starbucks was the gateway; the rest of the world just had to walk through it.

# 29

# THE TIGER'S CUP: THE SHIFT TO THE EAST

T he vibration of Seoul at 2:00 A.M. operates on a specific frequency, defined not by the hum of traffic but by a relentless LED glare that turns the night into a hyper-saturated day. In the district of Gangnam, the streets remain populated with the ppalli-ppalli (hurry-hurry) energy that reconstructed the South Korean economy from the devastation of the 1950s into a global powerhouse in two generations. Students carrying backpacks heavy enough to strain the spine, software engineers showing signs of fatigue, and fashion designers in oversized coats move toward a singular beacon: the café.

Inside the glass walls of a 24-hour Ediya Coffee, the atmosphere is library-deep, broken only by the mechanical actuation of keyboards and the turning of textbook pages. On nearly every table sits a plastic cup filled with ice and a translucent black liquid, the "Ah-Ah"—the Iced Americano. In South Korea, this drink has transcended the category of beverage to become a tool for endurance, consumed year-round, even when the winter winds off the Han River drop the temperature to -15°C (5°F). There is a local colloquialism that has become a generational motto: Eoljukah—"Even if I freeze to death, Iced Americano." It is consumed rapidly through a straw, utilized not for the flavor notes of jasmine or bergamot, but for the immediate, systemic delivery of pharmacologically active alkaloids. It serves as the metabolic fuel for a society that treats sleep as a variable to be minimized.

For three centuries, the history of coffee was documented primarily in the West, narrating the habits of Venetian merchants, Viennese intellectuals, Parisian revolutionaries, and American soldiers. The center of gravity for the coffee trade—the locations where trends were established, prices negotiated, and status conferred—was firmly anchored in the Atlantic axis of London, New York, and Hamburg. However, in the first two decades of the 21st century, the axis shifted. The trajectory of the industry is no longer being determined solely in the brick-walled roasteries of Brooklyn or the piazzas of Rome, but is increasingly influenced by the high-speed rail stations of Shanghai, the specialty labs of Tokyo, the tribal highlands of India, and the study halls of Seoul.

We are witnessing the rise of the "Tiger's Cup." The accelerated adoption of coffee by Asian markets represents a geopolitical realignment as much as a change in consumer demographics. This shift has fundamentally altered the supply chain, creating a competitive environment for the world's highest-quality beans and forcing Western markets to acknowledge that they are no longer the sole tastemakers of the world; they are merely one customer base among many, and in terms of growth potential, they are no longer the primary driver.

## THE REPUBLIC OF CAFFEINE

The scale of this shift is best measured by examining the density of technical expertise. The Q Grader license—created by the Coffee Quality Institute and, as of October 1, 2025, operated by the Specialty Coffee Association—functions as a calibration standard for the industry's sensory language. The course is an intensive multi-day gauntlet of triangulations, olfactory tests, and cupping calibrations designed to produce tasters who can score coffee with repeatable precision. South Korea, in particular, built an unusually dense culture of coffee certification; by mid-2010s reporting, it was widely cited as having around two thousand Q Graders, among the highest national counts in the world.

While coffee in the United States began as a commodity—a utilitarian fuel for the frontier—in Korea, it arrived as a marker of modernity and status, immediately jumping to a level of technical precision. The Korean consumer did not spend decades consuming low-quality instant coffee, although the "Maxim" gold mix sticks remain a nostalgic staple of the older generation; the modern wave arrived with significant momentum. The result is a café culture that is arguably the most sophisticated on earth.

In a specialized roastery in the Seongsu-dong neighborhood of Seoul, often referred to as the "Brooklyn of Seoul," the environment resembles a laboratory more than a rustic shop. The menu provides granular detail, listing not only the country of origin but the processing method (Anaerobic Natural, Carbonic Maceration), the altitude, the variety (Pink Bourbon, Sidra), and notably, the specific farm name. The clientele, often young and educated, understand these variables and are willing to pay 15,000 Won (approximately $12 USD) for a single cup of pour-over if the provenance is verified.

This sophistication exists alongside a strict utilitarianism. The rise of the *Cagongjok*—the "Cafe Study Tribe"—has reshaped the commercial architecture of the city. In a society characterized by intense academic pressure and high housing costs, young people often lack private space. With small apartments and multi-generational households, the café functions as a rented living room. Owners have adapted to this demand by installing individual study cubicles, high-speed power outlets at every seat, and occasionally enforcing silence policies. They are effectively leasing real estate by the hour, fueled by the "Ah-Ah." This dual nature of Korean coffee—high-end sensory appreciation coexisting with functional consumption—serves as the template for the Asian wave: a culture that demands high quality but consumes it at a volume that creates a supply vacuum for the rest of the global market.

## The Kissaten Legacy and the Third Wave

If Korea represents the engine of speed, Japan operates as the model of precision. It is a common misconception in Western markets that the "Third Wave" of coffee—the movement toward light roasts, single origins, and hand-pouring—was invented in the United States in the early 2000s. In reality, American entrepreneurs were importing a philosophy that had flourished in Tokyo for fifty years. Japan has been a significant coffee market since the Meiji Restoration, but it was in the post-war era that the culture crystallized into the *Kissaten*.

The *Kissaten* functions as a sanctuary, typically dark, wood-paneled, and filled with the scent of tobacco and the sound of jazz. The Master (*Masuta*) stands behind the bar, wearing a waistcoat and bow tie, operating with deliberate slowness. He utilizes a swan-neck kettle to pour a thin, continuous stream of water over a flannel cloth filter (Nel Drip), creating a mound of foam that rises but never breaks.

*The* Kissaten *master pours drop-by-drop into a flannel filter, a ritual of extreme patience and concentration.*

The extraction process can take five minutes, resulting in a cup that is small, dense, and chemically precise. When James Freeman founded Blue Bottle Coffee in Oakland in 2002, arguably catalyzing the global specialty movement, he explicitly cited the *Kissaten* of Tokyo as his primary inspiration. The minimalist aesthetic, the focus on single-cup brewing, and the obsession with freshness were Japanese exports.

However, Japan did not remain anchored in tradition; it industrialized quality. Japan is home to Hario, the glass company that invented the V60 dripper, and Kalita, the creator of the wave dripper, along with myriad high-end equipment manufacturers. They engineered the tools that the rest of the world uses to brew. Furthermore, Japan pioneered the "Ready to Drink" (RTD) market decades before Starbucks bottled a Frappuccino. In 1969, Ueshima Coffee Co. (UCC) launched the world's first canned coffee. Legend suggests that the company president, Tadao Ueshima, was forced to leave a cup of coffee unfinished to catch a train, leading to the realization that the modern worker required coffee that could travel.

Today, the vending machines of Tokyo—illuminated sentinels on every street corner—dispense millions of hot and cold cans of "Boss" and "Georgia" coffee daily.

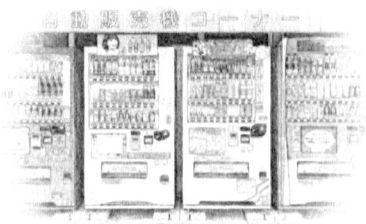

*Japan pioneered the Ready-to-Drink market, turning coffee into a ubiquitous convenience available on every street corner.*

This ubiquitous availability created a baseline of caffeine access that Western infrastructure is only now beginning to approximate. Japan demonstrated that a society could maintain the highest rituals of slow coffee, essentially the tea ceremony translated to the bean, alongside the ultimate convenience of the vending machine.

### THE LUCKIN SHOCK: ALGORITHMS OVER AROMAS

While Korea and Japan refined the culture, China expanded the scale. For five thousand years, China was the Empire of Tea, viewing coffee as a bitter, foreign medicinal soup. As recently as 2000, coffee consumption in China was statistically negligible, averaging three cups per person per year. The entry of Starbucks in 1999 introduced the "Third Place" concept—large, luxurious spaces where the rising Chinese middle class could perform their modernity. Holding a white cup became a signal of disposable income and connection to the global economy. However, the price point remained high; a latte cost roughly the same in Shanghai as in Seattle, despite the disparity in average income.

Then, in 2017, the market shifted with the arrival of Luckin Coffee. Rather than replicating the Starbucks hospitality model, Luckin treated coffee as a technology product. Their strategy was "New Retail." They constructed small, kiosk-style stores with no seating and eliminated cashiers. Transactions were processed exclusively through an app, which users utilized to order while in transit. Algorithms predicted the precise completion time of the drink. The customer would enter, scan a QR code, retrieve their blue cup, and exit without verbal interaction.

*Luckin Coffee replaced the cashier with the algorithm, streamlining the transaction into a purely digital interaction.*

The efficiency was absolute. Luckin utilized data from the app to map heat zones of demand in real-time, opening stores in locations indicated by the digital footprint of their users.

Their most significant innovation, however, was the "Coconut Latte." Luckin recognized that the bitter profile of dark-roasted coffee presented a barrier for the Chinese palate, which was accustomed to the sweetness of milk tea. Additionally, a significant portion of the East Asian population is lactose intolerant. They developed a proprietary coconut milk blend—sweet, creamy, and capable of masking the bitterness of the roast. The "Raw Coconut Latte" went viral on social media platforms like Douyin, becoming the flavor profile of a generation. In a single month, Luckin sold 10 million coconut lattes.

The company grew at a velocity that defied traditional retail logic. In two years, they opened 4,500 stores, surpassing the number of Starbucks locations in China, and went public on the NASDAQ in 2019. In 2020, a massive accounting fraud scandal revealed that Luckin had fabricated $300 million in sales. The methodology of the fraud was uniquely digital: they inflated the volume of digital coupons redeemed, creating a phantom revenue stream that existed only in the app's backend. This revelation caused the stock to collapse and led to the dismissal of executives and delisting from the exchange. Western analysts viewed this as proof that the Chinese coffee market was a mirage.

They were incorrect. While the financial reporting was fraudulent, the consumer addiction was genuine. Luckin restructured, paid its fines, and returned with renewed momentum. By 2023, Luckin had surpassed 10,000 stores in China, becoming the first coffee chain in history to reach that milestone in a single country. Luckin demonstrated that if friction—both in price and convenience—was reduced, the Chinese consumer would consume coffee at a volume that staggered industry projections. The "Luckin Shock" forced competitors to pivot; Starbucks had to partner with Alibaba to launch delivery services, scrambling to compete with the logistics of the Blue Deer. The center of innovation for coffee retail technology, including mobile ordering, delivery logistics, and auto-mated payments, is no longer Silicon Valley, but Shanghai.

### The Yunnan Pride

The rise of consumption in China spurred a parallel evolution in production. In the southwestern province of Yunnan, along the border with Myanmar and Laos, coffee has been grown for a century, originally introduced by French missionaries. For decades, it was treated as "filler" coffee. The region primarily grew the Catimor variety—a rust-resistant hybrid of Arabica and Robusta—cultivated for high yield and sold to multinational corporations for instant coffee production. The flavor profile was typically woody, herbal, and flat.

However, as cafes in Shanghai and Beijing began to demand "spe-cialty" coffee, a wave of domestic interest swept the industry. Young roasters began to question why they were importing coffee from Ethiopia when they could source it domestically. A new generation of farmers in Yunnan, often the children of the original growers, began to experiment. They moved away from strip-picking and adopted selective harvesting, built raised drying beds, and experimented with anaerobic fermenta-tion, using techniques borrowed from the Chinese *baijiu* liquor industry.

The results were significant. Yunnan coffee began to score 86, 87, and 88 points on the international scale, developing flavors of dried plum, black tea, and cognac. The *Guochao* (national trend) movement fueled the demand, making the consumption of Yunnan coffee an act of cultural pride. Today, the vast majority of high-quality Yunnan harvest is consumed domestically. It rarely leaves China. The Western buyer seeking a top-tier Yunnan microlot often finds the supply unavailable, as Shanghai roasters have already purchased it at farm gate prices that exceed the New York exchange rates. This represents an internal loop: China has achieved coffee independence, growing, roasting, and consuming the bean, thereby retaining 100% of the value chain within its borders.

## THE ROBUSTA RECLAMATION

Further south, in Vietnam and Indonesia, a different type of market evolution is occurring. For a century, these nations were the engine room of the global commodity market, growing Robusta—the bitter, high-caffeine species—to fuel the instant coffee factories of Europe and the United States. Western coffee standards often dismissed Southeast Asian coffee as "rubbery" or "industrial." However, the youth of Hanoi, Ho Chi Minh City, and Jakarta are reclaiming this heritage, rejecting the notion that Arabica is the only viable species for quality coffee.

In Vietnam, the *Cà Phê Sữa Đá* (strong Robusta dripped over sweetened condensed milk) has always been a staple. Modern cafes are elevating this tradition by using "Fine Robusta"—beans grown with the same agronomic care as specialty Arabica. These beans are revealing notes of dark chocolate, hazelnut, and whisky. In Jakarta, the Kopi Kenangan chain (literally "Memories Coffee") became a "unicorn" startup, valued at over $1 billion, by serving localized drinks utilizing palm sugar (*Gula Aren*) and local Robusta blends.

This movement proves that the Western definition of quality—characterized by high acidity, floral notes, and tea-like body—is not the sole standard. A distinct "Asian Palate" is emerging, one that values body, texture, sweetness, and intensity. It does not apologize for the bitterness but balances it with fat and sugar. This reclamation challenges the sensory dominance of the West, asserting that modernization does not require the adoption of Western tastes.

## INDIA: THE TRIBAL REVOLUTION

Perhaps the most striking example of de-colonizing the coffee trade

is occurring in the Eastern Ghats of India, in the Araku Valley. Historically, Indian coffee was a colonial enterprise. The British established
massive estates in the Coorg and Chikmagalur regions of Karnataka,
planting coffee in neat rows under silver oak shade trees. These estates
were integrated into the global auction system, feeding the commodity
markets of Europe with consistent beans.

Araku operates differently. Here, the farmers are not estate owners
but *Adivasi*—indigenous tribal people who have lived in the valley for
millennia. For decades, they were marginalized, living in poverty while
insurgency raged in the surrounding hills. In the early 2000s, the Naandi
Foundation, an Indian non-profit, initiated a radical experiment by orga-
nizing thousands of tribal families into a cooperative. They bypassed the
phase of chemical farming entirely, adopting regenerative agriculture.
They planted coffee under a canopy of native fruit trees—mango, jackfruit, and avocado—and used compost made from local sources.

The true revolution, however, was the route to market. The Naandi
Foundation recognized that selling this coffee through traditional Indian
Coffee Board auctions would result in commodity pricing, blending
away the specific *terroir* of Araku—spicy, full-bodied, and complex.
Consequently, they bypassed the auction and the importers, establishing
a direct link to Paris. In 2017, the cooperative opened a flagship store in
the Marais district. It was not positioned as a charity shop but as a
luxury boutique, selling coffee as a premium product competing with
French wine and truffles. The tribal farmers of Araku became share-
holders in the brand. The value added—the roasting, branding, and
retail margin—was captured not by a European multinational, but by
the cooperative itself. This model overturns centuries of extractive
economics, suggesting a future where the origin does not merely grow
the raw material but owns the prestige associated with it.

### The Economic Consequences: The Bidding War

This shift matters to the Western consumer because of the auction
mechanism. Every year, the finest coffees in the world—the top 0.1% of
the harvest—are sold at prestigious auctions like the "Cup of Excellence"
or the "Best of Panama." For twenty years, the winning bidders were

primarily Japanese, American, or Scandinavian. In 2023, the list of winners indicated a new reality. The record-breaking lots—selling for $2,000, $4,000, even $10,000 per pound—are increasingly going to buyers in China, South Korea, and Taiwan.

A notable incident involving the "Elida Geisha" from Panama, one of the most celebrated coffees in the world, illustrates this trend. When it broke the world record price, it was purchased by a consortium of Chinese buyers. The Asian market possesses capital, a desire for status, and a definition of luxury that aligns with high prices. In China, gifting a $100 bag of coffee is a rational social gesture, similar to gifting a bottle of Bordeaux or a box of high-end tea. In the United States, such a price point is often viewed with skepticism.

This economic reality creates a diversion of premium beans. The best coffees in the world are flowing East. The American roaster, accustomed to being the "buyer of choice," is finding that the farmer in Panama prefers to sell to the buyer in Shanghai who pays cash upfront without negotiation, rather than the buyer in Portland who requires extensive paperwork. The "West" is experiencing a slow demotion from being the primary market to being a legacy market.

### THE CONTAINER CRISIS

This shift is structural as well as high-end. During the global logistics crisis of 2021, when shipping containers were scarce, Brazilian exporters faced a difficult choice regarding limited slots on ships. They could send coffee to Hamburg (Europe) or to Shanghai (Asia). Historically, Europe was the reliable partner. However, Asia was growing faster and paying more efficiently. We witnessed the beginnings of a pivot. Trade routes are being redrawn. The "Pacific Rim" trade—Brazil to China, Vietnam to Korea—is becoming the dominant artery of the caffeine world. The Atlantic route, while still massive, has plateaued.

### THE DECENTRALIZED CUP

The rise of the Tiger's Cup marks the end of the colonial coffee model. The colonial model relied on a simple flow: The South grows, the

West consumes. That flow has ceased to be the only narrative. The South is consuming. The East is consuming. The loop is closing. The coffee world is now multipolar. There is a "Seoul Style" of roasting (fast, light, precise), a "Shanghai Style" of service (digital, delivery, sweet), a "Hanoi Style" of brewing (slow, strong, Robusta), and an "Araku Style" of business (tribal-owned luxury).

For the coffee drinker in the West, this represents a significant adjustment. The era of cheap, high-quality coffee was a historical anomaly, subsidized by the lack of competition for the beans. Now, the competition has arrived. As we look to the future, we must realize that the trends shaping our morning cup are no longer coming solely from Italy or the United States. The next great innovation in brewing, the next realignment in the supply chain, or the next leap in genetic breeding will likely have its origins in the Time Zone of the Tiger. The sun rises in the East, and now, the coffee does too.

# 30

# THE SENSORY PRIESTHOOD:
# CODIFYING THE INVISIBLE

T*he verdict is delivered by a sound rather than a gavel: the sharp, aspirated slurp of a silver spoon. It is a rapid, aspirated sound, something between a whistle and a sharp intake of breath, repeated in mechanical succession down a line of white porcelain bowls.*

*In a windowless, climate-controlled room in Long Beach, California, twelve individuals stand around a rotating table. They move with the synchronized precision of a surgical team, silent save for the auditory rhythm of the evaluation. Slurp. Pause. Spit. Slurp. Pause. Spit.*

*The environment is engineered for neutrality. The walls are a clinical white to prevent color reflection from altering the visual perception of the roast. There is no music, no perfume, and no distraction. The humidity is fixed at 50% relative humidity; the temperature is locked at 21°C (70°F). On the table, the coffee is stripped of its context. There is no milk, no sugar, no branding, and no origin story. It is merely ground particulates and hot water, steeping in open bowls. The participants hold silver spoons, shaped like deep ladles bent at an aggressive angle to facilitate the specific mechanics of the tasting. They dip the spoon, bring it to their lips, and inhale the liquid with enough velocity to vaporize it against the posterior of the oral cavity.*

*They are searching for volatile compounds—pyrazines, thiols, aldehydes— that exist for mere seconds before dissipating into the filtered air of the labora-*

*tory. One taster, a buyer for a massive European conglomerate, records data on a clipboard: Malic acidity, green apple, crisp finish. Another, a quality control lead for a boutique roaster, notes: Fermented, over-ripe strawberry, phenolic.*

*To the external observer, this ritual—known as "cupping"—may appear to be an affectation. However, in the global coffee trade, these individuals function as the Arbiters of Quality. The integers written on these clipboards determine the fate of entire harvests and the solvency of farming communities. A score of 88 points might enable a farmer in the Huehuetenango highlands of Guatemala to invest in concrete drying patios and fund higher education for their children. A score of 79 relegates the same crop to the commodity market, sold at a loss to a broker and destined for instant powder or high-volume gas station blends.*

*This represents the precise juncture where agriculture transforms into finance. It is the calibration point that transmutes a biological seed into a stock price, and the mechanism of that conversion is the standardized application of the human sensorium.*

### THE BIOLOGICAL HARDWARE

For centuries, coffee was judged by a binary metric: "good" or "bad," "strong" or "weak." As the industry modernized in the 20th century, it encountered a linguistic barrier. It is impossible to trade a product effectively without a descriptive framework. One cannot write a futures contract for a flavor unless that flavor can be quantified. The solution lay in the development of a new lexicon, a standardized map of sensory experience. But before the industry could standardize the language, it had to calibrate the instrument: the human mouth.

The human gustatory system is a biological marvel, yet for decades, education on the subject was fundamentally flawed. The "Tongue Map," suggesting distinct zones for sweet, sour, and bitter, persisted as a scientific myth. It was based on a mistranslation of a 1901 German thesis by D.P. Hänig and was never intended to be taken literally. In reality, taste buds sensitive to all five modalities—Sweet, Sour, Salty, Bitter, and Umami—are distributed across the entire dorsal surface of the tongue, housed within papillae.

However, the tongue remains a relatively blunt instrument. It acts as a primary gatekeeper, answering basic survival questions: Is the substance caloric? (Sweet). Is it toxic? (Bitter). Is it spoiled? (Sour). The tongue cannot perceive "Blueberry." It cannot detect "Roasted Hazelnut." It cannot identify "Jasmine." These are flavors, not tastes, and the perception of flavor occurs in the olfactory system.

Specifically, it occurs in the olfactory bulb. This biological reality dictates the physics of the "Slurp." When a cupper rapidly aspirates the coffee, the goal is not merely to cool the liquid. The objective is to create an aerosol. By spraying the liquid across the entire palate, the taster maximizes surface area, but more critically, they force vapors up the retro-nasal passage—the connection between the pharynx and the nasal cavity.

Here, the brain integrates the data. It combines the signal from the tongue (Sweet/Sour) with the signal from the nose (Volatile Aromatics) and the input from the Trigeminal Nerve to create the composite image perceived as "flavor."

Even with the retro-nasal passage engaged, the brain faces a formidable variable: temperature. The human perception of flavor is thermolabile—it shifts as the thermal energy of the liquid decreases. Consequently, cupping is not a singular event, but a longitudinal observation.

When the coffee is hot, at approximately 71°C (160°F), the human tongue is partially anesthetized to sweetness. The thermal intensity masks the perception of sucrose. At this stage, the taster perceives primarily "Aromatics" and "Body." As the coffee cools to a warm state, roughly 49°C (120°F), the anesthesia dissipates. The sweetness receptors activate. This is the "balance" phase, where the interplay between organic acids and sugars becomes most evident.

The definitive test occurs when the coffee reaches room temperature, around 21°C (70°F). In the trade, this phase is known as "reading the dregs." At this thermal range, there is no heat to mask defects. The volatile aromatics have largely evaporated, leaving only the basic taste structure. Defects become prominent. A coffee that presented as "caramel" when hot might reveal notes of "wet cardboard" or "medicinal astringency" when cool. Conversely, a high-quality coffee will "open up" as it cools, revealing a sparkling acidity previously muted by the heat. Q

Graders are trained to mistrust the initial impression; the truth of the bean is often found in the final sip.

*The cupping spoon is designed to hold a precise amount of liquid and facilitate the rapid aspiration required to spray the palate.*

Beyond temperature, the process must account for biological fallibility, specifically Anosmia. This "smell blindness" is more prevalent than commonly realized. Just as individuals may be colorblind to specific wavelengths, many are "odor-blind" to specific compounds. A cupper might be capable of detecting strawberry (ethyl methylphenylglycidate) but genetically incapable of perceiving vanilla (vanillin). To mitigate these biological blind spots, professional cupping panels utilize a system of redundancy, typically consisting of at least three certified tasters. This "Triangulation" ensures that one individual's sensory gap is covered by another's sensitivity. It is a system of redundant biological sensors, calibrated to minimize individual error.

There is also the risk of olfactory fatigue, or adaptation. When the olfactory receptors are exposed to a constant stimulus, the brain filters out the signal to prioritize new information. In a cupping room containing thirty samples, the air becomes saturated. To reset their sensory baseline, cuppers will often smell their own skin—specifically the unperfumed crook of the arm—or a glass of water. They must "zero out" their instruments before evaluating the next bowl.

.   .   .

## THE PHANTOM FEELING

Coffee possesses physical mass and texture, attributes detected by the Trigeminal Nerve. When a cupper describes a coffee as "syrupy," "buttery," or "astringent," they are referencing data from the fifth cranial nerve, which is responsible for sensation in the face. It detects pain, temperature, and texture. A high-fat milk registers as heavier than skim milk; a French Press coffee, rich in suspended oils and fines, registers as heavier than a paper-filtered brew.

"Astringency"—the drying sensation analogous to consuming red wine or an unripe banana—is a chemical reaction where tannins bind to the salivary proteins, stripping lubrication from the oral cavity. The Trigeminal nerve registers this friction as a tactile sensation. A superior coffee functions as a symphony played on three instruments simultaneously: the Tongue (Taste), the Nose (Aroma), and the Nerve (Body).

## THE PROTOCOL OF THE BOWL

With the biological variables understood, the ritual required strict codification. The "cupping" protocol was standardized by the Specialty Coffee Association (SCA) to eliminate every variable except the coffee itself. The physics of cupping are precise. The ratio is fixed: 8.25 grams of coffee to 150 milliliters of water. The grind must be calibrated slightly coarser than a standard paper filter drip.

This specific coarseness is a calculated defense against over-extraction. In a pressurized espresso machine, water passes through the matrix in thirty seconds. In a pour-over, it takes three minutes. In a cupping bowl, the water and coffee remain in contact for upwards of twenty minutes. If the grind were too fine—approximating table salt—the surface area would be excessive, causing the water to dissolve not only the desirable sugars and acids but also the structural cellulose of the bean. This results in "astringency" and "bitterness," masking the inherent character of the coffee. The cupping grind is calibrated so that roughly 70% to 75% of particles pass through a standard 20-mesh sieve, allowing for a slow, gentle extraction that plateaus rather than peaks.

The water temperature is equally critical. At 93°C (200°F), the water carries sufficient thermal energy to solubilize lipids and light volatiles but remains cool enough to avoid scorching the cellular structure. If the water were boiling (100°C / 212°F), it would instantly volatilize the delicate floral top notes, ejecting them into the ventilation system before detection. If the water drops below 90°C (195°F), it lacks the energy to dissolve the heavier, long-chain molecules that provide "body."

The mechanics of the pour constitute another variable. The stream must be forceful enough to create turbulence, ensuring full saturation of every particle, yet controlled to prevent splashing. This turbulence creates the "crust"—a thick, foamy cap of grounds that rises to the surface. This crust serves a dual function: it acts as a lid, trapping the aromatic gases, and as a thermal insulator, maintaining the slurry's temperature while the extraction stabilizes. For four minutes, the bowl functions as a sealed pressure cooker of flavor. If a cupper accidentally disrupts the table and breaks the crust prematurely, the sample is compromised; the thermal seal is broken, and the extraction curve is altered.

The process unfolds as a three-act sequence performed in silence.

**Act One: The Fragrance.** The beans are ground into the bowl dry. Tasters inhale the "dry distillation" notes—volatile gases trapped in the cellular structure during roasting. This phase reveals the heavier molecules: pine, spice, clove, walnut.

**Act Two: The Aroma.** Hot water is introduced. The crust forms. For four minutes, the room waits. Then comes "The Break." The taster uses the back of a spoon to displace the crust three times. As the seal is fractured, a cloud of trapped vapor escapes. This is the most intense olfactory moment, revealing the enzymatic notes—the florals, jasmine, rose, and coffee blossom—that evaporate rapidly.

**Act Three: The Slurp.** After the crust is skimmed, the coffee cools to a drinkable temperature (roughly 71°C / 160°F). This is where the retro-nasal collision occurs, and the scoring begins.

## THE TOWER OF BABEL

Prior to the 1980s, the vocabulary of coffee was chaotic. A roaster in Seattle might describe a bean as "snappy," while an importer in Hamburg described the same bean as "hard." A "winy" coffee could imply a pleasant fruit acidity or a defect resembling vinegar. There was no baseline. The wine industry had resolved this issue decades earlier, establishing rigorous systems for identifying tannins and varietal characteristics. Coffee remained linguistically isolated.

The issue is neurological. The human apparatus for perceiving flavor is disconnected from the language centers of the brain. The "tip-of-the-nose" effect makes communicating flavor notoriously difficult. In 1995, Ted Lingle, a founding figure of the SCAA, sought to codify the chaos. He aimed to create a tool allowing a buyer in Japan and a seller in Brazil to view the same document and agree on the sensory data. The result was the Coffee Taster's Flavor Wheel.

Modeled after Ann Noble's wine aroma wheel, it was a circular chart radiating with color. The center contained broad, primary categories: Fruity, Floral, Sweet, Nutty, Spiced, Roasted, Vegetal. As the user moved outward, the categories bifurcated. Fruity became Citrus, Berry, Stone Fruit. Nutty became Peanut, Hazelnut, Almond. The outer ring provided granular descriptors like Blackcurrant, Garden Peas, Pipe Tobacco, Rubber, and Hay.

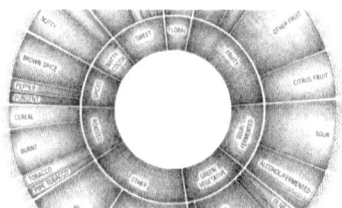

*The Flavor Wheel codifies the chaotic sensory experience of coffee into a standardized, hierarchical language.*

The Wheel acted as industry legislation as much as a graphic. It delineated "Taints" (chemical defects like phenol or rubber) from "Aromas" (positive attributes). It provided a shared syntax. A roaster could state, "This Kenyan has a distinct blackcurrant note with phosphoric acidity," and the description would be understood globally. It allowed value to be transmitted across borders alongside the physical commodity.

## THE Q GRADER'S GAUNTLET

With the Wheel and the Protocol established, the industry required certified interpreters. The Coffee Quality Institute (CQI) developed the "Q Grader" certification—a rigorous credential for professional tasting. In its classic form, the course spans six days and includes twenty practical exams across sensory, olfactory, triangulation, and cupping calibration. As of October 1, 2025, the Specialty Coffee Association operates the evolved Q Grader program, aligning it with its Coffee Value Assessment framework.

The failure rate is significant, serving as a filter for sensory precision. Candidates must navigate the "Organic Acids" test, which requires the identification of subtle chemical differences. They are presented with cups of clear water spiked with weak concentrations of specific acids and must identify them without visual cues:

- **Citric Acid:** Sharp, lemon-like, perceived on the sides of the tongue.
- **Malic Acid:** Lingering, smooth, reminiscent of green apple.
- **Phosphoric Acid:** Sparkling, dry, distinctively inorganic, similar to the bite of a cola.
- **Acetic Acid:** Vinegary, pungent, indicating fermentation.

The most formidable tool in the Q Grader's training is the *Le Nez du Café* kit. Created by French sensorialist Jean Lenoir, it consists of thirty-six glass vials, each containing a concentrated essence of a specific aroma found in coffee. Vial #1 is Earth. Vial #12 is Coffee Blossom. Vial #29 is Gingerbread. The kit also includes the scents of agricultural failure: Vial #34 is Leather; Vial #36 is Rubber. Candidates must memorize these scents blindly, reprogramming their perception to dismantle the generic concept of "coffee smell" and replace it with a high-resolution map of esters, aldehydes, and ketones.

The "Triangulation" test is perhaps the most demanding. In a standard cupping, visual cues can bias the taster—a "Halo Effect" where a dark bean primes the brain to taste smoke. To eliminate this, Q exams utilize the Red Room.

The room is illuminated solely by deep red light. Under this specific wavelength, all coffee appears as a uniform gray-brown, stripping the taster of visual data.

*Triangulation tests are often performed under red light to prevent visual bias from influencing the taster's judgment.*

Three cups are placed in a triangle. Two are identical; one is different. The candidate must identify the outlier. The difference is often microscopic—a variation in crop year or a slight shift in processing. In the silence of the Red Room, candidates are forced to rely entirely on olfactory data, overriding the panic of the brain. It is sensory deprivation combined with high-stakes testing.

### THE CHEMISTRY OF "BLUEBERRY"

The efficacy of sensory science is illustrated by the rise of the Ethiopian Natural. In the early 2000s, specialty coffee drinkers began encountering cups that presented an intense flavor of fresh blueberries.

Prior to the Flavor Wheel, this might have been dismissed as an additive or a defect. Sensory science allowed the industry to deconstruct the phenomenon. The "blueberry bomb" profile was the result of specific volatile compounds—primarily fruity esters and aldehydes—preserved by the natural processing method, where the coffee cherry dries on the seed. Chemists identified that the fermentation phase in natural processing created high levels of specific monoterpenes. The "blueberry" note was not a poetic exaggeration; it was a chemical reality.

This validation altered the economics of the trade. Coffees previously considered "unclean" due to their fermenty profiles were re-evaluated. If the fermentation tasted like "Rotten Fruit," it remained a defect. However, if it tasted like "Strawberry Jam," it was reclassified as a premium attribute. The distinction between waste and luxury was drawn not by the bean itself, but by the vocabulary of the taster.

## The Living Lexicon

By 2016, the original 1995 Flavor Wheel required updating. It was based on industry consensus rather than empirical data. The World Coffee Research (WCR) organization, partnering with sensory scientists at Kansas State University, sought to rebuild it.

They assembled a panel of professional sensory scientists—experts who analyze texture in food products—and provided them with hundreds of coffee samples. The objective was to create a "Sensory Lexicon" where every descriptor had a physical reference point available in a grocery store.

In the previous system, "Blackberry" was subjective. In the WCR Lexicon, "Blackberry" was defined precisely: *The aroma of Smucker's Blackberry Jam.* "Nutty" was defined by *Diamond brand chopped walnuts.* "Rubber" was defined by *a cut strip of bicycle inner tube.* This shift—from the poetic to the referential—marked the maturation of coffee analysis as a science. The 2016 Flavor Wheel became the global standard. It organized sensory descriptors according to chemical relationships rather than subjective taste categories, marking the maturation of coffee analysis from craft intuition into applied sensory science.

## THE POLITICS OF TASTE

The language of taste often presents itself as neutral. In practice, the determination of what constitutes "quality" is deeply political.

The SCA protocol and the Flavor Wheel originated in America and Europe. They prioritize attributes that Western palates historically value: clarity, acidity, sweetness, and "cleanliness." A "clean" cup is defined by transparency of flavor, free from "noise." This preference is the result of a specific industrial history. The wet-washing mechanical process, utilized in Latin America, was engineered to create this specific profile.

In other coffee cultures, "noise" is a desired attribute. In Indonesia, the traditional *Giling Basah* (wet-hulled) processing method creates a coffee that is heavy, earthy, spicy, and often tastes of damp forest floor. Under strict SCA protocols, these earthy notes can border on defects. A Q Grader trained in the Western tradition might penalize a Sumatran coffee for being "dirty," citing "phenol" or "moldy earth." Yet, for millions of drinkers in Indonesia and Japan, that earthiness constitutes the soul of the coffee.

The "clean cup" standard can function as a form of sensory imperialism, dictating that a washed coffee from Colombia is the "correct" expression of quality, while a funky, ferment-heavy natural from Yemen is "aberrant." This has financial consequences. A farmer in Sulawesi might produce a crop that is culturally perfect but fails the Q Grader exam, forcing them to sell it at a discount.

Recently, this hierarchy has been challenged by the rise of experimental fermentation. Producers in Colombia and Costa Rica are utilizing anaerobic fermentation tanks—technology adapted from wine-making—to create wild, boozy profiles that defy traditional definitions of "clean." These coffees polarize the priesthood. Traditionalists dismiss them as "defective"; modernists label them "innovative" and pay premiums for them. The definition of quality is fracturing under the pressure of innovation. The Flavor Wheel struggles to categorize market-driven flavors like cinnamon crunch or lactic yogurt—flavors that technically should not exist in coffee.

THE ECONOMICS OF THE SCORE

Despite these biases, the ultimate impact of the Flavor Wheel and cupping protocols has been the democratization of value. In the past, coffee value was determined by the brand on the tin or the relationship between buyer and broker. It was an opaque system.

For the first time, value began to follow flavor rather than reputation.

Consider a cooperative in Rwanda. During harvest, a farmer delivers parchment coffee to the washing station. Previously, the price was dictated by the weight of the cherry and the global commodity price (the "C-Price"). The farmer had no leverage. They did not know the flavor of their product; they only knew its mass.

Today, that cooperative operates a cupping lab. Inside, a young woman named Clarisse, the daughter of a farmer, works as a certified Q Grader. She roasts a sample of the farmer's lot, grinds it, and evaluates the fragrance. She detects orange blossom and black tea. She pours the water, breaks the crust, and slurps.

She records the score: 87.5.

That number acts as a financial weapon. It dictates that this coffee cannot be blended into the general container. It must be segregated as a microlot. Clarisse can contact a buyer in London or Seattle and state, "I have a distinct lot scoring 87.5 with floral intensity." The buyer understands the value proposition immediately.

The financial difference is stark. A score of 80 is "Commodity Grade." It trades at the C-Price (hypothetically $1.50/lb). A score of 84 is "Specialty Grade," trading at a differential, perhaps C-Price plus $0.50 ($2.00/lb). But a score of 87.5 enters a different economic tier entirely. It decouples from the C-market and trades at a fixed price, potentially $4.50 or $5.00 per pound. That variance—the difference between $1.50 and $5.00—is entirely dependent on the calibration of Clarisse's tongue and her ability to communicate that score to the buyer.

However, this democracy is fragile. Coffee is organic matter, and it decays. The score Clarisse awards in Rwanda is merely the first hurdle. Before the funds are transferred, the coffee must survive the logistics of the physical world.

The industry relies on a sequence of samples acting as checkpoints. First is the "Offer Sample"—the 300-gram bag sent via courier to the buyer. This represents the promise. If accepted, a contract is signed "Subject to Approval of Sample" (SAS).

Months later, after milling and bagging, a second sample is drawn: the "PSS" (Pre-Shipment Sample). This is the moment of risk. If the coffee was dried too rapidly, the internal moisture may be unstable. Over the eight weeks between the Offer Sample and the PSS, the flavor can "fade." A coffee that was vibrant may now taste of wet wood. If the PSS scores an 84 when the Offer Sample scored an 88, the contract is void. The buyer can retract the offer, leaving the cooperative with 18,000 kilograms of coffee that is effectively homeless.

Even if the PSS passes, there is the "Arrival Sample." The container spends weeks at sea, exposed to the humidity of the Indian Ocean or the chill of the North Atlantic. Condensation, known as "container rain," can drip onto the jute sacks, fueling mold. When the container opens in New Jersey or Hamburg, a final sample is drawn. If it tastes of mold or burlap (a defect known as "baggy"), the insurance adjusters are summoned, and the coffee may be condemned.

This creates a severe asymmetry. The farmer is paid based on the quality of the coffee after it has survived a global obstacle course over which they have no control. The "slurp" in the buyer's lab is the final verdict in a trial lasting six months—a summary judgment delivered in a fraction of a second that determines whether the farmer's season was a triumph of agriculture or a sunken cost.

The cupping score acts as the currency of the specialty market. It is the sound of coffee being stripped of its marketing, its packaging, and its romance, forced to testify on its own behalf. It is a rapid, mechanical, unglamorous ritual, but it remains the most honest moment in the industry. In that fraction of a second, when the liquid atomizes across the palate, the coffee reveals its true nature. It is either clean or dirty. It is either flat or vibrant. It is either a commodity to be burned, or a masterpiece to be savored.

# PART VI

## EMPIRES OF COFFEE

At a certain scale, coffee stops behaving like a drink and starts behaving like an empire.

In this section, the protagonist is not a person but a price: a number that moves lives across continents. We follow the C-market and its volatility, the shocks that can rewrite supply overnight, and the ethical promises—Fair Trade, sustainability, value—that strain against the cold logic of commodities. We examine who captures profit, who absorbs risk, and how geopolitics has repeatedly used coffee as both leverage and lifeline.

Coffee is comfort, yes. But it is also a contract.

# 31

## THE PAPER BEAN: THE CASINO OF THE C-PRICE

T*he trading floor of the Intercontinental Exchange (ICE) does not smell like coffee. For the vast majority of its history, the space known as the "softs" pit—where sugar, cocoa, and coffee were traded— smelled like a combination of recirculated air, floor wax, and sweat. It was a chaotic theater of bright jackets and shouting men standing on tiered wooden steps, flashing hand signals that moved millions of dollars in fractions of a second. Palm out to sell. Palm in to buy. A finger to the throat to signal a stop-loss.*

*To the figures in the pit, coffee was Ticker Symbol KC rather than a beverage or sensory experience. It was a data point. It was a standardized unit of 37,500 pounds (17,009 kg) of green Arabica beans, free-on-board at a recognized port warehouse. They were not concerned with the shade canopy in Ethiopia or the soil pH in Colombia. They focused on the spread, the resistance line, the moving average, and the margin call.*

*Three thousand miles away, on a steep, muddy slope in the department of Huila, Colombia, a farmer checks a smartphone. It is raining—a cold, relentless drizzle that threatens to knock the delicate white blossoms off the Castillo trees. He ignores the rain and stares at the number on the screen. The "New York Price" has fallen four cents in the last hour.*

*That four-cent drop was not triggered by a sudden change in global thirst.*

*It was not triggered by a bumper crop suddenly appearing in Vietnam. It was triggered because a proprietary weather model in Connecticut predicted a 20% lower chance of frost in Brazil over the coming weekend, causing a cascade of automated sell orders.*

*For the farmer, that four-cent drop is a physical blow rather than a data point. It means the labor of the last month has effectively been performed for free. He looks at his trees, heavy with cherries that need to be picked by hand, and performs the brutal mental math of the smallholder: paying the pickers the legal minimum results in a loss on every sack; failing to pay them means the fruit rots on the branch.*

*This invisible tether between the remote trading desk and the muddy slope is the C-Price. As the global benchmark for Arabica coffee, this ticker represents the single most important number in the industry. It determines the solvency of millions of families. Originally designed to manage risk, the C-Price has trans-formed into a mechanism where the futures market dictates the physical price.*

### Order from Chaos: The Panic of 1880

Why does a farmer's livelihood depend on a derivative contract? We must look back to the financial chaos of the late nineteenth century. Before standardized markets, the coffee trade was the Wild West. There were no standards, no regulations, and rampant speculation. Importers would purchase coffee from Brazil, hoping that by the time the ship arrived in New York three weeks later, the price would be higher. It was a blind wager on the speed of sail and the appetite of a city.

*Before algorithms, the price of coffee was set by the physical choreography of traders in the "softs" pit.*

In 1880, a massive syndicate of traders—known as the "Trinity," comprising the powerful firms of B.G. Arnold, Bowie Dash, and O.G. Kimball—attempted to corner the market. They bet heavily that supply would fail, hoarding inventory to artificially drive prices up and squeeze the roasters. They miscalculated. A massive, unreported bumper crop arrived from Brazil, shattering the artificial shortage. Prices crashed. The syndicate imploded, causing a cascade of bankruptcies that wiped out dozens of legitimate merchants who had nothing to do with the gamble.

The fallout was so severe that the coffee merchants of lower Manhattan decided they needed a system to stabilize the volatility. In 1882, inside a brick building at Hanover Square, they founded the Coffee Exchange of the City of New York.

Their goal was not to gamble, but to ensure stability. They wanted to create a centralized marketplace where buyers (roasters) and sellers (importers and farmers) could agree on a price for future delivery. This is the origin of the "futures" contract. The logic is sound; it functions as an insurance policy against time.

Consider the Roaster's Risk using a concrete example: Imagine a massive buyer like Starbucks needs to secure 100,000 bags for the Christmas rush. They fear a frost in Brazil could double the price by December. To "hedge" this risk, they buy a futures contract at today's price. If the frost hits and the physical price skyrockets, they pay more for the beans, but the value of the "paper" contract they bought also skyrockets. The profit from the paper cancels out the extra cost of the beans. Conversely, a farmer in Honduras fears prices will crash. He sells a contract today. If the price collapses, he gets less cash for his physical sack, but he makes a profit on the short sale of the contract. In theory, stability is achieved.

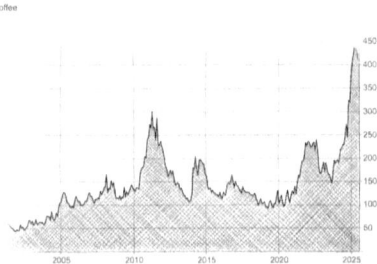

*The Cost of Stability: The peaks and valleys of the coffee market. While the Exchange was created to flatten these curves for farmers and roasters via hedging, the modern dominance of the "derivative function" keeps the price of coffee on a constant, jagged trajectory.*

For a century, this system functioned largely as intended. It smoothed out the inherent unpredictability of agriculture. But as the market evolved, the "insurance" role began to be eclipsed by the "derivative" role. The contract itself—the piece of paper—became more valuable and more frequently traded than the coffee it represented.

### THE ANATOMY OF THE "C" CONTRACT

When a trader executes a buy order, they are not just moving numbers; they are interacting with a highly specific legal document: the Coffee "C" Contract. It is essential to understand exactly what this document is, because the entire global industry is anchored to its fine print. Standardized by the exchange (now part of the Intercontinental Exchange, or ICE), the C-Contract is a promise to deliver a specific commodity.

The contract is a rigid set of constraints:

- **Quantity:** Fixed at 37,500 pounds (approx. 250 bags).
- **Quality:** Defined as "Exchange Grade." This is critical—it denotes coffee that is technically sound rather than "good" in the culinary sense. The contract allows for a specific number

of defects, such as broken beans, insect damage, or sour
beans.

- **Moisture:** Specified between 9% and 13% to prevent mold
  during shipping.
- **Size:** Mandates a "screen size" (bean diameter) of 15/64ths of
  an inch or larger for 50% of the lot.
- **Origin:** Accepts beans from a specific list of countries
  including Mexico, El Salvador, and Colombia. (Brazil was
  historically treated differently due to processing methods,
  though these distinctions have evolved).
- **Delivery:** The seller must deliver the coffee to a licensed
  warehouse in a designated port city like New York, New
  Orleans, or Hamburg.

Here lies the abstraction: almost no one takes delivery. In the futures
market, a fraction of 1% of contracts ever result in actual beans moving
from a warehouse to a truck. The contracts are "paper coffee." A trader
buys a contract on Monday and sells it on Thursday. They are trading the
price movement, not the commodity. The 37,500 pounds of beans exist
only as a theoretical obligation.

Yet, because the volume of "paper coffee" traded on the exchange
dwarfs the volume of physical coffee grown on Earth, the paper price
dictates the physical price. The tail wags the dog. The price of a physical
sack of coffee in Honduras is not determined by the cost of labor in
Honduras, but by the trading volume of paper contracts in New York.

### THE DAM BREAKS: 1989 AND THE END OF QUOTAS

For a brief era—specifically from 1962 to 1989—the volatility of the C-
Market was held in check by a geopolitical dam: The International
Coffee Agreement (ICA).

The ICA functioned as a quota system, similar to how OPEC
manages oil. Producing countries and consuming countries sat at a table
and agreed on export limits. The goal was explicitly political. The United
States, in the throes of the Cold War, feared that if coffee prices crashed,
poverty in Latin America would drive peasant farmers toward Commu-

nism. High coffee prices were viewed by the State Department as a cheaper and more effective alternative to foreign aid.

The system worked. It kept the price of coffee within a target band, dampening the "boom and bust" cycle. Farmers could plan. Governments in the Global South could budget for infrastructure. But by 1989, the geopolitical landscape had shifted. The Berlin Wall was crumbling. The fear of Soviet influence in Latin America was evaporating. In Washington, the economic philosophy had shifted toward the deregulation of the Reagan/Bush era. The "free market" was the new priority; quotas were seen as inefficient distortions.

On July 4, 1989, negotiations for the renewal of the ICA collapsed. The United States withdrew its support. The dam broke.

The result was immediate chaos. Without quotas, producing nations, desperate for foreign currency, dumped their stockpiles onto the market. Brazil opened the floodgates. Vietnam, a sleeping giant in coffee production, began its ascent. The price of coffee crashed by nearly 50% in a matter of months.

The "Free Market" had arrived. Since that day, the coffee market has been defined by extreme, rapid cycles of pricing. The safety net was gone, replaced by the raw mechanism of the ticker tape. The market became a "C-Price" regime, where the antagonist is the volatility itself.


THE FUNGIBILITY TRAP

The philosophical flaw of the C-Price lies in a single economic concept: fungibility. For a commodity market to function, the goods being traded must be interchangeable. A bar of gold is a bar of gold; a barrel of Brent Crude oil is a barrel of Brent Crude. The market assumes that one contract of coffee is essentially identical to another.

But coffee is not gold. It is an agricultural product with infinite biological variance. A sack of high-altitude Bourbon from Rwanda, grown by a cooperative on volcanic soil, is not the same as a sack of mechanized Caturra from a mega-plantation in Minas Gerais. One possesses complex acidity and floral aromatics; the other offers neutral, nutty baselines. One costs $2.50 per pound to produce due to steep terrain and hand-picking; the other costs $0.90 due to industrial efficiency.

The C-Market ignores these distinctions. It treats coffee as a widget. By forcing all "mild Arabicas" into a single pricing bucket, it drags the price of high-quality, labor-intensive coffee down to the level of the lowest-cost producer.

This creates a perilous reality for the smallholder. Brazil, with its massive, flat savannahs and combine harvesters, can produce coffee with incredible efficiency. When Brazil has a "super-harvest," they flood the global market. Supply skyrockets. The C-Price crashes. The smallholder farmer in Honduras, working two hectares of mountainside by hand, cannot compete with a Brazilian combine harvester. Yet, because the global market is pegged to the C-Price, the Honduran farmer sees the value of their crop destroyed by a harvest occurring in a different hemisphere. They are participants in a game where the rules are set by their competitors' geography.

### RISE OF THE MACHINES: FROM PIT TO SERVER

If the problem were merely supply and demand, the brutality of the market would be harsh but understandable. However, the C-Price is no longer just a reflection of physical inventory. Rather, it is a reflection of capital flow.

In the twenty-first century, the coffee futures market was colonized by participants who have no intention of ever roasting a bean: the Speculators. These are hedge funds, pension funds, and commodity index funds. To a macro-trader, coffee is an asset class, a line item in a diversified portfolio alongside copper, soy, and Treasury bonds. It is a tool for hedging against inflation or betting against the U.S. Dollar.

The transition from the "Open Outcry" pits to electronic trading accelerated this detachment. In the old pit, there was a human viscosity to the market. Today, High-Frequency Trading (HFT) algorithms execute trades in microseconds. These "black box" algorithms do not read weather reports from Huila. They read "technicals"—chart patterns, moving averages, and resistance levels.

A crash can happen in real-time without a single physical event occurring in the coffee world. If the price hovers near a "200-day moving average," and then dips slightly below it, algorithms managing billions of dollars interpret this as a bearish signal. They trigger automatic sell orders. Thousands of contracts—representing millions of pounds of paper coffee—are dumped onto the market instantly. The price plummets.

Down on the farm, the trees are the same. The cost of fertilizer is the same. Demand is the same. But because a server farm in New Jersey reacted to a chart pattern, the value of the crop in Ethiopia has evaporated. This financialization of the commodity means that price discovery is often divorced from physical reality.

### THE MYTH OF THE DIFFERENTIAL

Defenders of the system often point out that quality farmers do not sell at the C-Price. They sell at "C plus." This is known as the Differential or the Basis. If the C-Price is trading at $1.20, a buyer might offer a Colombian farmer "C + 40 cents," resulting in a final price of $1.60. The differential is intended to account for quality, certification (like Fair Trade or Organic), and the reputation of the origin.

But the differential is a floating premium on a sinking base. Imagine a house built on a raft in the ocean. The "differential" is the height of the house above the raft. It looks impressive. But if the ocean level (the C-Price) drops, the house drops with it.

In a scenario where the C-Price is $1.50 and the differential is $0.40, the total price is $1.90. The farmer makes a profit. But if the C-Price crashes to $0.90, the total price becomes $1.30. At $1.30, the farmer is likely operating below the cost of production. The premium did not save them. The industry often uses differentials to mask the structural crisis, celebrating high premiums while ignoring that the base price creates a poverty wage. It creates a psychological absurdity where farmers in Central America find themselves hoping for a drought in Brazil. They are locked in a zero-sum game where one region's misery is the requisite for another region's solvency.

.   .   .

## THE COYOTE ECONOMY

While the C-Price is set in New York and London, the actual transaction happens in the dust of the rural road. Most of the world's coffee is produced by smallholders—25 million families farming less than five hectares. They do not have export licenses. They do not have access to international buyers. They do not have 37,500 pounds of coffee ready at once. They have two bags.

While the C-Price is broadcast instantly via fiber optics to trading desks, it travels much slower to the farm gate—often arriving in the cab of a pickup truck driven by the middleman, known in Latin America as "The Coyote" or *intermediario*.

*The "Coyote" serves as the bridge between the remote farm and the global market, paying cash on the spot at a heavy discount.*

The Coyote drives up the unpaved roads to the farm. He has cash. He knows the C-Price, and he knows the farmer has few options. The math of the Coyote is a subtraction game.

Starting with the New York C-Price, one must subtract the export costs: shipping, insurance, and taxes. Then, subtract the milling costs: removing the parchment skin, sorting, and bagging. Then, subtract the Coyote's margin: gas, truck maintenance, risk, and profit. Finally, subtract the yield loss. Coffee loses nearly 20% of its weight when the parchment is removed to produce green beans.

By the time the calculation hits the farm gate, a $1.40 stock market price has become $0.80 in cash. The farmer stands there with their sacks. They need to buy food for the week. They need to pay school fees. They can argue, but the coffee is perishable. If they wait too long, humidity will ruin it. So they sell. This "Farm Gate Price" is the only number that matters, and it is almost always a fraction of the ticker price celebrated in the business news.

## THE STARVATION CYCLE

The math of the C-Price is often the math of insolvency. Extensive studies have pegged the average Cost of Production for washed Arabica in Central America at roughly $1.40 to $1.60 per pound. This includes fertilizer, labor, harvesting, and basic farm maintenance. Yet, for long stretches of the last decade, the C-Price hovered between $0.90 and $1.00.

When the market price is lower than the cost of production, classical economics breaks down. In a rational factory model, if it costs $1.50 to make a widget and it sells for $1.00, the factory closes. But a coffee tree is not a machine. You cannot switch it off. It is a perennial crop that takes 3 to 5 years to grow from seed to fruit. Once planted, the farmer is committed. The "sunk cost" is massive. If they stop tending it, the investment dies. Weeds take over. Pests invade.

So the farmer continues to harvest. They sell at a loss. To survive, they cannibalize their own equity. They stop buying fertilizer. They stop pruning. They take their children out of school to save on fees and use them as unpaid labor. They take out loans from local lenders at high interest, hoping that next year the price will recover. They become prisoners of their own land.

## LA ROYA AND THE MIGRATION

The consequences of this financial mechanism are not abstract numbers on a screen. They are visible in the migration patterns moving north from Central America. There is a direct link between the C-Price and the refugee crisis. It works through a biological mechanism known as *Hemileia vastatrix*—Coffee Leaf Rust, or *La Roya*.

Rust is a fungus that attacks the leaves of the coffee tree, choking off its ability to photosynthesize. It kills the yield. The only way to fight Rust is with expensive fungicides and rigorous plant nutrition. A healthy, well-fed tree can resist the fungus. A starving tree cannot.

When the C-Price crashes, the first thing the farmer cuts is fertilizer and fungicide. It is a discretionary expense they cannot afford. In Year 1, the price crashes, and inputs are cut. In Year 2, the trees are weak. Rust spores, carried by the wind, infect the farm. In Year 3, the harvest fails. The farmer has no crop to sell, even if prices recover. In Year 4, bankruptcy ensues.

In the highlands of Guatemala and Honduras, this dynamic has emptied entire villages. Farmers who have grown coffee for generations are removing their trees. They are replacing coffee with avocado, or illegal coca, or simply abandoning the land to migrate.

The irony is sharp. The consumer in the Global North is drinking better coffee than ever before, often paying a premium for quality. The industry is generating immense value. But the pipeline that transfers that wealth back to the producer is broken. The "value added" is captured by the roaster, the retailer, the landlord, and the taxman. The risk—the weather, the disease, the volatility—remains entirely with the producer.

## The Volatility Trap

The ultimate tragedy of the C-Price is that it discourages the very thing the industry claims to want: quality and sustainability. To grow exceptional coffee requires long-term planning. It requires planting shade trees, which take a decade to mature. It requires building drying beds and training pickers to select only the ripest cherries. This requires a multi-year horizon.

But the C-Price forces the farmer to live in a twenty-four-hour horizon. They are watching the ticker. They are gambling. Why invest in a new fermentation tank if the price might drop 30% next year because a hedge fund manager decided to short the KC contract? Why plant a shade canopy if the farm might be abandoned in two years?

Volatility is the enemy of investment. By turning the price of coffee into a rollercoaster, the C-Market makes sustainable farming irrational. It incentivizes the extraction of value from the soil—getting as much as possible out today with cheap inputs, because tomorrow is not guaranteed.

The "Third Wave" of coffee attempted to bypass this system through Direct Trade. The concept was to negotiate a fixed price directly with the farmer, ignoring the New York ticker. For the specific farmers who find a Direct Trade partner, this model is a lifeline. It restores dignity and predictability. But Direct Trade accounts for a tiny fraction of the global coffee supply. The vast majority of the world's coffee—the beans in the grocery store cans, the instant sachets, and the fast-food cups—is still bought and sold on the C-Market.

New technologies like blockchain are touted as solutions, promising "traceability" that allows the consumer to tip the farmer directly. But these are digital patches on a structural wound. You cannot tip your way out of a deficit. As long as the global trade infrastructure uses the C-Contract as its reference point—as long as the price of a hand-picked fruit is determined by an algorithm designed for high-speed speculation —the coffee trade will remain an extraction engine.

The C-Price was invented in 1882 to bring order to chaos. It succeeded in building a liquid, efficient, global market. But efficiency is not the same as justice. The machine works for the trader in New York. It works for the multinational roaster. But for the farmer in Huila, standing in the rain with a phone in their hand, the machine is broken. The financialization of coffee creates a volatility that small farmers simply cannot weather.

# 32

# THE BLACK FROST: ANATOMY
# OF A MARKET KILLER

T he meteorological event that would ultimately dismantle the existing order of the global coffee economy began as a silent, invisible anomaly in the Southern Hemisphere's atmospheric circulation. On the afternoon of July 17, 1975, a massive polar air mass detached from the Antarctic continent. It moved northward with unusual velocity, crossing the Andes mountains and descending toward the Tropic of Capricorn. By the time this thermal mass reached the state of Paraná in southern Brazil, it had lost nearly all of its humidity. It was a cold, dry wind—a phenomenon distinct from the typical winter patterns of the region, carrying a lethal potential that no farmer on the ground could see coming.

Paraná was, at that time, the undisputed engine room of the global coffee trade. The state's rolling hills, composed of the nutrient-rich, iron-heavy soil known as terra roxa, supported a monoculture of nearly one billion Coffea arabica trees. It was the height of the Southern Hemisphere's winter, and farmers monitored their thermometers with a practiced, anxious vigilance. A standard temperature dip to freezing was manageable, provided the air remained moist. In typical cold fronts, atmospheric humidity condenses on the leaves, freezing into a white rime that insulates the plant tissue. This phenomenon, known locally as the Geada Branca or "White Frost," acts as a *thermal barrier, keeping the internal temperature of the leaf just above the lethal threshold where cell death occurs.*

*The air mass arriving on the night of July 17, however, possessed a dew point far below the freezing level. It created a thermal void, stripping the landscape of protective moisture. At 3:00 AM on July 18, the temperature at the canopy level plummeted to -4°C. Because the air was desiccated, no protective ice formed on the exterior of the leaves. Instead, the cold penetrated the epidermis and attacked the cellular structure directly. This was the Geada Negra—the "Black Frost."*

### THE PHYSICS OF CELLULAR COLLAPSE

Grasping the scale of the economic devastation that followed requires that we first understand the botanical destruction at the microscopic level. *Coffea arabica* is an evolutionary product of the Ethiopian understory, a species with no genetic defense against deep freezing. Unlike temperate crops like wheat, maize, or even tea, which produce cryoprotectant proteins and solutes to lower the freezing point of their sap, the coffee tree's cells are chemically vulnerable. They are filled with water and dissolved sugars susceptible to crystallization.

As the ambient temperature dropped below the critical threshold, the phenomenon of intracellular ice nucleation began. The water inside the large central vacuoles of the leaf cells supercooled, remaining liquid below freezing for a brief period until the tension broke.

Microscopic particles within the sap acted as nucleation sites, triggering a rapid phase change from liquid to solid. Because water expands by approximately nine percent when it crystallizes, the fluid inside the cells had nowhere to go. In the darkness of the Paraná night, billions of microscopic ice crystals expanded inside the leaves, pressing against the delicate phospholipid membranes until they gave way. The expansive force severed the vascular bundles responsible for nutrient transport, quietly destroying the structural integrity of the trees from the inside out.

When the sun rose on the morning of July 18, the damage was not immediately visible to the naked eye. The leaves appeared green, held in place by their rigid cellulose walls. The farmers walking the rows likely felt a false sense of relief, seeing no white ice on the ground. However, as the morning temperature rose and the ice inside the leaves melted, the cellular disaster revealed itself. The cellular fluids—now uncontained by ruptured membranes—leaked into the intercellular spaces. The enzymes in the cytoplasm, exposed to oxygen and mixed with the vacuolar contents, began to oxidize rapidly.

*Why does a frost turn leaves black? It isn't just the cold; it is a violent biological event occurring at the cellular level. This image captures the aftermath of a thermal event where water expansion acted as "internal shrapnel."*

By noon, the emerald hills of Paraná began to shift in color. The leaves turned a sickly purple, the color of bruised biological tissue. By late afternoon, the oxidation was complete. The leaves blackened and curled, crumbling to ash when touched. The trees were not merely damaged; they were necrotic. In a span of six hours, 1.5 billion coffee trees were effectively mummified standing up. Brazil, responsible for supplying nearly sixty percent of the world's coffee, had lost two-thirds of its productive capacity in a single thermal event.

THE LIQUIDITY CRISIS AT 79 PINE STREET

In 1975, the transmission of agricultural data was analog and slow. There were no satellite feeds to broadcast the spectral analysis of crop health to New York or London in real-time. It took several days for surveyors to traverse the dirt roads of Paraná, assess the scale of the necrosis, and telex the findings to the major trading houses. When the reality of the supply shock finally reached the trading floor of the New

York Coffee and Sugar Exchange at 79 Pine Street, the reaction was a severe correction that bordered on market failure.

The benchmark price for Arabica coffee, the "C-Contract," had been trading quietly at approximately sixty cents per pound prior to the frost. As the reports were confirmed, the market entered a period of extreme volatility. The price gapped upward, hitting the daily "limit up"—the maximum price increase allowed by exchange rules in a single trading session. When a market locks "limit up," trading effectively ceases because no seller is willing to part with contracts at the capped price, anticipating further rises the next day.

For weeks, liquidity evaporated. The price rocketed toward three dollars and eight cents per pound (equivalent to nearly $18 today), a staggering increase that shattered the historical trading range. This price explosion triggered a phenomenon known as a short squeeze. Large speculators and hedge funds had been holding "short" positions, betting on a price decline due to what was supposed to be a bumper Brazilian harvest. They held "paper"—contracts obligating them to deliver coffee they did not own.

The physical holders of coffee—the importers and old-line merchant families who possessed actual bags of beans in warehouses in New Orleans, Hamburg, and Trieste—found themselves in a position of absolute leverage. The "basis," the differential between the futures price and the physical cash price, widened dramatically. The financial wealth transferred from the speculative accounts to the physical merchants was immense. The market dictated that paper derivatives are secondary to the physical commodity; those who held the inventory controlled the solvency of those who held the contracts.

The atmosphere at 79 Pine Street shifted from routine speculation to a chaotic scramble for coverage. The shouting in the pits wasn't just about price discovery; it was the sound of a market realizing that the underlying asset had vanished. The "C-Contract," usually a tool for hedging risk, became a weapon of financial destruction for those on the wrong side of the trade. Unlike modern electronic trading, where algorithms execute trades in milliseconds, this was a visceral, physical panic. Traders physically jostled for position, voices hoarse, trying to close out positions that were bleeding millions of dollars by the hour. The concept of "volatility" ceased to be a statistic and became a threat to the existence of some of the oldest trading houses in New York.

### THE GREAT ADULTERATION: ENGINEERING THE SUPPLY

For the "Big Three" American roasters—General Foods (Maxwell House), Procter & Gamble (Folgers), and Hills Bros—the Black Frost presented an existential threat. These corporations operated on a model of high volume and extremely tight margins. They were the gatekeepers of the American morning, and they were terrified that passing a four hundred percent cost increase to the consumer would destroy coffee drinking habits permanently. They feared a mass exodus toward the burgeoning soft drink market, which was aggressively targeting the youth demographic with sweet, caffeinated alternatives.

To protect their market share and maintain the price point of the "daily cup," the roasters turned to industrial chemistry. They initiated a period of quality degradation that industry historians refer to as "The Great Adulteration." Unable to control the cost of the raw material, they manipulated the physical properties of the bean to stretch the supply.

The primary innovation was "High Yield" roasting. In corporate R&D labs, chemists developed a method of steam hydrolysis. Green coffee beans were subjected to high-pressure steam before roasting. This process softened the cellulose structure of the bean, effectively pre-digesting the tough fibers. When these water-logged beans hit the high heat of the industrial roaster, the moisture inside flashed to steam, causing the cellular structure to expand violently. The bean "puffed" like popcorn, increasing its physical volume by up to fifty percent while reducing its density.

*Industrial roasters used steam hydrolysis to "puff" beans like popcorn,
filling the can with less actual coffee.*

This technological trick allowed roasters to fill a standard one-pound
coffee can with only eleven or twelve ounces of actual coffee matter.
Visually, the consumer saw a full can; chemically, they were buying air
and cellulose. The sensory cost was high. The puffing process increased
the surface area of the grind, accelerating oxidation and staling. Furthermore, the steam treatment interfered with the Maillard reaction, the
complex browning process that generates the sweet and nutty aromatic
compounds. The resulting beverage tasted hollow, metallic, and papery
—a ghost of what coffee was supposed to be.

Simultaneously, the roasters altered their blend compositions. They
aggressively replaced the expensive, frost-damaged Arabica with *Coffea
canephora* (Robusta). Robusta beans, which contain higher caffeine and
harsh pyrazines (compounds tasting of burnt rubber and earth), were
significantly cheaper. However, the traditional sources of Robusta were
also under strain; Angola, a major producer, was embroiled in a civil war,
further tightening supply. Roasters scoured the globe for any available
caffeine, sourcing harsh, low-grade beans from West Africa and Indonesia. A standard grocery store blend, which might have been ninety
percent Arabica in 1974, shifted to a mix containing fifty percent or even
sixty percent Robusta by 1977. To mask the rubbery off-notes of the
Robusta and the hollowness of the puffed beans, roasters darkened the
roast level, effectively burning out the flavor defects but creating a cup
characterized by bitterness and ash.

## THE MARKETING OF DECLINE

To sell this reformulated, chemically altered product, the industry relied on a massive advertising offensive designed to divorce the consumer's perception of quality from the actual sensory experience. Marketing campaigns moved away from describing the flavor of the coffee—because the flavor was objectively deteriorating—and focused entirely on the emotional utility of the ritual.

Folgers utilized the character of Mrs. Olson, a comforting neighbor figure who saved marriages by replacing a husband's "bad" coffee with "Mountain Grown" Folgers. The term "Mountain Grown" was a masterpiece of empty nomenclature; technically, most coffee is grown at elevation to survive, but the phrase implied a level of exclusivity that the contents of the can did not possess. The ads suggested that domestic tranquility relied on the brand of coffee served, leveraging social anxiety to sell a compromised product. Maxwell House countered with Cora, a general store owner, reinforcing the slogan "Good to the Last Drop" even as the chemical composition of that drop deteriorated into a slurry of puffed beans and Robusta.

Instant coffee brands, facing the same cost pressures, marketed heavy processing as a technological miracle. "Flavor Crystals" became a buzzword, framing the dehydration and freeze-drying process as a method of preservation rather than destruction. These campaigns were effective in the short term, maintaining sales volume despite the price spikes. However, they planted the seeds of a long-term demographic crisis. A generation of young Americans, the Baby Boomers, came of age drinking this bitter, diluted, high-yield product. Unsurprisingly, they rejected it, accelerating the shift toward sweetened carbonated beverages. The coffee industry effectively traded its future relevance for short-term survival, creating a flavor profile so poor that it would eventually necessitate the "Second Wave" rebellion of Peet's and Starbucks.

## THE CONSUMER REVOLT

By 1977, the retail price of coffee in the United States had reached historical highs, crossing four dollars per pound (adjusted for inflation, nearly twenty dollars). The elasticity of demand finally snapped. The

American housewife, the primary purchaser of household goods, organized a grassroots resistance that frightened the corporate giants as
much as the frost itself.

Boycotts erupted in major metropolitan areas. In New York, Elinor
Guggenheimer, the Commissioner of Consumer Affairs, became the face
of the movement. She urged Americans to stop drinking coffee entirely,
framing the high prices as price gouging by the roasters and the
Brazilian government. "It is a matter of discipline," she told the press.
"Tea is a viable alternative." Her rhetoric turned the coffee aisle into a
battleground of civic duty.

The boycotts were effective. Coffee consumption in the United States
dropped by nearly twenty percent in a single year. The drop in demand
eventually helped cool the overheated market, but the cultural damage
was done. Coffee had transitioned from a daily necessity to a luxury item
of questionable value. The industry had saved its margins but lost its
soul, creating a vacuum that would eventually be filled by the specialty
coffee movement decades later. The irony was palpable: in trying to
make coffee affordable enough to drink, the roasters had made it bad
enough to quit.

### THE GEOPOLITICAL BUTTERFLY EFFECT: THE RISE OF VIETNAM

The most profound consequence of the Black Frost, however,
occurred thousands of miles from Brazil, in a geopolitical maneuver that
would permanently alter the supply side of the global coffee equation.
The shockwaves of the price spike penetrated the Iron Curtain, destabi-
lizing the planned economy of East Germany (the German Democratic
Republic, or GDR).

In the GDR, coffee was a subsidized staple, a symbol of the state's
ability to provide a "Western" standard of living to its citizens. The
government spent significant sums of hard currency—specifically U.S.
dollars—to import green coffee. When the price tripled in 1976, the
GDR's budget could no longer sustain the imports. Coffee disappeared
from the shelves of East Berlin, replaced by a hated substitute known as
*Kaffee-Mix*, a blend containing fifty-one percent coffee and forty-nine
percent chicory, rye, and sugar beet.

*51% Coffee, 49% Filler, 100% Resentment. The* Kaffee-Mix *solution to the East German Coffee Crisis of 1977.*

The public reaction was furious. Workers rejected the ersatz coffee, leading to unrest and protests in factories—a dangerous level of dissent in an authoritarian state. This event, known as the "Coffee Crisis of 1977," terrified the Socialist Unity Party. Erich Honecker and the Politburo realized that relying on Western markets for a critical commodity was a strategic vulnerability. They needed a source of coffee within the socialist sphere of influence, one that could be controlled without the need for volatile Western currency.

The solution lay in Vietnam.

In 1977, Vietnam was struggling to rebuild after decades of war. Its economy was shattered, its infrastructure bombed, and it had little to export. However, the Central Highlands, specifically the province of Dak Lak, possessed deep, volcanic red soil and a climate suitable for agriculture. The GDR and the Soviet Union brokered a massive bilateral aid treaty with the Vietnamese government, a deal born directly from the frost-induced shortages in Berlin.

The terms were industrial and explicit: East Germany would provide heavy machinery IFA trucks, irrigation pumps, and hydroelectric equipment—along with agronomic expertise and medical supplies. In exchange, Vietnam would dedicate vast tracts of land to coffee production, paying back the investment with green beans over the next twenty years. It was a barter of industrial might for agricultural output.

Critically, the agronomic plan focused on *Coffea canephora* (Robusta) rather than Arabica. Robusta was native to the region, yielded significantly more cherries per tree, and was resistant to the rust fungus and higher temperatures of the lower altitudes. It was the perfect crop for a rapid, industrial-scale ramp-up. The East German agronomists and Vietnamese planners did not care about the nuance of flavor; they cared about yield, caffeine content, and the reliability of the supply chain.

This decision, triggered directly by the frost in Brazil, transformed Vietnam from a non-entity in the coffee world into a titan. In 1975, Vietnam produced almost no exportable coffee. By the late 1990s, the trees planted under this treaty matured, and Vietnam surged to become the second-largest coffee producer in the world. The flood of cheap Vietnamese Robusta that hit the market in the 1990s would eventually cause the price crash of 2001, proving that the frost's legacy was a permanent structural shift in global supply. The farmers of Central America in the 2000s, bankrupted by low prices, were the delayed casualties of a frost that happened in Brazil three decades prior.

### THE HUMAN COST: FROM COLONO TO FAVELA

In Brazil, the frost accelerated a painful social transition that reshaped the demographics of the south. Before 1975, coffee farming in Paraná operated largely on the *colonato* system. Workers lived on the plantations (fazendas) with their families, receiving housing and a small plot of land to grow their own food in exchange for tending the coffee trees. Though semi-feudal, it provided a degree of housing security and subsistence. The coffee harvest was the metronome of rural life, dictating the rhythm of the year.

When the trees died, the economic logic of the *colonato* collapsed. Landowners, facing bankruptcy and the need to replant crops that would not yield fruit for three years, could no longer afford to house and feed a standing workforce. They evicted the workers en masse. This triggered one of the largest internal migrations in Brazilian history. Millions of rural workers packed their belongings and migrated to the cities of Londrina, São Paulo, and Curitiba.

Lacking resources and skills for urban employment, these displaced agricultural workers settled on the outskirts of the cities, building informal shantytowns. The explosion of the *favelas* in southern Brazil can be traced directly to the unemployment shock of July 1975. The "boia-fria" phenomenon emerged from this displacement—day laborers who lived in the city slums and were trucked out to the countryside for seasonal work, bringing their "cold lunch" (*boia fria*) with them. The frost dissolved the traditional rural social contract, replacing it with a precarious, transient labor force that had no connection to the land they worked. The social fabric of the coffee regions was torn apart, replacing the community of the farm with the alienation of the urban periphery.

This migration also marked the end of the smallholder dominance in Brazilian coffee. As the industry recovered, it did not return to the labor-intensive model of the past. The capital required to survive such a disaster favored consolidation. Small farms were bought up by larger conglomerates, paving the way for the agribusiness model that characterizes modern Brazil. The romantic image of the small family farm was replaced by the reality of the corporate plantation.

## THE SHIFT TO THE CERRADO: INDUSTRIALIZING THE CROP

The Black Frost taught the Brazilian coffee industry a harsh lesson about geography. The risk of farming in Paraná, which sat at the southern limit of the tropical zone, was deemed too high for the capital investment required. The industry began a massive migration north-ward, into the state of Minas Gerais and the region known as the Cerrado.

The Cerrado offered a different climate profile: high altitude, distinct dry seasons, and crucially, a significantly lower risk of frost. However, the topography was different. Unlike the steep, rolling hills of Paraná which required hand-picking, the Cerrado was largely flat plateaus. This topographical feature allowed for the introduction of large-scale mechanization.

Farmers adopted industrial harvesters—massive machines that straddled the rows of coffee trees, using vibrating rods to shake the cherries onto conveyor belts. This shift from manual selection to mechanical harvesting fundamentally changed the economics of Brazilian coffee. It lowered the cost of production dramatically, allowing Brazil to pursue a strategy of volume over quality. The modern Brazilian coffee sector, a high-tech agribusiness powerhouse capable of dictating global prices through sheer scale, was built on the ashes of the Paraná disaster.

This shift also had botanical implications. The new monocultures in the Cerrado required intense chemical inputs to thrive in the different soil conditions. The soil was naturally acidic and required massive applications of lime to be suitable for coffee. The "Green Revolution" techniques of fertilizers and pesticides became standard practice to protect the massive investment required to open these new frontiers. Coffee farming became less about tending to nature and more about managing chemistry.


THE LESSON OF FRAGILITY

The Black Frost of 1975 serves as a definitive case study in the fragility of agricultural monoculture. The global economy had allowed the production of a critical commodity to become dangerously concentrated in a single, vulnerable geographic region. When the temperature dropped by a few degrees, the repercussions cascaded through the system: bankrupted hedge funds in New York, adulterated products in American supermarkets, riots in East Berlin, and the clear-cutting of jungles in Vietnam.

The event demonstrated that the coffee market is not merely a financial abstraction of numbers and contracts. It is a biological system, tethered to the soil and the weather. The "severe correction" was a reminder that despite the sophisticated mechanisms of the futures market, the entire industry rests on the metabolic stability of a delicate tropical tree. The frost forced the industry to diversify, scattering production across new latitudes and longitudes, but it also industrialized the crop, stripping away much of the romance and replacing it with the cold logic of risk management and efficiency. The frost proved that while the market can hedge against price, it cannot hedge against biology.

# 33

# THE MORAL LABEL: FAIR TRADE
# AND THE LIMITS OF A STICKER

T *he revolution began with a logo rather than a weapon.*

*In the autumn of 1988, in the fluorescent aisles of a Dutch super-market, a new package of coffee appeared on the shelves. It was named "Max Havelaar." To the average shopper in Rotterdam or Amsterdam, the name was not merely a brand; it was a historical signal. It referred to the protagonist of the 1860 novel by Multatuli—the pen name of Eduard Douwes Dekker—a fictional colonial administrator in the Dutch East Indies who had resigned his post rather than participate in the systematic exploitation of Javanese coffee farmers.*

*The book had been a literary bombshell in the 19th century, exposing the "Cultivation System" that forced farmers to grow cash crops for the colonial government while their own families starved. The name on the coffee bag was a ghost story brought to life, a reminder that the comfort of the European consumer had always been purchased at the expense of the tropical laborer.*

*The coffee inside this new 1988 package was not chemically different from the vacuum-sealed bricks sitting next to it. It was roasted to the same amber hue, ground to the same particle size, and sourced from similar altitudes. Yet, the price was significantly higher. The promise printed on the side was radical in its simplicity. For the first time in the history of the modern coffee trade, the price of this product had not been set by the supply and demand curves of the New York Stock Exchange. It had been set by a moral calculation.*

*The architects of this label, a Dutch priest named Frans van der Hoff and an economist named Nico Roozen, had analyzed the collapsing prices of the global coffee market and concluded that the market mechanism itself was flawed. They issued a challenge that would become the movement's manifesto: "Trade, not aid." They proposed a Floor Price—a minimum guarantee that would cover the cost of production and basic subsistence, regardless of how precipitously the global market crashed. Buying this specific bag was the purchase of an insurance policy for a family in Mexico as much as a caffeine transaction.*

*Four decades later, that singular Dutch experiment has metastasized into the most recognizable ethical certification in the world: Fair Trade. The blue and green logo is now ubiquitous, plastered on billions of dollars of merchandise, from bananas in London to cocoa in Berlin to coffee in Seattle. It has become the gold standard of conscientious consumption, a shorthand that tells the shopper, in the split second of a purchasing decision, that the supply chain is clean.*

*However, in the remote hillsides where the coffee is actually grown, the reality of the label is far more complex than the sticker suggests. What began as a tool for revolutionary justice has evolved into a massive bureaucratic apparatus—a system of audits, fees, and exclusions that can sometimes reinforce the very inequalities it was designed to dismantle. The label serves as a protection, but it has not proven to be a solution.*

### THE MATH OF SURVIVAL

Understanding the promise—and the structural limitations—of Fair Trade requires looking past the marketing and into the mathematics. The system is built on two specific financial levers: the Floor Price and the Social Premium.

The coffee market is defined by its volatility. It swings violently based on frost events in Brazil, droughts in Vietnam, or speculative shifts in Manhattan. For a smallholder farmer with two hectares of land, this volatility is not an abstraction; it is an existential threat. A price crash can wipe out a year's income in a single week, leaving a family unable to purchase food or pay for schooling.

Fair Trade was designed to act as a concrete floor beneath that chaos. The mechanism is rigid: if the global commodity price (the "C-Price") falls below a certain threshold—$1.80 per pound (0.45 kg) for washed Arabica (raised from the old $1.40 floor)—the Fair Trade buyer is contractually obligated to pay the minimum. If the global market rises above $1.80, the buyer pays the market price. The farmer receives the higher of the two.

On top of this base price, the buyer pays an additional fixed sum— the Social Premium, currently set at 20 cents per pound. This money is deposited into the communal bank account of the cooperative to be allocated democratically, rather than going into the individual farmer's pocket. It is designated strictly for "community development": building schools, improving roads, or investing in shared milling equipment.

In theory, this is a perfect model. It de-commodifies the coffee, transforming a ruthless market transaction into a stable social contract. In the late 1990s and early 2000s, when the global price of coffee crashed to historic lows—touching $0.45 per pound in 2001—the Fair Trade floor literally saved lives. While conventional farmers were abandoning their land or suffering from malnutrition, certified cooperatives remained solvent. The system worked as intended.

But time is a cruel variable. The floor price moves in slow steps, while the global economy is dynamic. For many years, the washed-Arabica floor sat at $1.40; today, it sits at $1.80. Since that older floor was set, the cost of nitrogen fertilizer has tripled. The cost of labor in Latin America has doubled. The price of fuel for transport trucks has skyrocketed. Inflation has eroded the purchasing power of the guarantee.

For a farmer in a low-cost region like Ethiopia or Uganda, $1.80 might still represent a viable living wage. But for a farmer in Costa Rica or Colombia, where the currency is stronger and the standard of living is higher, the "Cost of Production" might now exceed the floor. This creates a disturbing economic anomaly: A farmer can sell their coffee under the Fair Trade label—guaranteeing they are "paid fairly" according to the rules—and yet, because the floor has not risen in lockstep with global inflation, they are selling at a loss. The label certifies a price, but it no longer certifies a livelihood. The floor has effectively become a basement.


## INSIDE SOL Y CAFÉ

The other critical condition of Fair Trade is political: one cannot join the system as an individual. The certification requires farmers to organize into Cooperatives.

This was an ideological choice by the founders, rooted in the belief that individual smallholders were weak, but a union of smallholders was strong. By pooling their harvest, farmers could negotiate better contracts, purchase fertilizer in bulk, and share the cost of export licenses. The co-op was intended as the engine of rural democracy.

In the San Ignacio province of northern Peru, near the misty border with Ecuador, this engine is visible in motion. This region is a stronghold of certified organic coffee, a landscape of steep, green mountains where the morning fog clings to the canopy. Here, the cooperative Sol y Café operates as a massive logistical and social hub.

On a humid Tuesday morning, consider a farmer named Mateo, a member of the cooperative, navigating his motorcycle down a muddy track, balancing two heavy sacks of parchment coffee on the seat behind him. He arrives at the coop's warehouse, a cavernous structure made of concrete blocks with a corrugated metal roof. The air inside smells of dry dust and green vegetation.

Mateo unloads his coffee. A young accountant at a computer terminal logs the weight (in kilograms) and the humidity level. Mateo does not receive the full payment immediately. He receives a partial payment—an advance. The cooperative will aggregate his coffee with that of 500 other members, mill it, sort it, export it to a buyer in Hamburg or Oakland, and then, months later, pay Mateo the *reintegro* (the final adjustment) once the sale is finalized.

This system requires a profound level of trust. Mateo must trust that the managers will not embezzle the funds. He must trust that the German buyer will honor the contract. He must trust that the global price won't collapse before the container ships. But in exchange for this patience, he gains access to the cooperative's infrastructure.

He has access to the dental clinic the coop funds with the Social Premium, where his children can be treated without upfront cost. He has access to the staff agronomist, who visits his farm to teach him how to prune his Caturra trees to fight leaf rust. He has a guaranteed buyer for his harvest, even in a bad year. For Mateo, the system functions. He is not wealthy—his home has a dirt floor and his motorcycle is held together with wire—but he is part of a safety net. When he walks into the annual general assembly, he holds a voting card.

## Voting for Cash

However, the reality of that "vote" is often far messier than the marketing brochures suggest. The communal management of the Social Premium is a frequent flashpoint for internal conflict.

Imagine the scene of the annual assembly. Five hundred farmers sit on plastic chairs in the warehouse, the heat rising as the sun beats down on the metal roof. The air is thick with humidity and tension. The cooperative manager stands at the front with a microphone and a projector, announcing that the group has accumulated $50,000 in premium funds from the previous harvest.

"We should build a new wet mill," the manager proposes, pointing to a slide on the screen. "It will improve our quality scores, allow us to process coffee faster, and help us sell for higher prices next year." This is the rational, long-term business choice. It is an investment in the cooperative's future competitiveness.

But a farmer in the back row stands up, holding his hat in his hands. "My roof is leaking," he shouts, his voice shaking with frustration. "My children need school uniforms for the next term. I cannot wait three years for a mill to pay off. We should distribute the cash now."

*The Messy Reality of Democracy: Tension rises along with the humidity
as the cooperative debates how to allocate the harvest funds.*

A second faction argues for a fertilizer subsidy to combat the declining yields. A third group wants to repair the bridge that washed out in the last storm, cutting off the western sector of the village.

The label promises "Community Development," but "Community" is a collection of competing needs and desperate urgencies rather than a monolith. Often, the poorest farmers—those living closest to the financial edge—cannot afford the luxury of long-term investment. They vote for immediate cash payouts or tangible goods, like machetes, boots, or food subsidies, rather than infrastructure.

The democratic process, while noble in intent, can sometimes paralyze the business strategy. The cooperative becomes a miniature welfare state, struggling to function as a competitive export company while simultaneously attempting to fill the gaps left by a negligent government. The manager knows the mill is necessary for survival, but he is voted down by a membership that needs to eat today.

## THE COYOTE'S LIQUIDITY

Across the valley, on the ridge opposite Mateo's farm, lives Sofia. She grows the same variety of coffee in the same soil, under the same weather conditions. But Sofia is not certified.

Her exclusion could be due to several factors. Perhaps she cannot afford the "buy-in fee" to join the cooperative, which can amount to $200 —a fortune for a subsistence farmer. Perhaps her farm is located down a ravine that the cooperative's collection truck cannot navigate. Or perhaps she simply does not trust the politics of the coop managers, having seen a previous organization collapse due to corruption a decade ago.

Because she is outside the system, she cannot access the Floor Price. She cannot access the Social Premium or the technical assistance. When the harvest comes, she has only one option: The Coyote.

The Coyote is the local intermediary. Often cast as a villain in the narrative of ethical coffee, in the ecosystem of the coffee lands he provides a service that the virtuous cooperative often cannot: Liquidity.

The Coyote drives a battered Toyota Hilux, usually armed for protection, carrying a duffel bag filled with small-denomination bills. He drives up to Sofia's farm gate at dusk. He operates on a razor-thin margin based on real-time information. At 6:00 AM, he receives a text message from a large exporter in the city telling him the day's "street price" for parchment coffee. If the exporter offers him $1.00 per pound, the Coyote calculates his gasoline, his truck maintenance, and his risk of robbery.

He offers Sofia $0.70 per pound.

This price is 30% lower than what Mateo might eventually receive from the cooperative. It is a predatory rate. But the Coyote adds a crucial phrase: "Cash. Now."

He does not care about the moisture content of the beans. He does not care if the beans are ugly or slightly insect-damaged. He does not care about child labor rules, environmental audits, or shade coverage. He weighs the sacks on a handheld scale, hands Sofia the stack of cash, and drives away.

Sofia takes the deal. She has debts to pay today. The school fees are due tomorrow. She needs to buy rice and oil for the week. She cannot wait three months for a *reintegro* payment from a German buyer she will never meet. She trades value for speed.

*The "Coyote" provides immediate liquidity, purchasing coffee at a discount from farmers who cannot wait for cooperative payments.*

The Fair Trade label creates a binary world. It divides the farming community into the "Chosen" and the "Left Behind." The label on the supermarket shelf suggests that it solves poverty for the region. In reality, it often creates an island of slightly-better-off farmers (like Mateo) in a sea of desperate ones (like Sofia). The structural poverty of the region remains; the label simply selects a few winners who can navigate the bureaucracy.

## WHO IS EXCLUDED?

There is a deeper structural critique regarding who gets to be a "winner" in this system. Fair Trade certification rules are strict about organizational structure. To be certified, a group must be a Small Producer Organization—a cooperative of small family farms.

However, a significant portion of the world's coffee is not grown by smallholders. It is grown on medium-sized estates or large plantations. In countries like Brazil or parts of India, coffee is an industrial crop. On these large farms, there are thousands of landless laborers—pickers, pruners, and sorters. These individuals are often the poorest people in the entire coffee supply chain. They do not own land; they own only their labor.

Under the classic Fair Trade rules, a large private estate cannot be certified in the same way a cooperative can. The logic is that Fair Trade is designed to support the "small family farmer" against the corporate plantation.

This creates an arbitrary moral distinction. A landless laborer picking coffee on a private farm in Brazil might be destitute, earning minimum wage and living in a dormitory. But the coffee he picks cannot easily carry the Fair Trade mark because the farm is owned by a single landlord, not a cooperative. Meanwhile, a "smallholder" in a cooperative might actually be a relatively prosperous landowner with ten hectares and hired workers of his own.

The label fetishizes the structure of the farm—cooperative versus private—rather than the poverty of the worker. It protects a specific class of landowner, while often ignoring the proletariat of the fields. The system was built to save the peasant, not the employee.

## THE CLIPBOARD POLICE

For those who do manage to enter the system, the privilege of the label comes with a heavy price tag: Compliance. Fair Trade is not just a philosophy; it has become a bureaucracy. To maintain the certification, the cooperative must survive the annual Audit.

This is a moment of high anxiety for the cooperative management. An auditor, usually an educated professional from the capital city or from Europe, arrives in a 4x4 vehicle. They carry a clipboard—or increasingly, a ruggedized tablet—and a binder of criteria hundreds of pages thick. They are there to inspect the "Internal Control System."

They randomly select member farms to visit, looking for violations. Is the chemical storage shed exactly 50 meters from the water source? Are the empty pesticide containers triple rinsed and punctured to prevent reuse? Are the children attending school, and is there documentation to prove they are not working during school hours? Are the workers on the larger farms being paid the legal minimum wage?

These are all noble goals. No consumer wants their coffee to be grown by poisoning a river or exploiting a child. But for a farmer with a fourth-grade education, the documentation required to prove innocence is overwhelming. The "Binder of Evidence" becomes a fetish object.

Cooperative managers spend weeks panic-filing receipts and timesheets instead of managing the business strategies of the group.

If the auditor finds a "Non-Compliance"—say, a farmer who forgot to update their compost logbook or a chemical container left in the wrong shed—the entire cooperative can be suspended. The risk is collective. One negligent member can cost 500 families their export license.

*Certification requires rigorous documentation, transforming farm management into a bureaucratic exercise of audit compliance.*

Furthermore, the audit is not free. The cooperative must pay the certification body for the privilege of being inspected. The fees run into the thousands of dollars annually. This money comes directly out of the coffee revenue. It represents a wealth transfer from the poor to the "ethics industry."

This creates a perverse incentive. The cooperatives that are most successful at Fair Trade are often not the ones with the best farming practices or the neediest members; they are the ones with the best administrators. Success depends on the ability to manage a spreadsheet, not the ability to manage a coffee tree.

### FAIRWASHING AND MASS BALANCE

If the view from the farm is complicated, the view from the super-market is deceptive. In the early days, Fair Trade was a niche movement, sold in church basements and activist food co-ops. The coffee often tasted terrible—stale, dark-roasted, and woody—but people drank it to feel good. It was "Solidarity Coffee," where the bitter taste was almost part of the penance.

Then, the corporations woke up. In the mid-2000s, giants like Starbucks, Nestlé, and McDonald's realized that "Sustainability" was a valuable marketing asset. They began to purchase Fair Trade certified lots. This was undeniably good for volume; suddenly, millions of pounds of certified coffee were moving, and millions of dollars in Social Premiums were flowing to cooperatives.

But the corporations were savvy. They realized they didn't need to certify their entire supply chain. They could launch a specific "Ethical Blend."

Imagine a massive multinational roaster. They buy 95% of their coffee on the conventional market, paying the lowest possible price, squeezing the farmers for every cent. Then, they buy 5% of their coffee as Fair Trade. They launch a massive advertising campaign featuring the 5%. They put the logo on the website. They release a glossy "Corporate Social Responsibility" report full of smiling photos of farmers like Mateo.

This is Fairwashing. The label allows the company to purchase a moral halo for a fraction of the cost of actually changing their business model. The consumer sees the logo and assumes the company is "good," masking the reality of the other 95% of the business.

Even more opaque is the system known as Mass Balance. In some commodity markets (more common in cocoa and sugar, but increasingly present in corporate coffee supply chains), the physical separation of beans is logistically difficult.

Mass Balance works exactly like the electricity grid. If you pay for "Wind Energy" at home, the electrons coming out of your socket aren't necessarily from a wind turbine. You are paying to put wind energy into the grid *somewhere*, matching your usage.

Coffee works the same way. A company buys 10 tons of Fair Trade beans and 90 tons of conventional beans, mixing them all in one silo. They can't separate the "fair" beans from the "unfair" ones. So, the certifier allows them to put the Fair Trade label on 10% of their bags.

When you buy that bag, you aren't necessarily drinking the ethical beans. You are funding the *purchase* of ethical beans that went into the general mix.

The link between the drinker and the grower is severed, replaced by an accounting trick. The moral properties of the product have been decoupled from its physical reality.

## THE OVERSUPPLY CRISIS

The most crushing failure of the system, however, is a simple failure of market mechanics: Too many sellers, too few buyers.

Because the promise of a Floor Price is so attractive, thousands of cooperatives have rushed to get certified. They have paid the fees, done the audits, and followed the rules. But the demand from Western consumers has not kept pace. There are more farmers who want to sell Fair Trade coffee than there are drinkers who want to buy it.

This leads to a heartbreaking statistic: roughly 50% of the coffee grown by Fair Trade certified farmers is sold as conventional coffee.

Mateo might grow 100 bags of certified coffee. But his cooperative can only find Fair Trade buyers for 40 of them. The other 60 bags must be dumped onto the open market at the standard C-Price. Mateo paid the cost of certification for his entire crop—he did the paperwork, he paid the fees, he maintained the standards—but he only received the price benefit for a fraction of it. The label is a ticket to the dance, but it doesn't guarantee you a partner.

## THE PARADOX OF QUALITY

There is a final, subtle irony in the system. The Floor Price mechanism can sometimes accidentally punish Quality.

Recall the "Smile Curve" of value. The highest value in coffee today is found in the "Ultra-Specialty" sector—coffees that score 88 or 90 points on the quality scale. These coffees sell for $4.00, $6.00, or even $10.00 per pound—far above a Fair Trade floor of roughly $2.00 ($1.80 plus the premium).

If Mateo produces an incredible, 90-point microlot—a coffee that tastes of jasmine and peach—he shouldn't sell it as Fair Trade. He should sell it as "Specialty." The Fair Trade floor is irrelevant to him because the quality market pays more.

So, who uses the Fair Trade floor? Often, it becomes the destination for the minimum acceptable quality. If a cooperative has a lot of mediocre coffee—beans that score a passing 80 points but aren't exciting—they will try to sell that lot as Fair Trade. They need the floor price because the quality doesn't merit a higher price on its own.

This creates a reputation trap. Among high-end coffee buyers, "Fair Trade" is sometimes whispered to be a synonym for "boring coffee." It is seen as a charity purchase, not a culinary one. The mechanism that was designed to save the farmer ends up devaluing their product's reputation. It frames the farmer as a ward of the state needing protection, instead of an artisan capable of excellence.

A FLOOR, NOT A CEILING

Does this mean Fair Trade is a failure?

To say it failed is to ignore the thousands of clinics, schools, and roads that the Social Premium has built. It is to ignore the fact that in 2001, when the market collapsed, Fair Trade cooperatives were often the only organizations that didn't go bankrupt. It is a vital, necessary triage.

But we must recognize it for what it is: Triage.

Fair Trade is a tourniquet. It stops the bleeding. It prevents the absolute worst-case scenario of starvation wages. But a tourniquet is not a rehabilitation plan. It does not help the patient walk, run, or thrive.

The $1.80 floor—plus a premium earmarked for community projects—is still a poverty line. It keeps the farmer alive, but it often keeps them poor. It does not offer a pathway to the middle class. It does not solve the structural issues of land ownership, climate change, or the colonial trade tariffs that punish value addition at the source.

True justice in the coffee cup would not look like a sticker. It would look like value addition. It would look like Sofia having the capital to build her own small roasting facility, rather than selling raw beans. It would look like Mateo owning shares in the shipping company. It would look like the "Smile Curve" flattening out, so that the person who takes the risk of growing the crop shares in the wealth of selling it.

Until then, the label remains a paradox: a necessary moral invention that has become a bureaucratic trap. It allows the consumer to feel they have "done their part" for $5.50, while the structural machinery of the market grinds on, largely unchanged. The ghost of Max Havelaar still haunts the aisle, waiting for a revolution that the sticker promised but could not quite deliver. Ethical consumption labels often mask the need for deeper structural change, providing a comfortable illusion of progress while the fundamental inequities of the trade remain intact.

# 34

# THE COFFEE PARADOX: THE SMILE CURVE AND THE FOUR-CENT CUP

T he transaction occurs thousands of times a minute, executing a synchronized global rhythm that stretches from the rain-slicked pavements of London to the neon-lit districts of Tokyo. A customer in a beige trench coat approaches a white marble counter, taps a smartwatch on a glowing terminal, and authorizes a payment of $5.50 for an oat milk latte. The exchange is seamless, mechanical, and largely thoughtless. The price is accepted as the requisite cost of participation in the modern economy. The customer purchases warmth, a precise dose of alkaloids, high-speed connectivity, and fifteen minutes of shelter from the urban drizzle as much as a beverage.

Five thousand miles away, in the misty highlands of Huila, Colombia, a producer named Sofia stands at the receiving station of her local cooperative. Her boots are coated in reddish mud, the residue of the steep Andean terrain. She has just delivered two sacks (approximately 140 kg or 308 lbs) of parchment coffee—the physical result of four months of pruning, fertilizing, picking, depulping, and fermenting. The station manager, operating a calibrated moisture meter, hands her a printed receipt. Based on the current global price trading on the Intercontinental Exchange (ICE)—the digital marketplace where the world's soft commodity futures are bought and sold—her coffee has been valued at roughly $1.10 per pound ($2.42 per kg).

When the film of the global economy is paused and the mathematics of the *supply chain are dissected, a staggering disconnect emerges. A standard latte contains roughly 18 grams of ground coffee. At the selling price dictated by the commodities market, the value of the actual beans within that $5.50 cup is roughly four cents.*

*The remaining $5.46 has been redistributed into the complex machinery of the value chain. It has been absorbed by shipping container logistics, marine insurance brokers, natural gas for roasting drums, cellulose manufacturing for cups, commercial real estate leases, and the service labor required to prepare the drink. This structural imbalance, often termed the Coffee Paradox, represents the central tension of the modern industry. Never has coffee been more expensive for the consumer, yet for the producer, the real value of the crop has remained stagnant for decades. The industry currently operates in a Golden Age of consumption built upon a Bronze Age of agricultural economics, where wealth is generated at the end of the chain while risk is concentrated entirely at the beginning.*

### DISSECTING THE LEDGER

Why does the producer receive a fraction of the retail value? The latte must be analyzed with forensic precision. The consumer frequently assumes that the $5.50 retail price reflects the cost of the coffee itself, but they are primarily purchasing service, real estate, and logistics. In a typical specialty coffee shop in a Tier-1 city like New York, San Francisco, or London, the cost breakdown dissolves the illusion of a coffee-centric economy.

*The "Coffee Paradox" reveals that the agricultural ingredient accounts for less than 1% of the retail price of a latte.*

Labor is the single largest cost driver, often accounting for $1.75 or more of the drink's price. Economists call this "Baumol's Cost Disease." While a factory can automate to produce more widgets with fewer workers, the service sector hits a human limit. A barista can only steam milk so fast. To attract staff in a high-cost economy, wages must rise, driving up the price of the latte without any increase in speed.

Real Estate consumes another massive slice, approximately $1.25. Coffee shops require high-visibility corners to survive. When you buy a latte, you are effectively renting a chair in prime commercial real estate for twenty minutes. The coffee is merely the admission ticket.

The additives and vessel often cost more than the primary ingredient. The rise of alternative milks has distorted the margin further; oat or almond milk often costs the café double the price of standard dairy, adding roughly $0.60 to the cost of goods sold. The packaging—the compostable cup, the lid, and the cardboard sleeve—adds another $0.35. This represents a silent inflation where a manufactured paper product holds a higher market value than the agricultural seed it contains.

After taxes and profit margins are accounted for, the roasted coffee beans represent approximately $0.30 of the cost to the café owner. However, this figure is the wholesale price of roasted beans, which includes the roaster's margin, packaging, and shipping. The actual green coffee inside that roast profile accounts for the four cents identified earlier. The retail price has become effectively decoupled from the agricultural price. A coffee shop essentially sells a cup of hot, textured milk in a rented room, with coffee acting as the chemical catalyst. This reality creates a financial buffer that shields the consumer from the producer's volatility. If the price of green coffee doubles—a transformative event for a farmer like Maya—the cost of the latte might only rise by thirty cents. The consumer barely registers the change. Conversely, if the price of coffee crashes to historic lows, the latte price remains sticky at $5.50.

## THE SMILE CURVE

Economists trace this distribution of wealth to a structural concept known as the "Smile Curve," first proposed in the 1990s by Stan Shih to explain the personal computer industry, but devastatingly applicable to modern agriculture. Visualizing a graph shaped like the letter U, the vertical axis represents "Value Added" and the horizontal axis represents the stages of production.

On the left peak of the curve lies Research & Development. In the coffee sector, this corresponds to the high-value intellectual property of developing new disease-resistant F1 hybrid seeds, proprietary processing methods, or patentable brewing technologies. The companies that own the genetics or the patents sit high on the value chain.

On the right peak of the curve lies Marketing & Services. This encompasses the brand equity of major chains, the "lifestyle" marketing of specialty roasters, the ambiance of the café, and the craft of the barista. This is where the emotional connection with the consumer occurs, and therefore, where the margin is highest.

At the bottom of the curve—the deep trough of the U—lies Manufacturing and Production. This is the act of growing, harvesting, and processing the cherry. The global economy treats farming as generic manual labor producing an interchangeable raw material. The market assigns astronomical value to the act of branding the bean, while assigning minimal value to the act of cultivating it. This distribution is not accidental; it is a legacy of colonial design where the "Value Add" is systematically captured by the nations that process and consume the goods, rather than the nations that grow them.

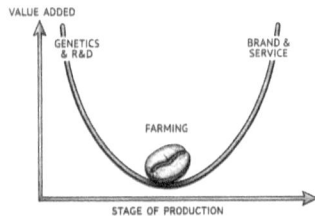

*The "Smile Curve" illustrates how value is captured by intellectual property and marketing, leaving the producer in the low-value trough.*

A bag of green coffee is treated as a commodity, mute and anonymous. A bag of branded "Single Origin" roast is a lifestyle product, vocal and distinct. The transformation from green to brown is where the capital accumulation occurs, and that transformation predominantly takes place in the Global North.

The question arises: why does a country like Colombia or Ethiopia not simply roast its own coffee and export the finished product directly to retailers in Europe or North America? By exporting finished goods, producing nations could capture the roasting margin, the packaging margin, and the branding margin, potentially multiplying the retained value by a factor of ten.

The barrier to this vertical integration is legal as well as logistical, maintained by a system of trade policy known as Tariff Escalation. Wealthy consuming nations—including the United States, the European Union, and Japan—have historically constructed their import codes to protect domestic manufacturing industries. Under these trade regimes, the import of green, unroasted coffee is typically duty-free or subject to negligible tariffs. The Global North requires the raw material because its climate cannot support the cultivation of *Coffea arabica* or *Coffea canephora*.

However, if a producing nation attempts to export roasted coffee, they are frequently met with significant tariffs, ranging from 7% to 30% depending on the specific trade agreement and the country of origin. This creates an artificial economic wall. If a Brazilian company attempts to export roasted coffee to the European Union, the tariff burden makes their product more expensive on the shelf than coffee roasted by a German or Italian company, even if the labor costs in Brazil are lower.

This system effectively rigs the game, ensuring that the industrial activity—the roasting, flavoring, and packaging—remains within the borders of the consuming country. It locks producing nations into their historical role as suppliers of raw ingredients and purchasers of finished goods. They function as the extraction sites of the caffeine world, digging up the fuel that powers an industrial engine located elsewhere. This asymmetry ensures that the "value add" of the Smile Curve remains geographically fixed in the developed world.

· · ·

## THE CANYON OF COSTS

Even within the specialized language of the coffee trade, a significant misunderstanding regarding price transparency persists. When a conscientious roaster publishes a transparency report stating, "We paid $2.50 per pound ($5.51/kg) for this coffee," they are almost invariably referring to the FOB Price (Free On Board). FOB is a maritime term indicating the price of the coffee when it is stacked in a container, on the vessel, and ready to depart the port of export. It represents the value at the water's edge.

However, the producer does not reside at the water's edge. Sofia lives in the mountains, often eight to ten hours away by truck. She does not receive the FOB price; she receives the Farmgate Price. Between the farm gate and the ship's rail, the coffee must navigate a gauntlet of deductions, service fees, and logistical costs that erode the final payout.

The coffee leaves the farm as "parchment"—seeds encased in a hard, protective hull. Before export, it must undergo dry milling at a facility known as a *beneficio*. Here, the beans are mechanically threshed to remove the hull, polished, and sorted by density. This process reduces the weight of the cargo by approximately 20%. The farmer is paid for the weight of the green bean, not the parchment hull, resulting in an immediate reduction in billable mass.

Following milling, the beans must be sorted to meet specialty standards. Optical laser sorters and gravity tables remove insect-damaged or broken beans. This further reduces the volume of sellable export-grade coffee. Inland freight presents another significant cost; moving heavy sacks through the mountainous terrain of the Andes or the Rift Valley consumes fuel and requires truck maintenance. In some regions, informal tolls or security costs further deplete the margin.

Additionally, national coffee federations or government bodies often levy export taxes and fees to fund marketing, research, or infrastructure. Finally, the exporter—the entity managing this complex logistics chain, handling the paperwork, and financing the coffee while it sits in the warehouse—requires a margin to operate.

By the time these dry mill costs and service fees are subtracted, a generous $2.50 FOB price may shrink to a $1.50 Farmgate price ($3.30/kg). If the producer lacks access to a transparent cooperative and is forced to sell to a roadside intermediary—often called a "coyote"—the price may be driven down even further. This distinction is critical because roasters often use FOB prices in marketing materials to signal virtue. While a price of $3.00 may appear revolutionary to a consumer, if the milling and export infrastructure in that specific country is inefficient or monopolized, the producer may still be operating near the cost of production.

## NITROGEN AND DEBT

Beyond the price of the bean, a hidden cost structure devours the producer's income: Input Dependence. In the 1990s, aiming to boost rural incomes, agricultural agencies and NGOs encouraged a shift from traditional shade-grown farming to "technified" systems. The logic was industrial and focused on volume. Traditional coffee grows under a canopy of native trees, where leaf litter composts the soil and birds control pest populations. Yields in these systems are low, but cash inputs are near zero.

Technified systems operate on a different philosophy. The shade canopy is removed, and dwarf, high-yield varieties like Caturra or Catimor are planted in dense rows exposed to full sun. This exposure triples the rate of photosynthesis and, consequently, the yield. However, biology extracts a toll for this acceleration. Without shade, the soil dries out rapidly. Without biodiversity, pests thrive. To sustain these high-performance trees, the farmer must introduce chemical inputs. They must purchase bags of nitrogen fertilizer and containers of fungicide.

A critical economic linkage exists here: nitrogen fertilizer is synthesized from ammonia, which is produced using natural gas via the Haber-Bosch process. This effectively pegs the cost of coffee farming to the price of crude oil and natural gas. When global energy prices spike —as they did following the geopolitical instabilities of the early 2020s —the cost of fertilizer can double or triple. A farmer may find themselves paying 200% more for urea while the price of coffee on the New York exchange remains flat. The producer is squeezed between a volatile input market (energy) and a volatile output market (commodities).

*"Technified" sun-grown systems maximize yield but trap farmers in a cycle of debt due to reliance on expensive chemical inputs.*

Many farmers operating technified systems are technically insolvent. They utilize loans against the future harvest to purchase fertilizer, to grow the coffee, to pay off the loan, and to buy more fertilizer for the next cycle. They have effectively become sharecroppers on their own land, working not for themselves, but to service the debt owed to agrochemical suppliers.

### THE MICROLOT PARADOX

Even when high prices are achieved, the mathematics of quality can be perverse. A specialty roaster searching for exceptional coffee will cup the harvest and identify a "Microlot"—the top 5% of the beans that score 88 points or higher on the SCA scale. They may offer a significant premium for this specific lot, perhaps $5.00 per pound.

While this appears to be a victory, coffee is an agricultural product rather than a manufactured widget. A single farm, or even a single tree, produces a bell curve of quality. Even on a well-managed farm, a significant portion of the harvest will be average. By selecting only the 88-point Microlot, the roaster removes the highest-quality beans from the main aggregate pile. This removal lowers the average quality score of the remaining bulk volume, making it more difficult to sell. The producer may be forced to offload the remaining 95% of the harvest on the local market at a distress price.

In many scenarios, the mathematics of selling the entire harvest at a mediocre but stable price (e.g., $2.00/lb) offers greater financial security than selling the top tier at a high price and being left with the devalued remainder. This is the Microlot Paradox: the pursuit of extreme quality for the few can sometimes destabilize the economic safety of the whole.

### "Authenticity" as Labor

In the "Third Wave" of coffee, Direct Trade was proposed as the solution to these structural failures. The narrative suggests that by bypassing the importer and building a relationship directly with the farmer, the value chain can be repaired. This model is seductive, replacing the cold bureaucracy of the commodity market with the warmth of human connection. However, it imposes a new, often uncompensated tax on the producer: Emotional Labor.

*Direct Trade often demands "emotional labor" from producers, who must perform authenticity for visiting buyers without guaranteed sales.*

When a buyer from a consuming nation arrives in a producing region, it constitutes a significant event. The producer feels the immense pressure of hospitality. They may use scarce resources to prepare meals, or take days away from the harvest—their most critical earning window —to guide the buyer through the farm, demonstrate processing methods, and pose for photographs. The producer is performing "authenticity." They are expected to be gracious, humble, and visually representative of the rustic ideal.

This represents uncompensated work. Frequently, the buyer is merely scouting. They may visit ten farms in a week, consuming time and resources at each, only to purchase coffee from one. For the other nine producers, the visit was a net financial loss. They expended capital and labor hosting a potential client who left nothing but a sticker with a roastery logo. Seasoned exporters now attempt to mitigate this by charging "farm visit fees" to screen out coffee tourists, but the power dynamic makes it difficult for a smallholder to refuse a potential buyer.


## THE DEMOGRAPHIC CLIFF

The long-term consequence of this value disconnect is not merely financial; it is existential. The coffee industry is facing a Demographic Collapse. The average age of a coffee farmer in Colombia is approximately 56. In Japan's coffee-growing regions, it approaches 70. The youth are exiting the sector.

If a twenty-year-old in rural Guatemala watches their parents work to the point of exhaustion for the equivalent of four cents per latte—weathering droughts, market crashes, and debt cycles—the choice is clear. They do not aspire to be coffee farmers. They aspire to be motorcycle mechanics, web designers, or migrant workers in the north. The "Brain Drain" of agriculture is in full effect. The most ambitious and educated young people are fleeing the coffee lands for the cities.

The question remains: who is left to prune the trees? Who is left to innovate? Who is left to manage the complex, data-heavy fermentation protocols required for modern specialty coffee? The industry is currently running on the momentum of the previous generation's labor. Large multinational corporations are increasingly alarmed by this trend, investing in "Next Gen" training programs not out of altruism, but out of the cold realization that the supply chain is about to age out of existence.

·   ·   ·

## CHARITY VS. COMMERCE

In response to this looming crisis, the technology sector has offered a new wave of solutions, often characterized as "Tip Jar Economics." Startups utilizing blockchain technology now allow consumers to scan a QR code on their latte cup, view a profile of the producer, and send a digital tip directly to their mobile wallet. It is presented as a seamless technological fix that bridges the gap between the consumer and the producer.

However, a distinction must be drawn between Charity and Commerce. By relying on tips to bridge the gap between poverty and solvency, the industry admits that the price of the product itself is structurally broken. This model shifts the burden of paying the producer from the corporation (which sets the price) to the customer (who pays the tip). It effectively transforms the farmer into a busker, dependent on the benevolence of strangers rather than the value of their labor.

True equity would require the price of the green coffee itself to cover the cost of living, the cost of sustainable production, and a margin for retirement, without reliance on digital gratuities. If the solvency of the farm depends on tips from consumers in Brooklyn or Berlin, the business model has failed.

## THE UNCOMFORTABLE MIRROR

The Paradox of Value forces a confrontation with the reality of consumption. The market claims to value the smallholder farmer, using their image to market products and construct narratives of quality. Yet, the financial structures prove that the market does not value their labor. The market values the barista's service, the café's ambiance, and the convenience of the transaction far more than the agricultural product itself.

The market acts as a voting machine, and every day, millions of consumers vote with their currency. The four cents that trickle down to the producer represent an accurate, ruthless reflection of how much the global economy values the act of farming relative to the act of retailing. Until that valuation changes—until the industry accepts that a sustainable cup of coffee may require a fundamental restructuring of the Smile

Curve to redistribute value from the brand to the soil—the asymmetry will persist. The Global North continues to consume the finished product, while the producers in the south navigate the precarious economics of the raw material, waiting for a redistribution that has yet to arrive.

# 35

## CAFFEINE DIPLOMACY: THE COLD WAR IN A CUP

The most consequential coffee meeting in history did not take place in a roasting plant, a cupping lab, or a trading pit. It convened in the East Room of the White House on a humid afternoon—March 13, 1961.

President John F. Kennedy stood before a gathering of Latin American ambassadors, his back rigid, his Boston accent cutting through the murmur of the assembled press corps. The air in the room was thick, charged not merely with the impending humidity of a District of Columbia spring, but with a palpable, silent anxiety. Two years earlier, Fidel Castro had marched into Havana, dismantling the old order and nationalizing industries. The specter of communism was no longer a distant theoretical threat in Eastern Europe; it was ninety miles off the coast of Florida, smoking a cigar and wearing fatigues.

Kennedy was there to propose the "Alliance for Progress," a ten-year, multi-billion-dollar plan to cement the bond between the United States and its southern neighbors. He spoke of "homes, work and land, health and schools." He spoke of a "vast cooperative effort, unparalleled in magnitude and nobility of purpose." While it appeared to be a speech about charity and development, a cold, hard calculation lay behind the soaring rhetoric.

The State Department's classified analysis was blunt: poverty was the

*breeding ground for revolution, and the economies of Latin America were frac-*
*turing because the price of their primary export—coffee—was in freefall.*

*In the late 1950s, a post-war glut of production had sent prices tumbling*
*from the historic highs of the early decade. In countries like Colombia, Brazil,*
*El Salvador, and Guatemala, where coffee accounted for up to 70% of foreign*
*exchange earnings, the crash was catastrophic. The State Department feared*
*that for every cent the price of coffee dropped, a new guerrilla unit was born in*
*the mountains. Kennedy understood what the Wall Street traders refused to*
*acknowledge: Coffee was not a widget. It was the geopolitical ballast of the*
*Western Hemisphere. If the United States wanted to stop the spread of the Red*
*Menace, it could not simply send munitions; it had to fix the price of the bean.*

*Thus began the era of Caffeine Diplomacy. For the next thirty years, the*
*global coffee market would be run by the iron fist of the treaty instead of the*
*invisible hand of capitalism. The United States, the world's largest consumer,*
*effectively agreed to overpay for coffee, transferring billions of dollars of wealth*
*to the producers. This was not altruism; it was a subscription fee for stability. It*
*was the largest commodity price-support scheme in history, a "benevolent*
*cartel" designed to keep the hammer and sickle off the coffee bag.*

### THE PRECURSOR: OPERATION FIBER

Why would the United States—the global champion of free enterprise—agree to manage a global cartel? Let's take a look back to a failed
Central Intelligence Agency operation that haunted the agency: Operation FIBER.

In 1954, nearly a decade before Kennedy's speech, the CIA was
already fixated on the link between coffee and communism in
Guatemala. The democratically elected government of Jacobo Árbenz
had begun an agrarian reform program that threatened the vast land-
holdings of the United Fruit Company. The CIA, fearing Árbenz was a
Soviet puppet, began plotting his overthrow (Operation PBSUCCESS).

But alongside the military coup, the agency devised a secret economic
warfare plan targeting the country's lifeblood. "Operation FIBER" was a
proposal to organize a boycott of Guatemalan coffee in the United States.
The Agency believed that coffee was the country's strategic vulnerability.

The logic was ruthless: if the U.S. could crash the price of Guatemalan coffee specifically, the resulting economic chaos would turn the elite coffee oligarchy against Árbenz and provoke a military coup from within.

The plan was technically sound but practically impossible. It failed largely because the American coffee roasters refused to cooperate. When CIA operatives approached executives from the National Coffee Association (NCA), they were met with confusion and resistance. The roasters were businessmen, not spies. They told the Agency that coffee was a fungible commodity—once beans were in a sack, one could not distinguish a "communist" bean from a "capitalist" bean. They warned that trying to selectively boycott one origin would disrupt their proprietary blends, alienate consumers, and likely damage their profit margins more than it would hurt Árbenz.

The refusal of the private sector to weaponize the market was a turning point. The lesson of Operation FIBER was burned into the State Department's institutional memory: You have to use a sledgehammer on the coffee market rather than a scalpel. By 1961, with Castro in power and guerrilla movements spreading to the coffee highlands of Colombia and Venezuela, Washington realized that crashing the price was the wrong strategy. To fight communism, they needed to raise the price. They didn't need a boycott; they needed a bailout.

## STRATEGY OF TENSION: THE FOCO THEORY

The urgency of this bailout was driven by a new tactical reality. Che Guevara, the architect of the Cuban Revolution, had popularized the *foco* theory of guerrilla warfare. It argued that a small group of committed revolutionaries—a *foco*—could create the conditions for a general uprising by embedding themselves in the rural peasantry.

The coffee lands were the perfect environment for *focoism*. Coffee is grown in the mountains, terrain that is notoriously difficult for regular armies to patrol but offers perfect cover for insurgents. It is grown by poor, landless laborers who are keenly aware of the disparity between their starvation wages and the wealth of the *fincas*. And, crucially, it is subject to wild price swings that create instant economic crises. When the price drops, the harvest wages vanish, and the starving picker becomes a willing recruit.

In Colombia, the bloody period known as *La Violencia* was winding down, leaving over 200,000 dead, but the rural peasantry remained destitute and angry. In Guatemala, CIA analysts warned that coffee pickers in the western highlands were beginning to organize into leftist militias. In Brazil, the erratic leadership of President Jânio Quadros—and later João Goulart—was openly flirting with the Soviet Union, trading coffee for Eastern Bloc machinery to bypass the American sphere of influence.

The U.S. needed a lever to pull these nations back into the fold. The traditional tools of diplomacy—aid packages and loans—were too slow. They needed an instrument that would put money directly into the veins of the Latin American economy, instantly and continuously. That lever was the International Coffee Agreement (ICA).

### Drafting the Straightjacket: 1962

The negotiation of the ICA was an act of economic heresy. The United States generally viewed price controls, quotas, and cartels as sins against the free market. Yet, in the summer of 1962, at the United Nations headquarters in New York, American diplomats sat across from Brazilian and Colombian delegates to engineer exactly that.

The agreement they hammered out was a market put in a straightjacket. It was a quota system designed to manage supply with precision. The mechanism was complex, relying on a sophisticated bureaucracy to function. Every producing nation was assigned a specific "Basic Quota," a hard cap on exports (in 60 kg bags):

- **Brazil,** the undisputed heavyweight, received a massive slice of the global pie—roughly 18 million bags (out of a total global quota of 45.8 million).
- **Colombia** secured the second-largest share, with approximately 6 million bags.
- Smaller nations like **El Salvador** and **Ethiopia** fought for the remaining allocation.

These quotas represented the maximum amount of coffee a country could export to the "member markets" (primarily the U.S. and Western Europe) in a given year.

*The International Coffee Agreement (1962) was a geopolitical tool designed to stabilize Latin American economies against communism.*

The organization set a "Target Price" band, typically hovering between $1.20 and $1.40 per pound (adjusted for inflation, significantly higher than modern prices). The system worked on a trigger:

1. **The Floor:** If the global indicator price dropped below the band, quotas were automatically cut. This tightened supply and forced prices back up.
2. **The Ceiling:** If prices rose above the band (threatening the American consumer with expensive breakfast), quotas were increased to cool the market.

But a quota is only words on paper unless it is enforced. Historically, producer cartels fail because a member always cheats—selling more than their share to capture revenue. This is where the United States made its unprecedented commitment.

The U.S. agreed to become the enforcer of the producer's cartel. The treaty stipulated that no bag of coffee could enter a U.S. port without an official Certificate of Origin document accompanied by requisite "export stamps" from the International Coffee Organization (ICO) in London.

*The quota system turned US Customs agents into market regulators, checking paperwork at the docks to enforce international price agreements.*

This tiny piece of paper changed the world. Imagine the scene at the Port of New Orleans in 1963. A Customs agent, paid by the U.S. Treasury, stands before a cargo ship from Santos. The captain offers him coffee at a bargain price, perhaps 20 cents below the market rate. In a free market, the agent—representing the consumer—should welcome the discount. Instead, under the ICA, the agent demands the certificate. If the shipment lacks the official ICO stamp, he turns it away. He effectively tells the market: "This coffee is too cheap. We will not buy it."

It was a remarkable act of economic self-sabotage by the U.S. government, deliberately keeping prices high for its own citizens to ensure that the checks kept clearing in Bogotá and Brasília. The "Washington Premium" was the difference between the free-market price and the quota price, a hidden tax paid by every American coffee drinker to subsidize the geopolitical order.

## THE 13-CENT WAR

However, the "Alliance" was not without friction. The brotherhood of the Americas was tested by the industrial ambitions of the South. The most dangerous moment came during the "Soluble War" of 1966–1968, a conflict that exposed the deep hypocrisy of the arrangement: The U.S. wanted Latin America to be prosperous, but not independent.

In the mid-1960s, Brazil decided it wanted to move up the value chain. For centuries, they had been the drawers of water and hewers of wood, exporting raw green beans while American and European companies roasted and processed them, capturing the vast majority of the profit. Brazilian companies began building factories to manufacture Instant Coffee (Soluble Coffee) domestically.

This strategy was brilliant. Brazil had millions of bags of "broken" or "black" beans—coffee that tasted acceptable when processed but was too physically defective to be exported as green coffee under the strict quality standards of the ICA. By turning this "trash" coffee into soluble powder in Brazil, they could add value, employ Brazilian factory workers, and export a finished product to the U.S. market.

The American coffee giants—General Foods (Maxwell House) and Nestlé—were furious. They viewed the manufacturing of instant coffee as their turf. They relied on buying cheap Brazilian "grinders" (low-quality beans) to make their profitable instant blends. If Brazil started processing those beans at the source, General Foods would lose its cheap inputs and face a new, lower-cost competitor on the grocery shelf.

The lobbying machine went into overdrive. The National Coffee Association descended on Washington. They invoked Article 44 of the agreement, which prohibited "discriminatory treatment." They argued that because the Brazilian government charged a heavy export tax on green beans (to fund the massive stockpiling program of the Brazilian Coffee Institute) but no tax on soluble exports, it was an unfair subsidy.

The dispute grew so heated that it threatened to dismantle the entire ICA. The State Department was torn. On one side was the geopolitical imperative: allow Brazil to industrialize and stabilize its economy against communism. On the other side were powerful American corporations who donated to campaigns and employed American voters.

In a tense showdown in 1967, the Johnson administration sided with the corporations. The U.S. threatened to walk away from the coffee agreement—effectively crashing the global price and bankrupting Brazil —unless Brazil agreed to tax its own instant coffee.

Brazil blinked. In a humiliating settlement, they agreed to impose a tax of 13 cents per pound on their own soluble coffee exports to the United States. This tax artificially inflated the price of Brazilian instant coffee, effectively protecting the profit margins of Maxwell House. It was a stark lesson for the developing world regarding the limits of Caffeine Diplomacy: You are allowed to grow the crop, but you are not allowed to cook the meal.

### THE ROSTOCK LOOPHOLE

Despite these skirmishes, the system worked for nearly three decades. From 1962 to 1989, despite wars, frosts (see Chapter 32), and oil crises, the price of coffee remained remarkably stable. This era is often remembered with nostalgia by older farmers in Latin America. It was a time when a coffee farm could support a middle-class life. The "Washington Premium" flowed into the rural sectors, building schools and roads, fulfilling Kennedy's promise in a roundabout way.

But no cartel is watertight. The Cold War context that created the ICA also created its biggest loophole. The agreement only bound its member nations. While the U.S. and Western Europe were members, the Soviet Union and its satellites in the Eastern Bloc were not. The socialist countries drank tea, mostly, but they bought some coffee. Because they were outside the quota system, producing countries could sell their "surplus" coffee—the beans they weren't allowed to sell to the U.S.—to the Soviets at deep discounts.

This gave birth to the phenomenon of "Tourist Coffee."

The scheme was an open secret in the port cities of Europe. It worked like this: A Brazilian exporter has 10,000 bags of coffee he cannot sell to New York because his country has hit its quota limit. However, he is allowed to sell it to East Germany or Poland, often at a 40% discount compared to the quota price. The beans are loaded onto a ship in Santos, the manifest stamping the destination as Rostock, East Germany.

But once the ship hits international waters, or pauses at a transshipment hub like Aruba or Panama, the alchemy of smuggling begins. The paperwork is doctored. The bags are transferred to a new vessel, or sometimes the same vessel simply changes its flag. The coffee, which was supposed to be drunk by a factory worker in Leipzig, suddenly diverts. It arrives in Hamburg or Amsterdam, disguised with forged stamps as "quota coffee" or as coffee from a non-member country.

*"The beans took a vacation." Supposedly bound for East Germany, this coffee stopped in Aruba just long enough to change its identity before entering the lucrative Western market.*

It was called "Tourist Coffee" because the beans took a vacation to a non-member country before returning to the lucrative Western market. It was smuggling, pure and simple, but for years it was tacitly tolerated. It acted as a release valve. If the producing countries were drowning in surplus coffee, the Tourist market allowed them to get rid of it without technically breaking the treaty. Everyone knew it was happening— traders in Hamburg whispered about the sudden influx of "Polish" Arabica—but as long as the volumes remained low, the diplomats looked the other way.

## THE AFRICAN CHALLENGE

While the U.S. focused its anxiety on Latin America, a new geopolitical force was rising: the post-colonial nations of Africa. In the 1960s and 70s, countries like Uganda, Ivory Coast, and Kenya gained independence. They were desperate for foreign currency to build their new nations, and they possessed the ideal climate for Robusta coffee.

They demanded a seat at the table. The diplomatic battles within the International Coffee Organization (ICO) headquarters in London shifted from a "North vs. South" conflict to a "South vs. South" conflict. The Latin American nations, who grew mostly Arabica, viewed the African Robusta producers as an existential threat. They argued that "quality" coffee (Arabica) deserved protection, while Robusta was just industrial filler that shouldn't be granted large quotas.

The U.S. State Department found itself in a double bind. It needed to keep Brazil happy (to stop communism in South America), but it also needed to keep the African nations stable to prevent Soviet influence in the post-colonial world. The quota negotiations became a proxy for the entire Cold War chessboard.

The African delegations proved to be shrewd negotiators. In the late 1970s, they threatened to flood the market with cheap Robusta if they weren't given a larger slice of the quota pie. The "Selectivity" battle raged for years: should there be separate quotas for Arabica and Robusta? If the price of mild Arabica went up, should the quota increase for everyone, or just the Arabica producers?

In the end, the U.S. often pressured the Latin Americans to cede market share to the Africans. Washington's logic was cold: Brazil was rich enough to take a hit; Uganda and Ivory Coast were fragile. The coffee agreement became a mechanism for managing the global economy, slicing the market share not by who was most efficient, but by who was most at risk of falling to the Soviets.

## INDEPENDENCE DAY IN LONDON: 1989

By the late 1980s, the glue holding the agreement together began to weaken. The threat of Castro-style revolutions was fading. The U.S. was more confident in its hegemony. But more importantly, the economic philosophy in Washington had shifted. The election of Ronald Reagan had ushered in the era of neoliberalism. The new guard at the State Department and the Treasury viewed the ICA not as a brilliant diplomatic tool, but as a distortion of the free market. They hated the quotas. They hated the price supports.

Simultaneously, the "Big Three" roasters were lobbying hard against the treaty. They pointed to the "Tourist Coffee" scandals as proof that the system was corrupt. They wanted cheap beans, and they wanted the freedom to buy them from anyone, anywhere.

The tension came to a head in the summer of 1989. The existing agreement was set to expire, and negotiations for a renewal were stalled in the windowless conference rooms of the ICO building on Berners Street in London.

The atmosphere inside the negotiation room was toxic. The delegates, usually paragons of diplomatic politesse, were exhausted and entrenched. The central figure in the drama was Jorio Dauster, the head of the Brazilian Coffee Institute (IBC). Dauster was a formidable negotiator, known for his sharp intellect and nationalistic fervor. He sat at the head of the Brazilian table, chain-smoking and refusing to budge.

Dauster's calculation was simple: Brazil was the "Saudi Arabia of Coffee." It was the most efficient producer. He believed that if the quota system collapsed, Brazil would survive the ensuing price war, while the smaller, less efficient producers in Central America and Africa would be wiped out. He refused to accept the American demand to reduce Brazil's quota share in favor of "Mild" Arabica producers. He believed the U.S. was bluffing—that they would never let the agreement collapse because the geopolitical risk was still too high.

But across the table, the U.S. delegation was not bluffing. Led by negotiators who were disciples of the free market, they presented a "take it or leave it" ultimatum. They demanded the elimination of the Tourist Coffee loophole and a significant redistribution of quotas toward higher-quality producers.

The deadline ticked closer. July turned to July 4th. The symbolism was lost on no one. In the final hours, Dauster held his ground. He refused to sign a deal that he viewed as humiliating to Brazilian sovereignty.

On July 4, 1989, the negotiations collapsed. The delegates packed their briefcases and walked out into the London drizzle. There was no handshake. The economic clauses of the International Coffee Agreement were suspended.


## THE CRASH

The timing was poetic. Four months later, the Berlin Wall fell. The Cold War was effectively over. The United States no longer needed to bribe the farmers of the Third World to stay loyal. The "Security Premium" evaporated overnight.

The market reaction was brutal. Without quotas to hold back the flood, every producing nation dumped its stockpiles onto the market simultaneously. The massive warehouses in Brazil—the "cathedrals of coffee" that had held millions of bags off the market—threw open their doors.

The price of coffee crashed by nearly 50% in a matter of months, dropping from over $1.34 to $0.77 per pound.

For the farmers, the 1990s were a lost decade. The devastation was not uniform; it struck the most vulnerable the hardest. In the high altitudes of Central America, smallholders who had relied on the stable prices of the 80s found themselves selling coffee for less than the cost of production. They abandoned their farms, migrating to the cities or north toward the U.S. border.

In Rwanda, the crash was an accelerant to a fire that was already smoldering. Coffee was the country's primary source of foreign currency. When the price collapsed in 1989, the government's revenue evaporated. The resulting economic desperation exacerbated the ethnic tensions between Hutus and Tutsis. While the causes of the 1994 genocide are complex, economic historians note that the collapse of the coffee economy destabilized the fragile peace, leaving a population of unemployed, desperate young men who were easily radicalized.

*The Deadly Substitution: When coffee prices dropped below the cost of production in the 1990s, many farmers in the Andes faced a stark choice. The same soil that grew coffee could grow coca, which offered a stable, high price guaranteed by drug cartels.*

In Colombia, the consequences were measured in cocaine. As the price of coffee fell below the cost of production, farmers in the southern departments looked for alternatives. A bush of coca grew in the same soil, at the same altitude, but it offered a stable, high price guaranteed by the drug cartels. The National Federation of Coffee Growers of Colombia (FNC) watched helplessly as thousands of hectares of coffee were ripped up and replaced with coca. The U.S. had stopped paying for coffee stability, and instead, it ended up paying billions for the "War on Drugs"—fighting the very crop that replaced the coffee they refused to subsidize.

### THE VIETNAM SHOCK

The end of the diplomatic era also opened the door for a new giant, one that would fundamentally alter the physics of the coffee world.

During the quota years, it was impossible for a new country to enter the coffee market in a major way. If a nation lacked a historical quota record, it did not receive an export license. The club was closed. But once the quotas were gone in 1989, the market was open to all.

Vietnam, recovering from its own wars and seeking an export crop to modernize its economy, launched a massive, state-sponsored coffee planting program in the 1990s, fueled by the *Doi Moi* economic reforms. They didn't focus on the finicky, high-altitude Arabica of Central America. They focused on high-yield, low-altitude Robusta.

The Vietnamese approach was agronomy as industry. They utilized high-density planting, aggressive irrigation, and heavy fertilizer inputs to achieve yields that were unheard of in traditional coffee lands. While a Brazilian farmer might get 15 bags per hectare (roughly 900 kg), Vietnamese farmers were pushing for 30, 40, or even 50 bags (up to 3000 kg).

The statistics of their rise are staggering. In 1990, just after the ICA collapse, Vietnam produced roughly 1 million bags. By 2000, they were producing nearly 15 million bags. They leapfrogged Colombia to become the second-largest producer in the world.

This surge of supply kept prices depressed for nearly fifteen years. Under the old ICA system, Vietnam's entry would have been managed— they would have been given a small "entry quota" that grew slowly. In the free market, it was a tsunami. The flood of cheap Vietnamese Robusta drove down the price of blends, pulling the price of Arabica down with it. It broke the backs of traditional farmers in Mexico and Guatemala, who simply couldn't compete with the efficiency of the new Vietnamese machine.

### Legacy: The Hidden Tax

Today, there is no Caffeine Diplomacy. The International Coffee Organization still exists in London, but it is a shadow of its former self. It acts as a statistical clearinghouse, collecting data on imports and exports, but it has no power to set prices or limit production. The market is ruled by the "C-Price," by the algorithm-driven hedge funds, and by the weather in Brazil.

There are occasional calls to bring back the quotas. Whenever prices crash, leaders in Latin America and Africa float the idea of a "new OPEC for coffee." But the geopolitical will is gone. The consuming nations have no interest in paying more, and the producing nations are too divided to form a cartel—Brazil and Vietnam would never agree on who cuts production first.

The history of the Cold War coffee agreements is a reminder of a strange, forgotten truth: The value of a cup of coffee has never been purely about its taste, its *terroir*, or its cost of production. For thirty years, the price on the ticker tape included a hidden tax—a tax paid by the West to purchase a specific vision of world order. When we stopped paying it, the coffee got cheaper, but for the farmers in the Global South, the world got much more expensive.

The end of the Cold War brought with it the end of the "political price" of coffee. The market was finally free, but the cost of that freedom was borne by the most fragile actors in the supply chain. The diplomatic shield was removed, leaving the smallholder farmer exposed to the raw, unbuffered volatility of global capitalism. The era of the "benevolent cartel" was over; the era of the "Crisis of Price" had begun.

# 36

# ENCAPSULATED: THE CLOSED LOOP

I nside the Café Sant'Eustachio, just steps from the Pantheon in Rome, the atmosphere is pressurized as much as scented. It is 1975, and this small espresso bar, located just steps from the Pantheon in Rome, operates as a theater of hydraulic intensity. The room is crowded with men in sharp Italian suits, their voices rising over the hiss of steam wands and the clatter of porcelain on marble. The noise is a cacophony of the morning rush, a symphony of caffeine intake that powers the Italian economy.

Standing in the corner, observing the chaos with the detached, analytical gaze of a Swiss engineer, is Eric Favre. He is ostensibly on a honeymoon with his Italian wife, Graziella, but his true focus is a technical problem that has plagued the Nestlé corporation for a decade: how to bridge the gap between the instant solubility of Nescafé and the rich, oily complexity of fresh Italian espresso. Favre watches the head barista, a man named Eugenio, work the machine. It is an old lever-piston model, likely a Gaggia, a machine that requires significant physical strength to operate. Most baristas of the era simply locked the portafilter and pulled the lever once, forcing hot water through the puck of coffee in a continuous, brute-force flow.

Eugenio is different. He pumps the lever multiple times—short, sharp bursts of pressure—before the final pull. Favre leans in, entranced by the mechanics. He realizes that Eugenio is aerating the coffee as well as extracting it. By pumping the piston, he forces oxygen into the hot water chamber, which then blasts into the coffee grounds. This oxidation initiates a crucial physical reaction: it emulsifies the oils, creating a thick, golden foam that traps the volatile aromatics in the cup. This foam is the crema. It serves as the lipid barrier that keeps the flavor from evaporating into the air, the signature of a correctly made espresso.

It is a moment of industrial epiphany. The difference between the thin, dark liquid produced by home machines and the viscous "espresso" of Sant'Eustachio is not just the bean; it is the interaction of air, water, and pressure. If Favre can replicate Eugenio's wrist action inside a sealed system—if he can build a machine that introduces oxygen into a pressurized capsule—he can allow an untrained novice in a suburban kitchen to produce a cup of coffee that rivals the best bar in Rome.

He returns to Switzerland, to the quiet order of the canton of Vaud, and retreats to his garage to begin the work of translation. He needs to convert the chaotic art of the Roman barista into a repeatable industrial process. He builds a prototype that looks more like a medical ventilator than a kitchen appliance, utilizing tubes, a compressor, and a small aluminum hemisphere to mimic the aeration process. He calls it Nespresso. When he pitches it to his bosses at Nestlé headquarters in Vevey, he expects a reception befitting a revolution. Instead, the board members look at him with confusion and skepticism. Nestlé is the king of instant powder; Nescafé is one of the most profitable products in human history. The executives view the machine not as an innovation, but as a threat —a parasite that would eat into their own lucrative margins for instant coffee.

Favre is sidelined, sent to the corporate wilderness in Japan to sell soy sauce. But the idea refuses to die. It sits in the patent archives, a dormant innovation that, once detonated twenty years later, will trigger the most vicious legal and commercial competition in the history of the beverage industry. This is the story of the capsule revolution—a shift driven not by the quality of the bean, but by the convenience of the plastic that encases it.

THE LUXURY PIVOT

For a decade, Nespresso is a commercial failure. Launched tentatively in 1986, the machines are clunky, resembling laboratory equipment more than domestic appliances. The capsules are prohibitively expensive, and the target market—corporate offices—does not care about crema. They want volume. The machines break down; the coffee is inconsistent. The project is nearly killed multiple times by the financial auditors at Nestlé, who see it as a vanity project bleeding cash. The turning point arrives in 1988 with Jean-Paul Gaillard, a marketing executive with the instincts of a luxury fashion house director. Gaillard looks at the failing Nespresso division and realizes the problem isn't the coffee; it is the context. They are trying to sell an appliance when they need to sell a lifestyle.

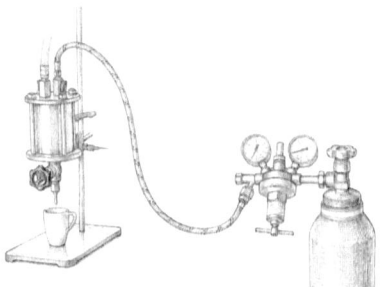

*Eric Favre's innovation was to replicate the barista's "aeration" pump inside a sealed machine to produce crema.*

Gaillard completely restructures the strategy. He stops selling to offices and starts targeting the wealthy homeowner. He raises the price of the capsules—a counter-intuitive move that increases their perceived value. He creates the "Nespresso Club," a direct-to-consumer model that bypasses the supermarket entirely. To get the coffee, one must be a member. One must order by phone or visit a "Boutique" designed to look less like a café and more like a high-end fashion retailer, complete with black walls, soft lighting, and staff wearing white gloves.

The masterstroke is the vocabulary. Gaillard bans the word "pod." These are capsules. They don't have flavors; they have Grands Crus, a term borrowed directly from the French wine classification system. The machine is sold as an affordable luxury, a way for the middle class to buy a piece of European sophistication for the kitchen counter. By the time George Clooney signs on as the global ambassador in 2006, creating an aura of suave, effortless cool around the brand, Nespresso is generating billions in revenue with profit margins that rival the pharmaceutical industry. The genius of the model is simple: Nestlé is selling a razor, and they have a patent on the only blade that fits.

The aluminum capsule is a closed system, a walled garden of caffeine that locks the customer into the Nestlé ecosystem.

## THE CURE FOR THE STALE POT

While the Swiss are obsessing over crema and aeration, two room-mates in Massachusetts are trying to solve a different problem: the bitter-ness of the American office breakroom. In the early 1990s, John Sylvan and Peter Dragone are tired of the "stale pot" phenomenon. In almost every office in America, a glass carafe of coffee sits on a hot plate for hours, slowly cooking into a sludge that tastes of battery acid and burnt rubber. The chemistry of this degradation is well understood: as coffee sits on heat, the chlorogenic acids break down into quinic acid, and the volatile aromatics evaporate, leaving behind a bitter, flat liquid. The first person to pour a cup gets something drinkable; the last person gets a cup of chemical regret.

Sylvan, a tinkerer by nature, is convinced there is a better way. He spends months in his kitchen, gluing filter paper inside small plastic yogurt cups. The engineering challenge is immense. The cup needs to be hermetically sealed to keep the coffee fresh, but easily penetrable by the machine. It needs to withstand the thermal shock of near-boiling water (93°C / 200°F) without melting or exploding. His health deteriorates as he becomes the primary test subject for his own invention. He drinks thirty to forty cups of coffee a day to test his prototypes, developing heart palpitations and severe hand tremors before eventually ending up in the emergency room, a victim of caffeine toxicity—a casualty in the pursuit of single-serve brewing.

His breakthrough is the "inversion" of the brewing process. Instead of water dripping down through the grounds as in a standard automatic brewer, his machine punctures the foil lid, injects hot water, and forces it out through a hole punched in the bottom of the plastic cup. He calls the machine the Keurig—derived from the Dutch word for "excellence"—and the container the K-Cup.

HOT WATER IN

FOIL LID

PAPER FILTER

COFFEE GROUNDS

BREWED COFFEE OUT

A Moreau

*The K-Cup reversed the brewing flow, injecting water through the top to filter through an internal paper cone.*

Unlike Nespresso, which operates as a closed garden of luxury, Keurig acts as a utilitarian workhorse. Sylvan targets the American office manager. The K-Cup is aesthetically utilitarian, plastic, and bulky, but it solves the social friction of the breakroom. No more fighting over who made the fresh pot. No more cleaning wet grounds. Everyone can have their own flavor—Hazelnut for the receptionist, French Roast for the boss, Decaf for the accountant—in sixty seconds.

In 2006, Green Mountain Coffee Roasters (GMCR), a Vermont-based company led by the visionary and aggressive Bob Stiller, acquires Keurig. Stiller realizes that the K-Cup is the perfect delivery vehicle for the American coffee habit. He licenses the technology to everyone: Starbucks, Dunkin' Donuts, Folgers, Newman's Own. He doesn't care whose coffee is in the pod, as long as Green Mountain owns the patent on the plastic cup. By 2013, nearly one in three American homes has a pod machine on their counter. The ritual of grinding, dosing, and brewing— a ritual that had defined coffee consumption for centuries, from the Sufi lodges of Yemen to the coffeehouses of London—has been replaced by a single button press. The skill of the barista has been encoded into a barcode.

## THE FIFTY-DOLLAR POUND

The pod revolution fundamentally alters the economics of coffee consumption, introducing the "Inkjet Printer Model" to the kitchen. In this model, the hardware (the brewer) is sold at a thin margin, or even a loss, to establish an installed base. The profit is entirely in the consumables. It is the classic "razor and blade" strategy, but applied to a commodity that people consume multiple times a day.

Consider the mathematics of the pod. A standard bag of specialty coffee beans costs roughly $15 to $20 per pound. That works out to about $0.50 per cup for fresh, high-quality beans.

A Nespresso capsule or K-Cup typically costs between $0.75 and $1.10. But the volume of coffee inside is tiny—only 5 to 6 grams, compared to the 20 grams used in a manual brew. If you perform the conversion, the markup is staggering:

- **Whole Bean Coffee:** ~$18 per pound.
- **Pod Coffee:** ~$60 per pound.

This makes pod coffee one of the most expensive food products in the household, pound-for-pound costing more than filet mignon. Yet, the consumer pays it willingly because the transaction cost is hidden in the single serving.

The consumer buys a "serving" rather than a pound of coffee. The mental accounting shifts from "grocery expense" to "café substitute." Compared to a $5.00 Starbucks latte, a $0.80 pod feels like a bargain. This decoupling of price from volume creates a river of cash for Nestlé and Keurig Green Mountain. Nestlé's Nespresso division becomes the company's most profitable unit, driving stock prices and financing global expansion. But where there are super-normal profits, there are legal challenges.

· · ·

### The Patent Fortress Crumbles

For twenty years, Nespresso and Keurig are protected by a fortress of intellectual property. Their patents cover everything from the shape of the pod to the angle of the puncture needles to the specific flow rate of the water. They sue anyone who tries to make a compatible capsule, protecting their monopoly with the ferocity of a cartel. But patents have a shelf life. In 2012, key Nespresso patents begin to expire, and the market sharks begin to circle.

The most dangerous challenger is none other than Jean-Paul Gaillard—the man who built Nespresso in the first place. After a falling out with Nestlé, he founds the Ethical Coffee Company. He knows the Nespresso machine inside out. He designs a biodegradable capsule that bypasses the remaining patents and undercuts Nestlé on price. Simultaneously, a massive consolidation occurs in the global coffee industry. A secretive German family office, JAB Holding Company, begins buying up coffee brands—Peet's, Caribou, Stumptown, Intelligentsia—with the goal of challenging Nestlé. They launch a plastic Nespresso-compatible capsule under the brand L'Or and flood French supermarkets. Suddenly, Nespresso's monopoly is broken. Customers no longer need to visit the "Boutique"; they can buy generic pods at the grocery store next to the dish soap.

Nestlé fights back with aggressive engineering. In a move reminiscent of industrial espionage, they tweak the design of their new machines—adding tiny hooks inside the brewing chamber or changing the angle of the injector blades—specifically to make the generic capsules jam or crush. It is a technological booby trap. Gaillard and others sue, arguing that Nestlé is engaging in anti-competitive behavior by modifying machines solely to block competitors' software. The legal battles rage across Europe. In France, the competition authority raids Nestlé's offices. The European courts largely side with the generics, ruling that a company cannot modify a machine solely to exclude a competitor's product. The walls of the fortress crumble.

Across the Atlantic, Keurig watches Nespresso's patent struggles with dread. Their own K-Cup patents are set to expire in 2012. They see the "private label" apocalypse coming—a future where cheap, generic pods erode their dominance. In 2014, Keurig decides to double down. They launch the Keurig 2.0. It is a machine designed with "Digital Rights Management" (DRM)—the same technology used to prevent piracy of DVDs and software.

The Keurig 2.0 features an infrared camera inside the brewing head. The new official K-Cups are printed with a special ink on the rim—a fluorescent tag invisible to the naked eye but readable by the camera. If a user inserts a generic, non-licensed pod into the machine, the screen flashes a message: "Oops! This pod isn't designed for this brewer." The machine refuses to brew. It is a technological lockout attempting to force the consumer to buy only authorized software (coffee) for their hardware.

They miscalculate the American consumer's tolerance for control. The backlash is instant and severe. Customers are furious, feeling they own the machine and should be allowed to put whatever they want in it. A cottage industry of "Freedom Clips"—small pieces of plastic that tape over the sensor to trick the machine—springs up on Amazon. These hacks are sold for pennies, defeating a billion-dollar R&D strategy. Competitors like TreeHouse Foods sue for antitrust violations. The "Keurig 2.0" disaster becomes a business school case study in corporate overreach. Keurig's stock plummets, and they eventually are forced to bring back the "My K-Cup" reusable filter, admitting defeat. They learn a hard lesson: one can patent a machine, but one cannot patent the customer's morning routine.

### THE IMMORTAL ARTIFACT

While the lawyers fight over patents and profit margins, a much larger problem is piling up in the landfills of the world: waste. The convenience of the pod comes at a heavy ecological price, one that is often hidden from the consumer who simply tosses the capsule into the trash can. To understand the scale of the problem, one must visit a Material Recovery Facility (MRF). Here, conveyor belts move mountains of trash at high speed, using magnets, optical sorters, and blasts of air to separate paper, glass, and plastic.

In this chaotic river of garbage, the coffee pod is a villain. A standard K-Cup is a composite nightmare: a plastic cup (usually #7 plastic, which is heat-resistant but difficult to recycle), an aluminum foil lid, a paper filter, and organic coffee grounds fused together. Because it is a mixed material, the optical sorters cannot identify it. Because it is small—less than three inches in diameter—it falls through the screens meant to catch bottles and cans. It drops into the pile of "residuals," the trash destined for the landfill.

Once in the landfill, the pod becomes an immortal artifact. It will sit in the dark, anaerobic mud for centuries. By 2015, it is estimated that the number of K-Cups sold in a single year could circle the Earth ten times. The image of billions of plastic cups accumulating in the strata of the Anthropocene becomes a public relations crisis. The city of Hamburg, Germany, famously banned coffee pods from all government buildings in 2016, citing them as an unnecessary waste of resources.

Nespresso fares slightly better because their capsules are pure aluminum, which is infinitely recyclable. However, the recycling process requires customers to perform a specific labor: collect the soggy capsules in special bags and return them to the store or a drop-off point. This requires a level of effort that negates the primary selling point of the system: convenience. The "Recycling Gap"—the difference between what can be recycled and what is actually recycled—remains vast. In a candid interview in 2015, John Sylvan, the inventor of the K-Cup, admits that he doesn't own one. "I feel bad sometimes that I ever did it," he says, referring to the environmental impact. The pod solved the problem of stale coffee, but it created a problem of permanent garbage.

## THE SPECIALTY SURRENDER

The final battlefront of the capsule revolution is fought on the tongue. Does the pod actually taste good? For the average consumer, the answer is "good enough." It is certainly better than the oxidized, burnt sludge of the office carafe. It is hot, it is brown, and it delivers caffeine. But for the coffee professional, the pod represents a flattening of the culinary curve, a regression in the pursuit of flavor.

To make a pod work, the coffee must be ground months in advance. Once coffee is ground, it loses 60% of its volatile aromatics within fifteen minutes due to increased surface area exposure to oxygen. To counteract this, manufacturers flush the pods with nitrogen to create an inert environment.

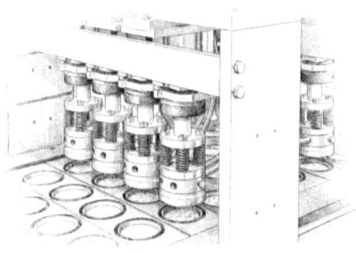

*Capsules rely on an inert nitrogen atmosphere to prevent the pre-ground coffee from staling (oxidizing) on the shelf.*

It preserves the coffee, but it puts it in a suspended state. The resulting cup is "stale-fresh." It lacks the high, vibrant acidity and the complex florals of a freshly ground pour-over. It is a standardized product. A Nespresso capsule tastes exactly the same in 2025 as it did in 2015. It is reliable, but it lacks the dynamism of a living agricultural product.

Furthermore, the mechanics of the machines limit the brewing parameters. A K-Cup uses roughly 10 to 12 grams of coffee for an 8-ounce cup. A specialty standard requires nearly double that ratio (roughly 1:16). To make the coffee taste strong enough with such a small dose, pod manufacturers often use darker roasts or add soluble coffee (instant) to the grounds to boost the body. Additionally, the physics of extraction inside a pod are prone to "channeling." Because the water is injected at high speed into a small, confined puck, it often finds the path of least resistance, boring a hole through the center of the grounds while leaving the edges under-extracted. This results in a cup that is simultaneously bitter (from the over-extracted channel) and sour (from the under-extracted edges).

For years, the "Third Wave" of specialty coffee—the artisanal movement led by roasters who treat coffee like wine—sneered at the pod. Blue Bottle, Stumptown, and Colonna Coffee viewed the pod as the antithesis of their craft. It was the enemy of terroir, the destroyer of nuance. But the economic gravity of the format proved too strong to resist. In the late 2010s, a shift occurs. Specialty roasters realize that if they don't put their coffee in pods, their customers will simply buy Nespresso on Tuesday mornings when they are in a rush, and only drink the "good stuff" on weekends. They are losing the majority of the customer's consumption volume.

Innovators like Maxwell Colonna-Dashwood begin to hack the pod. They work on grinding techniques that maximize extraction yield within the limitations of the capsule. They develop biodegradable, compostable pods made from cornstarch or wood pulp that can theoretically break down in a garden compost pile. They prove that if you put an 88-point Ethiopian Geisha into a capsule and flush it with nitrogen to keep oxygen out, it can taste genuinely good. In 2023, Blue Bottle—now majority-owned by Nestlé—releases a coffee developed for Nespresso's Vertuo capsule system. It feels like the final surrender. The artisans have joined the capsule economy. The barrier between "craft" and "convenience" has dissolved.

Today, the conflict has settled into a cold peace. The patents have expired. The supermarket aisle is a democracy of pods—Starbucks, Peet's, Dunkin', and generic brands sit side by side in compatible plastic cups. The machines are ubiquitous, found in hotel rooms, dorms, and boardrooms across the planet. Nespresso has pivoted to the "Vertuo" line, a new system with a new patent (using centrifugal force instead of pressure) to rebuild their walled garden. Keurig has merged with a soda giant to become Keurig Dr Pepper, diversifying away from just coffee. JAB Holding continues to consolidate the immense middle of the market.

But the legacy of the pod is permanent. It fundamentally changed the architecture of the kitchen. It took the skill of brewing away from the human and gave it to the machine. It prioritized speed over ritual. It turned coffee from a communal pot into a solitary, single-serve act. Back in Rome, the Café Sant'Eustachio still stands. The baristas still pump the levers, the steam still hisses, and the crema is still thick enough to hold a spoonful of sugar. It is a process that requires touch, smell, and timing. Eric Favre's vision of bringing this theater to the home was realized, but with a twist. He wanted to bring the skill of the Roman barista to the world. Instead, he created a world where the barista wasn't needed at all.

The capsule revolution was a victory for logistical efficiency. But as the plastic mountains grow in the landfills, and as we sip our nitrogen-preserved, standardized brews in the silence of our kitchens, the cost of that efficiency becomes clear. We have traded the communal ritual of the pot and the sensory complexity of the fresh grind for the certainty of a sixty-second extraction. The pod is the ultimate expression of the industrial age of coffee: a triumph of engineering that prioritized the consumer's seconds over the planet's centuries. It solved the problem of the morning rush, but in doing so, it created a mountain of waste that refuses to decompose. As we turn our eyes toward the future, the question is no longer whether we *can* engineer a more convenient cup, but whether the planet can afford for us to drink it. The era of extraction is ending; the era of adaptation must begin.

# PART VII

---

# NEW HORIZONS

The future of coffee will not be decided by taste alone. It will be decided by temperature.

This section moves from history into forecast: climate pressure, species resilience, laboratory experiments, new processing chemistry, and circular systems that treat waste as resource. Some of what you will read here sounds like science fiction, but coffee has always been an engine for invention. When a crop is loved this much—and threatened this much—human creativity becomes urgent.

The question is not whether coffee will change. The question is what kind of coffee world we are willing to build next.

# 37

# THE HEAT LINE: FARMING
# AT THE EDGE OF 2050

R ather than arriving on paper, the signs of stress appeared as a texture in the soil, a silence in the canopy, and a specific, sickly chlorosis on the leaf.

For three generations, a family like the Moraleses has farmed three hectares of *Coffea arabica* on a steep, mist-clinging hillside in the Huehuetenango department of Guatemala. This region, bordering the high granitic peaks of Mexico's Chiapas, was once considered a climatological sanctuary. The altitude of 1,500 meters acted as an invisible fortress, guaranteeing the cool nights and warm days that allow the coffee cherry to ripen slowly over nine months. This slow gestation is the biological engine of value; it is what allows the seed to develop the dense sugars, complex lipids, and citric acids that buyers in Seattle, Oslo, and Tokyo pay premiums to secure.

But in 2018, the rain stopped following the calendar. The rainy season, typically a reliable thermodynamic engine starting in May, stuttered. When the water finally arrived, it came not as a gentle, soaking nourishment but as a rapid accumulation, stripping the precious topsoil and exposing the white feeder roots of the trees to the solar radiation. Then came the heat. More than a warm spell, it marked a shift in the baseline. The daytime highs crept past 30°C and stayed there. The nights, crucial for the plant's respiration and recovery, refused to drop below 20°C.

*Standing in the rows today, the consequences are visible to the naked eye. The leaves are not the glossy, deep waxy green of healthy Arabica; they are matte, grayish, and drooping, clamping their stomata shut in a desperate phys- iological attempt to retain moisture. The cherries, which should be swelling with sweet mucilage, are "peppercorns"—small, hard, and failing to mature. The yield is down 60% compared to the 2000 average.*

*Jose Morales sits at his kitchen table, a piece of worn oilcloth covering the wood, with a notebook that details the logistics of contraction. He lists the inputs: nitrogen fertilizer, which has doubled in price due to global supply chain shocks; fungicides to fight the pests that thrive in the new heat; and labor costs that have risen as neighbors migrate north. Then he lists the income: a global "C-Price" that fluctuates wildly but often barely touches the cost of production. The math does not resolve. The farm is not an asset; it is a liability.*

*He debates migration rather than botany. He is calculating the cost of a coyote—currently running thousands of dollars per head—to take his eldest son to the United States. He compares this against the cost of a new drip-irriga- tion system that might cost $5,000 per hectare but might not function if the community aquifer runs dry. This is the "Climate Squeeze" in its most acute iteration: a specific farm, at a specific altitude, facing a specific threshold of viability.*

*The Morales farm is a single data point in a global trend that aims to rewrite the map of agriculture. We are witnessing the end of the "Goldilocks" era of coffee, a period of climatic stability that allowed a fragile, high-mainte- nance African shrub to become a global commodity. The heat line is moving uphill, and the adaptation required to chase it is forcing a total restructuring of the industry.*

### The Physiology of Two Degrees

To understand why a shift of 2°C matters, one must examine the biological architecture of *Coffea arabica*. It is an evolutionary snowflake, a species born in the cool, shaded understories of Ethiopian cloud forests. Unlike maize or soy, which have been bred for centuries to tolerate a wide variance of conditions, Arabica is genetically conservative. It has a preferred operating temperature range of 18°C to 21°C.

When the temperature exceeds this band, the plant's internal machinery begins to fracture. Above 23°C, the ripening process accelerates. The cherry matures too fast, rushing the development of the seed inside. The complex chemical precursors to flavor—the lipids, the sucrose, the amino acids—do not have time to form. The resulting cup is "flat," lacking the acidity and complexity that defines high-quality coffee. This is the first casualty of climate change: flavor profile. Before coffee disappears, it will simply become indistinguishable from low-grade commodities.

However, when the thermometer hits 30°C, the crisis moves from sensory to existential. At this threshold, photosynthesis slows dramatically. The tree enters a state of thermal shock. The enzyme Rubisco, essential for converting carbon dioxide into energy, begins to malfunction. The tree effectively stops eating.

Compounding the thermal stress is the weaponization of moisture and the disruption of phenology. Phenology refers to the timing of biological events—flowering, fruiting, and dormancy. Coffee trees are triggered to flower by the first rains after a dry period. In a stable climate, this happens all at once, leading to a synchronous harvest.

In the current climate, erratic "false rains" trigger the trees to flower early, often in February or March. If these rains are followed by a heatwave, the delicate white blossoms, which smell of jasmine, wither and drop without setting fruit. This is known as "flower abortion." Alternatively, erratic rains cause "scattered flowering," where the tree has flowers, green cherries, and ripe cherries on the branch simultaneously. This makes mechanical harvesting impossible and forces pickers to return to the same tree five or six times, destroying the labor economy of the farm.

Furthermore, a warmer atmosphere is a thirstier atmosphere. The "Vapor Pressure Deficit" (VPD)—essentially the drying power of the air —increases exponentially with temperature. This extracts moisture out of the soil and the plant simultaneously, creating a "hydro-thermal" trap. Even if rainfall remains constant in total volume, if it arrives in shorter, more intense bursts followed by longer droughts, the soil cannot hold it.

Scientific consensus has formalized what farmers were already observing: climatic suitability for coffee is retreating. Projections indicate that by 2050, the global area suitable for coffee production could be drastically reduced. This process acts as a vice. Unlike a single event such as a frost, it functions as a slow, suffocating tightening of physiological constraints.

## THE 300-METER CLIMB

If one cannot change the weather, the agronomic logic dictates that one must move the farm. Since temperature generally drops by about 0.6°C for every 100 meters of elevation gain, the most immediate adaptation strategy is vertical migration. Farmers who once planted at 1,000 meters are selling out and purchasing land at 1,200 meters. Those at 1,200 are looking at 1,500.

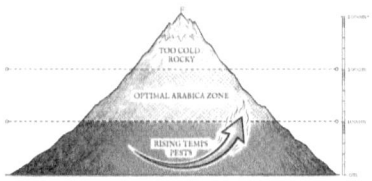

*As the tropics warm, the "Goldilocks" thermal zone for Arabica is migrating uphill, shrinking the available arable land.*

This is the "300-meter climb" required to maintain the current quality of production. However, geology imposes hard limits on this strategy. A mountain is a pyramid; there is significantly less surface area at the top than at the bottom. As the industry chases the cooling air uphill, the available acreage shrinks mathematically.

Consider the topography of Mt. Kenya or the Andes. The "coffee zone" is being pushed so high that it is colliding with other land uses. In Kenya, coffee is pushing into the tea zone, and the tea zone is pushing into protected forestry reserves. In Peru and Colombia, the "altitude ceiling" is often cloud forest, critical watersheds, or indigenous territories protected by law. The coffee farm cannot simply march up the slope without destroying the very ecosystems that regulate the local rainfall and hydrology.

Furthermore, altitude is not a perfect substitute for latitude. Higher altitude brings thinner air, different UV radiation levels, and steeper, more fractured terrain. The logistical cost of farming at 1,800 meters is significantly higher than at 1,000 meters. Roads are treacherous, mudslides are frequent, and mechanization is impossible. The vertical migration solves the temperature problem but creates a labor and logistics crisis.

The migration also creates a "Rust Paradox." As temperatures rise, the Coffee Leaf Rust fungus (*Hemileia vastatrix*), traditionally a low-altitude pathogen, is ascending. In the past, the cold nights at high altitudes acted as a natural fungicide, inhibiting spore germination. Now, farmers at 1,600 meters, who never had to spray for rust, are seeing the tell-tale orange dust on their leaves. They are being forced to apply copper fungicides in ecosystems that have never been exposed to them, altering soil chemistry and water quality.

## THE CARTEL OF THE AVOCADO

While scientists analyze the extinction of the plant, the market analyzes the economic defection of the farmer. A more immediate threat than the death of the trees is the farmer's decision to replace them.

In the state of Michoacán, Mexico, and increasingly in the coffee axis of Colombia, coffee is losing the war for land use. The primary antagonist in this land-use transition is the avocado. While thirsty, the "Green Gold" commands a profit margin that coffee cannot match. A hectare of avocados can yield five to ten times the net profit of a hectare of coffee, depending on the export window to the United States.

The agronomic comparison is stark. Avocado trees are voracious consumers of water, requiring roughly 2,000 liters to produce a single kilogram of fruit, competing directly with coffee for the dwindling aquifer. Yet, for a farmer looking at the debt ledger, the choice is rational.

But this pivot comes with a sociological consequence. In Mexico, the avocado trade has been thoroughly infiltrated by organized crime. Cartels demand "protection money" from avocado growers, seizing land and dictating prices. Coffee, with its lower margins and cooperative structures, has historically been less attractive to these groups. By switching crops, farmers are entering a high-stakes, high-risk economy.

*Economic pressure is forcing farmers to replace coffee with avocados, a
"thirsty" crop that offers higher immediate margins.*

This "Crop Migration" leads to a fragmentation of the coffee landscape. The continuous belts of coffee that sustained cooperatives and
processing mills are being broken up by patches of avocados, berries,
and cattle. This raises the logistical costs for everyone who stays in
coffee. If the wet mill closes because 40% of the neighbors switched to
avocados, the remaining coffee farmers have nowhere to process their
cherries. The infrastructure fractures before the climate kills the last
tree.

### THE BEETLE'S ASCENT

Heat is only one pressure point. The other is a creature no larger
than the head of a pin: the Coffee Berry Borer (*Hypothenemus hampei*).

For decades, altitude was the coffee farmer's natural pesticide. The
Borer beetle, an African native, thrives in warmth but becomes sluggish
and unable to reproduce in the cool air above 1,200 meters. Farmers in
the highlands could essentially ignore it. But as the heat line moves up
the mountain, the beetle follows.

The method of its destruction is mechanical and precise. The female
beetle drills a microscopic hole into the coffee cherry. She tunnels into
the seed (the bean) and lays her eggs. The larvae hatch and consume the
bean from the inside out. When the coffee is harvested and processed,
the beans are riddled with channels, lighter in weight, and prone to
fungal rot.

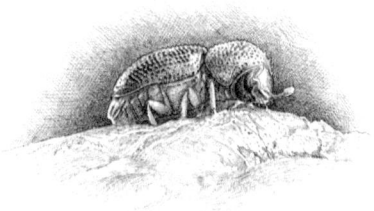

*The Coffee Berry Borer thrives in warmer temperatures, colonizing higher altitudes that were previously too cold for it to survive.*

In a 20°C world, the beetle might complete two reproductive cycles in a season. In a 22°C world, it can complete five or six. This exponential growth turns a nuisance into a biomass overwhelming the farm.

In Colombia, where the temperature has risen by roughly 1°C on average in coffee regions since 1980, the beetle has colonized altitudes that were previously safe zones. Farmers at 1,500 meters now find themselves in a chemical arms race. To save the crop, they must spray pesticides like Chlorpyrifos (often banned in the countries that buy the coffee) multiple times a season.

This creates a secondary crisis: pesticide resistance. The beetles are evolving faster than the chemical companies can develop new compounds. And for the smallholder farmer, the cost of these chemicals consumes the already thin margin. The beetle does not just consume the bean; it consumes the liquidity of the farm. A farm with a 10% infestation rate is manageable; a farm with 50% is a total financial loss.

### THE GREEN BUREAUCRACY: EUDR AND THE DIGITAL TWIN

As if the heat, the beetles, and the avocados were not enough, the coffee farmer of the 2020s faces a new, regulatory hurdle: European bureaucracy.

The European Union Deforestation Regulation (EUDR) represents the most significant shift in coffee trade policy in decades. The law is well-intentioned: to ensure that no product entering the EU has contributed to deforestation.

But the mechanism of enforcement is a technological shock. To comply, every single batch of coffee imported into Europe must be traced back to the exact plot of land where it was grown, verified by GPS coordinates accurate to six decimal places.

For a large plantation in Brazil, this is a spreadsheet exercise. They map their boundaries once and the compliance is complete.

For a cooperative in Ethiopia or Guatemala, comprising 5,000 smallholders who each own a fraction of a hectare on a misty mountainside, this is a crisis of data. Many of these farmers do not have smartphones. Their land deeds may be informal, ancestral, or communal. They do not have "digital twins" of their farms.

The "Consequence Layer" here is a bifurcation of the global market. Traders are already signaling that they may simply cease purchasing from complex, smallholder-heavy regions to avoid the compliance risk. They will source from the "safe," digital-ready plantations of Brazil and Vietnam.

The "untraceable" coffee—which often comes from the most vulnerable farmers—will not disappear. It will simply be diverted to markets with lower standards, likely China, Russia, or the Middle East, at a discount. The EUDR risks creating a two-tier world: a "Clean Tier" for the West, and a "Shadow Tier" for the rest, with the smallholder farmer paying the price of admission.

### The Genetic Ark: Hand-Made Trees

If the land cannot be moved, and the farmers are defecting, the plant must be fundamentally upgraded. This leads to the most high-tech and high-stakes sector of the climate fight: genetics.

For two hundred years, the coffee industry relied on a dangerously narrow genetic base. Most trees in Latin America are descendants of a handful of plants taken from Yemen in the 17th and 18th centuries. They are genetically almost identical. This homogeneity is a vulnerability in a changing climate.

Enter the F1 Hybrid.

In a nursery in Costa Rica, run by the World Coffee Research institute or private biotech firms, technicians are performing a tedious, manual procedure. Creating an FI (Filial I) hybrid is not a matter of simply planting seeds. It requires "emasculation."

The process is surgical. A worker must take a pair of tweezers and manually open the flower of the mother plant (often a high-quality variety like Geisha or Caturra) before it opens naturally. They must remove the anthers—the male parts—to prevent the plant from pollinating itself. Then, they must hand-pollinate the stigma with pollen collected from a specific father plant (often a robust, wild Ethiopia or Sudan landrace).

*Creating FI Hybrids requires the labor-intensive "emasculation" of flowers to prevent self-pollination.*

This must be done for every single seed produced for the initial breeding stock. It is labor-intensive, precise, and expensive.

But the result is "hybrid vigor" (heterosis). The offspring of this union —varieties like Centroamericano, Starmaya, and Evaluna—are biological accelerators. They grow 30% faster than traditional trees. Their root systems are massive, plunging deeper into the soil to find water that standard Typica roots cannot reach. They have higher leaf-to-fruit ratios, allowing them to photosynthesis more efficiently under stress. And crucially, they cup well, often scoring 85+ points, offering the flavor profile of the mother with the toughness of the father.

However, there is a catch—a cycle of dependency. FI hybrids are genetically unstable in the second generation (F2). This is basic Mendelian genetics: if two FI hybrids breed, their offspring will segregate. Some will be tall, some dwarf, some productive, some barren. The uniformity is lost.

This means a farmer cannot save the seeds from their harvest to plant the next year's nursery, as they have done for centuries. If they plant an F1 seed, the resulting tree will be a genetic lottery.

This biological reality shifts the economic power dynamic. To use these climate-resilient trees, farmers must return to the nursery every generation to buy clones or specialized seeds. The cost of an F1 seedling can be significantly higher than a traditional seedling. For a smallholder with 2,000 trees, this capital investment is often impossible without financing.

## THE DRAGON RISES: YUNNAN'S SUBTROPICAL PIVOT

As the "Bean Belt" disintegrates in the tropics, it is reforming in unexpected places. While Central America struggles, a new power is rising in the East, one that challenges the traditional geography of coffee: China.

For centuries, Yunnan was tea country. Then, for a brief period in the 20th century, it was opium country. Today, it is rapidly becoming coffee country. The Chinese government, identifying coffee as a strategic crop for rural development and a high-value export, has poured subsidies into the region. But the success of Yunnan is not just political; it is geographical.

Yunnan lies further north than most coffee regions—at roughly 24°N latitude, pushing the upper limit of the tropics. This latitude allows for cooler winters even at lower altitudes, mimicking the conditions of high-elevation Colombia but with easier terrain. It is a "latitude-for-altitude" trade-off that may become the blueprint for 2050 production.

The scale of the transformation is significant. In 1990, China produced fewer than 50,000 bags of coffee. By 2024, production had surged past 2 million bags—eclipsing longstanding producers like Costa Rica and Kenya.

Far from the romantic, small-plot farming of the Morales family, this is state-sponsored, consolidated agriculture. The hills of Pu'er are lined with neat, high-density rows of Catimor—a rust-resistant variety that is hardy but often considered lower quality. However, with massive investment in processing infrastructure, Yunnan is upgrading. The region now boasts wet mills that rival the best in Brazil, capable of processing cherries with consistent precision.

The rise of Yunnan signals a geopolitical shift. The Shanghai Coffee Exchange is growing in influence, aiming to set prices for the Asian market, decoupling from the volatility of New York. As the climate squeezes the traditional producers in the West, the East is positioning itself as the stable supplier of the future. It is a future where the center of gravity for coffee production moves from the fragmented, mountainous tropics to the consolidated, subtropical belts of Brazil and China.

### The Second Crop: Selling the Invisible

For the farmers who remain in the tropics, survival might depend on selling something other than beans: the invisible gas in the air.

Coffee, when grown correctly, is a forest crop. A shade-grown coffee farm can sequester significant amounts of carbon in the biomass of the shade trees and the soil. As global corporations race to meet "Net Zero" commitments, a new market has opened up: paying coffee farmers for the carbon they store.

The mechanism is seductive. A company like Microsoft or Delta Airlines buys "carbon credits" to offset their emissions. The money flows to a project developer, who verifies that a farmer in Peru has planted fifty Inga trees. The farmer receives a payment—a "second harvest."

In theory, this creates a virtuous cycle. The shade trees protect the coffee from the 2050 heat, and the carbon payments pay for the trees.

In practice, the "carbon market" is fraught with verification friction. How does one measure a tree on a remote mountain without spending more money than the tree is worth? For years, this required physical auditors with tape measures—a logistical bottleneck. Now, the industry is pivoting to LiDAR and satellite monitoring, attempting to measure biomass from space.

But the "human layer" of the transaction remains opaque. By the time the credit is verified, brokered, and sold, the leakage is massive. A credit might sell for $20 per ton on the open market, but the farmer often sees less than $2. For a smallholder with two hectares sequestering perhaps 5 tons of carbon a year, the total payout might be $10—hardly enough to prevent migration.

Furthermore, there is the thorny issue of "additionality." If a farmer was already growing shade coffee (as many indigenous farmers have for centuries), they typically do not qualify for credits because they aren't removing *new* carbon. This perversely penalizes the traditional stewards of the land while rewarding industrial farms that clear-cut and then replant.

### VIETNAM, 2030: THE WATER WARS

While carbon is the currency of the future, water is the currency of the present. Nowhere is this tension more visible than in the Central Highlands of Vietnam, the engine room of global Robusta production.

Vietnam built its coffee empire on irrigation. During the dry season, the landscape of Dak Lak province is crisscrossed with black hoses, pumping groundwater onto the flowering trees to trigger the bloom. This "hydro-shock" is what allows Vietnam to achieve the highest yields in the world—sometimes exceeding 3.5 metric tons per hectare.

But the aquifers are dropping. Climate models for the Mekong region predict more erratic monsoon cycles—longer, hotter dry seasons followed by violent, intense typhoons. The water table in some coffee districts has dropped by meters in the last decade. Farmers are drilling deeper wells, chasing the receding water.

This creates a zero-sum game between the coffee tree and the community. A single kilogram of green coffee requires roughly 100 liters of water for processing and thousands of liters for evapotranspiration during growth. As cities in the region grow and industrialize, the allocation of water to coffee farming becomes a political flashpoint. In the Mekong Delta downstream, the reduced freshwater flow allows saltwater from the ocean to intrude further inland, compromising rice paddies. The coffee upstream is essentially consuming the rice downstream.

### THE RETREAT OF INSURANCE: A PARAMETRIC SOLUTION?

Underlying all these physical risks—the beetle, the drought, the water table—is a financial risk that threatens to freeze the entire system: the retreat of insurance.

In the past, large agricultural insurers used the "Indemnity Model." A farmer bought a policy, the crop failed, an adjuster drove out to the farm, assessed the damage, and the bank wrote a check.

But as extreme weather events become "correlated" (happening everywhere at once) and "non-stationary" (the past is no longer a predictor of the future), this model is broken. The administrative cost of sending adjusters to thousands of small farms is too high.

The industry is pivoting to "Parametric Insurance" (or Index Insurance). This mechanism removes the human adjuster entirely. Instead, the policy is tied to a satellite data stream.

- If rainfall is below 50 mm in May (per satellite data),
- Then Farmer X receives an automatic $500 payout.

It is cold, algorithmic, and fast. It solves the speed problem. But it introduces "Basis Risk"—the disconnect where the satellite data indicates rainfall, but the specific microclimate of the farm remains dry. The algorithm indicates health; the trees indicate bankruptcy. The farmer is effectively betting against a satellite.

### THE LAB-GROWN FUTURE: COFFEE WITHOUT THE TREE

If the mountain becomes too hot, the water too scarce, and the insurance too robotic, a radical faction of the industry is proposing a final solution: abandon the farm entirely.

If the mountain becomes too hot, a radical faction of the industry is proposing a final solution: abandon the farm entirely. In industrial parks far from the equator, startups are beginning to brew 'molecular coffee'—a reconstruction of the beverage using upcycled plant waste rather than beans. The premise is that coffee is simply a collection of chemical compounds that can be mapped and synthesized in a lab, decoupling the caffeine fix from the dying ecosystem entirely.

Inside their facility, there are no burlap sacks, no roasters, and no smell of green beans. There are bioreactors and mixing tanks. They are not growing a plant; they are assembling a flavor profile. They can dial up the acidity, dial down the bitterness, and ensure a consistent caffeine content of exactly 100mg per cup.

The environmental pitch is compelling. In their lifecycle analysis, they claim to use 94% less water and emit 93% less carbon than conventional coffee farming. There is no deforestation, no fertilizer runoff, and no exploitation of labor in the Global South.

But the taste test is the battlefield.

Imagine a cupping table. On the left, a washed Ethiopian Yirgacheffe, grown by a cooperative at 2,000 meters. On the right, the molecular brew. The spoon breaks the crust of the Ethiopian: a burst of jasmine, apricot, and tea-like delicacy fills the nose. The spoon breaks the crust of the molecular coffee: it smells, simply, roasted. It smells like "coffee."

On the palate, the molecular brew is unnervingly close to a standard, medium-roast commodity coffee. It hits the nutty notes. It has the body. But for the specialty drinker, it falls into the "Uncanny Valley." It lacks the chaotic complexity of a true agricultural product—the weird, unpredictable fruit notes that come from a specific soil and a specific fermentation. It tastes like coffee, but it feels like an image of coffee—a high-resolution photograph of a meal rather than the meal itself.

The rise of lab-grown coffee poses a profound moral question. If the Global North succeeds in synthesizing the beverage, what happens to the 12.5 million smallholder families who depend on the crop? Technically, it solves the climate problem. It decouples the caffeine fix from the dying ecosystem. But economically, it threatens to sever the primary income stream for entire nations. If coffee becomes a software product manufactured in Seattle and Berlin, the "coffee lands" of the equator will lose their primary connection to the global economy. It is the ultimate form of gentrification: the product is retained while the producers are evicted.

### THE ZOMBIE SPECIES RETURNS

If the lab feels too sterile and the Arabica too fragile, nature may have one last card to play.

In the dusty archives of Kew Gardens and French botanical institutes, researchers have rediscovered coffee species that were abandoned a century ago. The most promising celebrity of this botanical revival is *Coffea stenophylla*.

Native to West Africa, *stenophylla* was farmed commercially in the 19th century and even served to coffee drinkers in London and Paris, who described it as excellent. But it yielded poorly compared to Robusta and was harder to process, so it vanished from commerce, lingering only in scattered wild populations.

In recent years, scientists led by Dr. Aaron Davis of Kew Gardens have tracked down these wild populations. The data they found was startling: *stenophylla* can grow and fruit in mean annual temperatures of nearly 25°C—significantly hotter than Arabica and similar to Robusta.

But unlike Robusta, which often tastes of burnt rubber and earth, *stenophylla* tastes like—of all things—Arabica. Blind taste tests suggest it has the complexity, acidity, and sweetness required for the specialty market. It is, effectively, a heat-resistant high-quality coffee provided by nature.

Other candidates are emerging from the shadows. *Coffea liberica*, the giant tree of the coffee world with leaves as big as fans and a deep root system, is seeing a renaissance in Malaysia and the Philippines. Its fruit is tough, its skin thick, and it thrives in heat and poor soils. Breeders are now rushing to sequence these genomes, hoping to either domesticate these wild species or cross them with Arabica to inject their hardiness into our morning cup.

## THE LEDGER OF DEBT

We return to Huehuetenango, to the kitchen table of Jose Morales. The high-tech solutions—the gene-edited hybrids, the digital twins, the parametric satellites, the zombie species—feel distant from his reality.

His reality is a ledger of debt.

The local cooperative is offering a renovation loan to plant rust-resistant Marsellesa trees. The interest rate is 12%. The trees will take three years to produce their first harvest. For those three years, Jose will have no income from that land. He will have to buy food, pay for his children's school uniforms, and service the interest on the loan.

If the price of coffee drops below the cost of production in 2028—a distinct possibility given the boom in Brazilian and Chinese production —he will default. He will lose the land.

This is the "Adaptation Gap". The technology to save coffee exists. We know how to farm regeneratively. We know how to irrigate. We have the genetics. But the financial mechanism to deploy it to the people who need it most is fractured. The market pays for the bean, but it does not pay for the resilience of the farm.

Jose closes the notebook. He looks out the window at the brown patch on the hillside where the rust has stripped the leaves. He is not waiting for a molecular scientist in Seattle to save him. He is waiting for a price that reflects the reality of growing a dying crop in a warming world. Until that price arrives, the migration north will continue.

## The Climate-Smart Cup

The future of coffee is not fixed; it presents a design challenge.

Imagine a single bean in the year 2050. It was grown on a tree in Yunnan, China, at 24°N latitude. The tree is an F1 hybrid, bred for heat tolerance. It was irrigated by a precision drip system triggered by a sensor in the soil. Its carbon footprint was offset by a bamboo grove planted nearby, verified by a satellite passing overhead. It was shipped to Europe with a digital passport proving it did not cause deforestation.

It tastes, unexpectedly, good. Not like the wild, chaotic floral explosion of a 2020 Ethiopian natural, but solid, chocolatey, and sweet.

This is the "Climate-Smart" cup. It is a triumph of engineering. But it is also a memorial. It is a memorial to the places like Huehuetenango that could not make the transition.

The machine of global coffee is massive, churning through millions of tons of beans a year. But its foundation is biological, and biology has hard limits. As the planet warms, we are learning that coffee is not a machine that can simply be dialed up. It is a partnership with a climate that is walking away from us. The question for the next decade moves beyond whether we can engineer a heat-resistant tree, to whether we can engineer a market that allows the farmer to survive the heat as well.

# 38

# THE GHOST IN THE MACHINE: BREWING THE POST-AGRICULTURAL CUP

D evoid of the roasted, caramelized heavy notes of a coffee production floor, the air in the laboratory in Espoo, Finland, smells faintly of yeast, ozone, and sterilized steel—a sharp, clinical olfactory profile that suggests a high-dependency hospital ward or a pharmaceutical clean room rather than a culinary origin point. Inside the high-security facilities of the VTT Technical Research Centre, the sensory markers of the traditional coffee trade are absent. There are no burlap sacks stacked in the corner, bleeding the earthy, vegetal scent of the tropics into the atmosphere. There is no particulate dust from dried husks floating in the light beams. There is no deafening rattle of green beans tumbling into a spinning metal drum.

The dominant acoustic feature is the rhythmic, low-frequency hum of a stainless steel bioreactor. This five-hundred-liter vessel is filled with a nutrient-rich broth that agitates back and forth in a hypnotic, mechanical wave. Suspended in the liquid is a slurry of beige biomass. To the unassisted eye, the substance resembles hummus, wet river sand, or a sourdough starter. Under a microscope, however, the identity of the slurry reveals itself. These are cells of Coffea arabica. They possess the genetic code identical to the plants growing on the slopes of Kilimanjaro or in the volcanic loam of Costa Rica. Yet, these cells have never been exposed to the sun. They have never been subjected to the trade winds, the bite of the borer beetle, or the soaking rains of the intertropical *convergence zone. They have never been part of a cherry, a branch, or a root system. They are undifferentiated plant cells, grown in a suspension culture, multiplying exponentially in a warm bath of sugars, nitrogen, minerals, and growth hormones.*

*Dr. Heiko Rischer, the lead scientist at VTT, opens a valve to draw off a sample of the liquid into a sterilized glass beaker. The fluid is thick, opaque, and creamy. This substance represents one potential trajectory for the coffee industry—a decoupling of the product from the plant. When this biomass is harvested, dried, and roasted, it will turn brown via the Maillard reaction. It will develop pyrazines and melanoidins. It will possess the aroma of coffee because, chemically speaking, it is coffee. However, it is coffee divorced from agriculture—a crop without a harvest, a stimulant without a season, and a commodity without a geography.*

*This marks the dawn of the "Post-Agricultural" era. As the traditional Bean Belt disintegrates under the pressure of the climate volatility—the "heat line" moving up the mountains—a high-stakes industrial race has begun to decouple the world's favorite beverage from the fragile biology of the coffee tree. In laboratories from Helsinki to Seattle to Singapore, scientists are attempting to replicate nature's output, but with accelerated timelines and without the requirement for a single acre of arable land. It is a technological ambition that promises to mitigate the environmental impact of farming, creating a buffer against a warming world, but it simultaneously threatens to render the livelihoods of twenty-five million farmers obsolete.*

### THREE PATHS TO THE SAME CUP

Let's take a closer look at the varying methodologies employed to solve the "coffee problem." In the public discourse, terms like "lab-grown," "synthetic," and "beanless" are often used interchangeably, but they represent three distinct technological philosophies. They are three separate avenues converging on the same goal: the separation of flavor from the farm.

*Cellular agriculture grows coffee cells in nutrient broth, decoupling the product from the plant.*

1. **Molecular Reconstruction ("Beanless Coffee")** Utilized by companies like Atomo, this method ignores coffee DNA entirely. Instead, it treats coffee as a chemical equation to be solved. Researchers analyze the molecular fingerprint of a cup—acids, oils, bitter compounds—and search the plant kingdom for matching building blocks. They identify lignin in upcycled date pits, bitterness in fenugreek, and caffeine in tea waste. These ingredients are combined and roasted—a synthetic assembly of nature's spare parts constructed to replicate the sensory experience.

2. **Precision Fermentation** This is the method of synthetic biology. Scientists do not grow plant cells; they utilize microbes as microscopic factories. Using gene-editing tools like CRISPR, specific DNA sequences are inserted into yeast or bacteria. These instructions program the microbes to produce specific target molecules—coffee fatty acids, floral esters, or lactones—rather than their usual outputs like alcohol. The microbes are fed sugar, and they excrete flavor compounds. These isolated compounds are then blended by flavor chemists, much like perfumers composing a scent.

3. **Cellular Agriculture** Pursued by VTT in Finland and California Cultured, this is the attempt to grow actual coffee cells in a bioreactor. It is the most technically complex path because it requires maintaining living plant tissue within a tank. However, it offers the biological material itself, grown in a nutrient broth rather than soil. It promises the full

complexity of the coffee genome without the need for the coffee tree.

## Reverse Engineering the "Black Box"

The audacity of the Molecular Reconstruction approach lies in its premise: that the coffee bean functioned as a delivery system for a specific set of sensations rather than a sacred object. For centuries, the coffee bean was treated as a "black box." It was subjected to heat, it turned brown, and it produced a desirable flavor. Modern gas chromatography-mass spectrometry (GC-MS) has allowed science to peer inside that box. We now understand that the "coffee" flavor is an orchestration of over 800 volatile compounds. We know that the mouthfeel comes from polysaccharides and oils. We know the acidity is derived from chlorogenic, citric, and malic acids. We know the roast flavor comes from the degradation of sucrose and the formation of pyrazines.

Founders of molecular coffee companies examined this chemical inventory and posed a provocative question: If the orchestra can be assembled from different musicians, will the audience discern the difference?

The logic is detailed in patents such as U.S. Patent 10,893,694, titled *Molecular Coffee and Methods of Making*. The document reads as an industrial manual for sensory replication. It outlines formulations comprising a substrate—seeds, pits, legumes, or grains—treated with a modulation agent comprising amino acids, sugars, and fats to produce a roasted coffee replicate. The patent explicitly lists the chemical targets: methoxypyrazines for earthiness, guaiacol for smokiness, and 2-acetyl-1-pyrroline for that quintessential "roasty" aroma.

The process often begins in the waste stream. Roughly 40% of the mass of a harvested coffee cherry is waste, but other industries generate waste that is valuable for this process. Date pits, for example, are a byproduct of the dried fruit industry. They are hard, dense, and rich in lignin—the structural material that gives plant cells their rigidity.

*"Beanless" coffee reconstructs the flavor profile using upcycled ingredients like date pits and seeds to mimic the chemical signature of coffee.*

When roasted, lignin breaks down into smoky, woody phenols, specifically guaiacol and 4-vinylguaiacol, that mimic the roast profile of coffee. By taking these date pits, granulating them, and soaking them in a "reaction liquid" containing proteins, amino acids, and sugars derived from other plants (like pea protein or grape skin extracts), manufacturers create a matrix. When this matrix is roasted, the amino acids and sugars interact via the Maillard reaction, just as they would in a coffee bean. The result resembles coffee grounds visually. It brews like coffee grounds. It contains caffeine (added exogenously).

However, the challenge lies in the "Uncanny Valley" of flavor. Early iterations of beanless coffee successfully mimicked the base notes—the roast, the bitterness, the nutty qualities. These are the chemically simple targets. The high notes—the delicate florals of a Geisha, the sparkling citrus of a Kenyan SL28, the winey fermentation of a Natural process— are exponentially harder to simulate. These flavors are the result of complex biological stress and wild fermentation in the field, processes that are difficult to replicate in a mixing bowl. Tasting a cup of first-generation beanless coffee can be a disorienting experience. The nose signals "coffee." The eyes perceive a black liquid. But the palate often detects a hollowness in the mid-palate, a lack of the structural complexity that thousands of distinct compounds create. It is analogous to listening to a symphony played on a synthesizer versus acoustic instruments; the notes are correct, but the resonance differs. The goal of the industry is to narrow this gap until the distinction is imperceptible to the average consumer.

## THE BIOPSY AND THE BIOREACTOR

While molecular reconstruction assembles the ghost of coffee from spare parts, the scientists at VTT are attempting to grow the body. The process of cellular agriculture begins with a biopsy. A technician takes a scalpel and slices a small explant—a piece of leaf or stem—from a living *Coffea arabica* plant. This tissue is sterilized and placed on a petri dish containing a gel nutrient medium infused with specific plant hormones, typically auxins and cytokinins.

In a natural setting, a leaf cell functions according to its location. It has a specific job: photosynthesis. However, the hormones in the petri dish trigger a process called "dedifferentiation." The cells lose their specialized function. They revert to a stem-cell-like state, forming a lump of white, amorphous tissue called a callus.

*The "Callus" is a mass of undifferentiated plant cells, the starter culture for the bioreactor.*

This callus serves as the starter culture. It is transferred into a liquid medium in a bioreactor. Here, the constraints of biology are removed. A normal coffee tree must endure the cycles of day and night; the bioreactor provides light or darkness on demand. A tree must forage for water; the bioreactor bathes it in constant hydration. A tree must defend against insects and fungi; the bioreactor is sterile.

Most importantly, a coffee tree spends 90% of its metabolic energy growing wood, roots, bark, and leaves—structures that are inedible to humans. In the bioreactor, 100% of the energy is directed into producing the target biomass. The speed of production is significant. A coffee tree requires three to four years to produce its first harvestable cherries. A bioreactor can produce a batch of harvestable coffee cells in approximately two weeks.

However, biology presents resistance. The biomass that emerges from the tank is not a green coffee bean. It is a paste. It lacks the complex cellular architecture of a seed. In a conventional coffee bean, the cells are tightly packed and encased in hard cellulose walls. When a natural bean is roasted, the heat causes moisture inside these cells to turn to steam. The pressure builds up—reaching 20 to 25 atmospheres (290 to 360 PSI) —essentially pressure-cooking the interior of the bean while the exterior chars. This miniature pressure-cooking environment is crucial for developing the complex acidity and flavor precursors of fine coffee.

The lab-grown paste, lacking this cellular pressure vessel, roasts differently. It dries out rapidly. It does not "crack" like a bean. As a result, early batches of cell-cultured coffee often exhibited "toasty" or "cereal-like" flavors, lacking the acidic snap of the agricultural product. Scientists are now experimenting with scaffolding—using plant-based structures to mimic the density of a green bean—to force the chemistry to behave as if it were inside a seed. They are engineering the "crunch" of the bean to ensure the Maillard reaction occurs under the correct thermal stress.

### THERMODYNAMICS: THE ENERGY TRAP

While proponents pitch lab-grown coffee as the ultimate sustainability solution    citing zero deforestation, 94% less water use, and localized production—there is a law of physics that cannot be edited: Thermodynamics.

Traditional coffee farming relies on a massive, free fusion reactor located 150 million kilometers away: the sun. Photosynthesis acts as free energy capture. Rain provides free irrigation. Soil provides free structural support. The farmer adds labor and fertilizer, but the primary energy input of the crop is gratuitous solar radiation. In a bioreactor, the sun must be replaced with electricity. Water must be pumped. Tanks must be heated and cooled to precise temperatures, typically around 25°C (77°F), as coffee cells are sensitive to thermal fluctuations. The steel tanks must be manufactured. Sterilization is constant and energy-intensive because the nutrient-rich broth is a paradise for bacteria; a single spore of wild mold can compromise thousands of liters of product.

This is the "Energy Trap" of cellular agriculture. Techno-Economic Analyses (TEA) of comparative bioproducts suggest that growing plant cell mass in steel vessels requires enormous energy input—estimates range widely, but can reach 200 to 400 MegaJoules per kilogram of dry biomass for complex tissue culture. By comparison, shipping a kilogram of green coffee from Brazil to Rotterdam consumes roughly 5 to 10 MegaJoules. Even factoring in fertilizer production and farm equipment, the "Sun-Grown" model is efficient at capturing energy. The "Foundry" model is energy-hungry.

*While land-efficient, bioreactors face an "Energy Trap," requiring massive electricity inputs to replace the free energy of the sun.*

If the electricity powering the Coffee Foundry comes from coal or natural gas, the carbon footprint of lab-grown coffee could exceed that of coffee shipped from Brazil. The sustainability claim is valid only if the bioreactor is powered by renewable energy—hydro, wind, or solar. Furthermore, there is the cost of the feedstock. Cells cannot be grown from nothing. They require a carbon source (sugar) and nitrogen. That sugar must be grown in soil—likely a field of corn or sugar cane. Therefore, the land footprint is displaced rather than eliminated. The trade-off swaps high-altitude tropical forests for monoculture cornfields in the Midwest or sugarcane plantations in Brazil.

Currently, the cost of producing complex plant tissue in a bioreactor is measured in dozens or hundreds of dollars per kilogram. Commodity coffee trades at roughly $4.40 per kilogram ($2.00 per pound). To compete, the lab-grown industry must reduce its costs by orders of magnitude. This requires scaling up from 500-liter pilot tanks to massive, 50,000-liter industrial vats—a scale of plant cell culture that presents significant engineering challenges regarding oxygenation and shear stress. Plant cells are larger and more fragile than bacteria; if the impeller stirs too fast, the cells shear and die. If it stirs too slow, the oxygen does not reach the center of the tank.

### RED TAPE AND LABELING WARS

Before cell-cultured coffee can reach the consumer, it must navigate a complex regulatory landscape. In the European Union, any food that was not consumed to a significant degree before May 1997 is classified as a "Novel Food" under Regulation (EU) 2015/2283. To receive approval, a company must prove—through extensive toxicology studies and allergen assessments—that its product is safe. The European Food Safety Authority (EFSA) requires rigorous data on the stability, nutritional value, and potential allergenicity of the new biomass. The process typically takes 18 months to 3 years and involves significant financial investment.

In the United States, the FDA's "GRAS" (Generally Recognized As Safe) pathway offers a route to market, but it remains rigorous. Beyond safety, there is the battle over nomenclature. The dairy industry provides a precedent. When oat and almond beverages began to capture market share, the dairy lobby litigated to prevent them from using the word "milk." The coffee industry is preparing for a similar defense. Traditional trade organizations are mobilizing to define "coffee" legally as the product of the *Coffea* tree grown in soil.

They will advocate for mandatory labels such as "Synthetic Caffeinated Beverage," "Imitation Coffee," or "Lab-Cultured Coffee Substitute." The terminology is critical. If VTT or Atomo is forced to use the word "Imitation" on the package, the product may remain a niche curiosity, trapped in the "uncanny valley" of consumer perception. However, if they can legally market it as "Sustainable Coffee" or "Brewed from Coffee Cells," it could achieve mainstream acceptance. The battle for the dictionary will be as significant as the battle for market share.

## "If They Can Grow It, We Are Dead"

Assuming the engineering challenges regarding texture are resolved, the energy grid becomes sufficiently green to address the carbon issue, and the regulatory hurdles are cleared, the industry arrives at the "Consequence Layer." The rise of the Coffee Foundry implies a radical bifurcation of the coffee world. The human cost becomes visible when one looks away from the sterile labs of Espoo and examine the reality of Dak Lak Province, Vietnam, or the Minas Gerais region of Brazil.

Dak Lak serves as the engine room of the global Robusta trade. Here, a farmer named Nguyen manages three hectares of coffee trees. He is not a "specialty" farmer. He does not market his beans on social media. He produces volume. His trees are fed heavy fertilizer, irrigated from dwindling aquifers, and harvested by strip-picking—removing every cherry, ripe or green, in a single motion. Nguyen's coffee is not destined for a boutique café. It is destined for the supply chain of a massive multinational corporation, where it will be steam-treated, freeze-dried, and transformed into instant coffee granules. This trade supports his family, funds his children's education, and sustains the local economy of fertilizer merchants, transport drivers, and mill operators.

Lab-grown coffee targets Nguyen directly. The slurry from the bioreactor is ideal for industrial applications. It is consistent. It is immune to bad weather. It has no defects. It is easily spray-dried into instant powder or mixed into sugary coffee drinks where the nuance of terroir is irrelevant. If the lab-grown industry succeeds, it could eliminate the market for Robusta and low-grade Arabica. While this might be framed as a victory for quality—removing low-grade coffee from the market—it represents an economic catastrophe for the Global South.

Vietnam, the world's primary source of Robusta, depends on this trade. Brazil's mechanized Cerrado region depends on it. Millions of smallholders in Uganda, Indonesia, and Honduras rely on selling their commodity beans to subsidize their livelihoods. If multinational giants switch to purchasing vats of biomass from a foundry in Germany or the United States instead of bags of beans from the tropics, the flow of capital to the developing world ceases. This is the "Vanilla Precedent." When synthetic vanillin was synthesized from wood pulp and petro-chemicals in the 20th century, the price of natural vanilla collapsed, decimating the economies of vanilla-growing regions like Madagascar. Natural vanilla became a luxury item, while 99% of the world consumed the synthetic version. Coffee faces a similar bifurcation.

This leads to a scenario of extreme inequality: The "Specialty" market remains as a luxury tier, a "Heritage Cup" consumed by those who can afford the inefficiencies of artisanal farming. The mass market consumes the "Tech Cup," grown in steel. The farmers who previously supplied the middle of the market are left with "stranded assets"—farms that are no longer economically viable. When presented with this possibility, an agronomist in Colombia bypassed the usual discussion of flavor notes or carbon footprints. He examined the data on funding for synthetic coffee startups and stated, "If they can grow it cheaper than we can pick it, we are dead."

## MARS AND THE INFINITE LOOP

The ultimate logic of the bioreactor is not found on Earth, but above it. NASA and the European Space Agency are monitoring the develop-ment of coffee labs closely. The coffee tree is a poor candidate for space travel. It has a low "harvest index"—it produces too much inedible wood and root mass relative to the edible seed. It requires significant volume and gravity for proper root orientation.

A bioreactor, however, is native to the spaceship environment. It is a closed-loop system. It recycles its own water. It is dense and volumetric. In a long-duration mission to Mars, the psychological comfort of coffee will be essential for crew morale. The first cup of coffee consumed on another planet will almost certainly be brewed not from a bean, but from a biomass paste, cultivated in a tank powered by a nuclear battery, millions of kilometers from the nearest soil.

This extraterrestrial vision clarifies the philosophical shift occurring on Earth. The industry is moving from an era of extraction—where resources are taken from the soil with the hope of recovery—to an era of synthesis, where necessities are constructed from elemental building blocks. It raises the question of whether the "terroir" of a coffee—the soul of the place—is a necessary component of the beverage, or merely a romantic inefficiency that we have learned to tolerate.

## THE SOUL OF THE BEAN

Standing in the VTT lab, observing the brown liquid swirl in the beaker, one is forced to confront the question that permeates the modern coffee industry: What is coffee?

Is coffee merely a chemical delivery system? Is it defined by the presence of caffeine, chlorogenic acid, and trigonelline? If so, the lab version is objectively superior. It is cleaner. It is free of mycotoxins. It can be engineered to possess higher antioxidant levels or lower acidity. It is coffee perfected, stripped of its biological variability.

Or is coffee a connection? Is it a ritual that binds the drinker to the earth, to the climate, and to the hands that harvested it? When a consumer drinks a cup of natural coffee, they are tasting the specific weather patterns of a season in Ethiopia. They are tasting the mineral composition of the soil in Antigua. The variations in the cup—the slight inconsistencies from batch to batch—are proof of its organic origin. They are evidence that the liquid is a product of a living world, not a sterile one. A cup of cellular coffee possesses no narrative. It has a batch number. It solves the problem of supply, but it creates a crisis of meaning.

The future of coffee likely contains both realities. The "Heritage Cup" and the "Tech Cup" will exist in parallel, separated by price and philosophy. The conflict will not be between Arabica and Robusta, nor between washed and natural processing. It will be a divergence between the Farm and the Foundry. Technology offers a necessary buffer against climate change. As the "heat line" moves up the mountain, synthetic coffee can fill the supply gap, ensuring that coffee remains affordable for the masses. However, this technological buffer comes at a potential cost to traditional livelihoods. As the tanks in Espoo hum their electric song, the farmers in the tropics watch the sky, wondering if the rain—and the buyers—will return. The "Ghost in the Machine" is now awake, and it is brewing.

# 39

# THE MONSTER: LIBERICA'S RESURRECTION IN A WARMING WORLD

T
he tree standing in the backyard of a smallholding in Lipa City, Philippines, does not resemble the polite, manicured shrubbery of a typical commercial coffee plantation. It possesses the architectural presence of a grand oak or a tropical mahogany, a massive canopy tree rising nearly fifty feet (15 meters) into the humid air, its trunk as thick as a utility pole. To harvest the fruit, the farmer cannot simply reach out a hand as one might with the accessible Arabica; the task requires a twenty-five-foot bamboo ladder and a willingness to climb into a dense, dark tangle of vegetation that resists the intruder.

The cherries themselves appear alien to the conventional eye. Unlike the small, uniform crimson berries of the high mountain slopes, these are massive, oblong, and resilient, resembling small plums or olives, turning a deep, bruised purple when they reach maturity. When they detach from the branch, they do not patter against the soil; they land with a heavy, audible thud.

This is *Coffea liberica*. For over a century, the industry has treated this species as a botanical outcast—relegated to the margins of the trade, dismissed by London cuppers as coarse, and ignored by the New York C-Market. In the established hierarchy of coffee, if Arabica is the refined aristocrat and Robusta is the industrial workhorse, Liberica has been viewed as the unkempt giant of the lowlands, considered too unruly and too bitter for the civilized palate.

Coffea liberica *is a botanical giant, requiring ladders to harvest and thriving in heat that would kill Arabica.*

*However, in the sweltering heat of the mid-2020s, the giant is being re-evaluated through the lens of botanical resilience rather than aesthetic noncon-formity. As temperatures in the traditional "Bean Belt" rise and the delicate Arabica plants of Latin America suffer from thermal stress, agronomists are examining this massive tree with a fresh perspective. They observe a taproot that drives deeper than standard agricultural machinery can plow. They measure leaves with a cuticle armor so thick that pests struggle to penetrate it. They realize that despite the punishing humidity of the Philippine lowlands— temperatures that would scorch an Arabica tree in three days—the Liberica is not merely surviving; it is biologically thriving.*

*For decades, the industry's search for a "Climate Savior" focused on breeding a tougher version of Arabica. The realization is now dawning that the solution may not lie in fortifying the aristocrat, but in embracing the resilience of a different species entirely. The resurrection of Liberica is not just a horticul-tural shift; it is a cultural reclamation. It is the narrative of how a species once critiqued for tasting of "jackfruit and wet wood" is being reimagined as a foun-dational crop for a hotter, harsher planetary environment.*

## THE ERA OF THE SILVER BEAN

Forecasting the future trajectory of Liberica requires first examine the scar tissue of its past. Liberica is not native to Southeast Asia; it evolved in the low-lying jungles of West Africa, specifically Liberia, where it developed defenses against heat and pathogens that would decimate other species. It arrived in the Philippines in the 19th century, carried by Spanish friars utilizing the Manila Galleon trade routes, but its moment of economic ascendancy emerged from a global biological crisis.

In the late 1880s, the global coffee industry faced a catastrophic disruption. *Hemileia vastatrix*—coffee leaf rust—had emerged from the Indian Ocean basin and was systematically dismantling the massive colonial plantations of Ceylon (Sri Lanka) and Java. The British and Dutch empires watched as their profitable Arabica monocultures were reduced to gray dust and leafless skeletons over the course of a few seasons. The "Wine of Islam," the commodity that fueled the London stock exchange, was vanishing from the ledger.

The Philippines, however, possessed a biological hedge. The farmers of Batangas and Cavite had planted Liberica alongside Arabica. When the rust pathogen arrived on their shores in 1889, the Arabica trees succumbed, but the Liberica trees remained productive. Their leaves, thick and waxy, repelled the fungal spores, allowing the tree to continue photosynthesizing while its neighbors withered.

For a brief, lucrative window between 1886 and 1890, the Philippines became the only major producer of coffee capable of meeting global demand. The town of Lipa became the epicenter of this supply shock. Prices on the world market escalated from 14 pesos per picul (a traditional unit of weight equal to roughly 63 kilograms or 139 pounds) to over 30 pesos. The capital that flowed into the municipality was transformative.

Historical accounts from the period describe a town undergoing a rapid and surreal economic metamorphosis, a period locally recorded as the "Era of the Silver Bean." The main thoroughfare was renamed Calle Real, serving as a display of newfound affluence that rivaled European capitals. Farmers who had subsisted on meager incomes were suddenly importing velvet from France, diamonds from Amsterdam, and mirrors from Vienna. They constructed two-story stone mansions (*Bahay na Bato*) using hardwoods so dense they sank in water—Narra, Molave, and Kamagong—fortifying their homes against typhoons and the passage of time. These structures served as fortresses of wealth as much as homes, built on the back of a single botanical anomaly.

The social restructuring was absolute. A new class of *ilustrados* (the enlightened ones) emerged, financing their children's education in

Madrid and Heidelberg. Local oral history preserves legends of families washing their floors with imported soda water because well water was deemed too plebeian, and using coffee beans as currency markers during long nights of gambling. One surviving account details a wedding feast where the soup was served in bowls fashioned from solid silver coins, melted down by local smiths to demonstrate the sheer liquidity of the region's wealth.

However, this economic boom was fragile. The rust eventually mutated, or perhaps the density of the monoculture allowed the pathogen to overwhelm even the Liberica defenses. By 1891, the trees began to show signs of stress. Concurrently, the geopolitical landscape shifted. The United States acquired the Philippines from Spain in 1898; the British abandoned coffee in Ceylon to focus on tea; and the Dutch identified a new, high-yielding species in the Congo called Robusta, which they planted aggressively across Indonesia.

The market correction in Lipa was severe. When the price collapsed, the mansions fell into disrepair or silence. The "Golden Era" of Liberica concluded in less than a decade. The massive trees in Batangas were felled to make space for housing or faster-yielding fruit orchards. By the turn of the millennium, Liberica accounted for less than 1% of global commercial coffee production. It had become a ghost crop, existing in the backyards of ancestral homes, unpicked and unmanaged, serving only as a reminder of the brief period when a small town in the Pacific controlled the global coffee supply.

ANATOMY OF A SURVIVOR

Biologically, *Coffea liberica* is built for endurance. While Arabica relies on high altitude and cool nights to develop sugar and maintain respiration rates, Liberica relies on structural engineering to survive hostile environments. It is defined by botanical resilience rather than delicacy.

The primary defense mechanism is the root system. A standard Arabica plant possesses a relatively shallow root ball, extending perhaps 30 to 50 centimeters (12 to 20 inches) into the topsoil. This architecture makes it highly sensitive to moisture variability; if precipitation ceases for three weeks, the Arabica plant enters a state of physiological shock. Liberica, by contrast, drives a massive taproot four to five meters (13 to 16 feet) into the subsoil, bypassing surface fluctuations entirely and accessing water tables that other plants cannot reach. This phenomenon, known as hydraulic lift, allows the tree to remain green and productive even during severe El Niño droughts that desiccate surrounding crops. It can thrive in heavy clay, in peat swamps, and in acidic soils that would compromise an Arabica seedling in days.

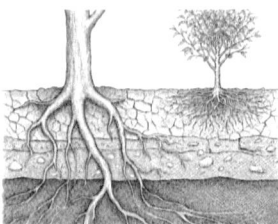

*Liberica's massive taproot allows it to survive severe droughts and poor soil conditions.*

The second layer of defense is the leaf architecture. A Liberica leaf is substantial—often twice the surface area of a human hand—and heavily reinforced. Under microscopic analysis, the cuticle (the waxy outer layer) is significantly thicker than that of its cousins. This acts as a shield against solar radiation and insect predation. The Coffee Berry Borer (*Hypothenemus hampei*), the beetle that plagues the global industry by drilling into the fruit to deposit eggs, finds the epidermis of a Liberica cherry exhausting to penetrate. Frequently, the beetle abandons the attempt, or the cherry's high pulp-to-seed ratio ensures the pest never reaches the bean itself.

This durability extends to the stomata, the microscopic pores on the underside of the leaf responsible for gas exchange. In Arabica, these pores are sensitive and prone to closing rapidly under stress, halting photosynthesis. Liberica's stomatal regulation is more robust, allowing the tree to continue carbon fixation even when vapor pressure deficits are high. It is a machine designed to function when the factory conditions are suboptimal.

The most critical trait for the 21st century, however, is the temperature threshold. Arabica begins to suffer physiological stress at 24°C (75°F) and ceases photosynthesis entirely at 30°C (86°F). Robusta can tolerate temperatures up to 30°C before showing signs of decline. Liberica remains metabolically active at 35°C (95°F) and can survive thermal spikes even higher. In a world steadily marching toward a +2°C or +3°C future, Liberica stands as the only commercially viable species already adapted to the projected climate baseline.

### Kapeng Barako: The Myth of the Stud

While the global market marginalized Liberica, the residents of Batangas maintained the species for domestic consumption. They assigned the coffee a name reflecting its character: *Kapeng Barako*.

The term *Barako* in Tagalog carries significant linguistic weight. Literally translating to "stud" or "wild boar," it implies intense masculinity, virility, and untamable strength. The mythology surrounding the beverage aligned with this nomenclature. It was reputed to be of such potency it could "make a dead man run." Traditionally, it was not brewed in delicate porcelain drippers but boiled in an iron pot for twenty minutes until reduced to a thick, black liquor, then sweetened with *panocha* (solid disks of raw muscovado sugar).

Designed as caloric fuel for laborers in the cane fields and ports, this beverage was rarely used for contemplative sipping. The flavor profile—heavy, smoky, anise-like, with a profound bitterness—became a marker of regional identity. Consuming Barako was a statement of resilience. Requesting milk or water to dilute the brew was viewed as a misunderstanding of its purpose, a rejection of the local custom.

However, this cultural reverence created a quality trap. Because Barako was valued for its aggressive strength and bitterness, incentives to refine the processing methods were non-existent. For decades, farmers stripped the branches indiscriminately, mixing ripe purple cherries with unripe green ones. They dried the fruit on concrete pavements exposed to local fauna and debris. The resulting cup was often harsh, medicinal, and tainted with mold, reinforcing the global perception that Liberica was a low-grade commodity. The challenge of the modern resurrection has been to decouple the species from the processing flaws—to demonstrate that the "Wild Boar" can be washed, groomed, and presented with sophistication.

## THE EXCELSA CONFUSION AND CLASSIFICATION

Complicating the Liberica narrative is the presence of its close relative, Excelsa. For the majority of the 20th century, Excelsa was categorized as a fourth distinct species (*Coffea excelsa*), completing the botanical quartet alongside Arabica, Robusta, and Liberica. In 2006, botanists led by Aaron Davis at Kew Gardens reclassified it based on genetic markers. Taxonomically, Excelsa is now considered a variety of Liberica (*Coffea liberica var. dewevrei*).

To a farmer standing in the field, however, the distinction remains vivid and practically relevant. Excelsa trees are large, though they rarely reach the gigantic proportions of pure Liberica. The leaves are smoother and less leathery. The beans are physically distinct—smaller, teardrop-shaped, and asymmetrical compared to the almond-shaped Liberica. Most importantly, the flavor profile is unique.

While pure Liberica leans toward dark chocolate, smoke, and jackfruit, Excelsa is renowned for a sharp, tart, fruity profile often described as "tartaric" or "tamarind-like." It possesses a higher perceived acidity than its giant cousin. This tartness makes Excelsa a crucial component in the modern blending strategy. In the context of the species' resurrection, Excelsa acts as a bridge. It is more palatable to the specialty drinker accustomed to fruity African coffees, spanning the gap between the familiar acidity of Arabica and the heavy, woody bass notes of Liberica. The reclassification has not erased the agricultural reality; farmers continue to cultivate them as distinct crops with distinct market applications.

## JACKFRUIT AND SMOKE: THE SENSORY BARRIER

If Liberica possesses such agronomic advantages, the question remains why it has not achieved ubiquity. The answer lies in the cup profile, or more accurately, in the disconnect between Western sensory expectations and Liberica's chemical reality.

For a century, Western traders described Liberica using adjectives ranging from "exotic" to "offensive." The most consistent descriptor is Jackfruit (*Langka* in Tagalog, or *Nangka* in Malay). To a Southeast Asian palate, jackfruit is a beloved, sweet, custard-like flavor. To an uninitiated Western palate, the specific volatile compounds—specifically the heavy esters and lactones such as ethyl 3-methylbutanoate—can present as over-ripe or fermenting fruit, sometimes compared to onions or durian.

This polarizing profile is partly genetic but largely a result of historical processing methods. Because Liberica cherries are voluminous and the skin is thick, they are notoriously difficult to pulp. Machinery designed for Arabica—disc pulpers and drum washers—often fails when processing Liberica. The machines jam, motors overheat, and beans are crushed, releasing enzymes that accelerate spoilage.

Consequently, farmers traditionally processed Liberica using the "Natural" method—drying the fruit intact on the seed. However, because the mucilage layer is so fleshy and thick (often double the pulp volume of an Arabica cherry), the drying time is extended. In the humid tropical air of the Philippines or Malaysia, this slow drying process often led to uncontrolled fermentation. The "funk" that international cuppers rejected was not necessarily intrinsic to the bean; it was the flavor of decomposition, a byproduct of insufficient infrastructure.

This prejudice was codified in the mid-2000s during a blind cupping session in London. A table of Q-Graders—the certified sensory analysts of the coffee industry—evaluated a set of mystery samples. After approving washed Ethiopian and Colombian lots, they reached the Liberica. The reactions were visceral. One grader characterized the flavor as "burning tires and wet wood." The score assigned was well below the 80-point threshold required for "Specialty" status.

For years, that score acted as a verdict. The graders, however, were unaware they were tasting a sample that had been strip-picked and dried on a compromised surface. They were judging the processing defects rather than the genetic potential.

Furthermore, the caffeine content created a market mismatch. Arabica contains roughly 1.2% caffeine by weight. Robusta, the industrial fuel, contains 2.2%. Liberica sits lower, ranging from 0.9% to 1.2%. It fails to provide the potent stimulant effect of Robusta, making it less attractive to instant coffee manufacturers who purchase beans specifically for caffeine extraction. Liberica was caught in a commercial limbo: not refined enough for the connoisseurs, yet not potent enough for the industrial factories.

## THE PROCESSING REVOLUTION

The trajectory of Liberica changed in the late 2010s, driven by a new generation of Southeast Asian coffee professionals who rejected the colonial assessment of their native crop. They recognized that Liberica was not ugly, merely misunderstood.

In the Philippines, pioneering groups such as the Kalsada Coffee collective began applying modern specialty techniques to these ancient trees. They treated Barako not as a bulk commodity but as a delicate fruit. They introduced raised drying beds constructed of bamboo and mesh to facilitate airflow, eliminating the earthy defects associated with patio drying. They experimented with anaerobic fermentation—sealing the massive cherries in oxygen-deprived tanks for 48 to 72 hours to control the ester development.

The results were transformative. When processed with clinical hygiene, the "rotting jackfruit" note resolved into "ripe cantaloupe" and "dried mango." The woody, smoky finish softened into "70% dark chocolate" and "sweet anise." The heavy body, previously perceived as muddy, became syrupy and coating.

Dr. Aaron Davis of Kew Gardens traveled to Uganda and South Sudan to cup wild Liberica and Excelsa in their native habitats. His findings corroborated what the Filipino millers were discovering: the species had been unfairly maligned due to processing failures. In 2021, a Liberica from the Philippines was presented at the World Coffee Roasting Championship. While it did not take the top prize, its presence on the table, scored by international judges who noted flavors of "violet" and "cognac," marked a paradigm shift.

This success sparked a "New Wave" of Liberica. Specialty roasters in Europe and the U.S.—motivated by curiosity and climate anxiety—began purchasing microlots. The narrative inverted. The "jackfruit" note was no longer a defect but a feature of terroir. In a market saturated with generic washed milds, Liberica offered a distinct primary color in the flavor palette, proving that diversity is an asset rather than a liability.

## MALAYSIA'S BUTTER ROAST: KOPI AND CHEMISTRY

While the Philippines focuses on artisanal, high-end Barako, Malaysia offers a different vision: the industrial engine. Entering a traditional *kopitiam* in Johor Bahru at 7:00 AM, the olfactory experience is not the delicate floral jasmine of a specialty café, but the robust scent of caramelized sugar, margarine, and charcoal.

*The traditional Malaysian "Kopi" roast involves caramelizing the beans with margarine and sugar to mask the woody fibers of Liberica.*

Malaysia is one of the few nations where Liberica is the dominant species, accounting for over 90% of commercial production. The method here is a masterclass in Maillard chemistry born of necessity. Historically, Liberica beans were considered too harsh and woody to consume as a standard roast. Consequently, the Hainanese immigrants who established the coffee shop culture developed a specialized technique: the "butter roast."

This technique is more cooking than roasting. Near the end of the cycle, when the beans are hot and porous (approx. 200°C), the roaster dumps margarine and sugar directly into the spinning drum.

It creates a thick, flammable smoke, but the chemistry is ingenious.

The sugar caramelizes instantly, creating a hard candy shell that seals in the aroma. The margarine adds a layer of fat that coats the tongue, smoothing over the harsh, woody fibers of the Liberica bean. It turns a rough product into a savory, bittersweet confection.

The resulting coffee, *Kopi*, is ground coarsely and brewed through a long cloth "sock" filter that is permanently stained black. It is mixed with sweetened condensed milk to create a beverage that is viscous and possesses the mouthfeel of melted chocolate.

*The slow-drip* Phin *combined with condensed milk creates a dessert-like intensity that balances the bitterness of Robusta.*

For decades, Western purists dismissed this as "adulterated" coffee. Today, however, the Malaysian government (via MARDI, the agricultural research institute) is funding research to modernize the crop while respecting this tradition. They are developing dwarf varieties of Liberica that can be harvested without the need for tall ladders, addressing the labor cost issue. If successful, this could position Liberica not as a specialty rarity, but as a global heavyweight—a bean cheaper than Arabica, sweeter than Robusta, and durable enough to withstand the century.

### THE "ZOMBIE" TREES: LIBERICA UNDERGROUND

Before Liberica becomes a standalone beverage on global menus, it may salvage the industry through a more clandestine method: grafting.

In Guatemala and Brazil, agronomists are utilizing grafting techniques adapted from viticulture. The logic is straightforward: the soil is becoming hostile, yet the market continues to demand the specific flavor profile of Arabica. The solution is to create a biological composite.

The process, often referred to as the Reyna method in Latin America, is a precise surgical operation performed in the nursery. It begins with the rootstock. A Liberica seedling is grown for roughly 75 days until its stem reaches the diameter of a pencil lead. Simultaneously, a high-quality Arabica variety (such as Geisha or Bourbon) is grown to match this diameter.

Using a scalpel, the nursery worker severs the top of the Liberica plant, leaving a 5-centimeter (2-inch) stump. A vertical slit, or "cleft," is cut down the center of the stump. The Arabica scion is cut into a wedge shape and inserted into the Liberica cleft. The wound is secured tightly with parafilm or a plastic clip to ensure contact between the vascular cambium layers.

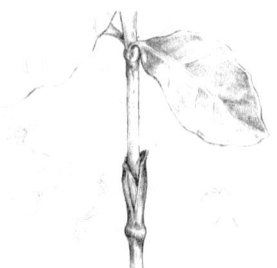

*The "Reyna Method" grafts delicate Arabica tops onto robust Liberica roots to combat nematodes and drought.*

The combined plant is placed in a "healing chamber"—a high-humidity tunnel that prevents the scion from desiccating while the tissues fuse. It requires weeks for the scar tissue to calcify. If humidity drops or the cut is imprecise, the graft fails. The mortality rate in the nursery can be high, driving the cost of a grafted seedling to three or four times that of a standard seed.

For farmers facing the twin threats of drought and nematodes, however, the investment is rational. Nematodes are microscopic roundworms that infest the soil, burrowing into coffee roots and causing them to knot and rot. Arabica roots are defenseless against them; a severe infestation can destroy a tree within two years. Liberica roots exude chemical compounds that repel nematodes, and their physical density makes them difficult to penetrate.

By grafting, the farmer creates a chimera. Below the soil, the plant is a monster capable of accessing deep water reserves and resisting pests. Above the soil, it produces the delicate, floral cherries demanded by the high-end market. It allows farmers to continue selling "Arabica" to buyers resistant to change, while relying on Liberica's biological engine to maintain the plant's viability. It is a silent resurrection—Liberica performing the essential labor underground, uncredited and unseen, sustaining the industry in a world becoming too hostile for the prince.


### BEYOND THE C-MARKET

Despite the agronomic potential, the Liberica Resurrection faces a massive structural barrier: the global trading infrastructure is calibrated for Arabica.

Industrial roasting facilities in Amsterdam, Seattle, and Tokyo are optimized for the density and physical dimensions of Arabica beans. Liberica beans are significantly larger and possess a different cellular density. If a roaster processes a batch of Liberica using a standard preset profile, the beans will scorch on the exterior while remaining raw and grassy in the center. Roasting Liberica requires relearning the craft— adjusting drum speed, airflow, and charge temperature to accommodate the bean's unique thermodynamics.

Furthermore, the C-Market implies a standardized contract. There is no futures contract for Liberica. It cannot be hedged. It is an "off-market" trade, negotiated directly between buyer and seller. This lack of financial instrumentation makes it risky for multinational corporations. Entities like Nestlé and Starbucks rely on the hedging mechanisms of the exchange to stabilize costs. Rewiring supply chains for a bean that varies in size and behaves unpredictably in the roaster presents a significant logistical hurdle.

Additionally, the industry must dismantle decades of prejudice. Coffee education has long been dogmatic: Arabica equals quality; Robusta equals caffeine; other species are weeds. The Specialty Coffee Association (SCA) cupping form was designed to penalize the very flavors that define Liberica. "Vegetal" and "Woody" are categorized as defects. Reversing this dogma requires re-educating millions of consumers and thousands of Q-Graders. It necessitates a shift in the definition of "quality"—from a singular target defined by acidity to a spectrum that includes the heavy, sweet, complex profile of the Barako.

### THE CLIMATE-PROOF BLEND

The most probable future for Liberica is not as a replacement for single-origin Ethiopian pour-overs, but as the savior of the espresso blend.

As climate change renders low-grade Arabica (the mild beans utilized in supermarket cans and fast-food coffee) increasingly difficult to cultivate cheaply, roasters will require a substitute. Robusta is the obvious alternative, but it introduces a bitterness that many consumers find unpalatable. Liberica offers a third path.

A blend comprised of 50% Fine Robusta (for body and caffeine) and 50% Clean Liberica (for sweetness and fruit) could create a palatable, affordable coffee that requires zero Arabica. This is the concept of the "Climate-Proof Blend." It is a product grown entirely in the lowlands, on trees capable of surviving heatwaves, requiring fewer synthetic fertilizers and pesticides than their delicate mountain counterparts.

This shift would represent a profound return to historical roots. The classic "Italian Espresso" profile was originally built on a mixture of species and origins. The fixation on "100% Arabica" is a relatively recent marketing invention, popularized in the 1990s. The resurrection of Liberica allows the industry to break that marketing spell and return to a more pragmatic, resilient definition of coffee.

.  .  .

## THE GIANT WAKES

Back in Lipa City, the farmer descends the bamboo ladder, his woven basket heavy with purple fruit. He is no longer felling these trees to plant bananas. He is planting seedlings. He holds orders from a boutique roaster in Manila and an inquiry from a Japanese importer eager to experience the "legendary Barako."

The tree above him is ancient. It has survived Spanish colonization, American occupation, the Japanese invasion of World War II, and the eruptions of the Taal Volcano. It has stood silently while the global market focused entirely on its delicate cousin in the mountains. It has endured agricultural neglect, deforestation, and a century of commercial obscurity.

The Liberica tree serves as a living testament to the fact that in evolution, success is not always defined by refinement or beauty. Success is defined by the refusal to die. As the planet warms, the mist retreats up the mountains, and the habitability zone for Arabica contracts, the future of coffee may not belong to the prince. It may belong to the giant. And perhaps, the industry will discover that the best method to tame this monster is not with fire, but with patience—extracting its sweetness slowly, adapted to a changing world. Diversity of species is the best defense against a warming climate.

# 40

# THE LONG COLD: TIME, NITROGEN, AND THE SAFETY PARADOX

Resembling a piece of laboratory equipment from the late nineteenth century rather than a conventional coffee maker, the apparatus stands in the window of Café de l'Ambre in the Ginza district of Tokyo. It is a tower of glass and brass, standing nearly a meter (three feet) tall, illuminated by the soft, sepia glow of the shop's vintage tungsten lighting. The shop itself serves as a preservation of the Showa era, smelling of aged mahogany and the faint, sweet residue of tobacco, but the machine in the window operates outside of any specific time period.

In a global industry where coffee is typically produced through high-energy phase changes—the roar of steam wands, the friction of burr grinders, and the hiss of pressurized boilers—this device operates in a hushed, hydraulic rhythm. It is a study in fluid dynamics rather than thermodynamics. At the apex, a globe of water hangs suspended, cold and clear. From a precision-machined brass valve, a single drop falls. Drip. The water strikes the bed of dark, coarse grounds in the middle chamber. It does not splash; it absorbs into the carbon matrix of the bean. Two seconds of silence pass. Drip.

The water slowly saturates the aggregate before winding its way through a spiral of glass tubing—a transparent conduit guiding the black liquid to a carafe at the bottom. There is no steam. There is no thermal shock. There is no urgency. The process is strictly governed by gravity and flow restriction; it will

*take twelve hours to produce a single liter of extract. This is the "Kyoto Drip"*
*method, known locally as Mizudashi, a technique that treats coffee not as a*
*culinary preparation, but as an act of slow-motion solvent extraction.*

*The Kyoto drip tower uses gravity and time to extract coffee drop-by-*
*drop, creating a liqueur-like clarity.*

For the majority of the bean's thousand-year history, heat was the non-
negotiable catalyst. Fire provided the energy required to drive flavor out of the
cellular structure. Hot water acts as a kinetic solvent; its molecules vibrate with
high-energy frequency, fracturing the cell walls of the ground coffee, dissolving
oils, acids, and solids in seconds. Heat is efficient. Heat is rapid. Heat is the
industry standard. However, the liquid collecting at the base of the Kyoto tower
possesses a fundamentally different chemical profile. Having never encountered
thermal acceleration, it is a product of duration rather than intensity.

When the liquid is tasted, the neurological response is often one of confusion. The brain, conditioned by decades of hot consumption, anticipates the
sharp, citric "bite" of black coffee—the phosphoric brightness that mimics a
crisp apple or a tart cherry. It is absent. The bitterness that usually triggers a
biological warning signal on the posterior of the tongue has been excised.
Instead, the liquid is viscous, heavy, and startlingly sweet. It carries the molecular weight of dark chocolate, liqueur, and molasses. By removing the variable
of temperature and substituting it with the variable of time, the chemistry of
the cup has been re-architected. This shift—from the hot and fast to the cold
and slow—did more than create a physiological preference; it transformed

*coffee from a perishable morning ritual into a stable, functional commodity that could be bottled, kegged, and managed like a soft drink.*

## THE THERMODYNAMICS OF THE LAZY SOLVENT

Why did cold brew conquer the modern palate? It has very much to do with the selective nature of solubility. A roasted coffee bean is a chemical vault containing more than a thousand distinct compounds. Some exist to please the human palate; others are the plant's original defensive chemistry, evolved to deter insects and predators.

When water heated to 93°C (200°F) contacts coffee, thermal energy acts as a powerful solvent. It rapidly dissolves highly soluble polar compounds—citric acids, malic acids, and volatile aromatic oils responsible for floral and fruity top notes. That same energy, however, also extracts heavier, less desirable compounds, including large molecular-weight tannins and chlorogenic acid lactones (CGLs). Under high heat, these CGLs degrade into phenylindanes, the primary chemical sources of harsh bitterness and astringency. Hot brewing extracts nearly everything, desirable and undesirable alike, in a compressed and chaotic rush.

Cold water behaves very differently. At refrigerator temperatures, water molecules move slowly, lacking the kinetic energy required to penetrate the denser cellular structures of the coffee bean or to dissolve waxy, hydrophobic oils. When cold water meets coffee grounds, extraction proceeds by passive diffusion rather than force. It readily dissolves simple sugars and caffeine, both of which are highly water-soluble, and it extracts polysaccharides that contribute body and mouthfeel. What it struggles to lift are the heavier oils and many of the acids that require heat to become soluble.

The result is a form of natural chemical filtration. Cold water selectively extracts sweet, nutty, and chocolate-forward base notes while leaving behind much of the sharp acidity and bitter tannins in the spent grounds. Laboratory analysis mirrors sensory experience: cold brew can exhibit as much as two-thirds less titratable acidity than hot-brewed coffee.

To the coffee purist, this is a flaw. Without acidity, coffee loses its sparkle—its clarity, its articulation of origin. A delicate Ethiopian

Geisha, prized for jasmine aromatics and bergamot brightness, surrenders its identity in cold water, collapsing into something generic and uniformly sweet. To a trained sensory judge, cold brew is a muted expression—a symphony performed with the treble section removed.

Yet for the mass market, and especially for the millions of drinkers with acid reflux or sensitive stomachs, this very muting was the breakthrough. Cold brew transformed coffee from a harsh stimulant—one that demanded milk and sugar for survival—into a smooth, self-contained beverage. It decoupled caffeine delivery from the acridity of poorly brewed hot coffee. Most importantly, it made coffee *sessionable*: a drink that could be consumed in volume, over time, without gastrointestinal penalty.

## THE DUTCH GHOST ON THE FIRELESS SHIP

While the Kyoto towers perfected the aesthetic of cold extraction, the commercial DNA of the method lies in the logistical desperation of the seventeenth century. The Dutch East India Company (VOC) controlled the flow of coffee from Yemen and Indonesia to Europe, orchestrating voyages that were long, arduous, and resource-constrained.

On a wooden vessel packed with gunpowder, hemp, and timber, fire was a managed risk. The ship's cook could only light the galley fire during calm seas and specific hours. Boiling water for a leisure beverage like coffee was a luxury the captain rarely permitted. Furthermore, fresh water stored in barrels for months often went stagnant, developing a green film of algae and a foul taste. The Dutch traders required a method to transport and consume coffee that did not depend on thermal energy and could mask the flavor of spoiled water.

They developed a method of soaking coffee concentrate in cold water, creating a potent, shelf-stable syrup—a "coffee essence"—that could be bottled, stored in the hold, and reconstituted with water later. This was functional brewing, treating coffee as a ration. When the Dutch established their trading enclave on the island of Dejima in Nagasaki in 1641, they brought this "Dutch Coffee" with them. Japan, operating under the isolationist policy of *Sakoku*, used Dejima as the sole aperture through which the outside world entered. The Japanese, a culture with a deep reverence for cold tea brewing (*Mizudashi Cha*) and methodical processes, observed the Dutch technique.

Over the next three centuries, Japanese artisans refined the crude Dutch concentrate. They moved the process from wooden barrels to glass. They realized that by slowing the flow rate, they could increase clarity and reduce sediment. The "Kyoto Style" towers were not merely brewing devices; they were kinetic sculptures that integrated perfectly into the *Kissaten* culture of the twentieth century—coffeehouses that served as quiet sanctuaries for listening to jazz and smoking tobacco.

However, the physics of the drop-by-drop Kyoto method differs significantly from the "immersion" method utilized by the Dutch. In immersion brewing (soaking grounds in a bucket), the water quickly becomes saturated with coffee solids. As the water fills with dissolved coffee, its ability to extract more flavor diminishes—a phenomenon known as the diffusion gradient leveling off. In the Kyoto tower, fresh, clean water constantly contacts the grounds at the top of the bed. This "fresh solvent" maintains a high diffusion gradient throughout the entire twelve-hour cycle, ensuring a clarity of flavor that immersion brewing can rarely match. For decades, this remained a regional specialty of East Asia. American "iced coffee" remained a primitive affair: hot coffee poured over ice cubes, resulting in a diluted, bitter, watery solution. It would take a chemical engineer in the Andes to translate the bucket method for the Western consumer.

## 1964: The Bucket and the Botanist

Todd Simpson was a man of science managing a sensitive constitution. A Cornell-educated chemical engineering graduate, Simpson found himself in the highlands of Peru in 1964. He was ostensibly there on a botanical expedition, hunting for rare plant species to import for his nursery business in Houston. However, in the misty, high-altitude villages of the Andes, he encountered a preparation method that would alter the trajectory of the industry.

Simpson observed that the local women did not brew coffee with boiling water. Firewood was a resource conserved for cooking beans and corn, not for beverages. Instead, they soaked ground coffee in cold

mountain water overnight in large vessels. The resulting dark liquid was
a concentrate. When a cup of coffee was desired, they would pour a
small amount of the concentrate into a cup and add hot water. Simpson,
who suffered from severe heartburn and had largely abandoned coffee,
sampled the liquid. He noted two distinct properties: the flavor was
exceptionally smooth, and hours later, he experienced no esophageal
irritation.

He returned to Houston with a directive. He was not interested in the
intricate glassblowing of Kyoto; he sought a solution that functioned in a
suburban American kitchen. He invented the Toddy Cold Brew System.
It was decidedly low-tech: a white plastic bucket with a rubber plug at
the bottom and a thick, reusable felt filter. The instructions were binary:
deposit 0.45 kg (1 lb) of coffee, add 2 liters of cold water, wait 12 to 24
hours, and remove the plug.

*Todd Simpson's cold brew system democratized cold extraction, using a*
*simple immersion soak to reduce acidity.*

The resulting filtrate was a "concentrate." It was opaque, resembling
crude oil, but it was chemically stable. Because the volatile oils had not

been oxidized by heat, the concentrate did not turn rancid within an hour like hot coffee. It could remain in the refrigerator for two weeks without significant degradation. For forty years, the Toddy was a niche product. It resided in the rear of the cupboard alongside the fondue set, utilized primarily by the elderly for its low acidity and by a small subset of coffee enthusiasts. It was functional, but it lacked cultural cachet. It was a domestic utility, not a revolution. It would require a roaster from Portland to convert this bucket sludge into a scalable industrial product.

### THE STUMPTOWN STUBBY: BREAKING THE CHAIN

In the late 2000s, Stumptown Coffee Roasters in Portland, Oregon, operated at the forefront of the emerging "Third Wave" coffee movement. The company emphasized quality, direct sourcing, and the precision of manual brewing methods such as the pour-over. Yet despite its craft focus, Stumptown encountered a persistent operational bottleneck.

During the summer months, demand for iced coffee routinely overwhelmed the espresso bar. Baristas were required to pull large volumes of hot espresso shots and pour them directly over ice. The workflow was inefficient. A single espresso shot takes roughly thirty seconds to extract; a line of twenty customers ordering iced lattes could easily produce a ten-minute delay.

The process also compromised the beverage itself. Espresso brewed at approximately 93°C (200°F) melted ice almost instantly, diluting the drink before it reached the customer. Rapidly cooling hot espresso further accelerated the formation of quinic acid, producing a bitter, stale aftertaste that developed within minutes.

The Stumptown team, analyzing the old Toddy method, recognized an opportunity for scale. They began brewing massive batches of cold brew in sterilized garbage cans, later upgrading to stainless steel wine fermenters. They realized the stability of the concentrate was the key to a new business model. If the coffee did not stale for two weeks, it did not require preparation à la minute. It could be bottled.

In 2011, Stumptown launched the "Stubby"—a squat, brown glass vessel identical to a beer bottle. They filled it with cold brew and capped it. This was the inflection point. Until the Stubby, specialty coffee had always been a service (something a human prepares in real-time) or a raw material (beans). The Stubby transformed specialty coffee into a Ready-to-Drink (RTD) consumer packaged good. Suddenly, high-end coffee could exit the cafe. It could be stocked on a shelf at a grocery store next to kombucha and craft beer. It could reside in an office refrigerator. It liberated the caffeine consumer from the queue. The "Cold Brew" category expanded rapidly, growing by 580% between 2011 and 2016, evolving from a cafe workaround into a billion-dollar grocery category.

*The "Stubby" bottle transformed cold brew from a café service into a packaged good, launching the Ready-to-Drink revolution.*

However, this shift required a massive logistical undertaking. Unlike carbonated sodas or canned beans, cold brew was a fresh product. It required a Cold Chain—refrigerated trucks, refrigerated warehouses, and refrigerated displays. If the chain broke, the product spoiled. This limitation kept cold brew expensive and regional. To achieve global scale, the industry needed to manipulate the texture. They needed bubbles.

### STOKES' LAW AND THE NITROGEN CASCADE

If cold brew functioned as the lager of the coffee world—crisp, accessible, and refreshing—then the industry required a stout. Cold brew, despite its smoothness, often suffers from a textural deficit. It can feel "flat" or watery on the palate because it lacks the emulsified oils (crema) that hot pressure extraction generates. Nate Armbrust, a food scientist at Stumptown, became focused on rectifying this gap in mouthfeel.

Armbrust first attempted to carbonate the coffee with Carbon Dioxide ($CO_2$), the gas utilized in soda and beer. The result was a sensory failure. When $CO_2$ dissolves in water, it forms carbonic acid ($H_2CO_3$). This added a sharp, metallic sourness that clashed dissonantly with the chocolatey notes of the coffee. It tasted of spoiled seltzer. Armbrust turned his attention to the brewing mechanics of Guinness. The Irish stout utilizes Nitrogen ($N_2$) rather than Carbon Dioxide. Nitrogen behaves differently; it is largely insoluble in liquid and creates no acid. Crucially, it generates bubbles that are vastly smaller and more stable than $CO_2$ bubbles.

Armbrust connected a keg of cold brew to a "restrictor plate"—a faucet with five microscopic holes that forces the gas into the liquid at high pressure. When the tap opened, physics took over.

Because nitrogen bubbles are microscopic, they lack the buoyancy to float immediately to the top like the CO2 bubbles in a soda. Instead, they get caught in the current. As the liquid pours into the glass, the friction against the glass walls creates a circular current that drags the bubbles downward. This creates the mesmerizing "Cascade Effect"—a wall of foam surging down the sides of the glass before slowly rising in the center to settle into a thick, creamy head.

*Nitrogen gas creates micro-bubbles that mimic the creamy mouthfeel of dairy without adding fat.*

The result was a transformative mouthfeel. The nitrogen bubbles deceived the tongue into perceiving "creaminess" without the presence of dairy or fat. It was velvety and rich. It appeared like a beer, poured like a beer, but tasted like sweet, black coffee. Nitro Cold Brew resolved the "sugar and cream" dependency. The nitrogen gas suppresses the tongue's bitter receptors slightly, enhancing the perception of sweetness. It allowed consumers who typically diluted their coffee with milk and sweeteners to consume it black. It was the ultimate functional beverage:

zero calories, high caffeine, and a texture that felt indulgent. But as kegs of coffee began rolling into bars and cafes across America, a silent, microscopic threat was germinating in the cans.

### ANAEROBIC MONSTERS: THE BOTULISM PARADOX

The transition from freshly brewed coffee to shelf-stable bottled products introduced a new and unfamiliar variable into the coffee world: biological safety. For centuries, coffee had been considered safe by default. Freshly brewed coffee is naturally acidic, typically registering between pH 4.5 and 5.0. In food science, the critical boundary lies at pH 4.6. Liquids below this threshold are classified as *high-acid* and are naturally hostile to *Clostridium botulinum*, the bacterium responsible for producing botulinum neurotoxin.

Botulism spores are ubiquitous. They exist in soil, on coffee cherries, and throughout agricultural supply chains. In oxygen-rich environments, these spores remain dormant and harmless. *Clostridium botulinum*, however, is an obligate anaerobe: it becomes dangerous only in the absence of oxygen.

Cold brew disrupted coffee's long-standing safety assumptions in two important ways. First, because cold water extracts fewer organic acids, cold brew often exhibits a higher pH—frequently measuring 4.9, 5.1, or even higher. This places it above the safety threshold. Second, in order to make cold brew shelf-stable, producers began sealing it in airtight containers—cans, bottles, and kegs—often purging the headspace with nitrogen to limit oxidation.

Together, these conditions formed a genuine biological risk: low acidity, an oxygen-free environment, and ambient temperatures. If refrigeration failed—for example, if a pallet of canned cold brew sat unrefrigerated on a loading dock during summer heat—dormant spores could activate and begin producing botulinum toxin. The toxin interferes with the release of acetylcholine at neuromuscular junctions, leading to progressive paralysis that begins in the face and can culminate in respiratory failure.

In 2017, this theoretical risk entered public view. Death Wish Coffee issued a nationwide recall of canned nitro cold brew products after a process review by Cornell University determined that the company's sterilization methods were insufficient for a low-acid beverage. No illnesses were reported, but the recall reverberated throughout the industry. The informal era—brewing cold brew in plastic containers and bottling it by hand—ended abruptly. Regulatory oversight increased, and safety standards tightened.

Today, producing shelf-stable cold brew requires industrial preservation techniques. One option is retort processing, in which sealed cans are pressure-heated to approximately 121°C (250°F) for several minutes to ensure sterility. While effective, the process thermally degrades flavor, often imparting cooked or rubbery notes. Another approach is flash pasteurization, which briefly heats the liquid to around 71°C (160°F) before packaging. This preserves more flavor but still demands strict refrigeration.

The most common solution is acidification. Producers add measured quantities of food-grade acids—typically phosphoric or citric acid—to force the pH safely below 4.6. The result is microbiological stability. The irony is unavoidable: many canned cold brews owe their safety not to cold extraction, but to the deliberate reintroduction of acidity. To make cold brew safe for the shelf, the industry was compelled to restore the very chemical property that cold brewing was meant to reduce.

### The Return of the Espresso Martini

The stability of cold brew concentrate did not merely facilitate the grocery aisle; it revolutionized the bar. For decades, the Espresso Martini was a logistical problem for bartenders. Invented by Dick Bradsell at the Soho Brasserie in London in the 1980s, the drink was born from a specific request by a patron for a drink that would "wake me up and f**k me up." Bradsell mixed vodka, sugar syrup, Kahlúa, and a fresh shot of hot espresso. It became a modern classic, but operationally, it was inefficient. To prepare it, a bartender had to leave the speed rail, approach the espresso machine, pull a shot, and then shake the scalding liquid with ice. This diluted the vodka and melted the ice too rapidly, creating a watery, lukewarm beverage with poor foam retention.

Cold brew concentrate resolved this friction. A bottle of high-intensity cold brew concentrate (often brewed at a 1:4 ratio) is shelf-stable and chilled. The bartender can pour it directly from the bottle, identical to the workflow for vodka or gin. This convenience fueled the massive resurgence of the Espresso Martini in the 2020s. It also spawned a new category: Hard Coffee. Companies launched "Hard Cold Brew"—canned coffee spiked with malt liquor or neutral spirits.

The chemistry of mixing alcohol (a depressant) and caffeine (a stimulant) is potent. It creates the "wide-awake drunk" effect. The caffeine masks the sedative effects of the alcohol, deceiving the brain into perceiving a higher level of sobriety than exists. While the FDA had banned pre-mixed energy drinks like Four Loko in 2010 due to health risks, "Hard Coffee" bypassed the regulation because the caffeine is natural, derived from the bean rather than added as a synthetic powder. It represented the ultimate commodification of the bean: coffee utilized not as a beverage, but as a functional drug delivery system, paired with another psychoactive substance for a specific physiological effect.

### FLASH BREW: THE TERROIR RESISTANCE

Not every segment of the coffee world embraced the rise of cold brew. Within the high-end specialty market, a counter-movement emerged: Japanese iced coffee, often referred to as flash brew. Its advocates argued that cold brew functioned as a blunt instrument. By limiting the extraction of acids and volatile aromatics, cold brewing tended to flatten distinction. A fruit-forward Kenyan coffee and a nut-driven Brazilian coffee, when cold brewed, could converge toward the same generalized profile—sweet, chocolate-leaning, and largely interchangeable.

Flash brew approaches the problem differently. The coffee is extracted using hot water, capturing the full range of acids and aromatic compounds, and then immediately cooled by dripping directly onto ice. The brewing ratio is adjusted so that the melting ice dilutes the beverage to its intended strength. The method depends on a simple physical principle: rapid cooling limits the loss of volatile compounds.

Aromatics evaporate readily at high temperatures—the fragrance rising from a hot cup of coffee is, quite literally, flavor leaving the liquid.

By dropping the brewed coffee from roughly 93°C (200°F) to near freezing in seconds, flash brewing dramatically reduces this evaporation. The volatile compounds lose the thermal energy required to escape, remaining dissolved in the drink.

The result is a cold coffee that preserves much of the structure of a hot pour-over: acidity remains present, floral and citrus notes are intact, and origin characteristics remain legible. The texture is lighter, more tea-like, and more transparent to terroir.

For years, this distinction fueled debate in specialty cafés. Cold brew offered smoothness and richness; flash brew offered brightness and definition. The market ultimately resolved the argument. Cold brew dominated. Consumer preference consistently favored chocolate-forward sweetness over citric acidity, comfort over complexity. The broader audience wanted a beverage that resembled a milkshake more than a tea, and cold brew supplied it.

## SONIC EXTRACTION AND THE SEASONLESS FUTURE

Today, cold brew is no longer produced in 20-liter buckets. It is manufactured in stainless steel silos that hold 40,000 liters. However, waiting twenty-four hours for a tank of that magnitude to steep is economically inefficient. In industrial food production, time is a liability. To accelerate the process, industrial food scientists have turned to Hydrodynamic Cavitation and Ultrasonics.

This technology utilizes high-frequency sound waves to bombard the mixture of water and coffee grounds. The sound waves create microscopic vacuum bubbles in the water. When these bubbles collapse (cavitate), they release tiny, localized shockwaves of immense energy and heat —temperatures reaching thousands of degrees for a fraction of a microsecond. These shockwaves fracture the cell walls of the coffee, forcing water in and solubles out. What requires twenty-four hours in a passive soak can be accomplished in twenty minutes with ultrasonic cavitation.

This is the mechanism behind the mass-market canned cold brew found in gas stations. It is "cold brew" by definition (no external heat was applied to the tank), but it was extracted with the force of sound. It allows for continuous production lines, pumping out rivers of black liquid to feed a global demand that no longer waits for the kettle to boil.

The ultimate impact of cold brew was the destruction of seasonality. Before 2010, coffee sales plummeted in the summer months. Hot coffee was a winter habit. Cold brew converted coffee into a year-round, all-day beverage. It competes now with carbonated soft drinks and iced tea. It is consumed at the beach, at the gymnasium, and at the nightclub. By stripping away the heat, the bitterness, and the ritual, cold brew distilled the bean down to its most consumable, commercial essence. It took a seed from Ethiopia, processed it with a method from the Dutch, refined it in Japan, scaled it in Oregon, and preserved it with the physics of nitrogen, creating a sweet, black fuel for a world that requires constant alertness.

# 41

# THE INFINITE LOOP: ALCHEMY, ENTROPY, AND THE END OF WASTE

I nside the Bio-bean processing facility in Cambridgeshire, England, the air presented a sensory paradox that defied the standard categorization of industrial spaces. Instead of the acrid scent of waste or the warmth of a café, it held the heavy, dense aroma of a bakery that was slowly, intentionally carbonizing—a complex layering of caramelized sugars, roasted proteins, and cellulose subjected to industrial heat.

Here, located in a sprawling industrial park fifty miles (80 km) north of London, heavy transport trucks arrived daily, delivering a cargo that modern civilization had collectively agreed was garbage. They carried the soggy, dense sludge of "spent coffee grounds"—millions of pucks knocked out of portafilters by baristas in Costa, Starbucks, and independent shops across the capital. For the majority of the last four centuries, this material represented the absolute end of the line. The journey of the coffee bean, having begun on a flowering tree in the tropics, crossed oceans, passed through roasting drums, and survived high-pressure extraction, terminated in a black plastic trash bag destined for a landfill. There, buried under tons of other refuse, the grounds would decompose anaerobically, starved of oxygen. In this suffocated state, coffee does not merely return to soil; it transforms into gas. Specifically, it releases methane, a greenhouse gas roughly twenty-eight times more potent than carbon dioxide over a century-long timeframe.

However, inside the Bio-bean facility, founded in 2013 by the entrepreneur Arthur Kay, the linear trajectory was bent into a circle. The sludge was dried, sifted, and processed. Oils were chemically extracted to make biodiesel. The remaining solids were compressed under high pressure into "Coffee Logs"— dense, heavy briquettes that burned hotter and longer than kiln-dried wood. This facility represented the intended evolution of the industry: the shift from a Linear Economy (take, make, waste) to a Circular Economy. It served as a proof of concept that the coffee industry's massive waste stream could be monetized, transforming a liability into an asset.

Compressed spent coffee grounds contain high calorific energy, burning hotter than wood.

Yet, the narrative of the circular economy is rarely a straight line of progress. In April 2023, Bio-bean entered administration, collapsing under the sheer logistical weight of moving wet, heavy sludge across a country. The chemistry worked; the physics of transport did not. Spent coffee grounds are roughly 60% water by weight. Transporting them requires burning diesel to move water that will eventually be evaporated. If the energy expended in collection exceeds the energy saved by recycling, the loop is not circular; it is broken. This failure illustrates the central tension of the "Infinite Loop." While the moral argument for zero waste is irrefutable, the economic reality is a brutal war against entropy. To understand why this battle matters—and why the industry remains focused on solving it despite high-profile failures—one must examine the mathematics of the harvest.

· · ·

ANATOMY OF AN ICEBERG

The concept of the 'Coffee Iceberg' helps visualize the scale of the inefficiency of coffee production. The cup of liquid consumed by the end user represents the tiny, visible tip of the production chain. Beneath the surface lies a mountain of organic matter that, in the traditional model, never leaves the farm. When a coffee cherry is harvested, the seed (the bean) accounts for roughly 20% of the fruit's volume. The remaining 80%—the skin, the fleshy pulp (mucilage), the parchment, and the silver-skin—is stripped off during processing. In the traditional "washed" process, this pulp is often dumped into heaps or washed into local waterways.

The environmental impact of this disposal is significant. Coffee pulp is rich in sugars, caffeine, and polyphenols. When dumped into rivers, a practice common in Central America throughout the late 20th century, the sugar triggers massive bacterial blooms. These bacteria consume the dissolved oxygen in the water to digest the sugar, causing the Biological Oxygen Demand (BOD) to spike. The river effectively suffocates, turning black and fetid, killing aquatic life instantly. In 1995, the Costa Rican government, recognizing that its coffee sector was degrading its ecotourism sector, passed strict environmental laws forcing mills to treat their water and manage their solids. This legislative pressure forced the industry to look for a solution. If they could not throw the pulp away, they had to sell it. Selling it, however, required a fundamental shift in perception: seeing "fruit" rather than "pulp."

This shift requires dismantling centuries of agricultural dogma. For generations, the coffee farmer was taught that the value lay exclusively in the seed. The fruit was merely a protective wrapper, a biological packaging to be discarded once the package was opened. Reclaiming the fruit requires not just new machinery, but a new agronomic philosophy that views the coffee tree not as a bean producer, but as a biomass factory where every gram of carbon captured from the atmosphere has a commercial utility.

· · ·

## THE RESURRECTION OF THE CHERRY

One of the most ambitious attempts to close the loop began not in a chemistry lab, but in a supply chain analysis. Dan Belliveau, a former engineer for Starbucks, observed the mountains of rotting cherry pulp at mills and recognized a caloric inefficiency. The coffee cherry is, botanically, a stone fruit. It is loaded with fiber, potassium, iron, and protein. Its fatal flaw is that it rots rapidly in the tropical heat. Within hours of depulping, mold sets in, rendering it useless.

Belliveau developed a proprietary process to stabilize and dry the pulp immediately after depulping, grinding it into a fine powder known as CoffeeFlour. The culinary profile of this substance is distinct; it does not taste like coffee. It possesses floral, citrusy notes with deep undertones of dried fig and tobacco. Nutritionally, it contains more fiber per gram than whole grain wheat, more iron than spinach, and more potassium than a banana. Belliveau's vision was to turn the waste stream into a secondary food source for the very nations that grow coffee. In countries like Guatemala or Ethiopia, where seasonal malnutrition is a persistent issue in coffee communities during the "thin months" before harvest, the caloric value of the crop was being discarded. By converting pulp into flour, local bakeries could produce nutrient-dense breads and tortillas.

While flour utilizes the whole pulp, the high-end specialty market focused on the skin. For centuries, farmers in Yemen and Ethiopia dried the skins to make a tea known as Qishr or Hashara. It was a drink for the farmers, while the beans were reserved for export. In the 2010s, the "Third Wave" movement rediscovered this practice. Enterprising farmers like Aida Batlle in El Salvador began drying their cherry skins on raised African beds, applying the same obsessive care used for their Gesha beans. This product was packaged and sold as Cascara (Spanish for "husk").

Cascara *(dried coffee husk) has evolved from a waste product into a high-value "coffee cherry tea.*

Cascara presents a flavor profile of hibiscus, tamarind, and dried cherries, naturally sweet and high in antioxidants. Suddenly, the "waste" had a market value of $10 to $15 per pound ($22-$33/kg)—rivaling the price of the coffee itself. However, the rise of Cascara encountered a bureaucratic wall that perfectly illustrates the friction of the circular economy. In 2015, the European Union halted sales, classifying Cascara as a "Novel Food." This regulation, designed to prevent potentially unsafe exotic foods from entering the European diet, created a regulatory paradox: the seed was legal, but the fruit that wrapped it was considered a mysterious, untested substance. It took massive coordinated efforts by trade bodies to submit the necessary toxicological dossiers proving that humans had been drinking coffee cherries for a millennium without adverse effects. It wasn't until February 2022 that the EU finally approved the sale of traditional coffee cherry infusions, a delay that cost farmers millions in lost potential revenue. This regulatory lag highlights a critical vulnerability in the circular model: innovation often moves faster than the legal frameworks designed to regulate the old linear economy.

. . .

## The Energy of the Mucilage

The deeper problem on the farm concerned the wastewater. In the wet mills of Colombia and Costa Rica, the sugary slime washed off the beans represents potential energy. Progressive mills have begun installing Biogas Digesters. These are large, sealed tanks where the wastewater is fed to anaerobic bacteria. In a controlled environment, these bacteria consume the sugars and release methane gas ($CH_4$).

In the open atmosphere, methane is a climate liability. Captured in a tank, it is fuel. This methane is piped back into the mill to power the mechanical dryers (Guardiolas) that dry the coffee parchment. In this closed loop, the waste from the coffee dries the coffee. The pioneer of this model is the Coopedota cooperative in Costa Rica. In the late 1990s, they overhauled their processing stream, and by 2011, they were declared the world's first "Carbon Neutral" coffee certification. They ceased purchasing diesel to run their dryers, running them instead on the byproducts of the harvest.

This alters the economics of the mill; energy is typically the second highest cost after labor. By turning a liability (toxic water) into an asset (free gas), the cooperative insulates itself from global oil price fluctuations. When the price of crude oil spikes, the bacteria continue to work for free. The engineering required for this is not futuristic; it is 19th-century chemistry applied to 21st-century sustainability goals. The limitation is capital. Building a large-scale biodigester requires an upfront investment that many smallholder cooperatives cannot afford, creating a "green divide" where only the wealthy can afford to be efficient.

## Pyrolysis: The Carbon Vault

The final frontier of agricultural circularity is Carbon Sequestration via Biochar. Coffee trees eventually age; after 20 to 25 years, their yield drops, and they must be "stumped" (cut down) or replaced. This generates massive amounts of wood waste. Traditionally, this wood was burned for cooking or left to rot, releasing stored carbon back into the atmosphere.

The emerging model utilizes Biochar. Farmers use simple kilns to burn the old coffee trees in a low-oxygen environment. This process, known as pyrolysis, is chemically distinct from combustion. Combustion turns wood into ash (minerals); pyrolysis turns wood into charcoal—a stable lattice of pure carbon. Because oxygen is restricted, the carbon cannot bond with oxygen to form $CO_2$. Instead, it locks into a crystalline structure that is incredibly durable. When this biochar is crushed and buried back into the soil, that carbon is removed from the atmosphere for centuries.

*Pyrolysis converts old coffee trees into biochar, locking carbon into the soil for centuries and improving fertility.*

Biochar functions not only as a carbon sink but as a habitat for soil microbiology. The charcoal is highly porous, possessing a massive surface area; one gram of biochar can have the surface area of a tennis court. When added to the soil, it acts like a coral reef, providing a home for beneficial bacteria and fungi, and increasing the soil's Cation Exchange Capacity (CEC)—its ability to hold nutrients. Companies like Microsoft and Stripe are now purchasing "Carbon Removal Credits" from coffee farmers who practice this, paying the farmer not just for the commodity (the bean) but for the ecosystem service (cooling the planet).

This represents a profound shift in the definition of a coffee farm. It becomes a climate amelioration facility as much as a producer of caffeine. The farmer becomes a steward of the atmosphere, monetizing the carbon stored in the structural tissues of the plant. However, the verification markets for these credits are still in their infancy, fraught with complexity regarding measurement and permanence. The promise is vast, but the mechanism for paying the farmer remains bureaucratic and slow.

. . .

## The Cup Crisis: The Poly-Lined Lie

While the industry learns to recycle the grounds, the wood, and the water, the vessel itself remains a structural failure. The paper coffee cup is a material deception. It appears to be paper, but to maintain structural integrity when filled with hot liquid, the paperboard is lined with a thin film of polyethylene plastic. Because the plastic is thermally fused to the paper, it cannot be recycled in standard facilities; the pulping machines cannot separate the layers, and the plastic clogs the filters. Consequently, the estimated 600 billion cups used globally each year almost entirely end up in landfills.

*The convenience of single-serve coffee created an environmental crisis,*
*generating billions of non-recyclable composite plastic shells.*

The industry attempted to solve this with "Compostable" cups lined with PLA (Polylactic Acid), a bioplastic derived from cornstarch. On paper, this appears to be the solution. In reality, it is often a "False Circularity." PLA does not decompose in a backyard compost heap; it requires an industrial composting facility maintaining a core temperature of at least 60°C (140°F) for several days to break down the polymer bonds. Most municipalities lack these facilities. If a consumer throws a "compostable" cup into a standard recycling bin, it contaminates the paper stream. If they throw it in the trash, it ends up in a landfill where, lacking oxygen and heat, it persists alongside petroleum plastics.

The only true circular solution is Reuse, which requires a behavioral revolution rather than a material one. Startups like HuskeeCup in Australia are attempting to build a "Cup-as-a-Service" network. They manufacture durable, reusable cups using a composite polymer made from coffee husks (waste) and polypropylene. The innovation lies in the system: a customer pays a deposit, buys a coffee, and walks away. Upon returning, they hand the dirty cup to any participating cafe, which exchanges it for a fresh coffee in a clean HuskeeCup. This model transforms the cup from a disposable product into a circulating asset. In 2019, the city of Freiburg, Germany, launched the "Freiburg Cup," a city-wide deposit scheme demonstrating that this could function at a civic scale. However, scaling this globally requires dismantling the "convenience culture" that the coffee industry spent the last fifty years perfecting. The friction of carrying a cup, or remembering to return one, battles against the frictionless ease of the trash can.

## THE MYCELIUM CONNECTION

Once the oils are extracted—or even if they aren't—the spent grounds have one final biological utility. They are rich in nitrogen and, crucially, they are a sterilized substrate. Because the grounds have been scalded by hot water during brewing, they are free of competing molds and bacteria, making them the perfect food for Mycelium.

In 2009, two UC Berkeley students, Nikhil Arora and Alejandro Velez, founded Back to the Roots based on the premise that mushrooms could grow on coffee waste. They began collecting waste buckets from Peet's Coffee and selling "Grow-at-Home" mushroom kits. The process utilizes the "Cascading Nutrient Cycle." The coffee bean serves three purposes: first as a beverage, second as a farm substrate for growing food (fungi), and third as a soil amendment. After the mushrooms are harvested, the remaining substrate (spent grounds plus the mycelium network) is broken down enough to be premium compost. The mushrooms "pre-digest" the tough lignin that usually makes raw coffee grounds unsuitable for immediate soil application. By cascading the resource through multiple kingdoms of life—Plant, then Fungi, then Soil—maximum value is extracted before it returns to the earth.

The biology here is elegant. The mushroom species typically used,

Pleurotus ostreatus (Oyster Mushroom), is a primary decomposer. It has the enzymatic ability to break down the complex carbon chains of the coffee cellulose, converting them into fungal protein.

*Spent coffee grounds are a sterilized, nitrogen-rich substrate ideal for cultivating gourmet mushrooms.*

What was once a waste product contributing to methane emissions becomes a high-value food source. Yet, like the Bio-bean example, this model faces the "logistics of wet waste." It works beautifully at a local scale—a cafe growing mushrooms in its own basement—but struggles when scaled to the industrial level due to the cost of moving the heavy substrate.

### THE TEXTILE SHIFT AND OIL EXTRACTION

The circular economy extends beyond food and energy into the realm of materials. Coffee grounds are granular and abrasive, but chemically, they are a complex matrix of lignin and oils. In Taiwan, the textile company Singtex developed S.Café, a technology that embeds post-consumer coffee grounds into polyester fibers. The coffee particles are processed at a nano-scale and polymerized into the yarn.

The functional benefits are derived directly from the physical properties of the coffee. The porous structure of the coffee grounds increases the surface area of the fiber, enhancing moisture-wicking capabilities and odor absorption. The coffee is not merely a gimmick; it provides UV protection and dries faster than cotton. Major outdoor brands have adopted this technology, meaning the shirt worn by a hiker might contain the espresso residue of a previous year's morning ritual. This is "Upcycling" at a technical level—taking a biological waste product and permanently fossilizing it into a high-performance material.

Furthermore, the oil within the grounds represents a "liquid gold" for other industries. Companies like UpCircle in the UK collect grounds from cafes to extract the oil for use in cosmetics. Coffee oil is high in linoleic acid and antioxidants, and the caffeine serves as a vasoconstrictor, useful in skincare products. This extraction demonstrates that the coffee bean is a chemical powerhouse that is rarely fully exhausted by the simple act of brewing. However, the sheer volume of waste far outstrips the demand for face serums or moisture-wicking shirts. These are niche solutions, valuable but not comprehensive.

## THE ECONOMIC PARADOX

The shift to the Circular Economy fundamentally changes the business model of the coffee trade, yet it encounters severe friction from the global commodity market. In the old model, the farmer sold one product (green beans) and paid to dispose of the rest. In the new model, the farmer sells a portfolio of products: Green Beans, Cascara, Coffee Flour, Biogas energy offsets, and Carbon Credits. This diversification makes the farm resilient; if the price of green coffee crashes, the farmer retains revenue from the other streams.

However, the infrastructure to support this does not exist in most regions. A farmer in remote Peru cannot easily sell cherry skins without a nearby processing plant to dry and sterilize them. The "Infinite Loop" is currently a luxury available primarily to well-capitalized estates or advanced cooperatives like Coopedota. Furthermore, the "Shadow Cost" of transport remains a barrier. As the Bio-bean example demonstrated, moving heavy waste to a central location often burns more carbon than it saves. This suggests that the future of circularity is not centralized mega-factories, but hyper-local loops. The waste must be used where it is generated: the farm uses its own pulp for fertilizer; the city cafe uses its own grounds for local mushrooms. The moment waste is placed on a truck, the mathematics begin to fail.

This localization of the loop challenges the globalized nature of the coffee trade. Coffee is the ultimate global commodity—grown in the south, consumed in the north. The "waste" is generated thousands of miles from the "farm." We cannot ship the spent grounds from a London cafe back to a Brazilian farm to be used as fertilizer; the carbon footprint of the shipping would be absurd. Therefore, the loop must be broken into two distinct circles: the Agricultural Loop (managing pulp and wood at the origin) and the Consumer Loop (managing grounds and cups at the destination). Bridging these two worlds requires not just technology, but a reimagining of responsibility. Who is responsible for the waste? The farmer who grew it? The roaster who sold it? Or the consumer who drank it?

### The Loop

Back in the industrial parks and the quiet mills, the machinery continues to run. The failure of specific companies does not negate the necessity of the concept. More than a machine, the conveyor belt that turns sludge into fire represents a philosophy of resource management. The "Coffee Log" that drops off the line is a physical manifestation of a closed loop. Tonight, it might burn in a fireplace, keeping a family warm. The heat it releases is the captured sunlight of a Brazilian hillside, absorbed by a tree three years ago, transported across the ocean, brewed into a stimulant, and finally resurrected as fire.

The story of coffee, as traced from the ancient forests of Kaffa to the high-tech labs of fermentation, this narrative is a story of transformation. It changes from a flower to a cherry, from a seed to a commodity, from a liquid to a drug. Throughout this book, we have examined the forces of biology, empire, market, and science that have shaped this liquid. We have seen how the desire for alertness built economies and destroyed rainforests. We have seen how the chemistry of a single molecule, caffeine, rewired the circadian rhythms of the human species.

Now, at the end of the industrial age, coffee is learning its final and most difficult trick: how to vanish without a trace. True sustainability is not about "saving" the coffee industry in its current form; it is about redesigning it so that it leaves no scar. The goal is a system where the water leaving the mill is cleaner than the water entering it, where the soil is richer after the harvest than before it, and where the cup does not outlive the drinker.

This conclusion is not a prediction of inevitable success. The economic hurdles are significant. The inertia of the linear economy is massive. But the experiments in circularity—from the mushroom farms of Berkeley to the biogas reactors of Costa Rica—offer a blueprint for a different relationship with the plant. The story of coffee continues in the circular systems we are beginning to build. The cup in your hand is the center of a global web, connecting you to the soil, the history, and the future of the planet.

# EPILOGUE

I

t began with a goat in a forest, vibrating with the agitated energy of a discovered alkaloid. It ends, for this moment, with the paper cup resting in your hand. Between those two points lies a distance that is difficult to measure in kilometers or miles. It is a journey measured in chemistry as much as geography.

As the reader holds this vessel, the liquid inside is already obeying the laws of thermodynamics. It is cooling. Volatile aromatic compounds —hundreds of distinct molecules released by the Maillard reaction and Strecker degradation during the roast—are dissipating into the ambient air. The acids, liberated from the cellulose structure of the bean by the thermal shock of hot water, are settling into a chemical equilibrium. The caffeine, that ancient botanical defense mechanism evolved to paralyze insects, has already begun its transit across the blood-brain barrier. It is currently docking into adenosine receptors, blocking the neurochemical signal for fatigue and borrowing energy from tomorrow to expend on the tasks of today.

But before the cup is finished, it is necessary to look at the liquid one last time, not as a beverage, but as an archive. Throughout the preceding chapters, the narrative has moved through distinct spaces: the Afromontane forest floor in Ethiopia, the hushed vigilance of a Sufi monastery in Yemen, the humidity of a glass Wardian case on a French naval vessel, and the frenetic digital noise of a futures exchange in New Jersey. We have stood in a roasting plant watching steel drums rotate, and we have analyzed the hydrology of a drip brewer. Now, at the conclusion, these disparate threads weave together. Rather than a linear progression from seed to cup, the story of coffee is a complex, recursive web of biology, empire, market, and science.

## THE BIOLOGICAL ARCHIVE

When one lifts the cup, they are lifting the weight of a biological history that stretches back millennia. The specific flavor profile— perhaps the sharp, wine-like acidity of a Kenyan SL-28 or the floral delicacy of a Geisha—is not an accident of nature, but the result of a relentless genetic struggle. We must recall the lessons of the forest. The coffee tree did not evolve to be a beverage; it evolved to survive.

The caffeine molecule itself, the "White Crystal" we examined as a pharmacological agent, began as a chemical weapon. In the dense competition of the understory, the *Coffea* genus developed this alkaloid to poison the larvae of beetles and slugs that sought to consume its leaves. When the plant eventually migrated from the forest to the farm, it carried this genetic memory. The flavor in the cup is literally the taste of the plant's stress response. The complexity of the bean is derived from the soil composition, the nitrogen fixation provided by companion shade trees, and the metabolic struggle of the cherry to ripen against the challenges of altitude and temperature.

We have seen how biological fragility defines the industry, from the specter of leaf rust to the vulnerabilities of monoculture farming. Every sip is a testament to the temporary victory of agronomy over entropy.

## THE IMPERIAL ECHO

Beneath the biological notes of fruit and acid, there is a heavier, darker undercurrent: the taste of empire. The fact that coffee grows in

Colombia, Vietnam, or Kenya is not a result of natural seed dispersal, but of imperial logistics. The global distribution of the coffee tree is a map of colonial ambition. We traced the movement of the "Seven Seeds" taped to the stomach of Baba Budan, and the "Glass Case" that protected the single genetic ancestor of the Americas during its fraught voyage across the Atlantic. These were acts of corporate espionage and statecraft as much as botanical expeditions.

The infrastructure that delivers the coffee to the modern consumer was built by the great trading monopolies of the seventeenth and eighteenth centuries. The Dutch East India Company (VOC) did not just trade spices; they terraformed islands in Indonesia to create a steady supply of caffeine for the European market. The French turned Saint-Domingue into a "Crucible" of production, engineering a landscape of irrigation and terracing that was fueled by the brutal machinery of the *Code Noir* and enslaved labor. The legacy of these systems remains dissolved in the liquid. The trade routes that move containers from Santos to Hamburg to New York are the modern iterations of the shipping lanes carved out by galleons and clippers.

Even the processing methods discussed in the "Controlled Decay" of fermentation are shadows of this history. The "washed" process, which uses vast quantities of fresh water to strip the fruit from the seed, was popularized to ensure that the beans would not rot during the months-long sea voyages required to reach the imperial capitals of Europe. The very clarity of the drink, its lack of fruit pulp and fermentation funk, is a technological adaptation to the tyranny of distance. When one drinks a clean, washed Arabica, they are tasting a flavor profile designed for export. The cup stands as a liquid monument to the era when coffee became the fuel of the industrial revolution, transforming from a social lubricant in the Ottoman coffeehouse to a caloric input for the factory workers of the West.

## THE THERMAL TRANSFORMATION

The transformation of the raw, green seed into the soluble brown fluid is the domain of science, a theme we explored through the lens of physics and chemistry. The cup is a feat of thermal engineering. The raw seed is chemically inert, a stone-like object with no aroma and a grassy, unpalatable taste. It requires the "Controlled Destruction" of the roasting process to unlock its potential.

We analyzed the violent thermodynamics of the roast, where temperatures reaching 200°C (392°F) complete the Maillard reaction, rearranging amino acids and reducing sugars into the complex melanoidins that give coffee its color and body. The roaster manages a rapid exothermic reaction, balancing the conduction of heat from the drum with the convection of hot air, navigating the "First Crack" where steam pressure fractures the cellular structure of the bean. This is thermal architecture instead of art.

The extraction itself is a study in fluid dynamics and solubility. Whether it is the high-pressure physics of the espresso machine, driving water at 9 bars (130 PSI) to emulsify oils into crema, or the gravity-fed percolation of a paper filter that removes the lipids cafestol and kahweol, the brewing method dictates the sensory experience. We learned that water is not merely a vehicle but a solvent, its hardness determined by the ratio of magnesium to calcium ions, which bond with specific flavor compounds to pull them from the ground matrix. The "grind geometry" dictates the surface area exposed to this solvent, a mathematical calculation of particle distribution that stands between a sweet, balanced cup and a bitter, over-extracted failure. The modern cup is the result of centuries of refinement in the "Sensory Priesthood," moving from the boiling pots of the clay hearth to the precision of the PID-controlled boiler.

### The Ledger of the Market

Finally, the cup tastes of the market. The price paid for the coffee—whether a commodity exchange value or a specialty premium—is determined by a financial mechanism that often bears little resemblance to the physical reality of farming. We have examined the Paper Bean, the futures contract traded on the exchange, where the price of coffee is dictated by hedging strategies, weather speculation, and macroeconomic trends rather than the cost of production.

The "Coffee Paradox" reveals the asymmetry of the value chain. The smile curve demonstrates that the majority of the profit is captured in the branding, marketing, and service sectors of the consuming countries, while the value retained at the origin remains a fraction of the retail price.

The efficiency of the "Green Mermaid's Empire" and the convenience of the "Encapsulated" pod system have democratized access to coffee, but they have also obscured the labor required to produce it.

The market has shifted the center of gravity. We are witnessing the rise of the "Tiger's Cup," as consumption in Asia accelerates, driven by a new generation of drinkers and tech-enabled retail models like Luckin. The West is no longer the sole arbiter of taste or the primary destination for the world's harvest. The market is dynamic, cold, and efficient, prioritizing scalability and consistency. The liquid in the cup is a commodity, stripped of its agricultural context and repackaged as an experience, a lifestyle, or a fuel. It is a product of the "Soluble Fuel" era, where the logistical necessity of shelf-life and transportability birthed the instant coffee industry and trained the global palate to accept convenience over complexity.

### The Horizon of Adaptation

But the story does not end with the consumption of the cup. The narrative is currently being rewritten by the forces of the "Heat Line." The climatic stability that allowed the coffee industry to flourish over the last century is eroding. The thermal belt suitable for high-quality Arabica is migrating uphill, forcing farmers to climb 300 meters higher to chase the cool nights required for sugar development. The "Black Frost" of 1975 showed us the volatility of supply shocks; the coming years will demonstrate the volatility of a systemic climate shift.

The future of the cup is uncertain. It may be found in the "Ghost in the Machine," the cellular agriculture startups growing coffee tissue in bioreactors, testing the Ship of Theseus paradox by decoupling the beverage from the plant entirely. It may be found in the "Monster," the resurgence of forgotten species like *Coffea liberica* and *Coffea excelsa*, with their deep taproots and heat tolerance offering a genetic buffer against a warming world. It may be found in the "Long Cold," the shift toward cold brew and ready-to-drink formulations that prioritize stability and mouthfeel over the delicate, fleeting acidity of a hot pour-over.

We are entering an era of necessary adaptation. The industry is beginning to understand that the linear model of "take, make, waste" is unsustainable. The "Infinite Loop" of the circular economy offers a path forward, where the pulp, the parchment, and the spent grounds are viewed not as trash but as resources for bioenergy, soil amendments, and new products. The seed must become a system. The extraction of value can no longer be a one-way street from the Global South to the Global North; it must become a regenerative cycle that restores the capital—natural, human, and financial—to the communities that steward the trees.

### THE CENTER OF THE WEB

This brings the focus back to the interaction between the human and the liquid. Coffee has always been a tool for attention. Its chemical function is to block the receptors of sleep, creating a state of alert consciousness. For centuries, civilization has utilized this borrowed energy to fuel the engines of progress. We used the clarity provided by the "Wine of Islam" to power the debates of the "Paper Parliament," to underwrite the risks of the insurance markets in the "Penny Universities," and to drive the code and commerce of the digital age.

Yet the attention generated by coffee has rarely been turned back upon its own origins. The beverage has been treated as a utility, a backdrop, a passive resource. The challenge of the next century is to extend that heightened awareness beyond the rim of the cup. It is to recognize that "quality" is a metric that extends beyond the sensory score awarded by a Q-Grader. True quality encompasses the dignity of the labor force, the health of the soil microbiome, the transparency of the transaction, and the resilience of the supply chain.

When the liquid touches the tongue, the drinker is participating in a ritual that binds them to the soil of the Ethiopian plateau, the hydrology of the Andes, and the volcanic loam of Indonesia. They are connected to the picker sorting cherries by hand, the miller monitoring the fermentation tanks, the trader watching the ticker tape, and the barista dialing in the grinder. The distance has been bridged by the supply chain, but the understanding of that distance requires an act of intellect and empathy.

The steam rises and fades. The cup cools to room temperature. The cycle of the seed is complete, yet it stands ready to begin again. The cup in your hand is the center of a global web, connecting you to the soil, the history, and the future that is already taking shape.

# PART VIII

---

# APPENDIX

# THE ART OF TASTING: A FIELD GUIDE FOR THE SENSES

Reading about coffee is only half the journey. To truly understand the complexity of the seed—to detect the altitude of the mountain, the nitrogen content of the soil, or the thermal curve of the roast—one must engage the senses with deliberate intent.

Most of the world drinks coffee passively, using it merely as a caffeine delivery system to wake up the brain. The professional taster (or *cupper*) does the opposite: they wake up the palate to evaluate the liquid. They slow down the biological process of consumption to catch the fleeting nuances—the volatile esters and organic acids—that the brain normally ignores.

Below is a comprehensive guide to conducting your own sensory analysis, based on the rigorous protocols used by Q-Graders and sensory scientists.

### I. The Setup

To taste effectively, you must eliminate variables. The focus must be entirely on the liquid in the cup.

- **The Environment:** Taste in a quiet room free of strong odors. Perfume, cologne, scented candles, and even the smell of cooking food will interfere with your retro-nasal olfaction. Use natural light if possible; the color of the brew (ruby, mahogany, amber) is a key indicator of roast development and clarity.

- **The Temperature:** Do not judge coffee while it is boiling hot. At 93°C (200°F), the human tongue's receptors are numbed by heat, perceiving only pain and steam. The sweet spot for evaluation begins at 70°C (158°F) and continues down to room temperature. As the coffee cools, the perceived sweetness increases and the organic acids (citric, malic) become more distinct.
- **The Palate:** Your mouth should be neutral. Avoid spicy food, toothpaste, or gum for at least thirty minutes prior. Room-temperature water or a slice of tart green apple act as excellent palate cleansers to reset your taste buds between cups.

## THE STORAGE COMMANDMENTS: STOP RUINING YOUR STASH

Coffee is not a shelf-stable staple like rice or pasta. It is a fresh agricultural product, biologically closer to toasted bread, fresh spices, or produce. It begins to die the moment it leaves the roaster. Follow these rules to keep it alive.

- **THOU SHALT NOT REFRIGERATE**
  - **The Science:** Refrigerators are humid environments filled with odors. Coffee beans are porous, hygroscopic sponges. If you store beans in the fridge, they will absorb the moisture and the aromas of your leftovers (garlic and onion notes are considered severe defects). Furthermore, when you remove cold beans, condensation forms on the surface, accelerating staling.
  - **The Fix:** Store beans in an opaque canister in a cool, dark cupboard, away from the heat of the oven or direct sunlight.
- **THOU SHALT EXCLUDE OXYGEN**

- The Science: Oxygen is the enemy of flavor. It causes the volatile oils (lipids) to turn rancid and the delicate aromatics to evaporate. Leaving a coffee bag open is the chemical equivalent of leaving a bottle of wine uncorked overnight.
  - The Fix: Use bags with one-way valves (which let Carbon Dioxide out but keep oxygen out) or dedicated vacuum-seal canisters. Squeeze the air out of the bag before resealing.
- **THOU SHALT GRIND ON DEMAND**
  - The Science: Whole beans have a very small surface area relative to their volume, protecting the flavor compounds inside. Ground coffee increases that surface area exponentially. Roughly 60% of the coffee's aroma dissipates within 15 minutes of grinding. Pre-ground coffee is essentially a "stale" product by the time you open it.
  - The Fix: Buy whole beans. Grind them immediately before you brew. It is the single most impactful upgrade you can make to your routine.

## II. The Ritual

1. **The Aspiration (Olfactory Analysis)** Smell occurs in two distinct stages in coffee. Do not skip the first.
   - **Fragrance (Dry):** Grind the coffee and immediately smell the dry grounds. Without water, you are smelling the heavier, woody, and spicy compounds. Look for notes of cedar, chocolate, nuts, or black pepper.
   - **Aroma (Wet):** Pour the hot water and smell again. The heat volatilizes the lighter, fruitier compounds. Cup your hand over the mug or carafe to trap the steam and inhale deeply.
   - **The Hunt:** Look past the generic smell of "coffee." Is it floral (jasmine, rose)? Fruity (blueberry, peach)? Herbal (tomato leaf, basil)? Sweet (caramel, molasses)?

2. **The Slurp (Auditory & Tactile Analysis)** This is the most famous and undignified part of professional tasting. Take a spoonful of coffee (or sip from the cup) and suck it into your mouth with a sharp, noisy, aggressive *slurp*.
   - **The Sound:** You want maximum aeration. This sprays the liquid into a fine mist, coating all the distinct zones of your tongue simultaneously and forcing retro-nasal aromas up the back of your throat into your olfactory bulb.
   - **The Texture (Body):** Before you swallow, assess the weight of the liquid. This is "Mouthfeel."
   - **Light Body:** Tea-like, delicate, juicy. (Typical of washed Ethiopian or high-altitude Latin American coffees).
   - **Medium Body:** Silky, round, like 2% milk. (Typical of Colombian or Guatemalan coffees).
   - **Heavy Body:** Syrupy, coating, creamy, like whole milk or heavy cream. (Typical of Sumatran, Natural Process, or Espresso blends).
3. **The Flavor Arc (Gustatory Analysis)** Flavor is not static; it evolves in a trajectory over time on the palate.
   - **The Head Notes (Acidity):** The first impact (0–3 seconds). This is the "sparkle" or "snap." Acidity is not sourness; it is structure. Is it sharp and citric like a lemon? Soft and malic like a red apple? Effervescent like a grape? Or is it harsh and acetic like vinegar (a defect)?
   - **The Body Notes (Sweetness & Depth):** The middle sensation (3–10 seconds). As the acidity fades, the deeper flavors emerge. This is the anchor of the cup. Look for the Maillard compounds: milk chocolate, toasted almond, caramel, brown sugar, or baking spices.
   - **The Tail Notes (Aftertaste/Finish):** The lingering sensation (10+ seconds). After you swallow, breathe out through your nose. What remains? A great coffee leaves a sweet, clean resonance that lasts for minutes. A poor coffee leaves a drying, astringent, bitter, or metallic sensation.

# THE CURATOR'S GUIDE: A CHECKLIST FOR THE CURIOUS

You cannot find the soul of coffee in a plastic pod or a jar of instant crystals. You must hunt for it. The spectrum of coffee flavor is determined by the intersection of three variables: **Genetics** (the specific variety of the seed), **Terroir** (the soil chemistry, altitude, and microclimate), and **Processing** (how the fruit was removed from the seed).

Most coffee drinkers stay within a narrow band of "nutty and dark." To truly understand the plant, you must explore the edges of the map. Use this checklist to explore the distinct archetypes of flavor described in this book.

1. **The "Gateway" Cup (Ethiopia Yirgacheffe)**
   - **The Profile:** Intense floral aromatics resembling jasmine, honeysuckle, and lemon blossom. The body is light, tea-like, and silky, often possessing the structural delicacy of Earl Grey tea or a white peach. It lacks the heavy, coating viscosity of darker roasts, trading weight for clarity.
   - **The Backstory & Science:** This is the coffee that usually breaks the "coffee tastes like coffee" paradigm for new drinkers. It proves that the coffee bean is, biologically, the seed of a tropical fruit. Grown at very high altitudes

(2,000+ meters above sea level) in the Gedeo Zone of Ethiopia, these beans mature slowly, allowing complex citric acids to develop. The "Washed Process" is critical here: the fruit flesh is mechanically stripped and the beans are scrubbed clean in water channels before drying. This removes the "mask" of the fruit, offering a pristine, transparent look at the seed's genetics.

- **Best Brew Method: Pour-over (Hario V60 or Chemex).** You need a paper filter to remove the coffee oils. Oils can coat the tongue and mute the delicate floral notes (like jasmine) that define this region. A French Press is too heavy for this delicate profile.
- **Look For:** The keywords "Washed Process" combined with "Yirgacheffe," "Sidama," or "Gedeo Zone." A "Light" or "City" roast is essential; dark roasting burns off the floral compounds immediately.

2. **The "Comfort" Cup (Colombia & Brazil)**
   - **The Profile:** The platonic ideal of coffee. Warm, round, and sweet, with dominant notes of milk chocolate, caramel, roasted peanut, red apple, and brown sugar. It has a medium, silky body and low, balanced acidity.
   - **The Backstory & Science:** This profile is driven by the **Maillard Reaction.** These coffees are typically roasted to a "Medium" or "Full City" level to caramelize the natural sugars without burning the cellulose.
   - **Colombia:** Look for beans from **Huila** or **Cauca.** The volcanic soils of the Andes provide a distinct sweetness and a touch of stone-fruit acidity (cherry/plum) that cuts through milk.
   - **Brazil:** Look for beans from **Cerrado Mineiro** or **Sul de Minas.** Brazilian coffee is often grown at lower altitudes and processed using the "Pulped Natural" method, which creates a heavier, nuttier body with very low acidity. It is the anchor of the global espresso market.
   - **Best Brew Method: Auto-Drip or Espresso.** These coffees have the structural integrity to stand up to milk and sugar.

They are the perfect "daily driver"—complex enough to be interesting, but approachable enough to drink every morning at 6:00 AM.

- **Look For:** "Huila" (Colombia), "Cerrado" (Brazil), "Supremo" (a Colombian bean size grade), or "Yellow Bourbon" (a Brazilian variety known for sweetness).

3. **The "Intense" Cup (Sumatra Mandheling)**
   - **The Profile:** Earth, wet cedar, pipe tobacco, clove, mushroom, leather, and dark bakers chocolate. The acidity is extremely low, but the body is massive—often described as "syrupy," "thick," or "coating."
   - **The Backstory & Science:** This flavor is not agricultural; it is mechanical. It is the direct result of the *Giling Basah* ("Wet Hulling") method unique to the Indonesian archipelago. Because of the constant humidity in Sumatra, farmers cannot dry their coffee efficiently. Instead, they strip the parchment skin off the bean while it is still wet (30–50% moisture), rather than waiting for it to dry (11%). This exposes the raw green bean to the humid jungle environment, creating a rapid bacterial fermentation that mutes acidity and creates those distinct savory, funky, forest-floor notes.
   - **Best Brew Method: French Press.** The metal mesh filter allows the heavy oils and microscopic sediments to pass into the cup, amplifying the massive body that is Sumatra's signature. Paper filters often strip away the heavy oils that make this coffee special.
   - **Look For:** "Sumatra," "Mandheling" (a trade name, not a region), "Lintong," or the specific phrase "Wet Hulled."

4. **The "Fruit Bomb" (Natural Process)**
   - **The Profile:** Blueberry jam, strawberry syrup, dried fig, red wine, and tropical punch. It can often have a "boozy" quality, reminiscent of port wine, sherry, or fruit liqueur.
   - **The Backstory & Science:** In the "Natural" or "Dry" process, the coffee cherry dries intact on the seed like a raisin. Over the course of weeks in the sun, the seed

absorbs sugars, esters, and alcohols from the decomposing fruit flesh. This migration of sugar creates a cup that is wildly sweet and fruit-forward. It is a high-wire act; if fermented too long, it tastes like vinegar or compost. If done perfectly, it tastes like fresh fruit juice.

- **Best Brew Method: AeroPress or Immersion Dripper.** These methods allow you to control the extraction time to manage the wild fruitiness without extracting the funky bitterness that can sometimes accompany naturals.
- **Look For:** "Natural Process," "Dry Process," or "Sun-Dried." **Ethiopia (Guji or Harar regions)** and **Costa Rica** (where they use the term "Black Honey" for a similar style) are the gold standards for this profile.

5. **The "Heirloom" Experience (Panama Geisha)**
   - **The Profile:** Honeysuckle, papaya, candied orange, vanilla, lemongrass, and bergamot. It possesses an "ethereal" quality—a flavor separation so distinct and clean that it feels more like a perfume than a beverage.
   - **The Backstory & Science:** The **Geisha** (or Gesha) variety is an ancient Ethiopian wild type that was brought to Central America in the 1950s but "rediscovered" in Panama in 2004. It is genetically distinct from commercial Arabica, with a root system that demands specific high-altitude microclimates. It is notoriously difficult to grow and produces very low yields, but the cup quality is unrivaled. It consistently shatters world auction records (selling for thousands of dollars per pound) because of its genetic purity and aromatic intensity.
   - **Best Brew Method: Pour-over (Kalita Wave or Flat-Bottom Dripper).** Precision is key here; you want to extract the delicate sweetness without crushing the florals. Use slightly cooler water (91°C / 195°F) to avoid scalding the delicate aromatics.
   - **Look For:** "Geisha" or "Gesha" variety. Panama is the most famous origin, but excellent (and more affordable)

examples are now coming from Colombia (Huila) and Ethiopia (Bench Maji).

6. **The "Savory" Cup (Kenya SL-28)**
   - **The Profile:** Blackcurrant (cassis), tomato vine, pink grapefruit, rhubarb, and blood orange. It is defined by a sparkling, intense acidity that hits the sides of the tongue, often described as "phosphoric" or "winy."
   - **The Backstory & Science:** Kenyan coffees are the most chemically potent in the world. The "**SL**" **varieties** (SL-28, SL-34) were developed by Scott Laboratories in the 1930s for drought resistance, but they accidentally selected for extreme flavor intensity. The volcanic soil of Mount Kenya is rich in phosphorus, which is absorbed by the plant and contributes to the savory, mouth-watering sensation (orthophosphoric acid) found in the cup—chemically similar to the acid found in sparkling cola.
   - **Best Brew Method: V60 Pour-over or Siphon.** The high heat stability of a siphon helps extract the complex acids that make Kenya unique.
   - **Look For:** "Kenya AA" (a screen-size grading indicating large beans) or specific varieties "SL-28" and "SL-34."

7. **The "Robusta" Renaissance (Fine Robusta)**
   - **The Profile:** Dark cocoa, roasted walnut, malt, savory soy/umami, toasted grain. It features a heavy caffeine kick (2x Arabica) and produces a thick, persistent, peanut-butter-colored *crema* that lasts for minutes.
   - **The Backstory & Science:** For decades, Robusta (*Coffea canephora*) was treated as an industrial weed, processed cheaply, and used only for instant coffee or tire rubber. "**Fine Robusta**" is a modern movement to treat this species with the same agronomic care as specialty Arabica selective hand-picking and careful fermentation. The result is a bean that lacks the "burnt rubber" defect of commodity Robusta but retains the massive body and low acidity. It is the future of coffee in a warming world.

- Best Brew Method: Espresso or Phin Filter (Vietnamese style). Robusta needs the pressure of an espresso machine or the slow, high-dose drip of a Phin to tame its intensity and bring out the chocolate notes.
- Look For: "Fine Robusta" or "Single Origin Robusta." **Vietnam (Central Highlands), India (Kaapi Royale),** and **Uganda** are leading the charge in this emerging market.

8. The "Experimental" Frontier (Anaerobic Maceration)
   - **The Profile:** Cinnamon, bubblegum, banana, lactic acid (yogurt), wild spices. The flavors often feel "synthetic" or candy-like in their intensity.
   - **The Backstory & Science:** This is the cutting edge of coffee processing, borrowed from the wine industry. Farmers place whole cherries in sealed, oxygen-deprived tanks (stainless steel or plastic) to ferment for days. Without oxygen, different microbial colonies dominate, producing unique esters and acids (like lactic acid) that do not exist in traditional open-air fermentation. It is controversial, risky, and distinct—some call it "adulterated," others call it "evolution."
   - **Best Brew Method: Pour-over.** These coffees are volatile and highly soluble; you want a gentle method to see what the fermentation did to the bean without extracting bitterness.
   - **Look For:** "Anaerobic," "Carbonic Maceration," "Co-ferment," or "Lactic Process."

# THE COFFEE PILGRIM'S GUIDE: MUSEUMS AND ARCHIVES TO VISIT

A global atlas for the obsessed. From the volcanic highlands of East Africa to the velvet-draped salons of Europe and the neon-lit precision of Tokyo, these are the holy sites of the bean. These locations are not just places to drink coffee; they are the physical landmarks where the history of the world was written in caffeine.

- **THE AMERICAS:** The Empires of Innovation
  - <u>**United States**</u>
    - **Pike Place Market (Seattle, WA):** The Birthplace of the Second Wave.
      - **The Draw:** 1912 Pike Place. It is easy to dismiss this as a tourist trap, but to do so is to ignore its immense historical weight. This is the "Plymouth Rock" of the American coffee revolution. While the company has since become a global ubiquity, this single storefront—with its original brown nautical logo, brass fixtures, and lack of seating—marks the specific moment in 1971 when the vocabulary of the United States shifted. Before this shop, America drank "coffee." After this shop, America

drank "Sumatra," "Kenya," and "Dark Roast." It represents the transition from coffee as a cheap commodity to coffee as an affordable luxury.

- **The Experience:** There are often lines stretching down the block. Inside, the baristas (often the company's most tenured "Coffee Masters") toss cups with theatrical flair. The air smells of dark-roasted beans and the sea salt from the Puget Sound fish market next door.
- **Must Try:** A double espresso or a short Americano. Strip away the syrups and the milk to taste the dark, smoky roast profile that Alfred Peet taught the founders, which defined the "Seattle Style" for forty years.

- **Peet's Coffee (Berkeley, CA):** The Mentor's Workshop.
  - **The Draw:** The corner of Vine and Walnut Streets. Opened in 1966 by Alfred Peet, a Dutchman with a background in the spice trade, this is the true ground zero of specialty coffee in the US. Peet was the man who taught the founders of Starbucks how to roast. While the rest of America was drinking weak, percolated swill, Peet was roasting dark, oily, pungent beans that tasted of "density and violence".
  - **The Experience:** The original shop still operates as a shrine to the "Deep Roast." It lacks the polished corporate sheen of its Seattle offspring. It feels like a neighborhood institution where professors from UC Berkeley debate politics over cups of sludge-thick coffee. The scent of roasting coffee here is so intense it permeates the entire block.
  - **Must Try:** The "Major Dickason's Blend" brewed on a French Press. It is the definitive taste of the Second Wave—smoky, spicy, and uncompromising.

- **Café Du Monde (New Orleans, LA):** The French Resistance.
  - **The Draw:** Established in 1862, this open-air pavilion stands as a monument to the "Empire" era of coffee history. It tells the story of the American Civil War and the French colonial legacy. During the Union naval blockades, coffee was scarce, so New Orleanians cut their coffee with roasted chicory root to stretch the supply. That survival tactic became a flavor profile that persists today.
  - **The Experience:** Open 24 hours a day, 7 days a week, it is a place of humidity, jazz, and powdered sugar. The waiters wear traditional white paper hats, and the floor is often sticky with humidity and sugar. It is one of the few places in America where coffee is still treated as a slow, sitting-down social ritual rather than fuel for the commute.
  - **Must Try:** A *Café au Lait* (half coffee-chicory blend, half hot milk) paired with fresh beignets. The chicory adds a woody, herbal bite that cuts through the rich milk.
- **Blue Bottle Coffee (Hayes Valley, San Francisco, CA):** The Garage of the Third Wave.
  - **The Draw:** In the early 2000s, a clarinetist named James Freeman grew tired of the commercial stale coffee market. He vowed to sell coffee "within 48 hours of roasting." He started in a potting shed in Oakland, but the kiosk in Hayes Valley (specifically the Linden Street location) became the icon of the "Third Wave." This is where coffee began to be treated like software—precise, minimalist, and expensive.
  - **The Experience:** There are no comfortable chairs or wifi. The focus is entirely on the extraction. It represents the shift from "coffee as comfort" to "coffee as culinary art." The aesthetic—clean lines,

Japanese brewing equipment, scales weighing water to the gram—set the visual template for every modern coffee shop in the world.
    - **Must Try:** A Single Origin Pour-over. Watch the barista weigh the water and time the bloom. Taste it black to understand the difference between the "Roast" flavor of Peet's and the "Origin" flavor of the modern era.
  - ○ **Argentina**
    - **Café Tortoni (Buenos Aires):** The Paris of the South.
      - **The Draw:** Founded in 1858, Tortoni is the grand dame of South American *cafeterías*. It represents how European coffee culture adapted to the New World, serving as the haunt of Jorge Luis Borges and tango legend Carlos Gardel.
      - **The Experience:** With Tiffany glass ceilings and marble tables, it feels like a church dedicated to conversation.
      - **Must Try:** A *Lágrima* (a "tear")—hot steamed milk "stained" with a single drop of espresso.
  - ○ **Brazil**
    - **The History of Coffee Museum (Santos):** The Cathedral of Commerce.
      - **The Draw:** Housed in the *Bolsa Oficial de Café* (Official Coffee Stock Exchange), this building is a testament to the era when coffee built nations. The architecture is eclectic, blending Victorian grandeur with Baroque excess. The centerpiece is the trading floor—a massive hall with marble floors, high stained-glass windows depicting the history of Brazil, and a dais made of jacaranda wood. From 1922 to 1957, the price of coffee for the entire planet was dictated here by the "Barons of Santos."
      - **The Experience:** Stand in the center of the trading pit and imagine the shouting of brokers that once

moved millions of sacks of green gold. The museum also houses archives of the immigrant labor that fueled the boom and the brutal history of the plantation system.

- **Must Try:** The museum café serves beans from different micro-regions of São Paulo state. Order a *cafezinho* (a small, strong black coffee) brewed from a Cerrado Mineiro bean to taste the classic chocolate-nut profile of Brazil.

o **Colombia**

- **Coffee Cultural Landscape (*Eje Cafetero*):** The UNESCO Heartland.

  - **The Draw:** This is not a single building, but a region comprising the departments of Caldas, Quindío, and Risaralda. It was designated a World Heritage site not just for the coffee, but for the unique culture of the *paisa* farmers who tamed the Andes. The landscape is vertigo-inducing; coffee trees cling to slopes so steep that mechanical harvesting is impossible.

  - **The Experience:** Stay on a working *finca* (farm) near Salento or Manizales. Wake up before dawn to the smell of mist and wet earth. Watch the *chapoleras* (traditional female harvesters) work the rows. The architecture here is distinct: colorful bahareque houses made of bamboo and adobe with clay tile roofs.

  - **Must Do:** Ride in a "Willys Jeep." These WWII-surplus vehicles are the mechanical mules of the region, often piled ten feet high with sacks of coffee and plantains, climbing vertical mud tracks that would defeat modern trucks.

o **Costa Rica**

- **Hacienda Alsacia (Alajuela):** The Laboratory of the Giant.

- The Draw: This is the only coffee farm in the world owned by Starbucks. It serves as their global agronomy headquarters, dedicated to breeding rust-resistant trees to save the industry (and their supply chain).
- The Experience: Unlike rustic farms, this is a polished, open-air educational facility. You can walk through the nursery where "F1 Hybrids" are being engineered and drink coffee overlooking the very fields where the science is happening.
- Must Try: A flight of "Alsacia Reserve" processed three ways (Washed, Honey, Natural) to taste the impact of processing on a single harvest.
- Jamaica
  - **Mavis Bank Coffee Factory (Blue Mountains):** The Old Empire.
    - The Draw: Before Panama Geisha, there was Jamaica Blue Mountain. This factory processes the beans that defined "luxury coffee" for the 20th century. It is a time capsule of the British colonial aesthetic—misty peaks, wooden barrels, and extreme prices.
    - The Experience: The drive up the Blue Mountains is harrowing. The factory itself smells of cedar wood and drying beans. It represents the old definition of quality: mild, smooth, and lacking bitterness, rather than the acidic fruit-bombs of today.
    - Must Try: A cup of 100% Blue Mountain, black. It tastes like history: polite, balanced, and incredibly expensive.
- Mexico
  - **Café de Tacuba (Mexico City):** The Colonial Kitchen.
    - The Draw: Established in 1912 in a 17th-century convent, this restaurant is a temple to Mexican

culinary history. It perfectly captures the
integration of coffee into indigenous traditions.

- **The Experience:** The walls are lined with
Talavera tiles and oil paintings. The atmosphere is
bustling, loud, and smells of spices.
- **Must Try:** *Café de Olla*. Coffee brewed in an
earthen clay pot (*olla*) with cinnamon (*canela*) and
raw dark sugar (*piloncillo*). The clay pot is said to
impart a specific earthy flavor that cannot be
replicated in metal or glass.

- **Panama**
  - **Hacienda La Esmeralda (Boquete):** The Vineyard
  of God.
    - **The Draw:** If Santos is the cathedral of volume,
    Esmeralda is the cathedral of value. This family-
    run farm in the chiriqui highlands is the site of the
    most important botanical discovery of the last
    century: the "rediscovery" of the Geisha variety in
    2004.
    - **The Experience:** Tours here are rare and treated
    like sommeliers visiting a Grand Cru vineyard in
    Burgundy. You are walking on holy ground where
    a single pound of green coffee has sold for over
    $1,000 at auction. The air is cool, misty, and smells
    of jasmine flowers.
    - **Must Try:** A private cupping of their "Special"
    reserve lots. It is the cleanest, most floral coffee
    experience on earth.
- **EUROPE:** The Coffeehouse Capitals
  - **Germany**
    - **The Speicherstadt (Hamburg):** The Warehouse of the
    World.
      - **The Draw:** This UNESCO World Heritage site is
      the largest warehouse district in the world, built
      on oak piles in the Elbe river between 1883 and
      1927. For over a century, this Gothic-Revival city of

red brick was the primary entry point for coffee into Europe. The smell of raw green coffee still lingers in the canals.

- **The Experience:** Visit the Coffee Museum Burg located inside one of the old warehouses. It houses a massive collection of industry artifacts, from vintage roasters to molds used for making coffee porcelain.
- **Must Try:** A cup of "Hamburg Blend" in the museum café, overlooking the canals where the barges used to unload the sacks.

- Italy
  - **Caffè Florian (Venice):** The Oldest Living Room.
    - **The Draw:** Opened in 1720 by Floriano Francesconi, this is the oldest continuously operating coffeehouse in Europe. It is a time capsule of the Venetian Republic. The interior is divided into small, intimate rooms (the Hall of the Senate, the Hall of Seasons) lined with red velvet, gold leaf, and blackened mirrors. This is where Casanova courted women, where Goethe wrote, and where Proust lingered. It represents the "Penny University" era, where coffee was the fuel for the European intelligentsia.
    - **The Experience:** It is unapologetically expensive, but you are paying for the ghost of the 18th century. A live orchestra often plays on the terrace in St. Mark's Square.
    - **Must Try:** The *Caffè Florian* house blend, served on a silver tray with a glass of water and a small jug of milk. Sip it slowly; you are renting the seat as much as buying the drink.
  - **Caffè degli Specchi (Trieste):** The Silicon Valley of Espresso.
    - **The Draw:** While Rome and Naples have the culture, Trieste has the science. This port city is

the historic entry point for coffee into the Austro-Hungarian Empire and the headquarters of **Illycaffè**. It is where the modern scientific approach to espresso—pressurization, inert gas packing, and chromatograph analysis—was pioneered.

- **The Experience:** Located in the grand Piazza Unità d'Italia, the "Café of Mirrors" is the living room of the city. The locals drink more coffee per capita here than anywhere else in Italy (approx. 10kg per year).
- **Must Try:** A *Capo in B*—a Trieste specialty. It is a mini-cappuccino served in a small glass (*bicchiere*), perfectly layered.

- **Sant'Eustachio Il Caffè (Rome):** The Theater of Espresso.
  - **The Draw:** Located in the Piazza di Sant'Eustachio since 1938, this shop is legendary for a single technical mystery: the *crema*. The espresso here arrives with a thick, moussy foam that you can almost chew. The baristas operate behind a stainless steel screen that hides the machines from view, protecting their "secret method" (rumored to involve whipping the first drops of sugar and coffee into a paste before adding the rest of the shot).
  - **The Experience:** It is chaotic, loud, and quintessentially Roman. There are no seats. You pay at the register, take your receipt to the bar, and elbow your way in. The floor is littered with sugar packets and napkins. It is a place of speed and intensity.
  - **Must Try:** The *Gran Caffè*. It comes pre-sweetened (unless you aggressively shout "senza zucchero"!) and is a masterclass in the heavy, chocolaty Robusta-Arabica blend style of Rome.

- **Gran Caffè Gambrinus (Naples):** The Soul of the South.
- **The Draw:** While the North (Milan/Venice) is polite, Naples is raw energy. Founded in 1860, Gambrinus is the belle époque palace of the city. It is famous for the tradition of *Caffè Sospeso* ("Suspended Coffee")— paying for two coffees but drinking one, leaving the other for a stranger who cannot afford it.
- **The Experience:** Naples espresso is different— shorter, darker, and often containing Robusta for a massive caffeine punch. The cups are kept boiling hot in water baths. You drink standing up, quickly.
- **Must Try:** *Caffè alla Nocciola* (Hazelnut Coffee), a frothy, sweet specialty of the Campania region.
  - **Austria**
    - **Café Central (Vienna):** The Intellectual Hub.
      - **The Draw:** If Florian is the living room, Central is the study. Opened in 1876 in the Ferstel Palace, this cathedral-like space features vaulted ceilings and marble pillars. It was the nerve center of late 19th-century thought. It is said that in 1913, Leon Trotsky, Sigmund Freud, Joseph Stalin, and Adolf Hitler were all patrons of this specific cafe at the same time. The "Viennese Coffee House Culture" is intangible heritage here: the right to sit for hours with a single cup, the selection of international newspapers on wooden sticks, and the grumpy, tuxedoed waiters.
      - **The Experience:** It is slow. Deliberately so. Coffee here is not a beverage; it is a mechanism for passing time.
      - **Must Try:** A *Wiener Melange* (a shot of espresso topped with half steamed milk and half foam, similar to a cappuccino but milder) and a slice of *Sachertorte* or *Apfelstrudel*.

- Norway
  - **Tim Wendelboe (Oslo):** The Laboratory of Light.
  - **The Draw:** This modest corner shop in the Grünerløkka district is the Vatican of the "Nordic Roast." Tim Wendelboe, a former World Barista Champion, pioneered the ultra-light roast style that treats coffee more like fruit juice than a roasted seed. This shop shifted the global palate away from bitterness and toward acidity.
  - **The Experience:** The aesthetic is mid-century modern, clinical, and precise. There is an on-site roastery that looks like a clean room. The baristas function like scientists, measuring Total Dissolved Solids (TDS) and extraction yields.
  - **Must Try:** The "Tasting Flight." A single Kenyan coffee served two ways: as a Cappuccino and as a filter brew, demonstrating how milk changes the perception of acidity.
- Sweden
  - **Vete-Katten (Stockholm):** The Institution of Fika.
    - **The Draw:** While Norway represents the *science* of light roast, Sweden represents the *ritual*. Established in 1928, this labyrinthine café is the guardian of *Fika*—the sacred, non-negotiable coffee break that fuels the Swedish workforce.
    - **The Experience:** It feels like a grandmother's parlor, with maze-like rooms and copper kettles. Coffee here is not analyzed; it is consumed by the liter, always paired with a cinnamon bun (*kanelbulle*).
    - **Must Try:** *Bryggkaffe* (batch brew) and a *Prinsesstårta* (green marzipan cake).

- **United Kingdom**
  - **The Oxford Coffee History Walk:** The Academic Roots.
    - **The Draw:** While London had the famous Exchange Alley coffeehouses, Oxford had the first. Visit the site of "The Grand Cafe" (established c. 1650) on the High Street. It was opened by a Jewish entrepreneur named Jacob, marking the moment coffee entered the English bloodstream.
    - **The Experience:** Standing on this spot, you are at the flashpoint of the Enlightenment. It was in these Oxford coffeehouses that the Royal Society was incubated, where Isaac Newton dissected physics, and where the "virtuosos" (early scientists) met to conduct experiments.
    - **Must Do:** Visit the nearby Queen's Lane Coffee House (established 1654), which still serves coffee, to feel the continuity of 370 years of student caffeine consumption.
- **France**
  - **Le Procope (Paris):** The Crucible of Revolution.
    - **The Draw:** Established in 1686, this is where coffee fueled the Enlightenment. Voltaire drank forty cups a day here, and Benjamin Franklin drafted alliance treaties at its tables. Napoleon's hat is still displayed in a glass case as collateral for an unpaid tab.
    - **Must Try:** *Café à l'Ancienne.*
- **Portugal**
  - **A Brasileira (Lisbon):** The Literary Salon.
    - **The Draw:** Opened in 1905 to sell authentic Brazilian coffee (a direct link to the "Empire" theme), it became the headquarters of the modernist movement. A bronze statue of the poet Fernando Pessoa sits permanently at his favorite table outside.

- **The Experience:** The Art Deco interior is stunning, but the real draw is the specific coffee culture. This is the birthplace of the *Bica* (an acronym for *Beba Isto Com Açúcar*, "Drink this with sugar"), a long, smooth espresso that differs from the shorter, punchier Italian shot.
- **Must Try:** A *Bica* and a *Pastel de Nata* (custard tart) from the bakery next door.

- **AFRICA & THE MIDDLE EAST:** The Origins
  - Egypt
    - **El Fishawy (Cairo):** The Mirror of History.
      - **The Draw:** Located in the Khan el-Khalili market, open continuously since 1773. It was the "office" of Nobel laureate Naguib Mahfouz.
      - **The Experience:** A narrow alleyway café lined with massive, tarnished mirrors. The air is thick with apple tobacco and history.
      - **Must Try:** *Ahwa Sada* (plain coffee)—black, thick, and brewed in hot sand.
  - Ethiopia
    - **Tomoca Coffee (Addis Ababa):** The Guardian of the Ritual.
      - **The Draw:** Established in 1953, Tomoca (TO.MO.CA is an acronym for the Italian *Torrefazione Moderna Café*) is the bridge between the ancient Ethiopian ceremony and the modern Italian espresso machine. The original shop in the Piazza neighborhood is small, wood-paneled, and smells intensely of frankincense, which is burned in the corner to sanctify the space.
      - **The Experience:** There are no chairs. You stand at high, chest-level counters, rubbing shoulders with diplomats, taxi drivers, and poets. The walls are lined with vintage grinders and trophies. It feels like a secret society.

- **Must Try:** A Macchiato. In Ethiopia, this is not the Italian version. It is a tall glass of extremely strong, dark-roasted Harar coffee, topped with a dense head of foam and filled to the very brim. It is viscous, sweet, and incredibly potent.
- ASIA & OCEANIA: The Future Frontiers
  - Japan
    - **Chatei Hatou (Tokyo):** The Temple of the Hand-Pour.
      - **The Draw:** Located just steps from the frantic energy of Shibuya Crossing, this shop is a portal to silence. It represents the *Kissaten* culture—the "Showa era" style of coffee shop that predates the Third Wave. The interior is dark wood, filled with dried flowers and ticking clocks. Behind the bar is a wall of hundreds of unique, bone-china cups. The barista selects a specific cup based on your clothing, mood, or personality.
      - **The Experience:** This is the antithesis of "fast coffee." The beans are roasted over *Binchotan* charcoal, giving them a distinct smoky sweetness. The barista uses a flannel drip filter (nel drip) and takes nearly five minutes to pour a single cup, water drop by water drop.
      - **Must Try:** An aged-bean blend (Old Crop), served black. Pair it with their legendary chiffon cake.
  - South Korea
    - **Gangneung Coffee Street (Anmok Beach):** The Modern Obsession.
      - **The Draw:** A mile-long strip of multi-story roasteries facing the Sea of Japan, representing the sheer speed and scale of Asian coffee adoption.
      - **Must Try:** *Einspänner*—strong black coffee topped with cold, sweet cream.

- Thailand
  - **Doi Chaang Village (Chiang Rai):** The Opium Replacement.
    - **The Draw:** A pilgrimage of ethics. In the 1980s, this region was the center of opium poppy production. A royal project successfully transitioned the Akha hill tribes to high-quality Arabica coffee.
    - **Must Try:** Honey-processed Arabica brewed in a bamboo filter.
- Indonesia
  - **Kopi Es Tak Kie (Jakarta):** The Survivor.
    - **The Draw:** Established in 1927 in the Glodok (Chinatown) district, this shop has survived colonial wars, independence struggles, and modernization. It represents the "Old World" of Java—where coffee was not about delicate notes, but about survival and strength.
    - **The Experience:** It is humid, loud, and unpretentious. Photos of generations of owners line the peeling walls. It feels like stepping onto a set of a 1940s noir film.
    - **Must Try:** *Kopi Es* (Iced Coffee). A blend of strong Robusta, condensed milk, and ice, served in a simple tall glass. It is the original energy drink.
- Vietnam
  - **The Old Quarter (Hanoi):** The Robusta Kingdom.
    - **The Draw:** Vietnam is the world's second-largest producer of coffee, mostly Robusta, and Hanoi is its spiritual heart. The "cafe" here is not a building; it is the sidewalk. The culture is built on low, plastic stools, constant humidity, and the roar of motorbikes.
    - **The History:** During the First Indochina War (1946), fresh milk was scarce. A bartender at the Sofitel Legend Metropole named Nguyen Van

Giang invented a substitute using whisked egg yolks, condensed milk, and cheese to create a cappuccino-like foam.
- **Must Try:** *Cà Phê Trứng* (Egg Coffee) at **Giang Café**, still run by the founder's family. It is rich, custard-like, and tastes like liquid tiramisu, proving that Robusta can be luxurious.

- India
  - **Baba Budangiri (Chikmagalur, Karnataka):** The Shrine of the Seven Seeds.
    - **The Draw:** This is perhaps the most significant historical site outside of Ethiopia. It is the mountain shrine where the Sufi saint Baba Budan allegedly planted the seven fertile seeds he smuggled out of Yemen in the 17th century, breaking the Ottoman monopoly.
    - **The Experience:** It is a pilgrimage site for both Hindus and Muslims (a Dattatreya Peetha). The surrounding hills are lush with coffee estates that trace their lineage back to those original seeds.
    - **Must Do:** Hike the trails of the Mullayanagiri peak to see the wild coffee growing in the shola forests, a living testament to the first successful coffee transplant in history.

- Turkey
  - **Fazıl Bey'in Türk Kahvesi (Istanbul):** The Return to the Source.
    - **The Draw:** Located in the bustling Kadıköy market on the Asian side of the Bosphorus, this shop has been roasting and grinding since 1923. It keeps the 16th-century Ottoman tradition alive in its purest form. The shop is filled with the mechanical whir of massive, antique brass grinders pulverizing beans into a powder as fine as flour.
    - **The Experience:** The brewing method here is archaic and beautiful. The coffee is brewed in

copper *cezves* (long-handled pots) often nestled in a bed of hot sand, which provides even, gentle heat. The service is a ritual of hospitality: the coffee, a glass of water to cleanse the palate, and a piece of Turkish delight (*lokum*) to sweeten the tongue.

- **Must Try:** *Damla Sakızlı Türk Kahvesi* (Turkish coffee with mastic gum). The resin adds a piney, herbal complexity to the brew. Remember: never stir the cup once served, and stop drinking when you hit the mud at the bottom. Flip the cup over on the saucer to read your fortune in the grounds.

  ○ <u>Australia</u>
  - **Pellegrini's Espresso Bar (Melbourne):** Patient Zero of the Flat White.
    - **The Draw:** Established in 1954, this is where the Italian heartbeat of Melbourne began. With its checkerboard floors and neon signs, it introduced the espresso machine to a tea-drinking colony.
    - **Must Try:** A Flat White—the ratio of double-ristretto to micro-foam that conquered the world.

# GLOSSARY OF COFFEE: A COMPENDIUM OF CULTURE, CHEMISTRY, AND COMMERCE

## A

- **Acidity:** Not to be confused with the pH level that causes stomach upset. In high-quality coffee, acidity is a prized sensation of brightness and vibrancy—the "snap" of a Granny Smith apple or the "zing" of citrus. It is the primary characteristic that separates specialty coffee from commodity coffee.
- **Adenosine:** The brain chemical responsible for making you feel tired. Caffeine works by acting as an antagonist, mimicking the shape of adenosine and blocking its receptors, effectively jamming the "sleep signal" from reaching the brain.
- **Aerobic vs. Anaerobic:** Refers to fermentation environments. *Aerobic* occurs in the presence of oxygen (open tanks). *Anaerobic* occurs in sealed vessels deprived of oxygen. The latter is a modern processing trend that forces yeast to work under stress, often creating wild, boozy, or "fruit-bomb" flavor profiles.
- **Agtron:** A spectrophotometer used by commercial roasters to measure the color of roasted beans using near-infrared light.

It assigns a number to the roast level—the lower the number, the darker the roast.

- **Alkaloid:** A class of naturally occurring organic nitrogen-containing bases. In coffee, caffeine and trigonelline are the primary alkaloids, contributing bitterness and physiological effects.
- **Arabica (*Coffea arabica*):** The noble species of the coffee family, accounting for about 60-70% of global production. Grown at higher altitudes, it is harder to cultivate and more susceptible to disease than Robusta, but it possesses four sets of chromosomes (tetraploid) and offers a vastly superior, complex flavor spectrum.
- **Aroma:** The smell of brewed coffee. Distinct from *fragrance* (the smell of dry grounds). It is carried by volatile organic compounds released by the heat of the water.

**B**

- **Bag:** The standard unit of trade. A "bag" usually refers to 60kg (132 lbs) of green coffee, the standard measure for the C-Market, though different origins vary (e.g., Colombia uses 70kg sacks).
- **Barista:** From the Italian for "bartender." A professional specialized in the preparation of espresso and coffee beverages.
- **Bean Belt:** The band of tropical latitude between the Tropic of Cancer and the Tropic of Capricorn where coffee thrives. It creates a global ring including Central/South America, Africa, and Southeast Asia.
- **Beneficio:** The Spanish term for a coffee mill or processing station. A *Beneficio Húmedo* is a wet mill (pulping/washing); a *Beneficio Seco* is a dry mill (hulling/sorting).
- **Bimodal Grind:** A distribution of ground coffee particles that has two distinct peaks: one of larger boulders and one of fine dust (fines). This is common in espresso grinding, where fines

restrict flow to build pressure while boulders provide flavor clarity.

- **Blend:** A mixture of two or more single-origin coffees. Historically used to lower costs or ensure consistency; in specialty, used to create a complex flavor profile (e.g., a chocolatey Brazilian base with a floral Ethiopian highlight).
- **Bloom:** The rapid release of carbon dioxide that occurs when hot water hits fresh coffee grounds. The bed of coffee puffs up and bubbles. A robust bloom indicates freshness; a flat bed usually means the coffee is stale or degassed.
- **Body:** The tactile sensation of the coffee on the tongue (viscosity/mouthfeel). Is it tea-like and watery? Or syrupy and coating? Body is largely determined by the presence of oils and colloids extracted from the bean.
- **Borer (Berry Borer):** The *Hypothenemus hampei*, a tiny beetle that drills into the coffee cherry and lays eggs inside the seed. It is one of the most economically devastating pests in the coffee world.
- **Bourbon:** A legendary heirloom variety of Arabica (a mutation of Typica) originally cultivated by the French on the island of Bourbon (now Réunion). It is prized for its sweet, buttery complexity and is the parent of many modern varieties (like Caturra).
- **Brix:** A scale used to measure the sugar content of an aqueous solution. Farmers use a refractometer to check the Brix of coffee cherry mucilage to determine the optimal moment for harvest.

# C

- **Caffeine:** A bitter alkaloid (1,3,7-trimethylxanthine) evolved by the coffee plant as a natural pesticide to paralyze insects. For humans, it is the world's most popular psychoactive drug, acting as a central nervous system stimulant.
- **Carbonic Maceration:** A processing technique borrowed from winemaking (Beaujolais). Whole cherries are placed in a

sealed stainless steel tank which is then pumped full of carbon dioxide. This triggers intracellular fermentation inside the fruit, creating distinct bubblegum, banana, or berry notes.

- **Cascara:** From the Spanish word for "husk" or "skin." It is the dried fruit skin of the coffee cherry. Historically discarded as waste, it is now often brewed as a tea, tasting of hibiscus, tamarind, and dried fig.
- **Castillo:** A rust-resistant hybrid variety developed by Colombia's research institute (CENICAFÉ). While agronomic gold for farmers, it was historically maligned by cuppers for having a "rubbery" taste, though quality has improved significantly in recent years.
- **Catimor:** A group of hybrids created by crossing Caturra (Arabica) with the Timor Hybrid (Arabica x Robusta). It offers high yields and rust resistance but often lacks the cup quality of pure Arabica.
- **Channelling:** A defect in espresso extraction where high-pressure water finds a weak spot in the coffee puck, rushing through a single path. This results in a shot that is simultaneously sour (under-extracted) and bitter (over-extracted).
- **Cherry:** The fruit of the coffee tree. It turns from green to yellow to a deep crimson (or sometimes yellow/pink) when ripe. It usually contains two seeds (beans).
- **Chlorogenic Acids (CGAs):** The compound responsible for the perceived acidity and antioxidant properties of coffee. During roasting, CGAs break down into quinic and caffeic acids. If the roast is pushed too dark, these degrade into unpleasant bitterness.
- **Cooperative (Co-op):** An organization of smallholder farmers who pool their resources to mill and market their coffee. Co-ops give small farmers access to the global market that they would not have individually.
- **Commodity Coffee:** Coffee traded on the C-Market,

indistinguishable by origin, usually used for blends, instant coffee, or mass-market grocery brands.

- **Coyote:** A slang term (often used in Central America) for an unregulated middleman who drives a truck to farm gates, paying cash for coffee at prices often well below market value, exploiting farmers who lack transport to a mill.
- **C-Price:** The global benchmark price for commodity Arabica coffee, traded on the Intercontinental Exchange (ICE) in New York. It is notoriously volatile and often drops below the cost of production, a major driver of poverty for coffee farmers.
- **Crack (First & Second):** Audible cues during roasting. *First Crack* sounds like popcorn (steam escaping) and signals the bean is edible. *Second Crack* sounds like rice crispies (cellulose fracturing) and signals the oils are migrating to the surface (Dark Roast).
- **Crema:** The reddish-brown, golden foam that sits atop a shot of espresso. It is composed of $CO_2$ bubbles suspended in emulsified coffee oils. While visually appealing, it actually tastes quite bitter; its presence is a visual marker of proper pressure and freshness.
- **Cupping:** The industry-standard method for evaluating coffee quality. Beans are roasted, ground, and steeped in small bowls, then slurped loudly from a spoon to spray the liquid across the palate. This allows Q-Graders to score the coffee objectively.

D

- **Decaffeination:** The process of removing caffeine from green beans. Methods include the *Swiss Water Process* (using solubility and osmosis, chemical-free), *Sugarcane Process* (using ethyl acetate derived from molasses), or *Methylene Chloride* (a chemical solvent).
- **Defect:** A flaw in the green bean (like insect damage, fungus, or souring) that negatively impacts the flavor. A "Specialty" grade coffee allows for zero "Primary Defects."

- **Degassing:** The process by which roasted coffee releases the carbon dioxide trapped inside the bean structure. If coffee is brewed too soon after roasting (before degassing), the escaping gas can prevent water from properly extracting the flavor.
- **Density:** The hardness of the bean. High-altitude beans are denser (Hard Beans) and can withstand more heat during roasting, usually resulting in better flavor clarity.
- **Differential:** The price premium (or discount) paid above or below the C-Price for a specific coffee based on its quality or origin.
- **Direct Trade:** A sourcing model where roasters buy directly from farmers or mills, bypassing traditional exporters and importers. The goal is to pay a quality-based premium directly to the producer, though the term is unregulated compared to "Fair Trade."
- **Dose:** The amount of dry ground coffee used to brew a cup. In espresso, typically 18–20 grams.

E

- **Elevation:** See *MASL*.
- **Endocarp:** The scientific name for the parchment layer—the tough, protective hull that surrounds the seed inside the cherry.
- **Espresso:** A brewing method, not a bean. Defined by brewing under pressure (9 bars) with a high coffee-to-water ratio, resulting in a concentrated, viscous liquid with crema.
- **Extraction:** The process of dissolving flavor compounds from grounds into water.
- **Extraction Yield:** The percentage of the dry coffee mass that ends up in the cup. Optimal extraction is generally considered to be between 18% and 22%. Below 18% is sour (under-extracted); above 22% is bitter (over-extracted).

- **F1 Hybrid:** The first generation offspring of two distinct parent varieties (e.g., crossing a wild Ethiopian with a rust-resistant Catimor). F1 hybrids often display "hybrid vigor," offering high yields and high quality, but they cannot be reproduced by seed; they must be cloned in a lab.
- **Fair Trade:** A certification designed to provide a safety net for farming cooperatives by setting a minimum price floor. While it protects against market crashes, it does not necessarily incentivize high quality in the same way the specialty market does.
- **Farm Gate Price:** The actual price paid to the farmer for their cherries or parchment, exclusive of milling, export, and shipping costs. This is often a fraction of the FOB price.
- **Fermentation:** The metabolic process where microbes (yeast/bacteria) consume sugars in the coffee mucilage. In coffee, it is primarily used to remove the sticky fruit flesh from the seed, but it also generates flavor precursors (esters and acids).
- **Fines:** The smallest particles produced during grinding. Too many fines can clog a filter, causing bitterness/over-extraction.
- **First Crack:** See *Crack*.
- **Fly Crop:** A secondary, smaller harvest that occurs in some countries (like Colombia and Kenya) due to their specific rainfall patterns, effectively allowing for two harvests per year (the Main Crop and the Fly Crop).
- **FOB (Free On Board):** A trade term indicating the price of the coffee once it is packed in sacks and loaded onto the ship at the port. It includes the cost of the coffee plus milling and transport to the harbor, but not the ocean freight.
- **Full City:** A roast level descriptor. It indicates a medium-dark roast where the beans have passed the First Crack and are on the verge of the Second Crack. The surface may show the first glimmers of oil.

## G

- **Geisha (or Gesha):** The "Champagne" of coffee varieties. Originally from Ethiopia but made famous in Panama, this elongated bean is prized for its ethereal, floral aroma of jasmine and bergamot. It consistently shatters price records at global auctions.
- **Giling Basah:** Bahasa Indonesia for "Wet Hulling." A processing method unique to Sumatra/Indonesia where coffee is hulled while still wet (30-50% moisture). This exposes the bean to the environment, creating the distinct earthy, spicy, tobacco notes of Sumatran coffee.
- **Green Coffee:** The raw, unroasted seed of the coffee fruit. It is hard, dense, smells grassy or vegetal, and can be stored for months or years before roasting.

## H

- **Hard Bean (HB / SHB):** A classification used in Central America to grade coffee by altitude. *Strictly Hard Bean* (SHB) indicates coffee grown at the highest elevations (usually 1,350+ meters), implying higher density and quality.
- **Heirloom:** A catch-all term often used for Ethiopian varieties that are wild or semi-wild and genetically distinct from the commercial cultivars used elsewhere.
- **Honey Process (Pulped Natural):** A hybrid processing method. The skin of the cherry is removed, but some of the sticky, sugary fruit flesh (mucilage) is left on the bean while it dries. It is often color-coded by the amount of flesh left: White Honey (less flesh) to Black Honey (more flesh).
- **Hulling:** The mechanical removal of the dried parchment skin (endocarp) from the green bean just before export.

I

- **Ibrik (Cezve):** A small, long-handled pot (usually copper) used to brew Turkish coffee. The coffee is ground to a powder and boiled with water and sugar, served unfiltered.

L

- **Leaf Rust (La Roya):** See *Rust*.
- **Liberica (*Coffea liberica*):** The "third species" of commercial coffee. Much larger trees and cherries than Arabica or Robusta, with a controversial flavor profile often described as smoky, woody, or like jackfruit. It is rare but gaining attention for its climate resilience.
- **Lipids:** The fats and oils within the coffee bean. They carry the volatile aroma compounds. Paper filters remove most lipids (creating a "clean cup"); metal filters or espresso let them pass through (creating "heavy body").

M

- **Maillard Reaction:** The chemical reaction between amino acids and reducing sugars during roasting (occurring around 150°C / 300°F). It is responsible for turning the beans brown and creating hundreds of savory, nutty, and malty flavor compounds—the same reaction that sears a steak or toasts bread.
- **MASL:** "Meters Above Sea Level." A crucial spec on coffee bags. Generally, higher altitudes (1,500+ MASL) create cooler nights, slowing cherry maturation and leading to denser, sweeter, more acidic beans.
- **Microlot:** A specific, small selection of coffee from a single farm, harvested from a specific plot of land or processed in a unique way to isolate a distinct flavor profile. These lots usually command the highest prices.

- **Monoculture:** An agricultural practice of growing a single crop species over a wide area. While efficient for industrial farming, it depletes soil nutrients and makes the crop highly vulnerable to pests and disease spread.
- **Mucilage:** The sticky, sugar-rich layer of pectin and glucose found between the coffee cherry skin and the parchment layer. In fermentation, yeast eats this layer to access the seed.

N

- **Natural Process (Dry Process):** The oldest method of processing. The entire coffee cherry is dried intact on raised beds or patios like a raisin. The fruit ferments slightly into the seed, imparting heavy body and flavors of strawberry, blueberry, or wine. If done poorly, it tastes like rot; if done well, it is a fruit bomb.
- **Nitro:** Cold brew coffee infused with nitrogen gas under pressure (like Guinness beer), creating a creamy, cascading texture and a perceived sweetness without sugar.

O

- **Organic Acids:** Acids formed during the plant's metabolic cycle or during fermentation. Key acids in coffee include *Citric* (lemon-like), *Malic* (apple-like), *Tartaric* (grape-like), and *Acetic* (vinegar-like).
- **Over-extraction:** When water dissolves too much material from the grounds, pulling out the slower-dissolving compounds like tannins and long-chain fibers. The result is a bitter, drying, astringent cup.

P

- **Pacamara:** A "Frankenstein" giant bean. A hybrid of the Pacas variety and the Maragogype (Elephant Bean). It is massive in

size and prized for its unique savory, herbal, and chocolate flavor profile.
- **Parchment (Pergamino):** The protective, papery hull that surrounds the green coffee bean. Coffee is usually aged and stored in this shell ("in parchment") to protect flavor until it is ready to be milled and shipped.
- **Peaberry:** A genetic mutation occurring in about 5% of coffee cherries where only one small, round seed forms instead of the usual two flat-sided seeds. They are often sorted out and sold at a premium, believed by some to roast more evenly and possess concentrated flavor.
- **Phenology:** The study of cyclic and seasonal natural phenomena (like flowering). Climate change is disrupting the phenology of coffee trees, causing erratic flowering and harvest times.
- **Picker:** The laborer who harvests the coffee. In high-quality specialty coffee, pickers must be skilled, selectively picking only the ripe red cherries while leaving the green ones for later passes.
- **Portafilter:** The handle and basket assembly on an espresso machine that holds the ground coffee. It locks into the "group head" to withstand the high pressure of extraction.
- **Pre-infusion:** The practice of gently soaking the coffee grounds with low-pressure water before full pressure is applied (in espresso) or before the main pour (the "bloom" in filter). This prevents channeling.
- **Pulping:** The mechanical process of squeezing the coffee cherry to separate the seeds from the skin and fruit flesh.

# Q

- **Q-Grader:** The coffee world's equivalent of a Sommelier. A certified professional who has passed rigorous sensory exams to grade coffee on the 100-point SCA scale.
- **Quaker:** A defective roasted bean that remains pale and blonde while the rest turn brown. It is caused by an under-

ripe cherry lacking the sugars needed for the Maillard reaction. A single quaker can make a whole cup taste like peanut skins or cardboard.
- **Quinic Acid:** An acid formed as chlorogenic acids break down during roasting (or as brewed coffee sits on a hot plate). It provides a clean finish in moderation but is the primary cause of the sour, bile-like taste in stale or burnt coffee.

R

- **Refractometer:** A laboratory tool used by baristas to measure the Total Dissolved Solids (TDS) of a brew. It works by measuring how much light bends as it passes through the liquid.
- **Resting:** The practice of letting roasted coffee sit for several days to allow excess carbon dioxide to off-gas. Brewing immediately after roasting can result in sharp, metallic flavors.
- **Robusta (*Coffea canephora*):** The hardy, lower-altitude sibling of Arabica. It contains nearly double the caffeine and produces a thick crema, but lacks nuanced flavor, often tasting of burnt rubber, earth, or grain. It is the backbone of instant coffee and traditional Italian espresso blends.
- **Roast Profile:** The specific "recipe" of time and temperature a roaster uses to bring out the best in a bean. It is often visualized as a curve on a graph (S-Curve).
- **Rust (Coffee Leaf Rust / *Hemileia vastatrix*):** A devastating fungal disease that appears as orange dust on the underside of leaves. It inhibits photosynthesis, causing the tree to drop its leaves and die. It is the single greatest biological threat to the Arabica species.

S

- **Screen Size:** A grading system based on physical bean size. Green coffee is shaken through metal sieves with holes of varying diameters (e.g., Screen 18 is larger than Screen 15). Larger beans are often sold at a premium (like Colombia Supremo), though size does not always correlate to flavor.

- **Second Crack:** See *Crack*.
- **Shade Grown:** Coffee grown under a canopy of other trees (Inga, banana, fruit trees). Shade slows the maturation of the cherry (increasing sugar) and provides habitat for birds, which act as natural pest control.
- **Silver Skin:** The wispy, paper-thin layer of chaff closely adhering to the green bean (under the parchment). It usually flakes off during roasting.
- **Single Origin:** Coffee sourced from one specific country, region, or cooperative, rather than a blend. Designed to highlight the *terroir* of that specific place.
- **SL-28:** A famous botanical variety created by Scott Laboratories in Kenya in the 1930s. It is drought-resistant and renowned for its intense acidity and notes of blackcurrant and tomato.
- **Slurry:** The mixture of hot water and coffee grounds during the brewing process.
- **Specialty Coffee:** Technically, any coffee that scores 80 points or higher on the 100-point scale by a Q-Grader. Culturally, it refers to the movement toward higher quality, transparency, and lighter roasts.
- **Strecker Degradation:** A chemical reaction that follows the Maillard reaction during roasting, where amino acids interact with carbonyls to create aldehydes and ketones—compounds responsible for the aromatics of the coffee.
- **Stripping:** A harvesting method (common in Brazil) where laborers strip the entire branch of cherries—ripe, green, and overripe—in one motion. It is faster/cheaper than selective picking but results in lower quality.

T

- **TDS (Total Dissolved Solids):** A scientific measurement of the "strength" of a cup of coffee—literally, how much coffee material is dissolved in the water. A standard cup is about 1.25% coffee and 98.75% water; espresso is roughly 8-12% coffee.
- **Terroir:** A term borrowed from wine. It refers to the environmental factors—soil composition, rainfall, shade, microbiome, and altitude—that give a coffee its unique regional flavor fingerprint.
- **Third Wave:** The historical movement (starting in the late 90s/early 2000s) that treats coffee as an artisanal foodstuff rather than a commodity. It focuses on lightness of roast, single-origin character, and manual brewing.
- **Typica:** The "Adam and Eve" of Arabica cultivars. It is the genetic base from which many other varieties mutated. It is known for clean, sweet cup quality but low yields and high susceptibility to rust.

U

- **Under-extraction:** When water flows too quickly through the grounds, failing to dissolve the sugars and balancing components. The result is a cup that tastes sour, grassy, saline, and lacks sweetness.

V

- **Varietal vs. Cultivar:** Technically, a *Variety* is a naturally occurring variation of the plant (like Geisha); a *Cultivar* is a variation created through human agricultural intervention (like Castillo). In the coffee world, the terms are often used interchangeably.
- **Volatile Organic Compounds (VOCs):** The aromatic molecules that evaporate from the coffee and enter the nasal

passage. Coffee has over 800 identified VOCs (more than wine), making it one of the most chemically complex scents in the world.

## W

- **Washed Process (Wet Process):** The method where fruit is mechanically stripped and the mucilage is fermented and washed off *before* drying. This results in the cleanest, most acidic, and most consistent flavor profile, highlighting the bean's genetics rather than the processing.
- **Water Hardness:** The measure of mineral content (magnesium and calcium) in brewing water. Magnesium helps extract fruity notes, while calcium buffers acidity. Without the right mineral balance, even the best coffee will taste flat.

## Y

- **Yield (Agricultural):** The amount of green coffee produced per hectare of land. High-yield varieties (like Robusta) are more profitable for volume; low-yield varieties (like Typica) are often higher quality.
- **Yield (Extraction):** See *Extraction Yield.*

# SELECTED BIBLIOGRAPHY

This bibliography acts as a map of the territory covered in *The Coffee Chronicles*. It includes foundational histories, scientific papers, and the specific primary source documents referenced in the narrative.

### General Histories & Reference Works

- **Allen, Stewart Lee.** *The Devil's Cup: A History of the World According to Coffee.* New York: Soho Press, 1999.
- **Courtwright, David T.** *Forces of Habit: Drugs and the Making of the Modern World.* Cambridge, MA: Harvard University Press, 2001.
- **Hoffmann, James.** *The World Atlas of Coffee: From Beans to Brewing — Coffees Explored, Explained and Enjoyed.* 2nd ed. Richmond Hill, Ontario: Firefly Books, 2018.
- **Jacob, Heinrich Eduard.** *Coffee: The Epic of a Commodity.* Translated by Eden and Cedar Paul. New York: Viking Press, 1935.
- **Koehler, Jeff.** *Where the Wild Coffee Grows: The Untold Story of Coffee from the Cloud Forests of Ethiopia to Your Cup.* New York: Bloomsbury, 2017.

- **Morris, Jonathan.** *Coffee: A Global History.* London: Reaktion Books, 2019.
- **Pendergrast, Mark.** *Uncommon Grounds: The History of Coffee and How It Transformed Our World.* Revised ed. New York: Basic Books, 2010.
- **Standage, Tom.** *A History of the World in 6 Glasses.* New York: Walker & Company, 2005.
- **Ukers, William H.** *All About Coffee.* New York: The Tea and Coffee Trade Journal Company, 1922.
- **Wild, Antony.** *Coffee: A Dark History.* New York: W. W. Norton & Company, 2005.

## Part I: Roots in Legend

*Focusing on Ethiopia, Yemen, the Islamic World, and the Early European Coffeehouses.*

- **Alpini, Prospero.** *De Plantis Aegypti liber* (The Plants of Egypt). Venice: 1592. [The first European botanical description of the coffee plant].
- **Arendonk, C. van.** "Kahwa." In *The Encyclopaedia of Islam*, vol. 4. Leiden: Brill, 1978.
- **Cowan, Brian.** *The Social Life of Coffee: The Emergence of the British Coffeehouse.* New Haven: Yale University Press, 2005.
- **Ellis, Markman.** *The Coffee-House: A Cultural History.* London: Weidenfeld & Nicolson, 2004.
- **Hattox, Ralph S.** *Coffee and Coffeehouses: The Origins of a Social Beverage in the Medieval Near East.* Seattle: University of Washington Press, 1985.
- **Naironi, Antonie Faustus.** *De Saluberrima Potione Cahue* (On the Wholesome Potation of Coffee). Rome: 1671. [The first written record of the Kaldi legend].
- **Paulli, Simon.** *Commentarius de Abusu Tabaci et Herbae Thee* (Commentary on the Abuse of Tobacco and Tea). Copenhagen: 1665. [Early medical critique of coffee].
- *Primary Source:* **The Women's Petition Against Coffee.** London, 1674.

- *Primary Source:* **King Charles II.** *A Proclamation for the Suppression of Coffee-Houses.* London, 1675.

## Part 2: Seeds of Empire
*Focusing on Colonialism, Slavery, and the Spread to the Americas and Asia.*

- **Clarence-Smith, William Gervase.** *Cocoa and Chocolate, 1765–1914.* London: Routledge, 2000.
- **Clarence-Smith, William Gervase, and Steven Topik, eds.** *The Global Coffee Economy in Africa, Asia, and Latin America, 1500–1989.* Cambridge: Cambridge University Press, 2003.
- **Dubois, Laurent.** *Avengers of the New World: The Story of the Haitian Revolution.* Cambridge, MA: Harvard University Press, 2004.
- **Multatuli (Eduard Douwes Dekker).** *Max Havelaar: Or the Coffee Auctions of the Dutch Trading Company.* Edinburgh: Edmonston & Douglas, 1868 (Original Dutch ed. 1860).
- **Mintz, Sidney W.** *Sweetness and Power: The Place of Sugar in Modern History.* New York: Viking, 1985.
- **Trouillot, Michel-Rolph.** "Motion in the System: Coffee, Color, and Slavery in Eighteenth-Century Saint-Domingue." *Review (Fernand Braudel Center)* 5, no. 3 (1982): 331–88.
- **Van Norman, William C.** *Shade-Grown Slavery: The Lives of Slaves on Coffee Plantations in Cuba.* Nashville: Vanderbilt University Press, 2013.

## Part 3: From Blossom to Bean
*Focusing on Botany, Agronomy, and Disease.*

- **Bertrand, B., et al.** "Breeding for Coffea arabica–Coffea canephora hybrids." *Euphytica* 151 (2006): 183–200.
- **McCook, Stuart.** *Coffee Is Not Forever: A Global History of the Coffee Leaf Rust.* Athens, OH: Ohio University Press, 2019.
- **Perfecto, Ivette, and John Vandermeer.** *Breakfast of*

*Biodiversity: The Political Ecology of Rain Forest Destruction.*
Oakland: Food First Books, 2005.

- **Rice, Robert A., and Justin R. Ward.** *Coffee, Conservation, and Commerce in the Western Hemisphere.* Washington, D.C.: Smithsonian Migratory Bird Center, 1996.
- **Talhinhas, P., et al.** "The coffee leaf rust pathogen Hemileia vastatrix: one and a half centuries around the world." *Molecular Plant Pathology* 18, no. 8 (2017).
- **Wintgens, Jean Nicolas, ed.** *Coffee: Growing, Processing, Sustainable Production.* Weinheim: Wiley-VCH, 2004.

Part 4: The Chemistry of Aroma
*Focusing on Chemistry, Roasting, Grinding, and Extraction.*

- **Buffo, Roberto A., and Cristina Cardelli-Freire.** "Coffee Flavour: An Overview." *Flavour and Fragrance Journal* 19, no. 2 (2004).
- **Colonna-Dashwood, Maxwell, and Christopher H. Hendon.** *Water for Coffee: Science Story Manual.* Bath: Pavilion Books, 2015.
- **Folmer, Britta, ed.** *The Craft and Science of Coffee.* London: Academic Press, 2017.
- **Illy, Andrea, and Rinantonio Viani, eds.** *Espresso Coffee: The Science of Quality.* 2nd ed. Amsterdam: Elsevier/Academic Press, 2005.
- **Lingle, Ted R.** *The Coffee Cupper's Handbook.* 4th ed. Long Beach, CA: Specialty Coffee Association of America, 2011.
- **Lockhart, E.E.** "The Soluble Solids in Beverage Coffee as a Measure of Cup Quality." *Coffee Brewing Institute Research Paper* (1957).
- **Petracco, M.** "Technology of Espresso Coffee." In *Coffee: Recent Developments.* Oxford: Blackwell Science, 2001.
- **Rao, Scott.** *The Coffee Roaster's Companion.* Scott Rao, 2014.
- **Runge, Friedlieb Ferdinand.** *Neueste phytochemische Entdeckungen* (Latest Phytochemical Discoveries). Berlin: 1820. [The isolation of caffeine].

## Part 5: Rituals and Revolutions

*Focusing on Consumption, The Second & Third Waves, and Global Coffee Culture.*

- Dickinson, Greg. "Joe's Rhetoric: Finding Authenticity at Starbucks." *Rhetoric Society Quarterly* 32, no. 4 (2002).
- Oldenburg, Ray. *The Great Good Place: Cafes, Coffee Shops, Bookstores, Bars, Hair Salons, and Other Hangouts at the Heart of a Community.* New York: Paragon House, 1989.
- Roseberry, William. "The Rise of Yuppie Coffees and the Reimagination of Class in the United States." *American Anthropologist* 98, no. 4 (1996).
- Schultz, Howard. *Pour Your Heart Into It: How Starbucks Built a Company One Cup at a Time.* New York: Hyperion, 1997.
- Segrave, Kerry. *Vending Machines: An American Social History.* Jefferson, NC: McFarland, 2002.
- West, Paige. *From Modern Production to Imagined Primitive: The Social World of Coffee from Papua New Guinea.* Durham, NC: Duke University Press, 2012.

## Part 6: Empires of Coffee

*Focusing on Economics, Trade, The C-Market, and Geopolitics.*

- Bates, Robert H. *Open-Economy Politics: The Political Economy of the World Coffee Trade.* Princeton: Princeton University Press, 1997.
- Daviron, Benoit, and Stefano Ponte. *The Coffee Paradox: Global Markets, Commodity Trade and the Elusive Promise of Development.* London: Zed Books, 2005.
- Fridell, Gavin. *Fair Trade Coffee: The Prospects and Pitfalls of Market-Driven Social Justice.* Toronto: University of Toronto Press, 2007.
- Jaffee, Daniel. *Brewing Justice: Fair Trade Coffee, Sustainability, and Survival.* Berkeley: University of California Press, 2007.
- Talbot, John M. *Grounds for Agreement: The Political Economy*

*of the Coffee Commodity Chain.* Lanham, MD: Rowman & Littlefield, 2004.

- *Institutional Data:* **International Coffee Organization (ICO).** "Historical Data on the Global Coffee Trade." London: Various Years.
- *Institutional Data:* **ICE Futures U.S.** "Coffee 'C' Rulebook and Contract Specifications." New York: Various Years.

**Part 7: New Horizons**
*Focusing on Climate Change, Innovation, and the Future.*

- **Ahmed, Selena, et al.** "Climate Change and Coffee Quality: Systematic Review." *Frontiers in Plant Science* 12 (2021).
- **Bunn, Christian, et al.** "A bitter cup: climate change profile of global production of Arabica and Robusta coffee." *Climatic Change* 129 (2015).
- **Davis, Aaron P., et al.** "High extinction risk for wild coffee species and implications for coffee sector sustainability." *Science Advances* 5, no. 1 (2019).
- **Davis, Aaron P., et al.** "Lost and Found: Coffea stenophylla and C. affinis, the Forgotten Coffee Crop Species of West Africa." *Frontiers in Plant Science* 11 (2020).
- **Johnson, Matt D., and Thomas Sherry.** "Insectivorous Birds Increase Growth of Coffea arabica Through Depredation of Coffee Berry Borer." *Condor* 111 (2009).
- **Moat, Justin, et al.** "Resilience potential of the Ethiopian coffee sector under climate change." *Nature Plants* 3 (2017).
- **Ovalle-Rivera, Oriana, et al.** "Projected shifts in Coffea arabica suitability among major global producing regions due to climate change." *PLOS ONE* 10, no. 4 (2015).
- **World Coffee Research.** *Annual Reports and Variety Catalogs.* 2016–2024.

# ABOUT THE AUTHOR

**Josh Lee** is an author, Silicon Valley executive, AI consultant, and father whose work bridges technology, storytelling, and craft. He is the author of *The Cacao Chronicles* and *The Coffee Chronicles*, long-form explorations of how food, science, and global systems quietly shape human culture. Educated in finance and psychology at Santa Clara University and Indiana University, he currently serves as a CFO, drawing on deep experience in venture capital as well as senior leadership roles as a finance executive and COO for high-growth technology companies.

Guided by a philosophy of continuous growth and experimentation, Lee founded Codebase Studio, an AI-driven media lab where he has created interactive applications, games such as *Astrocat*, and multiple podcasts—including *KidsNewsFlash*—reaching audiences in more than fifty countries. He is also the founder of the Menlo Park Chocolate Company, where he explores the history, science, and culture of food through small-batch creations. He resides in Menlo Park, California, with his two children, Tyler and Katie.

# ACKNOWLEDGMENTS

This book exists because of the positivity, love, and support of those closest to me. Without you, the motivation to continue creating, building, and growing simply wouldn't be there.

That includes my parents, who nurtured my curiosity and encouraged my interests, and my children, whom I love with all my heart and who inspire me daily with their enthusiasm, kindness, and earnestness.

I also want to thank Nana, who showed me that boundaries are often arbitrary and that you can do whatever you set your mind to. You thrived in the arts and in business at a time when it was far more difficult for women to do so, and I always admired you for that. I admired your sharp wit, your humor, your kindness, and your talent—and I miss you every day.

I hope you enjoyed the journey through the world of coffee, and that it gave you a deeper appreciation for the history, science, and nuance that often go unnoticed.